"Too much data and not enough insight? Fleisher and Bensoussan offer a fabulous solution to the problem. *Business and Competitive Analysis* provides a nice combination of theory and practice, including a comprehensive, wide-ranging description of analytical techniques. Providing a strong complement to their previous work, *Strategic and Competitive Analysis*, this latest work is a 'must read' for anyone analyzing strategic and tactical issues across the competitive landscape."

—Timothy J. Kindler, Director, Competitive Intelligence, Eastman Kodak Company and 2005 President, Society of Competitive Intelligence Professionals

"Baruch's Law reminds us that, 'when all you have is a hammer, everything looks like a nail,' a condition describing the single most difficult challenge facing both business analysts and consultants, novice and veteran alike. In 2003, Fleisher and Bensoussan delivered what all leading intelligence thinkers agree was THE definitive guide to analytics and interpretation for the first half-decade of the new millennium. With their latest collaboration, this expert duo has defined the second-half of this decade as one guided by knowing the tools appropriate for the cognitive task at hand while expanding the toolkit available to be even more complete, valuable, and useful through the actionable detailing of 24 all-new techniques. Plus, the unique FAROUT approach to tool selection equips analysts to quickly and easily apply the right techniques more reliably and scientifically to the range of outcomes anticipated in every business-decision support situation."

—Arik Johnson, Managing Director, Aurora WDC

"The realm of competitive intelligence has, in recent years, benefited from a profusion of books, handbooks, and essays, most of which deal with issues in intelligence collection: emerging techniques and technologies and general overviews of the business intelligence discipline. Fleisher and Bensoussan offer a choice of analytical models destined to narrow corporate course charting uncertainties and present a convincing case for matching science and art in the analysis process. This new book is an important addition to the definitive professional library on the art and science of business intelligence."

—Michael Belkine, Managing Director, Splendour Ltd

"Having been involved in information analysis and strategic information support to companies for many years, I found this book very helpful and full of insights addressed not only to the newcomer, but also to an experienced person. The in-depth review of each analysis technique actually brings new ways of looking at problems: Information analysis becomes an instrument in the hands of a thinking person; it's not an academic exercise or just a conceptual framework. Furthermore, in my experience usually some of the analysis techniques are known and used almost only by people working in a few functions inside a company. This book enters you in a fascinating multi-stage and multi-face analysis world: Everyone needs a way of organizing thoughts, and here you can find what you require to perform a good analysis and give insightful meanings to the information you manage, wherever you work in your company, whatever the problem you face is. Every day everyone needs to analyze information to understand phenomena and then act to achieve the best performance: hence you need to keep this book on your desk."

—Milena Motta, Managing Director, Strategie & Innovazione, Italy

"There are very few books I recommend as a must-read to the managers who come to us from all over the world for professional training in competitive intelligence. Porter, Fuld, Gilad (of course), and Fleisher and Bensoussan."

—**Dr. Benjamin Gilad, President, The Fuld-Gilad-Herring Academy of Competitive Intelligence, www.academyci.com**

"At last a comprehensive manual of tools and techniques for the business and competitive analysis professional! Fleisher and Bensoussan's second collaborative work builds beautifully on their first. It provides the specific guidance desperately needed by company analysts to ensure that decision makers receive the right information at the right time to make the right decisions."

—**Kirk W. M. Tyson, CEO, Perpetual Strategist Ltd., Chicago, USA**

"The dynamic collaborative team of Bensoussan and Fleisher has done it again. Expanding on their earlier text, *Strategic and Competitive Analysis*, the refined perspectives offered in their latest work, *Business and Competitive Analysis*, have raised the bar for essential literature in the profession of decision support. By artfully interweaving both pragmatic and theoretic principles, this book couples frameworks for critical thinking with practical operational guidance for the successful analyst. They never lose sight of the ultimate end game—sustainable competitive advantage through sound, evidence-based decision making. Very few enterprises seem capable of achieving this elusive objective in the hyper-competitive business environment of the 21st century. These thought leaders have built another pillar in the foundation of the business intelligence literature base that should be required reading in both academic and corporate settings."

—**Clifford Kalb, Vice President, Life Sciences, Wood Mackenzie, Inc.**

"*Business and Competitive Analysis: Effective Application of New and Classic Methods* from Fleisher and Bensoussan is 'the definitive must have' for anyone undertaking competitive analysis, irrespective of experience, practitioner, or third-party vendor. This practical and actionable set of techniques grows and develops the agenda of the first edition by extending the range of techniques, focusing on their actionability rather than a statement of their intent, and allows the practitioner to hit the nail on the head with at times complex problems and their recommendations. Through the consistent approach adopted with the techniques, it provides the guide to what can be achieved and how, and helps structure the problem from the very outset. The FAROUT methodology again helps the practitioner work out which ones to apply first given their own unique position and provides a development framework to seek out opportunities to apply the rest. Like the first edition, it becomes the most sought after next installment in defining competitive analysis' role in business for practitioner and user alike."

—**Andrew Beurschgens, Competitive Analysis Manager, Orange, UK**

"Bravo! Bensoussan and Fleisher have returned for an encore performance as your instructive desktop guides to thoughtfully assist analysts of all stripes in selecting and applying a wide-ranging array of frameworks, all designed to enhance analytical thinking, insight, and decision-making. This second volume, following their wildly successful first book, delivers exactly what it promises—to assist analysts in developing high value insights, to aid them in making sense of the competitive environment confronting their organizations, and to guide them in advising decision-makers—all contributing integrally to organizational performance. This book joins their first volume as a 'must have' addition to an analyst's toolkit. I highly recommend it."

—Cyndi Allgaier, Director, Strategic Analysis, AARP

"*Business and Competitive Analysis* by Fleisher and Bensoussan is an excellent complement to their earlier volume, *Strategic and Competitive Analysis*. Both books provide a comprehensive resource on analytical methods for the business and competitive analyst. I have found this book to be an excellent summary of many analytical tools commonly used by competitive intelligence, strategic planning, and marketing professionals, including some techniques that have not been well documented in the past. The standardized approach to describing methods is a welcome approach to showing how the methods work, as well as their history, applications, and strengths and limitations. Excellent references are also included. The detailed step-by-step descriptions of how to use the methods with realistic examples is especially valuable. I highly recommend this book for business analysis professionals seeking a basic reference on important tools or a readable source for learning about new methods."

—Dr. Brad Ashton, Concurrent Technologies Corporation

"Governments and businesses, whether the emphasis is on product or service development, are all looking for the same thing, that next great new idea that will help them position themselves effectively and successfully in the marketplace with consumers or with the voting public. Through technology development in the last 15 years, more data is available to and within organizations than ever before to help achieve this goal. The struggle, and indeed it is, is for organizations to mine this data in a meaningful way and find that 'insight' that will give them the strategic advantage over a competitor. In *Business and Competitive Analysis*, Fleisher and Bensoussan have provided the pathway for data to be taken and mined and to be combined to find those insights. They have also cleverly aided the reader and the practitioners of competitive analysis by giving strong definitions for clarity around the data mining area. Anyone who is charged with competitive strategic analysis and intelligence *must* read this book."

—Louise McCann, Chief Executive Officer, Research International, Australia and New Zealand

Business and Competitive Analysis

Effective Application of New and Classic Methods

Craig S. Fleisher
and Babette E. Bensoussan

Vice President, Publisher: Tim Moore
Associate Publisher and Director of Marketing: Amy Neidlinger
Acquisitions Editor: Martha Cooley
Editorial Assistant: Pamela Boland
Development Editor: Russ Hall
Marketing Coordinator: Megan Colvin
Cover Designer: Chuti Prasertsith
Managing Editor: Gina Kanouse
Project Editor: Betsy Harris
Copy Editor: Water Crest Publishing
Proofreader: Language Logistics, LLC
Senior Indexer: Cheryl Lenser
Compositor: Moore Media, Inc.
Manufacturing Buyer: Dan Uhrig

FT Press offers excellent discounts on this book when ordered in quantity for bulk purchases or special sales. For more information, please contact U.S. Corporate and Government Sales, 1-800-382-3419, corpsales@pearsontechgroup.com. For sales outside the U.S., please contact International Sales at international@pearsoned.com.

Printed in the United States of America
Third Printing May, 2008

ISBN-10:   0-13-187366-0
ISBN-13: 978-0-13-187366-7

Pearson Education LTD.
Pearson Education Australia PTY, Limited.
Pearson Education Singapore, Pte. Ltd.
Pearson Education North Asia, Ltd.
Pearson Education Canada, Ltd.
Pearson Educatión de Mexico, S.A. de C.V.
Pearson Education—Japan
Pearson Education Malaysia, Pte. Ltd.

Library of Congress Cataloging-in-Publication Data

Fleisher, Craig S.

   Business and competitive analysis methods: effective application of new and classic methods / Craig Fleisher, Babette Bensoussan.

      p. cm.

   ISBN 0-13-187366-0 (hardback : alk. paper) 1. Business intelligence. 2. Competition. I. Bensoussan, Babette E. II. Title.

HD38.7.F57 2007
658.4′032—dc22   2006030892

Table of Contents

Acknowledgments

I, Craig Fleisher, want to express my gratitude and thanks to a number of friends and colleagues without whose help the book could not be written. My first expression of gratitude goes out to my co-author Babette Bensoussan, who worked alongside me for the last few years in developing this text. Second, a big dose of thanks goes out to Sheila Wright, my colleague and fellow SCIP Board member who researches and teaches competitive intelligence and marketing courses at Leicester Business School (De Montfort University, UK), and who was a magnificent and timely help in polishing Part 1, as well as being a particularly helpful sounding board for my ideas. Go Tigers! My highly capable research assistant Jennifer White did a marvelous job in helping me uncover and organize the materials as well as develop PowerPoint slides for each of the technique chapters, and Sanjay Gupta assisted in reviewing and commenting upon several chapters—particularly the one on business model analysis, which he helped develop, as did my long-time research assistant Victor Knip, who was his usual hard-working self.

I also want to thank the many individuals who helped review these chapters and provided valuable advice. I'd particularly like to thank long-time competitive intelligence and related professionals Brad Ashton, Albert Cruywagen, Bill Fiora, Alex Graham, Arik Johnson, Timothy Kindler, Victor Knip, Martha Matteo, Rainer Michaeli, John Prescott, Pascal Savioz, Pat Shaw, Fred Wergeles, and Melanie Wing. Thanks to many excellent MBA students in my various CI courses at the University of Windsor, University of New Brunswick, and Wilfrid Laurier University. The book also benefited from feedback from students and workshop attendees at the University of Sydney and Sydney Graduate School of Management (Australia), Nihon University (Japan—special thanks to my friend and colleague Yoshio Sugasawa), Stellenbosch University, Graduate School of Business Leadership at UNISA (thanks to Peet Venter), University of Pretoria and North-West University in South Africa (special thanks to Wilma Viviers). They offered me a wonderful sounding board for discussing many of the book's ideas. Additionally, I want to acknowledge David Blenkhorn, who co-taught CI courses at WLU with me, where I also benefited from teaching related strategy courses with my colleague Kenneth Harling, and Conor Vibert of Acadia University, with whom I regularly discuss these concepts. Additionally, several valuable workshops and conferences held under the auspices of Society of Competitive Intelligence Professionals (SCIP), CBIA (South Africa) and its long-time leader Steve Whitehead, my friends Mike Kuhn and Marie Luce-Muller of IBIS South Africa, Frost & Sullivan, KMWorld, and Marcus Evans Conferences, in particular, have also allowed me many opportunities to hone these ideas. Last but not least, I want to express my appreciation to various agencies that provided funding and other forms of support along the way in developing this book, including the Canadian Council for Public Affairs Advancement, National Research Council (Canada), National Research Foundation (South Africa), Odette School of Business, Dean Allan Conway, and the Windsor Research Leadership Chair and Odette Research Chairs—University of Windsor.

I, Babette Bensoussan, readily acknowledge that I am right on the cutting edge of the still relatively new competitive intelligence market in Australia. This positioning has not only presented me with a multiplicity of challenges when compiling this book, but it has also placed me in a somewhat unique professional situation.

While I have been privileged to witness and indeed help create the emergence of this field in Australia and Asia over the past decade, the fact remains that relevant expertise is still very thin on the ground locally. This situation has, however, provided me with a wonderful opportunity to tread new ground, refine implementation frameworks and ideas, and help excite the Australasian business environment about the value that competitive intelligence can deliver when it is applied professionally and comprehensively.

Putting this book together in these market circumstances has been personally fulfilling and challenging at the same time. I have been propelled largely by my keenness to make competitive intelligence a more fundamental consideration in both Australian and Asian businesses. Turning that keenness into hard copy, however, would not have happened without the knowledge that everyone who knew about my efforts added a dimension and fully supported me—even with just a few words of encouragement to keep me focused during the tougher times.

There are several people and groups of people to whom I owe a note of thanks for their contribution—whether direct or indirect—to the existence of this book. May I firstly acknowledge and express my thanks to my co-author Dr. Craig Fleisher, who has shared my vision so completely in both this and our first book. I would also like to extend heartfelt thanks and appreciation to Dr. Graham Godbee, whose expertise in competitor cash flow analysis delivered that chapter with style. In addition, my continuing appreciation to my undergraduate and postgraduate students over the years at Sydney's Graduate School of Management both in Sydney and Guangzhou, China, and Queensland's Bond University who have—possibly unknowingly—given me additional impetus to commit my ideas to paper; to the SCIP organization for helping to build and consolidate my international professional profile and allowing me to test my analytical ideas in practical situations, and to the Australasian business community, who continue to provide the clay with which I work.

With everything in life, you do it all with a little help from your friends—and there are several who stand out. For support in getting this manuscript finalized, I owe heartfelt thanks to Kerrie Tarrant, Carolyn Schmidt, and Korina Ashbrook—what a team—thank you. To my dearest friends—Cyndi Allgaier and Christine Bull—ladies, without your ongoing encouragement, where would I be!

Last but certainly not least, we thank the excellent staff at FT Press and Pearson who helped us all along the way, particularly Martha Cooley, Betsy Harris, Russ Hall, Michael Ablassmeir, Paula Sinott, and Megan Colvin. It was a genuine pleasure to work with each of you.

About the Authors

Authors Fleisher and Bensoussan are uniquely placed as experts in the field of business and competitive analysis. They have extensive corporate consulting, research, and teaching experience in strategy and competitive intelligence and have both published and spoken internationally. Their collaboration also brings the book a healthy balance of both theory and application.

Craig S. Fleisher is the Windsor Research Leadership Chair and Professor of Management (Strategy and Entrepreneurship), Odette School of Business, University of Windsor, Ontario, Canada. He was the 2006 President of the Board of Directors of the international Society of Competitive Intelligence Professionals (SCIP), inaugural chairman of the Board of Trustees of the Competitive Intelligence Foundation (Washington, DC), founding editor of the *Journal of the Competitive Intelligence and Management*, is an SCIP Fellow, and is on several editorial boards of journals in the intelligence field. Author or editor of eight books and scores of scholarly articles and chapters, Craig has been recognized as one of Canada's top MBA professors by *Canadian Business* magazine, is named in the Canadian Who's Who, and has taught university and executive courses in the strategy, analysis, and competitive intelligence areas for nearly two decades. A well-traveled speaker, he regularly advises leading corporations, associations, and public sector agencies on CI and analysis.

Babette Bensoussan is the Managing Director of The MindShifts Group Pty. Ltd., a Sydney, Australia, based consulting firm specializing in strategic planning, competitive intelligence, and strategic marketing projects in the Asia Pacific region. Over the past 15 years, Babette has carried out over 300 intelligence and strategic projects in a wide range of industries and markets, including aerospace, information technology/computers, insurance, transport, financial services, waste services, pharmaceuticals, utilities, mining, and manufacturing operations—to just name a few. Babette was a Founder and Vice President for the Society of Competitive Intelligence Professionals in Australia (SCIPAust), a member of the *Journal of Competitive Intelligence and Management* and *Competitive Intelligence Review* editorial boards, and was awarded the CI field's highest individual honor by being named SCIP's Meritorious Award winner in 2006, as well as having been the first international recipient of the SCIP Fellows Award in 1996. She also has successfully taught undergraduate, MBA, and executive courses on competitive analysis and intelligence at the Sydney Graduate School of Management and Bond University.

Preface

This is a book about how individuals in organizations can turn data and information into insights that decision makers cannot and will not ignore. This book provides its readers with 24 commonly applied methods for helping generate actionable recommendations for decision makers, as well as a handful of detailed chapters that address the process of competitive analysis itself.

Given the priority of competitiveness in firms today, business managers need to have a benchmark about what business and competitive analysis is and how it works. More importantly, they need to be able to convert the wealth of available data and information into a valuable form for decision-making and subsequent actions. Collected data must be converted into intelligence. This is accomplished through analysis.

Business and Competitive Analysis (BCA) is a book about analysis. Analysis is one of the more difficult and critical roles a manager, consultant, functional specialist, strategist, or intelligence provider is called upon to perform. Although great strides have been made in recent years in terms of planning strategy and intelligence projects and collecting data, the same cannot be said for analysis.

Much of the background research we performed in developing this book was derived from practice and research in the larger field of competitive intelligence (CI). This field is not one most of our readers will have encountered during their formal education, and their current employers may not have anybody with that discipline in their job titles. Nevertheless, nearly every firm performs some of the CI functions, and most of them perform it on a regular basis in advance of making key decisions. Analysis is one of the key roles performed by individuals in the CI field, and it is the one that arguably generates the highest value for executives. In our view, business and competitive analysis can and should be a key weapon in the firm's arsenal for achieving competitive advantage.

Despite many advances and steady growth in the CI field, some areas of this growing field have received more or less attention than others. The growth of digital communication and information technology and especially the Internet has led to much attention being given to processes and techniques of data collection, as well as information and knowledge management. Planning competitive intelligence projects has also received a boost from the ever-present attention given more broadly to strategic planning and strategy development. Despite these areas of popular interest, two areas that have received disproportionately less attention are analysis and its communication. In fact, our own observations, experiences, and several studies underlie the authors' contention that many practitioners have limited understanding of the breadth and depth of the challenge underlying these areas.

We seek to remedy this situation by offering this needed book that is devoted entirely to the process, tools, and techniques for conducting business and competitive analysis. This is our second book in this subject matter area, with our first, called *Strategic and Competitive Analysis: Methods and Techniques for Analyzing Business Competition*, having been published several years ago and subsequently translated into half a dozen different languages. We received a lot of constructive feedback on that effort, particularly from managers and analysts who were using the techniques described in that book. Based on the feedback and reviews, readers typically found it to be an excellent, one-stop source for reminding and guiding them on the key steps of a particular tool to address a particular problem they were facing, as well as providing them with an enhanced idea of what was supposed to be accomplished by applying the tool. That book was used in many well-known enterprises to help train newly hired analysts and consultants. Finally, the book was used in business school courses in scores of countries to help students learn and apply these techniques to decision-oriented case studies and "real-world" projects.

We took the feedback we received and incorporated it into this book in the form of a wider range of proven techniques and a better background on the process and context of business and competitive analysis. This book is absolutely *not* a second edition and contains completely new content. Between the two books, we provide lengthy coverage of nearly 50 different techniques, which is surely the most detailed coverage of business and competitive analysis methods ever produced.

We recognize that there are literally hundreds of business and competitive analysis techniques that we could have included in this book. It was not our intention to offer an exhaustive list and detailed description of all these techniques. Instead, we have extensively reviewed the literature in the field, considered survey research and our own experiences in determining those techniques we view as potentially being the most applicable across a broad range of decision making contexts supported by the business and competitive analysis process.

Although we have tried to include both "classic" and evolving techniques, we recognize that some techniques that are being used in consulting and industry may not be included here. One reason for this is that some of these tools are and remain proprietary to the consultancies employing them. Another part of the reason we may not have included a useful tool here is that analysis is a process that requires both technical knowledge and creativity. We recognize and hope that managers and analysts will creatively develop techniques not included in this book that provide for better outcomes in their specific contexts.

The reader should also be alert to the fact that any listing of techniques is bound to run into a variety of problems of semantics and definitional confusion. Some of the techniques included in this book are known by multiple names. This may have occurred because the technique came to be associated with a particular originating organization or particular company's use (e.g., McKinsey 7S), a particular author (e.g., Porter's Five Forces Model), or has retained a generic name (e.g., benchmarking analysis). We recognize that some of the techniques included in this book have seen modifications in use over the years or are derivatives of other closely related techniques. In all cases, we have tried to include and describe the most popularly utilized versions of the techniques, as opposed to all of a technique's possible derivatives. Throughout our methods chapters, we have tried to alert the reader to where there is overlap between techniques by suggesting that the reader refer to the overlapping constructs elsewhere in the text.

Many of the techniques included in this book were created by leading economists, financial and cost accountants, futurists, sociologists, anthropologists, intelligence agencies, business professors, consultants, and other insightful practitioners or theoreticians. They often developed their ideas in an effort to solve pressing analytical problems that they faced. We are grateful to these individuals for enlightening our understanding of business and competitive analysis. We make a sincere attempt to acknowledge the originators of these techniques in the book.

We must also note to our readers that it was not our primary intention to "invent a new wheel" when it comes to analytical techniques. The techniques we have included all have a history, with some having been applied for several decades or longer. This book's techniques have been and are in use in real organizations and do not exist just in theory. However, we have included several techniques that are likely to be unfamiliar or novel to many readers, even those who have gone through graduate business, management, or marketing courses, as well as individuals who have been performing analysis in their enterprises for many years. We believe strongly that unfamiliarity is a particularly bad indicator of a method's value. We believe our readers will find that even some of the new techniques (to them at least) will be of high potential value in helping them make sense of their firm's business and competitive contexts.

How to Use the Book

To assist our readers, the majority of this book is self-contained, with the array of analytical techniques being supported by references for further reading for those individuals who want lengthier treatments. The book is organized into two main sections, with the first providing the reader with an understanding of what the evolving body of knowledge in the field has revealed about analysis in its real-world context and how analysis processes actually are supposed to work.

This book includes five detailed chapters that describe, define, and discuss the basic facts about analysis, how analysis can ideally be performed, avoiding analytical pitfalls, and communicating analysis results. The last chapter in the opening section describes our unique FAROUT method for understanding the application of the various tools. We strongly recommend that readers thoroughly review that particular chapter before progressing into the remaining sections of the book that contain coverage of the analytical techniques themselves.

We have tried to make the book easy for the reader to use. The basic structure of the chapters containing the analytical techniques is common throughout the second part of the book and contains the following format:

- **Short Description**—A brief definition of the purpose and objective of the analytical model to provide an analyst with a quick and handy reference guide.

- **Background**—To place the model in context of management, this section outlines a broad description of the history behind the development of the analytical technique.

- **Strategic Rationale and Implications**—Understanding the strategic thinking and implications associated with a particular analytical technique is important in order to evaluate the appropriateness of a particular tool. This section reviews the strategic issues inherent in each technique.

- **Strengths and Advantages**—Each model has its own strengths and advantages that need to be weighed in light of the purpose of the analysis. This section briefly reviews those strengths and advantages.

- **Weaknesses and Limitations**—Likewise, each model has its own inherent weaknesses and limitations. The weaknesses/limitations identified in this section need to be taken into account when performing the analysis.

- **Process for Applying the Technique**—This is the "how to" of the analytical technique and identifies the necessary steps required to use this tool. Case studies, figures, and tables are also provided to guide the analyst through the strategic thinking required for each model.

- **FAROUT Summary**—Unique to this book, the FAROUT Summary allows analysts, at a quick glance, to identify the ease of use, practicality, and usefulness of each model.

- **Related Tools and Techniques**—Each model of analysis is related to or supported by a number of other techniques that may aid or enhance the analyst's task. This section provides a useful guide of related tools and techniques that support the objective and purpose of each analytical model.

- **References**—For those analysts wanting to delve further into a particular technique, references for additional readings are provided at the end of each chapter.

Readers will benefit by becoming familiar with this template. This book was not designed to be read in one sitting—if nothing else, its length would probably make that an extremely tiring task and practically impossible for most individuals. Instead, we have designed it as a handy comparison and reference source. In this respect, it can be most effectively applied in a "just in time" fashion so as to proactively or concurrently meet an organization's analytical needs as they arise.

The book features conceptual ideas about business and competitive analysis, along with a strong bias toward practical application. Among the unique aspects of this book that readers should find valuable are the following:

- It provides in one easy location two-dozen of the most common and popular models of analysis used in business. Normally, executives and students would have to go to multiple sources to locate each model. Here, for the first time, the most commonly used models are defined and explained in *one* book.

- Every model is also uniquely evaluated using FAROUT—an evaluation process for identifying the ease of use, practicality, and usefulness of each model. FAROUT allows analysts or decision-makers to understand the strengths and weaknesses of the techniques.

- An easy-to-use, consistent format (i.e., template) is utilized to provide the reader with a faster understanding of how to apply the techniques.

- The book covers both the so-called "classic" strategy techniques, such as industry analysis, along with some of the newer popular techniques, such as business model analysis. Several of these models, such as win/loss analysis, strategic relationship analysis, driving forces analysis, and event and timeline analysis, among others, have never been treated this comprehensively in any other publication.

- It provides external techniques addressing the environments and industry that the organization competes in, along with the techniques for focusing internally on the organization.

- It provides references to more comprehensive treatments of the techniques for those who want to investigate them in greater depth.

We expect to stimulate others to begin closing some of the knowledge gaps in business and competitive analysis that we have explicitly and implicitly identified throughout this book's chapters. We also hope that this book encourages practitioners to further share their experiences and observations with researchers and teachers like us in the field. We anticipate that the book will compel our readers to question some, if not a large number, of their current analysis practices and understanding. Our ultimate aim is that this book be viewed as a valuable contribution to the knowledge and practice of business and competitive analysis. Whether or not we achieve our aim is left in your hands, our readers, as it should be. Please feel free to contact either of us if you would care to share your views.

Babette E. Bensoussan
The Mindshifts Group Pty. Ltd.
Level 6, 8 Help Street
Chatswood
New South Wales 2067
Australia
telephone: +(61-2) 9411-3900
fax: +(61-2) 9411-3636
email: babette@mindshifts.com.au

Craig S. Fleisher
Odette School of Business
University of Windsor
401 Sunset Avenue—508 OB
Windsor, Ontario, N9B 3P4
Canada
telephone: 519-253-3000 x3455
fax: 519-973-7073
email: fleisher@uwindsor.ca

Business and Competitive Analysis: Definition, Context, and Benefits

Business competition now comes in many different forms and from a great variety of competitors, and the challenges are increasing. Successfully positioning the enterprise, properly deciding on the correct allocation of resources, and deciding what an acceptable level of performance might be in such a competitive environment are key tasks of senior decision makers. Consequently, skillful business and competitive analysis (BCA) is critically important in determining how an enterprise can compete and deliver value to its stakeholders.

This book is designed to assist analysts to develop high value insights, to aid them in making sense of the competitive environment confronting their organizations, and to guide them in advising their decision makers. Our underlying premise throughout this book is that a good analyst, working in any environment, must have a robust and healthy repertoire of methods, tools, and techniques to help answer important questions on the enterprise's ability to compete, not only in the present, but also the future. For the most part, the end users of an analyst's output are decision makers, and as such, they will be the clients or customers taking action based on those results.

Uniquely, this book focuses specifically on analysis, analysis methods/techniques, and the analysis process. It is not designed to be another strategic management or strategic planning text. There are plenty of good titles of those genres available,[1] although the processes and techniques described herein will certainly benefit strategic planners and managers. We have decades of experience advising, consulting, instructing, practicing, and researching how BCA is used in all types of enterprises.

What surprises us about competitive and strategic analysis is the relatively limited number of tools and techniques used by most practitioners and how little genuine insight emanates from them!

These adverse results occur not only because some tools are badly chosen, outdated, or incorrectly used, but also because they are misunderstood and/or misapplied. This book provides comprehensive instruction on a range of constructive processes, tools and techniques that are available, direction on how the method was developed, analysis of its strengths and weaknesses, an outline of the process used to actually employ the technique as well as sample applications, and identification of complementary techniques, resulting overall in that vital ingredient—insight.

Our first text in this area identified 24 different techniques.[2] Since the first book was published, we have seen many instances and heard countless anecdotes from practitioners who wished to have an *"analyst's manual"* of BCA tools and techniques. We believe that this book goes some way toward meeting that desire.

Understanding the Terminology

This book emphasizes a handful of key words: *competitive, strategic, analysis*, and *intelligence*. These are all part of the normal business and management lexicon. As we use these words repeatedly, it is useful for us to clearly identify what we mean when we use them.

Competitive

In this book, we look at businesses that are in competitive markets and typically operate in a competitive mode. We are addressing the processes and means by which firms position themselves and their products or services against their rivals to win market share.

Competitive means that a contest is occurring between two or more parties. The sources of this can be multi-faceted, originating in product or service offerings, shelf-space negotiations, supplier contracts, and investor relations, to name just a few. Usually, competitive bouts end up with a winner, and no further contest is needed.

The focus of this book is on the market place, though, and this is quite a different proposition. Competition here is about achieving a sustainable winning performance, not delivering one action that simply wounds, but consistently beating the rest who are working, most likely, toward the same or very similar goals as your enterprise.

Strategic

Strategic is a word used today to describe almost every decision and/or action taken, when in reality there is a clear mix of the no less valuable, *tactical* decision making taking place. The generic use of a word such as "strategic" can diminish its real role and mask the impact that a true strategic decision has.

Strategic matters are a key focus of this book. Strategic decisions, as opposed to tactical, operational, or instantaneous decisions, have a unique set of characteristics to differentiate them. These distinctions occur along the dimensions of time, frequency, effort required, consequences, and impact. Strategic decisions typically:

- address at least a medium-term time horizon, at best long-term (time).
- occur infrequently or emerge from a formalized planning cycle (frequency).

- require significant input from key people (effort).
- require significant information input from key functions (effort).
- require substantial resources to formulate and implement (effort).
- affect the long-term direction of the organization (consequences).
- affect many, if not all, of the organization's activities (consequences).
- affect competitive dynamics (impact).
- involve major change to the firm's activities (impact).
- become the over-arching blue-print for subsequent decisions (impact).

If all or a significant number of the preceding elements are present, the greater the likelihood that the decision is indeed strategic. We want to make it clear that just because a decision is not strategic does not make it unimportant.[3] Many non-strategic decisions help to determine the performance of an enterprise in a marketplace, particularly in the shorter term. Decisions such as seasonal price discounting, direct mail campaigns, product enhancements, and ambush marketing are all examples of non-strategic decisions. They have a short-term lifespan and a short-term effect.

The key to our identification of a strategic decision is that they are the ones typically made by senior executives, managing directors, and/or the senior management team. Consequently, the enterprise that gets the strategic decisions "right" has a far greater chance of also getting the non-strategic decisions right.

Analysis

Where does analysis fit in with competitive understanding? Competitive analysis is the cornerstone of effective strategy formulation and execution.[4] Valuable analysis helps decision makers to understand and predict critical market-changing actions that may be taken by competitors and other competition-impacting stakeholders. These decision makers are charged with answering a small number of very powerful questions about their organization, including the following:

1. What is our current status or situation?
2. What are our options?
3. Which direction do we want to go?
4. Which direction should we go?
5. How can we get to where we have decided we are going?
6. How will we know that we have gotten there?

Many of the analysis tools in this book will be beneficial to strategic decision makers in their effort to address those critically important questions. Properly conceived analysis aids decision makers in generating, choosing, and validating appropriate strategic responses.

Analysis is a term that generates much controversy and disagreement. Before we provide our definition of analysis, it may be helpful to examine definitions put forth by others that are in common usage. These can be found in Table1-1.

Table 1-1
Common Definitions of Analysis as Used in Intelligence Contexts

Definition	Source
A critical evaluation, usually made by breaking down a subject (either material or intellectual) into its constituent parts, then describing the parts and their relationship to the whole.	Dictionary definition
The application of common sense and experience to raw information.	Fuld, 1995
A process where one does many of the following, in any order: observe, classify, count, compare, ask questions, role play (engage in war games, do scenarios, run simulations, etc.), and take action.	Halliman, 2003
The use of some methodology or technique to, first, find relationships between different pieces of information and then draw inferences from the relationships.	Halliman, 2003
A process where one converts information into actionable intelligence.	Halliman, 2003
A process where one asks, or answers, the "So What?" question.	Halliman, 2003
The application of individual and collective cognitive methods to weigh data and test hypotheses within a secret socio-cultural context.	Johnston, 2005
The process of evaluating data for reliability, validity, and relevance; integrating and analyzing it; and converting the product of this effort into a meaningful whole, which includes assessment of events and implications of the information collected.	Johnston, 2005
The primary output of the processing phase of the intelligence cycle is the human process of synthesizing pieces of information into finished intelligence.	Procycshn, 1998
The breaking down of a large problem into a number of smaller problems and performing mental operations on the data in order to arrive at a conclusion or generalization. It involves close examination of related items of information to determine the extent to which they confirm, supplement, or contradict each other and thus to establish probabilities and relationships.	Mathams, 1995
The heart of the intelligence process whereby meaning is derived from data.	IALEA, 2001

Although there is some value in these definitions, we find each of them to be lacking in some aspect. As such, in this book, analysis is defined as: *"The skilled application of scientific and non-scientific methods and processes by which individuals interpret data or information to produce insightful intelligence findings and actionable recommendations for decision makers."*

Like many developing fields of inquiry, business and competitive analysis is NOT purely art or science, but a combination of substantial portions of both in its effective application. As with the type of research formally taught to scientists, the analysis process can be viewed as holding much in common with the scientific method. Analysts will observe certain events, persons, or actions, develop a proposition or hypothesis that describes/ explains what they have observed, and then use the hypothesis to make predictions about what may subsequently occur. These predictions can then be further assessed through additional observations or data, and the hypotheses can be modified based on the results.[5]

This process, which can be applied in theory by analysts, gets complicated very quickly by factors present in the real world of business and market-place competition, as well as the politics and social nature of decision makers and enterprises. Analysts frequently work in groups or teams and benefit from the pooling of expertise. Hypotheses aren't always developed, tested, or reformulated, but are frequently modified in real-time by the evidence that is acquired. These factors point to genuine business and competitive analysis being more of a social scientific pursuit than that of physical or pure science.

The "real world" tends to bring out the "art" aspect of analysis. When conducting an experiment using control groups, we know that some percentage of a treatment group's analyses will not confirm the control group's analyses. Analysts in these two groups will weigh the same data or information differently, based on schemes that may be hard for others to accurately replicate. Even when analysts do substantively agree about the nature of the problems being addressed, they can still subsequently disagree about the proposed course of action. Consequently, analysts may never be able to "prove" they were right. It is these kinds of experiences that points to why analysis can sometimes be viewed as more akin to art than science. The following humorous parable helps point out some of the important differences between the two perspectives.

A Parable About the Artist and the Scientist

There were once two people, a scientist and an artist, sitting next to each other, traveling on a bus. They had never met before, and there wasn't much conversation between the two. The artist was minding her own business, looking out her window at the beauty of the passing terrain. The scientist was uptight, trying to think of things he didn't know so he could try to figure them out. Finally, the scientist was so bored, that he said to the artist, "Hey, do you want to play a game?" The artist, being content with what she was doing, ignored him and continued looking out of the window, humming quietly to herself. This infuriated the scientist, who irritably asked again, "Hey, you, do you want to play a game? I'll ask you a question, and if you get it wrong, you give me $5. Then, YOU ask ME a question, and if I can't answer it, I'll give YOU $5." The artist thought about this for a moment, but she decided against it, seeing that the scientist was obviously a very wise man. She politely turned down the scientist's offer. The scientist, who, by this time was going mad, tried a final time. "Look, I'll ask you a question, and if you can't answer it, you give me $5. Then you ask ME a question, and if I can't answer it, I'll give you $100!"

Now, the artist, who was not that smart academically, wasn't stupid either. She readily accepted the offer. "OK," the scientist said, "what is the EXACT distance between the Earth and the Moon?" The artist, obviously not knowing the answer, didn't stop to think long about the scientist's question. She took a $5 bill out of her pocket and handed it to the scientist. The scientist gladly accepted the bill and promptly said, "OK, now it's your turn."

The artist thought about this for a few minutes, and then asked, "All right, what goes up a mountain on three legs, but comes down on four?" The big smirk quickly vanished from the scientist's face. He thought about this for a long while, taking out his pencil and making numerous calculations on his books. When that didn't lead to an answer, he took out his laptop and accessed the Internet. After about an hour of this, all the while with the artist quietly watching the mountains go by, the scientist *finally* gave up. He reluctantly handed the artist a $100 bill. The artist accepted it graciously, turning back to the window. "Wait!" the scientist shouted. "You can't do this to me! What's the answer??" The artist smiled sweetly, pressed a $5 bill into his hand, and said "I don't know."

Business and competitive analysts are tasked with making sense out of often ambiguous, complex, and challenging matters that decision makers care about. Like the artist on the bus, they too have to weigh up the odds, work through the scenarios, work out what they know as opposed to their competition, and take action. They have to make sense of, or create meaning from, a typically constrained sample of data and information. In an often-confused and rapidly moving competitive landscape, they try to answer the three critical questions commonly asked of them:

1. "What?"
2. "So what?"
3. "Now what?"

Any of these three questions may be answered in a variety of constructive ways using replicable procedures and methods (science), as well as intuitive or creative ones (art).

Intelligence

It is important to understand the place of intelligence within the larger context of an enterprise. The need to generate competitive intelligence (CI) is certainly not new. Sun Tzu plainly stated the rationale for intelligence over two thousand years ago. He wrote, *"Now the reason the enlightened prince and the wise general conquer the enemy whenever they move, and their achievements surpass those of ordinary men, is foreknowledge."* [6]

Intelligence processes in business organizations have received significant attention in recent decades. The benefits gained by successfully anticipating a competitor's future plans and strategies are generally self-evident. The consequences of making decisions based on information that is incomplete, inaccurate, or late are as severe.

CI often engenders images of fictional secret agents such as James Bond using an impressive array of sophisticated gadgetry to eavesdrop on their business competition. In reality, CI can be exhilarating, but not because of illegal skullduggery. Modern CI practitioners are stimulated by using their unique set of skills, knowledge, abilities, and instincts to uncover relationships that enable their organizations to compete more effectively. Most CI practice includes a heavy dose of analytical capabilities. Analysts are prominent, central members of CI functions in today's successful, global enterprises.

There are numerous definitions of CI in contemporary practice and scholarship. Our current sense is that no single definition of CI is likely to be precise and universally accepted. As such, CI is generally viewed as *the process by which organizations gather actionable information about competitors and the competitive environment and, ideally, apply it to their planning processes and decision-making in order to improve their enterprise's performance.* CI links signals, events, perceptions, and data into discernible patterns and trends concerning the business and competitive environment. CI can be simple scanning, such as analyzing a company's annual report and other public documents, or elaborate, such as performing a fully digitized war gaming exercise.[7]

CI is not business espionage; it is ethical, legal, legitimate, and essential. Business espionage develops intelligence by illegal or cloak-and-dagger means such as breaking and entering, bribery, coercion, deliberate deception or advertising "phantom" job vacancies, electronic eavesdropping, bugging or tapping, network infiltration, or systems hacking.[8] CI practitioners use public, but not necessarily published, information. In other words, the information the CI practitioner seeks is readily available and identified through legal means of open sources such as public documents, interviews, and in-house expertise. It does not involve the theft of trade secrets.

One way to understand CI is to view it as a progression from raw inputs to finished outputs. In this perspective, CI begins with scattered bits of raw, basic data. This raw material is then organized by CI practitioners and becomes information. Information becomes intelligence when it is placed into a format useful to a decision-maker's unique or critical intelligence needs (CINs). Intelligence is therefore information that is analyzed, interpreted, and infused with developed implications—the basic focus of this book. Using this lens, CI is the refined intelligence product produced by an analyst that meets a decision-maker's unique needs for understanding a competitive aspect of the internal and/or external environment. Effective CI helps the decision-maker make a better decision!

CI can also be viewed as an organizational function ranging in scope between the broader area of business intelligence (BI) and the narrower version practiced as competitor analysis (CA). A CI function provides the foundation on which strategy and tactics are built, assessed, and modified. As a mostly staff-oriented function, CI will cut across and overlap other functions, in particular, those associated with marketing, planning, and strategy.

Competitive Intelligence Programs (CIPs) have goals such as proactively detecting opportunities or threats; eliminating or reducing blindspots, risks, and/or surprises; and reducing reaction time to competitor and marketplace changes. CIPs attempt to ensure that decision makers have accurate, current information about the organization's competitive environment, and a plan for using that information.[9]

Analysis as a Component in the Intelligence Cycle

Analysis is arguably that portion of the larger intelligence process in which the greatest value is generated.[10] Much organizational experience suggests it can also be more difficult to do than the resource-draining data and information collection efforts that most organizations have emphasized in recent years. Nevertheless, there is a long series of research and publications that suggests that business and competitive analysis serves a variety of important, longstanding needs for organizations.[11] Although we intend to explore this context in much greater detail in other parts of this section, here we will briefly describe how analysis fits within the intelligence process.

Analysis is just one step of a larger process for developing intelligence for an organization. Most depictions of the so-called "intelligence cycle" show a series of 4 to 6 steps in a stripped-down form. These steps describe the functions of an intelligence operation in an enterprise and are illustrated in Figure 1.1.

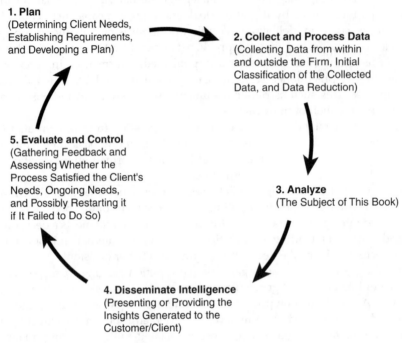

1. Plan
(Determining Client Needs, Establishing Requirements, and Developing a Plan)

2. Collect and Process Data
(Collecting Data from within and outside the Firm, Initial Classification of the Collected Data, and Data Reduction)

5. Evaluate and Control
(Gathering Feedback and Assessing Whether the Process Satisfied the Client's Needs, Ongoing Needs, and Possibly Restarting it if It Failed to Do So)

3. Analyze
(The Subject of This Book)

4. Disseminate Intelligence
(Presenting or Providing the Insights Generated to the Customer/Client)

Figure 1.1   A generic intelligence cycle

The analysis step in this cycle involves its own set of sub-tasks that need to be conducted in order to generate effective outputs and outcomes. Analysis works interactively with all the sub-processes of data classification and synthesis to produce a finished product such as a chart, graph, table, text, summary, visual, or other communicative aids appropriate for dissemination.

Analysis involves the skillful application of a variety of techniques. We are sharing many good ones in the upcoming chapters of this book. All of these will help decision makers make sense of intelligence.

Intelligence analysis is always context-specific in that it does not occur within a vacuum, a static condition, or under experimental conditions. Because analysis is performed by practitioners in active organizational and competitive conditions, it is important to identify the nature of competition that analysts examine as a part of their work task.

Competitive Analysis and Decision Making

Most organizations today are not structured or organized properly to make good decisions that will help them outperform their competition in the marketplace.[12]

It is commonplace for this book's authors to hear from decisions makers who lament in retrospect: "*If only I'd known that, I'd never have made that decision or taken that action.*" Such comments reflect an absence of intelligence supporting the decision maker and the lack of greater insight behind their decisions and subsequent actions.

There is no shortage of examples where poor decisions have adversely affected many stakeholders. Read the business section of your local paper, and you will hear of bankruptcies, down-sizing because of poor sales, over-optimistic new product revenue/volume predictions, wasted R&D efforts, or plant closures due to outdated technology or cheap imports. Intelligence failures relative to national decision making are also well publicized and again point to decision makers who were not properly prepared to make optimal decisions.[13]

Although it is often difficult to find decision makers who will publicly take the responsibility for having made poor choices, we all know of individuals who, with hindsight, would have done things differently. Unfortunately, we are unaware of anyone who has figured out how to either roll back the clock or to reverse time![14] Making better choices and decisions the first time creates a greater need for effective analysis and intelligence.

Today's managers face an abundance of information in their decision-making contexts, and sometimes this information abundance causes them to be paralyzed. Benjamin Gilad notes how information arriving to top managers is invariably biased, subjective, filtered, and/or late. Analysts have the means for helping reduce both the volume and rate of this information flow while simultaneously assuring the quality of the product being delivered. They can then greatly enhance the executive's actual ability and confidence in effective decision making.

Analysis has been revitalized in the "knowledge" era, or the era of intellectual capital. Whatever we should call it, knowledge is increasingly recognized as a key organizational asset that can distinguish between the winners and losers in many competitive marketplaces.[15] Organizations that can effectively generate, capture, disseminate, and apply knowledge better and faster than their competitors stand a higher probability of achieving successful performance. Analysts are a critical part of this knowledge-oriented process as they are among the primary directors of knowledge in an organization. One thing we hope to emphasize in this book is that analysts must provide direction and guidance to those individuals responsible for collecting data and information. They are the link to gathered data and the organization's key decisions.

Analysis is just as important because of the increased recognition and value on good thinking skills. Analysis cannot be conducted in the absence of thinking. Without it, we would have random choice and luck. This is not the best foundation for a considered outcome and is increasingly likely to suffer from "extinction by instinct." The other end of the continuum is from "paralysis by analysis." That is not to summarily discount the value of instinct, but it has to be measured alongside more reliable and tested methods of analysis.

As access to data or information has increased, the highest value is now placed on not just obtaining appropriate data, but more importantly, to making good sense of it. That's analysis!

The Competitive Context Facing Contemporary Enterprises

Beating competitors, in many industries, has become a necessity rather than a desirable goal. More insightful strategy development and execution has been needed since even a decade ago. We would suggest the following reasons are among the most critical ones underlying increased competition, all of which produce a greater need for improved business and competitive analysis.

Explosion of access to cheap and fast information: Whether it is employee mobility, greater access to higher education in both traditional and online formats, companies showing less loyalty to their employees, or those same employees showing less loyalty to their employers, the window on competition and competitive opportunities has grown wider and more transparent. Because of changing information and communication technology, as well as changing socio-cultural value systems, keeping key competitive information proprietary and out of the sight or hands of competitors has become more difficult than ever before.

Maturation of industries and businesses: Many industries that were prominent in the twentieth century were resource-based industries, such as forest products, manufacturing, steel, and so on. These have rapidly matured or have seen a dramatic slowdown compared to past rates of growth. Many have struggled to institutionalize innovation capabilities, resources, strategies, new resource inputs, new production processes, new product development challenges, new employee skill recruitment and integration, new distribution channels, and/or understanding new customer needs. These are quite different challenges to simply trying to build market share in an existing static and simple market space, and the potential for them to miss the disruptive forms of activity that may be occurring on the fringes of their still-lucrative markets is high.[16]

Loss of traditional means of competitive structuring and advantage: Traditionally, companies could achieve competitive advantage through scale economies, segment entrenchment, first-mover advantages, and other such industry level gains. While still existing in some sectors, these approaches are now so quickly and easily imitated that they no longer deliver sustainable advantage. While the generic strategies of *cost, differentiation,* and *focus* described by Michael Porter are still conceptually fruitful, they are hard to achieve and sustain in practice. In a later paper, Porter himself reconsidered the traditional approaches and concluded that the achievement of advantage is positioning, rather than resource-based.

Sophisticated and better-informed consumers: Customers are better informed than ever before and have access to significantly more information on which to base their purchasing decisions. As with B2B markets, buying habits are less ingrained, and purchases are increasingly based on specification, cost, and value. Today's consumer is less likely to be swayed by an emotional appeal and will do hard-nosed research before striking a deal, especially with big ticket items.

Companies that still think they can sell anything they like, at any price, to a gullible customer may well do so once, but not again. Bad news travels fast, and the presence of customer pressure groups, Internet blogs, and vociferous word-of-mouth channels will quickly damage a brand.

Dynamic and rapidly evolving technology: Physical strengths are being replaced by intangible assets such as intellectual property, knowledge, intelligence, brands, R&D teams, and market position, resulting in volume-based advantages being less prominent.[17] Even in industries where scale-based advantages still exist, typically manufacturing, the continual push by businesses across the globe to improve operational efficiency has made it harder to sustain such advantages.[18] This has made the development of effectiveness-based strategy and execution more critical than ever.

There is little doubt that competition compels organizations to respond, preferably in a proactive manner. Designing these responses and assessing their impact are the primary task of the business and competitive analyst. The context within which the analysis is undertaken and the organization within which the analyst is working, will, inevitably, produce unique demands. The following section elaborates on the unique contextual factors impacting business and competitive analysts.

Contemporary Context Facing the Analyst

Being an analyst in an enterprise facing a high degree of competitive rivalry is difficult, especially when inexperienced and/or lacking appreciation of analysis science. Analysts have always had to satisfy decision makers who want and need their assistance. If anything, the challenge for the analyst today is more daunting than in the past. We think there are several prominent reasons why this state of affairs exists, such as the following:

Lack of recognition that analysts are mission-critical: It is rare to find a student coming onto a business degree program who claims that he or she wants to be a competitive analyst. In contrast, hundreds, if not thousands, will say that they want to be a management accountant, financial analyst, a sales specialist, or a brand manager. Similarly, it is rare to hear a CEO or a CFO claim that their competitive advantage came from their analytical team or their capabilities. We know that analysis underlies many company's competitive advantages, but it is often called something else, or the process is embedded among other functional activities. Enlightened organizations recognize the unique value that analysis generates, and as a result, then put significant resources behind it to ensure that they continue to derive competitive advantage.

Decision makers cannot always articulate their decision needs: Analysis requires proper direction at the outset for the process to produce a satisfactory output. Unfortunately, decision makers may not ask the right questions of the analyst. They may not even know what the questions are. So it is up to the analyst to focus their decision-maker on the "must know," as opposed to the all embracing "like to know" style that we witness too frequently.

Pressure for a quick judgment: Competitors are moving fast, investors and shareholders want the quarterly performance targets on time, customers want solutions yesterday, and nobody is willing to wait. Time is the most precious resource for an analyst; consequently, time will always be in short supply. Decisions are often made on the basis of "what we know now" because the situation simply will not allow for more delay. As such, analysts need to constantly seek established data collection and classification systems that can provide reliable outputs quickly. They need to provide intelligence despite that being at a lower level of confidence than usually expected. Analysts and decision makers need to address the increasingly time-starved context within which they both work and assess its ramifications.

Highly ambiguous situations: Ambiguity comes in many forms for both the decision itself and the analyst. It can emanate from the nature of competition, the range of competitive tactics employed, key stakeholders' responses in a competitive arena, product and/or process enhancements, consumer responses to competitive tactics, and so on. These types of interjections have been studied by researchers who have recognized that ambiguity can be a potent barrier to competitive imitation[19] and allow for a competitor to sustain their advantage for a longer period.

Incrementally received/processed information: Rarely will an analyst get the information he or she needs, in time and in the format they require. The inability of traditional executive information systems to capture, classify, and rank rumors, gossip, grapevine data, and knowledge held by employees out in the field means that analysts lack the kind of primary source information that has always been the "jewel in the crown" element that makes analysis so valuable.[20]

Shifting Organizational Priorities for Analysts and Analysis

We know there has been a fundamental shift in the nature and sequence of organizational priorities for analysts. Though change is not uniform across sectors, it is possible to decipher the outline of a transformation toward improved analytical capabilities through the following principles.

Adding Value to Intelligence: A priority for analysts is to deliver a product that adds context and meaning to raw data and information. In today's information-overloaded environment, intelligence competes for the attention of the decision maker. John Gannon, former Deputy Director of the Central Intelligence Agency, commented, *"It is our challenging but rewarding job to keep telling these smart but overworked folks, decision or policy makers, what's happening in a complicated world."* Keeping ahead of the competition and keeping the attention of intelligence users cannot be taken for granted. Some commentators consider that the insufficient and poor training of analysts has been a primary reason for the low effectiveness of intelligence programs.[21]

One of the ways to stay relevant is to build and maintain subject matter expertise, continuity, and depth within the organization's analytical ranks. Information alone will not be useful to the consumer if it is not interpreted correctly and presented in a credible way by a recognized expert. This issue has been addressed in some organizations through the creation of a senior-level council that is responsible for strategic planning and addresses the areas of CI recruitment, assignments, core skills, standards, and training. Others have relied upon the continuous delivery of learning opportunities, through apprenticeships, traditional classroom, and virtual means, by which analysts can upgrade their capabilities. Finally, some organizations have outsourced to specialist companies who they believe can provide the needed services better than internal resources. The variety of ways that best practice CI organizations have attempted to address this need has been catalogued in several studies.[22]

Answering Questions in Real Time: Analysts have traditionally met intelligence needs through the regular briefings and overviews, usually tailored to the client's needs. These deliveries can also be supplemented with personalized electronic or paper memos that respond to incidental or supplementary questions. Analysts may provide daily or, when a crisis erupts, minute-by-minute support. While the vast majority of an organization's analytical tasks will be carried out in response to specific questions, over the course of a typical year, an analyst or analytical team will provide hundreds of ad-hoc briefings on virtually every aspect of the enterprise.

Concentrating Resources: Analysts must be vigilant about prioritization, and they are expected to use all the latest technology to stay ahead of the competition without wasting scarce resources. Consequently, there is a need to continually press for clarification of a critical intelligence need. Organizations have to find innovative ways to build in flexibility within their collection and analysis efforts so that new priorities can be addressed on as as-needed basis. This flexibility is seldom considered when devising a competitive analysis or intelligence system, but has become increasingly important in a resource-constrained context.

Forging Partnerships: Another priority is how the organization, its data collectors, and analysts relate with the broader community. Partnership is a concept that has taken hold as organizations seek to take advantage of others' specialized expertise and resources. Co-operative efforts between CI and other departments have built formal and informal networks of functional and subject experts throughout the organization. Rarely does all the expertise on any particular issue reside in one part of an organization or a single unit. Tapping into analytic expertise across the firm is important to overcome commonly experienced budget and personnel constraints.

Looking Over the Horizon: The focus on decision-tailored support helps make analysis more relevant and useful to the client. It also ensures that intelligence resources are going where they need to be. Providing such high-level support makes an enormous claim on resources, particular staffing and time. At worst, analysts risk becoming prisoners of their inboxes and unable to put daily events in a broader context, which is essential if they are to provide timely warning of emerging opportunities or threats. The challenge is to step back and consider what the organization might face tomorrow, next week, or next year. Analysts have to look beyond the immediate and the obvious, toward those forces that might be moving slowly but inexorably toward their organization. Giving decision makers a sense of the possible, rather than the probable, must be a key priority for analysts, and it is precisely this that sets them apart from others in the organization.

Providing Timely Support: Analysis is most relevant when it is provided directly to the decision maker. Analysts are at their best when deployed on-site and in regular contact with the organization's managers, negotiating teams, and front-line decision makers. This ensures a better understanding of shifting agendas, prime movers, and quick feedback on their outputs. This all helps to better target the intelligence effort. As mentioned already in this section, time is a luxury that few decision makers enjoy, so anything that puts the analyst closer to the problem can only speed up the solution identification process.

Summary

Excellent analysis is the key to successful insights and/or intelligence and can provide high-value strategic decision support capability in contemporary enterprises. Intelligence about customers, competitors, potential partners, suppliers, and other influential stakeholders is a company's first, and often only, line of offense/defense. Maintaining this capability into the future requires analysts and competitive intelligence practitioners to exploit every opportunity to provide their decision makers with analysis that is persuasive, relevant, timely, perceptive, and actionable. Analysts must provide their decision makers with the essential insight needed to preserve their organization's competitiveness and provide early warnings of market changes.

Contemporary analysts are expected to offer direct and immediate support to resolve different types of queries, work more closely with their counterparts responsible for human and technical collection, package their analyses in a variety of new forms, and deliver them through whatever means are best suited to the recipient.

In fulfilling this mission for the future, competitive intelligence-driven organizations and members of the analytical community face many fresh challenges. Success will be determined, at least in part, by how well these individuals and functions manage their scarce resources, balance frequently conflicting demands, produce longer-term analysis, continue to develop both broad and deep analytic expertise, and forge new relationships with others both inside and outside their organizations. This is not the time for analysts to be resting on their laurels. New ways of working and critical issues are appearing at a far greater pace than in the past. Analysts need all the help they can get to rise to the challenge of tomorrow's demands.

References

American Productivity and Quality Council (APQC) (2000). *Developing a Successful CI Program: Enabling Action, Realizing Results*. Houston, TX: APQC.

Chender, M. (2006). Comments from his speech given to the *KMWorld* webinar, "Creating a Predictable Advantage," January 19, found at www.kmworld.com.

Christensen, C.M. (2000). "Meeting the challenge of disruptive change," *Harvard Business Review*, 78(2), pp. 66–78.

Clark, R.M. (2004). *Intelligence Analysis: A Target-Centric Approach*. Washington, DC: CQ Press.

Dierickx, I., and K. Cool (1989). "Asset stock accumulation and sustainability of competitive advantage," *Management Science*, 35, pp. 1504–1511.

Dishman, P., Fleisher, C.S., and V. Knip (2003). "A chronological and categorized bibliography of key competitive intelligence scholarship: Part 1 1996-2003," *Journal of Competitive Intelligence and Management*, 1(1), pp. 13–79.

Fleisher, C.S., Knip, V., and P. Dishman (2003). "A chronological and categorized bibliography of key competitive intelligence scholarship: Part 2 1990-1996," *Journal of Competitive Intelligence and Management*, 1(2), pp. 11–86.

Fleisher, C.S. (2001). "An introduction to the management and practice of competitive intelligence," pp. 3–18 in Fleisher, C.S., and D.L. Blenkhorn [eds.], *Managing Frontiers in Competitive Intelligence*. Westport, CT: Quorum Books.

Fortune Magazine (2005). *Global 500* listing retrieved from the web on February 20, 2006 at http://money.cnn.com/magazines/fortune/global500/.

Fuld, L.M. (1995). *The New Competitor Intelligence*. New York, NY: John Wiley & Sons.

Gannon, J. (1996). "Intelligence analysis for the 21st century," excerpted from an address delivered November 18 to the Fletcher School of Law and Diplomacy at Tufts University. Source: http://www.cia.gov/cia/di/speeches/42826397.html.

Gilad, B. (1996). *Business Blindspots: Replacing Myths, Beliefs and Assumptions with Market Realities*. London, UK: Infonortics.

Hall, R. (1993). "A Framework Linking Intangible Resources and Capabilities to Sustainable Competitive Advantage," *Strategic Management Journal*, 14 (November), pp. 607–618.

Halliman, C. (2003). "A Look at How a Number of Business and Competitive Intelligence Professionals View or Define the Analysis Process," retrieved April 28, 2003 from http://www.InformationUncover.com/new.htm.

IALEA (2001). *Starting an Analytic Unit for Intelligence Led Policing*. Lawrenceville, NJ: International Association of Law Enforcement Intelligence Analysts, Inc. (IALEA).

Johnston, R. (2005). *Analytic Culture in the U.S. Intelligence Community*. Washington, DC: The Center for the Study of Intelligence.

Knip, V., Dishman, P., and C.S. Fleisher (2003). "A chronological and categorized bibliography of key competitive intelligence scholarship: Part 3 pre-1990," *Journal of Competitive Intelligence and Management*, 1(3), pp. 11–80.

Lackman, C., Saban, K., and J. Lanasa (2000). "Organizing the competitive intelligence function: A benchmarking study," *Competitive Intelligence Review*, 11(1), pp. 17–27.

Mathams, R.H. (1995). "The Intelligence Analyst's Notebook," in *Strategic Intelligence: Theory and Application*, 2d. ed., Washington, DC: Joint Military Intelligence Training Center, pp. 77–96.

McGonagle, J.J., and C.M. Vella (1990). *Outsmarting the Competition: Practical Approaches to Finding and Using Competitive Information*. Naperville, IL: Sourcebooks.

Porter, M.E. (1996). "What is strategy?," *Harvard Business Review*, 74(6), Nov/Dec., pp. 61–78.

Porter, M.E. (1980). *Competitive Strategy: Techniques for Analyzing Industries and Competitors*. New York, NY: Free Press.

Prescott, J.E., and P.T. Gibbons (1993). "Global competitive intelligence: An overview," pp. 1–27 in Prescott, J.E., and P.T. Gibbons [eds.], *Global Perspective on Competitive Intelligence*, Alexandria, VA: Society of Competitive Intelligence Professionals.

Prescott, J.E., Herring, J., and P. Panefly (1998). "Leveraging information for action: A look into the competitive and business intelligence consortium benchmarking study," *Competitive Intelligence Review*, 9(1), pp. 4–12.

Procyshyn, T.W. (1998). "The coming intelligence failure," a white paper found at http://bib.cfc.dnd.ca/irc/nh/nh9798/0069.html, Ottawa Canada: Department of National Defense (DND) Canada.

Rogers, P., and M. Blenko (2005). "The decision-driven organization: Making good decisions and making them happen," A white paper produced for Bain and Company, found at www.bain.com.

Shaker, S., and M. Gembicki (1999). *The WarRoom Guide to Competitive Intelligence*. New York, NY: McGraw Hill.

Tzu, S. (1988). *The Art of War*. Oxford, UK: Oxford University Press.

Waltz, E. (2003). *Knowledge Management in the Intelligence Enterprise*. Boston, MA: Artech House.

Werther, G. (2001). "Building an 'Analysis Age' for Competitive Intelligence in the 21st Century," *Competitive Intelligence Review*, 12(1), pp. 41–47.

Zahra, S., and S. Chaples (1993). "Blind spots in competitive analysis," *Academy of Management Executive*, 7(2), pp. 7–28.

Endnotes

[1] The field of strategy and strategic management is frequently covered in most university business or management curricula. The books used in these courses do a fine job in covering the processes and content of strategy. This book assumes some knowledge of these concepts, but does not require high levels of prior strategy knowledge to be applicable.

[2] Fleisher, C.S., and B. Bensoussan (2003). *Strategic and Competitive Analysis: Methods and Techniques for Analyzing Business Competition*. Upper Saddle River, NJ: Prentice Hall.

[3] We will distinguish between strategic, tactical, and operational decisions types in later chapters. This book's methods will be at least somewhat applicable to all three types, although admittedly it will disproportionately be focused on strategic decisions.

[4] Zahra and Chaples, 1993.

[5] Clark, 2004.

[6] Tzu, 1988.

[7] Shaker and Gembicki, 1999.

[8] Fleisher, 2001.

[9] McGonagle and Vella, 1990; Prescott & Gibbons, 1993.

[10] We recognize that there are likely key conceptual if not practical differences between the terms "business" and "competitive" intelligence. As explaining these differences would require far more detail than we can provide here, we refer readers to Fleisher's discussion of these terms in greater depth in Chapter 5 of the edited book (with D. Blenkhorn) entitled *Controversies in Competitive Intelligence: The Enduring Issues*, Westport, CT: Praeger Publishers (2003).

[11] Dishman, Fleisher, and Knip, 2003; Fleisher, Knip, and Dishman, 2003; Knip, Fleisher, and Dishman, 2003.

[12] Rogers and Blenko, 2005.

[13] For a poignant example of these, Robert Steele does a nice job of identifying the varying nature of the failures that occurred associated with the 9-11 events that dramatically affected the United States. See "What went wrong and why," pp. 3–10 in Steele, Robert David (2002). *The New Craft of Intelligence: Personal, Public & Political*, Oakton, VA: OSS International Press.

[14] This fact won't stop people from trying! This is another reason why strategic decisions need to be made correctly the first time, every time.

[15] Waltz, 2003.

[16] Christensen, 2000.

[17] Hall, 1993.

[18] Porter, 1996.

[19] Dierickx and Cool, 1989.

[20] Chender, 2006.

[21] Werther, 2001.

[22] Namely, APQC (2000), Lackman *et al* (2000), and Prescott *et al* (1998).

2

Performing the Analysis Process

Analysis is, arguably, the most important process underlying how decision makers make sense of their competitive and strategic environment. For analysis to achieve its aims and potential, analysts must be cognizant of this and appreciate how they can best contribute to meeting the organization's needs.

In this chapter, we explore the analysis step that is part of the larger intelligence process, as illustrated in Figure 2.1.

It is difficult to master the task of performing business and competitive analysis (BCA). Few actually can do it well without substantial development and experience. Even those who declare that they have been trained to do it may not be as skilled as they think they are at producing good output. In light of the many business decision-making failures we witness, the only conclusion that can be reached is that relatively few organizations have a well-developed analytical capability. Fewer still leverage that capability over time into achieving competitive advantage.

This chapter looks at the key success factors of performing BCA well. It is designed to help analysts better understand their tasks, their customers, the impact of their output, and the relationships they must build in order to get the job done. Due to their unique importance as part of the larger sense-making process, we discuss common analytical pitfalls in Chapter 3, "Avoiding Analytical Pitfalls," and how to communicate analysis results in Chapter 4, "Communicating Analysis Results."

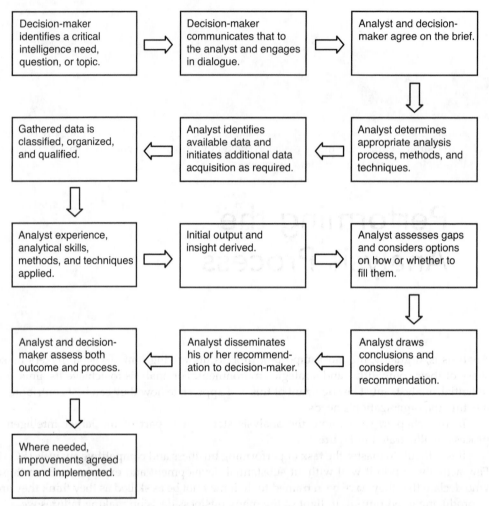

Figure 2.1   Analysis as a function of the larger intelligence project cycle

Understanding the Customers of Analysis

"Basically, the work that we do for our customers, which are our executive leadership, our sales forces, our product managers, and our strategy people, should help them with their customers . . . our approach is very customer-focused; how are we going to help our customers help their customers?"

—Bret Breeding, former Global Corporate Competitive Intelligence Manager for Compaq Computer

The first questions any analyst must answer are "Who are my analysis customers?" and "What are their critical needs?" These can sometimes be difficult to answer, especially if the customers themselves cannot effectively articulate what they want or there are multiple customers with differing agendas. The answers must at least be attempted because without those, the analyst cannot select the right methods. To be truly effective, analysts must understand how their outputs will eventually be used by the decision makers.[1] These individuals may well be one or more steps removed from the analyst's immediate customer.

An analyst's customers or clients[2] are those individuals in the enterprise who are in need of advice and guidance in advance of making an identified decision. We make no distinction here between the level at which a customer may be situated in the enterprise, as we know that analysts provide many decision makers with advice, whether they are working on a strategic, tactical, or operational problem.

The analysis process has a clear starting point when either the analyst identifies an issue himself or a customer makes a request. The process also has an end point when the satisfactory product is delivered to the customer. Having said that, good analysts will communicate with their customers throughout the entire process and will engage in many iterations to improve the final product. An open-minded attitude to the task is essential, as is the recognition that improvement can always be achieved. A delicate ego is a distinct hindrance to improving one's analysis.

Defining the Analysis Problem

Customer needs have to be interpreted before they can be acted upon. This is often the foundation to a successful analysis process. Analyst-customer interaction is critical at all stages of the process, but no more so than at the outset; consequently, time spent here will pay dividends later on. A genuine dialog is needed, as experience has shown us that the issuing of instructions in a one-way manner just does not produce effective results.

Most enterprises attempt to identify, relate to, and then satisfy market-place customers' needs and employ customer needs identification processes and (internal) customer relationship management (CRM) techniques. The relationship that an analyst has with his customer and/or decision maker is no less important. Symmetric, two-way communication is needed to identify an enterprise's actual, as opposed to perceived, intelligence needs.

Helping business and competitive analysts are government intelligence models for identifying national-level intelligence requirements, which have been adapted for commercial use. A popular adaptation is the Key Intelligence Topics (KITs) approach advocated by Jan P. Herring or using Key Intelligence Questions (KIQs). Essentially the same activity, this is a semantic terminology change that is preferred by some firms.

Although Herring suggests that KITs are not a simple management tool or a panacea for analysis efforts, the KIT process delivers three essential benefits:

- It facilitates the identification of legitimate intelligence needs and distinguishes between "need-to-know" and "fishing expedition" projects.

- An initial set of KITs provides a proper foundation for an intelligence program, eventually guiding the determination of CI resources, capabilities, and skills required.

- Being a user-driven model, the KIT process provides a foundation for operational planning to meet and understand both organizational and decision makers' dynamic intelligence needs.

In line with our suggestions in the previous paragraphs, the KIT/KIQ process centers on an interactive dialog between analysts and decision makers. A successful senior intelligence practitioner, Dr. Wayne Rosenkrans, Global Intelligence Director at AstraZeneca Pharmaceuticals, supported this view when he said: *"My advice usually is to spend whatever time is necessary on that KIT-KIQ process at the very beginning. That is so important, and if you get off on the wrong foot, or on a wild goose chase, you'll have wasted all kinds of time."*

Herring classified decision makers' intelligence needs into one of three, not mutually exclusive, categories:

1. Strategic decisions and actions
2. Early-warning topics
3. Descriptions of key marketplace players

The KIT process requires a high-level understanding of the intelligence needs as well as the various types of operations necessary to address them. Herring noted that when done effectively, analysts' use of the KIT process should result not only in identifying the organization's key intelligence needs, but also in creating the critical communication channel necessary to produce credible insight. It also helps to manage expectations.

Fiora, Kalinowski, and others offer help here by suggesting that the analyst assesses each task by addressing each of the following issues:

- Why is this project being proposed?
- Has anyone attempted it before?
- Are there any barriers I should know about?
- What data or information has already been gathered on this topic?
- What analysis process will be needed?
- Who has a stake in the outcome?
- What decisions will be made based on my work?
- How quickly is an answer needed or wanted?
- What are the customer's expectations of me?
- What does the customer want or not want to hear?
- What resources are available to support me?
- Can I do it?
- Is the potential decision worth more than the effort needed?

By managing expectations, analysts can develop mutual respect and trust with their decision makers, and each can better understand the inherent difficulties in the task. Any disconnect that exists between the intelligence analysis planning process and subsequent decision maker could be disastrous for the enterprise.

Identifying the Scope of the Analysis

In the field of BCA, it is crucial to understand the scope of the analysis effort.[3] We suggest that the following four main categories are relevant to the vast majority of analytical efforts conducted within profit-seeking enterprises (see Table 2.1).

Table 2.1
Categories of Analysis

Scope of Analysis	Specific Targets
Competitors	■ Product/brand level
	■ Product category level
	■ Needs-based/generic level
	■ Share of wallet
Environment	■ Competitive
	■ Customer
	■ Economic
	■ Political, legal, regulatory
	■ Social
	■ Technological
Technology	■ Innovation
	■ Product/process
	■ R&D
Decision Location and Decision Maker	■ Strategic decisions
	■ Tactical decisions
	■ Operational decisions

Competitors

Talking of his group's analysis work, Wayne Rosenkrans, Global Intelligence Director at AstraZeneca Pharmaceuticals, said: *"It's all about predicting competitors, either competitor behavior or competitive environment behavior."* The focus of most BCA projects will be on the type of competition and actual competitors present, which requires both art and science. Many new analysts will choose the easy route of letting others tell them what or who the competition is or will use industry and sector classification codes. Although these methods are convenient, they are not necessarily insightful.

Here we adapt the four areas identified by Donald Lehmann and Russell Winer:

■ *Product/brand level* is the narrowest perspective an analyst can take of competition and focuses only on rivals pursuing the same segment with essentially the same offering. An analyst employed by Coca Cola using only this perspective would only look at competing cola brands such as Pepsi, RC Cola, and Virgin Cola.

■ *Product category level* improves this situation by looking at products/services with similar features and attributes. Using our previous example, this would include not only cola brand drinks but other soft drinks such as cherry-flavored colas (Dr. Pepper, Cheerwine), lemon-lime flavored drinks (7-Up, Sprite, Fresca), diet colas, high-caffeine colas, and other varieties of soft drinks.

- *Needs-based/generic-level* competitors seek to satisfy the same functional need of a customer. Again, using our previous example, this would be the generic need to quench a thirst. Many beverages would be in this category, ranging from water, juice, tea, and coffee to beer, wine, and spirits.

- *Share of wallet level* is probably the broadest category of competition and considers any other product that a customer might choose to buy instead of ours.

There are many aspects of a competitor's activity that will attract the attention of a passionate analyst, but it is important to always be mindful of the task in hand and the time scale within which it has to be accomplished. While deconstructing a competitor's quarterly/annual report might be fascinating, if it does not help to answer the KIT/KIQ, then that is valuable time wasted.

Environment

Although we provided a detailed chapter in our last book on macro-environmental (STEEP) analysis,[4] David Montgomery and Charles Weinberg suggest that competitive analysis systems should ideally focus on the following main environmental sectors:

- **Competitive**—Both current and prospective competitors and the means by which they compete

- **Customer**—The firm's current customers, potential customers, and competitor's customers

- **Economic**—Issues such as GNP, inflation, financial markets, interest rates, price regulations, raw material sourcing, fiscal and monetary policy, and exchange rate volatility

- **Political, legal, and regulatory**—Institutions, governments, pressure group, and stakeholders that influence the "rules of the game"

- **Social**—Demographics, wealth distribution, attitudes, and social and cultural characteristics that determine the firm's purchasers

- **Technological**—Current and emerging technologies, product and process innovations, and basic and applied R&D efforts

Analysts often segment the competitive environment into two layers. The macro-environment embraces the largely uncontrollable STEEP factors, and the operational/internal or micro-environment includes the individual, sometimes unique, strengths and weaknesses of the enterprise.

Technology

Technology analysis is principally concerned with the technological base of new or emerging technological capacity.[5] Much technological analysis focuses on evolution of science and scientific activity, such as basic and applied research conducted within government laboratories, hospitals, innovation parks, and universities. One specialized area of competitive analysis falls under the rubric of Competitive Technology Intelligence (CTI). Brad Ashton and Gary Stacey identified three focal areas for CTI:

- **Innovation**—Identifying innovation and in particular, disruptive innovation. Decision makers in technologically driven industries experience rapid change. Consequently, new or different technologies will be needed within a short- to medium-term time period to compete.

- **Product/process**—Attempts to understand the nature and potential results of process improvements. For companies with technology intensive products and/or processes, technology is an important differentiating factor in product features, production steps, or pricing strategy. Those industries that are characterized by frequent product introductions must keep ahead of relevant emerging technologies.

- **R&D**—Many industries have a high proportion of companies with high R&D intensity. As such, they display higher-than-average ratios of R&D expenditures to sales. They are also firms whose R&D portfolio may contain a high proportion of large, long-range products and that are most active in developing innovation, as well as product and process improvements.

The intelligence needs of decision makers in technology environments will vary by industry and position. Ashton and Stacey also noted that scientists and engineers require detailed technical intelligence on technical objectives, manufacturing methods, R&D approaches, and technical contacts. Technical managers often need analysis related to competitors' program funding plans, IP portfolios, partnership approaches and arrangements, R&D strategies, and technology acquisition or transfer strategies. Senior decision makers are frequently concerned with the nature of emerging or potential business alliances, new product introductions, and technical breakthroughs. Marketing decision makers care about competitive product features, product sales, product benefits, and cost/performance/price insights. Last but certainly not least, public policy makers and regulators require analysis to help them establish reasonable policy and regulatory requirements. A flexible approach is therefore needed to respond to the needs of each and every customer.

Decision Location and Decision Maker

Management decisions differ depending on the level of responsibility on which they are made and who makes them. A brief overview is helpful here to put this into context:

- *Strategic decisions* have significant resource allocation impact, set the precedents or tone for decisions further down the organization, and have a potentially material effect on the organization's competitiveness within its marketplace. They are made by top managers and affect the business direction of an organization.

- *Tactical decisions* are less pervasive than strategic ones and involve formulating and implementing policies for the organization. They are usually made by mid-level managers and often materially affect functions such as marketing, accounting, production, a business unit, or product, as opposed to the entire organization. Tactical decisions generally have lower resource implications than strategic decisions and are typically semi-structured.

■ *Operational decisions* support the day-to-day decisions needed to operate the organization and take effect for a few days or weeks. Typically made by a lower-level manager, operational decisions are distinct from tactical and strategic decisions in that they are made frequently and often "on the fly." Operational decisions tend to be highly structured, often with well-defined procedure manuals.

Analysts must remain focused on the critical intelligence needs (CINs) of the decision maker, whatever their hierarchical level. Whether they are senior executives at the business unit or corporate level, middle managers from functional areas, or front-line personnel, each has different needs for the outputs the analyst provides.

The entire issue of geographic complexities can also be added here. In the past, the key focus of analysis would be constrained within national or nation-state boundaries. Today's enterprises increasingly compete in environments that require the analyst to consider all forms of geographical levels of competition, including national, multi-national, and global formats.

Multi-point competition, where a diversified company will compete across a variety of market sectors, is increasingly commonplace. Consequently, the analyst will need to examine how a business can best prepare to simultaneously compete against dozens of other businesses, across multiple segments, and in multiple countries. If a firm competes in fifteen different countries, there may be fifteen separate sets of competitive contexts and rules to which it must conform. When considering all these perspectives, it is perhaps not surprising that the analysis process is seen as a highly skilled and highly complex undertaking.

Intelligence Analysis at Differing Organizational Levels

Intelligence analysis takes place at multiple levels within an organization. The three most common are strategic, tactical, and operational. These match the decision location and decision-maker components discussed previously and as such, Table 2.2 gives guidance on the typical techniques used for intelligence analysis at each level.

Table 2.2
Levels of Intelligence Analysis

Level	Brief Description	Typical Techniques Used
Strategic Intelligence Analysis (SIA)	Provides a framework for the other decision levels and are long-term, mostly infrequently taken, difficult to reverse, resource-intense, and far reaching in nature. Also deals with competitive positioning issues.	■ Opportunity and threat assessments ■ Sector/competitor assessments ■ Trend analyses ■ Anomaly detection ■ Impact assessments
Tactical Intelligence Analysis (TIA)	Links macro-level analysis and micro-level focus on individual and specified matters. Supports decisions that are less pervasive than strategic decisions, typically involves formulating and implementing policies for the organization. Operates principally at the functional level.	■ Cluster and pattern analyses ■ Stimulus-response analysis ■ Value constellation analysis

Table 2.2 *(continued)*
Levels of Intelligence Analysis

Level	Brief Description	Typical Techniques Used
Operational Intelligence Analysis (OIA)	Supports the day-to-day decisions needed to operate the organization. These decisions affect the organization for relatively shorter periods of time.	■ Many of these will be similar to operational products, usually focused on shorter time frames and more immediate activity.

Strategic Intelligence Analysis (SIA)

SIA is arguably the most vital form of intelligence because it provides a framework within which other forms of intelligence collection and analysis take place. It helps to discern and make sense of important trends, to identify and extract patterns that would otherwise not be visible, and to provide an overall picture of the evolving opportunity and threat environment. SIA also provides guidance for tactical and operational assessments, and work done at these levels in turn helps to shape the strategic intelligence focus. As strategic analytic methodologies mature, they will also offer the basis for predictive or anticipatory assessments that can serve to provide warning of potential high-impact activities.

Treatments on the kind of specific techniques and tools that the business analyst might use exist,[6] but generic analytical initiatives that would fall under the rubric of strategic intelligence analysis include the following:

- **Opportunity and Threat (O&T) Assessments**—Used to assess the levels of dependence and vulnerabilities of critical issues, competitive changes that could cause significant impact, and the likelihood of such activities taking place.

- **Sector/Competitor Assessments**—Focus on emerging or threatening competitors that provide strong potential for impacting the competitive terrain.

- **Trend Analyses**—Baseline assessments to better recognize departures from current practice, especially those that shape the industry's future.

- **Anomaly Detection**—Requires systematic "environmental scanning," as well as the coalescing of tactical and operational intelligence reports that identify and highlight specific deviations from the norm.

- **Impact Assessments**—The macro-level view taken in SIA offers a good approach for assessing probable cascade effects of threatening competitive action and activity.

Tactical Intelligence Analysis (TIA)

TIA is a necessary and important complement to work done at the strategic level. It is the natural link between macro- and micro-level analysis. Although SIA provides the framework for TIA, these assessments in turn feed SIA. With a dynamic symbiotic relationship between the two, mutual strength is derived.

Typical techniques used in TIA are the following:

- **Cluster and Pattern Analysis**—Identifies the use of particular marketplace attack methods, commonalities of targets, and attempts to build profiles of competitors.

- **Stimulus-Response Analysis**—Identifies actions that could be taken by competitors in response to specific events. This analysis could be used both proactively to develop warnings or reactively to design future tactics.

- **Value Constellation Analysis**—Identifies the key stakeholders, important partners, allies, joint venture prospects, outsourcing potential, and agents that a company could utilize.

Operational Intelligence Analysis (OIA)

Unlike its two more broadly based IA cousins, OIA is often event-centric and single-case-oriented. It provides more immediate but lesser-lasting benefits and typically involves technological assessments of methods used for marketplace battles or investigations of competitive threats. It is frequently focused on helping the analyst understand in real-time a particular event; such as a competitor who is attempting to perform competitive intelligence efforts of your enterprise. This can be especially helpful for counter-intelligence and can keep your company's efforts from being prematurely disclosed.

An important component of OIA is vulnerability analysis and recommending how these can be minimized or eliminated. Vulnerability analysis can be used to look both at the enterprise's marketplace vulnerabilities as well as, more tactically, the competitive intelligence process being employed.

Evaluating the Inputs to Analysis

It is critical that analysts can credibly evaluate their data and information. In weighing the credibility of inputs, they have to consider the nature of their sources and reliability. In the intelligence community, this is often described as the process of determining "bona fides."

There are a series of questions that should be kept in mind when examining sources, as follows:

- **Reliability**—Can the source of the information be trusted to deliver reliable information to the analyst? Does the source have a "track record" for delivering credible inputs? The U.S. military uses the following information evaluation scale to assess reliability:[7]
  - ❑ "A" Completely reliable
  - ❑ "B" Usually reliable
  - ❑ "C" Fairly reliable
  - ❑ "D" Not usually reliable
  - ❑ "E" Unreliable
  - ❑ "F" Reliability unknown

- **Accuracy**—Have the data inputs been captured "first hand," or have they been filtered? Is there any reason to think that there might be any deception involved? Is the source able to communicate the data precisely? Is the source truly competent and knowledgeable about the information they provide? Do they have a known vested interest, hidden agenda, or other bias that might impact the information's accuracy? Can the source's data be verified by other sources or otherwise triangulated?

- **Availability**—Unavailable data is not going to help the analyst do his or her work. It is critical that the analyst does not rely solely on one source. Are there credible substitutes that can be used? Can sources be accessed quickly?

- **Ease of access**—What is the financial opportunity and time cost to access the source? Is this the best use of limited resources, or can equivalent data be gained with lesser expenditure? Does the source speak the right language, or will translation be needed? If so, what are the dangers of misunderstanding and/or incorrect reporting?

Once analysts have addressed their sources, they need to make sense of what has been gathered. The next section talks about the preliminary stage in sense-making—that of qualifying the raw data and information before it is subjected to analytical processing.

Making Sense of the Analysis

Analysts ultimately respond to decision makers' needs for knowledge. This brings up the key question of what we mean by the word "knowledge." In this book, we conceptualize knowledge as that which people in the enterprise either know they know or perceive that they know. Knowledge is definitely an asset of the enterprise and is referred to by analysts as evidence, the basis upon which they can perform further assessment.

Knowledge can be further broken down into five interrelated elements, all of which are important for analysts to understand in carrying out their responsibilities.[8]

Facts

Verified information, something known to exist or to have occurred. These are unambiguously true statements and are known to be so. Facts come in any form and will be found among virtually any source of data that enters an employee's awareness, or the enterprise's communication and information systems. It is surprising how few enterprises subject their collected data and information to fact checking and verification processes. This becomes even more important for strategy decision-making purposes because many of the facts about competitors and competition are time-sensitive. What may be accurate today may be dangerously incorrect tomorrow.

Perceptions

Perceptions are impressions or opinions that fall short of being facts, but which are supported to some extent by underlying data or logic. These are often expressed as thoughts or opinions in language such as: *"I think that . . ."* or *"My view is . . ."* It is important for the analyst to subject these thoughts and opinions to tests to establish which can be converted into facts and which have to remain as perceptions for the time being. There is nothing wrong in factoring perceptions into the analysis process, just as long as everybody knows that this is what they are. The error comes when perceptions are mistakenly regarded and treated as facts when they are not. The use of perceptions is perhaps the most exciting element to subject to subsequent analysis, especially when using scenario analysis, war-gaming, what-if analysis, and other such future-oriented techniques.

Beliefs

Beliefs are often drawn from a mix of facts and perceptions and commonly describe cause-effect relationships. They can be either explicit or implicit, but they too need to be subjected to verification and justification. Beliefs often color the way individuals understand their world and the way in which they think about the future. Therefore, it becomes critical in the analysis process for beliefs to be aired and made transparent to those individuals who are key parts of the process, whether these individuals are data gatherers, analysts, or decision makers.

Assumptions

This is the knowledge that individuals take for granted. These can come in the form of any of the previously described categories and may refer to things that have occurred in the past, present, or can be fairly safely predicted as going to happen in the future. Explicit assumptions are those that are consciously adopted by the analyst, are well understood, and are shared. Implicit assumptions are those that individuals in the analysis process do not consciously elicit, share, or articulate and may not even be aware of. Valuable as they are, as with perceptions and beliefs, assumptions need to be consistently and constantly challenged to reflect changing situations and a shifting competitive landscape.

Projections

Projections are composed of a mixture of facts, perceptions, beliefs, and assumptions. They are justified or substantiated judgments about the future. It is again important that the analyst be able to powerfully defend or justify their projections as they become a critical part of the knowledge base underlying the decisions made.

Synthesis

Having identified the type of knowledge in place, the analyst can proceed with greater confidence toward a high-quality output. Qualified inputs are then subjected to the real heart of analysis—the thinking processes, sifting, synthesis, induction, deduction, abduction, experimentation, mathematical conceptualization, experimentation, research, application of methods, techniques, and a vast array of other activities all designed to generate unique and actionable insights.

An important element to the analysis process is that of infrastructure support, or those technological parts of the analysis process that are complementary to the analysis and analysis process itself. The following section provides an overview of the key facets of analysis infrastructure that can encourage and permit the analyst to produce their best work.

Infrastructure to Support the Analysis Process

One facet of analysis infrastructure that has become more prominent in recent years is the growth of information systems support. When we refer to information systems in this book, we are specifically referring to combinations of software and hardware that are utilized to support information gathering, classification, synthesis, and dissemination. These are often referred to under alternative rubrics such as management information systems (MIS), decision support systems (DSS), enterprise information systems (EIS), enterprise resource planning systems (ERP), executive information systems (ExIS), business intelligence systems (BI), marketing information systems (MkIS), and knowledge management systems (KM), among others. Firms have also developed information support systems to which they refer by their own unique names. The function of each remains the same—providing support for the analysis process and enhancing sense-making.

The entire subject of system support would require book-length treatments to properly describe what we know and their ability to support the business and competitive analysis process. This book focuses on carrying out business and competitive analysis, and as such, we highlight what we deem to be the key elements that analysts should consider as they use these systems to support them in their work.

Intelligence Solutions

Unfortunately for most of the readers of this book, competitive analysts generally have not been well supported by the information systems introduced by organizations. Most were not purpose-designed to support BCA tasks, and as such, they have not and maybe cannot replace or substitute for the human cognitive and mental processes that analysts uniquely develop and employ.[9]

Successful analysts require the support of dedicated information systems, both formal, informal, human, and technical. These systems can, among other things, allow the manipulation of data for multi-dimensional visualization of phenomena and for mapping relationships. Effective systems also operate in real-time and have filters to make sure that the data and information the analyst works with is traceable, to provide the ability to assess validity and reliability.

Analysts are ordinarily uninvolved in the selection of management information systems and usually have to work with what is already there in the larger enterprise or what can be afforded. Fortunately, there has been an upswing in the nature and number of intelligence software solutions. Intelligence solutions have become one of the hotter topics in today's boardrooms. Recognizing their needs in this area, corporations have energized a burgeoning market for intelligence consulting, software, and services solutions.

Limitations of Intelligence Solutions

Essentially, decision makers want concise information they can act on. Typically, they get bits and pieces of data or stacks of undigested reports, leaving them to fill in the blanks. Effective intelligence solutions are designed not to create more information, but to create better information. Used properly, intelligence solutions can reduce the amount of information being transmitted; nevertheless, it is wise to be aware of their limitations.

Some commercial intelligence solutions have attempted to provide the "holy grail" of intelligence with artificial intelligence, knowledge trees, or executive decision support systems, which take the inputted information and perform a number of "tests" on it to alert the analyst to when certain data parameters have been triggered. Virtually all intelligence-related software provides the basic means for organizing and categorizing information, but precious few take it to the next step to where inferences can be drawn or insight achieved.

Nearly all commercial intelligence solutions fall short in the qualitative arena, which is what intelligence analysis has traditionally been about. There is little evidence of intelligence software that provides the kind of discovery through spatial, timeline, and relationship analysis that trained analysts routinely perform.[10] Analysis of soft data means seeing just around the corner, appreciating why a rival made certain visits to different competitors or provincial officials, or the competitor's CEO has voiced certain views. Few intelligence solutions are able to look around the corner, especially when that corner is on a different street or in a country where the written and spoken language differs markedly from the analyst's enterprise.

What the software industry generally has not grasped is that competitive intelligence is traditionally defined as information that has been analyzed to the point where a person can make a decision. Software generally does not analyze. It can perform rudimentary and even sophisticated statistical analysis on convenient data, but still requires interpretation. Reality dictates that most analysis is done on the less convenient data that employees encounter but mostly do not recognize to be an important piece of the intelligence puzzle. This highlights the importance of combining human/expert knowledge and organizational data with a sophisticated, purpose written, software product, to form an effective intelligence solution. These things can rarely be bought "off-the-shelf."

Organizations also use groupware or intranet-based technologies to organize and categorize the internal expertise of a company. These packages generally do an unsatisfactory job of relating one source to another and providing additional leads to the analyst who needs to locate another bit of data. Most packages fail to organize the data and simply generate long lists, crudely ranking the inputs by relevancy.

Managing the Internal Network

For the analysis process to succeed, analysts must be part of established networks aimed at facilitating intelligence sharing throughout the organization. This allows the analyst to access individuals who can provide bits of data or information that can often be the "missing piece" in their emergent analytic puzzles. Even if individuals in the internal network do not have the critical information, they can often point out those individuals who may have it. Other functions, such as human resources management, public relations, business development, and marketing and sales, also obtain important pieces of intelligence that needs to be shared.

For analysts in smaller enterprises or organizations that are lacking the financial resources to set up a dedicated analysis function, networks can be *the* most powerful way to accomplish their roles. Many smaller companies have established their intelligence networks with the purpose of providing a source for best practices, a repository of particular forms or types of data, or for helping to identify other key sources.[11] Figure 2.2 illustrates how an internal network can begin to take shape and the functions from where network participants are frequently drawn.

Analysts use their network partners to bounce their ideas, to test their insights, or to communicate initial findings. This helps to provide preliminary feedback on how the decision maker may react to the news. It is critical that these contacts take place in a mutually beneficial fashion, as the creation of "two-way" communication among members of a network is one of the best ways for ensuring that the network can be used for maximal benefit.[12]

When internal networks are created electronically and exist primarily in a digital format, it is critical that participation and contributions can be made conveniently and quickly. If they are not, then members will not use it.[13]

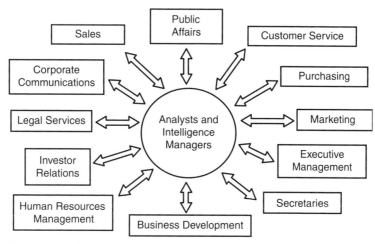

Figure 2.2   Participants of internal networks

Managing the External Network

External networks are also a key part of the analyst's contact universe. It is vital that analysts establish, maintain, and constantly qualify and update a set of contacts outside the firm, as certain types of research cannot be accomplished without them. Analysts must be able to access industry experts, industry associations, industry commentators, stock analysts, government experts, government departments, civil servants, respected journalists, subject specialists, and broadcasters to obtain needed data or access to other important stakeholders. Analysts that network with professionals from other non-competing or consulting firms can gain insight into effective practices.[14] It is important to note here that networks may not be viewed as providing immediate and obvious benefits. John Shumadine, Director of Competitive Intelligence for Deloitte and Touche, states it clearly when he says: *"But it sometimes takes years to develop a Rolodex within your own industry, a repository of information and a collection of individuals that you can network with. There's not an immediate payback."* Nevertheless, these networks are typically essential to long-term business and competitive analysis success.

Proactivity, Efficiency, and Perpetual Learning

Analysts need to be highly proactive, not only delivering the needed intelligence for their decision makers today, but also figuring out ways by which they can augment their organization's analysis capabilities for the future.

Developing increased expertise at searching, classifying, qualifying, and organizing data can be a very beneficial time saver for analysts. They also need to develop the ability to cut through the "noise" and get to the heart of an issue. They need to be able to remove the unnecessary trappings and keep only the essential bits that make the difference. The Pareto principle, whereby 20% of the information will provide 80% of the insight, nearly always rings true in analysis work. Better analysts also hone their project and time management skills over time. We know of few long-term analysts who are poor at this, and, in reality, it is one of the key competencies that effective analysts must eventually display.

Another key task for the analyst is to learn how to quickly deal with the flood of data and information that comes in on a daily basis. An analogy is considering how a quick keyword entry using any one of the many search engines available on the World Wide Web generates thousands of "hits" and how only a few of these will actually be relevant to the searcher's goals. By systematically capturing learning from prior projects, integrating their efforts across projects, building the capabilities of their supporting information systems, leveraging their networks more effectively, and last but not least, by educating their customers in ways that improves their mutual relationship, significant advances in business and competitive analysis can be made.

Summary

L.M. Fuld noted that three elements were part of the successful competitive intelligence operations that he had examined:

- **Constancy**—Information is gathered and analyzed constantly, not just during the traditional strategic planning cycle or on a just-in-time basis.
- **Longevity**—Intelligence program investments were for the longer term. Six months, one year, or even two years may not be enough to prove the worth of a program. The most successful and enduring intelligence systems had taken three to five years to mature.
- **Involvement**—The more people saw the development and use of intelligence as a key component of their jobs, the more readily available the intelligence was and the more it was used.

These three facets of success are not commonly experienced by competitive analysts. Most claim that they are not properly supported in terms of information systems, access to key decision makers, access to data or information, or most importantly, the time needed to effectively perform their tasks. Properly allocating resources is critical if the analysis function and individuals doing it are to be effective.

In examining analysis practiced in a number of organizations in the last twenty years, we have identified a set of characteristics that are present in those organizations that have maintained the greatest longevity. These are reflected in Fleisher and Bensoussan's 10 Commandments for Business and Competitive Analysis, and they provide a beneficial summary to the lessons that should be captured by analysts and their superiors from reading this chapter.

Fleisher and Bensoussan's 10 Commandments for Business and Competitive Analysis

1. Analysis should underlie and be an integral part underlying *every one* of your organization's important competitive and strategic decisions.
2. Decision-making customers shall use only *analyzed data* to direct competitive decision-making, planning, and subsequent actions.

3. Analytic processes should be performed in a timely manner and *products delivered to clients well in advance* of their need to use them in decision-making.

4. Analytic products must contain *conclusions and recommendations* effectively presented in the optimal format to customers for their consideration.

5. Analysts shall not confuse *data compilations*, digests, newsletters, static portals, or summaries with analysis.

6. Analysis must be *FAROUT©* and able to be relied upon to strike the best balance among these elements.

7. Analysis outputs (products, advice, services, etc.) will be negotiated based on the *client's specification* to ensure that the KIT is achievable.

8. Analysis should *reflect all relevant data* available, from all legitimate/legal means and sources.

9. Analysis should utilize the best and most current *methods, tools, and techniques* available (like the ones included in this book and beyond).

10. Analysis must be regularly *evaluated* by both its producers as well as consumers for its contribution to your organization's mission and goals.

References

Ashton, W.B., and G.S. Stacey (1995). "Technical intelligence in business: Understanding technology threats and opportunities," *International Journal of Technology Management*, 10(1), pp. 79–104.

Belkine, M. (1996). "Intelligence analysis as part of collection and reporting," pp.151–164 of Part B. in Gilad, B., and J. Herring [eds.], *The Art and Science of Business Intelligence Analysis*. Greenwich, CT: JAI Press.

Bouthillier, F., and K. Shearer (2003). *Assessing Competitive Intelligence Software: A Guide to Evaluating CI Technology*. Medford, NJ: Information Today, Inc.

Carr, M.M. (2003). *Super Searchers on Competitive Intelligence: The Online and Offline Secrets of Top CI Researchers*. Medford, NJ: Cyberage Books.

Chender, M. (2006). Comments from his speech given to the *KM World* webinar, "Creating a Predictable Advantage," January 19, found at www.kmworld.com.

Clark, R.M. (2004). *Intelligence Analysis: A Target-Centric Approach*. Washington, DC: CQ Press.

Fiora, B. (2003). "Applying consulting skills to CI projects—Part 1," *Competitive Intelligence Magazine*, 6(3), pp. 53–54.

Fleisher, C.S., and B. Bensoussan (2003). *Strategic and Competitive Analysis: Methods and Techniques for Analyzing Business Competition*. Upper Saddle River, NJ: Prentice Hall.

Fuld, L.M. (2003). *Intelligence Software Report 2003: Leveraging the Web*. Private report by Fuld & Company, Boston, Massachusetts.

Fuld, L.M. (1995). *The New Competitor Intelligence*. New York, NY: John Wiley & Sons.

Fuld, L.M., and K. Sawka (2000). "Money can't buy you smarts," *CIO Magazine*, 1 October.

Herring, J. (2002). "KITs revisited—their use and problems," *SCIP Online*, 1(8), May 2.

Herring, J. (1999). "Key intelligence topics: A process to identify and define intelligence needs," *Competitive Intelligence Review*, 10(2), pp. 4–14.

Kalinowski, D.J. (2003). "Managing expectations: Will clients ever fully understand?" *Competitive Intelligence Magazine*, 6(6), pp. 25–29.

Lehmann, D.R., and R.S. Winer (2002). *Analysis for Marketing Planning*, 5th ed. New York, NY: McGraw-Hill Irwin.

McGonagle, J., and C. Vella (2003). *The Manager's Guide to Competitive Intelligence*. Greenwich, CT: Praeger Books.

Montgomery, D.B., and C.B. Weinberg (1998). "Toward strategic intelligence systems," *Marketing Management*, 6 (Winter), pp. 44–52.

Nikkel, P. (2003), "How can we determine which CI software is most effective: A framework for evaluation," pp. 163–175 in Fleisher, C., and D. Blenkhorn [eds.], *Controversies in Competitive Intelligence: The Enduring Issues*. Westport, CT: Praeger.

O'Connor, T.R. (2003). "The skills of an intelligence analyst," North Carolina Wesleyan College, http://faculty.ncwc.edu/toconnor/392/spy/analskills.htm, March.

Page, A.M. (1996). "The art and science of collection management," pp. 181–206 of Part B. in Gilad, B., and J. Herring [eds.], *The Art and Science of Business Intelligence Analysis*. Greenwich, CT: JAI Press.

Ringdahl, B. (2001). "The need for business intelligence tools to provide business intelligence solutions," pp. 173–184 in Fleisher, C., and D. Blenkhorn [eds.], *Managing Frontiers in Competitive Intelligence*. Westport, CT: Quorum Books.

Senge, P. (1990). *The Fifth Discipline: The Art and Practice of the Learning Organization*. New York, NY: Currency Doubleday.

Skryzowski, L. (2003). "Building a CI network from scratch," *Competitive Intelligence Magazine*, 6(3), pp. 39–41.

Endnotes

[1] McGonagle and Vella, 2003.

[2] Similar to actual practice, we will use these terms interchangeably in this book, recognizing that there are subtle differences between the two terms.

[3] Clark, 2004.

[4] See Fleisher and Bensoussan, 2003, Chapter 17.

[5] See, in particular, Chapters 21 through 25 of this book, which focus on technological phenomena.

[6] Fleisher and Bensoussan, 2003.

[7] Page, 1996.

[8] Belkine, 1996; Fahey, 1999; O'Connor, 2003; Senge, 1990.

[9] Fuld, 2003.

[10] Bouthillier and Shearer, 2003; Fuld and Sawka, 2000; Nikkel, 2002; Ringdahl, 2001.

[11] Skryzowski, 2003.

[12] Skryzowski, 2003.

[13] Chender, 2006.

[14] McGonagle and Vella, 2003.

Avoiding Analysis Pitfalls

This chapter illustrates the common barriers or obstacles to business and competitive analysis (BCA) effectiveness in contemporary enterprises. Analysis of failure is an elusive concept, and research of analysts about their understanding and experiences of these terms have produced little, if any, consensus.[1] We, the book's authors, are typically uncomfortable when we hear analysts or their clients claim that, "I'll know it when I see it."

It hardly needs to be said that organizations and managers can learn from failures if individuals thoughtfully talk about and examine them, something that is rarely done except in cases of catastrophic, publicly visible failures[2] that cannot escape the media's glare. Unfortunately, by their very nature, adverse results and failures are rarely, if ever, discussed in the normal course of organizational affairs. Our premise in identifying the possibility and causes of analytical failure is that we believe that much can be learned by managers and practitioners from studying failures and that this learning can ultimately contribute to creating a more successful analysis function. As such, we begin with a discussion about what constitutes analysis of failure.

Analysis of Failure

Although analysis of failure is an accepted part of contemporary industry practice, its application to an enterprise's intelligence, planning, and decision-making functions is comparatively rare. There is a hierarchy of failure, though, and we examine this now.

Failure Location

We would regard the highest level of analysis failure to be that of business failure, whereby a business is no longer able to continue as a viable commercial entity. If failure is defined as "discontinuance of business," the percentage is likely around two-thirds of all start-ups will fail within their first ten years,[3] and at even higher rates in some particularly difficult sectors such as retailing and restaurants. Most of these business failures are commonly attributed to a general lack of effective planning and management skills exhibited by these firms' executives.

Beneath the level of the firm, we encounter planning, decision-making, and implementation failures. Because we are concerned in this book with the BCA function in contemporary enterprises, we recognize planning and decision-making failures as being at least partly composed of intelligence failures. These can be further disaggregated into failures along the traditional "intelligence cycle" functions of planning, data collection, analysis, and dissemination/communication.

Intelligence failures are distinguishable from more task-oriented intelligence errors, which are viewed as factual inaccuracies in analysis resulting from poor or missing data. Intelligence failure is defined by R. Johnston as "systemic organizational surprise resulting from incorrect, missing, discarded, or inadequate hypotheses." These failures may be due, at least in part, to failed analysis, but they can also be caused by other factors that interact with the analysis process. Attempting to disentangle or disaggregate the analysis portion of the process from other related processes is never an easy or straight-forward task. At a minimum, it is important that analysts and their decision makers always carry out a post-mortem on major projects to try and determine any areas for improvement.

Having suggested the need for post-task assessment of the analysis process, we recognize that there are a variety of problems associated with the evaluation of intelligence analysis and reporting that make this task more challenging.[4] For example, the range of cognitive biases impacting this process is outlined in greater depth in J.R. Heuer Jr.'s excellent book entitled *Psychology of Intelligence Analysis*. Briefly summarized, he notes that

- Analysts normally overestimate the accuracy of their past judgments.
- Intelligence clients or consumers normally underestimate how much they learned from analysis products such as reports or briefs.
- Overseers of intelligence production who conduct post-mortem analyses of an intelligence failure normally judge that events were more readily foreseeable than was, in fact, the case.

Suffice it to say, a variety of assessment methods must be used in evaluating the analysis and its complementary/supplementary processes to reduce the presence and impact of bias.

Sources of Failure

When analysis is ineffective, both the analyst and the decision maker often don't recognize it in time and frequently cannot identify the root cause(s) of the errors, problems, or failure. They must consider the following questions underlying the potential errors, some of which may also be causes of failure. Errors that we recognize as commonly occurring in performing the analysis task include the following:

- **Analysis problem definition**—Was the analysis problem, the key intelligence topic, or key intelligence question (KIT, KIQ) properly specified at the outset? Did the analysis process allow for any subsequent redefinitions of the problem?

- **Analysis project planning**—Did the analyst develop a project management plan or statement of work to perform the analysis process? Did they actually implement the process according to their plan or veer away from it mid-course?

- **Data-gathering error**—Was the appropriate data available to the analyst? If not, could the data have been efficiently acquired? Did the analyst properly account for data or information gaps? Was the analysis the cause of the failure, or was data collection the primary cause?

- **Tool- and technique-related error**—Did the analyst use the best available tools, techniques, and/or analysis methods? Were the right tools used and in the right sequence and combination?

- **Synthesis error**—Did the analyst arrive at the optimal conclusion or insight? Did they "connect the dots" in a logical and defensible manner? Would other experienced and successful analysts have connected them differently?

- **Communication transmission or channel error**—Did the analyst communicate their insights to their decision maker throughout the project in an optimal fashion? Was the analysis failure really a communication failure?

- **Communication reception error**—Did the decision maker have a complete and accurate understanding of the analyst's conclusions before the decision needed to be made?

- **Unsystematic development error**—Did (uncontrollable) events arise during the course of the process that derailed the analysis or analyst? What impact did unexplained variance or random factors have on the outcome of the analysis task?

Four-Level Hierarchical Model of Analysis Failures

Whatever the outcomes experienced for analysis errors or failures, it is valuable to identify the reasons why these happen. We have developed a four-leveled taxonomy for identifying the barriers to generating effective competitive analysis.[5] The four levels are as follows:

1. The individual analyst
2. The analysis task itself
3. The organizational context within which the task is conducted
4. The external environment in which the organization is ensconced

These four levels and the primary factors associated with each are illustrated in Table 3.1.

Table 3.1
Four-Level Hierarchical Model of Analysis Failures

Level	Nature of Problem
Individual Analyst-Level Failures	■ Different natural analytical abilities ■ Naturally limited mental capacities ■ Natural motivation ■ Cognitive biases and perceptual distortion ■ Insufficient understanding and application of analysis tools and techniques
Analysis Task-Level Failures	■ Part of larger task ■ Task discontinuity ■ Unsatisfactory data inputs ■ Disconnects from decision making ■ Imbalance among key task facets
Internal Organizational-Level Failures	■ Some decision makers don't understand and appreciate analysis ■ Clients cannot specify their critical intelligence needs or questions ■ Under-resourcing the analysis function ■ Lack of analysis-specific IT support ■ Lack of thinking time ■ Organizational culture and politics ■ Time and trust ■ Invisibility and mystery ■ Misconception that everyone can do analysis
External Environment-Level Failures	■ Growing range of competitive factors ■ Complexity and turbulence ■ Data overload ■ Globalization ■ Educational deficiencies

In the section that follows, we identify the most common problems we have found in our research at each of these four levels. We recognize that some of the factors may not be present in only the single category we ascribed it, but may also be present in one or more of the other levels. We have placed the factor at the level where we have most frequently observed it being an obstacle to effective analysis, recognizing that it may have secondary or tertiary impacts at another level.

Individual Analyst-Level Failures

The BCA task is fundamentally performed by individual analysts, although these analysts also need to cooperate and collaborate with others in their firm to get their tasks accomplished. We see the following hindrance factors as being primarily present at the level of the individual analyst. They are not listed in the order of occurrence or of perceived importance, but these are the half-dozen distinct items we have identified as being most commonly present.

Different natural analytical abilities: People rely on a limited set of mental models, have preconceptions on issues, and exhibit a wide range of cognitive bias when reviewing information. People also think differently. Some predominate cognitively in a right-brained linear fashion; others in a left-brained lateral fashion. This is important when viewed in light of analysis being a mixture of both scientific and nonscientific techniques.

Naturally limited mental capacities: The content and context facing most analysts has become more complicated, complex, and fast moving in recent years. Having said that, our brain's natural abilities to effectively process additional information hasn't evolved correspondingly to match this. The popular view that we only use 10% of our brain's ability is a well-worn myth, and one could argue with the figure, but we are confident that human beings still only use a limited percentage of their brain capacity, although scientific record still does not have a sense of what that true percentage might be.[6]

G.A. Miller suggested that the magical number describing our natural information processing capabilities is seven things at one time plus or minus two. This could be a major problem for analysts who often have a far higher number of issues to keep in their mental calculus at any one time. Although we now have better information technology systems to assist in the analysis task, we still mainly use our brains in the same ways as we have always done.

Natural motivation: Given a choice between a more difficult and a less difficult task with identical outcomes, the majority of people opt for the easier task. As we hope is already patently obvious by now, analysis is not an easy task. It can require the use or expenditure of tremendous cognitive, intellectual, organizational, and social resources to properly accomplish. One reason it is so difficult is because we have far fewer published heuristics or "rules of thumb" to use in performing analysis than we do in many other fields of organizational endeavor. Some analysts think that volume of analysis outputs is the answer, not their value. This form of sufficing behavior will probably fail to meet the needs of today's demanding decision-making clients.

Cognitive biases and perceptual distortion: In spite of the presence of the broad range of analytical techniques, some organizations still adopt poor strategies, and their decision-making processes are vulnerable to individual cognitive biases or "groupthink." Researchers have identified a variety of common cognitive biases that can enter into an individual's or group's process of analysis.[7] These include the following:

Estimation Bias—Over or under estimation of the magnitude of future events.

Escalating Commitment—The commitment of more and more resources such as time, effort, data, and funds to an idea, course of action, project, or program, even after there is growing evidence that it is failing.

Groupthink—This occurs when a group of decision makers embarks on a poorly determined course of action without thoroughly questioning the underlying assumptions of the decision. This is most prevalent in organizations with entrenched leadership, engrained cultures, and senior executives who dislike being challenged.

Illusion of Control—An individual with misplaced confidence in his or her ability to "always get it right" and to control things. Often found among senior executives who have been fortunate enough to get it right so far. Illusion of control and groupthink are common bed-fellows.

The Prior Hypothesis Bias—Beliefs about the relationships between variables, even when presented with contradictory analytical evidence. Individuals prone to this bias use data only when it confirms their beliefs while ignoring data that does not.

Reasoning by Analogy—Individuals will use simple analogies to make sense out of challenging problems. Oversimplifying complex problems is dangerous and can mislead an analyst to offer a detrimental judgment.

Representativeness—A bias that violates statistical law in individuals who tend to generalize from small samples to explain larger phenomena. Analysts are at risk of this when they hear from one or two influential individuals that an incident or action is taking place, and they immediately accept this as truth without further investigation.

The existence of cognitive biases and groupthink raises issues of how to bring critical intelligence to bear on organizational decision-making mechanisms so that the decisions made are realistic. It is important to understand the range of motives behind it. M.S. Feldman and J.G. March pointed out that people in organizations often tend to collect more information than strictly necessary for decision making, partly to influence others and partly to be seen as "rational." In other words, analysis is often used not just for objective decision-making but also for political or symbolic purposes.

Insufficient understanding and application of analysis tools and techniques: Studies on the use of analysis tools and techniques by business practitioners have consistently demonstrated that the individuals responsible will use only a very limited set of tools and techniques, usually those they know the best and have previously applied with some perceived success.[8] We previously illustrated this problem as a "tool rut."[9] Even when analysts are willing to acquire and then use an enlarged tool box and attempt tools and techniques outside their ordinary fare, they often lack the knowledge, understanding, and experience to apply it effectively. It is no surprise therefore, that they will stick to the safe but well-worn path of familiarity.

Analysis Task-Level Failures

A number of factors associated with the analysis task itself can be responsible for performance problems.

Part of larger task: In Chapters 1, "Business and Competitive Analysis: Definition, Context, and Benefits," and 2, "Performing the Analysis Process," we discussed how analysis was part of a larger number of processes that impact an organization's decision-making, policy development, and associated activities. We have seen many examples where the analysis process was short-circuited in favor of other activities, leading to the diminishment of the decisions made, as well as a reduced market performance. Research done on competitive intelligence processes have consistently found that more time should be spent on analysis and significantly less on data collection and gathering.[10]

Task discontinuity: Analysts can ordinarily go from task to task in the course of their day. They will frequently be working on any number of critical intelligence needs, questions, or topics at any single point in time. As such, benefits derived from the learning curve, which suggests that the efficiency if not the effectiveness of analysis performance should grow and accelerate over time, are seldom achieved. The learning curve is one reason why analysts in the public sector are often assigned to specific focal areas (e.g., country or regional "desks") for substantial periods of time, often between five to seven years. These long-term assignments allow for the analyst and their organizations to capture learning curve effects as experience is developed. Unfortunately, we find that most business or commercial enterprises do not have the defined internal career paths, the patience, or the plans to help analysts obtain the learning curve benefits of depth, breadth, and length of experience.

Unsatisfactory data inputs: The GIGO principle of "garbage in, garbage out" holds true in BCA. Many times, analysts will use data that is merely convenient, such as that generated by internal management information systems, which can be easily found on the World Wide Web, or that can be quickly gathered through discussions with colleagues. "Convenient" data seldom provides the analyst with critical insight or the "golden nugget" being sought. Convenience-based data gathering is an arch-enemy of effective analysis. There are a number of reasons why this state of affairs exists, including but not limited to the following prominent examples:

1. **Need to justify investments made in systems designed for other purposes**—Organizations make substantial investments in data-gathering systems and require evidence to justify their very existence. The problem with this is that most of the information systems established in enterprises today are not tasked to support competitive analysis and intelligence generation. They are good at gathering customer data, accounting data, production data, and financial data, but bad at gathering competitive and strategic data.[11]

2. **Differences in gathering versus analyzing/synthesizing information**—Many executives assume that web-based, electronic data subscriptions or media clipping services can generate intelligence. These things certainly generate volumes of data or information, but they do not, cannot, and are unlikely to perform the analysis and synthesis tasks that a human analyst can perform.[12] As we have noted previously, there are no systems of which we are aware that can perform analysis at a level anywhere near that of a successful analyst. Although systems can accelerate the reorganization, reclassification, or restructuring of data, they can do little beyond that. The continuing development of artificial intelligence (AI)-based collection systems will assist the analysis process in the future, but even these are typically only focused on a minor subset of typical business and competitive analysis problems.

3. **Extracting needed data from the heads of colleagues**—Sometimes the critical missing data the analyst needs can be found only within the heads of individuals either within or outside the organization.[13] It can be difficult to identify those parties that

are likely to be the best sources for needed information, and even if they could be readily identified, they would also have to be accessible and amenable to providing this on a "just-in-time" basis. Most organizations lack the systems to enable them to capture the critical information known by their own employees. Even though organizations have become more sophisticated in the application of knowledge management (KM) systems, these still require heavy investment, ongoing training, and constant human interaction to be effective.

4. **Separating the wheat from the chaff**—Many existing systems do not have the appropriate means for filtering or "grading" informational inputs as they enter the systems. As such, "bad" data, which may be corrupt for a bewildering variety of reasons, lives happily alongside the "good" data, and the analyst must still assess its suitability for the analysis tasks ahead.

Disconnects from decision making: The clients or customers of analysts are the ones who have the ultimate responsibility to use intelligence or not. Analysts do not make decisions, nor do they manage the processes by which an organization might implement their findings. As such, decision makers might simply choose not to use the intelligence, to ignore it, or to dismiss it for any variety of reasons. It is one thing for a decision maker to dismiss analysis because it is ineffective or unsatisfactory, but entirely another when it was indeed performed effectively.

This dilemma points out the difference between analysis and policy-making. Analysts can study the targets and potential outcomes of specific policy actions and can develop well-conceived rationales for decisions. At the end of the day, though, they are but one input among others in the client's decision-making calculus. We hope that the analyst's work will be a critical, if not *the* most critical, input. Nevertheless, we recognize that achieving the highest levels of trust from decision makers can only genuinely take place over time, supported with collaboration, regular interaction, achievement of successes, and a significant degree of mutual trust and understanding.

Imbalance among key task facets: Analysts must be ever-cognizant of and always striving toward maintaining any number of balances at any point in time. The ability to achieve this balance usually occurs after a number of years of analytical experience. The authors have seen and heard from some experienced analysts who have been doing the job for some time, and they still fail to properly balance the many conflicts that are associated with performing the analysis task. There are no simple solutions to this.

Internal Organizational-Level Failures

The internal organizational environment within which the analyst performs their task is also responsible for less effective analysis outcomes. The major organizational factors we see contributing to unfavorable outcomes are described next.

Some decision makers don't understand and appreciate analysis: In many organizations, decision makers neither understand the role or place of intelligence analysis nor recognize the value it can generate in improving decision-making quality. As more companies focus their attention and resources on understanding competition and the competitive environment, they are realizing that they are unsure of how to properly utilize the intelligence collected.[14] Insufficient understanding of the intelligence function leads to a deluge of poorly translated data, as departments request information, without filtering out the most relevant issues.[15] By churning out vast quantities of purposeless information, the analysts and their departments are unable to properly apportion their time to the accurate analysis and assembly of useable intelligence.

Clients cannot specify their critical intelligence needs or questions: The first critical step in the analysis process requires that the decision maker clearly articulate his or her needs to the analyst. This is frequently easier said than done. Many decision makers have difficulties briefing their analysts, struggle with explaining the decision that they are facing, or actually ask for the wrong thing. During the course of a project, the analyst will often uncover information that suggests the initial question needs to be modified. Unless the decision maker is fully familiar with the decision they are facing, they are unlikely to know if this new information has relevance.

Under-resourcing the analysis function: Because it is invariably a part of some larger organizational processes, analysis is typically under-resourced. The lack of resources in the form of data, information, databases, systems, people, and most commonly, time, are always mentioned in surveys of analysts. Indeed, time is seen as one of the primary barriers keeping them from being more effective in their organizational roles.[16] A large element of this problem is that it is difficult for those managing the analysis process to communicate the benefits derived from their activity in the format that executives ordinarily use in making their resource allocation decisions. Executives typically allocate financial and human resources on the basis of expected return on investment, net present value, or quantitative cost/benefit calculations. Putting a comparative quantitative calculation on the benefits of analysis has typically eluded most analysis managers and their clients.[17]

Lack of analysis-specific IT support: Organizations now have a plethora of information systems available for management, control, and planning purposes. Unfortunately, most of these systems are not designed to support the business and competitive analyst's roles and responsibilities in their organizations. Even when companies do employ so-called "intelligence solutions" or systems, these are mainly focused on facilitating the collection facet of the larger intelligence process rather than the analysis/synthesis tasks.[18]

Lack of thinking time: Thinking is a key component in producing analysis. It is rare for analysts to experience "blinding flashes" of insight[19] or to quickly obtain the essential and previously missing pieces of data that helps them arrive at confident conclusions. Instead, analysts spend substantial time thinking about their clients, data, models, networks, projections, targets, and work plans. There are times when this thinking just cannot be rushed, despite the perception held by many analysts that they need to produce ever more tangible products to more demanding clients.[20] This perception sometimes leads analysts to generate a lot of activity at the expense of insight.

Organizational culture and politics: In some organizations, the deliverers of "bad" or undesirable news to decision makers are punished. These punishments can range from admonishments, to the withdrawal of cooperation or resources, or ultimately, the elimination of the analyst's position. Unfortunately for analysts who find themselves reporting to easily offended decision makers in such organizational contexts, there is probably little they can do about it, except to hope for a change in those who act in this manner. If that behavioral change is not in the offing, analysts will often have to find more enlightened employing organizations.

Time and trust: Analysts and decision makers operate most effectively in an environment of mutual, shared trust. Unfortunately for some participants in the analysis process, trust usually takes some time to develop. Organizational realities demonstrate that many analysts or their decision makers are not in their posts long enough to allow for confidence, mutual respect, and trust to develop. In the absence of an appropriate level of trust, the analyst has to hope that they can develop this asset by carrying out effective analysis and convincing their clients that they can be relied upon to deliver the goods when asked.

Invisibility and mystery: Although analysis work is increasingly a social and network-oriented task, analysts frequently work in the background of organizations. They are not necessarily on the "front line" facing customers and can sometimes be invisible to the larger organization. Their work is also often part of larger research-related processes, so they are rarely singled out for attention. Analysts are not frequently in the organizational limelight for what they do, except in those cases where analysis failure was blamed for organizational mishap. Because an analyst's work and their function is sometimes viewed as mysterious or intellectually demanding, analysts are generally left to get on with their task without managerial interference. Unfortunately, this "invisibility and mystery" problem, at times, can be perpetuated by analysts themselves.

Misconception that everyone can do analysis: Randomly ask any recent MBA graduate whether they developed good analytical skills in their programs, and the answer you'll nearly always get will be "Yes." Most people do not recognize the differences between the process of analysis and their ordinary ability to think or "connect the dots." By this point in the book, it should go without saying that everyday thinking is not analysis, although an individual who does not think clearly cannot perform analysis. Analysis requires a unique and differentiated form of thinking and is encapsulated in the evolving analysis body of knowledge.

Most individuals have neither been formally trained nor have the natural ability to perform the rigorous and systematic type of specific thinking tasks that constitute competitive, enterprise, or strategic analysis as we know it. We know that analytical capability can be improved and enhanced through formal training, self-learning, mentoring, and coaching, as well as through regular review and evaluation of analysis processes and products.

External Environment-Level Failures

The external environment within which the organization operates can also be partially responsible for less-effective analysis outcomes. The major environmental factors we see contributing to these unfavorable outcomes are described next.

Growing range of competitive factors: The weapons used by enterprises in market-based competition have become more varied and better developed over time. Competition has historically occurred using the traditional marketing mix tactics along the "7Ps" dimensions of product, price, place, promotion, participants/people, physical evidence, and process.[21]

Today, competitive weapons can be found outside marketing in places such as the supply chain, human resources management, corporate culture, leadership, information systems, research and development, finance, operations, and production, among others. The growth of new knowledge, technological advances, and emerging public policies can all play a major factor in determining if an enterprise wins or loses in its marketplace.

Complexity and turbulence: Complexity has increased because there are more competitors and stakeholders, interacting in a variety of ways and in greater quantities, to produce more unpredictable and turbulent situations. Turbulence means that the competitive environment is subject to continuous or near continuous change. Emerging concepts such as chaos theory have been applied to the business context in both the popular and scholarly presses.[22] This further reinforces the point that the environment being analyzed today may well be more dynamic than it was yesterday.

Data overload: Because of the virtual explosion of resources that have been unleashed over the World Wide Web, the Internet, and in corporate intranets, analysts have more data and information than at any other period in history. Analysts commonly view this explosion of information as being akin to "drinking out of a fire hose." Unfortunately, much of this data is redundant, comes from dubious sources, is in foreign languages, lacks a paper trail, can be expensive to access, and/or turns out to be irrelevant to the analysts' concerns. Software engineers are recognizing this problem and are beginning to develop effective programs to assist organizations in filtering, organizing, and classifying incoming information into databases that better serve the organization's management information needs. Despite this, most analysts feel that they are drowning in information, yet starved of knowledge.

Globalization: This describes the nature of changes in societies and the world's economy from dramatically increased trade among different nation-states and increasing levels of socio-cultural exchange and interaction. Despite these sectors being intertwined and the blurring that occurs between markets, industries, and geographic boundaries, it is useful to distinguish economic, political, and cultural aspects of globalization. Globalization has also driven changes in technology, particularly in the transportation and communications sectors, where it is claimed there exists a global village with no recognized borders.

Educational deficiencies: Although there has been a natural and healthy evolution in the nature of BCA offerings available to individuals' intent on a formal education in the processes and competencies of analysis, not all educational developments in this area have been positive. We suggest that there are a number of prominent factors that have kept the number of offerings from mushrooming,[23] including:

1. **Lack of experienced faculty staff**—There is a dearth of experienced BCA staff in universities, colleges, and at the post-secondary level. Consequently, there are few programs offered in the subject. While being highly practical and of considerable value in a business management program, the area is not established as a major academic discipline. Few business or management schools have competitive intelligence or analysis courses, and it is mostly absent among the top-rated business schools.

2. **Scarcity of research**—The area of BCA lacks an agreed-upon body of knowledge, core texts, and case studies, all of which are the needed published record that helps professionalize a field. The larger area of competitive intelligence is served by few major journals, has virtually no chaired professorships, has a handful of disparate research centers, and has only a few programs dedicated to its study. A small number of institutions around the globe have the capability to offer doctoral level training in the field, so new researchers and scholars interested in BCA are produced only occasionally or drift into the area from an overlapping field.

3. **Scope ambiguity**—Ongoing struggles have occurred within a few universities about where to put a business or competitive analysis course—in business and management, library and information sciences, information systems, journalism, international studies, or military science/studies. Even within a business or management program, there are questions as to whether competitive analysis belongs in marketing, management information systems, or business policy/strategy. If they are asked at all, senior business or management administrators question whether business and competitive analysis or competitive intelligence is a legitimate discipline, practice, profession, field, or area of study. Nobody has yet produced a definitive answer.

4. **Economic trends**—Competitive intelligence appeared to be taking off in the 1990s as represented by a major growth in membership of the international Society of Competitive Intelligence Professionals (SCIP—www.scip.org). Since then, even this organization has experienced occasional periods of declining numbers. Similarly, past studies have demonstrated declines in the area during recessionary periods, when organizations reduce staff numbers of what they deem less-essential functions. Paradoxically, those working in analysis know that this is precisely the time when investment in such activity should increase, in order to better prepare the firm for the challenges ahead.

Despite the difficulties encountered in competitive analysis and intelligence gaining acceptance within the university context, CI and BCA education have had some positive developments, particularly in the offerings developed by consultancies and individuals. Fortunately, courses in business and competitive analysis can be found in most parts of the globe if individuals know where to look.

Overcoming the Barriers and Improving Analysis Performance

Besides employing simple and straightforward lists like Fleisher and Bensoussan's 10 Commandments for Business and Competitive Analysis described in Chapter 2 of this book, there are a number of additional things that can be done. To improve the performance and quality of BCA performed in contemporary enterprises, we recognize the following will help.

Provide Empowerment

Intelligence produced by effective analysis should be and is empowering to decision makers. A popular saying in the intelligence community is, "Without intelligence, a decision maker cannot take responsibility. With it, he or she cannot avoid taking responsibility." Clearly, the more that decision makers are equipped with insight, the better they will perform. This is why the importance of intelligence analysis needs to be recognized in its own right. Both analysts and executives need to promote the reality and truth that analysis is critical to an organization's competitive market success. Analysts and their clients should be comfortable with and publicize to others, that real benefit which emanates from analysis, that it is an evolving discipline in its own right, and that analysts are professionals in exactly the same way as others in the organization.

Realize the Value of Analysis

Even if the benefits and value of the process cannot be easily quantified by existing performance measurement systems, executives need to realize that effective analysis cannot be achieved through "quick fixes" or by the introduction of new software or hardware applications. The value of analysis comes from the insight it provides decision makers, which ultimately benefits their enterprise. When done well, analysis will become recognized implicitly, if not explicitly by decision makers for the value it provides.

Value the Link Between Analysis and Success

Providing managers with case studies and examples of good and bad analytical outputs can help powerfully demonstrate this relationship between analysis quality and decision-making effectiveness. Using analysis insights will significantly lower the number of controllable or perceived risks associated with decisions.

Ask the Right Questions

Consumers of analysis products must also be educated to know what to ask for from analysts and helped to understand what they can expect to receive. Executives and departmental managers, like many other employees within the organization, often misunderstand the true functions and proper operations of analysts or intelligence specialists. Decision makers will often ask for the wrong information and will then have difficulty in making sense of the analytical products they receive.

What matters to executives is "fact-based intelligence that makes a difference to their agendas, priorities, and needs as they perceive them," criteria that are important at the planning and directing phase of the decision-making process.[24] For intelligence to be useful and effective, managers should ask for and expect the items shown in the following list (adapted from Self [2003]). In general, analysts must provide products that are tailored not only to decision makers' specific information requirements but also presented or disseminated in their "language" and conform to their unique frames of reference.[25]

- Products that resolve their critical intelligence needs, questions, or topics.
- Analysis that utilizes the full and comprehensive range of available data within specified (budget, ethics, time, etc.) constraints.
- Analyzed data, information, and conclusions, not trivia or so-called "nice to knows."
- Timely delivery of products well in advance of the decision to which the analysis was targeted.
- Analysis findings that can play a central and vital role in their decision-making process.
- Conclusions that can enhance the positive effects of a chosen strategy or that can be used to diminish the adverse effects of competitor's actions.
- Recommendations that will enable the decision maker to make better decisions or more effective implementation of a chosen strategy or course of action.

- Logical, reasonable, and defensible support and explanations for why certain phenomena will occur and what future contingencies may arise.
- Feedback and post-mortems to improve future product quality.

Develop Recognized Analysis Training

Universities, employers, professional associations, and CI educators must develop dedicated courses and programs on analysis, not just the larger or broader CI process.[26]

These courses should include, at a minimum, the following items:

- Coverage of the techniques and methods of strategic, business, and competitive analysis.[27]
- Opportunities to practice performing analysis through case studies or supervised "on the job" experience.
- Processes to be used by analysts for helping their clients to clarify and articulate their KITs.
- Coverage of a range of philosophies and thinking styles such as those that would be gained through exposure to the basic tenets of epistemological science.
- Communication processes to deliver analytical outputs to the client.
- Exposure to methods of understanding the research on analytical failure, the pitfalls of analysis, and its associated psychological, social, and cognitive origins.

Courses can and arguably should be offered both in classrooms and through electronic and self-paced learning formats. Some courses should be designed to reinforce existing knowledge about the analysis process, while others should be designed to impart knowledge of newly emerged processes, tools, and techniques as they develop. Analysts should be encouraged to take these courses on a regular basis and be given incentives and recognitions for successfully upgrading their capabilities and knowledge.

Measure Performance Appropriately

The competencies, skills, and capabilities of an analyst can be measured, and what can be measured can be both managed and improved. The development of capability measurement tools and metrics to demonstrate improvement should be strongly encouraged. There is also a need to measure analysis products and processes against benchmarks. Best practices in the analytic field need to be identified and emulated.

Position the Analyst Correctly

Executives must place analysts in organizational positions where they can make a genuine difference and are secure. Analysts need to be actively involved in the networks of information collectors and their clients, but also be given the time needed to properly do their work. Also the longer that analysts can focus their efforts on particular specialties needed by the decision makers, the quicker they will move up the learning curve in terms of producing quality outputs.

As even the most effective analysts can provide inaccurate insight at times, decision-making clients need to give their analysts opportunities to fail and to demonstrate that they have learned from these undesirable experiences. This opportunity leads to the development of shared trust between an analyst and a decision maker. With security and the trust of their clients, analysts are at their most effective.

Provide the Right Tools

Enterprises need to provide analysts with the proper tools of their craft: analytic applications, proper data inputs, access to sources, time to think, advanced information and communication infrastructure, and so on. Analysts cannot be expected to provide insight without having access to rich sources of data, enabling technology, the open door of their organizational colleagues, and clearly articulated KITs/KIQs. The outputs must be focused to capture the client's imagination and provide assistance on complex issues quickly, yet in a comprehensive way. The analyst's job must not be to intimidate clients with information, but rather to entice them with it.

Differentiate the Task

Last but certainly not least, business and competitive analysts must differentiate the nature of analysis they perform from other forms of analysis concurrently being done within their enterprises. Business and competitive analysts and their decision-making clients should be careful not to overrate or overemphasize the analysis of organizations, industries, and markets that is provided by economists, financial analysts, or marketing researchers/analysts. These individuals are primarily concerned with short-term financial gains, customer satisfaction, product placement, and related concerns, not necessarily with long-term competitiveness and effective business or corporate strategy development. Executives who understand the reasons these functions vary and the respective benefits each generates will be far better served in their decision making.

Summary

Analysis is a critical component in aiding executives in their decision making. This chapter has identified much of what is wrong with analysis today, but it also suggests that there is much more that can be done to improve analysis. These problems can be fixed, although it will require the efforts of many stakeholders and institutions, some of which have been reluctant to-date to changing in the manner we have identified.

CI scholar Ben Gilad notes that intelligence is an insight about externally motivated change and future developments and their implications to the organization. Done well, analysis and the intelligence developed from it helps the organization to reduce its risk level in dealing with both threats and opportunities that exist outside. The absence of effective analysis will produce little insight to underlying key decisions. Without a good analysis capability, an enterprise is increasingly vulnerable to attack and will miss profitable opportunities in the dynamic, globalized, world economy of today.

References

Bazerman, M.H. (2002). *Judgment in Managerial Decision Making*, 5th edition. Hoboken, NJ: John Wiley & Sons.

Bernhardt, D. (1999). "Consumer versus producer: Overcoming the disconnect between management and competitive intelligence," *Competitive Intelligence Review*, 10(1), pp. 19–26.

Cohen, A. (1998). "The misuse of competitive intelligence," *Sales and Marketing Management*, 150(3), 13.

Edmonson, A., and M. Cannon (2005). "Failing to learn and learning to fail (intelligently): How great organizations put failure to work to improve and innovate," *Long Range Planning Journal*, 38(3), June.

Feldman, M.S., and J.G. March (1981). "Information in organizations as signal and symbol," *Administrative Science Quarterly*, 26(2), pp.171–186.

Fleisher, C.S. (2004). "Competitive intelligence education: Competencies, sources, and trends," *Information Management Journal*, 2004, 38(2), pp. 56–63.

Fleisher, C.S., and B. Bensoussan (2003a). *Strategic and Competitive Analysis: Methods and Techniques for Analyzing Business Competition*. Upper Saddle River, NJ: Prentice Hall.

Fleisher, C.S., and B. Bensoussan (2003b). "Why is analysis performed so poorly and what can be done about it?," pp. 110–122 in Fleisher, C., and D. Blenkhorn [eds.], *Controversies in Competitive Intelligence: The Enduring Issues*. Westport, CT: Praeger Publishers.

Fleisher, C.S., and D.L. Blenkhorn (2001). "Effective approaches to assessing competitive intelligence," pp. 110–123 in Fleisher, C.S. and D.L. Blenkhorn [eds.], *Managing Frontiers in Competitive Intelligence*. Westport, CT: Quorum Books.

Fuld, L.M. (2001). "Intelligence software: Reality or still virtual reality?," *Competitive Intelligence Magazine*, 4(2), pp. 22–27.

Gib, A., and R. Gooding (1998). "CI tool time: What's missing from your toolbag?," pp. 25–39 in the *Proceedings of the 1998 international conference of the Society of Competitive Intelligence Professionals*, Chicago, IL.

Gilad, B. (1994). *Business Blindspots: Replacing Your Company's Entrenched and Outdated Myths, Beliefs, and Assumptions with the Realities of Today's Markets*. Chicago: Probus.

Gladwell, M. (2000). *The Tipping Point: How Little Things Can Make a Big Difference*. Boston, MA: Little Brown.

Heuer Jr., J.R. (1999). *The Psychology of Intelligence Analysis*. Washington, DC: Center for the Study of Intelligence.

Johnston, R. (2005). *Analytic Culture in the U.S. Intelligence Community*. Washington, DC: The Center for the Study of Intelligence.

Kahneman, D., Slovic, P., and A. Tversky (1982). *Judgment under Uncertainty: Heuristics and Biases*. Cambridge, UK: Cambridge University Press.

Kalat, J.W. (1998). *Biological Psychology*, sixth edition. Pacific Grove: Brooks/Cole Publishing Co.

Kiel, L.D., and E.W. Elliott (1997). *Chaos Theory in the Social Sciences: Foundations and Applications*. Ann Arbor, MI: University of Michigan Press.

Marteniuk, J. (2003). "How do companies find the best balance between the technical and personal in effective competitive intelligence systems?," pp. 176–189 in Fleisher, C., and D. Blenkhorn [eds.], *Controversies in Competitive Intelligence: The Enduring Issues*. Westport, CT: Praeger Publishers.

McGonagle, J.J., and C.M. Vella (2003). *The Manager's Guide to Competitive Intelligence*. Greenwich, CT: Praeger Books.

Miller, G.A. (1956). "The magical number seven, plus or minus two: Some limits on our capacity for processing information," *Psychological Review*, 63, pp. 81–97.

Nikkel, P. (2003). "How can we determine which competitive intelligence software is most effective?," pp. 163–175 in Fleisher, C., and D. Blenkhorn [eds.], *Controversies in Competitive Intelligence: The Enduring Issues*. Westport, CT: Praeger Publishers.

Rafiq, M., and P.K. Ahmed (1995). "Using the 7Ps as a generic marketing mix," *Marketing Intelligence & Planning*, 13(9), pp. 4–15.

Rigby, D.K. (2003). *Management Tools 2003*. White Paper. Boston, MA: Bain & Company, Inc.

Rigby, D.K. (2001). "Putting the tools to the test: Senior executives rate 25 top management tools," *Strategy & Leadership*, 29(3), pp. 4–12.

Sawyer, D.C. (1999). *Getting It Right—Avoiding the High Cost of Wrong Decision*. Boca Raton, FL: St. Lucie Press.

Self, K. (2003). "Why do so many firms fail at competitive intelligence?," pp. 190–202 in Fleisher, C., and D. Blenkhorn [eds.], *Controversies in Competitive Intelligence: The Enduring Issues*. Westport, CT: Praeger Publishers.

Tversky, A., and D. Kahneman (1986). "Rational choice and the framing of decisions," *Journal of Business*, 59, pp. 251–294.

Waldrop, M. (1992). *Complexity: The Emerging Science at the Edge of Order and Chaos*. New York, NY: Touchstone.

Watson, J., and J. Everett (1996). "Do small businesses have high failure rates?," *Journal of Small Business Management*, 34(4), pp. 45–62, October.

Windle, G. (2003). "How can competitive intelligence practitioners avoid over-relying on the Internet," pp. 85–97 in Fleisher, C., and D. Blenkhorn [eds.], *Controversies in Competitive Intelligence: The Enduring Issues*. Westport, CT: Praeger Publishers.

Endnotes

[1] Johnston, 2005.

[2] Edmonson and Cannon, 2005.

[3] Watson and Everett, 1996.

[4] Fleisher and Blenkhorn, 2001.

[5] Fleisher and Bensoussan, 2003b.

[6] Kalat, 1998.

[7] Bazerman, 2002; Kahneman *et al*, 1982; Sawyer, 1999; Tversky and Kahneman, 1986.

[8] Fleisher and Bensoussan, 2003b; Gib and Gooding, 1998; Rigby, 2001; Rigby, 2003.

[9] Fleisher and Bensoussan, 2003b.

[10] McGonagle & Vella, 2003.

[11] Nikkel, 2003.

[12] Windle, 2003.

[13] Marteniuk, 2003.

[14] Cohen, 1998.

[15] Cohen, 1998.

[16] Johnston, 2005.

[17] Fleisher and Blenkhorn, 2001.

[18] Nikkel, 2003; Fuld, 2001.

[19] Achieving the elusive "a-ha" findings is sometimes known as the process of "abduction" in analysis circles.

[20] Johnston, 2005.

[21] Rafiq and Ahmed, 1995.

[22] Gladwell, 2000; Kiel and Elliott, 1997; Waldrop, 1992.

[23] Fleisher, 2004.

[24] Bernhardt, 1999.

[25] Bernhardt, 1999.

[26] Fleisher, 2004.

[27] Fleisher, 2004.

Communicating Analysis Results

One of the most difficult challenges facing analysts in organizations is effectively communicating the results of their work on a timely basis to their decision makers. This is important because analysis often underlies decisions, and decision makers cannot always wait for the analyst to complete their work. Also many of the decisions that are made about competitive business matters rely on data inputs that have a short shelf life. In other words, the intelligence generated about competitive actions is only useful to the enterprise for a short time period before it becomes out of date, at which point, it no longer has the ability to deliver competitive advantage. Analysts must place considerable attention on delivering their findings to, and gaining the attention, understanding, confidence, and ultimately trust, of their decision makers. Presenting results to decision-making clients is one of the vulnerable areas where intelligence and other strategy-related processes can fail.

The Art of Effective Communication

Individuals new to the field or those who remain ignorant of the art and science of communication will do their best to avoid the challenge of this element of the analyst's task. It is important to realize that the analyst's job is not over when the formal analysis process itself is concluded. Delivery of the findings to the decision makers, gauging their understanding of the analyst's recommendations, making sure that no critical intelligence was lost in the exchange of ideas, and understanding how the analysis product will be used are among the analyst's key communication task responsibilities. Failures in these final stages of the analysis process can devalue the analyst's work and can ultimately be a prime contributor to bad decisions and inappropriate actions taken by an enterprise in the marketplace. Additionally, the communication stage is a vital feedback mechanism for the analyst to understand how well he has done the job in hand. It also provides pointers on how he might improve his performance on the next one.

Within each enterprise, there will be established procedures for communicating with decision-making clients, writing a report, and presenting results. Many of these are generic across business or management professions, while others will be more specific to an enterprise and its particular culture. A major responsibility of analysts is to learn these procedures, particularly those associated with demonstrated and proven communication performance, and to pay close attention to them when communicating their own findings and insights.

A common theme regarding the relationship between communication and audience satisfaction is that the more confidence that the audience (decision maker) has in the ability of the communicator (analyst), then the more satisfied they are likely to be with what is being communicated (analysis product). Distortion, ambiguity, and incongruence in communication can all act to increase a decision maker's discomfort or uncertainty. Analysts who are able to lessen the amount of distortion in their communication will reduce their client's levels of discomfort and uncertainty, and ceteris paribus, achieve higher levels of satisfaction, and receive better feedback. These communication results are all beneficial in achieving successful analytical outcomes over time.

We want to state, for the record, that you will have difficulty becoming an effective analyst in an enterprise unless you demonstrate effective communication skills, knowledge, and abilities. Resources spent in supporting analysis efforts are wasted if the analyst's recommendations are not used. This is even more serious if the reason for non- or misuse is that the decision makers did not understand what was being provided to them, that the conclusions were not clear, or that the analysis product was delivered in an incomprehensible or inappropriate manner. Ineffective communication of results will negate what might otherwise have been outstanding work in all the other phases of the analysis process.

Over the past 20 years or more, the form in which competitive analysis is delivered has been dramatically altered. In the 1980s, most analysts' outputs were communicated through either occasional written reports, regularly written reports, and in a passive manner by making the contents of files available in a centralized location or database on an as-needed basis to decision makers.[1] Today, more active and regular delivery of results occurs through reporting, presenting, and pushing reports through electronic means to users.[2] What used to be contained in manila folders in large filing cabinets has now been shifted over to internal electronic databases or custom-developed intranet portals. Intranets have become a common means for communicating intelligence in most large organizations.

Packaging the Results of Your Analysis

How intelligence is presented and packaged affects the client's perception of its validity.[3] One thing the analyst must always consider is the need to inform versus the need to protect critical information from being shared beyond the persons for whom it was originally intended. Some analysis results are delivered through automated electronic means, while others are offered in face-to-face group settings or in-person. Regardless of the manner in which the analysis product is delivered to decision makers, the analyst must also address trade-offs between depth, breadth, speed, security, and convenience.

Similar to most forms of communication, analysts must always consider how each output format is likely to create the conditions necessary to influence the client of the importance of their insights. Analysts must also be cognizant of their own predisposition to particular formats. Properly factoring in these two considerations on the analyst and decision maker's communication preferences and taking account of these *before* communication takes place will strengthen the likelihood that the client will accept their recommendations.

Analysts who develop recognized levels of communication effectiveness are more likely to present results that

- are future-oriented with detailed predictions of the evolution of the phenomena of interest.

- contain well-articulated conclusions that are developed through comprehensive research and logical reasoning.

- include clear explanations of subjects that go beyond the reasonable technical grasp of their decision-making clients.[4]

Delivering the Message

By what methods does the analyst deliver these results? It should be reiterated here that the method(s) used should be mainly based on the decision maker's needs.[5] That premise does suggest, though, that the decision makers actually know what they need to know, and as previously mentioned in this book, that is not always the case. It is in these situations that the analyst has an even greater responsibility, not only to meet the decision maker's perceived needs, but to produce a back-up set of additional analysis product, recommendations, and/or communication channels. This added-value back-up set is where the analyst's communication skills, knowledge, and abilities become highly visible as it will address what the decision maker might have asked for, if only they had known what to ask for. It is in this role that the analyst acts more proactively, as a subject expert or an internal consultant, rather than as a reactive employee simply completing a task. At the end of every reporting event, the decision maker should always ask three questions of the analyst:

- "Is there anything else I should have asked you to do?"

- "Is there anything else you think you should have done?"

- "Is there anything else you want to tell me?"

The appropriate communication packaging of analytical outputs is essential. Analysts typically provide their outputs to decision-making clients in the following forms.[6]

Face-to-Face Briefings

One of the most effective two-way models of communication, face-to-face briefings allow the analyst to physically and orally present their findings to a client. This not only encourages discussion and exchange of understanding to take place in real-time, but it minimizes second-hand distortion or the effects that a time lag can have on the acquired understanding.

Written Reports and Briefings

Printed outputs are a cost-effective way of distributing results. Some executives still prefer to read items from the printed page rather than from a screen, particularly if a screen is not readily available or inconvenient (i.e., the decision maker is traveling on an airplane or his e-mail networks are not easily accessible). A problem with this form of communication is that there are many more pages of materials printed than are ever read, and much of the information that is read is not fully understood by its readers. It is not unknown, quite common even, for the readers of paper-based intelligence reports to be overlooked. Additionally, the report itself has the potential to fall into the hands of an unintended audience and can create undesirable vulnerabilities.

Presentations in Meetings, Seminars, and Workshops

These are a very effective way to deliver results to a group of decision makers and are a good way of gaining a group's attention. The main advantage in this format is that it provides opportunities for the analysts to discuss their findings in real-time, not only with those who may have initiated the task in the first place, but also more importantly with those individuals to whom it was designed to inform. It is important that the appropriate decision makers are available to observe and interact with the presenter, and this scheduling aspect is often an overlooked part of the analysis communication process.

One criticism of this method is that many times, analysts prepare PowerPoint slide decks whereby the aesthetics of their slides, the fanciness of their presentations, or the structure of their slide organization overpowers the important content or message, which then gets lost or missed because of the high reliance on the presenting technology.[7] Analysts need to be wary of spending too much time thinking about how snazzily they can present reports, at the expense of worrying about the robustness of content.

Seminars and workshops are two other forms of presentation-based communication. They can allow the analysts to present their ideas more formally while still allowing for the collective benefits of quality question and answer time. This encourages discussion among the collected group of executives in an audience and aids the exploration of solutions to competitive and strategic problems.

E-Mail/Instant Messaging

Digital communication is probably the most commonly used means for analysts to communicate with their decision-making clients. The major benefit of this format is the almost immediate attention and quick replies. E-mail and instant messaging are good ways to disseminate "alerts," regularly published newsletters, and other forms of analytical results that need to be acted upon in a quick manner. A drawback of this form of communication is that it makes it difficult to communicate the "richness" of the recommendation context and can limit the format of the results to mostly, if not entirely, text.

Intelligence Systems

Customized systems offered by specialized competitive intelligence vendors, or systems tailored for analytical use within the larger corporate communication system, are becoming more commonplace. These allow analysts' clients to either see their findings in refined and finished formats, which can include digital links to other materials, and/or in their original input such as documents, interview notes, articles, and so forth. Such systems nearly always allow for selective access and viewing by clients on a need-to-know basis, or they can be designed to send out various forms of information in the form of e-mails, instant messages, or fax to a selected numbers of recipients. The drawback to these systems is that they can be cumbersome, costly, complex, and do not always allow for two-way communication to take place.

Exercises and Planning Sessions

Many analytical tools require two-way interaction between analysts and their decision-making clients. Some of the tools in this book are best practiced in this way, including techniques such as war gaming (see Chapter 23, "War Gaming"), scenario analysis,[8] or shadowing (see Chapter 13, "Shadowing"). These frequently involve the analyst or designated individuals playing the role of one or more competitors. These techniques require a vast amount of data before anything is attempted and can be conducted in a one-off session, over an extended period of time in a person-to-person format, or can be conducted in teams in tightly planned and scheduled sessions aided by expert facilitators.[9]

Common Products and Reports Used by Analysts

Analysts ordinarily generate outputs in a variety of forms for use by their decision-making clients. Each of these has a typical audience, for which they are designed, are produced on a particular frequency, and are viewed to hold a certain level of perceived value in the eyes of the report recipients. They should always be tailored for the known and unique needs of the decision makers.

The most common types of analyst reports are given next and are discussed in greater detail with respect to their relative advantages and disadvantages.

News Bulletins and Newsletters

Targeted most frequently to field sales personnel, marketing, managers, sales managers, or other decision makers, these analysis outputs contain largely tactical and/or operational information and utilize data gathered from all sources. They can include both publicly available and internally available information. They frequently focus on current or immediate past events. They are rarely oriented toward the future.

Newsletters are typically of lower strategic value relative to other types of outputs.[10] Although these items may be seen as less valuable than other products in a comparative sense, their cumulative value can be higher and strategic in nature. This can be especially true if they raise the level of competitive awareness over time in the enterprise. When done well, newsletters and news bulletins can be catalysts for not only conversations and discussions between analysts, analyst groups, and their clients, but encourage new questions to be asked of the analyst group. One way of achieving this catalyzing effect is to ensure that newsletters do indeed include analysts' interpretations and insight, along with the informative "news" aspects of the bulletins.[11]

Assessments

These are fairly brief and regularly generated products that look at particular business decisions, providing an assessment of the current situation facing the decision maker, identifying the critical success factors associated with the situation, and suggesting likely outcomes in terms of probabilities. The content can range from a very general overview of broad issues to detailed answers to highly specific questions.

Competitor Profiles

Competitor profiles are produced as needed but are constantly updated and contain general information about the enterprise's competitors in the marketplace. They are valuable for field sales personnel, marketing, and sales managers, as well as other functional decision makers who not only benefit from their existence, but contribute to their augmentation and evolution. Seldom actionable in their own right, they are of lower strategic value relative to other types of analytic outputs, but can be combined with other types of outputs that have higher overall decision-making value.

Done well, competitor profiling is carried out at many different layers of the enterprise, addressing the competitive landscape and associated activities right across the value chain. Passive competitor profiles are simple historical commentaries, compiled from publicly available documents and as such, carry little or no analytical value or originality. Active competitor profiles are future driven, contain identification and assessments of critical success factors, deconstruction of published financial reports, qualitative and quantitative judgments on current/future capabilities, probabilities of competitor action taking place, and recommendations on how best to react to each and every one should it occur.

Strategic Impact Worksheets

Strategic impact worksheets are closely related to competitor profiles and are used to identify specific events that may potentially impact the enterprise. They are usually targeted at those individuals in the enterprise who will be most affected by the events, possibly including Strategic Business Unit or functional managers. Ordinarily issued on a regular basis, they are usually of moderate value to decision makers. However, if the analyst uses these with competitor profiles to develop an early-warning system, then they can take on increased value. Anything that helps the organization to avoid being surprised by competitor action, market shifts, or hitherto unforeseen events, can only be of great value.

Intelligence Briefings

Usually issued on a regular basis, in a highly condensed manner, these are reports to senior and other managers about strategic news. They are rarely used to address specific issues, but they do ensure that all concerned are kept as "aware" as possible of the shifting competitive landscape.

Intelligence briefings are increasingly offered electronically in broadcast formats over secure intranets, in *webinar* formats, or via secure video-teleconferencing facilities. They are typically of moderate value to the analyst's clients.

Situation Analysis

These are one of the more unique products produced by analysts on an as-needed or as-requested basis for key decision makers. The situation analysis report summarizes emerging and rising strategic issues. They usually provide background in the form of the detailed thinking and synthesis actually performed to generate the recommendations. Relative to other products, their shelf lives are short.

Special Intelligence Summaries

Special intelligence summaries are usually brief in length, not much more than one or two pages, and most frequently generated on an as-requested basis. They identify situations, summarize the key supporting analyses, and offer recommendations on desired actions to senior decision makers. They are among the most valuable outputs regularly generated by analysts and are often the most visible influencers of an enterprise's decisions.

Creating the Report

When creating reports, analysts should emphasize the following items:[12]

- Strategic versus tactical or operational information
- Decision-oriented information
- Inclusion of only relevant supporting data
- Distribution of reports to clients on a timely, need-to-know basis
- Multiple reports versus one large report for lower to middle levels of management

Analysts can enhance their decision makers' receptivity by using a variety of analysis outputs.

M. Dugal developed the idea of an analyst's portfolio, which comprised 10 key products. Each of these "products" differ in terms of shelf life, intended audience, processes used to generate them, sources underlying their development, analytical tools most commonly applied to generating them, their modes of dissemination, and the resources required to produce them.

1. *Current Intelligence* provides clients with the first identification of developments in the organization's competitive arena. This is typically light on analytical manipulation and, in cases where it is warranted, will later be assessed more thoroughly.

2. *Basic Intelligence* reports on analytical research that provides the up-to-date, systematic facts and understanding about the organization's environment, industry, and competitors.

3. *Technical Intelligence* helps the decision maker understand developments in both the scientific and technical areas that affect, or may potentially impact, their organization's competitive environment.

4. *Early Warning Intelligence* provides advanced warning of potential marketplace disruptions and environmental opportunities and threats.

5. *Estimated Intelligence* provides forecasts, scenarios, and likely developments relative to competitor's products, markets, customers, processes, and/or industry composition.

6. *Work Group Intelligence* is used in support of internal projects and teams especially those relative to possible merger and acquisition candidates, patent purchases, or acquisition of specialist expertise.

7. *Targeted Intelligence* offers one-time intelligence that targets narrow, specific, and focused needs of an intelligence client.

8. *Crisis Intelligence* is designed to assist the organization in managing its way through crisis events.

9. *Foreign Intelligence* focuses on competitors, industries, and companies that operate outside the nation-state domicile of the organization.

10. *Counterintelligence* assists the organization in addressing the intelligence threats posed by competitors.

Communication Difficulties Faced by Analysts

Despite the increased use of technology in communication between analysts and their decision-making clients,[13] the analyst's communication of their findings continues to be a trouble spot for decision support. Why is the effective communication of analysis results so difficult?

In our experiences, and through observation and surveys of hundreds of business and competitive analysts, their work context, and their organizations, we have identified a number of reasons that can be frequently associated with lower levels of analytical effectiveness.

Although we were tempted to prioritize these items, either by the frequency in which they occur or by their relative importance to the analysis process, we do not have access to systematic research in this field that would allow us to achieve this. We think that further examination and research of these reasons is warranted, and we usually suggest to managers that they audit their own operations to assess the prevalence of these problems in their context. In no particular order, we have observed that most analysts

■ Don't understand or think through basic communication transmission models that impact their daily work.

A basic model developed by C.E. Shannon and W. Weaver looked like this:

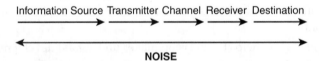

Information Source Transmitter Channel Receiver Destination

NOISE

Figure 4.1   Communication transmission model

Shannon and Weaver argued that there were three levels of problems in communication:

1. The technical problem: How accurately can the message be transmitted?

2. The semantic problem: How precisely is the meaning "conveyed"?

3. The effectiveness problem: How effectively does the received meaning affect behavior?

Subsequent research in human communication, most notably by Harold Lasswell,[14] was closely allied to behaviorist approaches, and this resulted in a verbal version of the former Source-Message-Channel-Receiver transmission model that essentially asked, "Who says what in which channel to whom with what effect?" Most analysts do not ask these questions of their communication products, and because of this, often misfire on achieving their aims of influencing the decision maker.

Although these models are far too simplistic to accurately reflect communication reality in today's complex world, having a communication model in mind such as these, at least provides an initial basis from which to think through the communication challenge. A widely known notion in physics that analysts should know about suggests that chaos or randomness always increases with time. This results in communication being increasingly distorted the more times it is passed along and through a channel. It would be seen as added noise or complexity and can occur at any stage or at multiple stages of the analysis process.

■ Have not received training and development in becoming effective communicators.

You cannot be an analyst and be a poor communicator, and you cannot be a successful analyst unless you are also an effective communicator. Unfortunately, reporting and presentation skills are not a focus of most business professionals' formal education or training.[15] Yes, companies will send graduate trainees on an "Introduction to Public Speaking" or "How to Use PowerPoint" type training course in their first year of employment, and in that respect, they can be useful. Functional managers and analysts at all other levels are generally assumed to have attained highly developed communication skills through some form of osmosis. The evidence contradicts this. Good analysts and good managers can sometimes be spectacularly bad at making presentations and delivering information, so much so, that the audience feels distinctly embarrassed and uncomfortable at their performance. This does not assist in the communication process and is an element that is entirely correctable.

Analysts use communication skills to negotiate with their clients for choices, time to decide, time to act, understanding, and to agree on how each can help to achieve better decisions. Analysts actually accomplish their jobs indirectly through the communication that is exchanged between the analyst and their clients.

What is important for the analyst to know is that communication can be exercised and improved. It can be broken down into its component parts and practiced. Analysts also need to know how and when to keep quiet. This is a highly developed talent used during information acquisition and most effectively by skilled negotiators.

Far from being seen as a one-off introductory type course for newcomers, advanced communication skills training should be a mandatory and ongoing requirement for all employees. Communication is a complex business, and it really is much more than talking.

- Rely upon the communication techniques that they are experienced and comfortable with, not necessarily those that are appropriate for a particular client and/or situation.

Analysts, who were trained to write reports in their earlier career responsibilities, will ordinarily continue to write them until someone suggests they stop. It is human nature for the analyst to fall back on what they know, but often what they *need to know* can be far more vital to them in achieving successful outcomes. This will require many analysts to undergo additional training, to learn new skills, to practice them, and to continuously develop their capabilities. Much of this will require an organizational and personal investment in time and money but will typically reap rewards in the form of more appropriate and effective delivery of the analysis product.

Many professionals, such as surgeons, pilots, engineers, and scientists, embrace the philosophy that they will never know all there is to know about their jobs. They also recognize that new developments are occurring every day. As such, they are legally required to learn about these and demonstrate their continued competence in order to remain employable. While not suggesting that this should be the case for analysts and their decision makers, it is perhaps a little strange that those involved in vital decisions about the future of an enterprise should be deemed as the "finished product" from day one in their job.

- Have not learned to pick up "silent cues" in communication.

Most analysts rely far too heavily on written data and information and discount or downplay other forms of inputs, including conversations, observations, and behavioral cues. This can be a critical skill for analysts since they need not only to communicate with the eventual recipients of their work, but also the gatherers of the data and information they are using. Much of this work will require the analyst to make judgments about the credibility of sources, the clarity of the gathered data, and/or the possible motivations of those involved. Better analysts will use not only the so-called obvious, published cues to conduct their work, but will also be cognizant of the informal, behavioral cues that are given off by individuals during communication.

- Lack a clear understanding of their client's (or sometimes their own) expectations and requirements.

Many analysts operate with a fuzzy understanding of how their clients will use their outputs and recommendations. A major problem is that many analysts work without an organized KIT/KIQ process and fail to do systematic debriefs and assessments with their decision makers.[16] If the analyst does not recognize when and why a client is dissatisfied with their work, they will have difficulties in identifying the means by which to improve it.

One means for avoiding this problem is to utilize the previously discussed KIT/KIQ process, supplemented by a "statement of work." D.S. Mockus has suggested that a statement of work should encompass, at a minimum, the following elements:

❑ Prioritized list of deliverables

❑ Primary contact and distribution list

❑ Anticipated timeframe of final report

❑ Format of final results

   i. Written (paper copy, digital, e-mail, instant message)

   ii. Verbal (face to face, over the phone, in meeting format)

❑ Anticipated frequency of status reports/updates

❑ Format of status reports/updates

   i. Written (hard copy, digital, e-mail)

   ii. Verbal (in person, over the phone)

❑ Anticipated audience (titles, positions)

Analysts also need to understand their own communication styles, tendencies, and biases. For example, many analysts will filter the results of their analyses by manipulating information in ways that they perceive it will be seen more favorably by the receiver. For analysts who have not rigorously determined their client's needs or requirements, this is likely to get them into trouble. The client may realize what has happened, and as a consequence, not believe, or trust, the recommendations offered.

Because intelligence is communicated via language, analysts need to recognize how important their choice of words, visuals, or voice will be, particularly if their decision-making clients are from different nationalities, cultures, genders, or experiential backgrounds. Words mean different things to different people. Cultural or social nuances need to be known and properly addressed. To one analyst's client, a "threat" may mean something imminent and urgent, while to another it may be viewed as something that is long-term, long distance, and unlikely to be problematic.

■ Do not develop a plan or strategy for communication or think through the choice of communication vehicles with the same level of rigor that they may think through the choice of analytical tools and techniques.

In far too many enterprises that we have advised, communication is treated as an afterthought. Strangely enough, executives frequently point to the communication process as being both important and yet a frequent source of organizational difficulties or failures. These facts point to the importance for analysts to consider communication as rigorously as they would any other key facet of their work. A facilitator of this is the development of communication plans and communication audits/reviews on a regular basis. These can then be linked to the overall strategic plan, group's analysis plans, or individuals' project plans.

Just like the analysis techniques we describe in this book, communication vehicles or modes all have different attributes. It is imperative that analysts think these matters through early in the process so that they can integrate the development of the final products into the intended delivery method. Communication, like most of the rest of the processes described in this book, can and should be planned, managed, measured, and improved.

- Do not make their recommendations "actionable."

  By "actionable," the analyst's recommendations must relate directly and obviously to the KIT/KIQ of the decision maker, the enterprise's relevant strategic, tactical, and/or operational plans, as well as the decision-making process itself. Actionable means that the analyst has made recommendations that walk the client through not only the decision itself but the likely organizational and competitive manifestations (i.e., contingencies) that would occur as a result of it being acted upon. Last but not least, actionable analysis usually includes an implementation plan, which can be scoped out in the form of a timeline, GANTT chart, project plan, or the like.

- Need to develop the synthesis skills to take volumes of complex data and information and convert them into brief and easy-to-understand outputs.

  A common reason many analysts fail is that they do not know how to summarize their thoughts and communicate them succinctly. One reason this occurs is that analysts may lack a deep understanding of the analytical techniques they are using. This book is intended to help put that situation right. Many decision makers have neither the time, patience, or desire to read through lengthy tomes or book-length backgrounders about a topic. This is one reason why we think the "Occam's Razor" rule[17] should always be applied to communication. This suggests that the analyst should communicate using the simplest and most parsimonious explanation that can fit the facts. All else being equal, it is better to communicate findings using simple and shorter formats as opposed to longer and more complex ways.

  Another related communication error made by analysts is not "cutting to the chase" or knowing how to differentiate between the "must have" and the "nice to have" intelligence. As one expert in the competitive intelligence field stated, *"effective analysts learn not to summarize but rather to synthesize."*[18] It is far too easy to produce volume, whereas synthesizing analytical findings down to their essential core messages is a skill that will always be valued by today's harried decision makers.

- Have not thoroughly examined the communication expectations, channel, and format needs/preferences of their decision makers.

  Some decision makers prefer to receive their intelligence via particular channels or in specific formats. Some will prefer to hear results in a private face-to-face, in-person manner; some will prefer a formal presentation; some will prefer to receive e-mails or access a special web area designed for the purposes; and some will prefer to receive written reports sent via the internal mail.

  It is common for analysis clients to exhibit selective hearing based on their own needs, motivations, experience, background, and other personal characteristics. Analysts should take account of and be sensitive to a client's work habits, personality, and schedule. If the client has an extremely busy day, it would be futile to try and arrange a 90 minute in-depth briefing for something that can wait until tomorrow. If an analyst really does have to *demand* a client's attention, then the subject matter and scenario had better be of sufficient gravity to warrant such an intrusion.

  Part of "managing a client's expectations" also compels analysts to profile themselves and their clients. D.J. Kalinowski suggests that clients have one of *four basic communication styles*—the first as a primary style and another exhibited less frequently as a secondary style, each of which indicates that the analyst should do specific things. This notion is expanded next.

Style 1: Analytical

Problem solvers, organized, logical, somewhat impersonal, typically cautious, and nearly always consistent. As such, it is important for the analyst to have done their homework. They should strive to communicate as accurately as possible, providing the level of background detail the client needs to gain confidence in the rigor and logic of their recommendations.

Style 2: Driver

Goal-driven, action-oriented, competitive, serious, strong-willed, controlling, and self-reliant. Analysts communicating with these clients must be efficient in their communication, cutting confidently and quickly "to the chase" and not providing much "fluff" or side-tracking in the presentation of their findings. It is important to stress the "bottom-line" implications of the findings, make clear recommendations, and answer these clients' questions quickly and directly.

Style 3: Amiable

Sympathetic, nurturing, cooperative, personal, adaptable, tolerant, patient, good listeners, and thoughtful. Analysts delivering their findings to these clients try and involve them in the communication, keep an open mind, are agreeable, and are willing to explore the many options they went through before coming to their actionable insight. Last but not least, they should be clear about the multiple types of benefits that can be generated from the recommendation.

Style 4: Expressive

Enthusiastic, intuitive, creative, inspirational, spontaneous, motivators, friendly, group-oriented, and energetic. Analysts delivering their findings to expressive clients should communicate with them often, be engaging, use multi-media, and be able to weave a captivating "story" together.

In a similar fashion, analysts need to look inwardly at their own personality and preferences to make sure that they are operating optimally in the communication process. Effective analysts recognize the different preferences and personalities and align them between the communicating parties.

■ Do not even know whether the right people are getting communicated to with the right results.

A surprising waste of analysis resources is common in those enterprises where analysts produce reports, develop web-sites, write briefings or newsletters, and distribute these items to readers who may never even know, or care, about receiving these items. We are aware of a great many firms where briefings would sit for weeks or months at a time before being read by the recipient, often rendering the content useless.

We find this communication error is made most commonly where analysts do not have regular, active meetings with their decision makers and become too heavily reliant on one-way methods such as newsletters, web-sites, intranet portals, or even bulletin boards. It is highly dangerous to assume that material disseminated in this fashion will actually be absorbed at all, let alone shortly after dispatch. Such a "scatter-gun" approach to communicating results ensures that little cross-fertilization of knowledge takes place—a vital ingredient in the rich mix of an analyst's appreciation of how information can impact in many ways, on more than one activity at any one time.

Effective Listening and Answering the Questions of Decision Makers

Analysts should also be competent in answering their client's questions and manage Q&A sessions effectively. One of the best things the analyst can do is to establish, up front, the guidelines and deadlines under which their presentation will operate. Some other tips analysts should demonstrate mastery of are the following:

- Never get into a debate, argue with, or criticize a questioner.

  Analysts who view every question as an attack on the integrity of their work or their personal integrity typically respond in defensive ways to questions. They will then attack the questioner, and this is unlikely to help them to become a trusted ally of the decision maker. Although some decision makers will commonly be argumentative with analysts, it will be important for the analyst to identify something the two parties can agree on, thank the arguer for their input, and move on to other facets of their dialogue.

- Answer questions succinctly.

  Most executives will quickly lose patience with an analyst who drones on and on about things without bothering to take a breath and assessing whether the client is still interested. Long-winded answers usually raise more questions than they answer. Short, concise, and "to the point" responses are generally favored by decision makers, and it is these that the analyst should aim to provide.

- Being able to admit they don't know something.

  Analysts cannot be afraid to say, "I don't know." It is surprising just how many people simply cannot say those three words when their client asks them a question. There is no way that you can have pre-empted and prepared for all the likely questions that can come from so many different perspectives. What they don't want to hear, though, after a dynamic presentation, is 30 seconds of mindless drivel while you try to make up a good answer to an unexpected question. Offer to find out the answer and get back to them by the end of the day. If you haven't found the answer by then, tell them so and keep looking unless, or until, you're told to stop.

- Start and end any meetings on time.

  Decision-making executives are well paid, and their time is highly valuable. One of the worst things an analyst can do in a communication activity is to either start a meeting after the appointed time or to end it late. Analysts should not let their poor attention to time management be the main thing their decision makers remember about their performance.

Conduct Communication Follow-Up and Gather Feedback

An element of most communication processes that is commonly overlooked is the gathering of feedback and subsequent measurement of the communication and client engagement process. Whenever possible, the analyst should take the opportunity to gain feedback from the audience, as close as possible to the event. Informal questions that can be asked might be:

- "Was that useful?"
- "Was there anything you'd like me to clarify or elaborate upon?"
- "Did I miss anything you would like me to have covered?"
- "Did you get what you needed?"
- "Was this information valuable?"
- "Did you feel confident about acting on my recommendations?"
- "Was there anything you'd suggest I do differently next time?"

It is essential, though, that this does not come across as the actions of a less than confident analyst, engaging in "approval-seeking" or "compliment-fishing" behavior that normally delivers only platitudes and not a truthful opinion on an individual's performance.

One thing that is often valuable to competitive analysts is to maintain a rolling audit of their outputs, their effectiveness in communicating these to their audience, and an account of any actions taken as a consequence. This will help them shape the overall process and enable all parties to identify any deficiencies.

Pragmatic Considerations

There are a variety of considerations that should always be taken into account when communicating across cultures or geographies.[19] This topic has received considerable treatment from many authors, but as a means of re-sensitizing analysts to the whole issue of cultural awareness and sensitivities when communicating, we offer a brief summary of the key points to consider in Table 4.1.

Table 4.1
Key Considerations When Communicating Across Cultures and Countries[20]

Factor	Consideration
E-mail	Recipients in many countries lack e-mail or enough bandwidth to accept long reports or attachments.
Hierarchical sensitivities	In some cultures, such as Indian or Japanese, the level and rank of the communicator and the audience is important. Therefore, it is the responsibility of the analyst to identify these factors before initiating discussion with hierarchically sensitive audience members.
Idiomatic expressions	Cats and dogs rain in the U.S. and UK, ropes rain in France, and it rains to the jugs in Spain. An analyst "rooting" for something to happen in the U.S. would be looked at askance by an Australian manager.

Table 4.1 *(continued)*
Key Considerations When Communicating Across Cultures and Countries[20]

Factor	Consideration
Local currency	Don't assume your unit of financial transactions is going to be properly understood elsewhere. Even the ubiquitous U.S. dollar doesn't easily convert to Chinese Remnibi and vice versa. Always help your audience by providing any financial data in familiar currency units.
Manner of communication	Some cultures prefer to receive communication in writing, others prefer face-to-face meetings, while others are most comfortable communicating electronically. It is critical that the analyst determines the most effective means before initiating the communication process.
Measurement units	Always convert measurements into the unit that is recognized and in common use by your audience.
Meeting times	North America, Europe, and most parts of Asia operate between 6 and 18 hours apart from one another. What is 5 p.m. on Thursday for an analyst in Chicago, Illinois, is early morning on Friday for the manager in Auckland, New Zealand. Also some cultures particularly value punctuality (Far East), while others are less concerned about it (Mediterranean).
Pace of speech	Reduce the pace of your oral communication when speaking to individuals whose first or native language is different from your own. This is not only polite but allows the recipient to hear all that you are saying, and provides them with time to mentally translate and understand the issues before responding.
Punctuation	Many nationalities have punctuation unique to their culture. Whether it is the chevron or the tilde, it is helpful to be aware of these before communicating with an audience that uses a language different from your own.
Use of color	White, red, and black have specific meanings to the Chinese people, whereas green is used for specific purposes in Islamic nations. Be very aware of such customs and practices to ensure that you do not unintentionally offend your audience
Written language structure	While English-reading audiences use a left to right structure, this is not so in others, where documents are read right to left across the page. Other groups, particularly Asian audiences, communicate vertically in the written word, not horizontally. This makes it important to pay attention to visual landmarks on the written page.

Summary

Just as analysts try to reduce the surprises experienced by their decision-making clients, they also need to apply the same principle to their own communication of results. M. Sperger put it succinctly when he said: "*How can we communicate intelligence so that it does indeed make a difference? We have to begin with a commitment: We will deliver intelligence at the right time, in the right form, with a message that compels action.*"

Analysts should have ongoing communication with their clients while they are engaged in the analysis process. This doesn't require them to report every small event, but it does require them to keep their clients informed of their progress, or equally important-ly, lack of progress. Maintaining open lines of communication and being able to give the client a "preview" of your findings before they are formally offered can minimize any adverse surprises. This also allows the decision maker to raise potential issues that the ana-lyst may not have thought of and still has time to address before the analysis process and project is brought to its conclusion.

Knowing when to begin the formal communication of results is also a delicate balanc-ing act that the analyst must master. Releasing results prematurely, possibly before the ana-lyst achieves a high enough degree of confidence in their findings, can result in poor deci-sions. Communicating one's results too late, possibly because the analyst wanted to be very certain of their insights, may render the findings obsolete and useless if the actions that needed to be taken were delayed unnecessarily by the analyst's reluctance to finish.[21]

Last, but certainly not least, in order to develop and keep their clients' trust, analysts must constantly acquire and enhance an in-depth understanding of their enterprise's busi-ness, industry, and markets. Additionally, they must always relate their key conclusions and recommendations back to what is important to their business. If they do not, they will have little ability to persuade their customers, build their influence, or impact business decisions.

References

Buchwitz, L. (1998). "*Monitoring Competitive Intelligence Using Internet Push Technology,*" available from http://home.eol.ca/~lillyb/CI_paper.html.

Clark, R.M. (2004). *Intelligence Analysis: A Target-Centric Approach*. Washington, DC: CQ Press.

DeSouza, K. (2001). "The communication of intelligence: Three lessons," *Competitive Intelligence Magazine*, 6(5), pp. 42–44.

Dugal, M. (1998). "CI product line: A tool for enhancing user acceptance of CI," *Competitive Intelligence Review*, 9(2), pp. 17–25.

Fehringer, D. (2001). "Hot off the wires: Improve the effectiveness of your CI Newsletter," *Competitive Intelligence Magazine*, 4(3), May–June, pp. 11, 14.

Herring, J.P. (1999). "Key intelligence topics: A process to identify and define intelligence needs," *Competitive Intelligence Review*, 10(4), pp. 10–19.

Kalinowski, D.J. (2003). "Managing expectations: Will clients ever fully understand?," *Competitive Intelligence Magazine*, 6(6), pp. 25–29.

Kopec, J.A. (1982). "The communication audit," *Public Relations Journal*, 38(5), May, p. 24.

Laalo, A.T. (2000). "Intranets and competitive intelligence: Creating access to knowledge," *Competitive Intelligence Review*, 9(4), pp. 63–72.

McGonagle, J.J., and C.M. Vella (2002). *Bottom Line Competitive Intelligence*. Westport, CT: Quorum Books.

Mockus, D.S. (2001). "Avoid the intelligence disconnect," *Competitive Intelligence Magazine*, 2001, 4(6), pp. 9–12.

Parker, D.A. (2003). *Confident Communication: Speaking Tips for Educators*. Thousand Oaks, CA: Corwin Press, Inc.

Sawka, K. (2000). The analyst's corner: Keep your messages short and sweet," *Competitive Intelligence Magazine*, 3(1), Jan–Mar, pp. 54–55.

Severin, W., and J. Tankard (1997). *Communication Theories*. 4th ed. New York, NY: Longman.

Shaker, M., and S. Gembicki (1999). *The WarRoom Guide to Competitive Intelligence*. New York, NY: McGraw-Hill.

Shannon, C.E., and W. Weaver (1949). *A Mathematical Model of Communication*. Urbana, IL: University of Illinois Press.

Sperger, M. (2005). "Managing the message: Communicating intelligence that makes a difference," *Competitive Intelligence Magazine*, 8(1), pp. 12–17.

Stanat, R. (1998). *Global Gold: Panning for Profits in Foreign Markets*. New York, NY: AMACOM.

Tyson, K.W.M. (2002). *The Complete Guide to Competitive Intelligence*. 2nd edition. Chicago, IL: Leading Edge Publications.

Waters Jr., T. (2001). "Special delivery: High impact presentation tactics for CI professionals," *Competitive Intelligence Magazine*, 4(6), Nov–Dec pp. 13–17.

Endnotes

[1] McGonagle and Vella, 2002.

[2] Buchwitz, 1998.

[3] DeSouza, 2001.

[4] Clark, 2004.

[5] Thanks to Melanie Wing for raising the importance of this premise in the communication of intelligence.

[6] See McGonagle and Vella, 2002; Tyson, 2002.

[7] Sawka, 2000.

[8] See Chapter 18 in Fleisher and Bensoussan, 2003.

[9] Shaker and Gembicki, 1999.

[10] Fehringer, 2001.

[11] A special note of thanks to Timothy Kindler for reminding us of the cumulative importance of communicating with decision makers.

[12] Tyson, 2002.

[13] Laalo, 2000.

[14] Severin and Tankard, 1997.

[15] Waters, 2001.

[16] Herring, 1999.

[17] Parker, 2003.

[18] Tyson, 2002.

[19] Sperger, 2005; Stanat, 1998.

[20] These factors were adapted from the cultural awareness data presented in Communicaid (www.communicaid.com), Sperger, 2005; Stanat, 1998; and www.WorldBiz.com.

[21] De Souza, 2001.

5

Applying the FAROUT Method

Choosing from an increasing array of techniques can be one of the most difficult tasks facing an analyst. Research of the use of conceptual tools and techniques suggests that executives heavily support the idea that executives who use the right tools will succeed, while simultaneously recognizing that most tools over-promise and under-deliver results.[1] We think one of the reasons this is believed is that the tools selected and used by analysts are frequently incorrect and inappropriate to their needs.

There are hundreds of analytical tools and techniques identified in the literature.[2] Some techniques are briefly referred to, while others are treated through book length treatises. Many more are applied in unique or proprietary ways by analysts in addressing their challenges. We are not surprised that "tools" are seen as over-ambitious and under-performing. The well-worn analogy that a worker with only a hammer sees every task as simply a decision on how many nails to use holds true in the case of competitive analysis. We might also suggest that just because a worker has hundreds of different tools, it does not mean that he can apply them all effectively. Most specialists have a handful that they prefer and can apply most effectively. Fortunately, we believe that there are some considerations that analysts can make to lessen the likelihood of using the wrong tool for the job.

Techniques have an important role to play in the larger competitive and strategic analysis process. Individuals who study for a Master of Business Administration degree (MBA) or other higher-level business program will be exposed to some of these techniques in their marketing or strategy courses. Among the benefits that analysts and their organizations gain from using techniques correctly are the following:

1. **Greater understanding of relationships and situations**—Virtually every technique and combination of techniques requires the analyst to ask numerous questions

including "what?," "how?," "when?," "who?," "where?," and most importantly, "why?." These questions lessen the likelihood that they will miss or overlook important facets of the analysis being undertaken.

2. **Initially focus the analyst on data and facts**—Most techniques require data and facts first and discourage the use of unqualified opinions, beliefs, rumors, or feelings. Although some techniques are highly qualitative, and others highly quantitative, nearly all of them require the analyst to maintain a keen understanding of the soundness of data input.

3. **Guide efficient data collection efforts**—On agreeing which questions are to be answered, the analyst can then consider which techniques will be of most use. This then drives the data collection effort and lessens the likelihood that time and resources will be spent on collecting unnecessary or redundant information.

4. **Encourages analysts to be rigorous**—Most techniques compel the analysts to consider a wider and deeper range of possibilities than they would normally accomplish alone. This is exemplified by the processes we outline in this book that can require multiple steps, which in turn require many checks and balances between these steps. Hasty analyses, badly organized information, and only using convenient data always leads to dissatisfied decision makers and short careers for the analysts who operate in this fashion.

5. **Forces analysts to think critically**—Analysts should consider the benefits and limitations inherent in looking at data and information in specific ways. Most of the techniques presented here, along with the information we urge analysts to consider, should help them to prepare defensible and well-reasoned insights that will stand up to the critical scrutiny of demanding decision makers. Many of these techniques are subsequently modified for particular proprietary applications in enterprises, which often then become part of the enterprise's analytical repertoire.

6. **Promotes a proactive attitude to analysis**—Most techniques require the analyst to consider the options and think through the relative value of each before use. Utilizing selection criteria to choose the best technique(s) for particular challenges causes analysts to think ahead in terms of the data they will need to operate each and the type of outcome each will deliver. This helps to determine their suitability to address the question(s) being asked.

Studies of the use of competitive analysis tools and techniques have demonstrated the extent of their use, as well as perceived judgments of their effectiveness. According to A. Gib and R. Gooding's survey of competitive analysts, the most-utilized tools included competitor profiling, product/market analysis, industry analysis, qualitative research methods, and customer satisfaction surveys. These tools all tended to be rated highly in terms of their perceived effectiveness, along with management profiling. The least-utilized tools included spire analysis, dialectic inquiry/devil's advocacy, gaming theory, force field analysis, and experience curve analysis.

As advisors and consultants in the area of competitive and strategic analysis, we are not surprised by the finding that a tool's extensive use and its perceived effectiveness would be highly correlated. Analysts will use tools they perceive to be effective and will shy away from ones they perceive to be ineffective. Having said that, we have no knowledge of how well trained the analysts were in applying the thirty tools that were rated, the nature of the questions or topics that their decision-making clients had asked them to address, the context in which they applied the tools, or the quality of the data/information used in employing the techniques.

Applying the Techniques

There is a process to properly identify analysis techniques, and analysts should think through a series of questions before they make their choice:

1. What is the full range of techniques that can be used to respond to the question asked?

2. What is the focus and scope of the competitive phenomenon being analyzed?

3. What are the constraints—personal, informational, organizational, resources, and contextual—that might affect the analysis process?

Every technique we detail in this book delivers certain things very well, but most also have drawbacks of which the astute analyst must be aware, and we draw attention to these individually.

In the "Background" section of each technique, we provide our readers with the context in which the tool was originally developed. A good number of the tools presented in this and our prior book[3] were developed decades ago by individuals who recognized problems at the time and sought a conceptual and/or methodological means for solving it. They often become popularized through a management guru or large consultancy practice.[4] Many of these tools have been in use, taught, and improved through the years to the point where they are now viewed as standard models for use by an analyst. These tools are also the most likely to have been customized or adapted for use by an enterprise, especially as they are more likely to be well understood and regularly employed in analysis work.

Other techniques have been developed more recently, often in response to new phenomena being encountered. These tools have not had the benefit of decades of critical scholarly scrutiny or improvement through practice and teaching and may yet still evolve dramatically. This does not make them more or less useful to the analyst, and time will be the best arbiter over whether they too become part of the standard competencies of the competitive analyst.

We try to point out the "strategic rationale" for the tool's development, and we demonstrate the important links the tool has to other strategic concepts. We also suggest what implications the analyst's application of the tool and the results that are generated from its application will have for the specific decisions being made.

In each section, we look at both the "strengths and advantages" and "weaknesses and limitations" of each tool identified. We caution readers against reading too much into the length or the number of strengths or weaknesses identified. It was not our goal to be exhaustive but to highlight the more prominent items that the analyst must consider. Readers should critically consider each of the points made in this section independently and factor them into their application of the tool. This will help to guide the level of confidence by which they communicate their findings.

Very few questions can be satisfactorily answered through the application of a single analytical technique. If it were that easy, then there would be no need for this book. Most strategic, business, and competitive questions are complex, dynamic, and cognitively challenging. This requires the analyst to identify the sequence and range of techniques that need to be applied, and every time that this is done, a different answer will emerge. Some application sequences will be more efficient and effective than others, sometimes, but not always. The analyst also needs to identify the nature and range of data that is already available or can be acquired before making a decision. Some techniques will have to be discarded simply because it is impossible to obtain the required information in a timely manner.

An Evaluation Scheme for Assessing the Adequacy of Tools and Techniques: FAROUT

Any form of intelligence generated must ultimately satisfy a decision maker and the organization's needs. An effective analyst needs to know how the intelligence generated by the application of a technique will be used. Although these principles may appear simple to apply on the surface, there are a variety of objective considerations that make the execution of an analyst's responsibilities far more difficult in practice.

After years of conducting strategic and competitive analysis projects, some authors realized that there were a limited number of key considerations common to all high-value analysis. [5]

A unique concept we have developed for analysts is the FAROUT approach. The FAROUT profile we developed for every technique can be beneficial in helping analysts make choices from the techniques we detail in this book. Applying FAROUT to their selection process will support analysts in selecting the particular technique or combination of techniques to best meet their unique situations. Having said that, we want to be clear that FAROUT is only a guide, and, as such, is only one input among many others that an analyst needs to consider in developing their craft. It is designed to assist analysts in knowing which techniques are appropriate for any given situation.

FAROUT is based on the premise that for analytical output to be insightful, intelligent, and valuable to business decision makers, it needs to meet a number of common characteristics. The output needs to be

*F*uture-oriented

*A*ccurate

*R*esource efficient

*O*bjective

*U*seful and

*T*imely

Failure to meet all these criteria to a satisfactory level will result in the analytical output being less than optimal and of lesser value to the decision maker.

The six components of FAROUT are described next.

Future-orientation: Relying on the past as predictor of the future can be dangerous. This is particularly true when innovation, science, and technology factors can quickly disrupt a market. This has been very evident in the rapid adoption and development of e-commerce causing disintermediation of entire industries. By definition, the intelligence resulting from an analyst's work must be future-oriented, looking both deeply and broadly at what might happen. They must be willing to take risks to some degree by being both inventive and predictive. Early warning, foresight, prescience, or prevision cannot be adequately generated by using historical data that are focused entirely on the past. The better analytical methods for developing intelligence are indeed future-oriented.

Accuracy: The effective analyst should develop outputs that aim for high levels of accuracy. This means that the insights gained are precise. Accuracy also means that the analyst's insights are as closely matched as possible to the actual conditions of the phenomena being analyzed. High levels of accuracy are difficult to attain in practice when the data underlying the analysis

- has come from only one source;
- has not been cross-validated against both hard and soft information;
- is collected under time constraints that restrict the comprehensiveness of the collection process;
- needs to be converted from sources in ways that it was not originally designed for; and/or
- comes from sources filled with high levels of bias in the first place.

Although achieving the highest levels of accuracy is theoretically desirable, the analyst usually has to trade-off against other conceptual and pragmatic considerations. Experienced practitioners have suggested that in a good proportion of competitive marketplace contexts, accuracy or precision may often be much less important than developing an enhanced understanding or perspective.

Resource efficiency: To produce effective analysis, data needs to come from sources that cost less than the resultant output is worth. This equation refers to the marginal value of gathering the additional information required. At the margin, the subsequent use of a tool is valuable to the extent that it will increase the value of the insights more than the resources expended by the enterprise's analyst in applying it. Executives commonly lament that their organizations gather enormous amounts of data, with the thought that it eventually may be needed. Their experiences suggest that much, if not most, of the data will likely lay dormant for years inside contemporary, high volume, digital storage devices. Although an Internet search may conveniently produce volumes of apparent "hits," one phone call to a well-placed and knowledgeable contact would most likely have produced far superior information in a fraction of the time.

Objectivity: The application of a given method affects the degree of bias held by the analyst, analyst groups, and/or organizations.[6] Too many otherwise "good" analyses can be clouded by cognitive or social biases ranging from *prior hypothesis bias* through *recentness* and *availability* to *groupthink*, all of which provide comfort in dealing with risk or uncertainty.[7] To minimize the potentially destructive nature of these common biases, data or information should be viewed by analysts in a dispassionate, impersonal, rational, and systematic manner. In other words, objectivity helps to minimize the destructive potential of analytical and decision-oriented biases. It is also essential for analysts to recognize the potential for and avoid the selective use of facts to provide support for pre-ordained or desirous conclusions. Experienced analysts recognize that delivering bad news is just as much a part of their job as delivering good news, and they will tackle each with equal skill and objectivity.

Usefulness: Almost by definition, valuable analytical outputs will meet the critical intelligence needs specified by a particular decision maker. The output of some techniques and models can be quickly understood, whereas others may be less easily digested and can require the decision maker to further engage with the analyst before they are confident of making decisions. It helps if the analyst and the decision maker can design a process that helps each of them to develop a clear understanding of the problems and intelligence needs, as well as a deep and broad appreciation of the decision context. This understanding does not always come easily, and for many, will only emerge over a lengthy period of time, which engenders trust and respect for the tasks and responsibilities of each. Ultimately, effective analysts strive to produce outputs that meet, or surpass, the requirements of the decision maker.

Timeliness: Strategic business information or competitive data frequently has a limited "shelf life," especially where those decisions are being made in dynamic, hyper-competitive, or turbulent environmental contexts. Consequently, raw data loses its value the longer it remains excluded from the decisions underlying organizational action. Some methods of analysis may provide the intelligence required by clients for decisions but take far too long to develop. This could happen when there is a need to subject the data to multiple phases of analysis, the need to gather a certain volume or variety of data that is not quickly accessible, or to employ other, less readily available individuals in the process. On the other hand, some methods of analysis may require little time to perform but do not deliver the other required features of objectivity, accuracy, utility, and resource efficiencies. Valuable analysis will provide decision makers with enough time to implement the course of action recommended by the analysis.

Using the FAROUT Rating System

Managing the analysis of business and competitive data is a challenging task, and we are not aware of any *Analysis for Dummies* books or magic software that can replace an analyst who knows how to employ a good balance of both science and creativity. We do know from experience, it is highly unlikely that good analytical output will be based on just one analytical method or tool. Rather, a combination of several techniques will be required.

Each analytical method has unique limitations, and these limitations multiply when placed in specific organizational contexts. The *FAROUT* system will enable the analyst to mix the appropriate tools to be applied in analysis tasks so as to maximize the insights generated for their decision makers. It is our view that the more successful analysts recognize and are sensitive to the limitations associated with any particular analytical method or technique. The sensitized analyst can address these issues throughout the whole of the competitive and strategy analysis process to overcome such limitations.

We utilize a five-point rating scale to assess each analytical technique contained in Part Two. The five-point scale ranges from low (1) to high (5) and is expanded in Table 5.1. Every technique is assessed against the six FAROUT elements. Our objective in offering the FAROUT framework is to assist analysts in assessing the outputs of different analytical methods to ensure high intelligence value. If the analysis delivers on all six characteristics, analysts and decision makers can be reasonably confident that the output will make a difference. All the techniques and their ratings are summarized for easy reference in Table 5.2.

Table 5.1
Assessment of Analysis Techniques Using the FAROUT Scheme

The *FAROUT* Scale	
Future orientation	1 = the model's output is not future-oriented. It may be too anchored in the past or present.
	5 = the model is highly future-focused.
Accuracy	1 = the level of accuracy for outputs using this model is low, taking into account the probable sources of data underlying its application.
	5 = the requirements of the model lead to the generation of highly accurate outputs.
Resource-efficiency	1 = this model requires a large volume of data, financial, and human resources, and is low in efficacy.
	5 = this technique is highly efficient in its use of resources and in deriving desired outputs from few inputs.
Objectivity	1 = a particular tool provides low levels of objectivity due to the presence of biases and mind-sets in its application.
	5 = that the potential for biases can be minimized.
Usefulness	1 = application of a model delivers less useful output and requires additional work by or on behalf of a decision maker.
	5 = tool provides a high level of valued output without requiring additional effort by a decision maker.
Timeliness	1 = an analysis model that requires a great deal of time to complete well.
	5 = this model takes little time to successfully complete.

Table 5.2
FAROUT Summary of Methods

	Analysis Method	Future-Orientation	Accuracy	Resource-Efficiency	Objectivity	Usefulness	Timeliness
	Section 1—Competitive						
6	Industry Analysis/ Nine Forces	4	3	4	2	3	3
7	Competitive Positioning	4	4	4	4	5	3
8	Business Model Analysis	3	3	4	3	4	3
9	SERVO Analysis	4	2	3	1	4	2
10	Supply Chain Analysis	4	3	3	4	5	3
	Section 2—Enterprise						
11	Benchmarking	3	3	2	3	5	2
12	McKinsey 7s Analysis	4	2	3	1	3	2
13	Shadowing	4	3	2	3	5	4
14	Product Line Analysis	3	3	3	4	3	2
15	Win/Loss Analysis	4	3	4	4	5	2
	Section 3—Environmental						
16	Strategic Relationship Analysis	2	4	2	4	3	3
17	Corporate Reputation Analysis	2	4	1	4	3	2
18	Critical Success Factor Analysis	3	4	3	2	5	3
19	Country Risk Analysis	3	2	3	3	3	3
20	Driving Forces Analysis	5	3	3	2	4	3
	Section 4—Evolutionary						
21	Event and Timeline Analysis	4	4	4	4	3	3
22	Technology Forecasting	5	2	3	2	4	2
23	War Gaming	5	3	3	3	5	1

Table 5.2 *(continued)*
FAROUT Summary of Methods

	Analysis Method	Future-Orientation	Accuracy	Resource-Efficiency	Objectivity	Usefulness	Timeliness
24	Indications and Warning Analysis	5	3	3	2	4	3
25	Historiographical Analysis	2	2	3	1	4	3
	Section 5—Financial, Probabilistic, & Statistical						
26	Interpretation of Statistical Analysis	1	4	3	3	3	2
27	Competitor Cash Flow Analysis	4	4	1	3	5	2
28	Analysis of Competing Hypothesis	1	3	2	5	3	2
29	Linchpin Analysis	3	2	3	4	5	2

References

Clark, D.N. (1997). "Strategic management tool usage: A comparative study," *Strategic Change*, 6(7), 417–427.

Fahey, L. (1999). *Competitors: Outwitting, Outmaneuvering, and Outperforming*. New York, NY: John Wiley & Sons.

Fleisher, C.S., and B.E. Bensoussan (2003). *Strategic and Competitive Analysis: Methods and Techniques for Analyzing Business Competition*. Upper Saddle River, NJ: Prentice Hall.

Gib, A., and R. Gooding (1998). "CI tool time: What's missing from your toolbag?," pp. 25–39 in the *Proceedings of the 1998 international conference of the Society of Competitive Intelligence Professionals*, Chicago, IL.

Harris, S.G. (1994). "Organizational culture and individual sense making: A schema-based perspective," *Organization Science*, 5(3), 309–321.

Hawkins, S., and R Hastie (1990). "Hindsight: Biased judgments of past events after the outcomes are known," *Psychological Bulletin*, 10(3), 311–327.

Hogarth, R.M. (1980). *Judgment and Choice: The Psychology of Decision*. New York, NY: John Wiley & Sons.

Hogarth, R.M., and S. Makridakis (1981). "Forecasting and planning: An evaluation," *Management Science*, 27(2), 115–138.

Mathey, C.J. (1990). "Competitive analysis mapping," *Competitive Intelligence Review*, 1(2), Fall, 16–17.

McGonagle, J.J. (2004). "Analytical techniques," *Competitive Intelligence Magazine*, 7(4), 51, 54.

Prescott, J.E. (1986). "A process for applying analytic models in competitive analysis," pp. 222–251 in King, W. and D. Cleland [eds.], *Strategic Planning and Management Handbook*. New York, NY: Van Nostrand Reinhold and Company.

Rigby, D.K. (2003). *Management Tools 2003*. White Paper. Boston, MA: Bain & Company, Inc.

Rigby, D.K. (2001). "Putting the tools to the test: Senior executives rate 25 top management tools," *Strategy and Leadership*, 29(3), 4–12.

Sandman, M.A. (2000). "Analytical models and techniques," pp. 69–98 in Miller, J. [ed.], *Millennium Intelligence: Understanding and Conducting Intelligence in the Digital Age*. Medford, NJ: Information Today.

Webster, J., Reif, W.E., and J.S. Bracker (1989). "The manager's guide to strategic planning tools and techniques," *Planning Review*, 17(6), Nov/Dec., 4–13.

Endnotes

[1] Rigby, 2001.

[2] For example—Clark, 1997; Fahey, 1999; Fleisher and Bensoussan, 2003; Mathey, 1990; McGonagle, 2004; Prescott, 1986; Sandman, 2000; Webster *et al.*, 1989.

[3] See Fleisher and Bensoussan, 2003.

[4] Rigby, 2003.

[5] Fleisher and Bensoussan, 2003.

[6] Harris, 1994; Hawkins and Hastie, 1990.

[7] Hogarth, 1980; Hogarth and Makridakis, 1981.

Industry Analysis (The Nine Forces)

Short Description

This chapter combines the two substantial topic areas of macro-environmental analysis with industry analysis and demonstrates the unique creativity that is part of the world of business and competitive analysis.

Organizations and the industries in which they operate are embedded in a broad environment, which can significantly impact the competitiveness of both industries and organizations.

The starting point then of any strategic analysis is some form of environmental analysis—generally STEEP/PEST analysis[1]—followed by Industry Analysis or Porter's Five Forces,[2] which together provide a structural framework outlining an industry and a unique and perhaps more holistic perspective on a firm's competitiveness.

Uniting these two techniques creates a powerful framework for not only identifying the forces operating in a particular industry, but the impact of environmental factors on these very forces. These two techniques combined provide a much broader approach to business and competitive analysis. The technique is called "The Nine Forces."

Background

A firm's environment is defined generally as the broad set of forces coming or operating from outside the firm that can affect its competitive performance. Firms are open systems subject to a range of external inputs and influences. They all "import" outside resources like finances, people, raw materials, and most "export" products or services back out into that environment. Because the environment influences the form and behavior of a firm, competitively successful firms must effectively evaluate that environment.

Most environmental analysis is based on the assumption that industry forces are *not* the sole explanation of all that occurs within the industry. The environment beyond an industry's boundaries can be a primary determinant or will in some way influence what actually takes place within that industry. External factors for change can be among the primary determinants of competition and competitiveness in a global marketplace or economy.

On the other hand, with industry analysis, the dominant aspects of a firm's environment are assumed to exist in and around the industry or industries in which the firm completes. An industry environment would consist of a particular set of competitive forces that create both threats and opportunities. Porter's Five Forces model addresses this perspective and is shown in Figure 6.1.

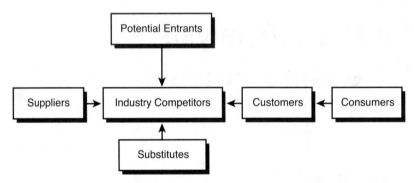

Figure 6.1   Generic framework of industry analysis

The definition of a firm's environment and the approach by which it may be strategically and competitively analyzed will often differ depending on the perspective the firm's members choose to pursue. By combining both analytical techniques, differing organizational perspectives can be taken into account through the broader analysis of nine forces.

To perform the Nine Forces analysis, an analyst needs to address the three basic levels of organizational environments: the general environment, the operating or industry environment, and the internal environment. Figure 6.2 illustrates the relationship of each of these levels with each other and with the firm at large.

General Environment

The general environment is that level of a firm's environment that is broad in scope and has long-term implications for managers, firms, and strategies. These are usually understood to be beyond the direct influence or primary control of any single organization. STEEP/PEST analysis is one way of addressing and studying the broader issues that affect the general environment in which a firm operates.

The acronym STEEP stands for *social*, *technological*, *economic*, *ecological*, and *political/legal* sectors. PEST represents the same approach and stands for *political/legal*, *economic*, *social*, and *technological* sectors (see Figure 6.3). Each sector operates over a large geographic area (e.g., global, international, multinational, regional, national, provincial/state, and local) and over time (i.e., past, present, and future).

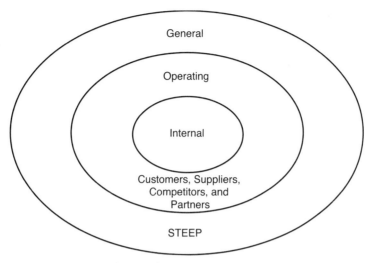

Figure 6.2   Three levels of the environment

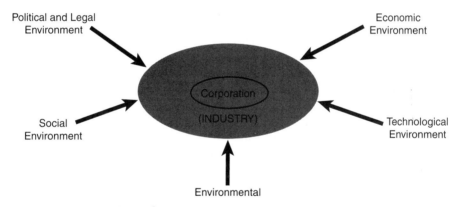

Figure 6.3   STEEP/PEST factors

Note: In PEST, ecological issues are often included across the other four sectors. These sectors are described as follows:

Political/Legal—The political component of the general environment relates to government and public attitudes toward various industries, lobbying efforts by interest groups, the regulatory climate, platforms of political parties, and (sometimes) the predisposition of politicians. The legal component consists of laws that members of society are expected to follow. In most nation-states, legal constraints in the form of public policies and regulations affect an organization's discretionary ability to act. Besides being a large consumer and producer in their own right, governments can legislate for greater or lesser competition and therefore become a critical focus of the competitive and strategy analyst's efforts in this sector. For companies such as defense contractors, educational institutions, health care organizations, and not-for-profits, the actions and mood of public policy makers are vital inputs to their competitive strategy development process.

Economic—The economic component of the general environment indicates the distribution and uses of resources within an entire society. By an entire society, we also mean the impact of the global economy on any market where international factors play an influencing role. This is important because consumption patterns are largely influenced by economic trends such as employment rates, exchange rates, interest rates, inflation rates, credit availability, fiscal and monetary policies, spending patterns, and levels of disposable income both locally and internationally.

In a rapidly changing global environment, events and economic issues that occur outside of one's market or country can still greatly impact the ability of a firm to remain competitive locally. Analytical tasks include the identification, monitoring, and forecasting of those economic variables to which the firm's strategic competitive efforts are most sensitive.

Ecological—This encompasses both the physical and biological environments within which firms operate. "Greening" of the environment illustrates the power that this factor can now exert on a firm's performance. Aspects of the ecological environment to include in this analysis are review of the global climate (e.g., effects of greenhouse gases), sustainable development (e.g., forestry practices), cradle-to-grave product life cycles, recycling, pollution, and biotechnological advances (e.g., genetic advances in agricultural products), among others.

Social—Characteristics of the societal context includes demographics, cultural attitudes, literacy rates, education levels, customs, beliefs, values, lifestyles, age distribution, geographic distribution, and population mobility. While the pace of change in this sector may be slow, its effects are quite profound and inescapable.

Technological—Digital communication, biotechnology, chemicals, energy, and medicine are only a few of the fields in which major technological changes have opened new areas to commercial competition. The technological component of the general environment is compounded by the impact of science and technology in product and process innovation as well. This includes new approaches to producing goods and services such as new procedures and new equipment.

The analytical task is to identify and monitor the effects of technological change as it affects competitive strategy. This can be seen not only in the final goods and services market, but also in new product and process innovation, and even communication, human resource attraction, and marketing methods. Interfacing with the organization's R&D functions is an obvious requirement for business and competitive analysts.

It is important to monitor and evaluate each of these nonmarket factors and their impact in terms of a firm's overall strategic directions.

Operating Environment/Industry Analysis

The operating environment, sometimes termed the competitive or market environment, is that level of the firm's external environment with components that normally have relatively specific and immediate implications for managing the firm.

The three main components of the operating environment are customers, suppliers, and competitors. Unlike the general environment, the operating environment can be influenced by individual firms.

The *Customer* component of the operating environment describes characteristics and behavior of those who buy or could buy the firm's goods and services. Customers are those who buy direct from a firm. They may not, however, be the final consumers of particular products or services. The customer component may therefore include direct buyers all the way to the end consumers. Analysts may want to break this group down into actual buyers (sometimes referred to as clients or customers) to retailers, wholesalers, or distributors, to end consumers.

The *Supplier* component refers to the role of external resources on the firm. Firms purchase and transform resources during production into goods and services, so issues like how many vendors offer specialized resources for sale, relative quality of material offered, reliability of deliveries, credit terms offered, and the potential for strategic linkages all affect managing the supplier component.

The *Competitor* component consists of rivals, present and prospective, that an organization must overcome in order to reach its objectives. Analysis and understanding of competitors is critical to developing an effective strategy. Competitor analysis should assist management appreciate the strengths, weaknesses, and capabilities of existing and potential competitors and predict their responses to both strategic and tactical initiatives.

The structure of key relationships in this operating environment, or environments when the firm operates in multiple industries, affects both profit potential and prospects for achieving competitive advantage.

Internal Environment

The firm's internal environment includes forces that operate inside the firm with specific implications for managing a firm's performance. Unlike externally derived components of the general and operating environments, components of the internal environment derive from the firm itself. The aspects of a firm's internal environment (production, marketing, and so on) include both trouble spots that need strengthening and core competencies that the firm can nurture and build. By systematically examining its internal activities, a firm can better appreciate how each activity might add value or contribute significantly to shaping an effective strategy. Michael Porter has proposed value chain analysis as a method for such an evaluation.[3] Value chain analysis can help identify internal core competencies, which in concert with an external industry structure, are seen as the critical elements of competitive advantage and profitability.

Strategic Rationale and Implications

Macro-environmental and industry conditions affect the entire strategic management process. Effective strategic management is about making organizational decisions that correspond positively with the entire business environment. While a firm may be able to shape elements of the environment to its advantage, it will also have to adapt and react in ways that disadvantage it less than its competitors.

Hence, the key purpose of the Nine Forces model is to provide an accurate, objective insight into the significant issues and forces that surround and impact on a firm, as shown in Figure 6.4. The Nine Forces lead executive thinking beyond current activities and short-time horizons. It provides sensible links to current and near-term activities while maintaining an appropriate balance between short- and long-term issues. However, unless a filtering process is developed, the abundant environmental and industry information available can weaken a firm's strategy formulation process.

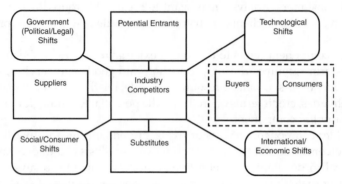

Figure 6.4   The Nine Forces

The Nine Forces technique provides a structured and systematic approach to the identification and analysis of relevant trends, events, and the influence and/or impact of each of the nine factors not only within themselves but across the other forces. Furthermore, this framework addresses the assumptions underlying strategy, which may lead to ineffective planning. Success or failure can depend on the accuracy and effectiveness of decision makers reading and responding to this more realistic environment.

Combining analysis of the broader business environment, with Porter's Five Forces, this technique enables the analyst to identify and analyze those major forces that will influence an industry's profit potential. Identifying the profit potential or attractiveness of an industry provides the foundation for building the strategy that bridges the gap between the firm's external environment and its resources.

Analysts can, within this framework, address Porter's "rules of competition,"[4] which are as follows:

- **Threat of New Entrants**—Entry barriers define the level of difficulty facing those firms considering competitive entry into the industry. When barriers are low, new competition will add capacity to the industry and increase demand and prices for inputs, resulting in lower industry profitability.

- **Bargaining Power of Suppliers**—This force refers to the ability of the suppliers to influence the cost, availability, and quality of input materials to firms in the industry.

- **Bargaining Power of Buyers**—The firm's customers have a major role in defining industry structure by virtue of their ability to force down prices via comparison shopping or by raising quality expectations.

- **Threat of Substitute Products or Services**—This force describes the risk of market displacement by existing or potential substitutes.

- **Rivalry Among Existing Competitors**—Intensity of competition within an industry. This force has been empirically demonstrated in a large number of instances to be the most influential of the five forces.

By combining STEEP/PEST and Porter's Five Forces, the Nine Forces technique provides a robustness to any industry and environmental analysis and delivers a unique combination of insights that are not apparent when doing either of these analytical techniques in isolation. The purpose then of this analytical technique is to help analysts to answer the following two questions: Based on this environment, how attractive is the industry? How can your firm best compete?

Strengths and Advantages

Research has demonstrated that companies in some environments can gain an advantage over their competition based on the quality of their environmental analysis.[5] Using the Nine Forces provides one way of integrating key personnel and cross-functional information into some facet of environmental and industry analysis. Further, this framework implies that managers should focus on broader environmental characteristics, and it encourages investment in understanding influencing industry factors and structure. This analysis can additionally identify existing and potential strengths, weaknesses, opportunities, and threats suggested by components of the firm's environment.

Throughout the firm, people can contribute to this analytical process. Various contributions can be important in and of themselves as they can create an evergreen forum for sharing and debating divergent views on relevant general environmental changes. The more individuals involved, the greater the opportunity to identify and challenge opportunities or threats in the environment. However, as the firm must gather and act on diverse information in a timely manner, cross-functional teams of internal specialists can often perform the Nine Forces analysis most effectively.

The Nine Forces analysis can assist in developing a firm's positioning strategy by matching a firm's strength and weaknesses within the current environment. Competitive forces analysis identifies sources and strengths of competitive pressures whether they be from within the industry or from the broader environment. To be successful, strategy must be designed to cope effectively with key competitive pressures to build a strong market position based on competitive advantage.

Unattractive competitive environments may exist when government plays a strong role, rivalry is intense, entry barriers are low, competition from substitutes is strong, and suppliers and customers have stronger bargaining power. Attractive competitive environments may exist when entry barriers are relatively high, no good substitutes exist, and both suppliers and customers have weak bargaining positions. In general, weak competitive forces mean greater firm profits. A company whose strategy and market position provides a good defense against these forces can earn better profits despite some or all of these forces being strong.

The Nine Forces model provides us with a broad analytical tool to develop strategies that will protect the company from competitive forces, provide a strong position from which "to play the game" of competition, and help create competitive advantage.

This technique can also be used to develop a proactive strategy influencing industry dynamics in a firm's favor. Industry evolution is an important component of the Nine Forces model since it allows us to identify windows of opportunity to capitalize on changes in force of industry structure or the influencing factors from the general environment.

The Nine Forces are interrelated to such an extent that a change in one force may impact the other forces. The essential tasks in this analysis are to identify the following:

- Forecasted changes in each of the nine competitive forces.
- How these changes impact other forces.
- How results of interrelated changes will impact future profitability of the industry.
- The predicted strength of the firm's position in this future scenario when employing the current strategy.
- How strategy might be changed to exploit changing industry structure and environmental factors by either reacting to competitor actions or by proactively seeking to secure competitive advantage through strategic change.

Because both the STEEP/PEST and Five Forces models place a strong emphasis on environmental and industry evolution respectively, they provide strong foundations for scenario analysis. By first examining each of the Nine Forces and then understanding the mutual dependency between the various forces, analysts can establish the proper mindset for long-range analysis.

The Nine Forces uniquely combines the strengths of both STEEP/PEST and the Five Forces analysis, while addressing some of the more common weaknesses of each technique.

Weaknesses and Limitations

Nine Forces analysis is not an easy analytical task because differing perceptions of the environmental context come into play. Apart from the identified weaknesses and limitations of both STEEP/PEST and the Five Forces, analysts may find that decision makers often have difficulty in defining what their environment is and in placing limits around it. Difficulties may also exist in interpreting the results and specific impacts, which in turn will affect choosing effective responses. Potential interpretation weaknesses include: structuring robust studies; showing financial impact; understanding both short- and long-term implications; insufficient senior management involvement in the analysis; difficulties in translating potential opportunities into action plans; and the time and resources required to do accurate analysis. As a result, the analytical output can be inaccurate.

With many firms also focused on the short-term perspective, executives may forestall the environmental analysis process. Many decision makers dislike spending "real" money today for speculative actions about tomorrow. Many firms also cut back their resources for in-depth analysis during tough economic times, viewing it as a luxury rather than a necessity. However, this is often when the analysis is most needed.

Many companies do not accept the value of the Nine Forces analysis and therefore do not take the time to do it well. It can be poorly understood and thus under-valued by management. The failure to link the Nine Forces analysis to competitive implications is common. The key goal of this process is the identification of competitive implications for the firm based on this broader environment analysis.

In his book, *The Fifth Discipline*, Peter Senge[6] stated, "More specifically, new insights fail to get put into practice because they conflict with deeply held internal images about how the world works, images that limit us to familiar ways of thinking and acting." Many decision makers hold narrow, limited, or invalid perceptions about the world in which they operate. For example, they think in local terms as opposed to global terms, or since this type of analysis was not covered in their formal training, it must be of lesser importance.

Finally, diversified businesses can bring great complexity for analysts, as they seek to grasp the implications of many environmental and organizational dynamics. Biases, prior experience, and human limitations will affect their approach. Particularly in multinational environments, home-country biases and attitudes often lead organizations to assume and superimpose their own experiences, views, and understandings on variables operating in other countries.

Process for Applying the Technique

Begin with the firm's decision makers defining environmental and industry boundaries to limit the breadth, depth, and forecasting horizon of the analysis. *Breadth* refers to the topical coverage of the environmental data that are collected. *Depth* determines the amount of detailed data sought and analyzed in the Nine Forces. *Forecasting horizons* span short, medium, and long terms, as dictated within the firm's specific environment.

To establish the boundaries of the firm, management may look at the organization's strategic posture with respect to its geographic diversity (i.e., where it does and does not compete), its product or service market scope, its return horizon on its fixed resource commitments, technology and innovation, sources of its resources (capital, human, other financial, and raw materials), regulatory mandate, and flexibility.

Once definition and delimitation have occurred, the process essentially involved three key steps. First, collect information to identify the characteristics of each force (refer to Figure 6.4). The objective is to understand each force being analyzed and its relationship to the other forces.

Questions that may be addressed include:

What are the interrelationships between trends? This requires the analyst to use his or her creative capacity in identifying interrelationships between environmental and industry segments. The analyst should be looking for areas where trends are suggesting redefinitions or changes from the expected evolutionary path or where trends are reinforcing one another.

What are the conflicts between trends? Trends often push in opposite directions. For example, people are becoming more committed to their work at the same time that they are seeking more family time outside of the workplace.

Not all trends are of equal importance to a firm or an industry. Some will have a direct impact, while others may have only tangential impact depending on how the trend interacts with the firm's strategy. It is crucial that the analyst identify those trends and trend combinations that are likely to have the highest impact on the firm's goal pursuits. Critical trends are "issues" for the organization.

Forecasting the future evolution of a trend or set of trends within the issue requires analysis of the driving forces behind the issue. It is critical to distinguish between symptoms and causes, but it may be very difficult. Often driving forces work against one another and push simultaneously in multiple directions. Once the causes are accurately identified, the analyst can then develop alternative projections of the issue's evolution.

The objective is to examine and assess the impact of all Nine Forces on the industry and/or firm. Secondary sources can provide much of the information in this step; however, primary sources should be consulted to improve objectivity.

The process for analyzing the nine competitive forces looks to identifying the main sources of power or competitive pressures among each force.

For the next step, the analyst needs to determine the relative strength of each force by ascribing a value to each, indicating if it is strong, moderate, or weak. Another way is to rank the forces using a scale of 1 to 10, with 10 indicating a strong force and 1 a weak force. Again, important to the analytical process is the need to determine a logical explanation of how each competitive force works and understand its role in the overall competitive picture.

Next, collectively assess and evaluate the nine forces in light of your firm's competitive ability. The ultimate goal is to identify the ability of your firm to successfully compete within this industry and environment, given the collective strength of these forces. Further, making a comparison between the firm's resources and strengths against the "fit," or gaps, with the Nine Forces will provide valuable insights to the firm's opportunities and threats. The need here is to integrate the entire analysis within the broader context of corporate strategy—find the tightest fit between the firm's resources and capabilities and the broad external environment.

This involves three types of strategic analysis: reactive strategy against likely competitor moves; proactive strategy to manipulate changing forces already in motion; and proactive strategy to explicitly force change in one or all of the Nine Forces.

To improve the usefulness of this technique, identify long-term environmental and industry trends and determine whether industry profitability is sustainable. Further, determine effects of long-term trends on your firm's competitive position.

Each competitive force should be constantly monitored for its impact on the current strategy and the opportunities it represents for extending competitive advantage. Finally, not all industries are alike. Therefore, for companies with product portfolios across numerous industries, this model must be repeated for each unique industry served.

Case Study: Rating the Nine Forces Model in the Australian Airline Industry

(10 = strong, 1 = weak)

Barriers to Entry—Weighting 9

- While deregulation reduced legislative barriers, the small size of the Australian market means great efficiencies must be achieved to make this a viable market for any player.

- Capital intensity offset to some extent by ability to lease aircraft and hire ground crews on contract.

- Limited availability of terminal slots in major capital cities.

Bargaining Power of Buyers—Weighting 6

- The Internet has made air travel a readily accessible commodity (i.e., price driven).
- Price sensitivity of consumers has not been significantly offset by loyalty programs.
- Market share warfare is the industry norm.
- Domestic travel within Australia almost always involves long distances.

Bargaining Power of Suppliers—Weighting 6

- Airport authorities, pilot, flight attendants, and other aviation unions have eroded economic rent associated with producer surplus.
- Aircraft manufacturing companies compete heavily for new sales providing alternative financing.

Government—Weighting 6

- Government ownership of many international airlines makes exit or capacity reduction unlikely due to conflicting sociopolitical considerations.
- Government protection policies impact the level of new entrants and their local operational effectiveness.
- Competition Commission, on the other hand, forces the establishment and maintenance of a competitive choice for travelers.
- Privatization of airport infrastructure management and services.

Social—Weighting 5

- Total growth is limited to the size of the Australian market and international tourism to Australia. Main growth appears to be in price-sensitive, low-cost economy travel class.
- The combined impact of terrorism, viruses, wars, and the heightened need for security has increased the reticence of travelers for particular destinations.

Competitors—Weighting 9

- Predominantly a duopoly—Qantas and Virgin.
- Majority of costs are fixed regardless of load. Resulting variable cost pricing through heavy discounting to maximize contribution margin from excess capacity.
- Growth in low-cost airlines results in substantial capacity increases and lower margins.
- Long history of Qantas as the major airline in Australia for both domestic and international travel.

Technology—Weighting 8

- The business travel market is being impacted by video conferencing and other technology, reducing the need for physical face-to-face communication.

■ New airplane technology allows for greater load capacity, better fuel consumption, and longer distances, reducing requirements for airlines to operate through hubs.

Substitutes—Weighting 3

■ Ships, trains, buses, and cars—with the time-pressed individuals of today, these substitutes have a weakened competitive position when it comes to travel across long distances. There is presently minimal loss of industry revenue to substitutes.

International—Weighting 6

■ Competitive international airfares and a strong Australian dollar has encouraged strong growth in outbound travel by Australians.

■ Australia is seen as a "safe" holiday destination increasing inbound travelers.

■ Conflicts in the Middle East and North Africa impact on the cost of airline fuel.

Conclusion: Competitive forces are strong and evolving. Profitability of the airline industry in Australia is not bad as a result of the duopoly and Qantas' long previous history as a government-owned entity.

This analysis can be represented diagrammatically, as shown in Figure 6.5.

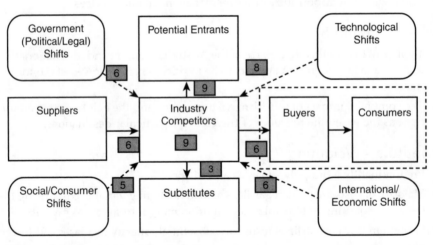

The Australian Airline Industry

Figure 6.5   Australian airline industry

FAROUT Summary

FAROUT SUMMARY

	1	2	3	4	5
F	███	███	███	███	
A	███	███	███		
R	███	███	███	███	
O	███	███			
U	███	███	███		
T	███	███	███		

Figure 6.6   Nine Forces FAROUT summary

Future orientation—Medium to high. Focuses on trends and driving forces. Their evolutionary development ensures that it is a highly anticipatory method. Because the forces are not static, analysis must be reviewed regularly.

Accuracy—Medium. The method requires understanding and tracking of a wide variety of interacting qualitative and quantitative elements. Accuracy depends upon sources of information used. Cross validation with industry experts will increase accuracy of the analysis.

Resource efficiency—Medium to high. Much information can be gleaned from secondary sources such as government agencies, specialist publications, consulting firms, and census data. There may also be some information already available in the firm. Cost of analysis will depend on the number and positions of analysts employed.

Objectivity—Low to medium. Depends on the information used. Use of subjective data reduces objectivity. There is also a high emphasis placed on qualitative analysis. Understanding of trend interactions and driving forces requires insight combined with useful and reliable data.

Usefulness—Medium. Valuable technique. Provides an overview of an industry and its environment; highlights key competitive factors and elements that require close monitoring for strategies to be successfully implemented. If effectively undertaken can provide opportunities to achieve strategic advantage.

Timeliness—Medium. Method requires firm to collect and track data. Time is required to undertake a close analysis of each of the forces, particularly if primary sources are addressed.

Related Tools and Techniques

- Competitor analysis
- Experience curve analysis
- Financial analysis
- Issue analysis
- Product life cycle analysis
- Scenario analysis
- S-curve analysis
- Stakeholder analysis
- Strategic group analysis
- SWOT analysis
- Technology forecasting
- Value chain analysis

References

Ackoff, R. (1981). *Creating the Corporate Future*. New York, NY: John Wiley & Sons.

Aguilar, F. (1967). *Scanning the Business Environment*. New York, NY: Macmillan.

Arrington, C., and R. Sawaya (1984). "Issues management in an uncertain environment," *Long Range Planning*, 17(6), pp. 17–24.

Bain, J.S. (1956). *Barriers to New Competition*. Cambridge, MA: Harvard University Press.

Bates, D., and D. Eldridge (1984). *Strategy and Policy: Analysis, Formulation, and Implementation*, 2nd edition. Dubuque, IA: Brown.

Black, J.A., and K.B. Boal (1994). "Strategic resources: Traits, configurations, and paths to sustainable competitive advantage," *Strategic Management Journal*, [Special summer issue], 15, pp. 131–148.

Black and Boal (1994), paraphrasing Porter, M.E. (1991). "Towards a dynamic theory of strategy," *Strategic Management Journal*, [Special summer issue], 12, pp. 95–117.

Carr, C. (1993). "Global, national, and resource-based strategies: An examination of strategic choice and performance in the vehicle components industry," *Strategic Management Journal*, 14(7), pp. 551–568.

Diffenbach, J. (1983). "Corporate environmental analysis in large U.S. corporations," *Long Range Planning*, 16(3), pp. 107–116.

Dill, W. (1958). "Environment as an influence on managerial autonomy," *Administrative Science Quarterly*, 2(2), pp. 409–443.

Fahey, L. (1989). "Understanding the macroenvironment: A framework for analysis," In L. Fahey, (ed.), *The Strategic Planning Management Reader,* Englewood Cliffs, NJ: Prentice Hall, pp. 38–43.

Fahey, L., King, W., and V. Narayanan (1981). "Environmental scanning and forecasting in strategic planning—The state of the art." *Long Range Planning,* 14(1), pp. 32–39.

Fleisher, C.S, and Bensoussan, B. E. (2003), *'Strategic and Competitive Analysis',* Prentice Hall, Upper Saddle River, N.J

Grinyer, P.H., and D. Norburn (1977/1978). "Planning for existing markets: An empirical study," *International Studies in Management and Organization,* Vol 7, pp. 99–122.

Lenz, R., and J. Engledow (1986). "Environmental analysis: The applicability of current theory." *Strategic Management Journal,* 7, pp. 329–346.

McWilliams, A., and D.L. Smart (1993). "Efficiency v. structure conduct performance: Implications for strategy and practice," *Journal of Management,* 19, pp. 63–79.

Miller, D., and P. Friesen (1977). "Strategy making in context: Ten empirical archetypes," *Journal of Management Studies,* 14(3), pp. 253–280.

Porter, M.E. (1979). "How competitive forces shape strategy," *Harvard Business Review,* 57(2), pp. 137–145.

—. (1979). "The Structure within Industries and Companies Performance," *The Review of Economics and Statistics,* 61(2), pp. 214–227.

—. (1980). *Competitive Strategy: Techniques for Analyzing Industries and Competitors.* London: Collier Macmillan Publishers.

—. (1980). "Industry structure and competitive strategy: Keys to profitability," *Financial Analysts Journal,* 36(4), pp. 30–41.

—. (1985). *Competitive Advantage : Creating and Sustaining Superior Performance.* London: Collier Macmillan Publishers.

Roquebert, J., Phillips, R., and C. Duran (1993). "How much does strategic management matter?," Presentation at the meeting of the National Academy of Management, Atlanta, GA.

Rumelt, R.P. (1991). "How much does industry matter?," *Strategic Management Journal,* 12(3), pp. 167–185.

Scherer, F.M. (1970). *Industrial Market Structure and Economic Performance.* Chicago, IL: Rand McNally.

Schumpeter, J.A. (1943). *Capitalism, Socialism, and Democracy.* London: George Allen and Unwin Ltd.

Senge, P. (1992). *The Fifth Discipline.* New York, NY: Currency DoubleDay.

Starbuck, W. (1976). "Organizations and their environments." In M. Dunnette (ed.), *Handbook of Industrial and Organizational Psychology.* Chicago, IL: Rand McNally.

Stubbart, C. (1982). "Are environmental scanning units effective?," *Long Range Planning,* 15(3), pp. 139–145.

Suutari, R. (2000). "Understanding industry structure," *CMA Management,* 73(10), pp. 34–37.

Thompson, J. (1967). *Organizations in Action.* New York, NY: McGraw-Hill.

Wilson, I. (1982). "Environmental scanning and strategic planning." In G. Steiner et al. (eds.) *Management Policy and Strategy* (Reading 7). New York, NY: Macmillan.

Endnotes

[1] See Fleisher and Bensoussan (2003), Chapter 17.

[2] See Fleisher and Bensoussan (2003), Chapter 6.

[3] See Fleisher and Bensoussan (2003), Chapter 9.

[4] See Fleisher and Bensoussan (2003), Chapter 6.

[5] Miller and Friesen, 1977; Grinyer and Norburn, 1977/78.

[6] Senge, P. (1992).

Competitive Positioning Analysis

Short Description

Competitive positioning analysis is conducted to enable a firm to make strategic plans in relation to its current competitive position: These may be to preserve an advantage, attempt an improvement, or withdraw from a market. The analysis assesses market share, client perception of products and service, current marketing strategies, prices, and costs. It also provides information about the relative market positions and strengths and weaknesses of a firm's competitors. The process identifies opportunities and points to strategies to exploit these opportunities in an industry or market.

Background

A firm's competitive position refers to its place in an industry or market in comparison with its competitors. The concept of "positioning" appears to have come from Jack Trout's 1969 paper,[1] "Positioning' is a game people play in today's me-too marketplace." At the time, it revolutionized the idea of communication with a market. Where traditional marketing had been based on the idea of telling clients about the benefits of your product in comparison with your competitors, positioning attempts to change the perception of your product in the mind of a target audience by giving your product a unique position.

Competitive positioning explores an industry in part by researching the perceptions of the clients serviced by it and looks for ways to improve perceptions of your firm overall. It also extends the positioning concept beyond product marketing and feeds information into the firm's strategic planning and strategic management.

Strategic planning and strategic management evolved around the same time as positioning. Linden Brown[2] notes that "corporate planning" employed by firms up to the 1960s was founded on reasonably steady expansion in a relatively stable financial environment. Corporate planning could not guide firms through the turbulent economic conditions and rapidly changing markets of the late 1960s and early 1970s. Strategic planning and strategic management evolved to provide firms with tools to review their performance and plan for the future in order to cope with increasingly competitive and volatile markets.

Competitive positioning is an umbrella term for a variety of different tools and processes designed to apprise a firm of its competitive position and inform strategic decisions made in relation to it. Competitive positioning is also the name given to the action of strategically changing a firm's position in the marketplace.

Competitive positioning analysis provides information with direct importance to the development of a strategic plan by giving a firm an overview of its industry and enabling it to apprise its own competitive position. Essentially, it assesses factors that impact on market performance and profit performance. It examines a particular industry and the participants within it to provide an understanding of the industry and the competition. It looks at who is competing and how, what market share they have, how clients perceive the participants in the industry, how the various participants operate in the marketplace, and their strengths and weaknesses.

Strategic Rationale and Implications

Competitive positioning is based on the truism that business is characterized by competition. Where more than one participant is involved in an industry, competition exists not only to win the business of clients by convincing them that they need your product, but to do so better than your competitors. This necessitates a marketing strategy for your products and/or services and also a competitive marketing strategy to differentiate your firm from its competitors.

Undertaking an analysis of your competitive position compares your firm's position in an industry or market with that of its competitors. Such an analysis should include information about the structure of the industry and the participants; outline their operating practices; cover customer satisfaction and profitability issues; and provide an overall appraisal of your firm's position.

The competitive positioning process requires a detailed analysis of a firm's own business and the various markets (or market segments) in which it competes. Competitive positioning analysis is designed to give you an understanding of your firm's competitive position within its industry and an overview of the industry as a whole. This is fundamentally important to developing an effective competitive marketing strategy as it broadens your outlook beyond your own revenue, products, and services, and gives an industry-wide perspective of your firm's performance and opportunities.

The most common structure found in a market is for there to be one clear market leader; a second major player differentiated from the leader; a substantial amount of lower-priced competition; and then niche specialists, who generally charge a price premium and cater to specific needs. One variation on this structure is the situation where a market is dominated by two firms of roughly the same size, which hold a large majority of market share (that is, a duopoly).

Using a variety of different tools and processes, a firm can address its current competitive position and inform strategic decisions made in relation to it. The key outcome of the analysis is some action of strategically changing a firm's position in the marketplace.

Porter's Five Forces Industry analysis and the Nine Forces Industry analysis, for example, are all sophisticated tools for identifying a firm's competitive position (see Chapter 6, "Industry Analysis (The Nine Forces)").

A variety of modeling concepts are also useful in analyzing competitive position. These include the BCG matrix, McKinsey matrix, and perceptual maps. By feeding the relevant information into one of these analytical models, a firm's competitive position may be readily visualized.

There are four basic directions for any competitive strategy, as follows:

- To develop and build on a firm's position
- To maintain and hold a firm's strong market position
- To defend a dominant position
- To withdraw from a market with minimal loss

Develop and Build on the Firm's Position

There are three broad situations where a firm may wish to develop and build its position. These are the following:

1. A niche firm looking to expand its business
2. A minor competitor seeking to become a dominant force
3. A firm in a position of joint dominance wishing to move to sole dominance

These three competitive positions may also be viewed as a progression of strategic position from niche to broad market dominance.

A firm in any one of these positions will be looking for weaknesses in its competitors, which can be easily exploited to its own advantage. A niche firm may be looking for unfulfilled segments in the market. These may be segments viewed as not profitable enough for the dominant firm to pursue but may be worthwhile for a niche firm seeking to consolidate its position as a force in the marketplace.

A minor competitor may try to focus on gaps in the market not properly serviced by the dominant firm.

Where a market is dominated by two or more major firms, competitive positioning analysis may give insight into how one of these may differentiate itself from its competitors or reposition its product/service within the market in order to gain a competitive advantage and market dominance.

Maintain and Hold the Firm's Strong Market Position

In this situation, a firm is not seeking dominance within a market, but wishes to hold onto its share of the market against all incumbents. Where a market is mature and no longer expanding, it is unlikely that there will be interest to invest in expanding market share. The ideal position for a firm in this market would be to preserve its market share (and revenue) for as long as the market remains profitable with minimal outlay of resources.

Defend a Dominant Position

A position of dominance in a market has advantages going beyond the immediate revenue stream and economies of scale that come with size. Market dominance allows a firm to manage the market and control competition to some extent. Often the dominant product in a market can be perceived as the standard by clients.

Apart from consolidating its position against its major competitors, the dominant firm should also be aware of any developing "third force" coming between it and its traditional competitors. The emergence of significant new competition can undercut profits for all existing players by siphoning away market share.

The dominant firm in the market generally has a variety of strategies available to it to fend off competition. It may choose to follow a price-cutting strategy, although this is costly and may have a negative affect on clients by changing cost expectations or perceptions of product quality. A dominant firm may launch new products in direct competition with any competitor that tries to fill in gaps in the market. These new products may trade on the high esteem in which clients hold the dominant firm or may simply dilute the profitability of new products for smaller firms, leading them to withdraw from the market.

Withdraw from a Market

There are times when it may be best for a firm's overall competitive position to withdraw completely from a particular market, leaving the firm to concentrate on more profitable markets. This may occur where the market itself is declining—for example, because technology is rendering it obsolete. A declining market is one where profits are falling and the costs of doing business will eventually outweigh possible revenue, even for the market leader. Ideally, where a market is declining, a firm should aim to get its clients to substitute the product being withdrawn with another product from the same firm or at least to withdraw the product with as little inconvenience to clients as possible.

Unsuccessful expansion or diversification by a firm into a new market may also leave the firm in an unprofitable position and thereby needing to withdraw. Additionally analysis of competitors may point to the likelihood of a market player being able to sustain the investment necessary to support the expansion/diversification in the face of defensive strategies from existing market players.

Once you have a detailed understanding of your firm's competitive position and the industry it is situated in, you are then equipped to design and implement strategic plans to defend or improve your competitive position or even to cut your losses and withdraw from the market.

Strengths and Advantages

Competitive positioning analysis provides detailed and practical information about the industry and markets in which a firm competes. It generates practical strategic information to improve competitive position that may be immediately incorporated into the firm's strategic plan.

The process will provide useful information to firms of all sizes and in many different competitive positions. Major firms with market dominance may use the results to consolidate their positions. Minor players in an industry may use the results to increase market share and expand the markets in which they participate. Established firms may use the results to keep up with changes in their industry or markets. New firms may get valuable information about how to go about establishing themselves within an industry or market. Gaps uncovered in a market may point to a need or desire in a marketplace for particular new products or styles of products or services.

Competitive positioning analysis may also provide information about the viability of particular products or markets within an industry, allowing informed decisions about developing or discontinuing products. It may further be used to provide information about competition in new markets and give guidance about how to best enter a particular new market.

Improving your firm's competitive position additionally puts it in a better position to attract investment and enter strategically desirable alliances.

Weaknesses and Limitations

The quality of the information obtained by conducting a competitive positioning analysis will depend on the design of the process. Care must be taken when defining the industry or markets you wish to study. The analysis will be compromised where the industry examined is defined too narrowly (and important or potentially important competitors are omitted), and where the industry is defined too widely (and meaningless comparisons are made with firms that are not relevant competitors).

It is important to take care in accurately and comprehensively identifying relevant markets and products for the same reasons.

Another limitation of competitive positioning analysis is its reliance on information about competitors. In some industries, competitor information is not readily available. In other industries, there may be individual firms that do make particular information available. It is also possible that a firm will not be able to gather meaningfully detailed information about the new products in development with competitors. It is also possible to find that competitors have been circulating misinformation specifically to confound any competitive positioning analysis undertaken by their market rivals. Gaps in the information you are able to gather may compromise the reliability of the analysis you conduct.

A firm that chooses to carry out its own competitive positioning analysis and draw its own strategic conclusions may find the final strategies are limited by internal biases. Incomplete briefing of a third-party analyst may result in a misdirected analysis and missing important nuances in the industry and/or market.

Process for Applying the Technique

Competitive positioning can be understood as a broad three-step process:

1. Identify the focus of your firm's current strategy and identify analysis parameters such as market or products to be assessed.
2. Conduct analysis with the following:
   (a) Undertake market segmentation to gain a better understanding of competitors and the breakdown of your industry.

(b) Undertake industry analysis to get a more detailed understanding of the competitive environment.

(c) Conduct market research to gain insight into client perceptions of the market, products, and competitors (including your own firm).

3. Derive insights from the preceding analysis and formulate a positioning strategy for your firm.

Both primary information (focusing on the needs and perceptions of clients) and secondary information (which looks at facts and trends) are used throughout the competitive positioning analytical process.

Secondary research should provide you with objective information about market share, market size, expected growth, and general economic conditions in the marketplace.

Although this information is available from publicly available sources, such as online databases and industry publications, it may be more expedient to get a professional researcher to undertake this part of the project, even if the rest of the project is being run in-house. Unless you have internal staff who regularly monitor this sort of information, tracking all the background information can be time-consuming.

A particularly interesting source of secondary information for competitive positioning may be the PIMS database, which provides market and competitive profiles and business results from some 3,000 firms arranged by industry category. The PIMS (profit impact of market strategy) project has been collating information since 1972 and aims to pool collective business experience for the benefit of other firms in similar industries. Although PIMS data has no accurate predictive power, it can give insight into how the structural attributes of a business may have an impact on its competitive position. The database may be accessed at www.pimsonline.com. It is a subscription service.

Identify Current Strategy and Market/ Product/Project Parameters

Assessing your current business and marketing strategies will provide you a background to your firm's current position in the market and a starting point from which to plan the strategies arising from the competitive positioning project. This is also the step in the process when you will be defining the scope of the project and what you hope to gain out of it.

One of the issues then to be addressed in this step is how you plan to use the information you obtain. This will have an impact on the depth of analysis you undertake throughout this process. For example, a project that is looking for competitive positioning strategies relating to distribution has a much narrower focus than a complete competitive positioning analysis. Whatever level of detail you are aiming for, you need to make early decisions about categories of information you will need to gather. The division of information into categories is arbitrary and is a fundamental part of the project design.

Another point that needs to be considered is the level of detail you plan to go into with your research itself. The level of analysis will depend on the size of any investment likely to flow from the competitive positioning process. For example, if a multi-million dollar refit of a manufacturing plant is contemplated, then a more expensive and detailed analysis is not only justified but advisable.

Linden Brown observes that the factors considered in appraising competitive position are basically all the factors that have an impact on market performance—for example, market share, revenue, brand image, and profit performance, including costs, margins, prices, and productivity. These factors may be examined at the industry level or at the level of individual niche product markets within an industry.

A preliminary investigation of your firm's current portfolio is often a useful place to start and might be typical of a product/market matrix, as shown in Figure 7.1.

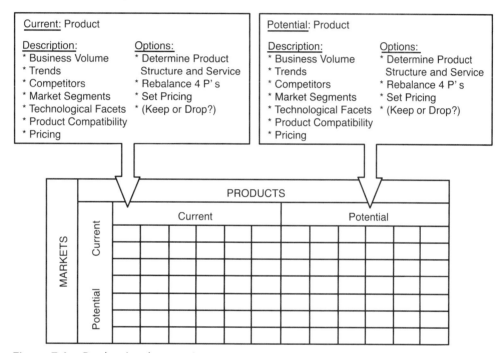

Figure 7.1   Product/market matrix

The Boston Consult Group (BCG) growth-share matrix[3] provides a graphic representation of markets, products and services, which can be useful in judging where to focus resources. Looking at your product and/or service range plotted on a growth-share matrix can provide an indication of what strategies may be appropriate for your various products.

Another method for assessing your own products and/or services is the GE/McKinsey attractiveness-competitive position matrix.[4] Plotting the strength of a business/product/service against the attractiveness of the industry for your firm will identify a potential course of action.

However, a note of caution: The BCG model vastly simplifies market conditions, which in reality can be very complex, and in some circumstances, there may be strategic value in treating products differently. In addition, despite the relative complexity of the GE/McKinsey model compared to the growth-share matrix, it can still miss some subtleties of a firm's business.

Another preliminary issue is who will run the project. A project team, which crosses departments within the firm, will ensure that the learning experience of those involved is distributed throughout the firm. Keeping the project out of the control of just one department may also diminish the likelihood of the project outcomes being skewed by internal politics. It will also ensure that the time taken by staff in gathering information is not all lost to one department. T.L. Louden[5] advises that while internal staff may gather most of the information used, independent third parties should be involved in the process of visualizing the final competitive positioning strategies arising from the competitive positioning analysis. These people will have experience in the process of identifying strategies from analysis and will be independent of any internal biases that may compromise the effectiveness of the final strategies.

Conduct Analysis

(a) Market Segmentation

Market segmentation is a process that divides your market into distinct groups of clients who share particular characteristics. A market segment is a way to conceptualize a target market. A market segment must be identifiable and measurable; accessible by communication/distribution channels; have unique needs (compared to other market segments); be relatively stable over time; and be large enough to be profitably targeted for its business.

These segments may be made up of individual consumers or industry consumers, and the basis for dividing them into segments varies slightly between the two client groups. Individual consumers are divided into market segments on four broad bases: geography (which includes not only location, but also population density and growth); demographics (age, gender, etc.); psychographic variables (including values, lifestyle, and attitudes); and client behavior (including brand loyalty, usage made of product, and sensitivity to price). An industry client segment will be identified by geography (concentration of clients, regional growth, and international considerations); client type (how big are client organizations, what industry are they part of); and how the clients behave (are they loyal to suppliers, and how big and/or frequent are their orders).

Segmenting your markets in this way will narrow your client base into smaller groups and make it easy for you to identify the competitors who also compete for each segment's business.

Segmentation is a valuable exercise from a planning point of view, as it will provide obvious categories of clients to target with specific products and/or specific marketing strategies.

As an alternative to market segmentation, Pankaj Ghemawat[6] suggests breaking your firm's activities into economically meaningful categories to allow close attention to the impact of costs and client willingness to pay for product. This can be done by undertaking value chain analysis.[7]

Another approach might be to focus on key assets and skills you judge to be essential to competition in your industry or individual product markets within your industry. In *Developing Business Strategies*, David Aaker[8] suggests four broad areas to concentrate on when you are determining what are the key assets and skills in your particular industry (or within a market): reasons some firms are successful and some are not; major motivations for clients in deciding who to do business with; major component costs; and the ease with which firms may enter or reposition themselves within the industry (or market).

(b) Industry Analysis

Areas you may focus on include investigating current and potential products and markets of your competitors. Additionally, you will need to understand the structural characteristics of the industry. For example, is it very competitive? How many competitors exist in the field? Is it subject to regulation? Is ownership of firms in the industry stable? Is the industry concentrated in one geographical area? Are there gaps in market coverage?

Industry analysis provides a strategic assessment of the competitive position of each of your competitors within a given market. This analysis considers the existing rivalry between suppliers in the market; the threat posed by new entrants; the bargaining power of clients in the marketplace; the power of suppliers; and any threat to the market posed by substitute products. It can also address the broader industry framework to identify the trends that will impact the long-term direction of a market. (See Chapter 6 for detailed information about how to conduct this type of analysis.)

A SWOT analysis[9] or competitor analysis[10] of your competitors may also be useful in identifying competitors' existing strengths and weaknesses and opportunities arising for your firm. It may also identify any threats to your competitors, which you may be able to utilize to your competitive advantage.

(c) Market Research

Traditional market research will give valuable insight into client perceptions of a marketplace and the suppliers servicing it (these are your firm and your competitors). Feedback may be sought on various product types, individual products, various services, various suppliers, and client desires in terms of improved product or service.

Market research may be undertaken via telemarketing or face-to-face interviews—preferably by an independent third party to limit internal firm biases. It may also use detailed surveys designed and administered by specialist researchers to generate statistically comparable empirical information.

The scope of your competitive positioning project as identified in the first step will inform your decision as to who and how to undertake this research.

Review Results and Formulate Positioning Strategy

A great deal of detailed information will be obtained in undertaking competitive positioning analysis. The simplest and most commonly used way to get an overview of the results of your research may be to use perceptual maps to give a quick graphic summary of the main findings.

A perceptual map plots the position of a firm or product in space generally using two axes. Information may be plotted using more than one axis; however, this may be difficult to represent as a two-dimensional graphic.

Perceptual maps plot perceptual information and may include vectors indicating the preferred performance for a product/service/firm across the two axes commonly attributed by clients. These maps can be generated by software.

a perceptual map addressing the pain relief tablet market. The axes
…ia as identified by clients.

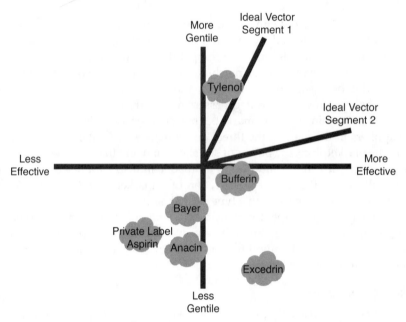

Figure 7.2   Perceptual map with ideal vectors in the pain relief market
Source: http://en.wikipedia.org/wiki/Perceptual_map (last accessed October 2006).

However, these are not accurate reflections of reality, being based on perceptions to start with and then subject to possible distortion in the process of converting verbal opinions into a numerically generated graph. Perceptual maps have attracted criticism for being no more than intuitive reflections of pre-existing biases.

It is important that perceptual maps should be interpreted in tandem with the detailed information from which they are drawn. Used with caution, perceptual maps can give a quick picture of competition in the marketplace from the point of view of clients.

Another way to conduct an appraisal of the analysis and to help formulate appropriate strategies is to compile evaluations of your firm's and each competitor's strengths and weaknesses in terms of a matrix. For each key business area or critical success factor, competitors can be evaluated in a matrix relative to your own abilities. This provides an overview and understanding of your position against key competitive factors in your industry. Figure 7.3 shows an example of a matrix relating to the quality of a marketing communications.

Compiling matrices or perceptual maps and referring back to the information gathered should enable the analyst and the project team to generate a list of opportunities available to not only improve the firms competitive positioning but to address specific problem areas for longer term competitive advantage.

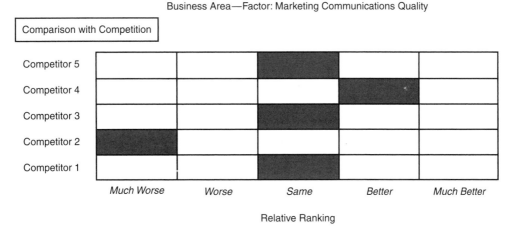

Figure 7.3   Strength/weakness evaluation matrix

T. L. Louden[11] advises that while internal staff may competently gather most of the information used, independent third parties should be involved in the process of visualizing the final competitive positioning strategies arising from the competitive positioning analysis. These people will have experience in the process of identifying strategies from analysis and will be independent of any internal biases that may compromise the effectiveness of the final strategies.

Summary

In essence, a complete competitive positioning analysis will put together the following:

1. A clear outline of your own firm's current and potential markets and products. Some options for management may start to be identified. The product/market matrix reproduced in Figure 7.1 may be a useful template.

2. Identify competitive practices in the industry, covering such areas as the principal relationships between costs, revenue, and profits; who has competitive advantage in which areas; the level to which the industry is tradition bound; opportunities for innovation; advantages arising for differing geographical/environmental factors; weaknesses to exploit; and strengths to overcome or avoid.

   Additionally, competitor profiles may expose an organization and management style; corporate goals; marketing, sales, and customer support strategies and practice; production processes (particularly productively and costs); technical and support systems; finance (including accounting and control systems); investment management (portfolio and performance); and staff (including turnover, level of remuneration, and personnel policies).

3. Review general and specific factors contributing to client satisfaction with their current suppliers (your firm and your competitors) including: quality of product (including whether products are perceived as meeting needs); client ability to

understand value of purchases; whether the market prefers one-stop suppliers or specialist sources; availability and convenience of products; quality of service; tendency to be loyal to their supplier or to shop around; whether short- or long-term performance of products will reflect on reputation of supplier; and effort required to change suppliers. Any customer dissatisfaction suggests an opportunity for your firm to step in and meet the unmet need.

4. Undertake an overall appraisal of the competitive environment to identify any strategies or tactics, which may improve your firm's competitive position and identified a set of strategies to take the firm where it wishes to go in an industry.

The detailed information gathered during the competitive positioning project give a comprehensive picture of the industry, markets, and products on which it focuses. Any gaps in market coverage, or potential weak points in the position of the dominant firm in the market, should be obvious. This information can be used to inform decisions about directions for new product development or provide clues as to what strategy might successfully attack the dominance of the market leader and steal away some market share.

The satisfaction or otherwise of clients served by any particular market or unmet needs perceived by clients should be apparent. This analysis may also give clues for strategic development of a new product or for more effective marketing and sales approaches in the market.

Case Study: Financial Services

Increasing competition and a slowdown in the economy prompted the capital mortgage division of a very large financial services firm to seek feedback from the market.

In particular, the division wanted some direct information of client perceptions of it and its key competitors. It also wanted to check the progress of its strategic plans and marketing in the marketplace and from that get an indication of how it was traveling in implementing its strategic vision.

It engaged a third party to conduct a competitive positioning study.

The first step in the process was a telephone survey developed and designed to hone in on the perceptions of intermediaries and borrowers as two key segments of the firm's market. The survey was presented to a sample of both existing and potential clients from various asset groups.

The interview began with a qualitative blind study. The questions asked respondents to do the following:

- Identify the most important factors in deciding where to borrow.
- Define selection criteria in terms of behavior and the consequences of the decision.
- Nominate which lender they considered to be the market leader in terms of each selection criteria.

The second half of the interview asked each respondent for their perceptions of the client firm, addressing both the factors discussed in the first half of the interview and the strategic marketing undertaken by the firm.

There were some surprise results from the survey, which showed that no one lender met all the criteria for choosing a lender.

While the client firm came out as leading the market in terms of the most important selection criteria, it was viewed much less favorably against other important factors. The firm received very favorable feedback about brand image and service; however, these factors were relatively unimportant to potential clients when deciding who to approach for finance.

The two segments of the market addressed in the study seemed unaware of the firm's current focus in the marketplace, possibly due to a series of recent acquisitions and some resulting restructuring.

The analysis pointed to opportunity to build on the firm's reputation by improving communication with the market. As a result, the firm adopted a strategy, which saw a single point of contact model adopted.

A follow-up study one year later indicated significant progress had been made.[12]

FAROUT Summary

FAROUT SUMMARY

	1	2	3	4	5
F	■	■	■	■	
A	■	■	■	■	
R	■	■	■	■	
O	■	■	■	■	
U	■	■	■	■	■
T	■	■	■		

Figure 7.4   Competitive positioning analysis FAROUT summary

Future orientation—Medium to high. Competitive positioning analysis identifies future strategies to improve competitive position.

Accuracy—Medium to high. Accuracy of the final strategies drawn from the analysis will depend on the accuracy and comprehensiveness of the information gathered. This may range from medium to high, depending on circumstances. Statistical research and publicly available financial information should increase accuracy. Primary information or word of mouth sources may be less accurate.

Resource efficiency—Medium to high. Where the work of gathering information is divided up into manageable portions, the process should not be a drain on the firm's resources.

Objectivity—Medium to high. The objectivity of the final strategies drawn from the analysis may be compromised by internal biases if carried out by firm staff. Objectivity should be higher where a third party is involved in the analysis.

Usefulness—High. Competitive positioning analysis should provide practical insights about the nature of an industry or market and opportunities available in it.

Timeliness—Medium. The implementation of competitive positioning analysis should be a simple process once the project has been designed.

Related Tools and Techniques

- BCG growth/share portfolio matrix
- Benchmarking
- Competitor analysis
- Customer segmentation analysis
- Financial ratio and statement analysis
- GE business screen
- Industry analysis
- Product line analysis
- Supply chain analysis
- SWOT analysis
- Value chain analysis

References

Aaker, D. (2001). *Developing Business Strategies*, 6th edition. New York, NY: Wiley.

Brown, L. (1990). *Competitive Marketing Strategy*. Melbourne: Nelson.

Fleisher, C.S, and Bensoussan, B. E. (2003). *Strategic and Competitive Analysis*. Prentice Hall, Upper Saddle River, N.J.

Gantz Wiley Research. "Competitive Positioning Study Capital Mortgage Lender," www.gantzwiley.com. Accessed June, 2006.

Ghemawat, P. (1999). *Strategy and the Business Landscape: Text and Cases*. Reading, MA: Addison-Wesley.

Louden, T.L (1991). "Take time out for competitive positioning," *Health Industry Today*, March issue.

Trout, J. (1969). "'Positioning' is a game people play in today's me-too marketplace," *Industrial Marketing*, 54(6), pp. 51–55.

Endnotes

[1] Trout, J. (1969).

[2] Brown, L. (1990).

[3] See Fleisher and Bensoussan (2003), Chapter 4.

[4] See Fleisher and Bensoussan (2003), Chapter 5.

[5] Louden, T.L. (1991).

[6] Ghemawat, P. (1999).

[7] See Fleisher and Bensoussan (2003), Chapter 9.

[8] Aaker, D. (2001).

[9] See Fleisher and Bensoussan (2003), Chapter 8.

[10] See Fleisher and Bensoussan (2003), Chapter 11.

[11] Louden, T.L. (1991).

[12] Adapted from "Competitive Positioning Study Capital Mortgage Lender," published by Gantz Wiley Research.

Business Model Analysis

Short Description

A business model has been defined as the "core logic by which a firm creates customer value." Organizations that take leadership positions in their industries succeed by having an outstanding business model and executing it masterfully.

Business model analysis (BMA) provides the tools to quantify the relative strength of an organization's business model to generate economic rents from a product or service. It acts as the link between the social domain, where economic rents are generated, and the creative domain, where products and services are conceptualized. With a detailed examination of the components of the business model, the analyst can determine what in particular makes one business model superior to another, thus creating an effective understanding of the linkage between rents and the raw product or service. However, a business model cannot exist in isolation and must be viewed thorough the lens of competition; it is in this analysis that the superiority of one model over another may be established.

The elements of the business model for companies to consider are the following:

- The value proposition in the positions it adopts.
- The market segments it chooses to serve or avoid.
- Its value chain and the resulting costs from the activities it performs or the resources it employs.
- Its revenue model (or models) and the resulting profit potential.
- Its position and strength in the larger upstream and downstream value network, including competitors and complementors.
- Its competitive strategy and how it seeks to gain a sustainable competitive advantage.

Understanding the elements of a model at a detailed level allows a firm to change it to potentially generate larger economic rents, disrupt competitors, or to use it to competitive advantage.

This analysis integrates the concepts of the value proposition, market segments, value and extended value chains, revenue models, value migration, disruptive innovation, competitive strategy, and economic value.

Background

Business models have existed since humans first traded goods in barter and have evolved to provide the means to deliver and capture superior customer value. The oldest model still used today is the shopkeeper model. It involves setting up shop where customers are likely to be and displaying a good or service for sale.

Business models evolved from the "single-celled" shopkeeper model to more readily deliver customer value and capture revenue. Such "multi-celled organisms" can be observed with tied products, such as the razor and blades model attributed to King C. Gillette, where the razor is sold at a low price and the blade is sold at a significant premium. This model is used today to sell not only razors and blades, but also items such as ink jet printers/cartridges and cell phones/air time. Other models leverage consumer density to deliver value—the telephone is an example of a network efficiency model where the value provided to customers increases with the number of subscribers. Other well-known models include a subscription business model, trade associations, co-operatives, and franchises, which all may be classified as "collective" business models.

The old style auction has embraced technology and is now conducted online with providers like eBay, resulting in an immense increase in the number of potential buyers.

But these models, if carefully considered, describe more how a firm will generate revenue—there is no market segmentation inherent in them.

Other examples of recent business model innovations are: McDonald's in the 1950s with their "Speedee Service System" for hamburgers; Toyota with its introduction of a sub compact, the Datsun, to the North American market at a time when American cars were big; and Wal-Mart in the 1960s, which provided branded high-quality products at discount prices in small towns. The 1970s saw new models from Toys "R" Us, which disrupted existing toy departments and discount department stores. The 1980s saw Dell and Intel introduce their business models, and in the 1990s, we had eBay and Amazon.

New business models are being introduced with great frequency, such as the technology of voice over Internet protocol (VOIP or voice over IP), which delivers telephone calls using the Internet, and threatens traditional telephone companies and their associated business models. Numerous carriers are competing for VOIP business offering to carry voice calls across the Internet for a fraction of the cost of the traditional switched networks. However, as magical as this technology seems, its widespread implementation will only succeed when a firm leveraging this technology as a disruptive force adopts a viable model. These introductions represent more than just the emergence of new competitors—the new concepts and new technologies embodied in these models will disrupt existing business.

The examples discussed previously represent only a small sample of well-known business models and represent a fraction of those in use today. Each successful new model has found a way to deliver greater value to customers and, equally importantly, successfully capture that value for the firm. Business models are not static constructs but undergo frequent changes in response to competition, the macro environment, and the introduction of new models.

The end of the twentieth century saw the rise of business models that leveraged technology offered by the Internet. These dot-coms were virtual companies, many existing only in cyberspace. Others followed what was known as a "bricks and clicks" model. Companies that used the bricks and clicks model had a physical location but looked to the Internet as another channel to generate sales.

The twenty-first century ushered in the "dot-com bust," where thousands of companies that described their business model as being "Internet-based" simply ceased to exist, in turn losing billions of dollars in venture capital. The pundits and the media told us that the old rules did not apply to these dot-coms. Stock valuations with price to earnings multiples that were unheard of 10 years previously were okay because of the rules of the "new economy." Critical examination of the models of "Internet" companies was often poor, with attempts at separating the "model" from "strategy." In fact, there was no alchemical transmutation to change the laws of business. The pundits were wrong! Until the dot-com bust of 2000/2001, the term "business model" was poorly understood and poorly applied.

Since then, academics and researchers have worked to understand, analyze, and clarify the definition of business models and study their respective components.

Strategic Rationale and Implications

The dynamism of the business world must be translated to the model for a firm to remain in a leadership position. Technology disrupts existing businesses, markets, and the macro environment. New business models are a source of disruption as well. These disruptions can be harmful not only to existing firms, but to entire industries and even nations. The model a firm uses must adapt to meet the challenge of competition and the opportunities and threats posed. It must also provide the means for a firm to act on opportunities and leverage strengths. A superior business model will allow the firm to maintain or gain a leadership position in its industry, while an inferior model can spell disaster—hence, it is imperative to understand the relative strengths and weaknesses of the firm's own business model through the lens of competition.

This analysis allows the firm to determine its value proposition, targeted market segments, value chain, relative position in the value network, and revenue model and place it in a superior position to deliver value to the customer. The firm can determine if it has a temporary or sustainable competitive advantage with its model and if the model lends itself to delivering factors critical to the firm's success. Moreover, the same analysis applied to a competitor's model will provide a broad understanding of the competition's strengths that can be neutralized and weaknesses that can be leveraged.

The Business Model

Definitions of business models range from "an organization's core logic for creating value" to "a story that explains how an enterprise works." Some researchers consider how the pieces of a business fit together, but these approaches typically lack the critical aspects of strategy, which considers competition. Others view the business model as the missing link between strategy and business processes. Alan Afuah[1] provides a more complete definition of a business model, as follows:

"A business model is the set of which activities a firm performs, how it performs them, and when it performs them, as it uses its resources to perform activities, given its industry to create superior customer value and put itself in a position to appropriate that value."

There is, however, no real consensus of what a business model and its components are. The purpose of every business is to satisfy a customer's need. This can only be done by looking at the business from the outside—from the point of view of the customer and the market.

Chesborough and Rosenbloom[2] proposed the definition of a business model as a link between products, services, and economic rents earned by the firm utilizing the model. They propose that a business model incorporates the following six elements:

1. **Value proposition**—The value of the product or service from the customer's perspective and how the product addresses customer's needs.

2. **Market segment**—With the recognition that consumers in different segments have diverse needs and will value the product or service in distinct ways, the value may only be unlocked if the right segment is targeted.

3. **Value chain and cost models**—This is the structure required to create and distribute the product or service and the resulting cost models from performing activities and utilizing resources to deliver its value proposition to its target market.

4. **Revenue models**—The revenue model and resulting profit potential.

5. **Value network**—This is the firm's position in the chain linking upstream and downstream activities to the final consumer of the product. It should include suppliers, competitors, complementors, and other downstream activities.

6. **Competitive strategy**—How the firm seeks to gain a sustainable competitive advantage.

Figure 8.1 defines the various elements of a business model and how they fit together. It considers competition, or the relative ability and activities of the firm to create and deliver *superior* value in satisfying a customer need or want, and it should justify the financial capital needed to realize the model.

Chesborough and Rosenbloom contrast the business model to strategy and suggest that there are three distinctions, as follows:

1. A business model's focus is on creating and capturing value. It seeks to define how that value will be created and the structure and method by which it will be captured. The strategic layer goes further by attempting to define how a firm seeks to generate a competitive advantage.

2. A business model is a construct for converting the product or service into economic value, but it does not consider how to deliver that value to the shareholders that must be considered by the strategic layer.

3. Strategy depends on knowledge of the wider environment the firm is to operate in. The business model does not require such knowledge and requires only a limited understanding of its surroundings. From a practical perspective, the business model needs to understand its target market and the web that makes up its value network.

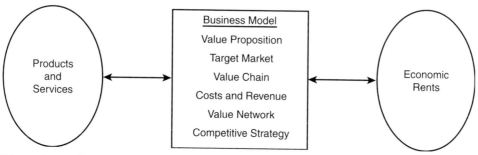

Figure 8.1   The Business model
Source: Adapted from Chesborough and Rosenbloom. "The role of the business model in capturing value from innovation: evidence from Xerox Corporation's technology spin-off companies," *Industrial and Corporate Change*, Volume 11, Number 3, pp. 529–555.

Classification of Business Models

Business models occur in an inestimable variety of shapes and sizes: One small disparity between two models—for example, with the target market and the value proposition—and they become substantially different. Extensive research has been directed at classifying the vast array of existing business models. With the boom of the Internet economy, one focus has been classifying models that use the Internet; another has attempted to determine if one business model sharing a set of common characteristics is superior to another.

Two general approaches to model classification can be found. The first approach attempts to group like models based on a set of shared characteristics. The resulting structure is most often a two-dimensional construct: with position in the value chain, source of revenue, core profit-making activities, pricing policy, value integration, degree of economic control, and others being considered along x and y axes. Following are two examples of such schemes.

Timmer's[3] 11 e-business models use the degree of innovation and the degree of integration as the characterizing dimensions, describing architecture for the product, service, and information flows.

Linder and Cantrell[4] propose a classification scheme based on a model's core profit-making activity and its relative position on the value chain. Linder and Cantrell's scheme is broader in scope and does not limit itself to e-models.

In determining the superiority of one business model concept over another, Linder and Cantrell concluded there is "no silver bullet," and one model in their classification system was not superior to another. Researchers from MIT classified models based on the type of asset and the rights to the asset being sold. Their classification and analysis of the 1000 largest U.S. firms along those dimensions state, "some business models do indeed perform better than others." The results from researchers are mixed; however, we do know some firms consistently produce better results than others in the same industry—for example, Southwest in the airline industry and Bristol Meyers Squibb in the pharmaceutical industry. In general, the profitability of a firm is determined by both firm- and industry-specific factors.

	Innovative			Integrative	
	Less	More		Less	More
E-Shop	✓			✓	
E-Procurement	✓			✓	
E-Mall	✓			✓	
E-Auction		✓		✓	
Collaborative Platform		✓			✓
Information Brokerage		✓		✓	
Third-Party Marketplace		✓			✓
Trust Services		✓		✓	
Value Chain Integrator		✓			✓
Value Chain Service		✓		✓	
Virtual Community		✓			✓

Figure 8.2   E-business models
Source: Adapted from Timmer's Classification Scheme (1998).

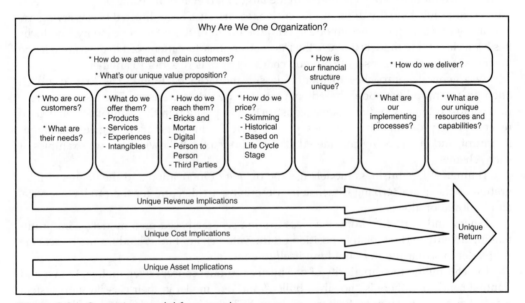

Figure 8.3   Operating model framework
Source: Adapted from Linder, J., and S. Cantrell (2000), "Changing Business Models: Surveying the Landscape," Accenture Institute for Strategic Change.

BMA provides a means for bridging the gap between a firm's prosperity and its products and services. For some firms, familiar business models cannot be applied, and new models must be devised. Adapting the models themselves serves to change the economic value of the products or service. In fact, changing any one of the elements of a model serves to change the economic rent derived from the good or service. Take, for example, the segment served in the airline industry—the business traveler versus the tourist. Consider the activities in that value chain and the costs and the revenue-generation models. Continental and Southwest have different structures in their value chain, yet they basically start with the same raw material. Their revenue generation models differ. They occupy the same location in the value chain. The various parts of the value net have differing ability to generate economic rents; for example, suppliers of aircraft based on the forces at work in that segment of the value net capture a differing level of economic rent from air travel than the airlines themselves. In order to generate superior rents, the organization must create superior value and avoid commoditization of its supply chain and distribution network to prevent value migration. Finally, competitive strategy determines how a firm creates a competitive strategic advantage over rivals. A superior business model will also ensure the value the firm appropriates from the customer is greater than the costs of the activities undertaken, resources employed, and positions adopted in delivering that value.

BMA provides a holistic framework to combine all the activities of the firm in the pursuit of competitive advantage and to maximize the value delivered to the targeted customer. It then becomes possible to deliver superior value propositions to the target market and receive higher prices for the product or service delivered.

The Dow Jones Industrial Average (DJIA) was introduced in 1896 to create an index from the leading firms of the day. Only one firm has survived to this day—General Electric. The mortality of firms is well understood, estimates for first-year failure is an astonishing 70–80%; however, more interesting is the fall-out rate from the S&P 500 and the Fortune 500, which is estimated to be between 2–6%. This effectively means that between 10 and 30 companies depart their leadership positions every year. Innovative business model introductions have caused the disruption of established firms. Kmart, whose business models sustained it for 103 years, filed for Chapter 11 bankruptcy protection early in 2002. Railroads, which were the basis of the Dow prior to the turn of the twentieth century, are minor players today. They saw their value migrate to other forms of transportation and their value proposition diminish along with their leadership positions.

In 1994, Japan had 149 corporations listed in the Global 500 with $3.8 trillion in total revenue; this fell to 82 corporations with $2.2 trillion in total revenue in 2004. This indicated that the business models they employed no longer allowed them to occupy leadership positions. In the same timeframe, 1994 to 2004, the total revenue generated by the Global 500 increased from $10.3 trillion to $14.9 trillion. The inability to adapt business models to changing competitive and macro-economic conditions can spell disaster for firms, industries, and nations.

As a result of this history, there are two subtly distinct philosophical directions regarding business models. Christensen and Raynor[5] focus on technological evolution disrupting business models. Mitchell and Coles[6] suggest, "Improved business models will replace technology as the most frequent and most powerful source of business disruptions." This is a powerful proposition—where the business model itself becomes a competitive weapon. It stands to reason that the ability to modify or construct a business model to disrupt competitors and avoid disruption can provide a significant advantage to a firm.

BMA will determine the viability of any business model for any type of concern, including those organizations using multiple business models. Those organizations that do engage multiple models will benefit by understanding which part of their business is driving revenue and which models need improvement. Additionally, conducting a BMA will allow a firm to understand its weaknesses and extend its advantages. BMA may also be used to disaggregate a competitor's position and understand where it is most vulnerable.

Strengths and Advantages

Comprehensive

BMA verifies the relationship of the firm's model—that is, its strategy, positions, activities, and resources—to the larger macro-environment, the industry, and its competitors. The value delivery mechanisms of the firm and their interaction with the customer and the environment are made evident with this analysis. BMA provides a comprehensive approach beyond strategic and operational effectiveness in describing why a firm is profitable or unprofitable.

Detailed Understanding

BMA allows a detailed understanding of the advantages and disadvantages of the firm's value delivery systems. This understanding makes it possible to modify part or all of a business model to create a competitive advantage. Those firms employing multiple models in multiple industries can quantify their relative strengths.

As a corollary, it is possible to examine the relative position of competitors by using BMA and to use the insights from this analysis to disrupt their business models.

Integration of Value Delivery Mechanism

BMA delivers the ability to integrate the value delivery mechanism of the model and charge superior prices for the value delivered. This in turn will lead to maximizing revenue generation and consequently increased profitability for the firm being analyzed.

Innovation

BMA can provide an impetus to innovate within the organization, either with the model itself, the services and products that the firm provides to customers, or along any dimension of the value delivery mechanisms of the firm. Identification of advantages at the target firm or identification of competitor weaknesses could enhance the innovation process.

Weaknesses and Limitations

Disruption from Outside the Industry

Firms may become blind to rivals offering innovative solutions or to those companies that are not considered direct competitors—this is a position detailed by Christensen and Raynor[7] as the primary means of business disruption. Firms must then consider not only direct competitors, as emphasized in this analysis, but must also avoid being blindsided by firms and industries that are not considered direct rivals.

Innovation

Although this technique may be used to correct business model inconsistencies, it does not *necessarily* provide the means to innovate and consequently to provide additional value to customers. If a firm defines its leadership position too closely with that of current rivals, it may become a follower by adopting models that are easily duplicated.

Market Orientation

This technique will only be useful to a firm that has a market orientation. It is irrelevant for a firm that is producing a product and trying to sell it by targeting a heterogeneous market with a homogeneous marketing strategy.

Process for Applying the Technique

Step 1: Articulate the Value Proposition

Value is determined by the customer—the firm needs to define the product or service it will provide and the forms in which a customer may use it. The value proposition will change depending on the target market specified, and there may be an iterative process between Steps 1 and 2, with a different proposition specified for each target segment.

The firm, through its value proposition, may choose to position its products or services as low cost, differentiated, or niche-focused.

Low-cost provider strategies work best in cases where:

- Price competition is especially vigorous.
- Competitive products are essentially identical.
- There are few ways to achieve product differentiation that are meaningful to buyers.
- Buyers incur low switching costs.
- Buyers are large and have significant power to bargain down prices.

Differentiation allows a firm to command a premium price for its product and/or increase unit sales. A firm can employ several differentiation themes; these can be based on product features, although they are the easiest for competitors to copy. Differentiation themes that are difficult for competitors to copy can provide a sustainable competitive advantage. Bases for differentiation that are more difficult to imitate include the following:

- Brand name or reputation. Coke, for example, is the best-known brand in the world.
- Where the good or service is available. An extensive and well-configured distribution network makes the product widely available to customers.
- Extreme positioning in levels of quality or delivery—a six-sigma or beyond level of quality may be difficult to imitate.

The situation may be complicated by the fact that a firm supplies multiple products or services, and the question is whether the firm is operating multiple models or a single model.

Consider the case of a bicycle shop: The basic business of this shop is to retail bicycles, accessories such as clothing, and bicycle parts, and to service bicycles. Bicycle service may account for 35–50% of revenue. Should this bicycle shop be considered two distinct businesses, a service business, and a retail business? Or is it a single business model with a sustainable competitive advantage in service over an online retailer who sells bicycles and accessories? What about General Electric, which is in the business of supplying power systems as well as aircraft engines? The technology in these two industries may well be transferable, partially answering the question: "Why are we one business?" However, the question of disaggregating a business model is best answered from a customer's perspective. A customer for a bicycle would definitely consider how their bicycle would be serviced when making their purchase decision.

The customer, in defining value, also provides guidance in the consideration of models. If the customer sees the business offering as a whole, the separate activities undertaken by a firm should be considered as sources of advantage, or where they are not offered, and should be, as sources of disadvantage.

Step 2: Specify the Target Segment

Unless the firm is a very specific niche player, it may serve multiple segments of the market, and it may need to specify the changing propositions for each segment it chooses to serve and from whom it will derive economic rents. Quite often, a business provides more than one service or product; our bicycle shop, for example, provides bicycles, clothing, accessories, and service. For somebody seeking to purchase a new bicycle, these may be viewed as a bundle of services offered by the whole firm, and the proposition presented to them may be quite different than to an individual already owning a bicycle who wishes to have it serviced.

Segments can be broken down broadly by: (a) customer characteristics unrelated to the product, generally known as demographics (i.e., geographic span, socioeconomics, etc.); and (b) product and/or service-related approaches that define user types, usage, and benefits generally known as psychographics. The analyst should pursue a detailed analysis of each market segments served by the firm—additional examples of segmentation bases are widely available[8]—and tie the value proposition to customers who may desire different aspects of the product or service.

The objective is that customers' needs must be understood, along with their growth potential; for example, with airline flights, business consumers demand frequent, inexpensive flights with minimal delays, no lost baggage, and polite courteous service. If a customer's needs are not well understood, analytical tools using customer focus groups, Kano model analysis, or quality function deployment (QFD) may be especially useful.

Step 3: Determine Competitors

A firm exists within its industry because it serves those customers who see its value proposition as superior to its competitors. Typically, firms serving the same customer segments with the same product or service are perceived as "the competition." These firms will occupy a similar position along the industry value chain and may have similar resource characteristics. However, there may be firms that provide substitute products; companies that operate in niche markets; and suppliers or customers that have a credible threat of forward or backward integration. Firms that cause companies to forfeit their leadership positions are rarely obvious and do not attempt to compete directly against established rivals; instead, they find new ways to deliver value to customers. Firms often surrender segments that have become unprofitable due to commoditization and later discover that those same competitors have moved up the experience and learning curves and now threaten another segment. Interviews with customers and sales staff and systematic, regular competitor analysis conducted by the firm will help identify current and future competition.

The analyst, after determining who the competitors are, will need to articulate the value propositions of those competitors and the target markets served by those firms.

Step 4: Evaluate the Value Chain and the Cost Model

With the ultimate goal of delivering value to, and capturing economic value from, the customer, it is imperative that the value chain be understood. To deliver the right value to the appropriate market segments, price it correctly, and position itself properly, a firm must undertake a specific set of activities. Using value chain analysis,[9] these activities can be analyzed to identify which step or steps provide economic advantage.

A value chain identifies a series of activities that must be undertaken to transform inputs into a product or service delivered to customers. Figure 8.4 identifies the activities of a classic value chain.

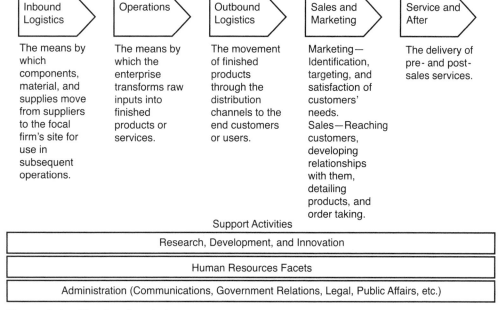

Figure 8.4   Classic value chain

On the other hand, a customer-focused activity value chain (AVC) emphasizes the activities that a firm engages in to learn about customer's needs and the work required with customers in design, development, delivery testing, and installation of the product or service. This type of value chain is better suited to firms that provide intangible products or services. The two value chains are complementary, and both may be used.

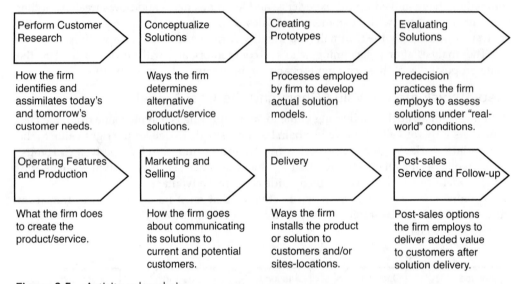

Figure 8.5   Activity value chain
Source: Adapted from Fahey, L. (1999). *Competitors.* New York, NY: John Wiley & Sons, p. 175.

The classic value chain facilitates an overview of what a firm does to access suppliers, its manufacturing, and service. A firm will pursue activities and employ resources to achieve its desired position and, as a result, will incur costs. Value chain analysis allows the analyst to determine the current advantage or disadvantage of the firm along each segment of the value chain and the resulting cost structure. The customer-focused AVC, on the other hand, identifies all the direct and indirect interaction with customers.

Conduct a classic value chain and/or AVC analysis of the target firm. Compare the two value chains to the firm's *direct* competitors, as determined from competitive positioning analysis. Firms that are competing using radically different positions may not pursue similar activities. Add the dimension of time to the value chain and AVC for both *direct* competitors and the target firm if appropriate. Use this analysis to extract where the firm has a competitive advantage or a competitive disadvantage. The time dimension should also include an understanding of experience curve effects.

For the business model being analyzed, determine which resources a firm is leveraging to deliver value to the customer. The resources may be tangible, such as plant and equipment, or intangible, such as patents, brands, or copyrights. They can be human, structural, or based on R&D. A firm's ability to turn its assets into customer value for different market segments is part of its competence or capability.

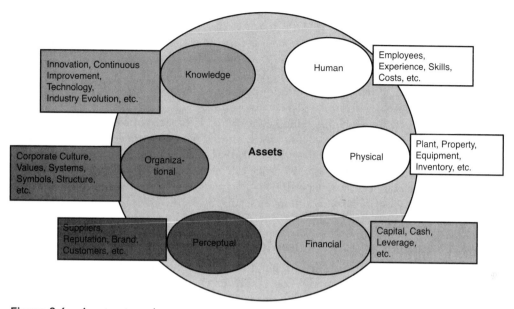

Figure 8.6   Asset categories

Source: Adapted from Fahey, L. (1999). *Competitors.* New York, NY: John Wiley & Sons, p. 300.

Using the six asset categories identified in Figure 8.6, evaluate the assets the firm is using. The analyst should look beyond the firm's own assets; it is not necessary for a firm to control or own the assets it leverages in pursuit of its model. Alliances, relationships, and networks may provide an organization with a competitive advantage by using assets that are owned or controlled by another entity. Assets vary between the following five attributes:

- **Availability**—Not all assets are equally available; capital, for example, is not available in unlimited quantities.

- **Specificity**—An asset is specific to place, time, and space. An asset physically located in North America may provide little to no advantage in the Chinese environment. The range of application technology is typically limited; for example, technology designed to improve the hardness of rubber tires cannot suddenly be used in electronics.

- **Sustainability**—Performance, for example, can increase the stock of capital available, and poor quality may diminish the brand of the firm.

- **Replicability**—Organizational culture, knowledge, and other attributes may be difficult to reproduce. These may provide a source of great competitive advantage.

- **Substitutability**—Can a given asset be trumped by another asset, thus reducing the value of that asset?

Step 5: Evaluate the Value Network

It is important to consider the value the firm is capable of capturing in its extended value chain or its relative position to its customers, suppliers, and rivals. The relative positioning of a product or service is critical. If a firm produces a product or service that it can supply to only one customer, it will be in an inferior position as its customer will have significant bargaining power.

A firm may have developed a value network that is capable of competing in dimensions where it has not been able to before; for example, Sony, to compete in the game console market, established relationships with both IBM and Toshiba to produce multi-core processor architecture for Playstation in order to compete with the Microsoft-Intel team, who had a clear lead in technical expertise.

This value network analysis should include suppliers, customers, complementors, and competitors.

Step 6: Determine the Revenue Model for the Firm

The ability to appropriate value will depend on the revenue model the business uses. Examples are: a subscription model commonly used with magazines; fee for service commonly used by realtors and agents; direct sales to end users; and so on. It is important to ensure that revenues are greater than costs. Analysis of the firm's and competitors' financial statements over time will reveal if the target firm enjoys an advantage over its competitors.

The revenue model should describe each revenue stream and how each stream brings in revenue; for example, a newspaper may have streams from direct newsstand sales, paper box sales, subscription, advertising, classifieds, and the Internet, and each of these revenue streams will incur a different cost. The evaluation of the revenue model should include an understanding of price compared to the competition, the value proposition, product quality, service, and the value customers perceive in the model.

The analyst should also be able to determine if the revenue/cost model at this stage is superior to that of the competition and is likely to produce better profits. The key here is also profit potential, and this may be determined from actual financial results, although they can be misleading if viewed from a point in time—a firm may not have matured and may be in its startup stage; the more important measure then becomes profit potential.

Step 7: Determine the Critical Success Factors for the Industry

Critical success factors (CSFs) are a limited set of aspects that are necessary to secure and gain a competitive advantage. CSFs represent those areas that are critical to a firm's success, providing a direct link to organizational performance (see Chapter 3, "Avoiding Analytical Pitfalls").

John F. Rockart[10] defined four basic sources of CSFs, as follows:

- **Specific industry characteristics**—The airline industry, for example, must provide frequent, on-time flights to successfully target business customers.
- **Those arising from the chosen strategy of the business**—High level of technical service is an important factor for companies seeking to differentiate themselves in the welding industry.

■ **Environmental characteristics or those resulting from economic or technological change**—For example, a telecommunications firm taking advantage of deregulation in the industry.

■ **Those arising from the internal needs of the firm**—An organic structure may be critical to a firm that has to compete in a highly innovative environment.

Critical success factors that relate to position, activities, resources, and costs will be used to determine the strength of the business model. Sources that may be useful in determining CSFs are management tools such as the balanced scorecard and benchmarking. Other tools, such as environmental analysis, industry structure analysis, internal analysis, competitor analysis, or using industry and business experts, are other sources for determining CSFs.

Step 8: Complete an Analysis Grid Detailing Each Element of the Business Model

The objective of this analysis is to detail where in its business model a firm is capable of producing a superior result. To complete the analysis, each element of the business model is placed in a grid, as shown in Table 8.1. Each element is ranked from 1 to 5 (superior) for the target firm and its competitors on an analysis grid.

Table 8.1
Business Model Analysis Grid

	Target Firm	Competitor A	Competitor B	Competitor C
Value Proposition	5	3	4	4
Target Markets	4	5	3	3
Value Chain Analysis and Cost Model	3	3	5	5
Value Network	1	3	4	4
Revenue Model and Profit Potential	3	5	4	5
Strategy	3	4	2	2

This grid should, at a glance, allow the analyst to determine which part of the business model is superior or inferior to its competitors.

Ultimately, the strength of firm's business model will be determined by its ability to convert the product/service domain to economic rents for the firm. The true value of this analysis lies in the ability of the firm to achieve a detailed understanding of the components of its business model and to make improvements in components of the model design. The firm may find ways to innovate along its revenue model, its value chain, or some other element, or disrupt its competition and generate greater economic rents. Because business models are not static constructs, the analyst will find it useful to generate both a current state and future state analysis and to review the analysis on a regular basis.

Case Study: Dell Computer and the Printer Market

Dell Computer has been the darling of the personal computer industry, gaining market share—reported at 18.2% of all units shipped worldwide in 2004—and reporting revenue growth in double digits, outstripping its rivals year after year. Dell is a competitor to IBM, HP, and other firms, not only in computers but also in areas such as printers, storage, hand-held devices, and increasingly in consumer electronics.

Dell has entered the low-end printer business using its direct model and threatens market leader HP. Can Dell's printer model propel it to success, allowing it to capture sufficient market share to disrupt HP?

Dell's competitors in the printer market are HP (the market leader), Epson, Lexmark, and Canon. HP by far has the largest share, with 60% of the existing market, Epson has 16% and Lexmark 12%. Dell has approximately 3% of the current market, selling a small number of printers to businesses while its most active market is the home consumer market. HP excels at R&D, rolls out new product lines to remain competitive, and expects to introduce digital printing, which could save corporations up to 30% in costs each year. HP earns 70% of its profits from sales of ink and printers.

Low-cost, high-quality, easy to use, readily available products win in the marketplace, and printers are no exception. However, innovative new printers that produce better pictures, use multimedia cards directly, and interface to other devices also sell. Highly differentiated products as a result of R&D, brand, and widespread distribution appear to be the driving CSFs for the printer industry, and Dell's brand cannot compete with HP's and Lexmark's.

Dell has adopted a low-cost direct sales approach to target business customers, which comprises 80% of its personal computer sales. Dell has licensed products from Lexmark, which it sells under its own brand name, that meet the needs of business customers. HP targets a larger spectrum of business printing with a broader range of products than Dell—for example, high-end color laser printers. Lexmark and Epson, while competing in the same range of products as Dell, offer customers dot matrix printers. HP and Lexmark have strong distribution networks and are readily available.

Dell has a well understood, sustainable competitive advantage along its activity chain that it has utilized to dominate the personal computer industry. Its cash conversion cycle, because of efficiencies, especially in inventory, has improved from minus 18 days in 2000 to minus 36 days in 2004. HP, however, has an advantage in R&D and the ability to launch new innovative products far more quickly than Dell. Dell must work with Lexmark, who manufactures its product. However, Dell could match this R&D capability by acquiring technology from a printer manufacturer and entering the market with product it manufactures directly and sustain its momentum by investing in R&D.

Both companies use the razor and blades model to generate revenue. However, Dell sells using its electronic model, while HP uses conventional distribution, which is significantly more difficult to manage. The advantage must go to Dell here.

Using an abbreviated form of the BMA, analysts can quickly determine where weaknesses or advantages might lie by comparing each element of the Dell and HP printer business models, as follows:

- **Value proposition**—Dell is competing on price with limited high-end printers available to large business that allows centralized management. It does not provide large printers with robust duty cycles. Advantage: HP.

- **Target markets**—The result of the value proposition and the product offering is that Dell's active market segment is the home consumer. In 2004, Dell sold some 31,000 laser printers, compared to over 2,000,000 for HP. Advantage: HP.

- **Value chain analysis and cost structure**—With Dell's value chain and cost structure and the complexity HP has in shipping product across the country for distribution, the advantage lies with Dell here.

- **Value network**—Dell purchases a number of its printers from Lexmark; however, both have a PC business and make storage devices. Consequently, neither have an advantage.

- **Revenue model**—Both companies use the razor and blades model, with neither having a significant advantage.

- **Strategy**—Dell has a sustainable competitive advantage with its revenue model; however, this does not seem to be well aligned in printers with the CSFs for the industry. HP printers are readily available for demonstration at stores and to distributors. Printers, in fact, may not lend themselves to Internet selling or distribution. Advantage: HP.

In examining the BMA grid in Table 8.2, we can see that HP indeed has an overall advantage with its business model, and Dell needs to seek a new value proposition, target market, and strategy if it is going to succeed. The printer market is extremely competitive, characterized by low prices and razor-thin margins. At this point in time, Dell has not been able to penetrate this market aggressively because of issues with its positioning, active market segments, and strategy.

Table 8.2
Business Model Analysis Grid—Dell Versus HP

	Dell	HP
Value Proposition		
Target Markets		
Value Chain Analysis and Cost Model		
Value Network		
Revenue Model and Profit Potential		
Strategy		

Darker = Superior

FAROUT Summary

FAROUT SUMMARY

	1	2	3	4	5
F	▓	▓	▓		
A	▓	▓	▓		
R	▓	▓	▓	▓	
O	▓	▓	▓		
U	▓	▓	▓	▓	
T	▓	▓	▓		

Figure 8.7   Business model analysis FAROUT summary

Future orientation—Medium. BMA provides a medium orientation, giving the target firm a comprehensive view of its own business model and its integration with the industry and macro environment. This integrated forward-looking view is mitigated by the erosion of customer value by potentially superior competitor offerings, or disruptive industry forces.

Accuracy—Medium. While the analysis is somewhat subjective, its accuracy is determined by the accuracy and skill of the analyst. This has been rated as "medium" but, depending on the quality of the analyst, this can vary.

Resource efficiency—Medium to high. Analysis of a firm can be completed rapidly; the research required and the complexity of tools used are limited. Medium-high resource efficiency should be expected.

Objectivity—Medium. The detailed nature of the analysis, while allowing for some subjectivity, forces structure on the analyst.

Usefulness—Medium to high. The analysis provides a comprehensive view of the business model and an opportunity to correct model irregularities and attack competitor's weaknesses.

Timeliness—Medium. Analysis can be completed readily but contingent on the detail required; in contrast to other analysis techniques, this is high.

Related Tools and Techniques

- Activity value chain analysis
- Competitor profiling
- Competitor segmentation analysis
- Customer value analysis
- Financial ratio analysis

- Functional capability and resource analysis
- Industry analysis
- Kano model analysis
- Quality function deployment
- STEEP analysis
- Strategic funds programming
- Strategic group maps
- Value chain analysis

References

Aaker, D. (2005). *Strategic Market Management*. Hoboken, NJ: John Wiley & Sons.

Afuah, A. (2004). *Business Models: A Strategic Management Approach*. New York, NY: McGraw-Hill Irwin, pp. 3, 5, 12, 173–209.

Chesbrough, H., and R. Rosenbloom (2002). "The role of the business model in capturing value from innovation: Evidence from Xerox Corporation's technology spin-off companies," *Industrial and Corporate Change*, Volume 11, Number 3, pp. 529–555.

Christensen, C.M., and M.E. Raynor (2003). *The Innovators Solution*. Boston, MA: Harvard Business School Press, pp. 56–65.

Drucker, P.F. (2001). *The Essential Drucker*. New York, NY: Harper Collins.

Fahey, L. (1999). *Competitors*. New York, NY: John Wiley & Sons, pp. 172–205.

Fleisher, C.S., and B.E. Bensoussan (2003). *Strategic and Competitive Analysis*. Upper Saddle River, NJ: Prentice Hall, pp. 104–121, 216–219.

Hjelet, P. (2004). "The Fortune Global 500," *Fortune*, July, p. 160.

Langdon, M. (2003). "Business Model Warfare: A Strategy of Business Breakthroughs," Innovations Labs white paper, Ackoff Center for the Advancement of Systems Approaches, University of Pennsylvania.

Linder, J., and S. Cantrell (2000). *Changing Business Models: Surveying the Landscape*, Accenture Institute for Strategic Change (www.accenture.com).

Hermes Newsletter by ELTRUN (The eBusiness Center for the University of Athens), October–November 2002, http://www.eltrun.aueb.gr/newsletters/1/18.pdf, p. 1 (referenced July 17, 2004).

Mitchell, D., and C. Coles (2003). *The Ultimate Competitive Advantage*. San Francisco, CA: Berett Koehler Publishers, Inc.

National Bicycle Dealers Association, "Industry Overview," http://nbda.com/site/page.cfm?PageID=34 (referenced July 13, 2004).

Quick MBA, "The Business Model," http://www.quickmba.com/entre/business-model/ (referenced December 11, 2005).

Osterwalder, A. (2004). "The Business Model Ontology" (PhD. thesis), http://www.hec.unil.ch/aosterwa/PhD/ (referenced October 19, 2004).

Rockart, J.F. (1979). "Chief Executives Define Their Own Data Needs," *Harvard Business Review,* March–April, 52(2), pp. 81–93.

Stalk Jr, G. (1988). "The Time Paradigm," Boston Consulting Group, http://www.bcg.com/publications/publication_view.jsp?pubID=300 (July 13, 2004).

Thompson, A., Gamble, J., and A.J. Strickland (2004). *Winning in the Marketplace.* New York, NY: McGraw-Hill Irwin, pp. 121–123.

Timmer, P. (1998). "Business models for electronic markets," *Electronic Markets,* 8(2), pp. 3–8. http://www.electronicmarkets.org/netacademy/publications.nsf/all_pk/949.

Weil, P., Malone, T., D'Urso, V., and G. Herman (2004). "Do Some Business Models Perform Better Than Others? A Study of the 1000 Largest U.S. Firms.," http://seeit.mit.edu/publications.asp (accessed July 11, 2004).

Wikipedia, the free encyclopedia. "Collective Business System," http://en.wikipedia.org/wiki/Collective_business_system (referenced October 24, 2004).

Endnotes

[1] Afuah, A. (2004).

[2] Chesbrough, H. and R. Rosenbloom (2002).

[3] Timmer, P. (1998).

[4] Linder, J., and S. Cantrell (2002).

[5] Christensen, C.M., and M.E. Raynor (2003).

[6] Mitchell, D., and C. Coles (2003).

[7] Christensen, C.M., and M.E. Raynor (2003).

[8] See Fleisher and Bensoussan (2003), Chapter 12.

[9] See Fleisher and Bensoussan (2003), Chapter 9.

[10] Rockart, J.F. (1979).

SERVO Analysis

Short Description

The SERVO (an acronym for *strategy, environment, resources, values, organization*) analysis framework model is a diagnostic management tool used to build and test a firm's strategic decisions and initiatives. Analysts examine the interactions and relationships among five critical elements to test the degree of consistency or fit between the firm's current and proposed strategies, its organization, capabilities, management preferences, and environment. It is a management tool designed to assess and facilitate the process of strategy formulation and implementation within the context of both market and organizational change.

Background

An analyst requires a way of organizing his or her thoughts, and conceptual models guide the analyst's thinking by focusing on the most relevant and important features of a phenomenon under consideration. Models are especially important in competitive and strategic analytical tasks because there are so many factors that need to be considered.

The SERVO model detailed in this chapter is a broad, integrative framework that helps the analyst hone in on the primary factors that need to be addressed in competitive response and strategy development situations. In addition to being integrative, SERVO allows for a depth of analysis to address many strategy development situations. SERVO is similar to other strategy models in terms of content but differs from most of them in that it is structured to emphasize the relationships among actions or decisions.

SERVO is useful for strategic analysis because it can be applied to many different situations and yet does not imply that every firm in a specific industry needs to compete in an identical fashion or have identical strategies. It attempts to achieve a beneficial balance between both internal (the S, R, V, and O elements) and external (the E element) dimensions impacting strategy. Each of the five elements in the SERVO model consists of several components that can be analyzed separately and in their relationships with each other.

The SERVO model explicitly addresses the need to build a tight, strategic fit between strategy, the environment, resources, values, *and* organization.[1] Successful formulation and implementation of strategy requires explicit management of the interrelationships among the five elements, of which structure and strategy—the main focus of much strategy advice during the early decades of strategy literature and practice—are only two.

"Fit" is a critical concept in the application of this model. It is a desirable and viable state that holds when all management decisions have produced consistency between the firm's resources and capabilities and the external environment. In other words, better fit leads to better performance; correspondingly, bad fit results in bad performance. In seeking to produce better fit, analysts try to identify the managerial decisions that bring about the necessary alignment over both short and long time frames. This requires that analysts recognize both static and dynamic dimensions of management decisions. See Figure 9.1 for a diagram of the "fit" concept.

Figure 9.1   Illustration of the "fit" concept

The reality of most organizational situations is that some inconsistencies will nearly always exist between the elements over time. This occurs because sometimes a firm will seek to pursue opportunities in the environment that put undue strain on it or its resources. At other times, a strategy or value that worked for many years may not hold up to environmental changes. The key for the analyst is to decide which inconsistencies the firm must strategically address through recommended actions and which ones it must overlook or accept.

Each of the five SERVO elements is important on its own and also in the corporate sense. These five elements are discussed in turn next.

Strategy

Among the many formal definitions of strategy, several dominant themes are common. Strategy is the set of competitive decisions and actions made in response to the firm's environment. Strategy aims to best position the firm's current capabilities and resources to secure competitive advantage over time. Because the firm's environment is constantly in a state of flux, so too must strategy change in order to protect existing sources of competitive advantage. In addition, strategy must seek out new opportunities and acquire or develop the requisite resources and capabilities to turn ongoing environmental changes into new sources of competitive advantage. In sum, an effective strategy will clearly identify the firm's goals and objectives, the product/service and market spaces in which it will compete, the business activities on which it will focus, the value it will offer to customers, and the approaches it will use to provide superior offerings to competitors.

For the analyst's purposes, strategy within the SERVO model can best be characterized as composed of four elements: the executive team's goals, scope, competitive basis/premise, and business model. These are discussed in greater depth in the following section:

1. **Goals**—What is the mission of the firm? What is the vision for the firm held by key decision makers and employees? What does the firm intend to accomplish vis-à-vis its stakeholders' expectations? What are top management's expectations (both in quantitative and qualitative terms) with respect to revenue growth, innovation, market share, quality, and profitability?

2. **Scope**—What products/services is the firm selling, and which ones would it like to sell? What customers is it aiming to provide value for? What markets will the firm compete in?

3. **Competitive basis/premise**—In what ways will the firm attempt to beat competitors? How will the firm build capabilities or resources to achieve competitive advantage over time?

4. **Business model**—Is the basic operating structure sound and reflective of appropriate choices and priorities between in-house and outsourced activities? Is there an economic explanation of how the firm can deliver value to customers at a price and cost that yields satisfactory profitability? Do the revenues and costs associated with the goals, scope, and competitive basis demonstrate viability over time?

The focus on strategy within the SERVO model is not necessarily on developing new strategies or protecting existing ones. Rather, its inclusion underscores a core theme demonstrated in many applications of the model that strategy conception and formulation is often done very well in most firms. However, inconsistency between strategy and the other more manageable elements (R, V, and O [resources, values, and organization]) are more often the cause of ineffective implementation and/or strategic failure.

Environment

Environment as a larger concept for competitive and strategic analysis is ordinarily classified into several strata. This is done to help reduce the level of complexity facing the analyst, as the environment can be simultaneously expansive, complex, dynamic, and ambiguous. Though each component has the word "environment" in it, there is only one environment with the components being simply different stratifications of the larger concept.

The first division of the environment is into the external and internal environment. The external environment includes all those things "outside" the legal boundaries of the firm; however, for the analyst's purposes, it is limited to those decisions (beyond the direct control of executives) made by stakeholders outside the firm that may have a significant impact on the firm's performance. The internal environment includes stakeholders, forces, and conditions within the firm. It will include, prominently, stakeholders such as the board of directors, decision makers, and employees, as well as the business functions, culture, organizational practices, processes, structure, and systems.

The environment can also be segmented into several components ordered in terms of proximity to the daily activities of the business. The internal environment is closest to the business, next is task environment, followed by the industry environment, and, finally, the macro-environment.

The task environment typically impacts strategy on a day-to-day basis, involves the specific competitive situation facing the business, and is populated by those specific organizations and groups that most directly influence the organization's strategy, including customers, competitors, partners, and suppliers, but it can also include government regulators and labor unions.

The industry environment deals with environmental factors and forces, which have the most impact on the performance of the firm and its competitors. The value chain stretches all the way from the raw materials used to produce products/services through to after-sale services and includes connected commercial activities in which the industry is ensconced.

The macro or general environment is the set of conditions and influences affecting economic activity and is ordinarily outside a typical firm's direct influence. One particularly valuable scheme for the analyst who needs to further classify the general environment is the PEST/STEEP method.[2] Finally, some classifications of the external environment also subdivide the first division geographically, usually by international, trans-national, national, regional, and/or local boundaries.

Resources

Resources are the assets and capabilities a firm uses to generate outputs (that is, goods and/or services) for the marketplace. One way of classifying resources is to use the value chain,[3] a concept that shows the linked set of value-creating activities a firm performs. Primary activities, such as raw materials acquisition, operations, outbound logistics, marketing and sales, and service, are the value-adding pursuits that best explain the primary business role of the firm. Secondary activities, such as communications, human resource management, management information systems, and government and public affairs, facilitate and enhance the performance of primary activities.

Similar to the environment, analysts also need to reduce the complexity associated with classifications of "resources." Business resources can usefully be grouped under several categories, as follows:

Financial Resources

A strategy that requires significant investment in new processes or products, distribution channels, production capacity, and working capital can place strains on the firm's financial resources and needs careful financial management. An examination of financial resources should include an assessment of existing resources, such as bank overdrafts, bank loans, cash balances, creditors, other loans, shareholders' capital, working capital, and the ability to raise new funds.

Human Resources

A firm's human resources are its skills base. The raw material of competitive advantage frequently lies in the intangible core competencies and skills of its people. Environmental change (the "E") infers not only a change in strategy but also a change in the skill set of a firm's human resources that will act on a new set of key success factors. Successful organizational change often requires increased investment to acquire or develop new skills along with reduced investment in the established skill set that was more closely attuned to the old business models. This transition toward new skill sets is a process that, if done poorly, will thwart the cultivation of conditions necessary to grow new organizational skills.

When assessing these skills, the analyst must consider the following types of questions:

- What skills does the firm already possess?
- Are they sufficient to meet the objectives of the desired strategy options?
- Could the skills base be enhanced, enlarged, or stretched to meet the new requirements?

Physical Resources

The category of physical resources covers a wide range of operational assets concerned with the firm's physical capability to deliver its strategy into the marketplace. Sometimes referred to as plant, property, and equipment (PP&E), they include, among others, the following:

- **Information technology**—Management information systems, information technology assets, databases, and integration of systems across the firm.
- **Production facilities**—Location of existing production facilities, capacity, investment and maintenance requirements, current production processes, and particularly their quality, method, and organization. Ultimately, the analyst examining this area must consider the extent to which production requirements of the strategy can be delivered by existing facilities.

Intangible Resources

It is easy to ignore the intangible resources of a business when assessing how to deliver a strategy—but they can be crucial. Prominent intangibles the analyst must consider include the following:

- **Brands**—Strong brands are often the key factor as to whether a growth strategy is a success or failure.
- **Goodwill**—The difference between the value of the tangible assets of the business and the actual value of the business (what someone would be prepared to pay for it).
- **Intellectual assets (capital, property)**—Key commercial rights protected by copyrights, patents, and trademarks may be an important factor in the firm's strategy.
- **Reputation**—The collective representation of the firm's previous actions and results that describe its ability to deliver valuable and valued outcomes to stakeholders.

Values

To understand values, the analyst must attempt to capture the human as well as the social sides of the firm's leading decision makers. Decision makers do not make their decisions in a vacuum; indeed, one of the purposes of this book is to emphasize how the analyst can support these decision makers with beneficial insight.

Executives' decisions are affected by personal, positional, and situational factors. Personal factors affect what the decision maker thinks, values, and prefers. Positional factors reflect what others expect of the decision maker as expressed through the demands they place personally on him or her. Situational factors are relevant to the lead up and time of the executive making a decision. Values are reflected both in the posture and managerial style of the decision maker when making business decisions.

Managerial preferences refer to the actions and behavior of (senior) executives rather than what they say. As such, the conduct of top management is an extremely valuable management tool that conveys and reinforces strong messages to stakeholders and particularly employees throughout the organization. One of the most important barometers of executives' behavior is the way in which they spend their time. By concentrating their individual and collective attention on managing critical success factors, executives can help their staff prioritize the essential activities that the organization must perform well.

Another important barometer of executive leadership is symbolic or signaling behavior that can be seen as constantly reinforcing the fundamental value system of the firm. By fostering a firm-wide "strategic conversation" composed of formal and informal symbols, executives can instill a positive culture consistent with the firm's strategic intent.

Sometimes also referred to as super-ordinate goals, shared values represent the collective value system that drives a firm's organizational culture. Often, shared values are informal and go beyond the firm's mission statement by encompassing intangibles such as strategic intent, underlying beliefs, mental mindsets, and future direction. Shared values are sometimes viewed as the most fundamental building block of an organization, thereby providing a foundation for the other elements. Often, shared values are short articulations of the essential meaning or driving force of the organization. The difficulty, and hence value, in creating strong shared values within an organization is exemplified by the observation that only exceptional firms are able to consistently leverage this phenomenon over time.[4]

Organization

The main components of organization in the SERVO model are culture, leadership, staffing, structure, and systems. *Culture* differs from firm to firm and refers to the character of a firm's work climate and personality. These are shaped by a firm's beliefs, history, modus operandi, stories, traditions, and values. Once established, a firm's culture tends to be perpetuated in a number of ways and can be resistant in the short term to managerial attempts to change it.

Leadership is a highly visible organizational role that involves motivating people to best perform their responsibilities. It is most directly exemplified by the actions and behaviors of the firm's top executives and decision makers.[5]

Staffing involves the attraction, development, motivation, retention, and training of the individuals, which a business needs to operate. These tasks are ordinarily managed by a human resources department but have broader firm-wide implications that go far beyond the auspices of only one responsibility center. Staffing can be among the most critical activities—explaining the strategic success of firms in the knowledge economy—and has clearly risen in prominence as a point of analytical focus since the 1980s.

Structure involves the allocation and division of responsibilities and the configuration of reporting relationships within a firm; it is frequently represented by an organizational chart. The choice of structure involves a myriad of tradeoffs; for example, a firm's structure may be centralized or decentralized, hierarchical or flattened, or specialized or integrated. The focus on structure within the "O" element of the SERVO model, however, helps concentrate the analyst's mind on two key aspects of structure. First is the idea of coordination of all of the aspects of structure in the support of strategy. Second, the SERVO model seeks to isolate those aspects of structure, which are critical to successfully negotiating change in light of industry evolution and new or revamped strategies.

Systems encompass the flow of both primary and secondary activities that are important to the firm's daily functioning. These include core processes (for example, product development and operations management), as well as support activities (for example, information systems, accounting, and human resources). An important distinction that the SERVO model offers is that changing systems can be a less disruptive and more effective route to enhanced organizational effectiveness as opposed to the more traditional levers of manipulating strategy or structure.

Figure 9.2 is a schematic representation of the SERVO model. True to the adage that "a picture is worth a thousand words," the diagram sheds insights not captured in the previous discussion of the other elements of organizational effectiveness.

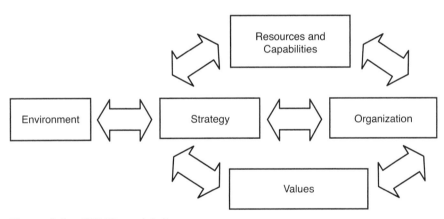

Figure 9.2   SERVO model diagram

The first insight from Figure 9.2 refers to the inclusion of three other elements comprising organizational effectiveness in addition to the traditional strategy and structure dualism—namely, environment, resources, and values.

The second insight refers to the dual arrow lines connecting each element. Decisions made in one element lead to a decision in another element, which complements the first decision, and so on. For example, look at the strategy element (S). A decision about strategy has implications for decisions in the E, R, V, and O elements. Having made a decision about strategy, the decision made by executives in a particular environmental context (E) must accommodate the business's strategic decision. Executives will have to make simultaneous as well as subsequent decisions so that resources (R) are in place to support the strategic decision and propel the necessary actions over time. The leaders in the business also have to make personal choices based on their values (V), which support and promote putting the strategy (S) in place. Finally, the strategic action/decision will dictate the nature and type of structure and systems of the organization (O) to perform those actions.

The third insight is the assertion that strategic failure may well be attributable to any one of, or a combination of inattention to, the five elements of strategic fit. The SERVO model can offer a corrective lens for the strategic myopia that often leads to bad structure or inappropriate strategy.

The fourth insight comes from its shape. The cybernetic consistency of the model is intentional. This focuses your attention on the total absence of hierarchical dominance or priority. It encourages you to reach the conclusion that no one element is more important than another. Each element is a necessary but insufficient condition for organizational effectiveness. This lack of precision and high level of abstraction makes the SERVO model quite flexible.

Taken together, these four insights have made an enormous contribution to modern strategy theory in a couple of powerful ways. First, the SERVO model introduces the importance of the qualitative factors of organizational effectiveness to counterbalance the almost exclusive focus on strategy and structure that pervaded previous management thought around the management of organizational change. Second, it rebalances the theoretical plane of strategy by shifting the fulcrum of consideration. It pushes the conceptual envelope away from an external environmental preoccupation to a more holistic appraisal that includes a realistic appreciation of the whole system—that is, both the organization strategically acting on its environment, as well as the environment acting on the organization and its strategy.

Strengths and Advantages

The SERVO model is unique in that it was one of the first strategy models to emphasize the balance between internal and external factors. The need for internal alignment as part of the strategy equation was often given short shrift or even ignored in preceding management theory. The SERVO model filled this analytical vacuum by suggesting that strategic success is equally dependent on organizational effectiveness. This counteracted the disproportionate emphasis of previous models on external economic factors. The SERVO model laid the groundwork for the increasing prominence of organizational dynamics in future models, such as core competency theory.

Further, this model developed the concept that organizational effectiveness was not dependent on just strategy and organizational structure—a radical and much-needed departure from the confines of the "structure follows strategy" idea. The inclusion of the three other elements of strategic fit broaden the analyst's scope to consider the possibility that strategy follows structure, management preferences, and resources. It identified that organizational change requires management of the relationships among ALL five elements of strategic fit, not just tinkering with only one or two of the elements (traditionally, strategy and structure).

Another strength of this model is its inclusiveness and holistic approach, which will do much to ensure that all possible variables are included in strategic analysis. Arbitrary diagnosis of organizational effectiveness in the absence of the SERVO model could lead to serious deficiencies in strategic analysis.

Weaknesses and Limitations

The main weakness of the SERVO model is its high level of abstraction. It offers only diagnostic guidance regarding the identification of challenges and barriers to organizational effectiveness. Methodological precision is decidedly absent. Although the model can assist with both formulation and implementation tasks, it does not provide specific guidance for either. Creative analysis is therefore important for the successful application of the model.

There are also some limits in the definition and level of specificity associated with each of the five individual elements. For example, although resources and organization are ostensibly separate in practice, there is bound to be some definitional overlap and confusion when trying to keep them distinctive. This is due, in part at least, to the way that firms are organized functionally and the ways they are structured to address work and marketplace tasks.

Another weakness is the difficulty in applying this model. Often, the subtle interrelationships between the five elements are extremely difficult to discern. In order to manage this complexity, managers are often predisposed to treat each variable separately, or only to look at two or three combinations that may lessen the influence of the other interactions present among all of the elements. This is more due to the difficulty in dealing with simultaneous multi-variable interactive complexity—one that is only exposed to the light of day through this model.

Last but not least, the SERVO model tends to be a static model. It is useful for looking at a snapshot of an organization's fit at any one time, but can be difficult to use when making longitudinal changes—unless it is developed and applied on a regular basis or with specific time periods built into the analysis. The model's ability to address the challenges generated by dynamic firms and marketplaces is more limited than those models that expressly account for time as a critical variable.

Process for Applying the Technique

The process for applying the SERVO model is deceptively simple. It can be tempting at times to overestimate the firm's ability to achieve alignment among all five elements. The SERVO model is amenable to testing both current and proposed strategy and, as such, assumes that these strategies have already been conceptualized and formulated.

Step 1: Evaluate the Current Performance of the Firm

The first step is to assess whether the firm's performance has met both internal and external goals. This means understanding what decision makers seek to achieve as well as what other stakeholders, such as customers, suppliers, strategic partners, and employees hope the firm will do. Performance should also be compared to external references, such as market competitors and similarly focused firms in related industries. These comparisons must also be done over designated time periods, usually including the last few quarters and years, with projections of competitors' performance being made at least several quarters ahead. Many organizational analysts predominantly do these tasks by using financial ratio and statement analysis.[6]

If the analyst determines that the firm is not performing as well as it should against either internal or external references, then he must diagnose the potential causes of these performance problems. This diagnosis can be performed by working through a fuller SERVO analysis, as described in Step 2. If the analyst determines that the organization is performing well, his responsibility will shift to assessing risks and vulnerabilities and to identifying strategies that can exploit emerging opportunities.

Step 2: Assess the Current Strategy and Discern Whether Change Is Necessary

Relationships among the SERVO elements create the interdependencies that impact the firm's strategic and competitive actions. For the analyst serving a decision-making client, this means that in making one decision, another decision has to be made to complement the first, either by supporting the prior decision, by adding features to it, or by lessening any adverse effects. When applying the SERVO model, the analyst must be mindful that the relationships among strategic actions or decisions are important because the actions/decisions should complement each other. Complementary action and decisions ordinarily work in conjunction with each other to produce desirable results. When actions are taken or decisions are made in isolation, there is a danger that they will not work together, sometimes even contradicting each other, and so produce inferior results.

The number of relationships to consider is enormous because, theoretically, every strategic action or decision needs to be considered in light of every other decision. Where does the analyst begin this task? This dilemma is resolved partially by SERVO itself. It deals with the "big" picture, thereby focusing the analyst on those relationships that are strategically important. If the rare, major, and direction setting (that is, strategic) decisions are correctly made, then the operational and tactical decisions made in response to them should follow. This is why the diagnosis begins with the macro relationships among the five SERVO elements. When this has been completed, the analyst considers the details within each of the five elements.

Even though there are only five elements in the SERVO model, 20 macro relationships exist if the actions and decisions in each element are related to actions/decisions in every other element. In addition to these macro relationships between the five elements, there are relationships among the components within each element. Within the resource element, for example, we can uncover relationships between financial and other functional decisions. The financial decisions made about the amount of equity and debt a firms uses to finance its operations may limit the potential for raising new capital for investments, even in earnings enhancing activities that are planned.

The most common way that the analyst determines whether the relationships are effective or not is to gauge their *fit*. The following section describes the nature and strength of various types of fit. These will help the analyst to determine where decisions first need to be made, as well as where executive attention must be focused. These are placed within SERVO grids to help the analyst organize and visualize the relational diagnosis (see Figure 9.3).

A. An Ideal SERVO Configuration

	S	E	R	V	O
S	XXX	T / n	T / e	T / n	T / n
E	T / n	XXX	T / n	T / n	T / n
R	T / e	T / n	XXX	T / n	T / n
V	T / n	T / n	T / n	XXX	T / e
O	T / n	T / n	T / n	T / e	XXX

B. SERVO Configuration at Current StateÑShowing Several Misfits

	S	E	R	V	O
S	XXX	T / n	T / n	L / d	T / n
E	M / n	XXX	T / n	M / d	L / e
R	T / n	M / n	XXX	T / n	M / n
V	M / d	L / d	T / n	XXX	T / n
O	T / n	L / e	M / n	T / n	XXX

Figure 9.3   SERVO grid showing fits among elements

Fit Types

There are a number of ways to characterize the nature and strength of the "fits" found to exist between elements. We recommend using a two-stage process to characterize fits. The first stage looks at the strength of the fit. Strength can be characterized as "tight," "loose," and "medium." These are usually identified in a SERVO grid by being shown in capital letters:

■ **Tight fit**—(Characterized as "T" in Figure 9.3.) This occurs when all decisions made in the related SERVO elements support and contribute to each other. This type of fit appears to be associated with the highest levels of firm effectiveness, and a good indication it exists can be found in the financial ratio and statement analysis evidence that a firm is demonstrating superior performance. Tight fit can be difficult to maintain over time because a number of factors will always be, to some degree, outside of management's direct influence or control. It is also one of the reasons why few organizations, if any, can truly achieve decades-long sources of sustainable competitive advantages.

■ **Loose fit**—(Characterized as "L" in Figure 9.3.) This occurs when decisions made in the related SERVO elements fail to support and contribute to each other. This type of fit appears to be associated with the lowest levels of effectiveness, and a good indication it exists can be found in the financial ratio and statement analysis evidence that a firm is performing inadequately. A minimal form of loose fit exists when a firm has achieved the minimal degree of fit needed for its survival. Like tight fit, loose fit can also be difficult to maintain over time because decision makers, and their associated firms, seldom last long in this state. Loose-fitting organizations move from crisis to crisis and are always in fire-fighting mode. Managing in a state of loose fit may require a different set of knowledge, skills, abilities, and experiences of a firm's decision makers than is required to manage a firm that is in a state of tight fit.

■ **Medium fit**—(Characterized as "M" in Figure 9.3.) This occurs when some decisions made in the related SERVO elements support and contribute to one another, while others do not. This is the most common state of fit evidenced in firms at any one time. The goal for the analyst is to help decision makers make choices and decisions that will lead to actions that will tighten the "loose" fits. Some medium fits may be more "fragile" (how vulnerable they are to change; how much resilience the firm retains in dealing with other related elements) than others, and this should be noted when characterizing the strength between elements as being a medium fit.

The second dimension to characterizing fit attempts to address the issue of time. In other words, fits change over time—some more quickly and some more slowly than others. It is rare in an organizational strategy context for a relationship to remain in a steady state for extended periods. There are essentially three forms of temporal fit: early, normal, or late fits. These are usually identified in a SERVO grid by using small letters.

■ **Early fit**—(Characterized as "e" in Figure 9.3.) This means that the firm has discovered and is creating a new pattern of fit between its SERVO elements before any other business. It is ordinarily driven by the relationship of its strategy (S) and a number or sequenced combination of the other elements. It can be a competitive advantage for the firm, especially if the pattern is hard for its competitors to imitate.

■ **Delayed fit**—(Characterized as "d" in Figure 9.3.) Achieving this temporal state means that the firm is/was among the slowest in a particular competitor comparison to respond to changing patterns among its SERVO elements. This particularly exists in the relationship of the other four elements to the environment (E). For example, a firm that is very slow to market with a product/service reflecting an accepted technological change would be characterized as having a "late fit" between its strategy (S) and environment (E) elements. A firm that was late to change its human resources policies to adapt to changing standards, mores, or laws would have a late fit between its values (V) or resources (R) and environmental (E) relationship.

■ **Normal fit**—(Characterized as "n" in Figure 9.3.) This means that the firm was neither fast nor slow to respond to changes among its elements of SERVO. In other words, it adapts or changes at about the same time as a "typical" firm under consideration.

Empirical studies of these forms of fit face three major challenges: to determine the ideal profile to be used as a base; to work out relative position from the ideal profile; and to relate the type of fit to performance indicators.

Step 3: Develop and Evaluate Strategic Options and Programs

After isolating the nature of fit and the strategic distance between the five SERVO elements, there are essentially three options. The firm can work to change the required components of each element so that they are consistent with strategy. Alternately, it may be wise to consider changing the strategy to fit the existing orientation of the other four elements of the model. Often, a compromise between each of these two options is the realistic alternative.

First, the analyst will generate a set of options to consider and then attempt to identify those options that will bring into best alignment the misfits among the five elements. To do this, the analyst must consider the comparative feasibility of the various alternatives. One means for helping achieve this is to prepare performance projections of the various options to be recommended. Those that offer the best projected performance should be considered the most attractive alternatives and be the options recommended to decision makers.

After the policy actions have been decided on and the recommendations made, it is then useful to generate a projected new SERVO alignment. After the firm employs the recommendations, the framework should reflect an improved, or even better, ideal alignment between each of the SERVO elements—that is, strategy, resources, values, and organization should be moving together in the same direction to best support the desired match with the firm's environment.

Figure 9.3 depicts two scenarios. The first grid, Figure A, depicts an optimal situation in which all of the five SERVO elements are aligned—creating a tight strategic fit. Figure B displays an organization whose strategic fit is in disarray; the five elements of strategic fit are not aligned, and hence the effectiveness of the strategy should be called into question. In this instance, the analyst will need to identify the specific causes of the relational misfits.

The SERVO model is a general analytical framework that addresses what is important to strategic thinking. This means that the analyst will need to consider the key factors associated with the firm, its strategy, and the environment in terms of the five elements, and then assess the relationships among those elements. A strategic problem is present when the fit among the elements is loose, fragile, or broken. The analyst's objective is to generate recommendations to decision-making clients that will tighten the fit among the loose-relating elements.

FAROUT Summary

FAROUT SUMMARY

	1	2	3	4	5
F	■	■	■	■	
A	■	■			
R	■	■	■		
O	■				
U	■	■	■	■	■
T	■	■			

Figure 9.4   SERVO analysis FAROUT summary

Future orientation—Medium to high. The SERVO model is forward looking in that it is oriented toward the future implementation of proposed strategy or the correction of existing organizational configurations in order to maximize effectiveness of current strategy.

Accuracy—Low to medium. Accuracy depends on the ability of the analyst to (a) correctly diagnose the five elements and their interactions, (b) correctly diagnose the key success factors, and (c) implement the required changes to close the distance between (a) and (b).

Resource efficiency—Medium. Depends on the depth of analysis and the number of analysts engaged. Similarly, the comprehensiveness of internal consulting will dictate resource efficiency. Organizations with only a few elements out of alignment will achieve higher resource efficiency.

Objectivity—Low. The requisite analysis is highly qualitative and subject to perception bias.

Usefulness—Medium to high. The explicit purview of this model is exactly what many other models ignore. As such, the SERVO model is compatible with, and complementary to, a good number of other management tools and techniques.

Timeliness—Low to medium. A comprehensive SERVO analysis is extremely comprehensive and covers all facets of the firm. Additionally, correctly examining the intricate inter-relationships between the five elements can require a substantial amount of time.

Related Tools and Techniques

- 7S analysis
- Competitive benchmarking
- Customer segmentation and needs analysis
- Customer value analysis

- Financial ratio and statement analysis
- Functional capability and resource analysis
- STEEP analysis
- SWOT analysis
- Value chain analysis

References

Andrews, K. (1980). *The Concept of Corporate Strategy*, rev. ed. Homewood, IL: Richard D. Irwin, Inc.

Baker, D., and J. Cullen (1993). "Administrative reorganization and configurational context: The contingent effects of age, size, and change in size." *Academy of Management Journal*, 36(6), pp. 1251–1277.

Chandler, A.D. Jr. (1962). *Strategy and Structure: Chapters in the History of the American Industrial Enterprise*. Cambridge, MA: MIT Press.

Collins, J., and J. Porras (2002). *Built to Last: Successful Habits of Visionary Companies*. New York, NY: Harper Collins.

Darden Graduate Business School Sponsors (1983). *American Telephone and Telegraph (A)*, Charlottesville, VA: University of Virginia.

Fleisher, C., and B. Bensoussan (2003). *Strategic and Competitive Analysis: Methods and Techniques for Analyzing Business Competition*. Upper Saddle River, NJ: Prentice Hall.

Fry, L., and D. Smith (1987). "Congruence, contingency, and theory building," *Academy of Management Review*, 12(1), pp. 117–132.

Harling, K. (1999). "Note on strategic management," comments prepared for The Maple Leaf Conference, retrieved from http://info.wlu.ca/~wwwsbe/MapleLeaf/Strategic_Management.html.

Hax, A.C., and N.S. Majluf (1983). "Organization design: A case on matching strategy and structure," *The Journal of Business Strategy,* Fall, 4(2), pp. 72–86.

Ketchen, D., Thomas, J., and C. Snow (1993). "Organizational configurations and performance: A comparison of theoretical perspectives," *Academy of Management Journal*, 36(6), pp. 1278–1313.

Meyer, A., Tsui, A., and C. Hinings (1993). "Configurational approaches to organizational analysis," *Academy of Management Journal*, 36(6), pp. 1175–1195.

Peters, T.J. (1984). "Strategy follows structure: Developing distinctive skills," *California Management Review,* Spring, 26(3), pp. 111–125.

Powel, T.C. (1992). "Organizational alignment as competitive advantage," *Strategic Management Journal,* February, 13(2), pp. 119–134.

Waterman, R.H. Jr. (1982). "The Seven Elements of Strategic Fit," *The Journal of Business Strategy*, 1982, 2(3), pp. 69–73.

Waterman, R.H. Jr., Peters, T.J., and J.R. Phillips (1980). "Structure is not Organization," *Business Horizons*, June, pp. 14–26.

Endnotes

[1] Andrews, 1980; Harling, 1999.

[2] See Fleisher and Bensoussan (2003), Chapter 17.

[3] See Fleisher and Bensoussan (2003), Chapter 9.

[4] Collins and Porras, 2002.

[5] As thousands of studies and books have been written on the topic of leadership, we will not dwell on this area of SERVO, but will suggest the analyst refer to our explanation of management profiling that is captured in Chapter 15 of our prior book (Fleisher and Bensoussan, 2002).

[6] See Fleisher and Bensoussan (2003), Chapter 25.

Supply Chain Management (SCM) Analysis

Short Description

The supply chain can be defined as a network of suppliers, manufacturers, distributors, retailers, and customers that are linked by information, wares, and capital that move among the participants.[1] Supply chain management (SCM) is the conduct of the interrelated elements among the supply chain's functions, like procurement, logistics, and inventory management, as well as the interactions between the firm and outside companies within the supply chain.[2] In a general context, SCM can be defined as

> . . . the systematic, strategic coordination of traditional business functions and the tactics across these business functions within a particular company and across these businesses within the supply chain, for the purposes of improving the long-term performance of the individual companies and the supply chain as a whole.[3]

In short, an effective supply chain will ensure that the right goods get to the right people, at the right time, at minimal cost, and maximum efficiency to the company.[4] It is important to note that this chapter will look at analyzing the management of supply chains. As such, analyzing their management will require the analyst to answer the following questions, among others:

- What is the relative bargaining power of suppliers to industry competitor's supply chains?

- Do competitors or one's own enterprise have too many different suppliers when a few well-managed relationships could ably fill capacity?

- How effective are your own enterprises, as well as competitors' supply chains, particularly compared to the analyst's enterprise?

- Where are the vulnerabilities and strengths in the management of a competitor's supply chain?

- How does your own supply chain compare to industry competitors' as well as benchmark practices?

Background

Throughout history, goods and the people who want them have been in different places. In the days before sophisticated transportation and refrigeration systems, communities sprung up close to food sources and abundant natural resources. Because people lacked a good way to bring resources to themselves, they brought themselves to the resources. However, as civilization advanced, communication and mobility improved, and trade allowed people to develop tastes for faraway commodities. Individuals also quickly realized they could ship their excess goods to people who otherwise would not have had access to them.[5] Over time, strong import and export markets began to develop among numerous nation-states.

Compared to conditions only a century ago, communication and transportation mechanisms have become easier, faster, and less expensive. As a result, companies can source products from all corners of the globe, communicate with partners in real time, and get sophisticated and specialized products to market in weeks—a task that would have been basically inconceivable only a generation ago.[6] All the while, many average families have shrunk in size, and many women are working outside the home, raising the level of disposable income available to consumers. This phenomenon has fueled the desire for varieties of complex consumer goods to be available to whomever wants them, whenever they want them—a transition that the contemporary, well-managed supply chain will support and delivers value to. It naturally follows that how well a company manages all of the components that go into its final product can determine how successful the product will be in the marketplace. How well your enterprise and your competitors are managing their supply chain can mean big opportunities or big challenges for your company.

The notion of supply chain management (SCM) emerged around the 1960s, with more attention being paid to the subject into the 1980s, although the popularity of SCM did not really take off until the 1990s. Up until this time, the predominant model for a company's supply chain was very company-centric, with little involvement from suppliers and customers. A good example of this is the development of a model combining supply chains understandings and operations research.

In the mid 1990s, consultants at Pittiglio Rabin Todd & McGrath (PRTM) sensed the need for a model that would help illustrate, and thus improve, the way companies in a supply chain work together. The result of their efforts and input from more than 75 manufacturers and the Advanced Manufacturing Research (AMR) firm was the Supply Chain Operations Research model (SCOR). Those 75 companies created an association called the Supply Chain Council (SCC) to further these efforts.[7]

Successful companies such as Wal-Mart, Dell, Best Buy, Procter & Gamble, and Volkswagen are all managing their supply chains in ways that allow these companies to compete more effectively in their relevant marketplaces. Supply chain management is increasingly seen as a source of competitive advantage for companies, and this area of competition is expected to be further leveraged in coming years.[8]

The field of SCM is still youthful and promises to evolve further as more sources of competitive advantage are realized through effective supply chain management. Many companies are now realizing that the new opportunity to add value and increase profits cannot be undertaken alone—cooperation with other members in the supply chain can optimize capabilities. Ultimately, the partners that make up the chain will be more successful together than they could ever be by themselves.[9] Astute firms realize that in the future, the competitive arena will witness chains competing against chains rather than companies competing against companies.[10] Figure 10.1 stresses the myopic, dated view of some companies that they are stand-alones, competing against only others in their industry.

Figure 10.1   Old model of competition

Figure 10.2 is a demonstration of the realization that an optimized value chain can be stronger than the sum of its parts. Gone are the days where companies can isolate themselves and expect to be able to maintain a competitive advantage.

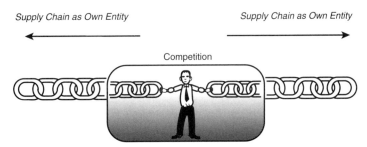

Figure 10.2   New model of competition

Strategic Rationale

As Henry Ford learned in the early 1900s, no company can operate completely independently. Henry Ford made it his automotive company's sole mission to be totally self-sufficient. His procurement efforts involved owning glass factories, coal mines, forests, soybean fields, and even an entire Brazilian rubber plantation in order to guarantee sources for raw materials. He invested in shipping lines, railroads, and roadways, and constructed his own harbor to ensure that materials and inventory had reliable transportation. His reach extended globally, so he could control all of his operations, including plants, dealerships, and service operations, throughout all countries where Ford products were produced and sold.[11] However ambitious, Ford learned that the laws of competitive advantage don't discriminate, and at the height of his vertical integration initiative, he was consistently being outperformed by smaller firms whose specialty could not be matched by his cumbersome regime. Ford learned a valuable lesson that is now part conventional business wisdom: *"No firm can be self-sufficient."*[12]

The pace of information and technology has lead to a marketplace that is dynamic, with ever-increasing customer expectations. The "bull-whip effect" refers to increased costs and inefficiencies that travel along the supply chain as a result of demand/supply incongruities and information disparities.[13] The effect can be reduced by effective supply chain management. This requires a paradigm shift from that of a reactive, myopic, ledger-driven organization, to that of a fully-integrated future-oriented, proactive, and agile supply chain member. The perspective is just the tip of the iceberg, however, and must be supported by technology, adequate and talented staff, and company-wide support.

A 2003 survey of over 500 manufacturers by Deloitte Consulting revealed the increasing complexities and challenges that companies are now facing in trying to optimize their supply chains. Although a majority of manufacturers have operations overseas, some with more assets in foreign countries than their home or headquarters country, most supply chain optimization efforts are directed at singular projects, facilities, and departments and tend to be local. Only about half of the surveyed manufacturers had a senior-level executive in charge of end-to-end SCM. Although many manufacturers cite flexibility as being very important, shorter cycle and lead times and pressure to reduce costs is making flexibility harder to attain. Managing supply chain risks is becoming more difficult as well, as many manufacturers say they continue to fragment their supply chains. Less than 8% of the surveyed executives said that they collaborate with customers on key initiatives. Fewer than 2% of respondents felt that they had a world-class supply chain, although more than 90% of respondents thought it was important.[14] These empirical findings highlight that effective supply-chain management is just now moving to the forefront of companies' collective consciousness, although there still remains a long way to go until the typical company is effectively managing its supply chain to achieve competitive advantage.

Strengths and Advantages

Effective Supply Chain Management analysis can ultimately lead to a competitive advantage due to decreased costs, increased efficiency, better product availability, and increased sales. Many companies are using their supply chains to beat their competitors at cost control, which can result in more pricing flexibility at the point where the goods interface with end customers. It can also result in higher profit margins if companies with effective SCM price their goods at relatively similar levels as their competitors with less effectively managed supply chains. As such, analyzing the management of supply chains can help the analyst pinpoint potential sources of competitive advantage that many other business or competitive analysis models may miss.

Effective supply chain management can translate to competitive advantage if the flow of information and products among the supply chain participants are synchronized and all parties' interests are constructively aligned. Proper alignment and information sharing between parties leads to a "win-win" relationship and allow the supply chain-related parties to minimize inefficiencies. Additionally, these sources of competitive advantage are often hidden "below the surface," meaning that companies using their supply chains for advantage may build large leads in the marketplace before their competitors realize what is actually the source of the advantage. These network-based advantages can also be difficult to spot using most other models of analysis, and SCM analysis allows for and encourages probing of resources, networks, and information sharing in ways that most other models do not consider.

For companies competing on a cost basis, effective SCM can be the difference between competitive success and failure. Many companies find that an analysis of their supply chains lead to changes that help them better manage their assets, therefore decreasing costs. In particular, accounts receivable, physical inventories, demand cycles, and infrastructure, including buildings, plants, warehousing, retail outlets, and transportation, can all be better managed. For example, Wal-Mart's asset turnover of 2.59 times in 2004 is a testament to the finely tuned supply chain for which they are famous. Target, a strong competitor in the competitive U.S. retailing market, struggled to catch them at 1.54 times.[15]

Today, effective supply chain management means building a product and information flow that will ultimately benefit the customer. Combined with notions of customer centricity that flow out of other approaches like product line analysis, customer segmentation approaches, and marketing research, SCM can be a powerful weapon that resists competitor imitation, a fundamental recipe of resource-based strategic advantage. Increased efficiencies and better asset management should lead to lower-cost goods without compromising quality. Information sharing and predictive modeling should mean that the product gets to market when the customer is looking for it. Principles like "Design for Supply"(where product designers understand the production costs and implications of their designs) utilize techniques like "postponement, commonality, and standardization"[16] to create products that are easier to customize to consumer group preferences without adding significant costs or steps in the supply chain. The result is a product that is more tailored to market groups. Ultimately, successfully analyzing a supply chain will reveal how in touch the supply chain is with customer needs and wants, a powerful equation for success in competitive marketplaces.

Weaknesses and Limitations

Supply chain analysis of both one's own enterprise, and more particularly of competitors, is not an easy task to accomplish. First of all, it requires a significant reservoir of comprehensive, timely, and accurate supply chain-related data, for which many companies will not have even for their own enterprises. For those companies that have experienced difficulties in analyzing the management of their own supply chains, imagine how difficult it will be for analysts trying to analyze the management of their competitor's chains.

One of the stranger limitations of SCM analysis is in how the analyst's decision-making clients may look at the evidence coming out of an SCM analysis. If supply chain management analysis reveals that a firm is missing opportunities and experiencing inefficiencies due to a lack of technology and integration, the firm is potentially looking at a very large financial and time investment to bring them into line with their competitors. Many decision makers may intrinsically already know this and be unwilling to authorize either an analysis of SCM or the recommendations that flow from one since it requires a risky, strategic decision. On the other hand, failing to improve one's own enterprise's SCM in the face of overwhelming evidence that competitors are using theirs to win in the marketplace is tantamount to managerial irresponsibility.

Analysts also need to have an understanding of some facets of the organization that require specialty expertise and knowledge. For example, the software that communicates supply chain dynamics to one's company uses complicated and sophisticated network modeling. Although they can add value and improve decision making, massive computer skill and programming are typically required. This process can be costly and time consuming, and as no standard set of network modeling tools has developed, firms run the risk of running into compatibility issues with supply chain partners. Integrating network modeling tools with the SCOR model could provide a framework for standardization at some point in the future.[17] Until or unless this standardization occurs, making "apples to apples" comparisons among the management of competitor's supply chains will remain a thorny issue among individuals performing SCM analysis.

Another existing limitation of most SCM analysis models also is brought about by the realities of today's business environment. Rapid advances in technology now allow companies to create strategic alliances with other companies in their supply chain. These partnerships allow information to flow freely between the organizations in real time. When this process is repeated in multiple organizations, networks are created. The current evolution of most SCM analysis frameworks or models have yet to allow for the comparative empirical illustration associated with *how* these supply chain networks compete against one another.

Process for Applying the Technique

We suggest that it is important to start this section with a look at the SCOR (Supply Chain Operations Reference) model developed by the Supply Chain Council (SCC). The SCOR model looks at SCM from a strategic, rather than operational or design perspective and should therefore be more helpful to analysts looking to analyze SCM for business and competitive purposes. Numeric and analytic modeling techniques, whose base is in engineering and day-to-day business principles can be used for operational and design decisions, but strategic decisions require that the supply chain be viewed as a whole.[18] Figure 10.3 demonstrates the traditional model for companies to view themselves as sole entities, rather than links in a larger chain.

The SCOR model helps executives see their part in the bigger chain by shifting the format away from the traditional supplier/manufacturer/customer perspective to four processes that each company must undergo in each link of the chain. *Planning* is the first of the four processes and is central to managing the other three processes, which are *source*, *make*, and *deliver*. Every time there is an exchange of goods between parties, all four processes are utilized. The SCOR model identifies three levels of process detail. Level I is the top level and deals with process types (SCOR Version 7.0 overview). It outlines the SCOR model and sets performance targets. Level II deals with process categories. The process categories are the basis for the supply chain to be custom configured, which in turn provides a format for the company to execute their operations strategy. Level III deals with process elements and is the level at which processes are developed, articulated, and translate into competencies. Best practices, performance metrics, and the necessary systems for support are articulated at this level.

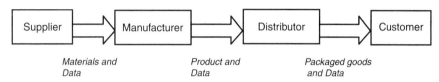

Figure 10.3   Old supply chain configuration

The model emphasizes that all processes must be planned and gives a collaborative tool to aid communication because all components of the chain are visible, as is the flow of information and materials. Figure 10.4 demonstrates how partners in the chain are linked and the planning process is central to all supply chain activity.

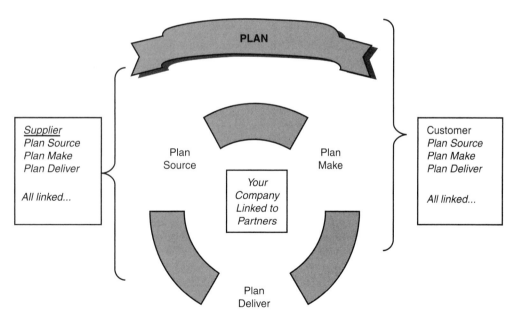

Figure 10.4   SCOR model of supply chain management
Source: Loosely adapted from SCOR Version 7.0 overview.

It is with this perspective in mind that we turn to some emerging and governing principles of effective supply chain management, which can aid in the process of analyzing supply chain management. The process of benchmarking is an important first step. Although we provide a detailed description of how to conduct a benchmarking analysis in Chapter 11, "Benchmarking," for the purposes of this chapter, we will include a brief summary here. In short, the process of benchmarking involves five steps. These are as follows:

1. Deciding what to benchmark
2. Forming a team that is capable and responsible to carry out the process
3. Identifying benchmark partners
4. Acquiring and analyzing benchmarking information
5. Implementing newly acquired best practices

We will show an application of SCM analysis using benchmarking by applying it to ten essential rules of supply chain management. This example will show the process of SCM analysis in action relative to two different competitors in the consumer electronics market place. First, we'll illustrate the ten essential rules. Next, we'll apply the rules through benchmarking the different the management of the different competitors' supply chains

Rules and Tools[19]

Rule #1: Effective supply chain management requires utilizing supplier and customer relationships to take advantage of scale economies when facing tough competition.

Tool: Create collaborative relationships that can create switching costs. Use incentives and align interests, share information with suppliers and customers, clearly define roles and areas of accountability for all parties, and apportion costs, risks, and rewards accordingly.[20] Companies are inherently self-interest seeking and will maximize their own interests if not aligned with partners in the chain. When reconfiguring their supply chain, printer RR Donnelley asked suppliers for their input in how to improve efficiencies and products, all the while offering to share in savings that resulted from the suppliers' ideas, thus using incentives to align interests.[21]

Rule #2: The supply chain network should allow access to global markets.

Tool: Supply chain analysis should reveal if competitors are beating you on price or innovation due to sources of supply or labor overseas. Additionally, moving operations overseas can open the supply chain to emerging markets.

Rule #3: Successful supply chain management means meeting customer needs, wants, and expectations. Customers are increasingly savvy and demanding. They have come to expect quality and features at competitive prices. Customers expect products to be in stock when they want them and are put off by having to make multiple trips for one purchase.

Tool: Design the supply chain from the customer backward, rather than the other way around. Engage market research firms to identify customer needs if necessary. This approach is known as "customer-centricity" and takes a holistic approach to designing the organization to optimize the customers' experience.

Rule #4: Global capacity and rapid turnaround times mean companies must drive costs out of chains and arrange access to supplies.

Tool: Maintain a stock of small, non-perishable parts whose absence could cause delays. For example, Spanish clothing manufacturer Zara keeps a supply of buttons and small fixtures so that garments can be completed even if shipments get inexplicably delayed or held up.[22] Logistics systems should allow a company to rally in the event of unanticipated needs. Rather than invest in expensive systems, it is useful to partner with a third-party logistics supplier.

Rule #5: While other companies are merging for muscle and under-performing, focus on agility instead.

Tool: Collaborative relationships are essential to achieving agility. Supply and demand changes should be communicated to partners perpetually so they can react promptly. This can only happen, of course, where collaboration and information sharing between partners is present. Lee illustrates the importance of having a supply chain that is agile, adaptable, and aligned. The agile supply chain is adept at handling short-term supply/demand changes and responds to crises with minimal interruption. Design should only differentiate product at the latter stages of production—this is called "postponement" and promotes agility because the product is completed only when the firm has information about end-user preferences.

Rule #6: Adopt a position pivotal to chain success in order to have visibility and awareness of changing integrations among partners.

Tool: Take a pro-active role in chain development. Identify strong executive level leadership whose job this is, and make sure they have the resources they need. When Whirlpool's supply chain was in need of an overhaul, then COO Jeff Fettig gave two executives—relative newcomer, Reuben Slone, and 25-year veteran, Paul Dittman—seven months and hundreds of man-hours to fix their supply chain problems. The result was a supply chain investment costing more than any supply chain initiative in Whirlpool's history. The pay-off has been a drop of $100 million in working capital in just one year, a reduction in supply chain costs of $20 million, all the while realizing an order fill rate of 96% and product availability of over 95%.[23]

Rule #7: Technology creates challenges if adoption is piecemeal.

Tool: The company's mindset must support a Digital Business Transformation (DBT), where every facet of every operation is examined to determine if it supports brand or product success. In DBT, technology should support customer value-maximizing processes, information sharing in real time, and customer-centric operations.[24]

Rule #8: Successful chains get products to market quickly.

Tool: Support real-time information exchange. Use time and cycles as metrics to which incentives are linked.

Rule #9: Collaboration and integration blur organizational boundaries.

Tool: Use supply chain risk management best practices:[25]

1. Promote top-level awareness of exposure: an environment where information can be shared at all levels will ensure that executives know which suppliers are struggling and why, creating an awareness of potential commodity shortages and the ability to create a contingency plan.

2. All suppliers should be continuously monitored. Companies with too many suppliers to monitor should consider overhauling the supply chain and focusing on relationships that can be leveraged.

3. Supplier information collection should be future-oriented—monitoring financial well-being and current performance rather than past performance.

4. Create an empowered culture: Benefits can be realized when those who operate closest to the suppliers have the ability to assess and intervene in cases where they may not be able to meet deadlines.

Rule #10: Pressure from stakeholders can mean conflict and little tolerance for growing pains.

Tool: Wall Street measures market value, rather than absolute value. A "Triple-A supply chain," one that is agile, aligned, and adaptable, will ultimately be successful.

The following Case Study demonstrates how to use these rules and tools to analyze competitors supply chains, or alternately, examine your own. When the ten areas are highlighted as strengths or weaknesses, areas for improvement or potential competitive advantage are easy to visualize. It is important to note that no amount of technology or resources will make a difference to supply chain performance without good leadership, good people, and a supportive corporate culture to follow it through.

Analysis of supply chain management is another effective technique in the tool-belt of the business and competitive analyst. Employed effectively, it can enable the analyst to uncover otherwise hidden sources of competitive advantage. In a global marketplace that increasingly values the ability to get goods to customers as quickly, cheaply, and effectively as possible, the management of supply chains will remain an important competitive weapon that requires insightful analysis for decades to come.

Case Study: A Tale of Two Supply Chains: Best Buy vs. Sears/Kmart

The retail market has become very competitive. The market is crowded with stores of all formats, catering to every segment, from broad to niche, all clamoring to capture a loyal clientele. Unfortunately for them, in the eyes of many customers, there is little other than price to differentiate one retail outlet from the next. Many retailers are now realizing that a smart supply chain will leverage more in terms of profitability than increasing sales. Effective supply chain management presents opportunities to better serve customers, reduce markdowns, and respond to changing market conditions.

Based in Richfield, Minnesota, Best Buy is the largest consumer electronics retailer in North America. When the company realized in the mid 1990s that mass market retailers Wal-Mart and Target were eating away at its customer base, and approximately one-third of their customers were leaving their stores unsatisfied, they knew something had to change. In 2004, its new CEO Brad Anderson had authorized and supervised the introduction of a new competitive approach called Concept VII, which he viewed as a revolutionary change. Concept VII was based on a strategic model of customer centricity and was supported by three strategic pillars known as "efficient enterprise," "win the home with service," and "win entertainment." One result of Concept VII is a new supply chain management system that is taking three years to implement and that has been designed from the customer back.

Sears is a venerable, mass-market retailer with a 100+ year history in North America. It offers home appliances, tools, lawn and garden products, consumer (home) electronics, and automotive repair and maintenance products. Sears' SCM strategy has been quite different from the one newly employed by Best Buy. Sears merged with Kmart in March 2005, and the result, for the most part, has been confusing.

Sears did not have strong asset turnover or return on assets (ROA) performance before the merger,[26] and Kmart's frail inventory management and technology deficiencies helped put that discounter into bankruptcy in the first place. Since the merger, the retail behemoth has yet to determine how it will position itself in the marketplace or how to merge the 37 software applications operating in both companies. Currently, the company seems focused on sales strategies[27] productivity and capital expenditure reduction rather than optimizing its supply chain.[28]

The following analysis of the two companies highlights the differences in supply chain management. The 10 rules of supply chain management are applied to current practices, and strengths and weaknesses are highlighted.

Table 10.1
Analyzing the Management of Competitors' Supply Chains

A Comparison of Best Buy and Sears

Rule #	Rationale	Sears	BB
1	Best Buy has learned that being a good customer is the best partnership with its shipping company—incentives are aligned based on costs that are within the carriers' control, and efficiencies are rewarded. At peak times, carriers are overloaded and are in a position to decide what they will deliver and to whom. Collaboration ensures that Best Buy gets their merchandise. Sears/Kmart, on the other hand, has yet to develop a logistics strategy. Currently, the company has 10 information systems devoted to SCM, 9 to data warehousing, 9 to logistics management, and 8 to inventory management. It's unlikely that any of these systems are aligned to each other, much less any of their carriers.	No	Yes
2	Sears needs to work with overseas suppliers, from designing private label merchandise forward. Best Buy sources most products from Asia, which are brought into two West Cost hubs and sent into a streamlined network, but is otherwise not vertically integrated.	Not yet	Yes
3	Best Buy's Supply Chain has been designed around customer needs. When Best Buy discovered they couldn't be all things to all people, they decided to focus on eight core groups of customers, emphasizing one or two in a particular store depending on the demographics of each market. Non-sales activities have moved up the supply chain to allow salespeople more time with customers. This "customer-centric" approach sees the store from the customer's perspective and allows empowered employees access to data on product logistics. Both Sears and Kmart struggled with defining their target market before their 2004 merger, and that has not changed. The company has yet to strategically identify who shops in their stores and what they are buying, much less what their needs are.	No	Yes
4	Part of Best Buy's SCM plan includes greater delivery frequency of smaller shipments. Sears is still turning merchandise slower than competitors and has yet to figure out to improve this markedly.	No	Yes
5	Sears is merging for muscle. Best Buy's new system focuses on agility—they share collaborative technology with 17 suppliers to share information in real time, and new predictive modeling technology actually recalls solutions to past problems when presented with like problems and adapts.	No	Yes
6	Sears' size and vertical integration mean it is in a position to influence supply chain generation, but that hasn't happened yet. Best Buy takes the initiative to work constructively with its partners.	No	Yes
7	At one time, Best Buy used internal forecasts as well as forecasts from suppliers and third parties. They now only use one forecast, which is a consolidation of information from partners and internal data. Sears still has 37 software applications being used.	No	Yes

Table 10.1 *(continued)*
Analyzing the Management of Competitors' Supply Chains

A Comparison of Best Buy and Sears

Rule #	Rationale	Sears	BB
8	Best Buy shares real-time information with 17 partners and has redesigned its channel so more smaller deliveries go exactly where they are needed, and the deliveries are sales-floor ready, so they are available for almost immediate sale. Sears technologies are not integrated and thus do not support one another.	No	Yes
9	Best Buy does have the technology to get instant information about delays and incidents, and predictive modeling technology, and an empowered work-force, but there has been little mention of continuously monitoring suppliers for well-being. Many of these suppliers are in Asia and hence not visible. There is little public indication given anywhere that Sears is using supply chain risk management best practices.	No	Partly
10	Overall: Best Buy has instituted the new scheme at over one quarter of its stores in its Concept VII roll-out, and those stores are already performing well—gains have been twice that of traditional stores. Sears has a lot of work to do, including identifying customer needs and positioning the business before designing a new supply chain and integrating partners and technology.	No	Yes

FAROUT Summary

FAROUT SUMMARY

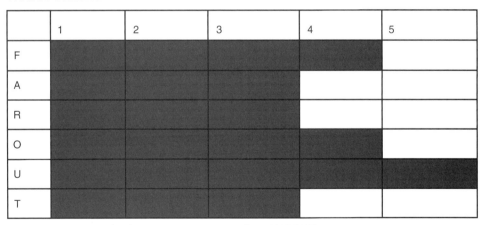

Figure 10.5   Supply chain management analysis FAROUT summary

Future-oriented—Medium to High. Supply chain management structure cannot be changed quickly; thus, movement in a certain direction will most likely remain stable.

Accurate—Medium. Competitors' supply chains may not be visible at all stages, leading to some speculation.

Resource efficiency—Medium. The technique is fairly simple to administer but requires substantial access to specialized supply chain knowledge and data to allow for comparisons.

Objectivity—Medium to High. Supply chain management analysis relies very little on subjective data.

Usefulness—High. Supply chain management is a big opportunity for many companies and will be a necessary skill for firms going forward.

Timeliness—Medium. With access to recent data, timeliness is increased.

Related Tools and Techniques

- Benchmarking
- Business process re-engineering
- Financial resources and statement analysis
- Key success factors
- Network analysis
- Value chain analysis

References

Ballou, R.H. (2004). *Business Logistics/ Supply Chain Management*, 5th edition. Upper Saddle River, NJ: Pearson Education, Inc., pp. 1–789.

Bowersox, D.J., and D.J. Closs (1996). *Logistical Management*. New York, NY: McGraw-Hill, pp. 1–725.

Bowersox, D.J., Closs, D.J., and R.W. Drayer (2005). "The digital transformation: Technology and beyond," *Supply Chain Management Review*, 9, pp. 22–29.

Brown, J.R., Dant, R.P., Ingene, C.A., and P.J. Kaufmann (2005). "Supply chain management and the evolution of the "Big Middle," *Journal of Retailing*, 81, pp. 97–105.

Cotrill, K. (2005). "Best Buy's customer facing supply chain," *Supply Chain Strategy*, 2, Dec–Jan.

Dewitt, W., Keebler, J.S., Min, S., Nix, N.W., Smith, C., and Z.G. Zacharia (2001). "Defining supply chain management," *Journal of Business Logistics*, 22, pp. 1–25.

Dignan, L. (2004). "Oh yeah, the computers," *Baseline*, 38, December, p. 24.

Fawcett, S.E., and G. Magnan (2005). "Beware the forces that affect your supply chain," *Supply Chain Strategy: A Newsletter from Harvard Business School Publishing and the MIT Center for Transportation and Logistics*. Harvard Business School.

Fiala, P. (2005). "Information sharing in supply chains," *Omega*, 33, pp. 419–423.

"Global supply chain management study" (2003). *Deloitte Touche Tohmatsu Global Homepage*. (Accessed January 23, 2006): http://www.deloitte.com/dtt/research/0,1015,sid%253D%2526cid%253D18503,00.html.

Huan, S.H., Sheoran, S.K., and G. Wang (2004). "A review and analysis of supply chain operations reference (SCOR) model," *Supply Chain Management*, 9, pp. 23–29.

Jorgensen, B. (2006). "How healthy is your supply chain?," *Electronic Business*, 32, pp. 16–18.

Kay, E. (2005). "Sears holding corp. faces massive supply chain," *Frontline Solutions*, 6, pp. 14–15.

"Lampert defends Sears" (2005). *Home Textiles Today*, 27, December 12, pp. 1–19, 2p.

Lee, H.L. (2004). "The triple-A supply chain," *Harvard Business Review*, 82, October, pp. 102–112.

Liker, J.K., and T.Y. Choy (2004). "Building deep supplier relationships," *Harvard Business Review*, 82(12), December, pp. 104–113.

Patterson, S. (2005). "Supply base optimization and integrated supply chain management," *Contract Management Magazine*, January, pp. 24–35.

"Putting an end to islands of manufacturers" (1998). *Modern Materials Handling: Special Report*, 53, pp. 40–41.

"SCOR version 7.0 overview" (2006). *Supply-Chain Council*, January 14: http://www.supply-chain.org/site/scor7booklet.jsp.

Slone, R.E. (2004). "Leading a supply chain turnaround," *Harvard Business Review*, 82, October, pp. 114–121.

Trunick, P.A. (2005). "Forecast 2006: In search of better practices," *Logistics Today*, 46, December, pp. 1–8.

Endnotes

[1] Fiala, 2005.

[2] Ballou, 2004.

[3] Mentzer, J.T., DeWitt, W., Keebler, J.S., Min, S., Nix, N.W., Smith, C., and Z.G. Zacharia (2001). "Defining Supply Chain Management," *Journal of Business Logistics*, Vol. 22, No. 2, pp. 1–25.

[4] Ballou, 2004.

[5] Ballou, 2004.

[6] Brown, Dant, Ingene, and Kaufmann, 2005.

[7] Modern Materials Handling, 1998.

[8] Lee, 2004; Liker and Choy, 2004.

[9] Bowersox, Closs, and Drayer, 2005.

[10] Patterson, 2005.

[11] Bowersox and Closs, 1996.

[12] Bowersox and Closs, 1996, p. 89.

[13] Fiala, 2005.

[14] Deloitte Global Supply Chain Management Study, 2003.

[15] Brown, Dant, Ingene, and Kaufmann, 2005.

[16] Lee, 2004, p. 9.

[17] Huan, Sheoran, and Wang, 2004.

[18] Ibid.

[19] All rules adapted from: Fawcett, S.E., and G. Magnan (2005). "Beware the Forces that Affect Your Supply Chain." *Supply Chain Strategy: A Newsletter from Harvard Business School Publishing and the MIT Center for Transportation and Logistics*. Harvard Business School.

[20] Lee, 2004.

[21] Lee, 2004.

[22] Lee, 2004.

[23] Slone, 2004.

[24] Lee, 2004.

[25] Jorgensen, 2006.

[26] Sears ROA was 8.4%, and asset turnover was 0.82 in 2002 (Brown, Dant, Ingene, and Kaufmann, 2005). By comparison, Best Buy had inventory turnover of 9.9 in 2002, rising to 10.1 in 2003.

[27] "Sears Inside" strategy moves Sears brands into Kmart stores; Sears Essentials concept gives Sears off-mall locale.

[28] Lee, 2004.

Benchmarking Analysis

Short Description

Benchmarking is a method by which an organization identifies and examines key facets of another entity and then implements the learning from the examination into its own operations. Almost anything can be benchmarked, such as a campaign, product, service, practice, process, or strategy, as long as it can be satisfactorily defined, measured, and compared to similar features in the comparison organization. Properly used, benchmarking can be a powerful learning tool and help the benchmarking organization to gain advantages over competitors, such as reducing costs, increasing productivity, and better aligning product/service features to customer needs.

Background

The first BCA application of benchmarking started in the mid-1950s through the practice of competitive financial ratio comparison. Comparative ratio analysis was often used as a component of industry analysis in order to determine the firm's relative financial performance as a gauge of the firm's competitive position. Comparing a financial ratio of the firm against that of its industry rivals, however, gives no indication regarding the underlying reasons for any performance divergence. As such, the value of comparative ratio analysis as a strategic tool proved to be limited.

Benchmarking was developed to fill this analytical vacuum offering a methodology to determine how and why some organizations achieve superior and sustained financial performance—the hallmark of competitive advantage. It provided the link between the result of competitive advantage (i.e., outstanding profits) and its root cause (i.e., excellent processes and practices).

One of the first firms to use benchmarking, or "industry tours" as the Japanese called them, was Toyota. This occurred when Toyota sent a number of their key people to the U.S.

to understand and monitor U.S. manufacturing processes after World War II. The Japanese executives took the ideas back to Japan and adapted and improved on them.

In the 1970s, Xerox realized that in order to stay competitive with rapidly strengthening foreign competition in copier markets, it needed to improve its manufacturing process. The improvements it achieved through the application of benchmarking led it to adopt the method as a corporate-wide practice.

Benchmarking involves examining firms with a world-class product/service, process, or strategy and incorporating the best ideas from them into your own business in order to gain a competitive advantage. Benchmarking is an ongoing process and should not be done as a one-off event to correct problems. Ideally, it should be employed as a proactive tool to stay one step ahead of the competition.

The original focus of benchmarking in the 1980s and early 1990s was more at the product level—comparisons of competitor's products within the same industry. It then evolved into benchmarking business processes, practices, policies, and corporate strategies in unrelated industries.

Benchmarking does not have to be done just on a competitor—it can also be done on another department or division within the same firm, or on the practices of a firm in a totally unrelated industry. For example, if a firm in the hotel industry has a billing procedure that is world-class, a construction firm might use it to improve their own billing procedure. Benchmarking generally involves the support of the entity that has the better process; this differs from competitor analysis, whereby the examining firm lacks the support of the entity.

As mentioned, an issue, practice, policy, product/service, process, or strategy can be benchmarked. Benchmarking products or services usually involves examining factors such as price, technical quality, ancillary product or service features, speed, reliability, and other performance characteristics through direct product or service comparison. Process benchmarking involves closely examining specific work processes, such as billing systems or production line processes. Benchmarking strategies involves examining the successful long-range planning and implementation techniques other firms use to be successful in the marketplace. Strategic benchmarking provides long-term benefits and may take time for results to show, whereas with the other two benchmarking categories, the results may show up immediately.

Strategic Rationale and Implications

Benchmarking gives the analyst many strategic benefits. The main advantage is that, properly employed, it can help a firm gain an advantage over its competition. It also allows for realistic targets and goals to be defined for an organization; for the validation of the strengths and weaknesses of a firm through hard numbers; and finally, the deciphering of future trends in the industry.

Benchmarking can provide an efficient and effective means for a firm to take the best ideas from other firms, integrate them into their own, and take actions that may provide it with a strong advantage over their competitors. For example, if two firms are competing fiercely with each other and one of them decides to benchmark an exceptional customer service model, it could win the battle for market share and leave its competitor scrambling to recover.

Realistic targets and goals can be set by an organization through the use of benchmarking because another firm has already demonstrated that it is able to achieve a performance level that is desired by the benchmarking organization, thereby giving it something tangible to work toward. Benchmarking efforts should focus on those projects that relate directly to the firm's overall strategy and provide the greatest room for improvement. For example, Federal Express ships packages across the world everyday. One of its main strategies is to ensure each customer receives their package on time and in good condition. Therefore, Federal Express spends most of their benchmarking efforts on ensuring that its customer service processes are the best.[1]

Another reason to use benchmarking is that it helps to validate an organization's strengths and weaknesses through the identification and uncovering of empirical data in the form of hard numbers. Usually analysts have a good idea of their firm's strengths and weaknesses; however, having hard numbers to back this up rather than just opinions increases confidence in the process. It shows how strong a strength or weakness is over competitors in a particular area, as the benchmarking data shows the actual degree to which the firm is performing against a standard.

Benchmarking can also assist the analyst to determine the future trends in the industry, which potentially can play a significant role in management's strategy. Management is constantly scanning the environment for trends five to 10 years in the future, and benchmarking gives managers another means for doing this. For example, when computers were becoming common in the workplace, an analyst who was benchmarking a firm with excellent response rates through direct mailing might have realized that one-to-one database marketing was going to be the trend and build this into her strategy. This shows how benchmarking can allow a firm to be proactive rather than reactive to trends.

Taxonomy of Benchmarking

There are four different types of benchmarking, each with different applications but with significant crossover potential around the same purpose:

- **Internal benchmarking**—Involves the measurement and comparison of best practices within the firm. For example, one division or strategic business unit may share information on best practices with another division in the same company. This is often the type of benchmarking that firms start with for several reasons. First, it is relatively easy, as the necessary data is in-house and cooperation is easier to attain than in external benchmarking. Second, it can serve as a pilot study for future external benchmarking projects providing a low-risk learning environment and securing motivational early successes or "quick hits." Third, internal benchmarking is an excellent way to gain a solid understanding of the firm's own value chain providing the necessary base from which to compare against best practices of other organizations. Fourth, it also provides information with which to strengthen the reciprocal relationship with future benchmarking partners discussed next. Despite these benefits, it is important for the firm to move out of internal benchmarking fairly quickly, as it can rapidly degenerate into a close cousin of the traditional insularity it was designed to ameliorate.

■ **Competitive/external benchmarking**—Refers to the benchmarking of competing firms in the same strategic group or in the same industry. In contrast to internal benchmarking, this type is the most difficult to perform because competitors are often understandably loath to share competitively sensitive information with direct competitors. Additionally, certain forms of external benchmarking by direct market competitors may be considered by regulators as tantamount to collusion. Despite these obstacles, competitive benchmarking is extremely valuable because it provides information on similar processes that the firm is directly competing on. There are two ways to effectively supplement any competitive benchmarking data that is secured. The first is to supplement any "hard" competitive data with "softer" qualitative data gleaned from customers and suppliers of the benchmarked competitor. The second method is to use anonymous benchmarking studies conducted by industry associations or consultants, as they often provide much valuable information on best practices while protecting against competitive and legal sensitivities.

■ **Other industry benchmarking**—Includes benchmarking organizations not in direct competition with the benchmarking firm. This type of benchmarking involves evaluating best practices of non-rival firms, evaluating best practices of potential rivals using similar processes in an unrelated industry, or evaluating best practices of potential rivals using different processes in an unrelated industry. The primary advantage of this method is that non-competing firms are much more willing to share information offering much greater potential for an extensive benchmarking analysis. Of course, this benefit is countered by the possibility that the processes of non-rival firms may not be applicable to the benchmarking firm.

■ **Global best practice benchmarking**—Concerns benchmarking against recognized world leaders in the relevant parameter regardless of the industry in which they are operating. For example, a restaurant chain seeking to increase customer satisfaction and dinner hour throughput may wish to benchmark the Disney Corporation, the recognized world leader in queue management. This type of benchmarking often yields the most significant performance gains because it truly benchmarks against the "best" rather than settling for "good" as in the previous methods. Additionally, global best practice benchmarking offers the highest chance of radical innovation as opposed to incremental improvement often associated with other types of benchmarking. Global best practice benchmarking is difficult because it forces management to adopt lateral thinking outside of industry best practices. However, this forced "out of the box" thinking alerts management to previously existing blindspots and discovers transferable innovation in the process.

Deciding on which type of benchmarking to use is often tempered by reality. Smaller firms may not be able to access global best practice firms to benchmark against or may not be able to afford the protracted time requirements and cost. Nonetheless, benchmarking against "good practice" or against firms that are relatively better at the chosen parameter process will still yield improvement opportunities.

Another useful approach to deciding which type of benchmarking approach to use is to keep in mind the strategic purpose of the benchmarking effort. This prevents the analysis from becoming clouded with tactical details. Figure 11.1 offers a useful conceptual framework that divides the purpose of benchmarking into three distinct but interrelated categories.

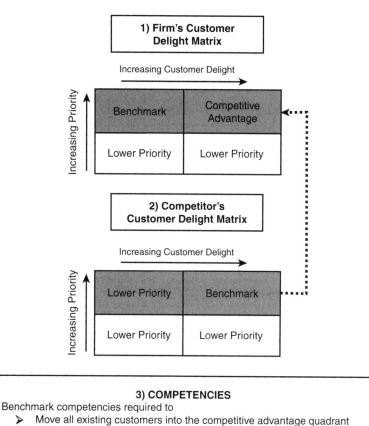

Figure 11.1   The three strategic purposes of benchmarking

First, customers are surveyed regarding which processes are important to their perception of value and which processes the firm is currently doing well. The firm's existing customers that are not being delighted around important processes represent significant benchmarking opportunities to improve internal performance (i.e., the "benchmark" quadrant in the Firm's Customer Delight Matrix). The strategic goal here is to move existing customers into the high priority/high delight quadrant.

Next, competitors are evaluated against the same criteria. Here, the ultimate goal to benchmark is to surpass competitors' process driven competitive advantage (hence, the location of the "benchmark" quadrant in the Competitor's Customer Delight Matrix).

The ultimate strategic goal of benchmarking here is to eventually offer a higher degree of customer delight around high priority processes in order to steal customers away from competitors. Of course, only profitable customers as dictated by the firm's customer segmentation should be targeted with these benchmarking initiatives.

Many of the internationally recognized quality awards offer guidelines as to which core competencies can be effectively benchmarked. Within each category are many detailed supporting processes that have not been included in the exhibit. Not all of these competencies will need to be benchmarked. Only those that will directly impact customer retention within the firm and customer migration from competitors will need to be benchmarked.

Framing the benchmarking process in such a strategic framework will help decide which of the four benchmarking types will yield results with the tightest application to the firm's strategy. It will also help the firm decide which parameter(s) to benchmark around.

Benchmarking can be conducted at three different levels in the firm's organizational hierarchy:

- **Strategic**—Benchmarks around the critical success factors that the firm must perform well in order to sustain its competitive position within its industry. Some examples include customer value monitors, hurdle rates of return, operational efficiency, market share, etc.

- **Functional**—Benchmarks around the processes specific to the various functional areas of the firm such as marketing, operations, finance, etc.

- **Operational**—Specific, tightly defined operational benchmarks that guide staff on the "shop floor" and the "front lines" to excellent operational performance. For example, defects per hour on an assembly machine or complaints per day in a service context may be chosen as operational benchmarks.

The three different purposes of benchmarking reflect the hierarchy that lies at the root of this management tool. At the top of the hierarchy are strategic benchmarks that culminate in firm-wide performance. The next lower benchmark level, functional benchmarks, support strategic benchmarks and are the culmination of the lowest level, the operational benchmarks. In this light, benchmarking can be seen as one way to operationalize organizational change within a learning context. Often, top management is directly concerned with strategic benchmarks, middle management with functional benchmarks, and staff with operational benchmarks. Not only does this properly engage everyone in the benchmarking process, it also ensures that all of the context levers are being pulled in the same direction.

Benchmarking is also often used as a vehicle for organizational change in concert with several other methods of organizational change; namely balanced scorecard, business process reengineering, and organizational learning. An extremely important aspect of the benchmarking philosophy is trust and open communication. As such, the integrity and ultimate success of benchmarking depends on adherence to the well-accepted bilateral codes of conduct. One of the best ethical codes has been developed by the American Quality and Productivity Center and can be found at http://www.apqc.org/free/conduct.htm.

Strengths and Advantages

Powerful Competitive Analysis Tool

Benchmarking offers an excellent tool for finding opportunities to maintain the relative competitiveness of the firm. It provides the analyst a methodology that, at a minimum, will offer a path to achieve competitive parity with rivals. Benchmarking results in increased self-knowledge of both the analyst's internal organizational strengths and weaknesses, as well as those of competitors. In today's turbulent competitive environment, benchmarking offers an effective coping mechanism for the firm to adapt to change by leveraging the knowledge of others.

Objective Stretch Goal Setting and Performance Measurement

Benchmarking heightens the firm's sensitivity to the fact that absolute improvements from internal historical performance may not be sufficient for competitive success. Rather, the explicit outward-looking orientation of benchmarking is an excellent prescription to correct strategic myopia. Often, benchmarking provides the motivation necessary to achieve stretch goals.

Flexibility

Benchmarking is an extremely flexible management tool in that it supports other equally important strategic change initiatives within the firm such as organizational learning and business process reengineering. It can be used to improve operations management, relative cost performance, and secure temporary competitive advantage.

Removal of Blindspots

Competitive benchmarking will alert the firm to at least two important elements that are commonly the source of blindspots. One, knowledge of rivals' process excellence and capabilities will help to prevent the firm from underestimating the potential competitive response to its own strategic initiatives. Two, knowledge of potential rivals' process excellence and capability will give the firm knowledge of the potential for industry migration. This type of knowledge is becoming especially important as many value chains are being reconfigured as a result of the liberating economics of information.

Improves Cost Efficiencies and Quality

By examining other firm's higher-performing processes, a firm will find better ways of performing their own processes. It could mean that it will find a better method of production that increases the number of items produced in a given day, an enhanced way to make a product last longer, or a better method of providing services to customers. The end result, however, will be a demonstrable improvement that can affect the firm's profitability.

Not Reinventing the Wheel but Redesigning It

The cost for any firm to develop a new product can be enormous, not to mention the level of risk associated with a particularly daring new product. Much research goes into developing original products and processes. Benchmarking has the advantage of examining what someone else has already done and fine tuning it to fit the needs of the firm. This provides an opportunity to come through with an incremental gain rather than a significant, green-field product innovation just to remain competitive.

Media Recognition

The media recognizes firms that excel at specific practices. Firms known to have "best practices" or outstanding practices often get these reported in industry publications, local media, or even in research papers, business cases, professional meetings, or through business school instructional channels. The media recognition that comes from benchmarking successes can help support improvement of the benchmarking firm's financial performance including share performance.

Requirement for Other Certifications

Firms are often required to employ benchmarking in order to achieve various forms of public certification, including many of the ISO series standards. For example, the Malcolm Baldridge National Quality Award in the U.S. is awarded to firms that have a strong benchmarking program in place, and it is the highest honor offered in the U.S. for quality and performance excellence. Other countries' national awards also require organizations to perform benchmarking in order to be eligible to receive their awards.

Creates an Innovative Culture Open to New Ideas

Benchmarking has the tendency to create a workplace that is always open to new ideas. It requires analysts and managers to think about how something may be done better elsewhere, thereby driving out the "NIH" (not invented here) syndrome from a firm's practices. If management is always emphasizing the importance of being the best, it requires frequent change to occur and results in employees devoted to always improving the firm.

Weaknesses and Limitations

Copycat Syndrome

One of the strongest critics of the benchmarking approach has been Porter. His main opposition revolves around the fact that operational effectiveness is not strategy. As such, he asserts that benchmarking should not be elevated to the status of strategic management. It should only be considered as a tactical management tool that is a necessary but insufficient condition for strategic success. The underlying rationale of benchmarking refutes one of the main tenets of sustainable competitive advantage—inimitability. Simply put, best practices are easily copied, granting all rivals absolute gains along the productivity frontier at the expense of relative gains in strategic positioning. The core argument of Porter is that benchmarking only allows a firm to mimic the processes of rivals. Legitimate strategy, on the other hand, rests on the ability to do the same processes differently or to pursue entirely different processes and practices. In industries where benchmarking is prevalent, strategy suffers two blows.

First, to the effect that benchmarking often becomes an industry-wide obsession, the attractiveness of the industry structure declines as gains from productivity translate into consumer and supplier benefits rather than producer benefits. Second, the strategic vision of participating firms becomes increasingly blurred as they focus on operational effectiveness to the exclusion of strategic positioning. As a result, the industry structure erodes even more, causing yet another "race to the bottom" as firms once again push out the productivity frontier with no accruing individual benefit. This reinforcing cycle represents a decidedly contrarian viewpoint to the acclaim that has embraced benchmarking from other corners. This is not to discredit benchmarking, but rather, to cast a reality check on its strategic function. Benchmarking only represents table stakes. Walking away with the kitty remains wholly contingent upon creative strategic thinking, not imitation.

High Rate of Failure

Formal benchmarking projects often fail because the proper amount of planning with regards to organizational readiness has not been done. Careful attention must be paid to such elements as forming a complementary mix of personnel composing the various benchmarking teams, psychological purchase, and demonstrable commitment of top management, reducing lead time before tangible results become visible, etc. Despite the fact that planning is the most critical success factor, it is often given short shrift as firms plunge headlong into the sexier aspects of the actual benchmarking process.

What Works Well in One Organization Might Not Work in Another

One of the weaknesses of benchmarking is that a firm may have a proven practice that works well for it, but its application may not produce similar results in another organization. Although a firm may be benchmarking a firm that is receiving extraordinary results through its best practice, the benchmarker may not be able to significantly improve its own process, if at all, due to a variety of factors. The firm's culture, history, markets, structure, leadership, or business model, among other things, may prevent the benchmarker from achieving desirable results. With benchmarking, it is particularly important not to merely copy the best practices of the benchmarked firm but, rather, to adapt them to uniquely fit into the benchmarker's firm.

Benchmarking Is Resource Intensive

There are many costs involved in benchmarking. These can include the direct costs of sending people out to observe other organization's processes, training staff to conduct the benchmarking process, as well as the costs needed to implement the identified changes throughout the firm. A multi-firm, cross-industry benchmarking consortium can require significant amounts of an analyst's or executive's time. It is therefore important to ensure that the organization has made the appropriate resource investments in order to properly perform the benchmarking process. There must be support from top management as well as the widely held belief of needing change in the organization. Benchmarking always works best when it is done over time and seldom delivers success when it is done as a one-off exercise or project.

No Firm Does Everything the Best

A firm may have a world-class process; however, that does not mean that all of its other processes are world class. Often, a benchmarking organization is tempted, usually due to resource constraints, to benchmark multiple processes of a single partner even though some of the target's processes may not have been demonstrated as outstanding. Therefore, it is recommended to find the best benchmarking partner for each practice needing significant improvement.

Low-Performing Firms Have a Disadvantage

Low-performing firms have been shown in some studies to be negatively impacted from benchmarking.[2] The reasons for this could be that low-performing firms may not feel comfortable approaching higher-performing firms and therefore settle on a mediocre firm to benchmark. In these cases, the resources needed to implement the change and perform the benchmarking end up being very costly for something that doesn't greatly improve performance.

Some High-Performing Companies May Not Be Willing to Share Information

Benchmarking involves receiving a lot of information from the benchmarking partner and, therefore, some firms may be unwilling to open their processes to scrutiny and share their sensitive information for fear it will be leaked to competitors. Also it may be hard to benchmark a competitor for obvious reasons, but if the competitor wants something in return from the benchmarker, then it may be possible to proceed.

Process for Applying the Technique

The process for applying benchmarking is fairly generic. Although some firms employ a four-step model, others may use 10 to 12 steps or more; however, there is a fair degree of commonality of the activities that need to be undertaken to conduct a successful benchmarking process. In this chapter's discussion, the benchmarking process we describe consists of six steps, as follows:

1. Identify the processes that need to be benchmarked.
2. Identify performance measures.
3. Evaluate your own firm's capabilities.
4. Identify firms to be benchmarked.
5. Conduct research from selected firms.
6. Analyze the collected data and develop an action plan.

Step 1: Identify the Processes That Need to Be Benchmarked

Benchmarking is a process that requires continuous monitoring of the environment for new and better practices, products, or services. Anything that can be observed or measured can be benchmarked. Areas of benchmarking include products or services, work processes, support functions, organizational performance, and strategies. Table 11.1 shows some key areas that can be benchmarked.

Table 11.1
Common Areas for an Analyst to Benchmark

1.	Customer service performance
2.	Product/service performance
3.	Core business process performance
4.	Support processes and services performance
5.	Employee performance
6.	Supplier performance
7.	Technology performance
8.	New product/service development and innovation performance
9.	Cost performance
10.	Financial performance

Some questions that managers should ask themselves are the following:

- Is the topic important to customers?
- Is the topic consistent with the mission?
- Is the topic significant in terms of costs or key non-financial information?
- What processes are critical to our success?
- What problems do we need to overcome?
- Is the process resource intensive?
- What factors are causing the most problems?
- Does the project have a high potential for improvement?
- What functions have the greatest effect or potential for differentiating the organization from its competitors?

Benchmarking tasks should be prioritized for their importance to the overall mission of the firm, department, or unit seeking performance improvement.

Step 2: Identify Performance Measures

Once the topic to be benchmarked has been identified, measures of how well the current process, service/product, or strategy are performing need to be defined. This allows for the establishment of indicators of how well a function is performing and for comparisons between it and the world-class function.

In order to identify these measures, develop a detailed list of factors, then cut down the list to key steps for those that will have the greatest impact. It is important to identify key measurements and not to make the list too long, as it is very costly if there are too many factors. Furthermore, the benchmarking partner does not have a lot of time to provide large amounts of data.

It is important to understand the critical success factors in the process that will help to identify key drivers and measures of performance. It is also important when defining key performance measures that the data can be obtained from the benchmark partner. Ensure that the data retrieved from competitors is in the same format so that apples can be compared to apples. Figure 11.2 outlines some measures that might be considered for the benchmarking topics outlined in Step 1.

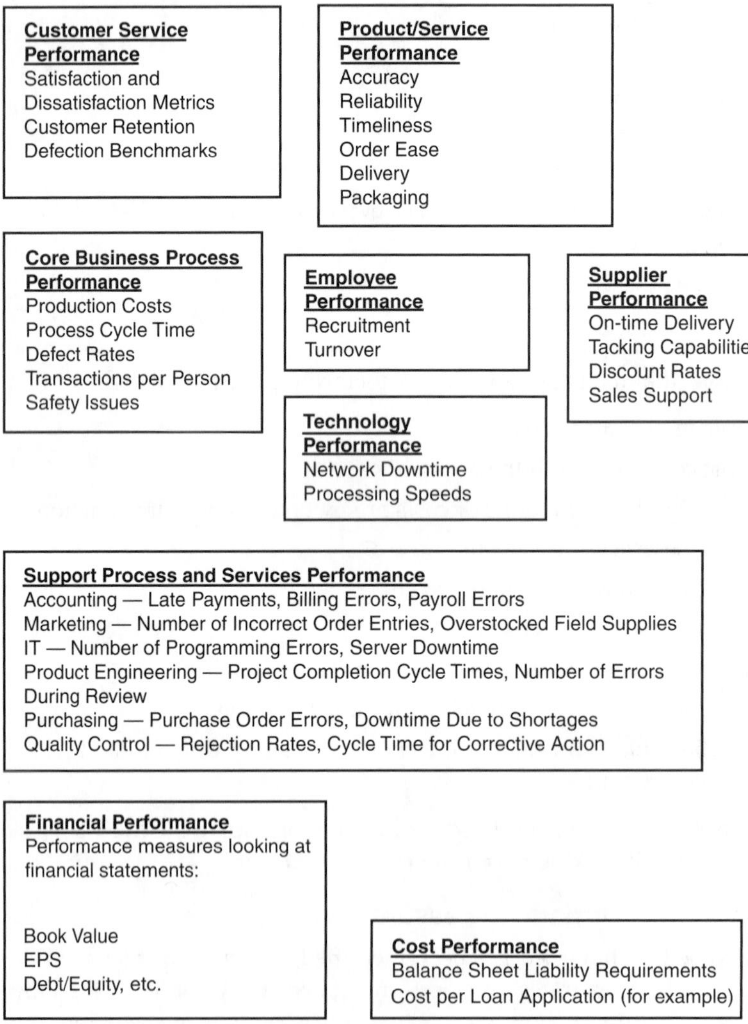

Customer Service Performance
Satisfaction and Dissatisfaction Metrics
Customer Retention
Defection Benchmarks

Product/Service Performance
Accuracy
Reliability
Timeliness
Order Ease
Delivery
Packaging

Core Business Process Performance
Production Costs
Process Cycle Time
Defect Rates
Transactions per Person
Safety Issues

Employee Performance
Recruitment
Turnover

Supplier Performance
On-time Delivery
Tacking Capabilities
Discount Rates
Sales Support

Technology Performance
Network Downtime
Processing Speeds

Support Process and Services Performance
Accounting — Late Payments, Billing Errors, Payroll Errors
Marketing — Number of Incorrect Order Entries, Overstocked Field Supplies
IT — Number of Programming Errors, Server Downtime
Product Engineering — Project Completion Cycle Times, Number of Errors During Review
Purchasing — Purchase Order Errors, Downtime Due to Shortages
Quality Control — Rejection Rates, Cycle Time for Corrective Action

Financial Performance
Performance measures looking at financial statements:

Book Value
EPS
Debt/Equity, etc.

Cost Performance
Balance Sheet Liability Requirements
Cost per Loan Application (for example)

Figure 11.2   Key performance measures

Step 3: Evaluate Your Own Firm's Capabilities

In order to be able to evaluate a benchmarking partner's capabilities, it is important that the benchmarker know its own processes first. There are three important reasons for this:

- The extent for improvement opportunities may not be fully realized.
- Your own capabilities may be overestimated or underestimated.
- It allows for greater productivity when conducting the collection of data from the benchmarking partner.

Opportunities may be missed if you do not know your own process, as you might not consider a factor when doing the benchmarking process that might have been evident if you had first evaluated your own process. Also if you do not look at your own operations, you may not know how you compare on factors to the partner—you may feel you are strong in that certain function, when really, you are very weak. Finally, knowing your own operations allows you to easily identify performance gaps and therefore spend time on those areas that need to be corrected, rather than on those that are already strong.

Step 4: Identify Firms to Be Benchmarked

As it can be costly to perform the benchmarking process, it is important to select firms that are world-class leaders in a certain area. The benchmarking partners could be in the same industry or in a different industry. In order to select firms to benchmark, create a list of potential partners by looking at media releases, literature from professional associations, talking to consultants or experts in the field, reading through company literature, or looking for special award winners such as the Malcolm Baldrige National Quality Award.

When you have a long list of firms, you need to narrow it down to those with whom you would like to benchmark. Table 11.2 provides a list of some criteria that a firm may consider when searching for benchmarking partners.

In order to select a firm, the analyst may use a pass/fail elimination system, whereby if the firm does not meet a certain criteria, then they are automatically eliminated; or by a weighting system, whereby each criterion is assigned a weighting and the firms with the most favorable ratings are selected. If the weighted rating system is used, the analyst must be aware of the halo effect, whereby if the firm rates favorably on one criterion, although it may not be the best in another, it is still given a high mark because it excels in one of the criteria. The weight that each firm is given for each criterion differs based on the goal of the benchmarking process and the type of benchmarking being done. For example, a firm with a similar product may be given a low-importance weight for its product if the item being benchmarked is the billing process.

One of the most important criteria in selecting a firm is that it is willing to provide you with the required information.

Table 11.2
Criteria to Select Benchmarking Partners

1.	Is the firm willing to provide information to us, and, if so, will there be enough data to draw conclusions?
2.	Is the firm culture similar, or will the benchmarking topic work in our organizational culture?
3.	How similar is the firm's product or process to ours?
4.	Is their organizational structure similar to ours, or will the benchmarked process be able to work with our organizational structure?
5.	Are the demographics of the firm similar in terms of revenue, employee size, and market capitalization? Will we have the resources to implement their best practice?
6.	Does the geographic location of the firm have any effect on their best practice? Do we have the same geographic advantages that they do?
7.	Will we be able to replicate the technology used by these firms?

Other factors that may help determine which firms to benchmark include the following:

- Process technology
- Financial performance indicators
- Distribution channels
- Manufacturing approach and volume
- Decision-making style of management
- Travel costs involved
- Type of business

Step 5: Conduct Research of Selected Firms

Once you have determined the performance measures that will be researched from Step 2, the actual collection of data can begin. It is important to plan ahead for this stage in order to ensure that the collection of data flows smoothly. The major concern is for the data to be reliable, accurate, timely, cost efficient, useful, and usable.

Data can be found from many sources and can be primary or secondary in nature. The collection of secondary data is the first source that should be used, as it is much cheaper than collecting primary data. Secondary data may include, but is not limited to, newspaper or magazine publications, archival research, annual reports, industry journals, professional association reports, conference minutes, 10-K filings, experts, and universities. If the information that the firm is looking for is not found in this first step, then primary research can be done. In order to conduct primary research, the following resources are valuable: personal or onsite visits, telephone interviews, surveys, and focus groups.

Step 6: Analyze the Collected Data and Develop an Action Plan

This is the stage where a firm is able to identify the gaps between their performance and their benchmark partners. It also helps identify where a firm's strengths lie. Although the main goal is to identify the strengths and weaknesses of the process, it is also important to project what the world-class standard will be in the next five to 10 years in this stage as well.

The data analysis method should already be decided on before it is collected, leaving this stage to the actual analysis of the data. Having the analysis methods in place will make the analysis go much smoother. One way to do this is to create a data matrix, as seen in Table 11.3.

Table 11.3
Benchmarking Data Organization Matrix
Example: Factors Impacting Insurance Agent Productivity

	Benchmarking Company	Company 1	Company 2	Company 3	Company 4	Comments
Average Number of Customers/ Agent	50	60	75	70	65	
Number of Agents/ Manager	4	8	6	7	9	
Average Years of Agent Experience	7	9.5	10	4.5	3.5	
% Commission	10%	5%	0%	10%	20%	
Number of Support Staff/ Agent	1.2	0.8	1.5	1.0	1.8	

This matrix should help the analyst to identify patterns in the data for both similarities and differences.

Once the gaps between the benchmarking processes have been identified, their causes need to be understood so that the analyst can find out what the two firms do that is similar and different.

It is important that the analyst ensures that the data is accurate. There could be many errors in the data collection process that could dramatically affect results, such as differences in the makeup of a certain set of data or inaccuracies caused by different sources collecting the data.

One of the most important components of this stage is to set a well-defined process to implement the improvement initiatives and to monitor projected vs. actual progress on gap closure over time. Often, the source of improvement comes from adapting the best practices of the benchmarked firm to the unique circumstances of the benchmarking firm.

Despite the length of time and effort required of benchmarking, it is critically important to realize that benchmarking is a snapshot in time. Dynamic competition necessitates constant monitoring of any changes in the competitive environment to determine any impact on the benchmarked parameters. In keeping with the continuous improvement ethos, future performance needs to be projected and existing benchmarks will have to be periodically adjusted and re-benchmarked in line with evolutionary change or performance slippage. Perhaps more importantly, innovative revolution will necessitate new benchmarking around entirely new competitive processes.

Case Study: Delivery of Packages by Federal Express

Step 1: Identify the Process That Needs to Be Benchmarked

The question that must be answered in one area of FedEx's operations is, "How can we improve our customer service between Toronto and Ottawa?"

Step 2: Identify Performance Measures

- How many packages arrived at the wrong destination last year?
- How many packages arrived late last year?
- How many deliveries do we make each day from Toronto to Ottawa?
- How long on average does it take to request a delivery through a customer service agent?
- How many customers complained about the delivery of their package last year?
- How many packages were damaged last year?
- How much revenue was generated from packages shipped between the two cities?
- What costs did we entail in shipping these packages?

Step 3: Evaluate Own Firm's Capabilities

See the matrix developed in Step 5. This matrix incorporates the firm's capabilities as part of the whole process of identifying the performance measures and benchmarks.

Step 4: Identify Firms to Be Benchmarked

- United Parcel Service
- DHL
- Canada Post
- United States Postal Service
- Purolator

Step 5: Conduct Research from Selected Firms

The following is a sample table demonstrating hypothetical performance data collected for the period from November 1–30, of the prior year.

	Federal Express	UPS	Purolator
Avg. # of daily packages delivered to correct destination	300	200	100
# of packages arriving late (total)	50	20	10
Avg. # of mass deliveries each day from Toronto to Ottawa	2	3	7
Avg. speed of placing an order (in minutes)	2	1	5
# of customer complaints recorded	7	4	1
# of damaged packages last year	20	30	50

Step 6: Analyze the Collected Data and Develop an Action Plan

The analyst would look at the matrix identified in Step 5 and ask a number of questions, the answers to which can help focus his attention on the key facets of what differentiates the highest performers from the lesser performers:

- What system does Purolator have in place that allows it to achieve higher accuracy in delivery of their products to the correct destinations?

- Why do more FedEx packages arrive later compared to the others? How does the presence of the other performance data help us to explain this?

- Purolator takes longer to take a customer order, while UPS can do it quickly. Why is this? Could this be a reason for the level of customer complaints experienced? Maybe our competitor's order-taking processes contains more or less information that impacts delivery accuracy levels.

The number of damaged packages for FedEx is lower. This may support an internally held view that FedEx are the best among its direct competitors in this area. This information could be used for customer communication and marketing purposes.

There are many other questions and issues that the analyst could address. This may lead to the gathering of additional data or to the "testing" of different propositions. No matter what the outcome of this particular exercise, the analyst must consider how to gain synergies from this benchmarking exercise and how it can create value for the organization both in the short and long term.

FAROUT Summary

FAROUT SUMMARY

	1	2	3	4	5
F	██	██	██		
A	██	██	██		
R	██	██			
O	██	██	██		
U	██	██	██	██	██
T	██	██			

Figure 11.3   Benchmarking analysis FAROUT summary

Future orientation—Medium. Benchmarking is forward looking in that it is oriented toward the future implementation of a proposed best practice or the correction of existing processes in order to gain a competitive advantage. However, benchmarks remain valid only for the duration of the productivity frontier function upon which it was based.

Accuracy—Medium. Accuracy depends on the ability of the analyst to (a) correctly diagnose the processes to be benchmarked, (b) correctly diagnose the key performance measures, and (c) implement the required changes to close the distance between (a) and (b).

Resource efficiency—Low to medium. Depends on the number of processes identified, the depth of analysis and the number of personnel engaged in the benchmarking process. Resource efficiency depends in large part on the extent of data collection and analysis.

Objectivity—Medium. The analysis and establishment of performance measures is subject to perception bias, particularly in defining the process to be measured and the evaluation criteria.

Usefulness—High. Benchmarking provides not only improved costs efficiencies and quality for products and services, but also enhances the outward focus and innovation practices within organizational cultures.

Timeliness—Low to medium. Benchmarking can be extremely comprehensive and covers all facets of the firm. Identifying the key processes that would benefit from benchmarking may take some time for a consensus to be established. Additionally, correctly examining the intricate inter-relationships between different processes in an organization can take some time.

Related Tools and Techniques

- Blindspot analysis
- Competitor analysis
- Customer segmentation and needs analysis
- Customer value analysis
- Comparative cost analysis
- Functional capability and resource analysis
- Industry structure analysis
- Strategic groups analysis
- SWOT analysis
- Value chain analysis

References

Aaker, D.A. (1998). *Strategic Market Management, 5th Edition.* New York, NY: John Wiley and Sons.

American Productivity and Quality Center (1994). *The Best of Benchmarking: A Best Practices Guide.* Houston, TX: American Productivity and Quality Center.

Bhote, K.R. (1989). "Motorola's long march to the Malcolm Baldridge National Quality Award," *National Productivity Review,* Autumn.

Bogan, C.E., and English, M.J. (1994). *Benchmarking for Best Practices: Winning Through Innovative Adaptation.* New York, NY: McGraw-Hill, Inc.

Boxwell, R.J. (1995). *Benchmarking for Competitive Advantage.* New York, NY: McGraw-Hill.

Camp, R. (1994). *Business Process Benchmarking: Finding and Implementing Best Practices.* Milwaukee, WI: ASQC Quality Press.

Cook, S. (1995). *Practical Benchmarking: A Manager's Guide to Creating a Competitive Advantage.* London, UK: Kogan Page.

Deming, E.W. (1982). *Quality, Productivity and Competitive Position.* Center for Advanced Engineering Study, Cambridge, MA: Massachusetts Institute of Technology.

The Economist Intelligence Unit (1993). *Global Benchmarking for Competitive Edge.* London, UK: The Economist Intelligence Unit.

Fuld, L.M. (1989). *Monitoring the Competition: Find Out What Is Really Going on Out There.* New York, NY: John Wiley and Sons.

Garvin, D. (1991). "How the Baldridge Award really works," *Harvard Business Review,* November/December, pp. 80–93.

Hammer, M. (1990). *Reengineering Work: Don't Automate, Obliterate,* July/August, 68(4), pp. 104–112.

Harrington, H.J., and J.S. Harrington (1996). *High Performance Benchmarking: 20 Steps to Success.* New York, NY: McGraw-Hill.

Jennings, K., and F. Westfall (1992). "Benchmarking for strategic action," *Journal of Business Strategy,* Fall, 13(3), pp. 22–25.

Keehley, P., and S. Medlin, et al (1995). *Benchmarking for Best Practices in the Public Sector.* San Francisco, CA: Jossey-Bass, Inc.

Main, J. (1992). "How to steal the best ideas around," *Fortune,* October, 126(8), pp. 102–106.

National Institute of Standards and Technology (2004). "President and Commerce Secretary announce recipients of nation's highest honour in quality and performance excellence," in the Award Recipients section at Baldridge National Quality Program Web site.

Porter, M. (1996). "What is strategy?," *Harvard Business Review,* 74(6), pp. 61–78.

Spendolini, M.J. (1992). *The Benchmarking Book.* New York, NY: AMACOM.

Society of Management Accountants of Canada (1993). *Implementing Benchmarking.* Hamilton: Canada.

Society of Management Accountants of Canada (1995). *Tools and Techniques for Effective Benchmarking Studies.* Hamilton: Canada.

Thor, C.G. (1995). *Practical Benchmarking for Mutual Improvement.* Portland, OR: Productivity Press, Inc.

Tucker, G.F., Zivian, S.M., and R.C. Camp (1987). "How to measure yourself against the best," *Harvard Business Review,* January/February, 65(1).

Watson, G.H. (1993). *Strategic Benchmarking.* New York, NY: John Wiley & Sons, Inc.

Xerox Corporation (1988). *Competitive Benchmarking: The Path to a Leadership Position.* Stamford, Connecticut.

Endnotes

[1] Bogan and English, 1994, p. 46.

[2] Harrington and Harrington, 1996, p. 134.

12

McKinsey 7S Analysis

Short Description

The McKinsey 7S framework model is a diagnostic management tool used to test the strength of the strategic degree of fit between a firm's current and proposed strategies. It is a management tool designed to facilitate the process of strategy implementation within the context of organizational change.

Background

Implementation has always been the difficult aspect of strategic management. Often the best-laid long-range plans have remained unimplemented because the organizational structure and culture have been lacking. Although modern strategy theory offers the analyst a plethora of different models from which to choose, there is a dearth of implementation methodology. The McKinsey 7S model was designed to fill this vacuum with a conceptual framework to guide the execution of strategy.

In 1978, several consultants at McKinsey & Co.[1] codeveloped the McKinsey 7S model. They recognized a circular problem central to their client's failure to effectively implement strategy. The long-held conviction developed by Alfred Chandler in 1962 that organizational structure will follow strategy had been a prominent concept in modern strategy theory.

Most strategies implicitly incorporate the assumption that structure follows strategy but offer no execution guidance with regard to organizational structure. Because implementation is equally important as conception, many strategies failed.

The McKinsey 7S model challenged this implicit assumption by suggesting that the "structure follows strategy" paradigm was not that at all; rather, not only must structure be actively managed, it must be supplemented with equal concern for organizational effectiveness as a whole.

The McKinsey 7S model specially addresses the need to build a tight strategic fit between strategy, organizational structure, and five additional components of organizational effectiveness. Successful implementation of strategy requires explicit management of the interrelationships between these seven elements. These seven elements of organizational design and effectiveness are discussed next:

1. **Structure**—The familiar organizational chart is a suitable proxy description of structure. Structure involves the reporting of relationships within a firm as well as the division and integration of tasks. The choice of structure involves a myriad of tradeoffs. For example, a firm's structure may be centralized or decentralized, hierarchical or flattened, specialized or integrated, or autonomous or outsourced. The focus on structure within the McKinsey 7S model, however, concentrates especially on two aspects of the realm of structure. First, the idea of the coordination of all the aspects of structure in the support of strategy is prominent. Second is the need to isolate those aspects that are critical to successfully managing and negotiating change in industry evolution and new or revamped strategies.

2. **Strategy**—Among the many formal definitions of strategy, there are several common, dominant themes.

   Strategy is the set of competitive responses manifested through decisions and actions in response to the firm's environment. Strategy aims to best position the firm's current capabilities and resources in a competitive marketplace to secure competitive advantage over time. Because the firm's environment is constantly in a state of flux, so too must strategy change to protect and project existing sources of competitive advantage.

   In addition, strategy must be designed to seek out new external opportunities and acquire or internally develop the requisite resources and capabilities to exploit these environmental changes into new sources of competitive advantage. The focus on strategy within the McKinsey 7S model is not on developing new strategies or protecting existing ones; rather, its inclusion underscores the core theme of the model that asserts that strategy conception and formulation has been well managed in many firms due to its emphasis through decades of reinforcement in business schools and in the now-voluminous strategy literature. Problems in the other six elements are more often the cause of ineffective implementation.

3. **Systems**—Systems encompass the flow of both primary and secondary activities that are important to the firm's daily functioning. These include core processes (for example, product development and operations management), as well as support activities (for example, information systems, accounting, and human resources). The important distinction that the McKinsey 7S model makes with regard to systems is that changing systems is often a much less disruptive and more effective route to enhance organizational effectiveness, as opposed to the more traditional levers of manipulating strategy or structure.

4. **Style**—Style refers to the actions and behavior of senior executives, rather than what they say. As such, the conduct of top management is an extremely valuable man-

agement tool that conveys and reinforces strong messages to stakeholders, and particularly employees, throughout the organization. One of the most important barometers of executives' behavior is the way in which they spend their time. By concentrating their individual and collective attention on managing critical success factors, executives can help their staff prioritize the essential activities that the organization must perform well. Another important barometer of style is symbolic or signaling behavior that can be seen as constantly reinforcing the fundamental value system of the company. By fostering a firm-wide "strategic conversation" composed of formal and informal symbols, top executives instill a positive culture consistent with the firm's strategic intent.

5. **Staff**—The human resources of a firm are its most valuable strategic asset. The staff element includes both remuneration (compensation, incentives, and reward) and softer, more qualitative, motivational considerations. Specifically, in the 7S model, management attraction, recruitment, and development of employees are important to organizational effectiveness. Equipped with the organization's culture and core values, managers will hopefully spend fruitful careers fostering these attributes to staff located in all parts of the firm. In this regard, putting young managers in positions of authority close to the executive suite, with legitimate responsibility for some critical aspect of the firm's business model and opportunities for advancement, will positively impact long-term organizational effectiveness. By paying special attention to engaging the firm's future executives in all seven elements of the model, the firm's future organizational effectiveness can be successfully propagated.

6. **Skills**—The raw material of sustainable competitive advantage often lies in the intangible core competencies or skills of its people. The McKinsey 7S model focuses on skills because environmental change infers not only a change in strategy, but also an accompanying change in the skill set of a firm's human resources. Successful organizational change often requires increased investment to acquire or develop new skills, along with reduced investment in the established skill set that was more closely attuned to the old business models. This transition toward new skills is a process that, if done poorly, will thwart the cultivation of conditions necessary to grow new organizational skills.

7. **Shared values**—Sometimes also referred to as "super-ordinate goals," shared values represent the collective value system that drives a firm's organizational culture. Often, shared values are informal and go beyond the company's mission statement by encompassing intangibles such as strategic intent, underlying beliefs, mental mindsets, and future direction. Within the 7S model, shared values are commonly seen as the most fundamental building block of an organization, thereby providing a foundation for the other six elements. Often, shared values are short articulations of the essential meaning or driving force of the company. The difficulty, and hence value, of creating strong shared values within an organization is exemplified by the observation that only exceptional firms are able to consistently leverage this phenomenon over time.

Figure 12.1 is a schematic representation of the McKinsey 7S framework. This diagram identifies the significant cross relationships of the seven elements of organizational effectiveness.

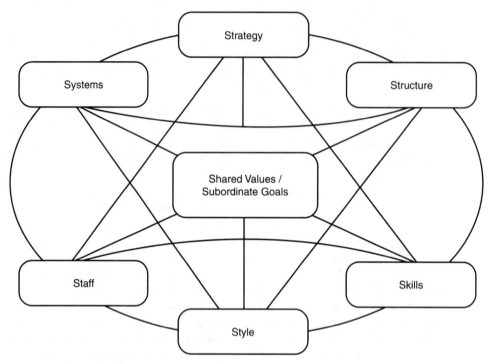

Figure 12.1   The 7S framework model[2]

There are four key insights that can be derived from this model. First, Figure 12.1 identifies the five other elements comprising organizational effectiveness in addition to the traditional strategy and structure dualism; namely, systems, style, staff, skills, and shared values.

Second, the lines connecting each element identify the mutual dependency between each element of organizational effectiveness. Pulling one lever, as it were, will cause a ripple effect across the whole system. It is this concept of holistic interrelationships that runs through the most fundamental units of the organization.

The third insight is the assertion that strategic failure may well be attributable to inattention to any one, or a combination of, the seven elements of strategic fit. This framework provides a corrective lens for the strategic myopia that often leads to inappropriate structure or poor strategy in the first place.

The fourth insight comes from the shape of the diagram—the circular consistency of the model focuses the analyst's attention on the absence of hierarchical dominance. It encourages the analyst to conclude that no one element is more important than the others—each element is a necessary but insufficient condition for organizational effectiveness. However, in some scenarios, one factor may figure more prominently than the rest. This lack of precision and high level of abstraction makes the McKinsey 7S model very flexible.

Taken together, these four insights have made an enormous contribution to modern strategy theory in two powerful ways. First, the McKinsey 7S model introduced the importance of the qualitative factors of organizational effectiveness to counterbalance the almost exclusive focus on strategy and structure that pervaded previous thought around the management of organizational change. Second, it pushed the conceptual envelope away from an external environmental preoccupation to a more holistic appraisal that includes a more realistic appreciation of the whole system—that is, both the organization acting on its environment, as well as the environment acting on the organization.

Strengths and Advantages

The 7S model pays particular emphasis to a firm's strategy implementation. This key facet of the traditional strategic management model was often given short shrift or even ignored in many preceding management constructs. The McKinsey 7S model filled this analytical vacuum by suggesting that strategic success in the competitive marketplace is also dependent on organizational effectiveness. This counteracted the disproportionate emphasis of previous models on external, economic, and marketplace factors. The McKinsey 7S model laid the groundwork for the increasing prominence of organizational dynamics in future models, such as core competency and resource-based theories.

Further, the 7S model developed the concept that organizational effectiveness was not dependent on just strategy and structure—a radical and much-needed departure from the confines of the decades-old (although admittedly still vibrant) "structure follows strategy" paradigm. The inclusion of the other elements of strategic fit broaden the analyst's scope to consider the possibility that for select firms, the reality of their context will be that strategy follows structure. At any rate, the analyst will soon realize that organizational change requires strategic management of all seven elements of strategic fit, not just tinkering with one or two of the elements (traditionally only strategy and structure).

The greatest strength of the 7S model is in its comprehensiveness. Because the analysts must consider each of the seven broad-ranging constructs, as well as how each of them interacts with one another, they are unlikely to miss any potential gaps that may arise out of changed strategies or their implementation. This model is also one of the first to actually compel the analyst to consider strategy implementation simultaneously with strategy development. These issues tended to be separated before the time of this model's introduction and popularization.

The 7S model was also one of the first to meld consideration of the "hard" (e.g., strategy, structure, and systems) and "soft" (i.e., shared valued, skills, staff, and style) aspects of the enterprise. Most models before this one tended to focus most heavily on one side or the other, to the exclusion of the ignored side of the equation. The 7S framework is valuable in supporting management thinking when implementing strategy and facilitating needed organizational changes.

The 7S model also emphasizes to the analysts and their managers the need to coordinate key tasks within the organization. The challenge lies in focusing on those dimensions that are important to the organization's evolution. The organization must be able to refocus and reallocate efforts as crucial dimensions shift.

The 7S model was also one of the first to help connect academic research with managerial practice. In particular, it emphasized how important shared values or corporate culture were in keeping the organization in synch and in driving the successful execution of smart strategies. A critical result of this model was that enterprises could be viewed as independent social systems—whose artifacts in the form of rituals, stories, symbols, and stated and exhibited values—create a powerful influence on employee behavior and can be the difference between an organization operating in an empowered fashion versus one that requires additional layers of bureaucracy to achieve its aims. This model would lead to a stream of subsequent academic research that has continued to inform consultants and managers to this day.

Weaknesses and Limitations

The primary weakness of the 7S is directly related to its greatest strength. Because the 7S requires the analyst to consider not only the seven independent constructs, but also their interrelationships, the analyst may miss some fine-grained areas in which gaps in strategy conception or execution can naturally arise.

There is little empirical support for the model or of its originator's conclusions.[3] Indeed, several years after the model was popularized by Peters and Waterman in their best-selling 1982 book *In Search of Excellence*, most of the companies that were highlighted had suffered from poor performance and were no longer the paragons of excellence that had been originally touted.

Despite the model's clear emphasis on looking inward at organizational factors and fits, it remains difficult to properly assess the degree of fit, particularly between strategy and the other elements. Strategy is the clear linking pin that should align the other elements, but this is far more complex to achieve in practice than a single construct can suggest.

It is also difficult for analysts to explain, in practical terms, just exactly what should be done for implementation in terms of using the model. The model encourages the analysts to consider the many interactions, but does not require them to consider the many different options available for changing interrelationships among the seven concepts or most importantly, specify what order or sequence within which the needed changes should be made.

The 7S is mostly a static model. It is useful for looking at a snapshot of the fit among the seven constructs at any single point in time; consequently, it can be difficult to use in recommending changes to relationships among the constructs over time, unless the model is developed, analyzed, and applied on an ongoing basis—something that is rarely, if ever, done in practice due to the pragmatic considerations of time and effort required to effectively accomplish this outcome. As such, the model's ability to address the challenges generated by dynamic enterprises and marketplaces is more limited than those models that expressly and explicitly account for time as a critical variable.

Process for Applying the Technique

The process for applying the McKinsey 7S model can be quite simple. However, it is easy to overestimate the firm's ability to achieve alignment among all seven elements of organizational fit. The 7S model can also be used to test both current and proposed strategy and, as such, assumes that these strategies have already been conceptualized and formulated.

The first step is to analyze the individual components of the McKinsey 7S model—that is, to closely examine each "S." The key success factors for each element as they pertain to the firm's current and/or future strategy need to be identified. Some experts recommend that a 7 × 2 matrix be composed, with the top row containing the critical features of each "S" that the company does extremely well. Correspondingly, the bottom row would contain the elements of each "S" in which the company is achieving subpar performance. This matrix can be extremely useful in organizing the analysis. It forces the analyst to not only explicitly isolate key action variables but also to determine the distance between what the company is currently doing well and what it needs to do well in order to successfully implement the strategy.

After isolating the strategic distance between the seven elements of strategic fit, there are essentially three options:

1. The firm can work to change the required components of each "S" so that they are consistent with strategy.

2. It can change the strategy to fit the existing orientation of the other six elements of the model.

3. Often, a compromise between each option is the realistic alternative.

After the choice of actions have been decided upon, the model should reflect an alignment between each of the seven elements of organizational effectiveness—that is, strategy, structure, style, skills, staff, systems, and shared values should be moving forward in the same direction.

Figure 12.2 depicts a prototypical application of the 7S framework. The boxes that are shaded the darkest are ones in which the two common elements are in alignment. Boxes shaded in gray are ones in which there is a partial alignment between the two conjoined elements. Boxes that are unshaded (i.e., white) exhibit misalignment between the two elements. The McKinsey 7S model asserts that organizations should seek alignment between all of the elements, and the areas identified as being misaligned (i.e., the white and grey shaded boxes) become the prime targets for managerial intervention and correction. The 7S model asserts that this alignment is a necessary condition for the successful implementation of strategy.

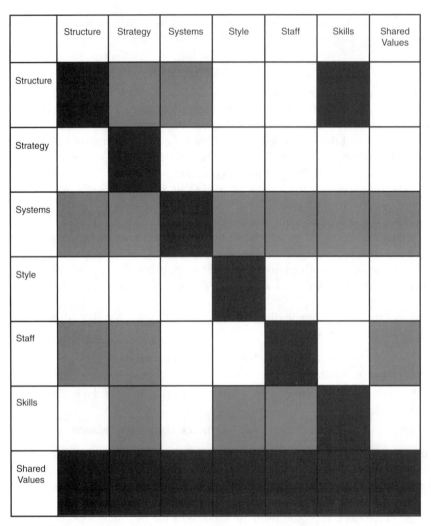

Figure 12.2   Grid showing state of "fit" between seven "S" elements at one point in time

Case Study: Privatization of Kenya Airways in the New Millennium

The 1960s were supposed to be a time of betterment and growth in Sub-Saharan Africa. The area was completing the decolonization process, and governments were creating new state-owned enterprises (SOEs) to lead their respective economies in major industrial, structural, and social improvement. However, these optimistic visions failed to materialize, as most SOEs were poorly run and almost never profitable. By the 1980s, problems stemming from massive state intervention and a lack of market forces led to economic disaster.

Consequently, external pressures have forced these countries to fight against dictatorship and authoritarianism in favor of democracy and privatization.

Kenya Airways was originally established in 1977 as a corporation owned by the Kenyan government. Senior management was appointed by politicians and had virtually no airline experience. The company lacked structure and direction, had very little equipment (seven planes), and was burdened with high interest foreign currency loans. By 1991, the airline was losing market share due to poor service and unreliable flight schedules, and its debts were an enormous strain on the Kenyan government. The only way to turn the fledgling airline toward profitability, it seemed, was to privatize it.

In 1991, the commercialization process began in order to prepare the airline for privatization. A new and capable management team was hired and given complete autonomy to restructure the company. Research was conducted to identify the needs of all stakeholders, and an IT department was created to introduce new, consistent systems and controls for accounting, scheduling, operations, management, and ticketing. By 1994, the airline recorded its first profits and in 1995 created a strategic alliance with KLM Royal Dutch Airlines. In 1996, the Kenyan Government sold 26% of its stock to KLM, and most of the remainder of its stock to the Nairobi Stock Exchange, leaving only a 22% minority ownership block held in the airline.

Privatization had forced Kenya Airways to become a self-sustaining profit-generating firm. It could no longer rely on government protection or bail-outs.[4] To successfully negotiate these challenges, Kenya Airways was required to assess threats and determine how to manipulate the seven elements of strategic fit to first survive the turmoil, and second to eventually prosper in a new competitive environment (see Table 12.1).

Table 12.1
McKinsey 7S Comparison of Pre- and Postprivatized Kenya Airlines

Before	After
Strategy	**Strategy**
■ Lack of strategy. ■ No market direction. ■ Mainly unprofitable. ■ Unreliable and rarely on time. ■ Government pricing policies dictated to low fare schema.	■ Goal to "achieve world-class standards in service delivery, product quality, and performance." ■ Deliver profitability consistently. ■ Always be safe. ■ Be the "airline of choice in Africa." ■ Anticipate industry change factors. ■ Operate a modern fleet of aircraft. ■ Create alliances with other respectable airlines.
Shared Values	**Shared Values**
■ Not suited to commercial profit-driven firm. ■ Very little attention paid to managing firm-wide human factors.	■ Identify needs of internal staff, customers, and travel agents. ■ Change culture to be service-oriented by taking every employee through customer service training program.

Table 12.1 *(continued)*
McKinsey 7S Comparison of Pre- and Postprivatized Kenya Airlines

Before	After
	■ Increase shareholder value. ■ Aim to become Africa's leading airline. ■ Keep product offerings consistent and of the highest quality.
Structure ■ Bloated workforce. ■ Bureaucratic. ■ Lack of accountability in governance.	**Structure** ■ Workforce reduction. ■ Managers expected to be responsible and accountable for their units. ■ Decentralized with offices or agents in every region the airline serviced.
Systems ■ Lack of measurement for operations. ■ Imprecise financial reporting. ■ Lack of accountability. ■ Technical skills misused and underutilized. ■ No means to measure productivity. ■ Computer systems not sufficient to sustain business.	**Systems** ■ New financial control and accountability systems. ■ New budget planning and reporting systems. ■ Creation of IT department. ■ New program to continuously improve operations and reliability.
Style ■ Politically influenced. ■ CEOs rarely held the station longer than a couple of years and lacked adequate time to implement strategies.	**Style** ■ Profit-oriented culture. ■ Hiring of upper management with airline experience. ■ Executives expected to re-vamp budget planning, sales and marketing, control, and reporting systems.
Staff ■ Employees were friends and relatives of politicians. ■ More employees were employed than needed. ■ Unused talent and energy at almost every level. ■ Low standards of customer service.	**Staff** ■ Reduction of staff. ■ All staff get customer service training. ■ Increased productivity. ■ All staff expected to be responsible and accountable.
Skills ■ Large market share of regional routes. ■ Decent share of international routes. ■ Technical skills misused and underutilized. ■ Weak sales and marketing. ■ Efficient use of fleet.	**Skills** ■ Strategic alliance with KLM. ■ Stakeholder-driven culture. ■ Attracting business-class customers. ■ Consistently profitable.

Source: Tiller, 1997; Debrah and Toroitich, 2005; Major Milestones: Kenya Airways Global Website, 2006.

FAROUT Summary

FAROUT SUMMARY

	1	2	3	4	5
F	■	■	■	■	
A	■	■			
R	■	■	■		
O	■				
U	■	■	■		
T	■	■			

Figure 12.3   McKinsey 7S analysis FAROUT summary

Future orientation—Medium to high. The McKinsey 7S model is forward looking in that it is oriented toward future implementation of proposed strategy or correction of existing organizational effectiveness to maximize the effectiveness of current strategy.

Accuracy—Low to medium. Accuracy depends on the ability of the analyst to: (a) correctly diagnose the seven elements and their interactions; (b) correctly diagnose the key success factors; and (c) implement the required changes to close the distance between (a) and (b).

Resource efficiency—Medium. This depends on the depth of analysis and the number of analysts engaged. Similarly, the comprehensiveness of internal consulting will dictate resource efficiency.

Objectivity—Low. The requisite analysis is highly qualitative and subject to perception bias.

Usefulness—Medium. The explicit purview of this model draws attention to what many other models ignore. As such, the McKinsey 7S model is compatible with, and complementary to, a good number of other management tools and techniques.

Timeliness—Low to medium. A comprehensive McKinsey 7S model analysis is extremely comprehensive and covers all facets of the firm. Additionally, correctly examining the intricate interrelationships between the seven elements can require a substantial amount of time.

Related Tools and Techniques

- Competitive benchmarking
- Customer segmentation and needs analysis
- Customer value analysis

- Functional capability and resource analysis
- SERVO analysis
- SWOT analysis
- Value chain analysis

References

Chandler, A.D. Jr. (1962). *Strategy and Structure: Chapters in the History of the American Industrial Firm*. Cambridge, MA: MIT Press.

Darden Graduate Business School Sponsors (1983). *American Telephone and Telegraph (A)*. Charlottesville, VA: University of Virginia.

Debrah, Y.A. and O.K. Toroitich (2005). "The making of an African success story: The privitization of Kenya Airways," *Thunderbird International Business Review*, 47(2), pp. 205-230.

Hax, A.C., and N.S. Majluf (1983). "Organization design: A case on matching strategy and structure," *The Journal of Business Strategy*, Fall, 4(2), pp. 72–86.

Major Milestones at a Glance, Kenya Airways Global Website, accessed September 28, 2006 at http://www.kenya-airways.com/kq/kqdispinfo.aspx?colm=69.

Pascale, R. *Managing on the Edge*. London, UK: Penguin.

Peters, T.J. (1984). "Strategy follows structure: Developing distinctive skills," *California Management Review*, Spring, 26(3), pp. 111–125.

Peters, T.J., and R. Waterman (1982). *In Search of Excellence*. New York, NY: Harper and Row.

Powel, T.C. (1992). "Organizational alignment as competitive advantage," *Strategic Management Journal*, February, 13(2), pp. 119–134.

"Privatization of Kenya Airways" (2005). *Thunderbird International Business Review*, March–April, 47(2), pp. 205–230. http://www.kenyaairways.com/root/pages/English/Home.asp (September 8, 2005).

Tiller, M. (1997). "A first for Africa: The privatization of Kenya Airways," Economic Perspectives: USIA Electronic Journals, 2(1), January, accessed September 28, 2006 at http://usinfo.state.gov/journals/ites/0197/ijee/ej5case.htm.

Waterman, R.H. Jr. (1982). "The seven elements of strategic fit," *The Journal of Business Strategy*, Winter, 2(3), pp. 69–73.

Waterman, R.H. Jr., Peters, T.J., and J.R. Phillips (1980). "Structure is not organization," *Business Horizons*, June, pp. 14–26.

Endnotes

[1] Waterman, R.H., Peters, T.J., and J.R. Phillips.

[2] Based on Peters and Waterman (1982).

[3] Pascale, 1990.

[4] Tiller, 1997; Debrah & Toroitich, 2005; Major Milestones: Kenya Airways Global Website, 2006.

Shadowing

Short Description

Shadowing is one of the newer analytical techniques that monitors specific competitors or markets in a high degree of detail to learn how a specific competitor might think, reason, and react. It means learning as much as possible about a competing firm's managers in order to predict what they might do. The competitive knowledge afforded by shadowing will allow a firm to make reasonably accurate inferences regarding the strategic and tactical intentions of rivals.

Background

Shadowing is the commercial application of a concept long used by opposition politicians in the British parliamentary system and throughout the Commonwealth. Opposition members of legislative assemblies or Parliaments regularly form "shadow cabinets," wherein each member of the opposition party follows and/or forecasts policy developments in each ministry or government department. For example, one opposition member of Parliament might be assigned to "shadow" the Ministry of Finance. In this position, he or she would be given responsibility to do the following:

- Monitor all changes in relevant policies such as tax, deficits, debt, and spending
- Track all changes in personnel within the Ministry of Finance, departments, and bureaucracy
- Develop proprietary policy for her/his affiliated party as an alternative to the party in power
- Offer rebuttals and critiques in response to recently developed initiatives to the party currently in power

- Forecast important issues in order to predict the government's response and to proactively develop opposition policy
- Be prepared to assume the portfolio in the event of a change in power

All of these individual shadow members working together are known as the "shadow cabinet." This strategic tactic has proved to be very effective in achieving the ultimate goals of opposition political parties. It has allowed political entrepreneurs to simultaneously counter the strategies of the incumbent government, as well as prepare for a hopeful electoral victory in the future by capturing a majority of the political "market."

Since the late 1980s, shadowing has become an increasingly popular technique within the competitive intelligence tactical toolkit. Many companies are now shadowing their competitors at a level of detail that is of an order of magnitude higher than traditional environmental scanning and even competitor profiling.

Shadow teams today provide a mechanism for accessing internal resources, scanning the competition and/or external environment, and integrating the insights to create new organizational learning. Fahey[1] asserts that shadowing is useful when one or more of the following conditions prevail within a firm:

- Managers have become complacent due to a firm's marketplace performance.
- A firm has become strongly committed to a set of assumptions underlying its historic strategy (and appears unwilling to evaluate them even in the face of significant marketplace change).
- The strategy planning process has largely degenerated into a routine (to be completed as quickly as possible and reviewed maybe once a year).
- Little effort is being expended to search for new marketplace opportunities.

However, shadowing does not need to focus on existing direct competitors. One can address secondary or non-direct competitors or, even as Fahey suggests, one can create "invented" competitors. An invented competitor is a rival that could appear in the future but does not exist today. This approach may serve to explore what strategies might be possible at some future time; anticipate potential new customer needs as well as the solutions required to satisfy them; identify possible marketplace opportunities that might otherwise be overlooked; and challenge your own firm to be more radical in thinking about its potential future strategies, both how they might be developed and executed.

Today when a cross-functional team focuses specifically on information about a major competitor or market, a shadow team has formed. The objective of shadowing is then to learn everything possible about a competitor—its people, processes, networks, and services—or a market, so that a firm can begin to think, reason, and react like the competitor.

Strategic Rationale and Implications

Shadow teams perform as a think tank, operating between working on special projects and creating a storehouse of knowledge to draw from when special needs emerge. Using analytical, team dynamic and communications techniques, shadow teams can evolve into smoothly operating entities with strong competitive and analytical skills.

They collect and organize information and become an identified knowledge base. With strong analytical skills, shadow teams can prove to be one of the greatest assets for the power brokers in a firm.

The fundamental premise underlying shadowing comes from the belief that strategy is a result of organizational structure and design. By closely monitoring the organizational structure and design of rivals, it is suggested that a firm can gain valuable insights into their strategic intentions.

In order to conduct this type of analysis, you must become intimate with every element of rival firm. Every minute detail, regardless of its apparent obscurity or immediate applicability, is taken into consideration. Often these details can be gleaned directly from your own firm's internal sources or by analyzing publicly accessible information. In addition, the actions and behaviors of rivals will often yield important information.

More important than the detail, however, is the holistic interpretation and analysis of the sum of the detailed information gathered from shadowing. Shadowing yields important clues as to the future plans of rival firms. Hence, the objective of shadowing is to be able to predict with reasonable accuracy the strategic intentions of competitors in order to develop proactive strategy.

To facilitate this goal, two approaches to shadowing offer two distinct but related courses of action:

1. **Shadow planning**—This technique involves the continuous monitoring of all of the relevant components of a rival's strategy. For example, the goal of shadow product planning is to equip the analyst with such an intimate knowledge of rival's product development plans so as to develop a reasonably accurate understanding of its competitive mindset. This will allow you to analyze contingencies in your firm's own product planning. The analytical output is a continuous stream of market intelligence necessary to strategically negotiate dynamic markets and intense competition.

2. **Developing a shadow market plan**—This technique differs from the previous one in that it is a one-off project with a limited timeframe for completion. Its objective is to develop an accurate proxy for the actual marketing plans of rivals. The analytical product is a document with a finite shelf life that closely resembles the formal marketing plan of a competitor.

These two approaches are not mutually exclusive, as shadow planning is used to build shadow market plans. The continuous stream of shadow planning information provides a solid intellectual foundation from which to develop actionable recommendations and launch strategy—think of the shadow market plan as the intelligence vehicle, and shadow planning as the maintenance that tunes it up regularly, making the engine run more effectively.

Not only are these two tactical manifestations of shadowing closely integrated, but should be closely integrated into the firm's broader corporate strategy. A recurring debate in the field of strategy is the question of identifying the true source of the firm's competitive advantage. Does it lie inside the firm in the form of resources, core competencies, capabilities, organizational structure and business processes, or does it lie outside the firm in the form of superior competitive position within markets, strategic groups, and industries? As with many arguments that attempt to delineate ambiguous or circular constructs to their core, the answer to these questions is not black and white but, rather, several shades of gray. In reality, the location of the firm's competitive advantage is both internal and external. It is in this gray area where shadowing, if employed correctly, can shed much light onto the challenge of crafting strategy.

In order to fully leverage the power of shadowing within a firm, it is important to bridge the link between the internal and external sources of a firm's competitive advantage. By having a number of analysts explicitly charged with learning as much as possible about rivals, the firm incorporates several legitimate sources of strategic challenge inside itself.

Shadow analysts with an accurate read on the competitive mindset of competitors, function in several ways to integrate the internal and external view of corporate strategy by

- Testing the validity of the firm's own strategies
- Identifying potential weaknesses of rivals that the firm may exploit
- Protecting against weaknesses in the firm's current and future strategies
- Predicting the contingent reaction of competitors to the firm's planned marketing strategies
- Identifying potential new competitive threats or opportunities in the broader market framework

Given that the goal of strategy is to find the best match between the firm's resources and opportunities to provide superior customer value, the knowledge that shadowing can bring to this process is extremely valuable. The competitive value of a firm's resources and the definition of superior customer value are contingent upon competitive response. Shadowing provides reasonable inferences regarding such contingent competitive response. Hence, shadowing is one of several effective methods to bridge internal and external views of strategy.

Often, the role of shadowing is seen as duplicating the market research function. Certainly there is an overlap, but shadowing is much more in-depth. A leading expert in this area, Rothberg[2] asserts that while traditional market research excels in securing knowledge of consumer research and the "Four Ps" of the marketing mix, it stops short of securing the breadth of knowledge required for strategic success. Shadowing supplements market research by providing insights into the entire value chain of competitors.

Shadowing is especially necessary for the heightened levels of competition that characterizes modern markets in which globalization is threatening once-secure markets. Similarly, technology is fostering market migration by unraveling traditional linkages in many value chains.

Strengths and Advantages

A valuable benefit of shadowing is the removal of blindspots that commonly develop inside of the strategic decision-making process. Without shadowing, firms often make incorrect assumptions about the future direction of rival strategies. Similarly, firms often neglect to adequately consider the contingent competitive reaction to the firm's planned strategy. Adopting the competitive mindset of rivals through shadowing allows the firm to counter these two common blindspots.

Shadow teams also become a firm's eyes and ears on a whole range of strategic and competitive matters. This means they are in a position to help a firm adjust to changes in its environment by attending to such matters as (to name a few):

- Facilitating new product development
- Adjusting existing products and services
- Interpreting market signals
- Investigating rumors
- Identifying new technology

A well-constructed and nurtured shadow team can become an invaluable organizational asset. First, through sharing, collaboration, and analysis, the firm's knowledge assets increase. Second, a shadow team can operate as investigators of competitive rumors and market signals, or they can serve as general think tanks, providing unfiltered analysis directly to the strategic players. As a result, shadowing allows for a firm's learning to improve, as well as enhancing its ability to respond to its competitive environment.

The key contributions and value of shadow teams are identified in Table 13.1.

Table 13.1
Characteristics and Contributions of Shadow Teams

Characteristics	Contributions
Cross functional.	Multitude of knowledge both internally and externally to the organization.
Think-tank team.	Able to interpret and analyze competitive information, reflecting competitor's ability to act, react, or change strategy.
Operate as investigators of information.	Discover strategic relevance; conduct comparative study.
"Devil Advocate" role.	Break assumptions and biases regarding the firm's own view of the competitor.
Facilitates organization learning.	Improves the firm's ability to respond effectively to the competitive environment. Cross sharing of information across the team and their respective departments.
Strategically focused.	Answers "so what" issues, not just tactical responses.

Source: Adapted from Rothberg, H.N. (1997). "Fortifying Competitive Intelligence with Shadow Teams," *Competitive Intelligence Review*, 8(2), p. 4.

Weaknesses and Limitations

Critics of shadowing argue that the strategy may not necessarily always follow structure. As such, shadowing may not be able to adequately predict new strategic directions undertaken by rivals, especially when past intelligence garnered from shadowing is premised on the structure and strategic infrastructure of rivals. A new strategic direction may blindside shadow team members who are myopically assuming that rivals are operating from a base of established resources and strategy. Often, when rivals are pursuing entirely new directions, strategy *will* precede structure.

Like many other strategic tools, blind application of shadowing does not handle discontinuity very well.

Shadow teams may also fail due to organizational issues such as the firm's culture, politics and role of senior management. Table 13.2 below identifies the issue and reason for the failure of competitive intelligence teams within a firm.

Table 13.2
Reasons Why Shadow Teams Fail

Issue	Reason
Supervisor fails to direct and encourage	Participating in a shadow team requires that time be taken from other activities.
	Direct supervisors can make a team member's existence difficult by not appreciating the importance of the shadow team and providing little time for participation.
	Supervisors have been known to hold the annual review over a team member's head to guarantee that his/her timetable is met. Members experience competing time demands and often give priority to the most urgent job.
Composition	Forcing people to join a shadow team for political or visibility reasons can result in a member who is not interested, motivated and/or capable of participating. This person can become a team liability instead of an asset.
No exposure to senior management	A shadow team by its very nature requires a direct line of communication to senior management. This ensures the delivery delivery of unfiltered, and at times, "china breaking" analysis —that is, identifying management held beliefs or blind spots.
	Additionally, exposure to senior management is a reward to team members and is an asset to senior managers. Not having direct contact with decision makers will severely retard the execution of analysis.
Employees lack regular training and development	Teams take time to develop, and the majority of participants —whether small teams, or champions or rings of experts— may need training of some kind in either business, marketing, or competitive and financial analysis, as they may not have had exposure to them.

Source: Adapted from Rothberg, H.N. (1997). "Fortifying Competitive Intelligence with Shadow Teams," *Competitive Intelligence Review*, 8(2), p. 10.

Shadow teams take time to develop and build rapport among themselves and senior management. They develop across circumstances and with experience. Individual members bring with them their own specific weaknesses and blindspots, which may in turn impact the team dynamics. Without management's ongoing commitment and support, the output of shadowing can be littered with biases, blindspots, team conflicts, and analytical naivety.

Process for Applying the Technique

Shadow Teams

Before the process of shadowing can commence, the establishment of a shadow team or teams that can operate outside the structural confines of a firm needs to be put into place. The specific guidelines for the effective operation of a shadow team need to be explicitly agreed to by senior management. The team needs to be able to report directly to senior management without editorial input from gatekeepers. They need to be relatively fearless.

Members of shadow teams need to be cerebral independent thinkers, self-starters, and tenacious.[3] Recruiting individuals with the skills, knowledge, and guts to conduct investigations and generate reports based on real data is one of the keys to developing a high-performance team.[4]

Teams will also require the following:

- A clear, unifying purpose
- Challenging goals
- Work that is meaningful with collective products and challenging performance criteria[5]
- Ongoing training and coaching in such areas as team dynamics and analysis

Special attention must be given to three key performance issues for shadow teams, as follows:

1. Team composition
2. Team structure
3. Performance goals

Team Composition

The objective is to create a balanced group of individuals who bring a combination of skills, diversity, knowledge, networks, disposition, personality mixed with creativity, out-of-the-box thinking, and analytical ability. Rothberg suggests selection of team members could address the following criteria:

1. **Intellectual capability**—The ability to secure relevant information; relate and compare data from different sources; identify issues and relationships; and to be conceptual, analytical, and creative
2. **Results-oriented**—The ability to work toward outcomes and complete what one starts

3. **Interpersonal skills**—The ability to relate to the feelings and needs of others and to convey interest and respect

4. **Planning and organizing**—The ability to schedule time and prioritize for one's self and/or others, to handle multiple activities, and to meet deadlines

5. **Team-oriented**—The ability to work collaboratively within a complex organizational structure

6. **Maturity**—The willingness to be open and act responsibly when dealing with people and situations

7. **Presence**—The ability to create a positive first impression and stand out tactfully (includes verbal and nonverbal communication)

Team Structure

High performance shadow teams are small yet provide a representation of the required skills. (Note: large teams tend to take on the characteristics of a group, which may impede a cohesive approach to the issue at hand and the timely delivery of the project goals and objectives.)

Shadow teams are composed of the best and brightest in a firm and are made up of volunteers who decide to take on this work in addition to their usual work responsibilities. A facilitator needs to be identified to serve as an administrative and communication hub for team members and as a liaison point between management and the team.

Performance Goals

Without focused, measurable goals and a belief that the goal is worthwhile, teams never achieve high performance.[6] Without clearly defined goals, members can become unfocused, politicized, lose their urgency, or become irrelevant.

In essence, when establishing a shadow team, the following guidelines should be observed. The teams operate within a learning climate. They have the opportunity to learn from each other. They also have some latitude for analysis to miss the mark as long as it is based on unfiltered information and demonstrates analytical thinking:

- Teams are comprised of diverse and cross-functional people who reflect the texture of the company.
- There are clear, meaningful, and measurable goals.
- There is management support.
- There is exposure to senior executives and executive strategic decision makers.
- Appropriate tools and training are available.

Shadowing

Once teams are in place, the process of shadowing and developing a shadow market plan can be commenced; however, the process cannot be described adequately by a formal sequential or step-by-step procedure. In general, the process is characterized by collection, analysis, and dissemination of strategic recommendations. However, these general stages are usually performed simultaneously and often become intertwined through a complex web of formal and informal iteration.

The first step is for the shadow team to learn as much as possible about every aspect of the rival firms. The goal of this knowledge will be to enable the shadow team to think like the competition. In order to achieve this, several methods are offered by two experts in the field of shadowing:[7]

- **Personnel hiring**—An examination of the personnel changes in the executive suite, as well as the functional areas in the firm, will often yield valuable insights on the strategic focus of rivals. For example, hiring marketing staff may indicate an expansion of marketing effort. Likewise, hiring research scientists may indicate that a rival is beefing up its innovation and internal product development capacity.

- **Personnel departures**—Monitoring the firings and resignations of key personnel can often shed insight into which functional areas are receiving the most attention at rival firms. For example, the resignation of an operations manager and senior R&D personnel may indicate that other areas of the firm are being pursued more aggressively. One may surmise that technical innovation may be taking a back seat at this particular rival; possibly, the real decision-making power may now rest in the finance function with a strategic focus on cost cutting.

- **Full text of news releases and speeches**—The full text of relevant sources will often provide hints of strategic intent by allowing you to place the document in a fuller context and to search for meaning by "reading between the lines."

- **Hometown media**—Often minute but nonetheless significant, details are included in press coverage of the newspaper or local business magazine published in the rival's hometown. Local press digs deeper and provides more detail due to the importance of the company to the local economy. Other, more distant, press sources may leave out this detail due to detachment.

- **Trade shows**—Participants at trade shows involve members of the competitor's entire value chain (that is, suppliers, customers, and distributors). Additionally, trade shows offer the chance to meet members of rival firms. Face-to-face contact may offer you the best opportunity to evaluate the human resource capability of rivals. Conversations with them may also yield clues as to their resources, industry outlook, priorities, or even veiled references to their current or planned strategies.

- **Corporate literature**—This includes company newsletters, technical brochures, and product support material.

- **Online databases**—The Internet provides a cost-effective source of information in the form of general press coverage, hometown press coverage, and online databases. Additionally, the perceptions of the shadow team can be tested, and if needed objectified, by reading material written by a wide variety of sources from official security firm analysts to the meandering "off the cuff" unguarded comments in chat rooms and forums.

- **Technological tracking**—This is done through professional society papers, industry trade association articles, and articles written by technical personnel of rivals.

- **Background checks**—This is done by assessing the totality of executive backgrounds including education, previous positions, career track, past successes and failures, and hiring tendencies.

- **Management personality profiling**—This provides an understanding of how decision makers at rival firms are psychologically hardwired (what makes them "tick").

- **Debriefing**—Talking to employees who have previously worked with rivals either directly through an employment contract or indirectly through industry associations. Additionally, other valuable sources of information include members of a rival's value chain, including salespeople, distributors, customers, suppliers, and advertising agencies.

- **Regulatory tracking**—This involves monitoring regulatory procedures with which competitors are involved, such as patents pending, licensing, consumer, or environmental regulation.

- **Financial statement analysis**—Learning of the financial strength of rivals, as well as any financial constraints facing rivals (for example, debt capacity, cash flow, and liquidity) may yield insights into the success of their past strategies, as well as their propensity to intensify or change strategies.

  Financial statement analysis is intentionally placed at the bottom of the list because the whole point of shadowing is to determine the future strategic plans of rivals before they materialize into financial results. This placement underscores the ultimate goal of shadowing to function as a leading rather than lagging indicator. Nonetheless, a solid understanding of a rival's financial situation provides a necessary foundation for shadowing.

Once all of this information has been collected, analyzed, and internalized, the shadow team should be ready to assume the role of strategic challenger. By functioning as a proxy for the competitor, shadow teams should be able to objectively filter any assumptions about rival firms that other decision makers in the firm may harbor. Similarly, shadow teams will be well placed within the firm to infer the future strategic decisions and directions that rival firms may pursue.

In order to maintain the integrity of this strategic capacity, this process should be continuous, or at least updated regularly. Nothing stands still, and new forces may change the dynamics of the marketplace very quickly.

Equally important, when conducting shadowing, you must be able to consciously divorce yourself from the firm's own decision-making processes, frameworks, and biases/blindspots; that is, in order to be an effective and legitimate strategic challenger, you must act as the rival firm in order to challenge the thinking within the firm. In the event that individuals with these capabilities cannot be found within the firm, external analysts may be considered. Table 13.3 outlines the various pros and cons of outsourcing the shadowing analysis to external experts. In general, the pros of developing shadowing capabilities in-house overpower arguments for outsourcing. Individual firm circumstances may, however, refute this generalization.

Table 13.3
Issues Around Outsourcing Shadowing Capability

In-house	Outsourcing
■ Risk of bias due to internal cultural influences; more susceptible to blindspots.	■ Objective appraisal of rivals.
■ Cost-effective as an ongoing process.	■ Cost constraints prevent full-time consultation for most firms.
■ Strategic services and responses available to management at any time.	■ Strategic services and responses available only during consultation period.
■ Possible training delays.	■ Shadowing can start right away.
■ Knowledge of shadowing efforts radiates throughout firm.	■ Fewer people see actual competitor report due to confidentiality.
■ May "sugar coat" discomforting findings.	■ Easier for consultants to disclose "bad" news.

Source: Adapted from Vella, C.M., and J.J. McGonagle, Jr. (1988). *Improved Business Planning Using Competitive Intelligence.* Westport, CT: Quorum Books.

Developing a Shadow Market Plan

Intermittently, throughout the shadowing process, a shadow market plan is drawn up from the analysis. A *shadow market plan* is essentially a document that captures all of the knowledge obtained to date, which has been analyzed to derive some insight. Its purpose is to provide a proxy of the official marketing or business plans of rivals. Competitive analysis is essential in estimating the capability of rivals, and specific analytical tools appropriate to the team's objectives are used at this time as a foundation for strategic decisions yet to be made. This analysis may be the first level of iteration of the shadow plan, with ongoing analysis occurring as further information is collected.

A shadow market plan views the resources, competencies, capabilities, processes, strategies, strengths, weaknesses, opportunities, and threats from the perspective of rivals. As such, it attempts to view all of the parameters of strategic decision making made by the rival. This detached perspective allows the firm to establish with reasonable accuracy the current marketing and business strategy of rivals. It will also enhance the firm's ability to project the future strategic direction of rivals or their likely reaction to strategic initiatives of the firm conducting the shadowing. An informal and qualitative sensitivity analysis is then conducted to predict different outcomes to various competitive scenarios.

A useful supplement to the shadow analysis plan is to conduct a reverse shadow market plan. Vella and McGonagle[8] suggest that firms may find it helpful to develop an analysis of how the rival actually views your firm. Often the results can be quite disconcerting.

The final step in the shadowing analysis process is to continuously monitor rivals and revise and adjust the shadow plans as required. If substantial enough, these revisions and adjustments will then influence subsequent strategic decisions. In this respect, labeling this step as the final one is a misnomer, as the shadowing process is more circular than linear in design and function.

Case Study: Illuminating Strategy by Shadowing

A hypothetical example is outlined next, which shows how the process of shadowing could improve strategic decision making at a large insurance firm. Suppose that the objective of the shadow team was to develop a shadow market plan for a large competing insurer, Mega Insurance. Summarized here is an itemization of what each stage in the proposed shadowing process may look like:

Specified objective—Delineate the analysis into the potential expansion of commercial lines by Mega Insurance in the Mid-Atlantic market.

Sources of Information

Insurance industry publications include the following:

- Mega filings with the Securities Commission
- Trade publications of industries to which Mega sells commercial insurance
- Commonly reported Mega press releases
- Full texts of Mega press releases
- Regional business publications
- Newspapers covering the city in which Mega headquarters is located
- Internet marketing and financial reports of Mega by securities analysts
- Coverage of Mega's new facilities in computer industry trade publications
- Interviews of Mega executives in local business publications
- Evidence of zoning application or permissions for new Mega facilities at relevant municipalities
- Evidence of expansion from industrial development authorities regarding public financing
- Mega's own Web site
- Other Internet sources

Inferences

- Mega is planning to initiate a new commercial line starting in Ohio.
- Mega has engaged a contractor to build a new office in New Jersey.
- Mega has recently recruited an executive from a rival firm to manage the NJ office.
- Marketing materials distributed by Mega to target customers, agents, and brokers reveal current distribution, target market, and sales of new commercial lines.
- Shadowing also uncovers the planned grand opening of the NJ office to coincide with the market launch.
- Management profiling reveals background, experience, and past successes and failures of the new NJ office executive.

Confirmation

These sources and inferences are then confirmed and cross-referenced with existing information of Mega's strategy, past affiliations, and actions in the Mid-Atlantic market area. Next, these tentative conclusions are meshed with an environmental analysis of the market conditions in the relevant areas.

Tentative Conclusions

A shadow market plan is built consisting of several prominent strategies, including the following:

- Mega is planning a major expansion of its commercial lines.
- A regional marketing approach will initiate the product launch under the auspices of the new executive in the NJ office.
- The pioneering product will be the new commercial line.

Monitoring

The same sources discussed previously are used to monitor the progress of Mega's shadow market plan. In addition, several additional sources are added, such as:

- Monitoring new policies and rates of the new commercial line via records at state insurance offices in Mid-Atlantic states
- Determining the target market from advertisements placed in regional business publications[9]

Mini Case Studies

Case 1—Deregulating Utility

A shadow team at a large utility company in the midst of deregulation warned senior management about activities indicating a key competitor's acquisition intentions that would result in shrinking the utility's current market and tilting market power in the competitor's direction.

Result

Senior management responded quickly by pre-empting the competitor's offer with one of their own. The threat of a loss in market share was thwarted and actual market power increased.

Case 2—Packaged-Food Multinational

A new product development group in a multinational packaged food corporation was planning to develop a challenger to a rival product category leader. The competitor shadow team was brought into the process to "war game" the potential rivalry with the group's new product offering. The shadow team knew the rival's operations down to product P&L, had profiles on senior management (one who had his corporate roots in the product category), and possessed a clear understanding of their marketing mentality.

Result

The two-day simulation revealed that the rival could and would retaliate against all market moves and had a cost structure enabling it to win any ensuing price war. At the game's conclusion, the decision was made to abandon the product line before investing further in its development.

Case 3—Ready-to-Eat Foods

A leader in "ready-to-eat" foods was gearing up to produce a new product for test marketing. While visiting a remote out-of-state facility, a manufacturing employee noticed an unusual structure in a nearby town owned by a rival. An internal search by the shadow team identified a recently hired employee who had worked for the rival and was familiar with the facility. Apparently, the rival employed the site as a testing ground for the manufacture of new products that the market had not yet proven worthy of full-scale operations. The shadow team's comparative financial analysis of the firm's new product manufacturing process versus a flexible testing facility demonstrated that the rival was saving millions of dollars. The shadow team was also familiar with the rival's equipment engineers and suppliers.

Result

Information leveraged from these network contacts increased the shadow team's contribution by recommending a rudimentary test facility design of their own.

Case 4—Pharmaceutical Firm

A medium-sized American pharmaceutical firm structured shadow teams around ailment classifications. During scanning activities, a shadow member heard a rumor from a Federal Drug Administration (FDA) contact, which was corroborated by a field salesperson, that a new drug positioned to rival the firm's market leader was close to receiving approval. An upcoming conference gave the shadow team the opportunity to gather intelligence and validate—or refute—the rumor. Network connections identified the academic institution conducting the competitor product trials. During an evening cocktail party, shadow team members independently engaged scientists in discussion about chemistry and related topics. In time, they learned about the trials (although the product or sponsor was never noted by name), confirmed the FDA rumor, and, importantly, identified the new procedures employed in clinical testing.

Result 1

The firm leveraged this information and launched a campaign to bolster its product's market share. During this time, the shadow team was charged with finding out why competitors were constantly beating the firm to market with new categorical drugs. The team's experience with competitor scientists at the conference influenced their decision to launch a counter-intelligence investigation of their own firm. They learned that their own scientists, both in-house and those contracted to run clinical trials, behaved similarly.

Result 2

A program was created to generate awareness for protecting intellectual property and competitive information throughout the organization. The shadow team drove home the importance of not only learning, but also of guarding knowledge.[10]

FAROUT Summary

FAROUT SUMMARY

	1	2	3	4	5
F	■	■	■	■	
A	■	■	■		
R	■	■			
O	■	■	■		
U	■	■	■	■	■
T	■	■	■	■	

Figure 13.1   Shadowing FAROUT summary

Future orientation—Medium to high. One of the primary purposes of this model is to forecast with reasonable accuracy the future strategic plans and contingent reactions of rival firms.

Accuracy—Medium. To the extent that strategy follows structure, this tool is reasonably accurate. To the extent that strategy precedes structure, accuracy is compromised. Additionally, qualitative inference is fraught with potential inaccuracies.

Resource efficiency—Low to medium. Shadowing requires a dedicated team of internal analysts conducting analysis on a daily or weekly basis. Outsourcing introduces painful and often costly tradeoffs.

Objectivity—Medium. The idea that analysts can fully and objectively adopt the competitive mindset of rivals may be questionable in principle. Bias can be introduced by the analyst's internal affiliation and exposure to the firm's strategic decision-making processes and blindspots.

Usefulness—High. Having an in-house team of strategic challengers is very useful in rooting out blindspots. The usefulness of this strategic challenge is enhanced by the fact that the analytical ammunition of this model is externally sourced and cross-referenced.

Timeliness—Medium to high. A shadow market plan can be drafted fairly quickly.

Related Tools and Techniques

- Blindspot analysis
- Competitor profiling
- Functional capability and resource analysis
- Growth vector analysis
- Management personality and profiling
- Scenario analysis
- Strategic group analysis
- SWOT analysis
- Value chain analysis

References

Fahey, L. (2002). "Invented competitors: a new competitor analysis methodology," *Strategy & Leadership*, 30(6), pp. 5–12.

Fleisher, C.S., and D.L. Blenkhorn (2003). *Controversies in Competitive Intelligence: The Enduring Issues*. Westport, CT: Praeger Publishers.

Gilad, B. (1994). *Business Blindspots*. Chicago, IL: Probus Publishing Company.

Gilad, B. (2003). *Early Warning: Using Competitive Intelligence to Anticipate Market Shifts, Control Risk and Create Powerful Strategies*, AMACOM.

Katzenbach, J.R., and D.K. Smith (1993). *The Wisdom of Teams*. New York, NY: HarperCollins Publishers, Inc.

McGonagle, J.J. Jr., and C.M. Vella (1996). *A New Archetype for Competitive Intelligence*. Westport, CT: Quorum Books.

McGonagle, J.J. Jr., and C.M. Vella (1999). *The Internet Age of Competitive Intelligence*. Westport, CT: Quorum Books.

Rothberg, H.N. (1997). "Fortifying competitive intelligence with shadow teams," *Competitive Intelligence Review*, 8(2), pp. 3–11.

Rothberg, H.N. (1999). "Fortifying strategic decisions with shadow teams: A glance at product development," *Competitive Intelligence Magazine*, April/June, 2(2), pp. 9–11.

Rothberg, H.N., and G.S. Erickson (2005). *From Knowledge to Intelligence: Creating Competitive Advantage in the Next Economy*. Elsevier, Inc.

Vella, C.M., and McGonagle, J.J. Jr. (1987). "Shadowing markets: A new competitive intelligence technique," *Planning Review*, September/October, 15(5), pp. 36–38.

Vella, C.M., and McGonagle, J.J. Jr. (1988). *Improved Business Planning Using Competitive Intelligence*. Westport, CT: Quorum Books.

Young, G. (2004). "Using shadowing to build creativity and continuity," *KM Review*, July/August, 7(3), pp. 20–23.

Endnotes

[1] Fahey, 2002.

[2] Rothberg, 1999.

[3] Larson and LaFasto, 1989.

[4] Rothberg, 1997.

[5] Katzenbach and Smith, 1993.

[6] Rothberg, 1997.

[7] Vella and McGonagle, 1988.

[8] Vella and McGonagle, 1988.

[9] Adapted from Vella, C.M., and J.J. McGonagle, Jr. (1988).

[10] Rothberg, H.N. (1999).

14

Product Line Analysis

Short Description

Product line analysis is the process of examining a company's product line to determine if the line is maximizing the company's use of resources and is able to meet its strategic goals. The process involves assessing whether the correct volume and type of products are present in the line, an awareness of the life-cycle stages products are in, the manner in which product markets are segmented, the methods by which products are marketed to those segments, how the product is perceived by customers in the marketplace, and how a company allocates resources to products within its line.

Background

There were considerable advancements in products being made available in the marketplace after the Second World War that made a difference in how people lived. All a company essentially had to do was present the products with their fabulous features to waiting customers, and the growing marketplace would flock to purchase the item. Disposable razors and nylon pantyhose were products launched during this time and were readily adopted. However, by the 1960s, the competition had intensified, and managers became mindful of the fact that in order for a firm to prosper, a simple "build it and they will come" approach was not going to be sufficient. As competition for customers' favor intensified, the scope of managers' responsibilities—particularly marketing, brand, and product-related managers—started to include understanding the needs and wants of the customer and designing products to meet their actual (and not just assumed) needs. By the 1970s, concepts like segmentation, perceptual mapping, consumer behavior, and the product life cycle had been formulated and generally accepted, and the constructs aided in the product line analysis process.

Strategic Rationale

For those enterprises competing in global markets, the world's population is only growing at a little more than one percent per year.[1] Managers increasingly recognize in industry after industry that market share will not grow unless it is being taken from competitors. Products can achieve sales growth by out-performing or under-pricing competitors' offerings. In order to do this, it is important for managers to understand a product's potential, as well as the potential of all products that the company has in the competitive marketplace. For example, discerning managers will need to know where the product is in its life cycle, what market the product is in, how that market is segmented, and how profitable the product is to the firm.

The reality of just-in-time delivery systems, efficient value chains, and shorter business cycles means that product line managers are under increasing pressure to get products to market faster and have fewer margins for error with steadily empowered and newly enlightened customers.[2] "Design for postponement" strategies allow last-minute customizations to suit customers' preferences.[3] These are among the reasons that customers' expectations of products' abilities and features offered are at historically high levels, putting more pressure on managers to get the product mix right the first time.

Product line analysis is a beneficial tool used in both business and competitive analysis. Decisions about whether or not to add or subtract products can have large consequences. Many apparently well thought-out new products have gone awry—wasting time, wasting money, and destroying careers along the way. Experiencing adverse consequences such as these leads many company executives to adopt a fast follower strategy, thus avoiding the risks, and rewards that are associated with new product development.[4]

In a competitive sense, knowing where a competitor's products are vulnerable can be a key facet of understanding what tactics might be employed by your company in exploiting these vulnerabilities. Turned on its head, knowing where your own company's products are vulnerable to competitive attacks allows you the opportunity to shore up the product's defenses or to employ cross-product or cross-line tactics and methods to maximize the return of the entire line of products in any given market space.

Strengths and Advantages

A critical tenet of economics suggests that competitive firms have limited resources. Product line analysis (PLA) is a valuable tool in determining where and which products should be the recipient of scarce, valuable organizational resources. The product life cycle can help in the forecasting process and in the ability to compare firms' products in terms of past and future to other products in a company's product line, and to competitors' products as well.[5] Realistic expectations of profits, growth, and market share can be developed for the firm if each product and brand is viewed objectively within the context of the entire product portfolio offering. This objectivity is important if the manager who is evaluating a products' viability is, in some way, emotionally attached to the product. If the manager helped develop a product or spent a great deal of time resurrecting or marketing it, s/he may be less likely to cut it loose or alter it without persuasive empirical evidence of why the resulting business decision is beneficial.

Tools like the product life cycle (PLC), which are used in doing product line analysis, enable marketers and managers to see product life stages for what they are. Profits can be forsaken for market share in the beginning stages, and profits will follow in later stages when managers see the "big picture." Profit maximization for the life cycle can be most effectively realized when managers are not focused on the myopia of profit realization for the quarter or year.[6]

The ability of PLA to help the analyst categorize markets and position products according to segments ensures maximum efficiency in an overall product line. The process of analyzing the product line can reveal actual or potential cannibalization, duplications, met or unmet customer needs and wants, and availability or shortcomings of market size or structure. The overall strategy of a company's product line is improved when viable segments are identified, and resources are allocated with the intent of satisfying needs and communicating product attributes effectively.

Weaknesses and Limitations

A limitation of product line analysis is that the outlook tends to be limited to organizational phenomena, and external, less organizationally controlled factors like economic, social, and political circumstances are not taken deeply into consideration. Potentially significant macro-environmental conditions like recessions, demographic shifts, exchange rate fluctuations, and other risk factors outside the immediate control of the firm are frequently neglected; consequently, contingency plans for maximizing profitability from a product line facing these conditions may not be put in place.

From a business analysis perspective, there is a risk that product line analysis may lead to a too quick abandonment of some products or brands because they may appear to be at the end of their life cycle, even though they may have a loyal and still profitable (albeit less so than in the product's heyday) following for years to come. Product life cycles are not something that exists in absolution. They are metaphorical tools used to classify certain stages that many products or brands potentially pass through over a given period of time. If a manager views all products and brands through the product life cycle lens, there is a risk that some products' longevity will therefore be thwarted simply because the manager is looking for them to expire. Many classic products are simply exempt from the construct or run an atypical cycle.[7] For example, combinations of nostalgia, technological developments, and/or good marketing have saved many toys from the scrap heap. Long-standing products like Hasbro's "My Little Pony," "Transformers," and "G.I. Joe" have all been resurrected from the PLC-prescribed phase-out in time to regain popularity with the original market's children. Mattel's "Barbie" line and Hasbro's "Monopoly" line of games use landmark anniversaries to build momentum, rather than lose it.

Another business-oriented risk inherent in product line analysis is that management become "product-focused" rather than "customer-focused." Entire industries have failed as a result of that very perspective. Theodore Levitt noted decades ago that had the railways seen themselves in the transportation industry (providing service that clients were actually looking for) rather than the railway industry (in the business of operating rail transportation), rail companies would be in a better position today.

The result of the product line analysis is the risk that some managers will use these concepts as hard and fast rules to develop or eliminate strategies, without taking into consideration the many unquantifiable nuances that can result from product line changes. A good example of this was the elimination of 25-cent coffees at Nordstrom stores. The Seattle-based retailer has built a reputation for legendary customer service over its 100+ year history. For decades, coffee has been available in the Nordstrom Café for a quarter. Payment is based completely on the honor system, and the product is there for anyone who wants it, customers and employees alike. In the late 1990s, Nordstrom share price was taking a beating in the stock market, and the company wanted to build a much more cost-conscious culture in order to help improve profitability. Some of the cost-cutting measures made a lot of sense—vastly reducing bloated inventories and speeding cycle times, as well as training employees to be more aware of the true cost of sales. One cost-cutting measure, however, was the elimination of the quarter coffee. Overnight, the cup of coffee was raised to a dollar! The outrage that resulted from the elimination of one little gesture, a coffee for 25 cents, and the nostalgia that was lost along the way, left a bitter taste with many loyal customers and employees, and may have ended up costing the company more money than it saved.

Process for Applying the Technique

Ideally, at the time of analyzing a product line, the analyst (or product manager) has firmly defined the goals of the product(s) in questions, and these are checked for consistency with the overall corporate strategy. It is also worthwhile to identify whether the target market has been identified and the marketing, pricing, and promotion strategies are consistent with the goals. The process of analyzing the product line will identify if the products are able to meet these goals given their current position, if the products need to be replaced with newer options, improved, or if market opportunities are being missed because the firms lacks a certain offering.

Step 1: Initial Product Audit

Volume of products in a line: The goal of maximizing profit over the long term is complicated when numerous products exist in a line. If a company is looking to exploit a low-cost strategy, they may choose to try and drive out costs by eliminating products that in any way duplicate or cannibalize sales of other products in the line. Alternatively, if a company is pursuing a differentiation strategy, they may seek to have more products in the line, which are tailored for and customized to different market segments. In a perfect world, any company product would not cannibalize the sales of other products within the company; nevertheless, cannibalization does occur to varying degrees where similar products are offered, and it is important for managers to be able to assess the impact of this phenomenon. Likewise, they must be able to assess any potential cannibalization that may occur to existing products if a new product is being introduced. Customer information systems, like CRM software, can be used to track how many mature-product sales are being lost to new products.[8]

However, cannibalization by itself, even if deemed at an intolerable level, is not a sufficient reason to eliminate products without properly evaluating alternatives. Data optimization techniques can use sophisticated mathematical modeling to generate revenue projection based on objectives and constraints. Programs like Excel Solver, Crystal Ball, and others use programming techniques, like linear, non-linear, dynamic, and stochastic techniques to attach a fiscal value to competing options.[9] Ideally, these optimization techniques will identify a range where long-term goals and profits can both be realized, which helps managers decide how to apportion resources to different products. The process should aid in incremental analysis. Basically, for each additional unit produced, how much profit can the enterprise expect to realize?

Raw data alone cannot be the full extent of this step of the analysis. Each product must be viewed within the context of where it is in its expected life. In the same way that we would not expect a five-year-old child to perform the way we would expect a 15-year-old child to perform, organizations should have different expectations of products at different stages in the life cycle.

Step 2: Assess the Product Relative to Its Position in the Product Life Cycle

The product life cycle (PLC) is a marketing construct that applies a stylized life span to brands or products. The idea is that generally speaking, a product will experience four stages during its life, measured in terms of sales, profit, market share, or some combination.[10]

During Stage 1, the product will experience introductory minimal sales and slow growth in its infancy, while the product is still "catching on" and glitches are worked out. Depending on the product, marketers will choose a "price skimming" strategy with a very high introductory price to discourage demand that the company is unable to fulfill or a "penetration pricing" strategy, selling the item at a low price in order to gain market share and then slowly raising the price in the growth stage. In Stage 2, the product will start to gain momentum and experience the greatest sales growth of the cycle. Stage 3 will see maturity and saturation, reflected in consistent sales, followed by Stage 4, the period of sales decline. Figure 14.1 is a summary of some of the trends that are represented in each stage of a traditional product life cycle.

There are variations of this traditional cycle. As many as 11 different types of life cycle patterns have been identified in the literature, and probably more exist than this number.[11] Life cycle performance can partly be determined by market demand (external, outside the direct control of firm) and partly by marketing efforts (i.e., internal locus of control). Not only will managers want to know where their or their competitor's products are in a life cycle at any given time, they will also want to know what sort of cycle the product is likely to experience and how sensitive the product's market is to expansion efforts. It is important to note that products' fates are not necessarily at the whim of pre-determined cycles—many elements will combine to determine products' longevity.[12]

Once one is familiar with the product life cycle, product line analysis will include examining data on all products, keeping in mind each product's holistic revenue and profit implications for each stage in the life cycle.[13]

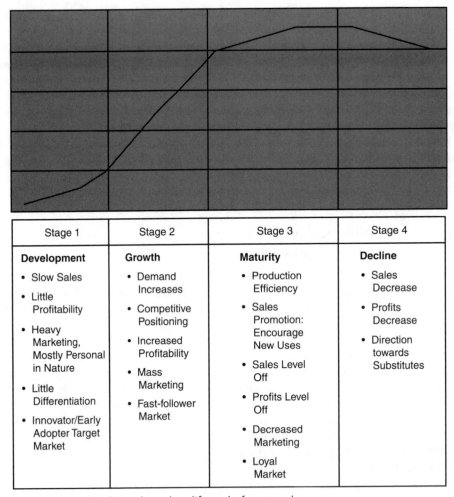

Stage 1	Stage 2	Stage 3	Stage 4
Development	**Growth**	**Maturity**	**Decline**
• Slow Sales	• Demand Increases	• Production Efficiency	• Sales Decrease
• Little Profitability	• Competitive Positioning	• Sales Promotion: Encourage New Uses	• Profits Decrease
• Heavy Marketing, Mostly Personal in Nature	• Increased Profitability	• Sales Level Off	• Direction towards Substitutes
• Little Differentiation	• Mass Marketing	• Profits Level Off	
• Innovator/Early Adopter Target Market	• Fast-follower Market	• Decreased Marketing	
		• Loyal Market	

Figure 14.1   Traditional product life cycle framework

Cost and revenue projections should be developed for the product at each stage of the product life cycle, particularly those in the future. Product success using this conceptual lens can be evaluated not based on comparisons between products, but how each product performs or has performed at the various stages. Product substitutions, extensions, sequels, and improvements can also be planned or projected by stage. Last but not least, the product life cycle can highlight profit contribution of the product, sales trends, and customer migration patterns within a valid construct.

Product Market Segmentation

A key to product line analysis is to develop an understanding of how the product is actually segmented among customers in the market. After all, the customer has to see the product in terms of features that matter to them and meets their needs, be it on price, quality, service, or other attributes. Being able to segment the market means being able to identify relatively homogeneous groups of customers, understanding what matters to these groups and how they behave. Apart from understanding the groups, product line analysis is also aided by segmenting because the process can identify if the segment is big enough to be served in a cost-effective manner.

Segments can be broken down into two types: customer-related and product-related. A segmentation perspective assumes that competition comes from other products in the same product category. For example, a company may see mint-flavored toothpaste products as competing against one another, but not competing against baking soda, a product that, aside from doing other things, can clean teeth. A customer segmentation approach, however, might see mint-flavored toothpastes as competition against baking soda, if the target group is being segmented based on their values and self-image. A customer may value baking soda over mint-flavored toothpastes if they see it as environmentally friendly, less expensive, creative, and/or it satisfies a customer segment's desire for a multi-use, all-natural product. Table 14.1 gives an example of how markets can be segmented within these categories. The answers to the product or customer-market questions in Table 14.1 can aid analysts in developing an understanding of products' overall strategies, based on needs, wants, preferences, and motivations that are revealed by this process. The answers can also provide an idea of the proportion of products purchased by segments and shed light not only on the segment where marketing may be directed, but how they are being communicated with and whether there are problems in the process that can be addressed through insightful tactics or strategies.

Table 14.1
Product- versus Customer-Related Perspectives on Segmentation

Product Related	Customer Related
Usage: How frequently is the product used?	Geographic: Local, regional, national, etc.
Benefits Desired: What are special features sought ?	Demographic: Age, gender, etc.
Price: Is the buyer price sensitive or not?	Psychographic: What customer behavior can one expect given their self-image? (For example, an "innovator" sees himself as adventurous and a risk taker and will want to be the first to adopt a new product.)
Brand Loyalty: How loyal is the product's following?	Orientation: What are customer needs in individual, work, family, or recreational profiles?
User Type: Who uses the product?	Socio-Economic: What class structure does the customer belong to, and how much disposable income is the social class expected to afford them?
Application: What is the product used for?	Family Life Cycle: What life stage is the customer in (i.e., "empty nesters" or "retirees")?

Table 14.1 *(continued)*
Product- versus Customer-Related Perspectives on Segmentation

Product Related	Customer Related
Competitor: Are customers locked in with a competitor (i.e., cellphone users)?	Psychological Segmenting: How far up is the customer on "Maslow's hierarchy of needs"? (Hierarchy of needs dictates that once our basic needs for food and shelter are met, our needs become increasingly more sophisticated.)[14]

Once this process is complete, managers should know if their or their competitors' strategic goals and product offerings are aligned. They should know if they are offering too many or not enough products to customers and which of those products are meeting the needs of desirable segments.

Understanding Positioning

Along with product positioning comes the more elusive task of deciphering how customers relate to a product's image and how that image compares with competing brands in the marketplace. The key to successful positioning is that a product delivers real desired benefits to the consumer in a form that they can easily understand and relate to.[15]

An assumption underlying most businesses is that in order to be viable, the company's goal is to grow and prosper over time. The growth can occur in profits, market share, geographical reach, and the like, but fundamentally, a company's overall product strategy in order to realize these goals will fall into the differentiation or low-cost strategy categories. Porter's Generic Strategies, as they are known, are attractive because they can be applied to one-product firms or multinational corporations. In short, the low-cost strategy seeks to gain competitive advantage by bringing a product to market, which is equivalent to competitors' in features and quality, at a lower price than the competitor. The differentiation strategy is where the company seeks to gain market share by offering a product that has superior features, quality, or services than the competitors. The low-cost and differentiation strategies can further be segmented by the scope of the product's market. The product's target can be broad (mass) or narrow (niche). The result is four generic strategies that can be applied to companies, product lines, and products. In summary, these four strategies are discussed next.

Cost Leadership

This is where enterprises try to provide low-cost products that have a mass market appeal. This requires these enterprises to employ very strict management controls and drive out costs at every level from production and distribution to sales and marketing. Examples of products in this category include the so-called "house brands," which are found at nearly every major supermarket chain. Companies using this generic strategy use their lower-cost edge to under-price competitors and attract price-sensitive buyers in great numbers to their products as a means of increasing their total profits. Alternatively, they can avoid price reductions and maintain an average price in the marketplace and use their lower cost edge to earn a higher profit margin on each unit of the product actually sold.

Differentiation

A product or business with a differentiation strategy appeals to the mass market but seeks to set it apart by offering a product that is better than the competitors in some way that matters to the customer, like features or quality. Procter & Gamble's Tide is an example of a product that appeals to a mass market and charges a premium based on its ability to fight stains, which is something that is important to people when they wash their clothes. This strategy has also pushed the Tide brand to develop innovative products like the Tide-to-Go Pen, Tide Coldwater, and Tide for High Efficiency washing machines. Consumers are typically willing to pay more for these products because of the convenience and effectiveness that they offer.

What sets the two focused strategies, discussed next, apart from cost leadership or differentiation strategies, is that the enterprise's focus is on products aimed at a narrow slice of the total market. The target segment or niche can be defined by geographic uniqueness (e.g., a restaurant chain that focuses on only the major cities of the UK), by specialized requirements in using the product (e.g., portable game playing units like the Nintendo Game Boy or Sony PlayStation Portables that are able to be played anywhere by their owners), or by special product attributes that appeal only to niche members (e.g., banks that offer certain financial products and services only to their wealthiest customers).

Generic focus strategies gain in their overall attraction as more of the following conditions are met:

- The industry has a wide variety of customers and different customer needs, thereby providing the opportunity to target products at many different segments.
- The focused segments are not being targeted by strong rivals.
- The focuser has built up unique capabilities or resources that allow it to serve the targeted niche in ways that are difficult for rivals to match.
- The niche targeted by the enterprise's products is large enough to be profitable and may also grow over time.
- The market share leaders in the larger product category don't perceive the niche as one that is crucial to their profitability.

Cost Focus

This is a low-cost strategy that targets a particular pre-determined group of buyers. Companies employing a cost-focus strategy are focused on securing a competitive advantage by serving customers in the targeted market niche at a lower price than rival competitors. An example of a company employing this strategy is Motel 6, a provider of overnight lodging in the U.S., which caters to price-conscious travelers seeking a clean, no-frills room for a night.

Differentiation Focus

A focused strategy based on differentiation aims at securing competitive advantage by offering the targeted niche customers something they perceive is more closely aligned to their own unique needs or preferences compared to the products offered by rival sellers.

This strategy focuses on a narrowly defined segment and seeks to differentiate the product based on product features, service, or convenience. The philosophy is that the focused strategy can serve the unique needs of the market better than any generalist. Local wineries often successfully employ this generic strategy.

The number and type of products offered in a product line will depend on what category the product is in. If a category is dominated by value brands with little differentiation, a variety of product types with innovative features will not be appreciated in the marketplace. Differentiation and innovative features should be saved for categories dominated by high-end niche markets where consumers are willing to pay more for product quality and features.[16]

Categories dominated by house brands where products are hard to differentiate between one another should focus on cost reduction and efficiencies, resulting in less SKUs and economies of scale.

A perceptual map can be a useful tool to understand where the consumers see firms in the market place in terms of image and product offerings. Not only can a perceptual map help managers understand where their product stands relative to other products in the marketplace, it can reveal holes or openings in the marketplace, where a company may want to direct future efforts.[17] In order to construct a perceptual map, we must know the following:

1. What criteria customers use to evaluate competitive product offerings

2. How important this criterion is in the marketplace

3. Where our product is perceived in the marketplace relative to competitors

Because positioning has an external locus of control (it is in the mind of the consumer), market research is a good way to obtain this information. Sometimes companies will conduct surveys or focus groups as a way of understanding customers' priorities and how well their product is performing in the areas that matter. Companies can also hire third-party market research firms to get unbiased feedback through surveys and data mining.

Figure 14.2 is an example of a perceptual map for laundry detergents available to customers in North America. In this example, a company would have determined on their own, or by purchasing research, that price and innovative product offerings, like special detergents for dark colors, high-efficiency washers, or organic stains, are important to the majority of purchasers. Then the company or researcher would determine how the product in question and those of the closest competitors are performing in meeting price and innovation expectations in the mind of the customer. In this example, Tide is perceived as more expensive than most competitors and most innovative as well. Persil products manufactured in Germany are the highest priced and are distributed in the U.S. by Miele, a high-end appliance company. For that reason, Persil targets a niche market of high-end customers and is not widely available.

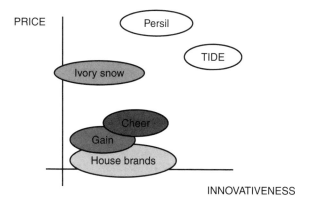

Figure 14.2   Perceptual map of laundry detergents

Resource Allocation and the Product Line

Resource allocation is tantamount to product line success. Under-capitalization will choke a product before it is able to succeed, and over-capitalization can waste valuable resources if they are better spent elsewhere. At this point in the analysis, managers will know where their product is in the expected life cycle, how the market is segmented, what is important to consumers, and how well the product is positioned to meet the needs of the target segments. From here, three factors remain that are important in determining resource allocation:

1. What are the incremental sales and profits that can be realized per unit of capital injection?

2. What are the inter-relations and dependencies that exist between products in the line?

3. How cohesive are the cost and design structures that bring the product to market?

In its simplest form, modeling techniques can be used to create sales projections based on different levels of resources allocated to a product. Modeling programs are designed to determine the optimum combination of resource allocation that is needed to maximize profits. Unfortunately, in all but the most straightforward cases, products in a line have relationships with one another that will create some sort of interdependence. For example, when a printer is discontinued, sales of cartridges that fit that printer will also be affected. If the product line was designed to minimize this affect, then multiple printers will use the same type of cartridge, and cartridge sales will be less affected.

In order to maximize supply chain performance, many companies design products that share common components. Where possible, products are also created that share the same assembly process and are made to be different at the latest possible stage. If a product is eliminated from the line, other products in the line may therefore become more expensive on a per-unit basis. Manufacturers may lose some advantage of economies of scale, like discounts on components bought in volume. It is important for the analyst and decision-making client to understand how profitability will be affected. On the other hand, the cost of bringing a new or replacement product to market can be reduced if it is designed to share the cost structure with existing products.

Case Study: eBay, Inc. in 2004

This case study provides an illustration of how you perform product line analysis along the lines just described. The analysis looks at online auctioneer eBay's product line and shows how the process described previously can answer key questions about its product lines.

eBay is a person-to-person, business-to-person, and B2B online auction service provider. eBay's mission is "to provide a global trading platform where practically anyone can trade practically anything." eBay has created the world's largest online auction community where people buy and sell goods of all kinds, including collectibles, artwork, memorabilia, and increasingly larger ticket items like cars, boats, and real estate.

eBay has some considerations in product line development:

1. Should eBay continue to grow by securing a global presence?
2. Should eBay grow their fixed price format and go toe to toe with e-tailers like Amazon.com and brick and mortar stores with online selling?

eBay will start with a product audit, examining the products in their product line, looking at sales trends, and customer migration patterns. Currently, eBay's platform supports three formats, or products in their line:

1. Online auction format, where buyers bid on items.
2. Fixed price format, where buyers have the opportunity to submit a best offer or pay a fixed "Buy it Now" price.
3. Store inventory format, where registered users have their own store pages and can manage and showcase their inventory, combine shipping, and create their own marketing plan or incentives.

eBay's sales trends are tremendous. The company's 41,000 registered users in 1996 grew to 94,900,000 registered users by the beginning of 2004, realizing a compound annual growth rate of 202%.[18] In 1996, eBay reported $7 million in merchandise sales, which grew to $24 billion in 2003, representing a compound annual growth rate of 220%. This seems to demonstrate that the value of merchandise sold is increasing even faster than the number of users, meaning that existing users are increasing their usage, while new users are being attracted. Since eBay's inception in 1996, the users have shifted in focus from collectors to bargain hunters. The fixed price format is increasing in popularity, and this could represent a migration away from the auction format toward a general e-tailing format, changing the nature of eBay's competitive landscape. This shift would bring eBay into direct competition with e-tailers and traditional retailers with online presence like Amazon.com, Staples, Best Buy, and Wal-Mart. However, eBay's CEO, Meg Whitman, is wary of abandoning the core business too soon.

The online auction industry is in a tremendous growth stage, with eBay enjoying approximately 88% market share. Figure 14.3 reveals that eBay's products have reached Stage 2, or the growth stage.

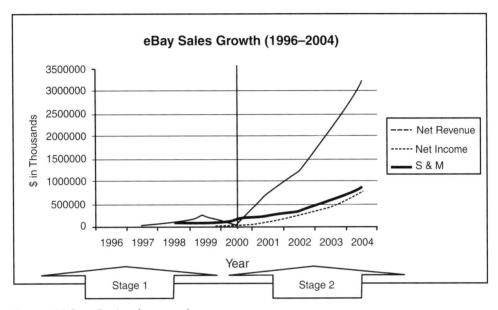

Figure 14.3   eBay's sales growth

eBay employed a first mover strategy in Stage 1. During that time, eBay avoided mass media in favor of careful PR and a community building approach. The user-friendly format attracted users who then touted eBay's benefits, and the company is now enjoying the affects of being the first to many markets and accumulating the critical mass that is creating global dominance. During Stage 2, or the growth stage, eBay's revenue is soaring, and sales and marketing costs are decreasing on a per-user basis. eBay started to use more mass-marketing techniques after 2002 and acquired many more auction formats in international markets. Stage 2 is typically when competitors will adopt a fast follower strategy and is crucial for positioning.

eBay's culture is unique in that the users have a sense of bonding with the company and other users. This phenomenon can translate to a core competence when the critical mass has been accumulated and their needs are continually anticipated and met. Although switching costs to other platforms are low, the feeling of comfort with a different platform would be hard to replicate, and the credibility that users have gained over time through eBay's rating system is not transferable to other sites.

eBay's position in the marketplace is consistent with the differentiation positioning strategy. The global Internet retail sector is very fragmented. Only 5.7% of the global sector value belongs to the top-five companies. The nature of the Internet lends itself to segments that are niche—focusing on one industry segment—but eBay has gone against the grain and resisted the urge to chase growth through traditional methods. Figure 14.4 demonstrates eBay's valuable positioning in the marketplace on the perceptual map, being the brand with the most awareness and greatest geographical scope.

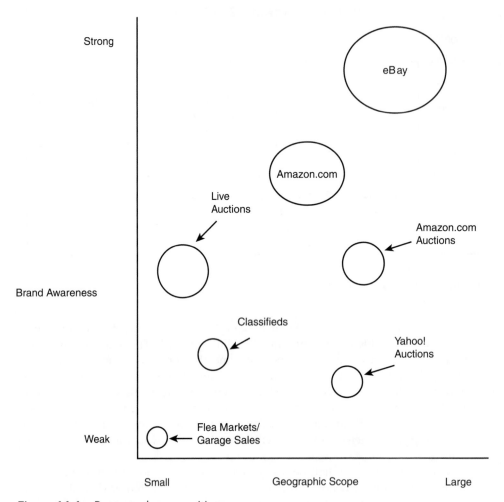

Figure 14.4   Perceptual map positions

eBay's first mover strategy meant that it beat Yahoo! Auctions and Amazon Auctions to many markets. Amazon.com is a competitor in the fixed price segment and may continue to be a closer competitor if the fixed price segment grows at eBay. Live auctions and flea markets cannot touch eBay's presence or scope, but the advantage that local outlets have is that they allow the purchaser to view the merchandise before buying.

The company is fortunate to be in a good financial position, having close to $2 billion to fund growth as of 2005. Nonetheless, the incremental sales growth per investment unit in marketing dollars appears to be quite small. Currently, there is significant inter-dependence between the formats because three of them will turn up in a search for any given item. For example, if one searches for a Burberry handbag, some sellers will have listed a fixed price, some will be auctioning the item, and some will have stores with other styles or brands of handbags for sale as well. The fact that all three are available to a buyer when they are considering making a purchase is a big part of what makes eBay attractive to many users.

The wiser money would be spent continuing international expansion and executing the first mover strategy or acquiring existing online auction houses in new markets, particularly where Internet usage is increasing. Many cultures worldwide are much more comfortable with bargaining than North American culture and may be even more receptive at first blush to eBay's platform. New markets also present opportunities to move into bigger ticket auctions, like cars and boats, which generate bigger fees, once the market is established. The fixed price format is attractive, but eBay would face fierce competition from traditional e-tailers and face a significant departure from its format and culture.

FAROUT Summary

FAROUT SUMMARY

	1	2	3	4	5
F	■	■	■		
A	■	■	■		
R	■	■	■		
O	■	■	■	■	
U	■	■	■		
T	■	■			

Figure 14.5   Product line analysis FAROUT summary

Future orientation—Medium. The focus of product line analysis is more current than future.

Accuracy—Medium. There are many factors that influence product performance, some of which include social and political forces, and not within the scope of the technique.

Resource efficiency—Medium. A lot of information is required in order to do a thorough analysis of a product line.

Objectivity—Medium to high. The process of analyzing the product line is meant to lessen some of the subjectivity that managers, particularly those with a vested interest in seeing certain results become a reality, project onto products.

Usefulness—Medium. This normally needs to be done in addition to a variety of other analyses, and as such, in and of itself offers only moderate utility.

Timeliness—Low to medium. It can take a while to conduct a very thorough product line analysis.

Related Tools and Techniques

- Customer segmentation analysis
- GE Business Screen/portfolio analysis
- Porter's Five Forces
- Product life cycle analysis
- Strategic group analysis
- SWOT analysis
- Value chain analysis

References

Buchalter, A., and H. Sakhnini (2006). "Fighting cannibalization," *McKinsey Quarterly*, 1, pp. 12–13.

Cox, W.E. (1967). "Product life cycles of marketing models," *The Journal of Business (University of Chicago)*, 40, pp. 375–384.

Dhalla, N.K., and S. Yuspeh (1976). "Forget the product life cycle concept!," *Harvard Business Review*, 54, pp. 102–111.

"eBay Canada: About eBay: Company overview." *ebay.ca*. Accessed Feb. 28, 2006: http://pages.ebay.ca/aboutebay/thecompany/companyoverview.html.

Fleisher, C.S., and B.E. Bensoussan (2003). *Strategic and Competitive Analysis: Methods and Techniques for Analyzing Business Competition*. Upper Saddle River, NJ: Prentice Hall.

Jones, M.C. (2004). "eBay lays its cards on the global table," *Brand Strategy*, September, pp. 12–13.

Lee, H.L. (2004). "The triple-A supply chain," *Harvard Business Review*, 82, October, pp. 102–112.

Lefton, L.A., Brannon, L., Boyes, M.C., and N.A. Ogden (2005). *Psychology,* 2nd edition. Toronto: Pearson Education Canada, pp. 1–757.

Levitt, T. (1960). "Marketing myopia," *Harvard Business Review*, 38, pp. 45–56.

Levitt, T. (1965). "Exploit the product life cycle," *Harvard Business Review*, 43, pp. 81–94.

Marino, L., and P. Kreiser (2006). "eBay: In a league by itself," pp. C322–C352 in Thompson, A., Gamble, J.E., and A.J. Strickland III. *Strategy: Winning in the Marketplace*, 2nd edition, New York, NY: McGraw-Hill Irwin.

Porter, M.E. (1985). *Competitive Advantage*. New York, NY: Free Press, pp. 317–382.

Quelch, J.A., Farris, P.W., and J. Olver (1987). "The product management audit: Design and survey findings," *The Journal of Consumer Marketing*, 4, pp. 45–58.

Sellers, P. "eBay's secret." *Fortune*, Oct. 18, 2004, March 2, 2006: http://money.cnn.com/magazines/fortune/fortune_archive/2004/10/18/8188091/index.htm.

Shewchuk, J. (1992). "Life cycle thinking," *CMA Magazine*, May, pp. 34–36.

Swan, J.E., and D.R. Rink (1982). "Fitting market strategy to varying product life cycles," *Business Horizons,* 25, pp. 72–76.

"The World Factbook: United States." *CIA—The World Factbook*. January 10, 2006. February 21, 2006: http://www.odci.gov/cia/publications/factbook/geos/us.html.

Tractinsky, N., and O. Lowengart (2003). "E-retailers' competitive intensity: A positioning mapping analysis," *Journal of Targeting, Measurement, and Analysis for Marketing*, 12, pp. 114–136.

Vishwanath, V., and J. Mark (1997). "Your brand's best strategy," *Harvard Business Review,* 75, pp. 123–129.

Endnotes

[1] 2005 estimate of 1.14% comes from the CIA *World Factbook*.

[2] Quelch, Ferris, and Olver, 1987.

[3] Lee, 2004, p. 105.

[4] Levitt, 1965.

[5] Cox, 1967.

[6] Shewchuk, 1992.

[7] Dhalla and Yuspeh, 1976.

[8] Buchalter and Sakhnini, 2006.

[9] Buchalter and Sakhnini, 2006.

[10] Cox, 1967; Fleisher and Bensoussan, 2003.

[11] Swan and Rink, 1982.

[12] Fleisher and Bensoussan, 2003.

[13] Shewchuk, 1992.

[14] Lefton, Brannon, Boyes, and Ogden, 2005.

[15] Tractinsky and Lowengart, 2003.

[16] Vishwanath and Mark, 1997.

[17] Tractinsky and Lowengart, 2003.

[18] Marino and Kreiser, 2006.

Win/Loss Analysis

Short Description

Win/loss analysis (WLA) is a cost-effective, insightful, and ethical method for gathering and analyzing information about your market, customers, and competitors. WLA identifies your customer's perceptions of specific sales situations and how you compare to your competitors. It provides a window as to why a customer is buying or not buying your products and/or services. The analysis provides information about the performance of both your firm and your competitors. This information can then be actively used to focus sales staff more effectively in the marketplace and also to inform research and development of products.

Background

Many companies believe they are already doing WLA, as they do keep track of their wins and losses and do conduct post mortems. However, these results are generally not shared across the firm; only salespeople are involved, and a history of "lessons learned" is lost.

WLA is a management tool that allows managers to understand the effectiveness of their sales team and the effectiveness of competitors. It is an analytical tool that sits well in the competitive intelligence framework, providing knowledge about a firm's sales performance. If you know yourself and your competitors from a customer perspective, then your ability to improve your sales success is increased.

WLA requires the gathering of direct feedback from a client or potential client about why you won or lost a specific sale or contract. It must include both wins and losses. The wins commonly highlight your firm's strengths and your competition's weaknesses, while the losses typically highlight your firm's weaknesses and your competition's strengths.[1]

The feedback obtained from a number of these interviews is analyzed. The results illustrate your firm's position in the market and that of your competitors. WLA provides information you can actively use to improve both the performance of your sales force and your existing products, and to guide your firm in the research and development of new products.

To be most effective, a win/loss program should be established as an ongoing process conducted on a regular basis by a third-party supplier for maximum objectivity. Key elements suggested by Schulz[2] include the following:

- Ongoing (not a temporary event around a particular client, product, or sales representative)
- Uses customer feedback (rather than or in addition to sales representative feedback)
- Timing (within a reasonably short time following the buying decision)
- Employs a consistent methodology
- Consists of clearly defined users

The feedback incorporating the preceding elements and obtained using the WLA process provides more detailed and useful information than the traditional sales post mortem. A sales post mortem involves your sales team discussing its experience of the sale after it is won or lost. WLA directly involves the decision maker with the client firm responsible for the sale or non-sale. It provides access to information your client may use in deciding whether or not to do business with you that your sales team may not aware of; for example, internal budget constraints or the nature of deals offered by your competitors. It gives insight into the client's relationship with both your own sales team and your competitor's sales team and into the market perception of your products and after sales service.

Strategic Rationale and Implications

WLA is a unique tool that brings together all the elements of strategy—information about customers, competitors, and your own firm—within the context of a most critical element for a business, the buying decision. As a market listening tool, it is designed to provide a firm with information that can actively be used to increase its sales. By seeking feedback directly from the target market and subjecting this to analysis, a firm can gain a more objective understanding of its place in the market and use this to improve its position.

From win/loss interviews, a firm can identify how a competitor is developing their products and/or services or whether they have or have not delivered on promises. It can provide an avenue to re-open doors with former clients. As a tool, it makes existing and potential clients realize the commitment your firm has to maintaining good customer relationships.

However, the strategic implications of WLA are highly dependent on the quality of the raw data. The raw data gathered from clients should be free from any political or strategic bias and subjective perspective—particularly where employees within a firm may distort information. Sales staff, for example, are not the best group to conduct WLA, as they often may be too biased or emotionally involved with their accounts to be objective when conducting a WLA. Many firms employ third-party interviewers to gather the feedback for

WLA specifically to avoid subjective influences from tainting the data and conduct parallel interviews with relevant sales staff, as well as clients, to allow comparison of these differing perspectives of the same sale/non-sale.

The results of WLA performed on feedback interviews will give information about sales performance, sales opportunities, market perception of your and your competitors' products, and your competitors' strategies. It can provide a measurement of how your firm is positioned with decision makers and key influencers within a client's firm. When acted on, this information can enable your firm to improve sales, increase market share, understand the market to maximize business opportunities, and focus marketing and sales resources to increase revenue.

Naylor identifies tactical and strategic benefits flowing from WLA. Tactical benefits tend to focus on sales performance, while strategic ones flow beyond the sales team to assist with product management, mergers and alliances, and product research and development. These are summarized in Table 15.1.

Table 15.1
Tactical and Strategic Benefits of WLA

Tactical Benefits	Strategic Benefits
■ Improve sales results by helping the sales team win more business.	■ Increase firm profits and revenue over a longer period of time.
■ Improve client retention by following up on sales wins to identify how/why you win business.	■ Forecast revenue streams more accurately.
■ Identify regularly why/how you lose against each of your competitors and devise ways to enhance your sales positioning.	■ Enhance the product/service offering and mix.
■ Establish an action plan to address gaps in perceptions that may exist between clients and the sales force.	■ Influence more timely product/service development.
■ Change behavior and culture to improve client service, maintenance programs, or delivery based on accurate, timely feedback from clients.	■ Alter the firm's culture to a more client service/needs focus.
■ Identify traits of your successful salespeople. Conversely, identify traits of unsuccessful salespeople.	■ Select appropriate market alliances with increased confidence.
■ Predict likelihood of winning/losing a sale more accurately and therefore identify when to walk away from business.	■ Support the firm's early warning system.
■ Change the sales mindset from one of making excuses for sales loss.	■ Identify competitor trends over time to enable action.

Source: Adapted from Naylor, E. (2002). "Increasing sales through win/loss analysis," *Competitive Intelligence Magazine*, 5(5), pp. 5–8.

WLA must not be confused with typical sales post mortems. First, analysts have the opportunity to learn about customers' perceptions. Customers' perceptions are the basis for their decision-making processes and ultimately impact a firm's sales performance. As Ritchie points out, "widely held perceptions, or misconceptions, must not be discounted. Instead they must be managed or changed in future sales encounters."

Second, WLA should be an independent evaluation and conducted regularly to allow medium- and long-term trends in the market to be identified. Most firms adopt a monthly or quarterly cycle.

Third, when conducted systematically and regularly, WLA enables a firm to keep a close eye on its market, to monitor its own performance, and to gain timely feedback on its strategies and practices.

Strengths and Advantages

WLA is a systematic analysis of nominated sales results—both wins and losses. It encompasses feedback from strategically important existing clients, former clients, and potential clients.

Conducting win/loss interviews is a direct demonstration to your clients and potential clients that your firm values its relationship with them.

Interviews are conducted as close as possible to the actual sale or non-sale being investigated to ensure accurate recall of the circumstances. Because interviews are conducted by an independent third-party interviewer, information bias is limited, and particular issues relevant to its business are covered in a more transparent way. Obtaining information that addresses specific issues ensures meaningful comparison can be made when analyzing the responses obtained at individual interviews.

Regular and systematic WLA processes provides not only immediate feedback, but can also be used to compare and uncover trends over time.

The WLA process allows for direct feedback on what the decision-making criteria employed by your clients, in awarding your firm their business or taking it to a competitor, are. An expert interviewer can go beyond the standard questionnaire to probe a client and give him or her a chance to directly express their needs and preferences. This in turn gives your firm the opportunity to make meaningful changes acting on customer advice to improve practices and win new sales.

The benefits of conducting WLA extend beyond providing tactics to improve sales. WLA also has an impact on marketing, product improvement, and research and development. Information coming out of WLA can be distributed throughout the firm to aid in overall performance improvements. The results obtained from WLA may be used to inform other strategic programs within a firm. For example, it may assist in the development of training programs for sales staff or assist in product improvement projects.

The WLA process will give an indication in real time of the market's response to new business strategies and products. It will enable the firm to identify and respond to trends over time in the market and assist in sales forecasting. If undertaken in a systematic way, it will assist in growing revenues both in the short and long term.

In summary, WLA establishes a market listening and positioning tool with consistent analysis allowing for improved and informed decision making in an organization by

- Helping decision makers understand the customer's perspective.
- Providing objective input into sales and marketing strategies.
- Identifying opportunities, including target markets, key sales propositions, and winning attitudes.
- Improving business performance at the expense of competitors.

Weaknesses and Limitations

WLA is based on data obtained from interviews arising out of sales results. It is to that extent reactive and event-driven. Care must be taken to ensure that a good mix of sales results is followed up. Results will be skewed, for example, if in one round of WLA, only successful sales to existing clients are analyzed.

A key weakness of this process is that interviews are only as good as the interviewer conducting them. When an interviewer is inexperienced or has not been thoroughly briefed on the sensitivities of the market in question, the quality of the data obtained will be compromised. An inexperienced interviewer may lack the confidence to ask questions beyond those contained in the standard questionnaire developed for the WLA process. Even the most experienced interviewer will be unable to gain all the useful information potentially available if they are not sufficiently aware of the issues in the market to know when to probe for further detail in an interview and when it is not relevant.

There is no value in information gathered if it is not systematically disseminated to those who can act on it. As is a danger with any information-gathering process in a firm, it is possible for the results of WLA to end up being fiercely guarded rather than distributed. On the other hand, it is possible to undermine the process by giving all of the results to everyone and no one having time to read them, let alone act on them.

The value of WLA will only be as good as the system set up to inform interested parties of the results. Information taken out of context—for example, in an attempt to extrapolate widely from one individual analysis—will not be reliable. The true value of WLA is in the ongoing process.

WLA must be conducted systematically and in a timely fashion. Interviews must be organized and followed up as soon as possible after the sale is won or lost. Delay in interviewing may result in inaccurate recall, so the analysis performed does not reflect the real reasons behind the decision to do business with your firm or with your competition. WLA itself should be conducted regularly to give truly comparable results. The analysis must not, for example, be shelved while more important issues are dealt with, as sporadic WLA will not give reliable information.

The fact that WLA focuses on sales results may lead to a politicizing of the process within a firm. The sales team may be reluctant to cooperate fully with the process if they feel they are being singled out unfairly. Other parts of the firm may try to ambush the process to push their own agendas. The team responsible for running WLA must be very carefully chosen and trained to ensure the members fully understand the WLA process and are prepared to implement it properly.

Process for Applying the Technique

Numerous writers in the field suggest that there are up to seven steps to consider in creating and implementing a WLA process. These steps are shown in Figure 15.1. Each of the steps in the WLA process are described next.

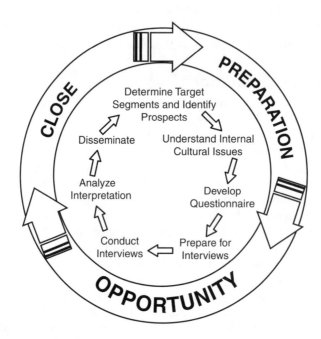

Figure 15.1   The win/loss process

Step 1: Determine the Target Segments and Identify Prospects

Target the right accounts to analyze and the right interval to conduct analysis. A good starting point is to look at the accounts that generate most of your firm's revenue (the 80/20 rule—80% of a firm's revenue comes from 20% of its customers). However, other considerations in choosing whom to interview may include whether your firm wishes to pick up business from particular potential clients or ex-clients or whether there are plans to introduce new products to the market. Specific companies that meet the firm's chosen criteria need to be identified and singled out and reviewed to ensure that the targets are worth the investment.

Powell and Allgaier suggest that one needs to start by segmenting the specific market group or target, particularly if the purpose of WLA is to identify sales sources. Once target segments and their criteria are identified, key information needs to be collected to qualify potential prospects.

The interval over which you run your WLA will depend on your firm's requirements. Monthly analysis requires a greater commitment of time and money but will provide very quick market feedback. Some firms prefer to run a large win/loss study annually. The interval chosen will also be affected by how quickly you wish to be able to act on the information you obtain as well as the frequency of sales opportunities experienced.

Step 2: Understand Internal Cultural Issues

Understanding your firm's culture will provide a guide as to how information will be used. For example, in a learning and consultative culture, sales representatives and their managers might become highly involved in both the collection and evaluation of information.

It is also important to ensure that involvement in the process extends beyond the sales team. Other key stakeholders need to be clearly identified, and creating cross-functional teams may be a way of addressing the differing needs of critical groups.

The results of WLA have implications that go beyond increasing sales. To get the most out of the process, the team running the program should include members from other departments and have the support of senior management. Schulz points out the wisdom of involving senior management (even up to the CEO) to help to keep internal politics out of WLA. The objectives of the program must also be well defined. The roles of designing and implementing the program should be clearly understood, as these may be assigned to different people.

Those who are likely to be affected by the information obtained from the WLA program should be educated about the process to ensure they support it. This should reduce internal resistance to WLA. Some staff, particularly in sales, may feel that their performance is being unfairly singled out for attention by the program. Staff should be reassured that the WLA program has wider implications for the firm than simply monitoring the performance of individuals in the sales team.

The decision must be made whether to use an independent third party to conduct the interviews or whether to use your sales team. Use of a third-party interviewer has cost implications. It will also require a commitment of time from internal staff to brief the interviewer. The use the firm intends to make of the information will also direct the decision of who conducts interviews. When the results of the interviews will be used in part to evaluate the performance of members of the sales team, Schulz suggests keeping sales staff involvement in the interview process to a minimum. However, parallel interviews of client and sales representative can reveal valuable information about the different perceptions they have of the same sales negotiations.

Step 3: Develop the Questionnaire

A WLA questionnaire needs to cover a number of broad areas. Naylor suggests four, as follows:

- **Sales attributes**—This will cover the professionalism of your sales team, the quality of the relationship your firm has with the client, and the esteem in which the client holds your firm compared to your competitors.

- **Company reputation**—This includes questions about the perception of your firm's and your competitors' image in the marketplace, the stability of your firm, and its reliability as a supplier and the quality and performance of your products.

- **Product attributes**—This is a wide area basically covering whether your products actually perform as promoted and covers issues of price and technology.

- **Service issues**—These questions will cover the delivery and implementation, maintenance/after sales service, and training provided to clients.

Depending on the purpose of the WLA, other areas that might be included in the questionnaire could address matters relating to how the purchase decision will be made. Will it be made by a group or individual? What are the decision criteria? When will the decision be made? Are there other stakeholders involved?

Another consideration will be the sophistication of the analysis you plan to carry out on the results. When analysis will stop at the quick identification of market trends, numerous detailed questions may not be necessary. When statistical analysis is the aim, the information must be sufficiently detailed to address the required level of analysis and still be of practical value.

Standard issues need to be identified in the questionnaire to ensure that the data from multiple interviews can be effectively analyzed together. At the same time, some flexibility in the interview process will enable valuable exploration of individual situations.

Step 4: Preparation for the Interviews

The interviewer now needs to be briefed about the significance of winning or losing each sale. To get the most out of the interview, the interviewer must be aware of all relevant details and sensitivities of the sale/non-sale being investigated.

When an interviewer does not fully understand the background of a particular sale negotiation, he or she is unlikely to be able to stray from the standard form questionnaire to probe for detailed situation-specific feedback. Specific and detailed information can greatly enhance the overall value of the WLA process.

Step 5: Conducting Interviews

Carefully consider how you wish to go about conducting interviews. This decision will depend to an extent on whether you plan to use a third-party interviewer or your own sales team. Experts in this field highly recommend the use of an independent third party to avoid interview results being skewed by any pre-existing relationship between a salesperson and his or her client. For example, the interviewer may direct the responses they receive with unintentional body language cues.

One option is to conduct interviews by telephone. This is a common practice in the U.S. and is quite time and cost effective. However, in some situations—for example, for big-ticket purchase items—it may be preferable to conduct face-to-face interviews in order to obtain optimal results in a particular situation. Here you will need to rely on your sales team to advise when face-to-face interviews would be better. It should be noted that face-to-face interviews provide a much greater opportunity to garner in-depth information and to build on customer relationships than do telephone interviews.

Interviews should be conducted as close in time to the actual sale/non-sale so to avoid memories of the negotiations fading. Some firms may also interview the salesperson involved in the particular sale/non-sale to investigate differences between the firm's own internal perception of the negotiations and those of the client.

Step 6: Analysis and Interpretation

Once the interviews are completed, the results need to be tallied and analyzed. The interviewer will generally summarize each completed interview and provide an analysis of key trends or issues identified as a result of the interviews in a report. If the interviews are carried out by internal staff, then training and support must be provided to carry out these tasks effectively and to aid with the report development. WLA must be given clear priority over other duties when analysis is due to be done. The value of WLA can be compromised by sporadic rather than regular analysis.

As the WLA program continues over time, trends will emerge from the analytical results. These need to be interpreted in light of the firm's strategic and competitive intentions.

Further, over time, WLA becomes more valuable in identifying trends that impact product development and sales forecasting. Companies have been known to adjust their product plans in light of client feedback from WLA.

Step 7: Dissemination

The report and results can now be disseminated. There will be information arising out of WLA that is relevant to different departments in the firm such as research and development, marketing, and sales. The program team should ensure that each department receives the information relevant to it. This should hopefully increase the likelihood that the information is read and supports decision making in the appropriate department. The results may be presented in different forms depending on preferences.

Different staff will have different preferences for how the WLA results should be communicated to them—from verbal presentations at the completion of interviews to half-yearly reports. Schulz highlights a WLA program where senior management received a monthly report summarizing quantified results, while the sales team had results incorporated into their regular e-mail alerts.

Properly conducted WLA is one of the most valuable tools for sales account strategies. WLA helps firms understand the value of customers and the cost of retaining them versus acquiring new ones. Simultaneously, it allows firms to capture best practices in sales and identify trends to enhance future revenue streams.

Case Study: Microsoft Business Solutions

Microsoft Business Solutions (now known as Microsoft Dynamics) provides a line of financial, customer relationship, and supply chain management solutions to help businesses improve their performances. Delivered through a network of specialized partners, these integrated business management solutions work with Microsoft software to streamline processes across an entire business and include applications and services for retailers, manufacturers, wholesale distributors, and service companies, doing business domestically or in multiple countries.

At the time of this case study, Microsoft Business Solutions was well positioned to be the dominant player in the mid-level financial software market with its Great Plains solution. This solution provides a financial, analytics, and business management system that unifies data and processes across a business, integrating easily with other solutions, and connecting employees, customers, and suppliers regardless of time or location.

With a strong product and a large sales force, Microsoft had the potential of winning the majority of competitive opportunities.

The challenge facing Microsoft Business Solutions was to understand the competitive environment in order to leverage its strengths and capitalize on the weaknesses of its competitors with the goal of winning the lion's share of opportunities.

Understanding the Environment

Primary Intelligence conducted a win/loss assessment of Microsoft Great Plain's previous 100 opportunities, comprised of 50 wins and 50 losses. Information was gathered on purchase selection criteria, primary competitors' strengths and weaknesses, the efficacy of various marketing activities, and customer satisfaction.

Analysis of the gathered information yielded a clear picture of the competitive environment, focusing on areas of differentiation—both in product and in sales methodology. It became apparent that Microsoft Business Solutions had clear advantages in certain areas that had not been previously identified and that although the competition was strong in most areas, they exhibited specific weaknesses that contributed to Microsoft wins.

Learning from Their Losses

Two important, related things Microsoft Business Solutions learned from their losses were that: a) prospects didn't perceive that they or their partners understood their needs; and b) one of the ways prospects expressed this was in lower marks for industry experience and knowledge.

Because of the knowledge gained in the win/loss report, Microsoft Business Solutions subsequently announced industry-focused strategies in four major industry sectors that they believe will help them and their partners be more successful in the mid-market.

Leveraging the Data

As part of the Primary Intelligence solution, senior analysts helped Microsoft Business Solutions leverage the data in the report to improve their competitive position in the marketplace, provide even further insight into the competitive sales cycle that Microsoft Business Solutions' channel partners currently face in today's market conditions, and gain important insight into potential new strategies and programs that could be implemented to ultimately help the partner win more business in competitive situations.

Keeping Current

Another valuable tool for Microsoft Business Solutions was the comparison Primary Intelligence provided with the previous year's win/loss study. Analysis of the differences showed that certain shortcomings had been addressed, while new potential problems had surfaced. It also showed the progress, or lack of progress, of the competition, making it possible to assess new threats and exploit new opportunities.

This ongoing assessment made it possible for Microsoft Business Solutions to track the dynamics of the industry, respond quickly to change, and stay one step ahead of the competition.[3]

FAROUT Summary

FAROUT SUMMARY

	1	2	3	4	5
F	■	■	■	■	
A	■	■	■		
R	■	■	■		
O	■	■	■		
U	■	■	■	■	■
T	■	■			

Figure 15.2   Win/loss analysis FAROUT summary

Future orientation—Medium to long term. Each time WLA is conducted, information will be obtained about how to improve sales by optimizing the focus of sales resources. Over the long term, market trends are revealed and can be used to fine tune strategic planning, research, and development.

Accuracy—Medium. Accuracy will depend on the integrity of the interviews conducted. Use of an independent third party will improve accuracy.

Resource efficiency—Medium to high. A third party specialist will be able to run a firm's WLA program very efficiently, albeit in a more costly manner. When internal staff take a greater role, there will be a decrease in the resource efficiency due to the utilization of staff time.

Objectivity—Medium to high. When interviews are conducted by a third party, objectivity should be high. However, use of staff to conduct interviews will probably result in a lowering of objectivity as internal biases creep in.

Usefulness—High. WLA provides useful practical and insightful information on customer perceptions and competitors' activities.

Timeliness—Low to medium. The timeliness of the information obtained will depend on the interval chosen for the WLA process and how often it is repeated.

Related Tools and Techniques

- Benchmarking
- Blindspot analysis
- Comparative cost analysis
- Competitive positioning analysis

- Competitor analysis
- Customer segmentation and needs analysis
- Customer value analysis
- Functional capability and resource analysis
- Scenario analysis
- SWOT analysis
- Value chain analysis

References

Gale, B. (1994). *Managing Customer Value: Creating Quality and Service that Customers Can See*. New York, NY: Free Press.

Levy, S. (2003). "A call to integrate: CI, customer relationship management, and sales force automation," *Competitive Intelligence Magazine*, March–April.

Naylor, E. (2002). "Increasing sales through win/loss analysis," *Competitive Intelligence Magazine*, 5(5), pp. 5–8.

Powell, T., and C. Allgaier (1998). "Enhancing sales and marketing effectiveness through competitive intelligence," *Competitive Intelligence Review*, 9(4), pp. 29–41.

Powell, T., and C. Allgaier (2003). "How high is your sales IQ?," *Competitive Intelligence Magazine*, 6(6), pp. 30–35.

Prescott, J., and C. Miree (2000). "TAP-IN to strategic and tactical intelligence in the sales and marketing functions," *Competitive Intelligence Review*, 11(1), pp. 4–16.

Ritchie, J. (1992). "Competitor assessment tools: win/loss analysis," *Competitive Intelligence Review*, Winter, pp. 18–19.

Schulz, S. (2002). "Seven steps to building a successful win/loss program," *Competitive Intelligence Magazine*, 5(5), pp. 9–12.

Web sites (all accessed March 12, 2006):

www.graffgroup.com/winlossarticle.html

www.lassiterassociates.com/winloss_casestudy.html

www.marketing-intelligence.co.uk/resources/competitor-analysis.htm

www.primary-intel.com.solutions/winloss.aspx

www.webpronews.com/ebusiness/sales/wpn-9-20041209HowWinLossAnalysisCanImproveYourSalesPerformance.html

Endnotes

[1] Ritchie, 1992.

[2] Schulz, 2002.

[3] Source: Web site: http://www.primary-intel.com/solutions/winloss.aspx, Primary Intelligence (accessed March 12, 2006).

16

Strategic Relationship Analysis

Short Description

Strategic relationship analysis (SRA) involves the study of strategic inter-firm relationships to determine their present and potential future competitive impacts. Strategic relationships (SRs) are found in the form of alliances, consortia, joint ventures, networks, and partnerships. They are all cooperative arrangements in which the competitive success of the partners is bound together to some degree.

Background

Strategic relationships were studied by international business scholars in the early 1970s. Most of the mainstream economics and industrial organization research struggled to fit SRs within the predominant "theory of the firm" that had guided knowledge development to that time. By the 1990s, inter-firm relationships began to be addressed as part of the quickly developing organizational economics field.[1]

Since the early 1990s, there has been an explosion of research into all forms of SRs, using approaches such as historical industrial marketing, negotiation analysis, organization economics, organizational sociology, population ecology, resource-based view of the firm, social network theory, and strategy and general management. Researchers have mostly assessed how SRs are formed and managed, with some more recently trying to understand how they relate to various performance outcomes.

Scholars have attempted to classify SRs across a range of variables, including but not limited to duration of commitment, extent of joint decision-making, nature of contract, degree of interdependence, degree of resource sharing, and degree of overlap among their value chains.[2] One way of illustrating the range of relationships is to examine many of the popular forms of relationships, as shown in Figure 16.1.

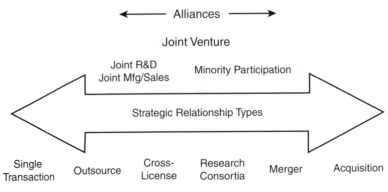

Figure 16.1   Common forms of SRs

In this instance, we are particularly interested in inter-firm relationships between business organizations. This is not to discount the value of management network analysis, which examines the relationships between individuals within and around an organization. Indeed, many of the concepts developed at the micro-level of network analysis are adaptable for use at the more macro-level of inter-organizational or inter-firm analysis, and vice versa. Common forms of strategic inter-firm relationships include, but are not limited to, those described next.

Consortia—An association of firms who cooperate for some definite purpose. Cooperation is normally formed through contracts. Each party retains its separate legal status, and the consortium's control over each participant is generally limited to activities involving the joint endeavor, particularly the allocation of profits. A well-known consortium is Airbus Industrie, one of the world's premier airplane manufacturers that operates mainly in Europe. Airbus is owned by EADS and British Aerospace. EADS itself is a merger of France's Aeropspatiale-Matra, Germany's Daimler-Chrysler Aerospace, and Spain's Construcciones Aeronauticas, all of whom were originally separate partners in the consortium. Airbus' status as a consortium means that profits accrue to the partner firms relative to their ownership interests.

Constellations/alliance groups/strategic networks—A *constellation* is a set of firms linked together through alliances that compete in a particular competitive domain, business, market, or technology. These are portfolios of alliances that come together either formally or informally within a larger network. Popular examples of these constellations are the global airline relationships that compete under the Star Alliance global partnership, OneWorld, or SkyTeam Global Alliance umbrellas.

Joint ventures (JVs)—Contractual agreements bringing together two or more organizations for the purpose of executing a particular business undertaking. The contracting parties form a new legal entity and agree to share in the profits and losses of the JV. These can be either operating or non-operating forms. Operating JVs create a new firm with its own facilities to perform designated functions. Non-operating JVs are purely administrative or legal entities that contract with their parent firms for certain activities.

Licensing agreements—The granting of permission by a firm to use intellectual property rights, such as patents technology, or trademarks under certain defined conditions. The sponsor is typically a larger and more established partner that provides the smaller party with needed capital to develop a promising product. These can include simple product development funding agreements with or without options to acquire the resulting output or non-specific development funding that was targeted to help the sponsor obtain access to more preliminary developmental work or research that may not be immediately applicable to its business.

Mergers and acquisitions (M&As)—Sometimes viewed as an alternative strategy to an alliance because the relationship involves a complete transfer of ownership of one organization to the other (that is, the relationship essentially ends after the acquisition is completed). These need to be considered and compared as strategic options for one another.[3] M&As are especially well suited for situations where the popular forms of SRs do not go far enough in providing a firm with access to the resources it needs to compete more effectively. Many M&As are driven by strategies to achieve one of the following objectives:[4]

- Allow the acquiring firm to immediately gain more market share.
- Eliminate surplus capacity in an industry by removing the "fat" from bloated operations.
- Facilitate a firm's entry to new geographic territories or international markets.
- Extend the firm's business into new product or service categories.
- Provide speedier access to developing technologies as opposed to performing time-consuming R&D.
- Lead the convergence of existing industries whose boundaries are being blurred by disruption and new market opportunities.

Minority investments—A relationship in which one firm makes an investment in the shares of another, but whose ownership of the firm is less than 50 percent of its outstanding shares. These are often made by large, established businesses that make purchases in high-potential businesses at an early stage of those businesses' development.

Networks—An intricately connected system of firms. Derived from social network analysis, this is the study of the structural form of the ties that link organizations or individuals.[5] It is a particularly useful tool for mergers and acquisitions, JV analysis, and interfirm relationships.

Outsourcing—Work is performed for a firm by people other than the firm's full-time employees. The two big drivers behind outsourcing are that outsource providers can provide services better, cheaper, or more quickly than the firm can or that it allows the firm to focus its capabilities on what it does best in the marketplace.

Strategic alliances (SAs)—Agreements between organizations in which each mutually commits resources to achieve shared objectives. Firms may form strategic alliances with a wide variety of players: customers, suppliers, competitors, universities, or divisions of government. Through strategic alliances, firms can improve competitive positioning, gain entry to new markets, supplement critical skills, and share the risk or cost of major development projects. When these cut across national boundaries, and depending on how many boundaries are involved, they are sometimes referred to as cross-national, multinational, or global strategic alliances. Others define these more restrictively; for example, Professor Benjamin Gomes-Casseres of Brandeis University views them as open-ended, incomplete agreements with shared control that create value by combining the capabilities of separate firms. An "incomplete" agreement means that the full terms or conditions of the alliance are not fully established at its conception because if they were, the need for a strategic alliance would not exist. Professor Gomes-Casseres summarizes why these are used when he states, "With an alliance, you can pinpoint where the greatest value creation potential lies and form the partnership around those specific areas only."

Strategic Rationale

Over the last few decades, firms across nearly every industry and in all parts of the world have elected to form SRs to help them accomplish their strategic initiatives and enhance their competitiveness in domestic and international markets. There is evidence that firms are increasingly looking to SRs as a way of achieving greater scale, incorporating new expertise, or quickly moving into a new geographic region, particularly if they view the complexity and resources required to merge with, or acquire another, firm to be too daunting. Gomes-Casseres notes that we now understand better about how firms and alliances are organized, but are still lagging in understanding how these relationships impact marketplace dynamics; nevertheless, there are a number of reasons why organizations pursue these relationships as a means of enhancing their competitiveness.

Purposes Served by SRs

SRs can mean different things to different organizations. Relationships, like alliances and JVs, serve many strategic purposes; in other words, helping the organization position itself for the longer term, making uncommon marketplace moves, enhancing its competitiveness, and allocating significant resources. The competitive attraction of relationships is in allowing firms to bundle competences and resources in a joint effort that is more valuable than when they are kept separate.

SRs have become a more prominent tool in supporting a firm's pursuit of competitiveness. There are a number of reasons for this increased popularity of SRs; the prominent ones are identified in Table 16.1.

Table 16.1
Reasons for Engaging in Strategic Inter-Firm Relationships

Ability to access resources or enter new markets—particularly in gaining participation in new geographic regions or territories in globalizing marketplaces.

Competitive complexity has grown, and no single firm can acquire and manage the needed resources and capabilities to always best serve their current and prospective customers.

Exchange information—this is related to a desire to reduce risk and lower information search costs.

Expedite new products or services to market more quickly—SRs can accelerate a firm's ability to speed up its entry when a partner has further developed capabilities or resources.

Table 16.1 (continued)
Reasons for Engaging in Strategic Inter-Firm Relationships

Exert collective lobbying and political strength—this is particularly important in cross-border policy and regulatory decision making matters.

Improve access to new technology—strategic cooperation is a much-favored approach in industries where new technological developments are occurring at a rapid pace along many different paths and where advances in one technology spill over to impact others.

Improve production, sales, research, and development efforts.

Inhibit competitors—particularly through things like the formulation of industry standards of activity or conduct.

Lower costs by achieving economies of scale in things like manufacturing or marketing, improving supply chain efficiency, or improving the productivity of certain functions.

Lower the risks of new product development or research and development activities through pooling of expertise.

Organic growth is typically no longer sufficient to appease executives' and shareholders' demands for steady and impressive growth.

Shortened product life cycles mean that firms need to accelerate their ability to generate return on products, and SRs can be the best means for "stepping on this accelerator."

Firms have a range of options for achieving enhanced growth and competitiveness. In fact, there is empirical evidence that points to the substantial financial and strategic value of SRs, including but not limited to the following:

- A 1999 survey on global alliances by Accenture Consulting showed that strategic alliances accounted for an average of 26 percent of Fortune 500 firms' revenue, which was up from 11 percent only five years earlier, and that alliances accounted for 6 to 15 percent of the market value of the average firm.[6]

- Firms, such as Cisco, which use acquisitions and alliances appropriately, grow faster than rivals do.[7]

- Studies demonstrated that the 15 most successful strategic alliances increased shareholder value by $72 billion, while the 15 least successful ones generated a loss of market capitalization of around $43 billion.[8]

- American firms announced 74,000 acquisitions and 57,000 SAs between 1996 and 2001. During that period, the acquisitions' combined value was driven upward by $12 trillion.[9]

Developing and maintaining successful relationships in a variety of forms with other firms is critical to achieving competitive advantage for many firms.[10] Firms like Cisco, HP, IBM, Oracle, and Procter & Gamble, among others, are increasingly looking to alliances to enhance their competitive capabilities and win new marketplaces. Relationships have also become more critical to the successful execution of business strategies, particularly in the global marketplace. They are a flexible alternative to acquisition or growing organically and can provide better access to resources and capabilities. With the growing number and complexity of relationships, however, most firms are not as process focused and disciplined as those whose relationship successes are commonly heard about in the general and business media.

There is always an element of co-operation present in the realm of competition; even long-time rivals form relationships to achieve common aims. Notable examples are the Airbus consortium of European aircraft manufacturers described earlier, different banks working together to launch Visa and Mastercard, the Sematech consortium of U.S. semiconductor manufacturers, and milk and dairy farmers using the Dairy Farmers of America organization to achieve cooperative marketing, distribution, supplies purchasing, and market access in that agricultural sector. The development of trust and commitment in these collaborative and competitive relationships will usually lead to more beneficial outcomes.[11]

SRs take on a greater role for multinational corporations in a rapidly globalizing marketplace. A firm that seeks global market leadership requires relationships to assist it in accomplishing what it cannot easily do alone. For example, SRs can help a firm get into critical country markets more quickly than it can alone, acquire inside knowledge about unfamiliar markets and cultures through its relationships with local partners, or access valuable skills and competencies that are concentrated in particular geographic locations.[12]

Two Key Strategic Relationship Processes

All SRs will compose at least the following two critical processes that will be of prime interest to the business and competitive analyst:

1. The process of forming the strategic relationship
2. The process of managing the relationship

Each of these processes should be studied by the analyst as they can offer clues that can impact a rival's, or your own firm's, competitiveness.

Although successful SRs can be prime vehicles for future growth and increase the shareholder value of the participating parties, many firms are finding it increasingly difficult to capture the full value of their relationships. It is commonly accepted that a majority of strategic alliances under-perform or end prematurely, and a number of the failed relationships have resulted in dramatic decreases in market capitalization.[13] Two primary reasons for relationship failure are insufficient attention to the working relationship between partners and lack of a corporate alliance management capability. Firms that have demonstrated the best performance in alliance management are those for whom relationship competencies are a corporate capability and the relationship management process is viewed as a central feature to their firm's success.

Gomes-Casseres identified 10 factors to be critical to success in both alliance formation and management processes:

1. Alliances must serve a clear strategic purpose that is related to the larger business strategy of the firm.
2. Partners must have complementary objectives and capabilities.
3. Partners must be able to work on those tasks in the relationship for which they are uniquely qualified.

4. Incentives must be structured to encourage co-operation among the partners.

5. Areas of potential conflict between the partners must be identified in advance and minimized.

6. Communication must be active, two-way, and candid to encourage the development of shared trust.

7. Personnel must move in both directions between partners.

8. Partners need to retain a focus on their long-term shared objectives and sometimes be willing to suffer inconvenience or pain in the short term.

9. Partners should try and develop a number of projects on which they can collaborate together so that all their eggs are not in one risky basket.

10. Partners should retain and build in as much flexibility into their arrangements as feasible in order to evolve with changes in the environment.

Despite the many benefits that have been achieved by partners in SRs, there is growing evidence that overall performance in relationships may not be as positive as was initially thought.[14] Many SRs become unstable, break apart, and are discontinued. The longevity of an alliance depends on how well the partners work together, their success in responding to and adapting to changing internal and external conditions, and their willingness to renegotiate the bargain if circumstance so warrant.

There are also dangers for firms that rely too heavily on SRs. A key vulnerability is one party becoming dependent on other firms in their relationships for essential expertise and capabilities over the long term. Because of these varied performance outcomes, it is critical that you be able to understand and decipher the signs of changing competitiveness within relationships affecting the firms, their industries, and their rivals.

Strengths and Advantages

SRs have grown in prominence in recent years and are expected to continue this trend. Because of the competitive importance and sheer value of these inter-firm combinations, business and competitive analysts need techniques that allow them to draw insights into the decisions and actions their own firms need to take to improve their competitive context. Effectively combined with other tools, SRA can be a powerful weapon in the analytical arsenal of the analyst.

SRA assists the analyst in focusing on competition in the way that it is increasingly being structured. It helps you to understand the nature of competition as it is conducted by different combinations of firms. It can also be used to provide insights into competition at a more micro-level (for example, relationships at a particular stage of an industry's value chain) than some other techniques.

SRA can be supported by software applications expressly developed for the purpose of helping you visualize competition as it occurs in networks or constellations. These applications have grown in both availability and functionality in recent years. Combined with the growth of data available on the World Wide Web, these techniques can uncover relationships that would have previously gone unnoticed.

SRA is one of the newest and fastest-developing fields of analysis. Analysts can apply and use this technique in ways that were not even considered a few years ago. As such, an analyst's ability to develop new insights and to better support decisions and actions could be a strategic advantage for the firms who are successfully employing this method.

Weaknesses and Limitations

The application of SRA does not provide ready-made insights or provide immediate decision-making support, but it does provide a wealth of newly organized data and information, often in complex and intricate graphic forms. In order to accomplish the task of developing strategic insight, SRA must be combined with other techniques to get actionable insights. It must also be combined with the growing body of knowledge in this area since there are still no ready-made guidelines that can be universally applied to help you understand competition within strategic inter-firm relationships.

Many SRA efforts, especially those supported through task-specific software applications, quickly become exercises in developing complex network diagrams that provide little practical insight. Most decision makers will not easily or quickly appreciate these visualizations, as they are not the type of data (that is, ordinarily condensed, synthesized, and succinctly summarized) that usually cross their desks. The analyst must make sense of these diagrams in ways that the decision maker will appreciate. This is an area of competitive analysis that is only now receiving attention, and there remains a lot to learn.

SRA requires specific forms of data to be effective. Much of this data will not be easily or inexpensively available or will not be available in a format that will promote the application of SRA techniques. This will require analysts to work with their firm's information specialists and be included when information communication and technology purchasing decisions are being made. Even these decisions will be difficult for analysts and their firm's IT specialists, since many of the applications that would support the gathering and organization of data for studying relationship-based competition are in the development phase, and there are few lengthy track records of experience about the vendors of these systems.

Process for Applying the Technique

There are two major processes that an analyst needs to understand in analyzing SRs. The first requires you to assess the firm's strategic relationship readiness and capability. The second requires you to assess your rival's relationships, relationship resources, and capabilities. Each of these is discussed in turn in the following section.

1. Studying Your Own Firm's Relationship Formation Readiness

In forming a strategic relationship, firms should begin by assessing their readiness to be involved in a relationship. Among other things, this includes having in place negotiation skills, change management expertise, relationship management competence, interoperable systems and processes, support from senior executives, and governance in the form of a relationship management structure.

Relationship-seeking firms should also define their business vision and strategy in order to understand how an alliance fits their objectives. Establishing goals and objectives for the relationship is usually the best place to start, followed by figuring out how closely matched they are to the firm's larger business and strategy goals. This stage of the formation process should also include an understanding of the benefits and costs that will potentially be generated within the relationship. Intangible benefits in the form of risk reduction, increased visibility or publicity, knowledge transfers, rival inhibition, and customer goodwill need to be considered.

Alternatives to a strategic relationship, including building the capabilities or seeking the benefits through the firm's own (that is, organic) activity, or mergers and acquisitions, should also be considered to determine if a relationship is a superior means of helping the firm meet its goals. The firm can usually proceed to the next step if it determines at this step that the goals of the potential relationship fit neatly with its larger strategy, the net gains of engaging in the relationship outweigh the estimated losses, harms and/or risks, there are no unacceptable risks, and a relationship is a superior option to the others available to achieve its goals.

The next step is for you to evaluate and select potential partners based on the level of mutual benefit that can be generated and the perceived ability of the firms to work well together. Analysts should consider: the complementariness of the partner's operational/production and technical capabilities; whether it has been involved successfully in any prior relationships and if it has the capabilities to manage the relationship; and whether it has the resources to make a good "go" of the relationship. It usually also helps to understand the partner's reputation in the marketplace, as the new relationship will be based at least partly upon that facet. Finally, it is useful to work through several of the so-called soft "S" elements of the McKinsey 7S framework (see Chapter 12, "McKinsey 7S Analysis"), such as shared values, leadership style of decision makers, and skills in order to determine whether the potential "fit" of these elements will be supportive to the proposed relationship. Assuming the responses to all of these areas are positive, you can recommend pursuing negotiations.

What occurs next in the relationship formation process is a meeting with the top prospective relationship partner to discuss the future of the potential relationship. This ordinarily begins by specialists in the firm developing a working relationship and mutual recognition of opportunities with the prospective partner. The firm should have confidence in its ability to negotiate reasonable, if not mutually favorable, terms with the partner. It should also have confidence in its ability to resolve any potential differences in establishing the relationship objectives, gaining agreement on the allocation of resources, melding different communication and information infrastructures, creating shared human resource policies and plans, gaining exclusivity on forming relationships with other firms, and establishing performance management and measurement systems, as well as developing controls to assure both parties that the relationship is operating according to both parties' wishes.

Once the relationship is agreed and established, the next task is to provide the appropriate level and quality of management to the relationship. Like most other organizational forms, relationships can evolve over time in a life cycle pattern. A relationship life cycle would include stages of pre-relationship (identification of potential partners), negotiation, introduction (the launch of the relationship), relationship management, and the latest stage of dissolution or restructuring. The life cycle concept can help you understand the phases of the relationship and may provide some keys as to what the partners in the relationship might do in terms of future investments, resource allocations, and other tactical options.

Relationship management is a unique facet of the SR process and requires the partners to demonstrate they have the capabilities to effectively manage their relationship with one another. Some firms designate particular individuals or groups to take on this responsibility. Here are some of the tasks at which an analyst needs to become adept when assessing SRs:

- Assessing the degree of fit between the relationship portfolio and the firm's business or corporate strategy, goals, and objectives

- Assessing the overall performance and value in the firm's portfolio of relationships

- Assessing the performance of individual relationships

- Reviewing all relationships to identify current and potential synergies

- Removing underperforming relationships from the portfolio

- Identifying the fastest-growing relationships for additional resource allocation and funding for greatest return

- Evaluating prospective partners and offering negotiation consultation and assistance

- Defining the parties' roles and responsibilities in the originating and originated relationship

- Facilitating the launch of new relationships by establishing appropriate governance structures and operating protocols

- Re-launching poorly performing alliances

- Assessing the health of the working relationship between your firm and your partners

- Comparing alliance management capability against demonstrated and proven practices (see Chapter 11, "Benchmarking," for more on this task)

- Facilitating the creation of knowledge and performance management systems to facilitate the sharing of lessons and learning across the relationship portfolio

Having done the preceding tasks, the analyst should be in a better position to provide insights to decision makers who need to make determinations about relationships as a means for accomplishing their strategies. The next task will be to study the relationships maintained and potentially sought by market rivals. This is done in order to identify opportunities and threats facing your firm so you can make decisions and take actions to improve your competitive position.

2. Studying a Rival's Relationships

There are a variety of techniques for studying a rival's relationships. The method we recommend is a fairly typical three-step process, which includes the following:

1. Identify relationships.
2. Map relationships.
3. Assess and analyze the relationships.

These are discussed in order next.

1. Identify Relationships

Many relationships are subtle and unannounced; others are bold and "in your face." For publicly traded rivals with highly visible products targeted at consumers, it is generally easier to identify their relationships. A big part of this process involves taking the results of the rival's business model analysis (see Chapter 8, "Business Model Analysis") and SWOT.[15] A business model analysis has, for example, shown that two firms in the operating systems marketplace took very different approaches to leveraging their primary products. Microsoft had a closed platform and deliberately made it difficult for others to partner with them unless it was squarely on Microsoft's terms. Red Hat took the opposite approach with its Linux systems and essentially tried to leverage its open platform through relationships with whatever parties could benefit from a relationship with it.

It is also important at this stage to identify the nature of the relationships. Does the rival tend to prefer using strategic alliances? Has it been dependent on JVs? Does it have relationships with certain consortia that it relies upon for its competitiveness? The analyst should try and uncover the rival's choice of relationships in the recent past, as this may indicate its predilection toward the future. A historiographical approach (see Chapter 25, "Historiographical Analysis") can be used to facilitate this examination of past relationships.

2. Map Relationships

Where the nature of a rival's relationships are predominantly in network forms (for example, constellations, strategic alliances, and consortia), it is usually best at this point for you to employ mapping techniques so that these relationships can be studied visually. These maps can be developed in two primary ways: by using whiteboards and markers/pen and paper, or by using digital mapping, modeling, and/or visualization software. Because of the overwhelming volume of data associated with a rival's relationships, analysts need "maps" of the pathways between firms, especially in complex industries or marketplaces. These maps can provide a sense of context that is absent from most hierarchical presentations of data in linear text form. The map can also help you to quickly get an adequate overview of the relationships in an unfamiliar area to guide the efficient use of conventional analysis methods.

One of the newer ways of understanding relationships is to do an analysis of relationships using information available on the Internet. Search engines such as HotBot, Google, and Alta Vista provide the "reverse link look-up" for links that lead into a firm's main Web site. The links indicate either official or unofficial relationships. Using this form of hypertext link analysis, you can often uncover relationships between firms that may not have been as clearly uncovered through traditional methods of human source or media analysis collection. Reid extensively describes how this form of Web link analysis can uncover otherwise hidden relationships within the World Wide Web, particularly as the relationships may provide you with competitive analysis insights.

In this book, we are mainly looking at the relationships between firms. Although we focus our comments to this level, this does not preclude you from looking at the nature, type, and directions of individual or personal relationships. Each of these levels of analysis can help you gain a richer understanding of the firm's rivals, its relationships, opportunities, and vulnerabilities.[16] Corporate relationships are the formal and informal relationships that a rival has with other organizations. Most relationships are created because there are some important exchanges of resources (funds, expertise individuals, and assets) occurring between the related organizations. These exchanges ordinarily leave a trail of visible evidence that is among the easiest for good intelligence practitioners to locate and gather.

3. Assess and Analyze the Relationships

Once the analyst has mapped the relationships that rivals maintain, he needs to examine the structure, developmental and managerial process, and context of these relationships for a variety of factors. Among the factors are the following: [17]

Age or timing of the relationship. SRs have been known to follow a traditional life cycle pattern,[18] and the age of the relationship can provide clues as to what might transpire with the SR in the near future. SRs tend to go one of two ways after a number of years: They either disband due to the failure of the relationship to accomplish the partners' goals, or they are restructured to create a new, independent entity or a different organizational form to maximize the ability of the relating partners to succeed in the marketplace. On the emergent side of the life cycle, Eisenhardt and Schoonhoven argue that firms exhibit a higher propensity to enter into alliances in markets with many competitors, as well as in markets that are in an emergent life cycle stage. Some industries—for example, biotechnology—also exhibit patterns whereby high levels of relationships are formed at an early stage of technology evolution.[19]

Location of the relationships. You need to assess whether the rival tends to use its relationships in certain geographic markets (that is, it has JVs in Asia, but not in Western Europe), or whether the relationships are located at a particular point in the rival's value chain (for example, some firms in chemicals, biotechnology, and pharmaceutical industries are known to rely heavily on SRs to help them perform their research and development activities; auto manufacturers rely heavily on relationships in the purchasing and sourcing areas, as well as the development of advanced technologies).

Management's relationship capacity and expertise. Many firms active in pursuing and participating in relationships will have individuals (for example, relationship portfolio managers) and structures (for example, an alliance management function) designed to manage their portfolio of relationships; this is usually a sign that it views this activity as important to its success. Relationship management capabilities have become increasingly important in firms that simultaneously manage a large number of relationships. These firms are essentially forced to institutionalize relationship management practices. Due to the strategic importance of relationships in many of these firms, relationship management capabilities have the potential to be a source of competitive advantage. On the other hand, firms that have no history of being in relationships before may experience greater difficulties in developing these relationships.

Market context of relationships. In order to determine whether a relationship will actually impact the profitability or market share of your firm, you should attempt to answer the following questions:

- What is the size and relative attractiveness in terms of profit potential of the market targeted by the relationship?

- What share of the market do the potential partners currently hold?

- How quickly is this particular area of the prospective partners' business growing?

- Have prospective partners been improving their capability in the targeted relationships' market area?

Combining these questions with already conducted techniques, such as critical success factor analysis (see Chapter 18, "Critical Success Factors Analysis"), industry analyses (see Chapter 6, "Industry Analysis (The Nine Forces)"), competitor analyses,[20] and/or SWOT can be highly beneficial in answering these questions.

Mix of relationships. This requires you to look at the types of relationships the rival has. Does the rival primarily use strategic alliances, or do they rely heavily on licensing agreements or co-activity (that is, co-marketing, co-production, and co-purchasing) arrangements? Assuming the rival offers products or services across a range of markets, does it use certain forms of relationships in some markets, while using different forms in others? The mix of relationships it uses may provide you with insight into what it is trying to achieve and the next steps it may choose to make.

Number of relationships. Some firms are known for making heavy use of relationships in the way they approach their marketplaces; others are known for avoiding them. The number of relationships a rival has, particularly as it compares to other rivals in similar marketplaces, can give helpful insights into the approach, resources, and capabilities of the rival.

Position in the relationship. The positions of members in the relationship, particularly in networks or consortia, can indicate much about the behavior of firms or the entire relationship. Firms positioned at the center of a relationship often display a greater ability to influence the outcome. Networks or consortia with a powerful, centrally positioned firm will often take on these attitudes and behavior, as opposed to the characteristics of the more peripheral parties.

Potential for knowledge spillovers. SRs are often formed to capitalize on knowledge, two types of which are of particular interest to the analysts since they signal different things: migratory knowledge, often technical in nature, which can be transferred easily between people or organizations in a formula or product; and embedded knowledge, which defines how a particular firm organizes itself to do business.[21] SRs take place between myriad organizations in many industries, and large multinational corporations can be involved in hundreds of relationships simultaneously.[22] Therefore, it is often important not only to identify your rival's partners but also its partner's relationships as well. A rival's partner may also be your competitor or collaborator in another relationship, so care must be taken that information or knowledge shared in one relationship doesn't leak over to your rival through another relationship.

Size of the firms in the relationship. The research remains unclear about the relationship between the size of firms and the likelihood to either form or behave in certain ways in relationships. Gomes-Casseres suggests that absolute size may be less important for the partnering behavior of small firms compared to their relative size with direct rivals. He notes that firms that lead their market segments and are large compared to their direct competitors are likely to have less incentive to seek alliances.

Strength and positions of the parties in the relationships. Some relationships are more important to a rival firm than others; for example, one in which the rival is benefiting unevenly or is in a sector that it considers to be critical for its future or growth will be more closely guarded and given more managerial attention than relationships that are at the periphery of their strategy. Eisenhardt and Schoonhoven suggest that firms are more likely to form alliances if they are in a vulnerable strategic position. They define strategic position through the number of competitors, the stage of market development and the strategy of the firm. Another key facet to the strength of the relationships is to look at the resources strength and capabilities of the partners involved. Well-managed relationships between strong partners can often result in more powerful rivals in the marketplace.

Clusters of relationships. As opposed to only assessing micro-level dyadic relations between firms, you also need to look at multi-level relationships in the form of alliance blocks, clusters or constellations. Competition between alliance blocks is a form of rivalry in which groups or clusters of firms that link together for a common purpose by means of SRs, is superimposed on competition between individual firms.[23] Driving forces and competitive pressures often favor some clusters while hurting others. The profit potential of different clusters varies due to strengths and weaknesses in each cluster's market position. A good example of clusters of relationships is the constellation of relationships present among air transportation firms. Table 16.2 shows the constellation of relationships that constitutes these relationships as of 2006.

Table 16.2
Major Constellations in the Air Transportation Industry Circa 2006

	N. America	S. America	Asia Pacific	Africa/MidEast	Europe
Star Alliance (24% market share)	Air Canada, UAL, USAir	Mexicana, Varig	AirNZ, ANA, Asiana, Singapore, Thai	South African Airways	BMI, LOT, Lufthansa, SAS, Tyrolean, Austrian, Spanair, Swiss
SkyTeam (21% market share)	Continental, Delta, Northwest	AeroMexico	Korean Air		Air France, Alitalia, CSA Czech, KLM, Aeroflot
OneWorld (14% market share)	American	LAN	Cathay Pacific, Qantas		AerLingus, British Airways, Finnair, Iberia

Source: Market shares are of all air passengers as of end 2004 and were drawn from data in the IATA 2005 annual report.

After having studied the relationships and worked through these questions, you should be in a good position to make sense of the competitive impact of the rival's relationships. At this point, it will be important to recommend insights to decision makers that can leverage them. For example, a recommendation might be to fund opportunities to weaken a rival's position by weakening its relationships or to strengthen one of your own firm's relationships as a means of precluding a rival from gaining an advantage. The kinds of recommendation that can emanate from SRA are often high level and of high value and therefore should be most appealing to the senior decision makers and executives in your firm.

FAROUT Summary

FAROUT SUMMARY

	1	2	3	4	5
F	■	■			
A	■	■	■	■	
R	■	■			
O	■	■	■	■	
U	■	■	■		
T	■	■	■		

Figure 16.2   Strategic relationship analysis FAROUT summary

Future orientation—Low to medium term. Projecting the nature of SRs into the future is not an easy task, and most forms of SRA have yet to build in the ability to extrapolate relational behavior into anything beyond the short term.

Accuracy—Medium to high. Most SRA requires sophisticated mapping, mathematical modeling, and statistical skills, assuming the presence of the appropriate data underlying these applications.

Resource efficiency—Low to medium. Gathering the data needed to perform a sophisticated SRA can require substantial digital as well as human resources. The establishment of databases for this purpose can require a significant amount of cumulative effort over time.

Objectivity—Medium to high. To the extent that this analysis is not supported through sophisticated models and databases, there can be a high degree of subjectivity involved in interpreting the results of the relationship analysis.

Usefulness—Medium. SRA is most useful when combined with other tools. It can answer some tactical questions easily and quickly, but to help promote strategy development, it needs to be usefully combined with other techniques.

Timeliness—Medium. This depends on the presence of the appropriate data, the nature of SRA applications employed, and the nature of the decision-making task to which it is being applied.

Related Tools and Techniques

- Industry analysis
- Issue analysis
- Management network analysis
- Stakeholder analysis
- STEEP/PEST analysis
- Strategic group analysis
- SWOT analysis

References

Badaracco Jr., J.L. (1991). *The Knowledge Link: How Firms Compete Through Strategic Alliances*. Cambridge, MA: Harvard Business School Press.

Bamford, J.D., Gomes-Casseres, B., and M.S. Robinson (2003). *Mastering Alliance Strategy: A Comprehensive Guide to Design, Management and Organization*. San Francisco, CA: Jossey Bass.

Borgatti, S.P., and J.L Molina (2003). "Ethical and strategic issues in organizational network analysis," *Journal of Applied Behavioral Science*, 39(3), pp. 337–350.

Borgatti, S.P., and P. Foster (2003). "The network paradigm in organizational research: A review and typology," *Journal of Management*, 29(6), pp. 991–1013.

Cainarca, G.C., Colombo, M.G., and S. Mariotti (1992). "Agreements between firms and the technological life cycle model: Evidence from information technologies," *Research Policy*, 21, pp. 45–62.

Churchwell, C.D. (2004). "Rethink the value of joint ventures," *Harvard Business School Working Knowledge* newsletter, May 10 edition.

Cross, R., Parker, A., and S.P. Borgatti (2002). "Making invisible work visible: Using social network analysis to support strategic collaboration," *California Management Review*, 44(2), pp. 25–46.

Cross, R., Parker, A., Prusak, L., and S.P. Borgatti (2001). "Knowing what we know: Supporting knowledge creation and sharing in social networks," *Organizational Dynamics*, 30(2), pp. 100–120.

Cross, R.L., Parker, A., and S.P. Borgatti (2000). "A birds-eye view: Using social network analysis to improve knowledge creation and sharing," *Knowledge Directions*, 2(1), pp. 48–61.

De Man, A.P. (2002). "How to analyze alliance networks," *Competitive Intelligence Magazine*, 5(4), pp. 14–16.

Doz, Y.L., and G. Hamel (1998). *Alliance Advantage*. Cambridge, MA: Harvard Business School Press.

Dyer, J.H., Kale, P., and H. Singh (2004). "When to ally and when to acquire," *Harvard Business Review*, July, pp. 108–115.

Eisenhardt, K., and C.B. Schoonhaven (1996). "Resource-based view of strategic alliance formation: Strategic and social effects in entrepreneurial firms," *Organization Science*, 7, pp. 136–150.

Fleisher, C.S., and B.L. Bensoussan (2003). *Strategic and Competitive Analysis: Methods and Techniques for Analyzing Business Competition*. Upper Saddle River, NJ: Prentice Hall.

Gary, L. (2004). "A growing reliance on alliance," *Harvard Management Update*, April, article reprint U0404B.

Gomes-Casseres, B. (2005). "How alliances reshape competition," Ch. 3 in Shenker, O., and J.J. Reuer (eds.), *Handbook of Strategic Alliances*. Newbury Park, CA: Sage Publications.

Gomes-Casseres, B. (1998). "Strategy before structure," *Alliance Analyst*, August, online text available at http://www.alliancestrategy.com/MainPages/Publications/Managerial.shtml.

Gomes-Casseres, B. (1997). "Alliance strategies of small firms," *Small Business Economics,* 9, pp. 33–44.

Gomes-Casseres, B. (1996). *The Alliance Revolution*. Cambridge, MA: Harvard University Press.

Gompers, P.A. (2001). "A note on strategic alliances," note 9-298-047, Boston, MA: Harvard Business School.

Gonzalez, M. (2001). "Strategic alliances: The right way to compete in the 21st century," *Ivey Business Journal*, 66(1), Sept/Oct, pp. 47–51.

Jagersma, P.K. (2005). "Cross-border alliances: Advice from the executive suite," *Journal of Business Strategy*, 26(1), pp. 44–50.

Kassler, H. (2000). "Competitive intelligence and the Internet: Going for the gold," *Information Outlook,* 4(2), pp. 37–42.

Khanna, T. (2001). "Inter-firm alliances: Analysis and design," *Administrative Science Quarterly,* 46(3), pp. 582–585.

Krackhardt, D., and J. Hansen (1993). "Informal networks: The firm behind the chart," *Harvard Business Review*, July/August, pp. 104–111.

Kuglin, F.A., with J. Hook (2002). *Building, Leading, and Managing Strategic Alliances*. New York, NY: AMACOM.

Lorange, P., and J. Roos (1993). *Strategic Alliances: Formation, Implementation, and Evolution*. Malden, MA: Blackwell.

Lyles, M.A. (1988). "Learning among joint venture-sophisticated firms," pp. 301–316 in Contractor, F., and P. Lorange (eds.), *Cooperative Strategies in International Business.* Lexington, MA: Lexington Books.

Mockus, D. (2003). "Do you REALLY know what the competition is doing?" *Journal of Business Strategy*, 24(1), Jan/Feb, pp. 8–10.

Park, S.O., and G.R. Ungson (2001). "Interfirm rivalry and managerial complexity: A conceptual framework of alliance failure," *Organization Science*, 12(1), pp. 37–53.

Reid, E. (2004). "Using web link analysis to detect and analyze hidden web communities," in Vriens, D.J. (ed.), *Information and Communications Technology for Competitive Intelligence.* Hershey, PA: Idea Group Publishing.

Segil, L. (2004). *Measuring the Value of Partnering: How to Use Metrics to Plan, Develop, and Implement Successful Alliances.* New York, NY: AMACOM.

Segil, L. (2003). "Relationship management as a corporate capability," *The CEO Refresher* (an e-magazine), retrieved from the Web on March 10, 2006 at http://www.refresher.com/!lscapability.html.

Thompson, A.A., Gamble, J.E., and A.J. Strickland (2006). *Strategy: Winning in the Marketplace*, 2nd edition. New York, NY: McGraw-Hill.

Vanhaverbeke, W., and N.G. Norderhaven (2001). "Competition between alliance blocks: The case of the RISC microprocessor technology," *Organization Studies*, 22(1), January, pp. 1–30.

Walker, G., Kogut, B., and W. Shan (1997). "Social capital, structural holes and the formation of an industry network," *Organization Science*, 8(2), pp. 109–125.

Wallace, R.L. (2004). *Strategic Partnerships: An Entrepreneur's Guide to Joint Ventures and Alliances.* Chicago, IL: Dearborn Trade Publishing.

Yoshino, M.Y., and U.S. Rangan (1995). *Strategic Alliances: An Entrepreneurial Approach to Globalization.* Boston, MA: Harvard Business School Press.

Endnotes

[1] Gomes-Casseres, 2005.

[2] Bamford, Gomes-Casseres, and Robinson, 2003; Gomes-Casseres, 1996.

[3] Dyer, Kale, and Singh, 2004.

[4] Thompson, Gamble, and Strickland, 2006.

[5] Krackhardt and Hansen, 1993.

[6] Gonzalez, 2001.

[7] Dyer, Kale, and Singh, 2004.

[8] Gonzalez, 2001.

[9] Dyer, Kale, and Singh, 2004.

[10] One bit of evidence that relationships have become more prominent among business professionals has been the formation of associations dedicated to meeting the needs of those individuals who perform in strategic relationship roles—for example, the Association of Strategic Alliance Professionals (ASAP), Inc., headquartered in Massachusetts (see http://www.strategic-alliances.org). This association assists both those involved in developing alliances, as well as those executives who must manage them.

[11] Lorange and Roos, 1993.

[12] Badaracco Jr., 1991; Jagersma, 2005.

[13] Dyer, Kale, and Singh, 2004; Gonzalez, 2001.

[14] Churchwell, 2004; Park and Ungson, 2001.

[15] See Fleisher and Bensoussan, 2003, Chapter 8.

[16] For literature and guidance on conducting this form of network analysis at the level of individual to individual relationships, see Borgatti and Foster, 2003; Cross, Parker, and Borgatti, 2002, 2000; Cross et al., 2001; and Krackhardt and Hansen, 1993.

[17] de Man, 2002; Gomes-Casseres, 2005; Mockus, 2003.

[18] See Fleisher and Bensoussan, 2003, Chapter 24.

[19] Walker, Kogut, and Shan, 1997.

[20] See Fleisher and Bensoussan, 2003, Chapter 11.

[21] Badaracco Jr., 1991.

[22] Doz and Hamel, 1998.

[23] Vanhaverbeke and Norderhaven, 2001.

17

Corporate Reputation Analysis

Short Description

Corporate reputation analysis (CRA) identifies a firm's or industry's perceptual image among key stakeholders based on a given set of factors. The CRA process sets out to give strategic managers a solid understanding of the firm's current image with their stakeholders to enable it to improve its relations with them in the future, ultimately increasing the firm's performance. The results of CRA provide a solid foundation to plan effective reputation management.

Background

In 1983, *Fortune Magazine* published their first edition, featuring its list of America's Most Admired Companies. In many regards, this was the first real introduction of CRA to the general public.

Since then, many variations and modifications have been made to the general idea of what is "admired" in firms, and CRA has emerged as a process to be used for analysis over various different specific criteria. Corporate reputation became recognized as a valuable asset.

Popular media organizations used CRA to create "most admired" or "top ten" lists of firms that reflected the interests of their target audiences, whether these are gender-specific or based on broader concerns such as diversity, the environment, etc. These lists were, and still are, usually constructed using opinion sought from CEOs and industry analysts.

Over time, CRA moved beyond media organizations and was adopted by many consulting firms, communications agencies, as well as internal marketing departments who conducted the analysis and used the results for reputation management.

It was not until 1999 that a systematic attempt was made to standardize CRA and make the process less subjective. Charles Fombrun, who founded The Reputation Institute, developed, with Naomi Gardberg and Joy Sever, a standardized formula for CRA, which they called the Reputation Quotient. The article they published about it in 2000 notes that their aim was to broaden CRA, taking it beyond the narrow range of opinion traditionally sought by the media and open the process to encompass the perceptions of multiple stakeholder groups. Their plan was to develop CRA into a robust analytical instrument that was both statistically valid and reliable.

While this standardized process was a great advancement for the analytical technique, many firms continue to construct their own CRA processes to meet their own specific purposes. Reputation management can be shown diagrammatically as follows in Figure 17.1.

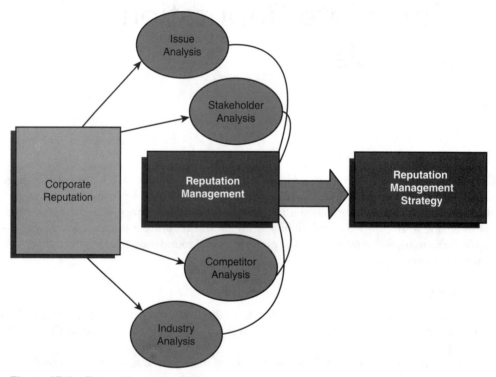

Figure 17.1   Reputation management

In recent times, a number of firms throughout the world sadly have damaged their corporate reputations through the behavior of their senior executives. Increasingly reputation risk management is becoming an agenda item for directors and in boardrooms.

So whatever method they employ, individual firms that actively monitor their reputation among stakeholders can use the information they obtain to strategically manage their reputation on a continuous basis.

Charles Fombrun and Christopher Foss quote Alan Greenspan's commencement speech as Chairman of the U.S. Federal Reserve—"In today's world, where ideas are increasingly displacing the physical in the production of economic value, competition for reputation becomes a significant driving force, propelling our economy forward. Manufactured goods often can be evaluated before the completion of a transaction. Service providers, on the other hand, usually can offer only their reputations."

Strategic Rationale and Implications

According to Grahame Dowling: "When strategy involves either growth or innovation, a company puts its corporate reputation into play. Growth involves stretching the company's operations, sometimes to the breaking point. Innovation involves doing something new."[1]

CRA seeks to identify and possibly enhance a firm's, or group of firms', image(s) among their stakeholders. The process may be undertaken by an individual firm to obtain information about its current reputation and help it design strategies to improve its reputation. The process may also be applied across an industry to accurately gauge how a firm's reputation compares to those of its competitors. Comparative information can then be used to differentiate the firm from its competitors.

While the particular reputation factors examined in a given analysis may vary, they all relate to the reputation of the firm in the eyes of stakeholders and should give an indication of the success or otherwise of the firm's reputation management strategies.

Dowling suggests that the major sources of corporate reputation risk fall into six broad areas:

1. The industry in which a firm operates.
2. Identifying strategies.
3. The culture and daily operations of the firm.
4. The comments and behavior of senior executives.
5. Managing stakeholder relationships.
6. Response to a crisis.

Firms that can effectively monitor their reputation among selected stakeholders across the six board areas mentioned previously will have a useful view of what type of strategic initiatives might be required to enhance their image. It will give the firm direct feedback of its reputation as perceived by stakeholders after the affects of public relations and advertising (both by the firm and by its competitors), media exposure, and any other external influences (for example, market speculation) are taken into account.

Successfully managing a company's reputation on a continuous basis is referred to as *reputation management* and is becoming increasingly important to senior management. Reputation management is usually a function of the public relations department and requires every aspect of a firm's operation to be consciously communicated with an overall strategy of improving or maintaining reputation. It may entail differently constructed messages tailored for specific groups of stakeholders—for example, more technical information being made available to industry analysts than is provided in press releases to general media outlets.

The image a firm communicates can heavily influence the actions of key stakeholders of the firm, including customers, employees, investors, and so on. The result of this is that the firm's reputation also has an impact on the overall value of the business, in dollar terms and also in terms of its value as a potential business partner in strategic alliances. The management of corporate reputation, then, can be seen to be an important part of the successful management of a firm overall.

Strengths and Advantages

Universal

The main advantage of CRA is that the process can be applied to any firm, no matter what type of industry it operates in or what size it is. The need to be aware of the image portrayed to key stakeholders is universal to all business. Small businesses may earn a good reputation in the eyes of the general public in a variety of ways—for example, by sponsoring local events, through the build up of customer loyalty and resulting word-of-mouth recommendations, or a network of friendships linking many people within the community directly to those participating in the business. Similarly, large firms earn their reputation in many ways (for example, sponsoring events or supporting charity), but quite often the image of the top executive has a very strong affect on the firm's overall reputation. For example, firms such as Apple, Ford, and GE have very prominent CEOs.

Although small and large firms can both use the CRA very effectively, the analysis process would generally be quite different for each of them. The inherent flexibility of CRA makes it easy to customize it to any specific situation based on the firm in question or industry in which it operates. Unlike many other analytical techniques, there is no given set of attributes or factors that *must* be included. In practice, there are many factors that reappear continuously in CRA throughout the world, and its ability to transform a firm is a major strength. The technique may be scaled up or down in complexity to allow it to be easily administered and managed by any type of strategic manager. Many small business planners might balk at the notion of using (and funding) complex analysis techniques or paying for market research that could investigate various reputation factors. However, they might engage in simpler versions of CRA.

The simplicity of the concept also gives it a universal appeal. Very few other strategic competitive analysis techniques are as widely recognized within non-business institutions or the general public as CRA. This makes CRA a useful tool for reaching stakeholders outside an industry itself—for example, shareholders.

Bottom Line

A firm that can effectively use CRA will see the results impact its bottom line. A great product is a good starting point for making a sale, but a firm's reputation is becoming increasingly important as it directly affects purchasing decisions. Consumers shop on more than just the product at hand. A firm's reputation is increasingly directly affecting the purchase decision. Customers, usually one of the most important of a firm's stakeholders, are crucial to the success of any firm and must be monitored and managed continuously. A firm that can consistently maintain a positive reputation with its customers reap positive financial rewards, not only by avoiding client attrition, but also with positive word-of-mouth publicity that can result in loyal customers.

The perceptions of other stakeholders of a firm can also have major implications on the bottom line. A firm's financial reputation will affect investment in that firm. If returns are significant and well distributed, more investors will be attracted, and the share price and the markets will look favorably on the firm as well.

Another important factor in relation to a firm's bottom line is whether or not the employees of that company are working diligently and effectively in order to generate profits. CRA can be used to gain insight into employees' perceptions of their employer. Employees who have a positive perception of their employer are more likely to work productively and to the best of their ability in an effort to move the firm forward, whether in an administrative or sales-oriented role.

Competitive Differentiation

Depending on which factors or attributes are used for conducting CRA, a firm can use the results to effectively plan strategies to differentiate itself from its competitors in the marketplace. CRA can easily generate rankings on various attributes for any given set of firms. A firm requiring this information could also use independent industry reputation analysis. Industry reputation analysis usually analyzes only a given set of firms on a given group of attributes. It could be the case that one firm is viewed as very community minded, while its direct competitors might be viewed as being more environmentally friendly. Either image has its advantages and could be used as part of a detailed differentiation strategy.

Using CRA for differentiation purposes involves the adoption of reputation management as a strategic function within the firm. The information generated by CRA can be used by a firm to analyze its existing strategies and create specific new strategies to maintain or develop a desired reputation position. There is no right way to manage reputation, nor is there any specific reputation that is perfect for every firm.

Healthy competitive differentiation could reach beyond the firms themselves and strengthen the industry in a 1 + 1 = 3 type of growth pattern. The total industry-wide effect of all firms' actively managing their reputations may be greater than the sum of individual firm efforts alone.

Qualitative

Although CRA uses statistical methods to interpret data and sometimes includes financial performance as an evaluation factor, the information given by CRA is frequently qualitative rather than quantitative, even when the Reputation Quotient is used. Where quantitative methods can provide insightful ratios and numeric analysis, qualitative analysis can usually provide more practical information in terms of future strategic planning so far as reputation is concerned.

Firms in various industries all over the world actively communicate certain information to their key stakeholders. These messages may become distorted by unusual circumstances or events and end up being heard by their audience as something entirely different from what was originally intended. CRA taps into the perceptual image formed by the final message recipient, giving the firm a clear grasp and understanding of its reputation.

Weaknesses and Limitations

Practical Uses

Simple CRA on its own, aside from enabling reputation management, provides little actionable information for the strategic analyst. The qualitative information so useful to reputation management does not provide the hard figures needed for wider strategic planning. This limits the technique as far as its usefulness to strategic planning is concerned. Many other qualitative analysis techniques, such as scenario analysis, issue analysis, and so on, can provide direct input into the strategic planning process. CRA, however, simply identifies a firm's image and can only provide analysis of current perceptions from their key stakeholders.

More complex versions of CRA can deliver a wide variety of reputation feedback based on a great number evaluation factors. However, where a large quantity of the factors are utilized, the set of results may be far too large to clearly convey any actionable recommendations.

At the board level, where reputation management responsibility should reside, there are two major weaknesses with CRA. The first one is that the board may be the last to receive early warning signals about factors affecting the firm's reputation. Second, the information they receive is filtered through managers and/or external service providers. This then impacts the practicality of the CRA output for the board.

Reliability of Results

Generally CRA begins with the use of focus groups to select the appropriate factors for analysis. The inherent weakness in using focus groups is that the research analysis can never be replicated. The results of CRA must be taken for what they are—that is, a record of the perceptions of the stakeholders questioned at the particular time of the analysis.

The second step of the CRA process frequently involves the use of private information to evaluate the firm on the selected factors. This private information usually comes from internal research done by private institutions, for example through personal interviews, Internet or telephone surveys. These methods not only provide information, which may be subject to privacy regulation by law, but they are not necessarily verifiable information sources either.

Because CRA results in information that cannot be verified or replicated, any changes in any given factor over repeated application of CRA cannot be proven to be significant. Statistically, the only way to show that a change is significant is to show that the research can be verified and repeated.

Return on Investment

After conducting CRA, executives within a firm must use the information obtained in some form or another. Usually the public relations department of any given firm will be directly responsible for the management of a firm's reputation. Any action taken on the basis of information obtained by CRA may, however, be limited by funding. Generally, then, it is difficult to guarantee specific returns from spending funds on public relations activities.

As a general rule, investing more equates to realizing more value; however, any public relations exercise is subject to extraneous information interfering with its message, and so spending on public relations cannot guarantee positive results for corporate reputation.

Process for Applying the Technique

Unlike many forms of strategic competitive analytical techniques, CRA can be very simple or quite complex. Simple CRA can be done virtually by anyone interested in a firm's image among its stakeholders. However, more complex forms of CRA—ones that evaluate an extended number of factors—require knowledge of and experience in descriptive research methods. Expertise is needed in all areas of the process, including data collection, coding, and interpretation. Mistakes in any one part of the process may compromise the integrity of the entire exercise.

Because the method is so simple as a concept, there are many different processes that can be used to effectively conduct CRA. These processes include the following:

- Reputation Quotient
- Focused CRA
- Media ranking and monitoring
- Reputation management

A single firm looking to gain insight into its reputation may use one form, while the popular media rankings, which rank several firms in various industries, use another. These media rankings require the CRA to be much more standardized because of its application over a wide selection of firms and the need to communicate results to a wider audience.

Reputation Quotient

The Reputation Quotient was developed in 1999 to try to standardize CRA. The need for the Reputation Quotient arose from the wide range of non-standard methods that existed prior to its formation and the narrow bases used in some corporate reputation research. Marketing research firm, Harris Interactive, worked with Charles Fombrun to create a standardized process that would overcome the inherent biases of different rating systems in use at the time.

The first step in developing the Reputation Quotient was to ask focus groups from a variety of industries to nominate the firms that they either had very positive or very negative perceptions of. The results were analyzed, and it was discovered that these selections were based mainly on 20 attributes from six given dimensions.

These six core dimensions can be described as follows:

- **Emotional appeal**—Evaluators tend to rate a given firm very well if they have gained some sort of emotional attachment with the firm. The results are based on how much the firm is liked, admired, and respected by each given stakeholder.

- **Products and services**—Better-regarded firms appear to earn reputation by offering better quality and more innovative products and services. Their reputations may suffer when they produce controversial products (for example, tobacco, alcohol, nuclear energy, weapons, or unhealthy foods).

- **Vision and leadership**—Better-regarded firms are those demonstrating clear vision and strong leadership and are also expected to establish an organizational infrastructure that supports not only equality of opportunity and diversity, but also one that stimulates improved ethical behavior.

- **Workplace environment**—Evaluators favor firms that offer greater job security, better relative pay and conditions, have good labor relations, employee stock ownership, and profit sharing. Employees demonstrate pride in their work and have regular and close contact with top management.

- **Social responsibility**—Firms with a good reputation for their community involvement appear to make more charitable contributions, are more philanthropic, encourage more employee volunteer programs, and have greater local economic impact (tax revenues, jobs, and investments).

- **Financial performance**—Evaluators attempting to judge a firm's social responsibility generally recognize the importance of the firm's financial health. Specific criteria used to judge financial health include profitability, earnings growth, earnings per share, and return on investment data.

Table 17.1 illustrates the six dimensions with the 20 attributes.

Table 17.1
The Reputation Quotient

Dimension	Attributes
Emotional appeal	- I have a good feeling about the firm. - I admire and respect the firm. - I trust this firm.
Products and services	- Stands behind its products and services. - Develops innovative products and services. - Offers high-quality products and services. - Offers products and services that are good value for money.
Vision and leadership	- Has excellent leadership. - Has a clear vision for its future. - Recognizes and takes advantage of market opportunities.
Workplace environment	- Is well managed. - Looks like a good firm to work for. - Looks like a firm that would have good employees.
Social and environmental responsibility	- Supports good causes. - Is an environmentally responsible firm. - Maintains high standards in the way it treats people.

Table 17.1 *(continued)*
The Reputation Quotient

Dimension	Attributes
Financial performance	■ Has a strong record of profitability.
	■ Looks like a low-risk investment.
	■ Tends to outperform its competitors.
	■ Looks like a firm with strong prospects for future growth.

Source: Adapted from Charles J. Fombrun, Naomi A. Gardberg, and Joy M. Sever (2000). "The Reputation Quotient[SM]: A multi-stakeholder measure of corporate reputation," *The Journal of Brand Management*, Vol. 7, No. 4, pp. 241–255.

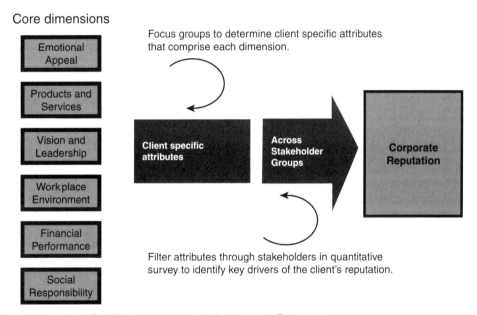

Figure 17.2   The CRA process using Reputation Quotient

This process can also be visually represented as in Figure 17.2.

The type of CRA that utilizes the Reputation Quotient is directed more toward competitive evaluation of an industry or to compare the reputations of a nation's largest firms (across a variety of industries). The Reputation Quotient was not developed for individual firms undertaking simple reputation research. The aim of the Reputation Quotient was to allow for multiple evaluation criteria and introduce statistically valid and reliable analysis.

Since its introduction in 1999, the Reputation Quotient has been used all over the world and has been used to survey hundreds of thousands of people.

Focused CRA

A firm wishing to use CRA for its own strategic planning or competitive research will not require such detailed evaluation as the Reputation Quotient. As a general rule, the first step in conducting this type of CRA would be to identify which specific attributes to base the CRA upon. To do this, the consultant or team responsible for running the CRA would select a focus group to nominate key attributes or factors for the research.

A starting point for this process might be the list of 26 items that are consistently used in CRA, compiled by Craig Carroll and Maxwell McCombs. The items are basically derived from the core dimensions in the Reputation Quotient and could be used as a guideline for the focus group. Table 17.2 displays these popular factors, ranking them from most popular to least.

Table 17.2
Consistently Used Attributes in CRA

1. Quality of products and services.	10. Strong and consistent profit performance.	19. Maximizing customer satisfaction and loyalty.
2. Financial soundness.	11. Being honest and ethical.	20. Overall admiration.
3. Ability to attract, develop, and retain top talent.	12. Best practices—markets.	21. Overall awareness of company.
4. Quality of management.	13. Business leadership.	22. Overall leadership.
5. Social responsibility.	14. Companies that other try to emulate.	23. Potential for growth.
6. Innovativeness.	15. Contribution to local economy.	24. Quality of marketing.
7. Long-term investment value/future potential.	16. Globalization of business.	25. Robust and humane corporate culture.
8. Ability to cope with changing economic environment.	17. Innovativeness in responding to customers.	26. Strong and well thought-out strategy.
9. Use of corporate assets.	18. Long-term financial vision.	

Source: Adapted from Craig E. Carroll and Maxwell McCombs (2003). "Agenda-setting effects of business news on the public's images and opinions about major corporations," *Corporate Reputation Review*, Vol. 6, No. 1, pp. 36–46.

The selection of the specific attributes by the focus group is the most critical step in the CRA process because it determines the grounds on which the firm is evaluated. If the wrong factors are selected, the end result, while not actually wrong, may not provide the type of strategic information the firm is looking for.

After a list of particular attributes has been finalized, the next step is to conduct a survey among the firm's key stakeholders. The individuals approached would be asked to rank each factor according to their own perceptions. Often statistical software will be used to interpret the data after a sufficient quantity of surveys have been carried out. This sort of statistical analysis allows the researcher or analyst to both filter and weigh the attributes and identify the key drivers of the firm's reputation.

Media Ranking and Monitoring

Media rankings of top-performing firms are still published every year. While these may not have a direct impact on the reputations of other firms, the information made available about leading firms may reflect on the general reputation of an industry and by extension on all participants in it. These media rankings are compiled using feedback from heads of industry and influential analysts.

Another form of reputation analysis available to firms is via subscription to a media monitoring service. Media monitoring sits somewhere between CRA and reputation management with the services it provides. These services provide information to firms about their reputation by monitoring mentions of the subscribing firm in the media and inferring the effect these will have on stakeholders. The service may also provide information comparing the subscribing firm's profile with that of its competitors. Usually the service will provide feedback on the effectiveness of particular public relations campaigns.

This sort of media monitoring role may also be undertaken within a firm. It will usually be undertaken by a firm's own public relations or communications department and often in conjunction with ongoing reputation management.

Increasingly, this style of monitoring extends beyond the traditional media and encompasses monitoring of the Internet, including blogs.

The information obtained from media monitoring is used to help focus future communication and public relations strategies on areas requiring reputation improvement and/or on differentiation strategies.

Reputation Management

Once reputation analysis has been carried out, the next step is to translate the findings into action by developing a longer-term strategic management plan to maintain/improve corporate reputation based upon the results. Ongoing reputation management is usually the responsibility of the company's public relations or communications department and will include both management and monitoring functions. Other strategic competitive analytical techniques may also contribute valuable information to the reputation management process.

There are five principles that have arisen in the conduct of CRA, noted by Fombrun and Foss, which may be used as a guide to implementing effective reputation management. These guiding factors are as follows:

1. *The principle of distinctiveness.*

   This is also called differentiation. A firm that owns a distinctive position in the minds of stakeholders will have a strong reputation.

2. *The principle of focus.*

   A firm that concentrates its communication with stakeholders around one central theme will have a stronger reputation. The firm may choose to emphasize its national loyalty, its financial strength, or perhaps its trustworthiness.

3. *The principle of consistency.*

   A firm that is consistent in its actions and communications to all stakeholders will have a strong reputation. This means a holistic approach should be taken to the image of the firm communicated by each internal department to all different groups of stakeholders.

4. *The principle of identity.*

   A firm that wants a strong reputation must ensure that it always acts in ways consistent with the identity it communicates. Spin is anathema to reputation building, and in time all efforts to manipulate external images that rely purely on advertising and public relations fail when they are disconnected from the company's identity.

5. *The principle of transparency.*

   A firm with a strong reputation tends to be visible across all media, communicating in ways that show they are transparent in the way they conduct their affairs. Transparency requires a lot of communication, and firms must be willing to disclose more information about themselves and be more willing to engage stakeholders in a dialog.

These five principles give scope for the management of a firm's reputation. While each of the principles relates to reputation, principle 1 contemplates traditional competitive positioning in the marketplace; principles 2 and 3 focus on the unity of a firm's communications; and principles 4 and 5 look to ethics.

The scale of the reputation management undertaken by a firm will depend on a variety of factors—for example, how big is the firm and how many resources can be devoted to the reputation management function? The internal complexity of the firm's organization will also have an impact on how reputation management will work in practice. For example, where a large firm has separate public relations, marketing, sales, customer service, human resources, and purchasing departments, each of these will have a direct role in and impact on reputation management (see Principle 3).

It should be noted that not only will internal staff be responsible for managing the corporate reputation of their employer firm, but that the firm also needs to be managing its reputation with its internal staff.

In summary, reputation management is an ongoing process and includes

1. Measuring the reputation of the firm across key stakeholder groups
2. Prioritizing the reputation risks and developing protocols to handle these risks
3. Equipping and empowering line managers to deal with these risks
4. Creating ways to listen and communicate with stakeholders on an ongoing basis

Case Study

In 1995, Royal Dutch/Shell found its reputation in tatters after two publicity disasters.

Shell had planned to get rid of the Brent Spar, a disused oil storage platform, by sinking it in the North Sea. In 1995, Greenpeace protested the decision. Shell found itself the center of worldwide protests and boycotts, which cost the firm millions.

Also in 1995, nine environmentalists were hanged by the government of Nigeria because they had spoken out against the government and Shell for the exploitation of the Ogoni people in the Niger Delta as a result of oil extraction there. Initially Shell publicly refused to intervene for clemency on behalf of the environmentalists. It eventually did make an appeal to the government, but this was ineffective. Again Shell was the subject of costly international product boycotts.

The affects of these disasters not only cost the firm money, but also reputation.

In 1996, Shell started a process of consultation involving 7500 members of the public in 10 countries and 1300 opinion leaders in 25 countries. The review was to explore two issues:

- Shell wanted a better understanding of what the public expects from transnational companies (like itself).

- Shell wanted to understand what people thought of them. What was the standing and reputation of the firm?

The focus groups showed that a small but significant group of people thought that Shell was "wanting in its care for the environment and human rights . . . We had looked in the mirror and we neither recognized nor liked what we saw," Shell concluded in its 1998 report from the review: *Profits or principles—does there have to be a choice?*

As a result of the review, Shell took several steps to improve its reputation.

Shell redefined its corporate mission, strengthened management and reporting to prioritize social performance. Another strategy was to improve its communications with the public. Shell acknowledged it had misjudged public sentiment in the past and sought to avoid repeating its mistakes.

In 1997, Shell initiated a 12-member Social Accountability Committee, which put together a human rights "primer" for Shell managers to refer to.

The 1998 *Profits or principles* report put forward a plan by Shell to incorporate social responsibility into its corporate strategy. A follow-up report in 1999 reiterated this plan. It began to publish an annual *People, Planet, & Profit* report to communicate its social responsibility agenda and actions.

Shell's investigation into and management of its reputation has resulted in its rehabilitation in the public view and an improvement in its profitability. It has also positioned the firm as socially responsible, differentiating it within the oil market as a firm that is authentic and transparent in its communication.[2]

FAROUT Summary

FAROUT SUMMARY

	1	2	3	4	5
F	■	■			
A	■	■	■	■	
R	■				
O	■	■	■	■	
U	■	■	■		
T	■	■			

Figure 17.3   Corporate reputation analysis FAROUT summary

Future orientation—Present to medium term. CRA only represents current views among stakeholders.

Accuracy—Medium to high. The statistical methods used in CRA can usually form a fairly precise depiction of the perceptions and images.

Resource efficiency—Low. CRA frequently requires the use of private panels, focus groups, and private information that cannot be verified or replicated.

Objectivity—Medium to high. Emphasis is placed on systematizing research methods.

Usefulness—Medium. The information that is generated is useful; however, only in terms of strategic plans to manage corporate reputation.

Timeliness—Low to medium. Basic CRA can be done in a very short period of time; however, reputation management is an ongoing process.

Related Tools and Techniques

- Competitive positioning
- Competitor analysis
- Critical success factor analysis
- Driving force analysis
- Industry analysis
- Issue analysis
- SERVO analysis
- Stakeholder analysis
- SWOT analysis

References

Carroll, C.E., and M. McCombs (2003). "Agenda-setting effects of business news on the public's images and opinions about major corporations," *Corporate Reputation Review*, Vol. 6, No. 1, pp. 36–46.

Coupland, C. and A.D. Brown (2004). "Constructing organizational identities on the Web: A case study of Royal Dutch/Shell," *Journal of Management Studies* 41(8), pp. 1325-1347

Dowling, G. (2006). "Corporate reputation risk," *Company Director*, April, Vol. 22, No. 3, pp. 42–43.

Fombrun, C.J., and C.B. Foss (2001). "The Reputation Quotient," *The Gauge*, Vol. 14, No. 3.

Fombrun, C.J., Gardberg, N.A., and J.M. Sever (2000). "The Reputation Quotient[SM]: A multi-stakeholder measure of corporate reputation," *The Journal of Brand Management*, Vol. 7, No. 4, pp. 241–255.

Henderson, T. and J. Williams (2002). "Shell: Managing a corporate reputation globally," in *Public Relations Cases: International Perspective*, eds. D. Moss and B. DeSanto, London, UK: Routledge, pp. 10-26

Skinner, P. (2003). "Shell's bid to rebuild its reputation: Group Director Paul Skinner discusses the need for trust," *Strategic Direction*, 19(7), pp. 9-11.

Yearly, S. and J. Forrester (2000). "Shell: A sure target for global environmental campaigning?", in R. Cohen & S. Rai (eds), *Global Social Movements*, London, UK: The Athlone Press.

www.reputationinstitute.com

www.fni.no/pdf/FNI-R0103.pdf

Endnotes

[1] Dowling, 2006.

[2] Sources used for case study: Coupland & Brown, 2004; Henderson & Wlliams, 2002; Skinner, 2003; Yearly & Forrester, 2000.

18

Critical Success Factors Analysis

Short Description

Identifying critical success factors (CSFs) is a valuable and necessary part of strategy development. "Critical success factors are the few things that must go well to ensure success for a manager or an organization and, therefore, they represent those managerial or firm areas that must be given special and continual attention to bring about high performance."[1] The CSF concept emphasizes the importance of ongoing industry monitoring. The CSF method helps the analyst to identify the key factors that have to be performed well in order to achieve a superior level of competitive performance in an industry.

Background

Although the CSF concept apparently stems from military psychologist John Flannagan's "Critical Incident Technique," its use in business was likely introduced by McKinsey consultant J. Ronald Daniel in his article, "Management Information Crisis," published in the *Harvard Business Review* in the fall of 1961.[2] Daniel noticed the problem of managers who were over burdened with information, with much of it distracting their attention and focus away from the most important factors affecting the firm's competitive success in the marketplace. Daniel discussed the importance of senior managers to have correct and useful information for competitive success. In particular, Daniel noted it was usually three to six factors that distinguished successful competitors in an industry from their less-successful peers.

The use of CSFs evolved in conjunction with the rapid growth in business planning efforts by firms in the late 1960s. The concept was further defined in the late 1970s and early to mid-1980s. The application of the CSF concept was boosted by John F. Rockart, who showed how the method could be used as a tool for senior executives to identify where their priorities should lie and develop measures to test how well the organization was performing. Although primarily looking at the application in the context of information technology (IT) decision-making, Rockart defined CSFs as "the limited number of areas in which satisfactory results will ensure successful competitive performance for the individual, department, or organization."[3] His recommended technique involved a multi-stage interview process as a means for discovering the factors, followed by a performance monitoring process matched to the uncovered CSFs.

The technique was later refined by both Christine Bullen and John Rockart as an aid in developing computer information systems that would effectively focus and measure work effort. By the mid-1980s, Anthony Boynton and Robert Zmud gained notoriety for applying the technique primarily in the MIS planning context. Through the 1980s, the technique was expanded to the strategic planning area, focusing on key areas to achieve performance goals. Because of these developments, it essentially became a framework for senior managers and stakeholders to monitor their strategy processes and results.[4]

Some key writers[5] outline methods for identifying differing levels of CSFs. Because this book focuses on strategy and competition of firms in the marketplace and in providing analysis that benefits the decision makers, this chapter focuses exclusively on industry-level CSFs that best explain competitive success at this level, and not at the application on the micro-level for examining the functional, product/service and unit-level, or project-focused techniques as an example.

Analysis by human nature tends to favor the known and the familiar. For those analysts who are unfamiliar with the CSF concept, we have seen a tendency for them to project firm-level CSFs onto those of the industry. If the focal firm is the industry leader or exists in a monopolistic context, there may be some validity in doing this, but if the firm is in any other position, the efficacy of extrapolating this analysis in this fashion is lessened. The extrapolation of firm-level CSFs to the industry can be misleading and is likely to be more problematic than first identifying the industry level CSFs and assessing how the firm, its strategy, and its performance compares against them.

The process of developing CSFs at the industry level will assist executives in understanding how their organization matches up against these factors. The typically inclusive process of determining CSFs enables managers from different areas and levels to partake in crafting the strategic direction of the company; consequently, they will have a greater ownership in the developed strategy. Allowing the company as a whole to understand and embrace the strategy presented by sharing in the agreement of the CSFs will enable the company to direct its efforts at succeeding in the key areas of the business that matter the most.

A benefit of identifying CSFs is to be able to view one's business in a larger industry context and to be able to assess your own firm's strengths and weaknesses in relation to the industry's CSFs. This comparison will not be properly done if you compare your firm and its CSFs against itself. We would agree that it is important to be aware of what a firm is doing well within its own purview, but that determination is better defined by specific internal analysis techniques, such as McKinsey's 7S Framework (see Chapter 12, "McKinsey 7S Analysis"), SERVO analysis (see Chapter 9, "SERVO Analysis"), or functional capabilities and resources analysis.[6] Last, the concept, as we discuss it at the industry level, can be readily adapted for use in more micro-level applications, like requirement analysis and project management. Indeed, the original evolution of the concept as previously described occurred in just this fashion.

Strategic Rationale and Implications

Most competitive enterprise and strategic business analysts clearly recognize the growing gap created by the volume of information being generated for managers in typical firms and the level to which they can make efficient use of that information. This information explosion has, to at least some degree, adversely influenced the rate at which companies make decisions, modify strategies, take actions, and react to market forces and key players. Contemporary decision makers need mechanisms to aid strategic planning that are concentrated on those areas that are the most crucial to their firm's success. The CSF methodology described in this chapter helps identify what those factors are and which of those among a much larger set of potentially viable competitive factors are most important. Figure 18.1 represents the cyclical and ongoing nature of CSF identification and monitoring as they are used in the strategy function of a typical enterprise.

Figure 18.1   CSF identification and monitoring

By presenting CSFs to the decision makers, analysts can facilitate their understanding of the rationales for adopting particular competitive strategies. An organization-wide understanding of the competitive environment will help direct effort toward areas that are necessary for success in this limited number of critical areas. It is important for managers to communicate to their employees how the firm's strategy matches up against the industry's CSFs. The more employees understand about this, the less arbitrary will be the resulting expectations, goals, and urgency of senior managers in helping employees attain certain performance levels in the firm's most critical activity areas or processes.

It follows then, that the top-level strategies and executives' priorities will trickle down to the operational and tactical levels. It seems obvious, but has not always worked out that way in real-world business practice. For example, Robert Cooper outlines that the product development process still showed strains despite the fact that the CSF method had been regularly used in many firms. He suggested that this outcome was caused either by many businesses simply not being in tune with their customers or that they did not adopt cogent understandings of the industry's critical success factors.

One means for better employing the CSF method concept is to break it down into those process areas that help define competitive behavior in an industry. For example, CSFs can be broken down into the following segments:[7]

- **Technology related**—CSFs in this area can include expertise in particular research or developmental processes, innovative production processes, access to potential partners with basic and applied scientific research expertise, and/or use of alliances or partnerships with universities or research consortia. Industries that tend to demonstrate the presence of these CSFs would include, for example, pharmaceuticals, advanced materials, chemical manufacturing, semi-conductor and electronic component manufacturing, and aerospace product and parts manufacturing.

- **Manufacturing related**—Expertise in quality management systems, Six Sigma processes, access to low-cost production inputs, high levels of employee productivity, low-cost or fast-cycle design and engineering, and so on. Industries that would tend to demonstrate the presence of these CSFs would be electrical equipment manufacturing, motor vehicle manufacturing, instruments manufacturing, and so on.

- **Distribution related**—This would include how products are moved from the manufacturer to the end-user, providing local inventory, technical product support, and sales and service. As such, CSFs may be found in supply chain management expertise, well known dealer networks or wholesale distributors with the ability to secure shelf space at the retail level and with strong internal sales capabilities. Industries that would tend to demonstrate the presence of these CSFs would be those in which distribution activities account for a higher than average proportion of total costs, those involved in most vertical markets, and other aspects of distribution including but not limited to operations, accounting, sales and marketing, purchasing, inventory, and profit management.

- **Marketing related**—These would be related to any of the "4 Ps" of marketing (price, promotion, place, or product). As such, marketing related CSFs could include respected brand names, well received products/services, breadth or depth of product/service line, product/service consistency, penetrating marketing research and an understanding of consumer behavior, effective product/service assistance, valuable guarantees and warrantees. Mass market, customer-oriented industries, such as those specialized retailing, consumer products, and/or entertainment and media tend to be ones in which these CSFs are most commonly found.

- **Skills and capability related**—Historical advantages, such as location or large scale contracts, short production or delivery cycle times, effective supply chain management capabilities, uniquely skilled or experienced employees, and strong e-commerce capabilities, adaptive corporate cultures, and flexible structures.

- **Other CSF types**—Locational convenience, historical monopoly protection in particular regions, having patent protections, or strong balance sheets.

CSFs vary from industry to industry, as well as over time. By considering the example of a number of industries, it is easy to see how certain processes can be most significantly related to competitive success. This is demonstrated by Table 18.1.

Table 18.1
Key Processes That May Constitute CSFs in Particular Industries

Industry	Potential CSF
Airline	▪ Load factor—air travel is a high fixed-cost business, and high-load factors are critical in achieving profitability.
	▪ Easy-to-use reservation systems—travelers often purchase their own travel and want good choices at fair prices on their own computers at their convenience.
	▪ Attractive routes and routing/airport slots—being able to get quickly (non-stop is ideal) from one popular place to another to generate volume.
Brewing	▪ Capacity utilization—this helps to lower production costs.
	▪ Strong network of wholesale distributors—allows brewers to gain access to retail outlets.
	▪ Appealing advertising—this helps sway beer drinkers to purchase specific brands or to stay loyal.
Bottled Water	▪ Access to extensive distribution—shelf space is limited, and there are many products vying for this limited yet valuable real estate.
	▪ Image—since the product can be viewed as a commodity, this attracts the buyer at the site of purchase to select one bottle over another. Consumer-perceived purity is a key sub-component.
	▪ Low-cost production facilities—allows the manufacturer to achieve an acceptable margin.
	▪ High sales volume—this must be in the millions of cases to justify the needed marketing expenses to differentiate the product.
Business Schools	▪ Active alumni relations—promotes hiring of current students and the development of resources for investing in current and future products/ programs.
	▪ Attractive and leading-edge programs—popular and in-demand subjects of study.
	▪ Effective career services—allows employers to connect with students and vice versa, resulting in satisfied alumni.
	▪ Popular instructors—improves the experience in the classroom as well as attracts top students.

Table 18.1 *(continued)*
Key Processes That May Constitute CSFs in Particular Industries

Industry	Potential CSF
Video Game Software Industry	■ Availability, retention, and motivation of talented game developers—these are key human resources needed for success in the industry.
	■ Ability to consistently develop and produce "hit" games for sizable market segments—this generates customer demand and recognition.
	■ Cross-platform backward-compatible game development capability (e.g., Sony PlayStation 3, Nintendo Wii, Microsoft Xbox 360)—enlarges the sales potential for the games.
	■ Relationships with forward channel partners including major console developers and retailers—makes games widely available to end consumers.

For example, Table 18.2 offers a summary of CSFs for the banking industry in the wake of government de-regulation in Taiwan.[8] We have added the CSF area from the preceding list that each factor would fit in to.

Table 18.2
CSFs and CSF Areas for the Banking Industry in Taiwan

Critical Success Factor	Includes	CSF Area
Management of bank operations	Internal management issues such as staff kindness, speed of transactions, and the bank manager's skill, strong internal auditing and control, and asset and liability management.	Skills/capability related.
Marketing	Long-term relationships with loyal customers, acquiring deposits and providing sufficient staff incentives.	Marketing related.
Bank image and visibility	Bank reputation and image and location and number of bank branches.	Marketing and distribution related.
Ability of financial market management	Quantity and contents of service items, government deregulation policy, and the prosperity of the stock and securities market.	Skills/capability related.

Source: Adapted from Chen, T. (1999). "Critical success factors for various strategies in the banking industry," *International Journal of Bank Marketing*, 17(2), pp. 83–91.

Note that the first three CSFs in Table 18.2 are "controllable" by the participants in the banking industry, but the fourth CSF, "Ability of financial market management," is an item that tends to defy any particular firm's influence, which is not unusual in cases involving government policies and the aggregate performance of a stock market. Our own view of CSFs would suggest that the fourth factor may not be a CSF at all since it is not a variable that management can influence through its decisions.

Correctly identifying CFSs in those areas of industry competition can provide a competitive advantage or be a distinctive competency for a firm[9] and, therefore, should be of keen interest to analysts. The idea behind this is that a firm is likely to be successful if it is competitively better than its competitors in one or more industry-level CSFs. If it is better than its rivals in all the CSFs, it has a powerful competitive advantage and should earn higher levels of profitability than its rivals. The key facets that the analyst needs to identify are the sources of those advantages that align so well with the industry's CSFs.

The top-down nature of the CSF methodology provides a mechanism to direct the entire organization toward common goals and understand what the firm's priorities are. It is also important to align CSFs with key individuals in the organization who will have responsibility in areas determined as most important to achieving CSFs. Consistency and synergies are easier to achieve when upper- and lower-level managers alike understand the firm's priorities and are measured on the corresponding criteria. As such, the firm's information and measurement system should naturally support these CSFs as well.

An important component of CSFs that must be emphasized is that they are dynamic. Because of the changing nature of the environmental context, customer, and competition impacting a marketplace, a key factor needed for industry success in the past or the present may not be as important in the future. Constant monitoring and revision are necessary to be able to identify future CSFs and develop a strategy for building long-term competitive advantage. It is essential that analysts always be on the lookout for emerging and changing CSFs. This is particularly important for markets experiencing high growth.[10]

For example, as product-based industries move along the life cycle, they will often move from stressing "product technology" to "process technology." One thing this suggests that as "fast followers" enter a market and competition substantially increases, cost control becomes increasingly important, regardless of whether or not the firm is a low-cost provider. Another change is in the trend toward shareholder activism and increasing attention to governance matters. CSFs may be used increasingly in the future by financial analysts or investors assessing a firm's performance in their given industry.

Identification of CSFs is important both for big corporations competing for global domination and small businesses. Dickinson et al, makes the point that some characteristics of small businesses are scarce resources and tight cash flows, and knowing where to direct those resources can be critical to survival.[11] Also note that this concept has wide application in government agencies and organizations and is often linked to the establishment of their key performance indicators.[12]

Strengths and Advantages

There are a number of strengths of the CSF method that account for its acceptance and popularity. As previously discussed, senior managers are plagued by too much information. The CSF methodology is appealing to both analysts and decision makers because it forces them to identify which information is important and where to focus their planning efforts. The concept is quite easy for decision-making customers to grasp and is viewed as being relatively more trustworthy than other more complex industry level focused concepts.

Because the CSF method helps focus attention on a small number of key factors that can best leverage action in a marketplace, it helps managers to prioritize their investment and resources allocation decisions. As such, the process is likely to lead to a better return on investment in analysis, and information gathering and collection activities, and a better level of success in generating positive returns on investments supported by the keener understanding of the CSFs themselves.

Another primary appeal of the concept is the top-down structure and the focus it provides to senior managers.[13] Because being better than competitors in one or more CSFs can be the difference in achieving competitive success, they should always be incorporated into sound strategic decision making. The method provides analysts or the firm's decision makers the focal context from which to recommend/design strategies and direct resources toward a common goal or set of goals. The method also stresses and encourages continuous monitoring of the organization's pursuit of these goals. This is a key reason why the method is intuitively understood and generally accepted by senior managers.

Another strength is that the process exposes the critical bits of information the analysts and decision makers need in order to direct strategic activity. As such, information systems can then be developed that will monitor proficiency in the areas identified as CSFs, rendering the use of these systems more accurate and comprehensive. This can lead to more tightly aligned information systems strategy processes, which should benefit all levels of decision making.

Weaknesses and Limitations

At a philosophical level, the CSF concept in strategy formulation has been criticized by some strategists. Pankaj Ghemawat has said that " . . . the whole idea of identifying a success factor and chasing it seems to have something in common with the ill-considered medieval hunt for the philosopher's stone, a substance that would transmute everything it touched into gold."[14] The biggest weakness here is that either the CSFs will be so obvious that they will not necessarily provide any informational advantage to the firm or that they will be so elusive that they will defy any decision making or action being taken to exploit them in the marketplace.

The CSF concept has a limitation at a tactical level as well. CSFs must be developed by individuals who have unique and specific training in this area. The level of the analyst's knowledge, skills, industry experience, and prior applications of the technique will likely influence the quality of their CSF understandings. Some of the concept's biggest advocates note that it is difficult for the layman to use, thereby rendering it inappropriate for firms that do not have access to qualified analysts. Also the ability to think creatively in the identification and development of CSFs may be a limitation for some analysts.

There is also the problem of staying focused at a particular level of analysis. Identification of brand, product/service, functional, firm, or firm-specific CSFs are often confused with *industry-level* CSFs, which we know are not necessarily the same and are amenable to added layers of analytic complexity. The broader outlook of identifying CSFs for an entire industry is a harder view to conceptualize for those not adept at using the techniques.

Even in the event of an experienced analyst using the technique, it has also been criticized for potentially being subjective. By definition, this is an inherent risk in any process that requires the communication and interpretation of outside information. Where interview processes are used to uncover CSFs, this weakness can be minimized by having skilled interviewers who can isolate and circumvent prevalent informational biases.

Process for Applying the Technique

There is a basic two-step process for performing the CSF methodology.

- First, the analyst must creatively, comprehensively, and accurately identify the set of CSFs in the industry, emphasizing the generation of proactive and forward-looking CSFs created by driving forces in the industry.[15] Some studies have identified as many as 25 CSFs, but typically the number that will be identified will be somewhere between three and eight, with five being the most frequently occurring number in our experience and a general rule of thumb we suggest initially.

- Once the CSFs are identified, it helps to determine which two or three of the larger set are the most important.[16] Remember that the whole purpose of identifying CSFs is to help focus the allocation of the firm's resources and to direct its strategy efforts, so it is important to choose the ones that are as close as possible to the center, not periphery, of success in the industry.

There are varying depths to which one can go to identify CSFs. One helpful starting point is outlined by Thompson, Gamble, and Strickland. They suggest that the analyst proceeds by asking a series of three questions, as follows:

- On what basis (attributes, characteristics) do buyers of the industry's product or service choose between sellers' competing brands?

- Given the nature of competitive forces and rivalry, what capabilities and resources does a firm require in order to be a competitive success?

- What limitations or shortcomings among product/service attributes, competencies, capabilities, or historical market achievements are almost certain to put a firm at a significant competitive disadvantage?

An effective viewpoint for the analyst is to examine the industry from the customer's, rather than the competitor's, stance. Using market research and customer-derived data, the analyst tries to answer the following:

- Why does the industry exist?
- For what purpose and to serve whom?
- What do those customers desire/demand?
- What don't customers know they want/need?

Leidecker and Bruno suggest a variety of different methods for identifying CSFs. They note that individually, they may not be sufficient to identify a CSF, but by combining two or more methods, the risk is lowered that the analyst will miss a CSF or the relative importance of one. A triangulated approach may verify the authenticity of the CSF because several different applications support its existence and priority.

Leidecker and Bruno outline eight CSF identification techniques that span three levels of analysis. Those three levels are as follows:

1. Environment or socio-political
2. Industry
3. The firm-level

ın the "Background" section of this chapter, we presented our reasons for focusing exclusively on the industry level of CSF identification. As industry level analysis ordinarily follows from analysis of the environment, a look at environmental identification techniques will commonly act as a prerequisite for industry analysis. Figure 18.2 is our adaptation of Leidecker and Bruno's identification techniques and subsequent explanation of their eight techniques. It is useful to recognize that five techniques are oriented from macro to more micro levels of analytics for identifying CSFs at the industry level.

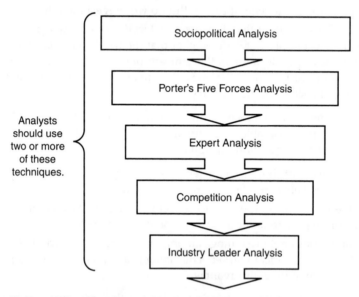

Figure 18.2 Popular industry level CSF identification techniques
Source: Adapted from "Identifying and Using Critical Success Factors," by Joel. K. Leidecker and Albert V. Bruno, 1984, pp. 25–29.

We will take a brief look at each of the five identification techniques and examine some of the strengths and weaknesses associated with them.[17] It is important to reiterate that any of these steps on their own is not sufficient to identify a CSF—at least two or more need to be used.

Leidecker and Bruno's Identification Techniques

Socio-Political/Environmental Analysis

This technique is often called PEST or STEEP analysis.[18] In the context of understanding its relationship to identifying CSF, we'll stress again that doing a PEST/STEEP analysis is ordinarily a prerequisite to understanding the industry, as it forces the analyst to thoroughly examine the environment within which the industry operates. Industries that are heavily regulated or whose survival depends on forces over which it has little or no control will be particularly affected by environmental factors. Some of these include inflation, exchange rates, government regulation, or de-regulation and politics. Some sources for macro-environmental forces identification include environmental scanning, econometric modeling, census and other government statistical information, and independent consultants who specialize in providing this sort of information, among others. The advantage to this outlook is that it is broad and can provide a comprehensive understanding of the industry's context. The disadvantage is that it is not usually sufficient to identify more micro-level industry CSFs. Looking at environment and socio-political factors merely presents a starting point. Environmental analysis will reveal forces affecting all companies in a particular industry, but it does not distinguish between how individual companies deal with these forces through their unique strategies, nor does it focus on the performance aspects of these firm's competitive efforts.

Porter's Five Forces Model

Porter's Five Forces model[19] is widely known as a tool for performing industry structure analysis. Viewed together, all five forces provide an excellent lens through which to consider the intensity of industry competition, as well as the pressures being applied to industry participants by buyers, suppliers, new entrants, and substitutes. Being able to understand how the five forces relate to one another is another asset of this framework, and gives the analyst a tool to gauge the potential for growth and profitability in the industry. Porter's Five Forces model is best used by analysts at several points in time (for example, 2004, 2006, and 2008) in order to facilitate the detection of movement and trends in an industry's attractiveness and its profitability profile.

The key to using Porter's Five Forces model and related industry analysis for CSF identification is to target those forces and underlying factors that are creating the greatest pressures on industry profitability. Once they are identified, it will enable the analyst to identify those product/service characteristics, competencies, resources, or processes that can most significantly lessen the impact of these pressures. It is within these areas that CSFs usually can be identified.

Industry/Business Experts

The analyst needs to compile the views, experiences, and insights of individuals or experts with in-depth knowledge of the industry. Some good places to locate industry experts include industry, trade or professional organizations, consultants to the industry, financial analysts, and industry veterans. They are often a good sounding board to either verify CSFs or play the "devil's advocate" role to the traditional wisdom or beliefs about competition in the industry. Industry experts can also expose nuances of an industry that only experience can provide. The obvious weakness of this technique, apart from the fact that it may cost the firm more in funds or time to acquire the expert's advice, is that it is more subjective than other methods, depending on the unique positioning and analytical prisms applied by the experts themselves; therefore, on its own application, using experts is precarious as a means to identify CSFs. Having said that, the method can be helpful when used in conjunction with more objective techniques, including some of the others described in this section (for example, Porter's Five Forces and competitive analysis).

Analyze Competition

Analyzing competition focuses solely on the "how firms compete" facet of industry dynamics. Using competition as an identifier of CSFs isolates it from the other four of Porter's industry structure components (that is, bargaining power of buyers, bargaining power of suppliers, threat of new entrants, and threat of substitutes). Some sources to understanding industry competition are industry consultants and line or department managers. Some tools we discuss that aid the analyst in performing competition analysis are weighted competitive strength assessment charts and strategic group maps.[20]

An advantage to taking a detailed look at the competitive nature of an industry is that it stresses the importance of competition in it, rather than diffusing its influence among other forces. The ability to quickly focus in on players in an industry and identify their relative positions and strengths is frequently beneficial. However, this technique can cause analysts to be myopic if it is not used in conjunction with other methods, primarily because it doesn't take any of the other forces, whether competitive or driving ones, into consideration. It also leaves out the possibility that CSFs have changed at the margins of an industry in which disruption is occurring, changing the scope and boundaries of the industry itself.

Industry Leader Analysis

By definition, dominant firms in an industry are likely to be skillful in at least one industry CSF and possibly more. Identifying why and where they succeed and how they achieve these superior performance levels can be a useful gauge to assess one's own firm's strengths and weaknesses—this is a form of reverse CSF analysis.

This technique is the narrowest of those we present and is by no means sufficient to use on its own. It may suggest a causal relationship that is overly simplified or invalid and prevent the discovery of CSFs not related to a particular firm. It can also be complex because many firms are parts of larger organizations (for example, corporate ones), and trying to isolate a particular set of CSFs attached to a firm in a particular industry may mean disaggregating a large number of other factors that may contribute to the existence of the industry-level CSF. Although some studies have attempted to link the success of one generic strategy (for example, low cost, differentiation, niche focus) and industry CSFs, it is commonly recognized that there is room for more than one successful generic strategy in an industry, and attempting to relate dominant firm success factors with CSFs can be fallacious in some circumstances.

Table 18.3 summarizes the five techniques discussed previously and highlights some of the strengths and weaknesses associated with each technique.

Table 18.3
Summary of Identification Technique Advantages and Disadvantages

Identification Technique	Advantage	Disadvantage
Socio-Political/ Environmental (PEST or STEEP) Analysis	Very broad view identifying factors outside of industry's control.	Broad nature of the technique may not point to specific CSFs for an industry.
Industry Structure Analysis	Very thorough method. Acknowledges all forces effecting industry and relationships between them.	Frequently done in static fashion. May miss driving forces or trends. Can ignore disruption.
Industry Experts/Consultants	Exposes nuances of industry. Good for use in conjunction with Industry Structure Analysis. Insights borne in experience.	Not as thorough as some techniques. Subjective. Can be expensive. Experts can help competitors too.
Competition Analysis	Stresses importance of competition rather than diffusing it.	Myopic if used on its own. Neglects other forces outside competition.
Industry Leader Analysis	Accessible view of what success looks like. Best practices today can be benchmarked.	Narrow and potentially misleading. What works today may fail tomorrow.

Source: Adapted from "Identifying and Using Critical Success Factors" by Joel. K. Leidecker and Albert V. Bruno, 1984, p. 26.

Determining Critical Success Factor Importance

Once CSFs have been identified and narrowed down to a handful of factors (for example, between three to eight factors), the next step is to identify which, relatively, are the most important ones. There are three characteristics that will help identify which sample of CSFs of a larger population are the most crucial. The three criteria outlined by Leidecker and Bruno are helpful in this regard. They stress that profit impact analysis is a key to identifying relative factor importance. They go on to note that the three characteristics to consider when determining the relative importance of potential CSF candidates include the following:

Major Business Activity

Typically, a CSF exists in an area or activity that is central to the business and its success, rather than being peripheral. For example, in the auto parts or steel production industries, manufacturing and operations are central business activities and will frequently have a CSF associated with it, but CSFs will generally not be associated with marketing processes or capabilities. For luxury hotels or prestige brands industries, on the other hand, marketing resources and capabilities probably are a good place to look for a CSF.

Involvement of Heavy Monetary Resources

An important CSF will probably have a substantial amount of financial resources attached to it. For example, inventory is a major cost for most retailers. It stands to reason that the ability of a retailer to quickly and efficiently acquire popular goods at a reasonable cost might be a CSF, as it should improve profit margins. Major air carriers or airlines, because of the high fixed-cost nature of the business, will have a CSF around their load factors (that is, an indicator that measures the percentage of available seating capacity that is filled with passengers—the higher, the better).

Major Profit Impact

This speaks to the sensitivity of certain business activities to related forces. CSF-related activities tend to be particularly sensitive to major change. For example, a change in the price of raw materials will have a major profit impact in a manufacturing-based industry like housing construction, whereas a significant change in the price of advertising services will not be likely to have a significant impact on a housing developer's profit.

Summary

The purpose of this chapter was to demonstrate the value and use of CSF analysis in strategy development and decision making. CSFs remain a popular and easily communicated method by which analysts and decision makers can work with others in the firm on focusing attention on a limited set of factors that can help achieve success. Properly performed, CSF analysis can assist decision-making clients in allocating resources to those places that require their greatest attention.

FAROUT Summary

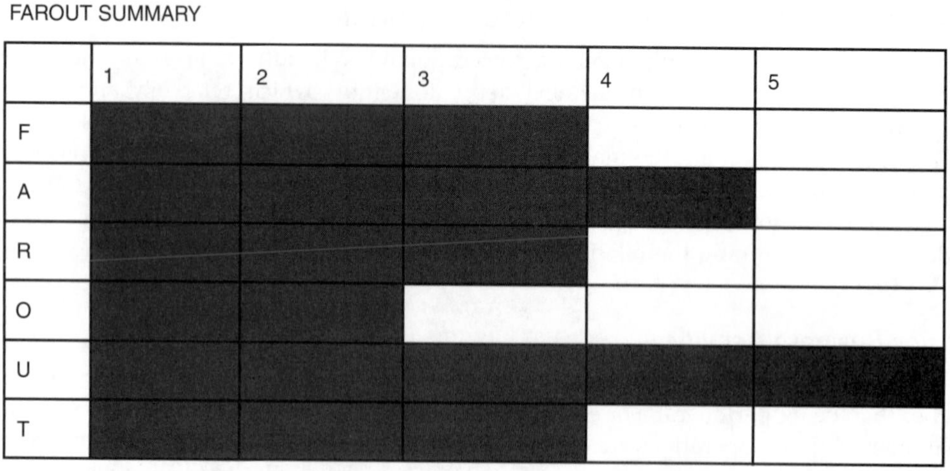

FAROUT SUMMARY

Figure 18.3   Critical success factors analysis FAROUT summary

Future orientation—Medium. The emphasis on continued monitoring and strategic planning infer a future orientation, but CSF analysis is often done in a static manner in actual practice.

Accuracy—Medium to high. Used correctly, with more than one supporting/complementary technique being applied, a skilled analyst as the executor, the potential for accuracy improves, but a subjective element will remain.

Resource efficiency—Medium. This depends on the form of data gathered and the manner in which it is collected. If experts are used, the interview process can be time consuming. If the industry is heavily populated by privately owned firms, performance metrics may not be easily accessible.

Objectivity—Low to medium. The degree of objectivity will depend on which discovery methods have been used. If an analyst has relied primarily on secondary sources or non-proprietary expertise, the objectivity will be lower.

Usefulness—High. The notion of a critical success factor links performance measurement and strategic planning with an emphasis on directing resources to the most important areas of the organization. The holistic and structured nature of the concept is highly organized and usable.

Timeliness—Medium. The initial process of identifying and determining the importance of critical success factors can be time-consuming, but once they are identified, they are quick and easy to use unless the industry environment undergoes a drastic change.

Related Tools and Techniques

- Balanced scorecard
- Benchmarking
- Cluster analysis
- Functional capability and resource analysis
- Porter's Five Forces analysis
- Product line analysis
- Strategic group mapping
- Weighted competitive strength analysis

References

Aaker, D.A. (2001). *Strategic Market Management*. Hoboken, NJ: John Wiley and Sons, Inc.

Anthony, R.N., Dearden, J., and R.F. Vancil (1972). *Management Control Systems, Text Cases, and Readings*. Homewood, IL: Richard D. Irwin, Inc.

Boynton, A.C., and R.W. Zmud (1984). "An assessment of critical success factors," *Sloan Management Review*, 26(4), Summer, pp. 17–27.

Bullen, C., and J.F. Rockart (1981). *A Primer on Critical Success Factors*. Boston, MA: Sloan School of Management, Massachusetts Institute of Technology.

Byers, C.R., and D. Blume (1994). "Tying critical success factors to systems development," *Information & Management,* 26(1), pp. 51–61.

Chen, T. (1999). "Critical success factors for various strategies in the banking industry," *International Journal of Bank Marketing,* 17(2), pp. 83–91.

Cooper, R.G. (1999). "From experience: The invisible success factors in product innovation," *Journal of Product Innovation and Management,* 16, pp. 115–133.

Daniel, D.R. (1961). "Management information crisis," *Harvard Business Review,* 39(5), September–October, p. 111.

Dobbins, J.H., and R.G. Donnelly (1998). "Summary research report on critical success factors in federal government program management," *Acquisition Review Quarterly,* Winter, pp. 61–81.

Fleisher, C.S., and B. Bensoussan (2003). *Strategic and Competitive Analysis: Methods and Techniques for Analyzing Business Competition.* Upper Saddle River, NJ: Prentice Hall.

Garner, L. (1986). "Critical success factors in social services management," *New England Journal of Human Services,* VI(1), pp. 27–31.

Grant, R.M. (1999). *Contemporary Strategy Analysis.* Oxford, UK: Blackwell Publishers Ltd.

Jenster, P.V. (1987). "Using critical success factors in planning," *Long Range Planning,* 20(4), pp. 102–109.

Leidecker, J.K., and A.V. Bruno (1984). "Identifying and using critical success factors," *Long Range Planning,* 17(1), pp. 23–32.

Leidecker, J.K., and A.V. Bruno (1987). "Critical success factor analysis and the strategy development process," pp. 333–351 in King, W.R., and D. Cleland (eds.), *Strategic Planning and Management Handbook.* New York, NY: Van Nostrand Reinhold Co.

Lester, D.H. (1998). "Critical success factors for new product development," *Research Technology Management,* 41(1), pp. 36–43.

Lilley, W. (May 27, 2005). "We're not gonna take it," *The Globe and Mail,* retrieved June 29, 2005 from http://theglobeandmail.com/servlet/story/LAC.20050527.RO6TAKEIT/PPVStory/?DENIED=1.

Porter, M.E. (1980). *Competitive Strategy.* New York, NY: The Free Press, MacMillan Inc.

Rockart, J.F. (1979). "Chief executives define their own data needs," *Harvard Business Review,* March–April, p. 85.

Thompson, A.A., Gamble, J.E., and A.J. Strickland (2006). *Strategy: Winning in the Marketplace,* 2nd edition. New York, NY: McGraw-Hill.

Westerveld, E. (2003). "The Project Excellence Model: linking success criteria and critical success factors," *International Journal of Project Management,* 21, pp. 411–418.

Endnotes

[1] Boynton and Zmud, 1984:17.

[2] Daniel, 1961; Anthony et al., 1972.

[3] Rockart, 1979: 85.

[4] Boynton and Zmud, 1984.

[5] Leidecker in particular—see Leidecker and Bruno, 1984.

[6] See Fleisher and Bensoussan (2003), Chapter 14.

[7] Thompson, Gamble, and Strickland, 2006: 76.

[8] Adapted from Chen, 1999: 88.

[9] Thompson, Gamble, and Strickland, 2006.

[10] Aaker, 2001: 91.

[11] Leidecker and Bruno, 1987: 347.

[12] See Dobbins and Donnelly, 1998; Garner, 1986.

[13] Boynton and Zmud, 1984: 18.

[14] Grant, 1999: 79.

[15] Leidecker and Bruno, 1987.

[16] Strickland, page 72.

[17] Leidecker & Bruno, 1984.

[18] We describe this technique as PEST/STEEP analysis in Chapter 17 of our previous book and provide a detailed explanation of its background and how to perform this technique.

[19] The Porter's Five Forces model is covered thoroughly in Chapter 6 of our previous book.

[20] See Fleisher and Bensoussan, 2003, Chapter 7.

Country Risk Analysis

Short Description

Country risk assessment (CRA) deals with how a firm addresses the risks involved in making investments in a foreign country. *Country risk* is the risk that economic, political, or social conditions and events in a foreign country will adversely affect a firm's financial and strategic interests. Decision makers need to weigh any potential loss of invested capital that could result from troublesome circumstances in a foreign country. CRA as a discipline seeks to identify these risks and determine the degree to which they will negatively impact their return on investment (ROI). Country risk can be segmented into the following six distinct, yet interrelated, categories:

- Economic risk
- Transfer risk
- Exchange rate risk
- Location or neighborhood risk
- Sovereign risk
- Political risk

Background

Risks are generically viewed as the potential damage or harm that may arise in the present or future. Risks are often mapped to the probability of some future event or current process, which may result in an undesirable outcome. CRA is primarily used for business analysis, although it can also be used to assess the vulnerability associated with rivals' foreign investments and market entry.

CRA became popular in the 1970s and was refined in subsequent decades. Its first manifestations were designed to help private investor banks make educated decisions about lending money to entities in foreign countries. Following the oil crisis in the 1970s, CRA took a more quantitative approach. Risk assessment forecasting services from agencies such as the International Monetary Fund, the *Economist's* Economic Intelligence Unit, and the Wharton Economic Forecasting Associates (WEFA) grew and became more sophisticated, often with the assistance of analytical models that had benefited from years of empirical testing and experience.

Indices that rated country risk began to be developed, often with data collected from vast and knowledgeable sources. These services typically used a combination of qualitative and quantitative measures to regularly rank over 200 different countries. A range of experts from universities, government, and organizations would be surveyed by the respective indices developers to produce an individual score and or ranking.

Unfortunately, there were often differences in ratings/rankings between indices because experts' definition and conversion of the data into measurable actions and behaviors could differ. Thus, there was an element of subjectivity in the models. Additionally, they were often too general for most business people and decision makers to use in their planning considerations because they were primarily prepared for banks and institutional lenders for a fee. They also commonly lacked the specificity of which risks were more prevalent in different types of investments or market entry activities. With such international events as the change of governments in Iran and Nicaragua in the late 1970s, the models became more refined in the 1980s and 1990s and began to make use of more types of quantitative measures and the inclusion of investment limits and statistical significance for commercial CRA services and indices.

Strategic Rationale

Today's reality is that firms interested in becoming industry leaders must seek global, not local, market dominance. Global expansion is becoming increasingly attractive for firms whose home markets have reached maturity or are simply too small to allow exploitation of economies of scale or learning curve advantages.[1] Multinationals are locating manufacturing facilities in foreign countries, outsourcing, joint venturing, and exploring licensing opportunities to gain access to developing markets.[2] All of these situations will present risks that the firm may not have experienced in its home country.

The term "investment" covers a range of actions that a firm can take to extend its operations into a foreign country. A strategy as simple as selling products in another country can represent a risk in the short term. These risks include not getting paid for the full cash value of the goods, or getting paid in a valueless currency.[3] Many expansion strategies require longer-term investments and a correspondingly longer period over which a risk may be experienced, such as the construction of manufacturing facilities or development of strategic alliances.

Although international expansion or investments can provide many positive opportunities to generate profitability and wealth, the risks associated with investing in a foreign country are numerous. Some of these risks include a foreign entity defaulting on its debt;

renegotiating or rescheduling obligations in order to alleviate problems associated with the financing instruments or processes; and the transfer of risk, which includes losses to the home country firm that emanate from foreign exchange rates and controls.[4] Firms will want to assess the potential that their ROI may fall short of what might be reasonably projected.[5] Firms' or governments' financial positions in the foreign market are affected by changes in taxation, exchange rates, and exchange controls.

In the twentieth century, there were numerous situations where domestic debtors were relieved of obligations to foreign investors, leaving foreign investors few options for recourse to compensation. One reason for this was because the laws of independent countries were outside the bounds foreign courts. Even with a ruling by the International Court of Justice (the World Court or ICJ) in The Hague, if the situation would even qualify, firms receive little more than moral vindication if the guilty country refuses to act on the ruling.

Strengths and Advantages

Foreign markets enable firms to gain access to less-developed markets, capitalize on economies of scale, and develop more cost-effective value chains. For firms looking to expand abroad, it is important to be educated about the potential risks and create contingency plans where possible. CRA is important to enhance the firm's understanding of the kind and degree of risks that are associated with a potential foreign investment. Firms that have a realistic grasp of risks stand a much better chance of achieving success with their investments over the long term.

CRA also helps you to identify not only the nature of the risks inherent in making investments abroad, but may also allow you to identify remedies to minimize or even eliminate taking on all of the risk. In addition, certain risks can be insured against or hedged— for example, exchange rate risk, which can help firms weather the tough times that they would not experience in their home market.

When a firm has an investment choice among several countries, CRA can help it make relative determinations and prioritize those places, which are likely to generate the most favorable return/risk trade-offs. Analysts can help their decision makers gain confidence in their investment decisions by choosing countries that have lower risk levels.

CRA may also help you identify other firms, particularly those in non-competing markets, which have previously invested in risky countries. This can help you to identify the actions those firms took to lessen country risk. As such, this becomes a form of benchmarking that can help the firm adapt practices that have been successful elsewhere (see Chapter 11, "Benchmarking," for more about benchmarking).

Finally, CRA is part of the cultural awareness a firm must develop for long-term success when investing and operating in a foreign country. A comprehensive CRA helps to educate analysts, managers, and decision makers about a country's political system, history, economic, judicial, and commercial factors in advance of making a major investment. Hence, it accelerates the firm up the "learning curve" and can potentially also facilitate an adjustment into a foreign country after a decision to invest has been made.

Weaknesses and Limitations

Concerns arising from data collection, lack of objectivity, looking to past events to predict the future, and lack of specificity are problems that plague the CRA discipline. Many attempts by CRA experts and advisory agencies to standardize and quantify dynamic, simultaneous events and isolate them are conducted upon a shaky foundation of causal and affective relationships. Ultimately, CRA tries to assign quantitative measures to human events, actions, and concepts that are themselves constantly developing and unfolding.[6] As such, analysts need not only to understand how to interpret the various country risk ratings or rankings they encounter, but also to have a reasonable conceptual understanding (meaning that they can explain it in common sense terms to their decision makers) of the modeling that underlies and provides the computational foundations of these results. To increase confidence in their findings, analysts will need to focus on the root causes of the problems, not just on the more visible symptoms of these problems. However, even with the elaborate techniques and models used by many firms, research has shown the results are often subsequently wrong.[7]

A CRA model based on substantial volumes of historical data may also be flawed. This occurs because past actions may be unreliable indications of future behavior. A country with a high level of risk in the past may have taken actions to reduce these factors, while countries with lower levels may have become riskier in recent years. This is one reason why data gathering for CRA purposes must be kept active and regularly updated.

The data collection efforts that provide the raw data to calculate country risk scores are often flawed. Political risk assessment models are often comparative, and it is difficult to procure the same data for different countries when it is subjective. Much of the data is based on opinion, which is highly subjective, and can be biased. An interviewee that is an "insider" (that is, a resident or citizen of the country in question) may be biased toward the country or biased against the home country of the interviewer. As such, different studies of the same country will often deliver dramatically different results. Apart from potential respondent biases, expert interviewees and interviewers may simply attach different meanings to a variable or interpret questions or answers differently, thereby introducing an additional bias.[8]

In underdeveloped or slowly developing countries, much of the economic data needed to accurately calculate risk scores using today's sophisticated quantitative models may not be published. If this data is published, it may not reflect the actual state or an accurate picture of the market in the global economy. Many countries have well-developed black markets where the exchange of cash, bribes, and goods, both legal and illicit, go unrecorded, and the data captured about economic activity is corrupt, or suspect at best.

Finally, CRA is helpful in illuminating the risks of investing or establishing operations in a foreign country, but it is not so helpful in providing an understanding of the other side of the risk and reward/return equation—that being the benefits to be generated for the firm from making these investments. You will need to employ different techniques, particularly those associated with modeling financial returns over time, and even more economic models like Porter's Diamond of National Advantage, in order to have a strong sense of the entire risk/reward equation.

Process for Applying the Technique

The investment decision-making process for a firm looking to enter a foreign market often follows a common pattern, and it can be adapted to a large or smaller scale project. Country risk ratings are commonly used to summarize the conclusions of the CRA process. The ratings provide a framework for establishing country exposure limits that reflect the firm's risk tolerance and willingness to balance potential rewards against these risks.

Business and competitive analysts can play a prominent role on a CRA effort. This will become more evident once we describe the organizational process for performing CRA. The following fairly standard methodology is adapted from one recommended by D.H. Meldrum:

1. Create a foreign country market risk assessment team. The team will be responsible for assessing risk in terms of the specific kind of investment being contemplated. For example, if the firm is considering locating a plant in a foreign country, longer-term risk factors, like economic risk, will be viewed as more important. If it is to be financed by the home firm, sovereign risk will not require consideration. If a firm is looking at a shorter-term investment, for example, selling goods in the private sector, economic outlook and exchange rate risk may reflect more pressing issues.

2. Analysts should help executives decide how important or potentially influential each of the different risk categories will be to the decision under consideration. The most influential receive the highest relative weight, and the least influential receive the lowest relative weight. These weights must be established for a particular time period because they will not likely be fixed at the same weights over long periods of time.

3. The team should select appropriate measures or metrics for each of type of risk. At this point, focus on a small number of quantifiable indicators (say between five and 10, which appear to be particularly relevant), such as GDP and debt service ratios, and determine if those indices are falling within a desirable range. Each index is given a score between 1 and 5, according to how closely the measure reflects low risk. Some samples of indicators for each type of risk are outlined in the risk descriptors described in subsequent paragraphs of this section.

4. For qualitative indicators, analysts should canvas risk experts (or the consensus of several experts) for their opinion on conditions in the country in question, and those outcomes are given a score from 1 to 5.

5. The resulting values can all be combined for each risk factor.

6. Each risk factor's score can then be multiplied by its weight, and all weighted scores can then be aggregated to create a total country risk score. If different countries are being compared, it is important to use the same weighting scheme consistently for all countries in order to get a relative assessment of country risk. Although this step results in a quantitative score, it is important not to attribute any spurious accuracy or confidence intervals to the results.

Assessing country risk ordinarily requires the use of a variety of sophisticated quantitative techniques. In many typical country analysis or planning situations, the analyst will begin with an index acquired through subscription or fee payment from a country risk consultancy or reporting body. Country risk reports can be purchased from the Business Environment Risk Intelligence (BERI) S.A., Control Risks Information Services (CRIS), Economist Intelligence Unit (EIU), Euromoney, Institutional Investor, Moody's Investor Services, Standard and Poor's Rating Group, and Political Risk Services: International Country Risk Guide (ICRG), among others. These reports are generated by groups that continually monitor and assess country risk and publish them on a regular and systematic basis.

The advantage of commercial reports is the vast resources and knowledge they have at their fingertips. Most, like the WEFA, IMF, and EIU reports, provide timely and regularly updated information on over 200 countries as well as periodic global reports. It is almost impossible for any other than the most resourceful firms to attempt to match the reach and capabilities that these commercial services provide. That said, the commercial reports are general overviews, not tailored to any particular type of investment or situation and not necessarily designed to answer the kind of investment oriented questions that a firm might be called upon to address. That is why a combination of commercially available material, adapted to and complemented with other analysis that apply to a firm's specific investment situation, is a preferable country risk assessment method for most firms looking to expand and invest abroad.

Acquiring these reports is a helpful but not a sufficient step in doing CRA for competitive or strategic decision-making purposes. None of the indices is sufficient to predict the array of social, political, and economic factors that can align to create a good or bad environment on any given day or at the time your firm is planning to make its investment. Very generally, the more stable a country is, the easier it is to make predictions about the nature and level of risk that will be experienced.

As assessing country risk for the strategic analyst is as much "art" as it is "science," the technique can vary according to the practitioner. Most CRA researchers will use their best judgment and knowledge to select a mix of social, economic, and political measures that will allow them to develop confident insights into the relative risk of a potential investment. In any case, it is pretty much impossible, if not impractical, to include every risk factor in any analysis; the range of economic, political, social, infrastructure, and other variables that can potentially be combined is too extensive for any single model.

A more desirable approach will involve a model being tailored to the strategy or competitive analysis needs of the firm, focusing on the factors that pose the greatest risk for the specific situation under analytical consideration. Although intertwined, country risks will fall into one or more of the following six categories described in Table 19.1.

Table 19.1
Common Types, Sources, and Indicators of Country Risk

Risk	Sources	Indicators
Economic	■ Disadvantageous shifts in policy goals, including fiscal and monetary. ■ Disadvantageous shifts in demographics, natural, or other resources and industry.	■ GDP growth rate. ■ Tax system stability. ■ Government debt levels. ■ Financial security.
Transfer	■ Movement of capital is restricted by agents of government. Can happen at any time and for a variety of reasons.	■ Having trouble attracting foreign currency. ■ Debt service payments/exports ratio. ■ Amount and type of foreign debt/income. ■ Foreign currency reserves/different import categories. ■ Current account status.
Exchange Rate	■ Unpredictable, unfavorable exchange rate movement or change in type of exchange rate (fixed to floating, or vice versa).	■ Pegged currency ranges. ■ Recent change from floating to fixed rates or vice versa.
Location/ Neighborhood	■ Instability in a neighbor, similar country, or region infects the country where you have invested.	■ Geographic location and proximity to hot or trouble spots. ■ Instability in strategic partner or ally.
Sovereign	■ Inherent risk that a government may default on obligations, either by choice or necessity.	■ Similar to transfer risk indicators. ■ Track record: Has government repaid in the past?
Political	■ Risks that result in loss of profit, expropriation, or repudiations due to changes in the political environment.	■ Qualitative expert opinion.

Economic Risk

Economic risk is the risk associated with less than expected rates of return or performance to an investment stemming from changes in economic policies or growth rate. Economic risk can occur most commonly when:

- Economic policies change.
- The goals underlying economic policies change.
- The market growth rate changes.
- An economy's strengths or advantages are somehow compromised.

Material changes in a country's natural or human resources, demographics, or industry performance can all result in economic risk. Political risk and economic risk may be closely intertwined. Some models for assessing political risk will put economic risk under the political risk umbrella, as government economic policies affect both the political and economic climates.

Economic Risk Indicators

There are numerous ratios that can be used to determine the relative level of health of a country's economy. A simple and accessible indicator is the gross domestic product (GDP) growth rate. A high growth rate can frequently indicate a developing country whose economy is experiencing rapid change, whereas a slow growth rate can indicate a mature market. In order to determine the amount and burden of external debt, one can look at the ratio of Net External Debt (NED) to GDP or the ratio of Net External Debt to exports of goods and services. These ratios give an indication of the country's ability to service its debt. As a rule of thumb, a debt service ratio under 10 percent is a positive sign, while anything over 20 percent is a negative sign. The amount and growth of GDP and the current tax system are also factors you should consider examining.

Transfer Risk

Transfer risk is the potential for a government, public agencies, or its officials to confine or hinder capital movement from their country to another. This can make it difficult or impossible for a firm to shift (or transfer) profit or capital assets back to their home country or elsewhere. Countries can hinder capital movement at any time through a variety of measures. Generally, countries that are having a hard time attracting foreign currency are more likely to enact capital restrictions. Like economic risk, some models for assessing political risk put transfer risk under the political risk umbrella, as political policies can also affect the flow of goods.

Transfer Risk Indicators

Imbalances in quantitative figures can expose the risk of transfer restrictions. It is more important to look at the trend of consistency or inconsistency in these figures than the absolute figures themselves. Some ratios to examine to determine transfer risk are: debt service payments to exports, foreign debt to income ratios, foreign currency reserves to imports (in categories), and relative current account status. Adverse imbalances in accounts could create a situation where governments will restrict capital in order to cover up deficits.

Exchange Risk

Exchange risk generally entails a quick or unexpected movement in the exchange rate between countries that causes detrimental investment results. This can include a country switching from fixed to floating exchange rate systems or vice versa. Currency traders and analysts are trained in making longer term predictions and can be a valuable source of information in assessing exchange rate activity. Short-term exchange risk can be mitigated by the use of hedging tactics. For the longer term, the firm will want to look at whether costs and revenues in the same currency match up or build in safety nets to cushion against currency fluctuations. The structure of the exchange rate policy is also an indicator. Floating rates, particularly when the country is an active participant in global trading regimes and its currency is regularly traded and exchanged, often produce less-unexpected movements. Managed floats, the situation in which governments are trying to keep their currency's rate of exchange pegged within a certain range, often increase this risk.

Exchange Risk Indicators

Transfer risk indicators can also be useful in determining exchange rate movement because over valuation of a currency can lead to increased imbalances that increase transfer risk. Alternatively, a currency devaluation can decrease these kinds of imbalances.

Location/Neighborhood Risk

These risks exist by virtue of being physically close to an unstable environment. They can occur wherever there are problems in a particular region: problems with a geographically near trading partner, with a neighboring country, or a country with similar traits or characteristics. For example, religious or racial persecution can lead to a flood of refugees to neighboring countries and cause disruption in commerce and trade.

Location/Neighborhood Risk Indicators

The best indicator for neighborhood risk is geographic proximity. Proximity to superpowers, troubled nations, unstable, warring, or impoverished countries can increase the levels of this risk. The number of borders (particularly pertinent for land-locked nations within larger continents), border disputes, and membership (or lack thereof) of alliances or trade agreements can also have an effect on this form of risk.

Sovereign Risk

The unique characteristic with sovereign risk is not so much the risk of loss, but the lack of repercussions in the event of loss, due to the sovereignty of nations. Any form of investment or partnership by a private investor with a government or one of its designated agencies runs the risk of default due to an inability or refusal by a country's government to honor its commitments. An inability to pay is related to economic and transfer risk, and a refusal to cooperate may be politically motivated. International law states that a private investor cannot sue a sovereign government without the government's permission.

Transfer risk indices are helpful in determining if a country will be able to honor financial commitments. Willingness to pay is a little trickier. It can be helpful to look at the historical record of payment by a particular nation and its respective governments. Although past actions are no guarantee of future behavior, an historical trend of not paying is a track record to be mindful of. The analyst must also consider the consequences to the nation/its government and the firm if the government does not pay. Could the nation experience potentially damaging consumer boycotts or receive strong pressure from other nations?

Political Risk

Generally speaking, assessing political risk is another elusive and varied task. Briefly, these are risks that result from political changes. Macro- and micro-risk can be further divided into two categories: societal and governmental.

Societal macro-risk refers to instability caused by civil wars, terrorism, coups, dramatic shifts in societal values, pressures by powerful unions, religious disagreements, revolutions, national work stoppages, or any other politically charged civil event that is detrimental to the activities of a foreign firm.

Governmental macro-risk encompasses all actions by the host government that can have negative effects on foreign businesses. These include nationalization and expropriation, limits on the repatriation of assets and profits, a dramatic change in leadership, and/or general bureaucracy. A less extreme, though far more common, example is the incongruence that results from high tariffs in countries that are trying to attract foreign business.

Societal micro-risks include boycotts, activism, some acts of terrorism, and competition from other multinationals.

Governmental micro-risks are those that are directed toward a specific foreign country or industry. They include selective nationalization, prejudicial tax systems, equity, content and hiring regulations, supporting indigenous competition, disregarding contracts, and putting controls on pricing.

In most cases of political risk analysis, either a business or political risk assessment service will interview experts (academics, business people, politicians, and consultants) and quantify the results into a numerical score or index in order to evaluate the country in relation to other countries. These political risk scores have been criticized as being inconsistent, subjective, and lacking future orientation.

Other techniques for gauging political risk include the "grand tours" technique, whereby a firm representative investigates the investment site and interviews local officials and businesses. Another method is the "old hands" technique, where the firm seeks out country experts and veterans in order to gather their views and insights.

This six-step process is best demonstrated via an example. The case study in this chapter is for a fairly standard application of the CRA process and will provide you with a better understanding of the process just outlined.

Although the nature of the CRA process and the level of analytical resources devoted to it will vary from firm to firm depending on the size and sophistication of its international operations, a number of considerations are relevant to evaluating the process:

- Is there a quantitative and qualitative assessment of the risk associated with each country in which the firm is operating or planning to conduct business?

- Is a formal analysis of country risk conducted at least annually, and does the firm have an effective system for monitoring prominent developments in the interim?

- Does the analysis take into account all aspects of the broadly defined concept of country risk, as well as any special risks associated with specific groups of counterparties the firm may have targeted in its business or market strategy?

- Is the analysis adequately documented, and are conclusions concerning the level of risk communicated in a way that provides decision makers with a reasonable basis for determining the nature and level of the firm's exposures or potential exposures in a country?

- Given the size and sophistication of the firm's international activities, are the resources (that is, data gathering, analysts, processes, systems, and time) devoted to the CRA process adequate?

- Have analysts checked with their decision makers to assess their satisfaction with previous country risk analyses? Did decision makers make use of the provided CRAs? Were the results provided credible? Have decision makers been surprised by an adverse event occurring in a country where an analysis was performed?

- As a final check of the process, are the analyst's conclusions concerning a country reasonable in light of information available from other sources, including external research and rating services?

CRA is important in an increasingly global marketplace, particularly for small- to medium-sized firms that are planning to make investments abroad for the first time. Conclusions about the level of country risk provide an evaluation of prevailing (and possible future) economic, political, and social conditions, which reflect on a country's ability to meet its obligations, as well as the credit risk on individual counterparties located in the country. CRA should be combined with other tools to improve the firm's ability to make better decisions about its international business activities.

Case Study: Zyboldt Metals (ZMC) Expansion into Eastern Europe

Zyboldt Metals Corporation (ZMC), headquartered in the mid-western part of the U.S., is a spin-off of a large American conglomerate that had gone through a massive restructuring and divesture initiative in order to focus on its core businesses of metal and plastics. ZMC, a firm with close to $130 million in sales in 2004 (nearly all of which were in Canada and the U.S.), viewed home canning products as a key part of the firm's product offering. The firm hoped to achieve at least a 50 percent growth in its home canning sales within the next three years, and an expansion into Eastern Europe, the first investment the firm would make outside of North America, would potentially be part of the strategy.

An observant CEO, Arthur Rieden, noticed some interesting things while on a six-week pleasure trip to several nations in Eastern Europe during July and August 2005. He observed that many people in the bed and breakfast facilities, as well as small hotels he stayed in, had their own vegetable gardens, with the Hungarians, Poles, Romanians, and Ukrainians having sizable vegetable gardens. When he asked his hosts about the produce from their gardens, he discovered that most of the people repetitively used the same jars to store their vegetables, and many of these jars lacked the proper seals; hence, they had to use a large volume of various preservatives in the canning process to avoid the contents being spoiled when bacteria, enzyme, mold, and yeast grew out of control.

Rieden knew that his canning products, properly applied, would control the spoilage, allowing the canned food to be kept for a substantially longer time. Market research the firm had authorized some years ago also showed that families in this part of the world generally preferred the ZMC canning process and its preservative-free taste.

With this information and forecasted market potential of around 60 million jars per year, expansion into Eastern European markets looked promising. While lids would be imported from Canada, upwards of eight million dollars for the glass jars molds and production, carton design and production, and an extensive multi-media advertising campaign would be invested directly in the country of entry. Based on his visits, the views of some of his well-traveled employees, and some sparse country data he was able to acquire, Rieden considered Hungary and Ukraine good entry points to establish an Eastern European market.

Before making the investment, Rieden asked his firm's analysts to perform a CRA, along with a number of other complementary market, competitor, and partner analyses of the two countries. For the CRA, he wanted to know if the potential benefits of investing in these countries would outweigh the associated risks. He asked the analyst to compare Hungary and Ukraine and their relative country risk. This study was carried out in late 2005.

Step One: What kind of investment is ZMC making? Which types of country risk will ZMC potentially be exposed to?

As the firm is outsourcing suppliers for jars, packaging, distribution, and advertising, the expansion into Eastern Europe can be classified as "Direct Investment—Private Sector." Therefore, the risk impact would be as follows:

Risk Category	Direct Investment Private Sector*
Economic	High
Transfer	Moderate
Exchange	High
Location	High
Sovereign	Moderate
Political	High

Source: Adapted from Meldrum, 2000.

Step Two: Choose weighting for each risk type, as follows:

Risk Category	Direct Investment Private Sector*
Economic	2
Transfer	1
Exchange	2.5
Location	2
Sovereign	1.5
Political	2

Step Three: Select indicators:

Grading Guide: A = 0 points, B = 1 point, C = 2 points, D = 3 points, F = 4 points, +/− = add/subtract .25 points.

Hungary

Hungary is a landlocked country in Central Europe bordered by Austria, Slovakia, Ukraine, Romania, Serbia and Montenegro, Croatia, and Slovenia. Hungary fell under Communist rule following World War II. In 1956, a revolt and announced withdrawal from the Warsaw Pact were met with a massive military intervention by the USSR. Under the leadership of Janos Kadar in 1968, Hungary began liberalizing its economy, introducing so-called "Goulash Communism." Hungary held its first multiparty elections in 1990 and initiated a free market economy. It joined NATO in 1999 and the EU in 2004. In mid-2005, the population was just above 10 million.[9]

Basic Economic Facts

- GDP (purchasing power parity, or ppp): USD$149.3 billion (2004)
- GDP (ppp) per capita: USD$14,900
- GDP (ppp) real growth rate: 3.9 percent (2004 est.)
- Inflation rate: 7 percent (2004 consumer est.)
- Debt (external): USD$57 billion

Economic Risk Indicators

This points to a very high debt service ratio (23.5 for 2004) and total debt increasing over the next two years. Hungary maintains large fiscal and external deficits. However, domestic spending is getting stronger, and a cut in the VAT will help keep inflation down.
Score = B = (1).

Transfer Risk Indicators

Current account balance was –8.8 percent of GDP in 2004 and is projected to remain around 8 percent in 2005 and 2006. The country's debt-service ratio paid is over 20 percent, averaging around 22 percent between 2004 and 2006. Foreign investment has been a key to Hungary's economic success. With about $55.44 billion in foreign direct investment (FDI) since 1989, Hungary has been a leading destination for FDI in this part of Europe. Slightly over 25 percent has come from U.S.-based firms. Foreign firms have helped modernize Hungary's industrial sector and created thousands of new, high-skilled, high-paying jobs. Foreign firms account for over 70 percent of Hungary's exports, 33 percent of GDP, and about 25 percent of new jobs.
Score = B = (1).

Exchange Rate Indicators

In 1995, Hungary's currency, the forint (HUF), became convertible for all current account transactions and subsequent to it gaining OECD membership in 1996 for almost all capital account transactions. In 2001, the Government lifted the remaining currency controls and broadened the band around the exchange rate, allowing the forint to appreciate by more than 12 percent in a year. Conflicting fiscal and monetary policy in the summer of 2002 caused confusion in the market, with the forint surging against the Euro for several months. In attempts to reassure the market, the Medgyessy Government repeatedly said the coun-

try would join the ERM II as soon as possible, with hopes of adopting the Euro by 2008. This issue remains on hold until the next elections (in mid-2006), which may settle direction and timing.
Score = B– = (1.25).

Location Risk Indicators

There are no significant location risks in the near future, although the surrounding area has been tumultuous within the last decade.
Score = A– = (.25).

Sovereign Risk Indicators

Hungary has not had any problems in this area since becoming a liberalized economy and shows no obvious signs of sovereign risks in the near to mid-term.
Score = A = (0).

Political Risk Indicators

There will be another election in mid-2006, after several rounds of governments have been unable to hold power for long periods. The current ruling party was trailing badly in the polls at the end of 2005. Both the government and opposition have populist platforms, so there is unlikely to be much in the way of structural reform until the election concludes.
Score = B– = (1.25).

Hungary Country Risk Summary

Risk Type	Weight	×	Grade	=	Total
Economic Risk	2	×	1	=	2
Transfer Risk	1	×	1	=	1
Exchange Risk	2.5	×	1.25	=	3.125
Location Risk	2	×	0.25	=	0.50
Sovereign Risk	1.5	×	0	=	0
Political Risk	2	×	1	=	2
			Total	**=**	**8.625**

The analyst concluded that Hungary did not have high levels of country risk for the firm's Eastern European expansion. Nevertheless, the charge by CEO Rieden was to compare the relative risk levels of Hungary to Ukraine. The next section performs the same CRA process on Ukraine.

Ukraine

Situated in East-Central Europe, Ukraine is bordered by Poland, Slovakia, Hungary, Romania, and Moldova to the West, by Belarus to the North, and by the Russian Federation to the North-East and East. To the south of the country lies the Black Sea. The capital is Kiev.

Ukraine became independent in 1991 with the dissolution of the USSR. Since that time, democracy has remained elusive as the legacy of state control and endemic corruption stalled efforts to improve civil liberties, achieve economic reform, and accelerate privatization. A peaceful mass protest (the "Orange Revolution") toward the end of 2004 compelled the authorities to overturn a rigged presidential election and to allow a new internationally monitored vote. This election swept into power a reformist slate under Viktor Yushchenko. The population was around 47.4 million in the middle of 2005.[10]

Basic Economic Facts

- GDP (ppp): USD$299.1 billion
- GDP (ppp) per capita: USD$6300
- GDP (ppp) growth: 12 percent (2004)
- Inflation rate: 12 percent (2004 est.)
- Debt external: USD$16.4 billion (est. 2004)

Economic Risk Indicators

Ukraine has many of the components of a major European economy—rich farmlands, a well-developed industrial base, highly trained labor, and a good education system. The country experienced a sharp period of economic decline in the 1990s, and the standard of living for most citizens declined steadily, leading to widespread poverty. Beginning in 2000, economic growth has averaged almost 9 percent per year, reaching 9.4 percent in 2003 and 12.5 percent in 2004. The GDP in 2000 showed strong export-based growth of 6 percent (the first growth since independence), and industrial production grew 12.9 percent. The economy continued to expand in 2001 as real GDP rose 9 percent and industrial output grew by over 14 percent. Growth was driven by strong domestic demand and growing consumer and investor confidence. The rapid economic growth in 2002–4 was largely attributed to a surge in steel exports to China, and personal income levels have been rising. The macro-economy is stable, and high inflation level is gradually coming under control. While economic growth continues, Ukraine's long-term economic prospects depend on the acceleration of market reforms. The economy remains burdened by excessive government regulation, corruption, and lack of law enforcement, and while the Yushchenko Government took steps against corruption and small and medium firms have been largely privatized, much remains to be done to restructure and privatize key sectors such as energy and telecommunications.
Score = B = (1).

Transfer Risk Indicators

Ukraine has been encouraging foreign trade and investment. The foreign investment law allows non-citizens to purchase businesses and property, to repatriate revenue and profits, and to receive compensation in the event that their property is nationalized by a future government. On paper, there is no legal distinction between domestic and foreign capital; in practice, large local firms—mostly state-owned firms in the industrial sector—have considerable political and legal influence. However, complex laws and regulations, poor corporate

governance, weak judicial enforcement of contract law, and corruption inhibit large-scale foreign direct investment in Ukraine. Contracts are difficult to enforce, and regulation is neither impartial nor clear. Although it is possible for foreign firms to win court cases, particularly at the higher levels, the judicial process remains slow and inefficient. Ukraine is dominated by powerful local players who have successfully prevented foreign investment. The risk that foreign investors' assets will be de facto expropriated is low, but recent examples exist. While there is a functioning stock market, the lack of protection for minority shareholders' rights severely restricts portfolio investment activities. Total FDI in Ukraine was approximately $7.72 billion as of October 1, 2004, which, at $162 per capita, was still one of the lowest figures in the region.
Score = C = (2).

Exchange Rate Indicators

Ukraine's currency, the hryvnia, was introduced in September 1996 and has remained stable until quite recently. There has been increasing volatility in the rate since 2000, and successive governments have stated their aim was to enact policies that increased outsiders' confidence towards the economy as well as its credit rating. These actions remain in flux.
Score = C = (2).

Location Risk Indicators

The region surrounding Ukraine is mostly stable and appears to be entering a period of stable adjustment to the global economy. The only remaining location risk issue is inside the country, as crime is a serious problem in Ukraine, and a higher than European average number of racially motivated assaults and incidents of harassment to individuals of African or Asian descent have been reported in recent years.
Score = C = (2).

Sovereign Risk Indicators

Ukraine has a recent history of defaults and therefore may have higher than average levels of sovereign risk. There are still some trends on the horizon to suggest the retention of higher than average levels of risk in this indicator.
Score = D+ = (2.75).

Political Risk Indicators

A new democratic constitution was adopted on June 28, 1996, which mandates a pluralistic political system with protection of basic human rights and liberties. Recent elections have been challenged, and there remains some skepticism over the long term stability of the government.
Score = C– (2.25).

Ukraine Country Risk Summary

Risk Type	Weight	×	Grade	=	Total
Economic Risk	2	×	1	=	2
Transfer Risk	1	×	2	=	2
Exchange Risk	2.5	×	2	=	5
Location Risk	2	×	2	=	4
Sovereign Risk	1.5	×	2.75	=	4.125
Political Risk	2	×	2.25	=	4.5
			Total	=	**21.625**

Recommendation

Based on the calculations performed, it was clear to the analyst that at the end of 2005, Ukraine held a far higher degree of country risk in the short and medium term than Hungary. This raised a number of "yellow flags" that the analyst knew would require further analysis. When the results of the CRA were combined with the firm's examination of customers, market, and financial projections, the analyst was confident to make an insightful recommendation to CEO Rieden about the firm's preferred choice for locating its new Eastern European operations.

FAROUT Summary

FAROUT SUMMARY

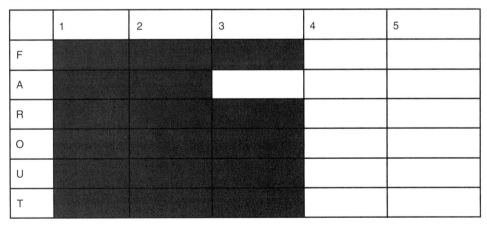

Figure 19.1   Country risk assessment FAROUT summary

Future orientation—Medium. The technique can be somewhat future oriented if projections and the assumptions upon which they are based are prudently constructed and clearly communicated, but analysts who rely too heavily on data that is historical or stale in nature will compromise the future orientation.

Accuracy—Low to medium. The nature of any form of risk (including country risk) is that there is always an element of unpredictability, and no method will ever consistently and accurately predict outcomes.

Resource efficiency—Medium. Depending on the extent to which one is undertaking the analysis, the process of gathering extensive data from experts, weighting, and aggregating outcomes, can be time-consuming and expensive, whereas buying reports from country risk forecasting advisors or services can be more efficient.

Objectivity—Medium. CRA will always rely at least partly on subjective data, despite the common efforts by consultancies and advice vendors to quantify the method.

Usefulness—Medium. Country risk and the concepts discussed to forecast it can be applied in many areas of business strategy and decision making.

Timeliness—Medium. If the process is ongoing and a part of a firm's ongoing operations, the information should be developed and delivered on a more timely basis. If the data needs to be gathered, the process will be slower to complete.

Related Tools and Techniques

- Investment valuation analysis
- Outsourcing analysis
- Political risk analysis
- Porter's Diamond of National Advantage
- Scenario analysis
- STEEP/PEST and related macro-environmental analysis
- Strategic relationships analysis
- SWOT analysis
- Value chain analysis

References

Alon, I., and M. Martin (1998). "A normative model of macroeconomic political risk assessment," *Multinational Business Review*, Fall.

Bartlett, C.A., and S. Ghoshal (1998). *Managing Across Borders: The Transnational Solution*, 2nd edition. Boston, MA: Harvard Business School Press.

Bremmer, I. (2005). "Managing risk in an unstable world," *Harvard Business Review*, 83(6), June, pp. 51–62.

CIA World Factbook (2005). U.S. Dept. of State Country Background Notes (Source Date: 08/05). Retrieved Oct. 10, 2005 from http://www.odci.gov/cia/publications/factbook.

Coplin, W.D., and M.K. O'Leary (1994). *The Handbook of Country and Political Risk Analysis*. East Syracuse, NY: Political Risk Services, International Business Communications.

Desta, A. (1993). *International Political Risk Assessment for Foreign Direct Investment and Investment Lending Decisions*. Needham Heights, Massachusetts: Ginn Press.

Ghose, T.K. (1988). "How to analyze country risk." *Asian Finance*, October 15, pp. 61–63.

GlobalEDGE (2006). Country insights section, retrieved from the web on March 18, 2006, from http://globaledge.msu.edu/ibrd/countryindex.asp.

Meldrum, D.H. (2000). "Country risk and foreign direct investment." *Business Economics*, 35, January, pp. 33–40.

Merill, J. (1982). "CRA." *Columbia Journal of World Business*, 17, pp. 88–91.

OCC (Office of the Controller of the Currency) (2001). Country Risk Management. Administrator of National Banks. Washington, DC: U.S. Department of the Treasury.

Perlitz, M. (1985). "Country-portfolio analysis-assessing country risk and opportunity," *Long Range Planning*, 18, pp. 11–26.

Porter, M.E. (1990). *The Competitive Advantage of Nations*. New York, NY: The Free Press.

Robock, S.H. (1971). "Political risk: Identification and assessment," *Columbia Journal of World Business*, 6, pp. 6–20.

Sethi, P.S., and K.A. Luther (1986). "Political risk analysis and direct foreign investment: Some problems of definition and measurement," *California Management Review*, 28, pp. 57–68.

Simon, J.D. (1982). "Political risk assessment: Past trends and future prospects," *Columbia Journal of World Business*, pp. 62–71.

Thompson, A.A., Gamble, J., and A.J. Strickland (2006). *Strategy: Winning in the Marketplace*, 2nd edition. New York, NY: McGraw-Hill.

Ting, W. (1988). *Multinational Risk Assessment and Management*. New York, NY: Quorum Books.

Wells, R.K. (1997). "Country risk management: A practical guide," *Business Credit*, 99, Nov/Dec, pp. 20–24.

Endnotes

[1] Thompson, Gamble, and Strickland, 2006.

[2] Ting, 1988.

[3] Wells, 1997.

[4] Ghose, 1988.

[5] Meldrum, 2000.

[6] Bremmer, 2005.

[7] Alon and Martin, 1998; Sethi and Luther, 1986.

[8] Desta, 1993.

[9] Sources: GlobalEDGE, 2006; *CIA World Factbook*, 2005.

[10] Sources: GlobalEDGE, 2006; *CIA World Factbook*, 2005.

20

Driving Forces Analysis

Short Description

Performing an industry analysis (see Chapter 6, "Industry Analysis (The Nine Forces)") can reveal much about the current state of an industry and the potential for it to generate profitability for its incumbents; nevertheless, change and uncertainty are ever present in the competitive environment. Driving forces analysis (DFA) is a way of understanding and accounting for change at the industry level. "Drivers" are clusters of trends that create influences on changes to an industry's structure and a rival's competitive conduct.

Background

Change, particularly longer-term change, became a topic of interest to researchers, managers, and policy makers following the First and Second World Wars. DFA was developed in the 1950s as a means for helping organizations and individuals deal with changes in the business environment. Techniques such as force field analysis (FFA), developed by Kurt Lewin in 1951, included the concepts of driving and hindering forces. FFA was used to analyze the conditions that support or restrain a given outcome and was seen to be an effective way both to analyze an existing set of conditions and determine the most effective methods to achieve a desired outcome. This work captured the fancy of economists and set the stage for the further development of DFA within the competitive industrial context.

So what are driving forces (DFs)? There are forces in every situation that cause things to remain as they are or to change. Forces that push toward change are called "driving" or "helping" forces. Forces that resist change are called "restraining" or "hindering" forces. When these forces are balanced, no change is likely to occur. When the net effect of these forces is altered and moves away from balance, change occurs in either a helpful or obstructive manner.

Change is not the only factor associated with DFs that firms need to take into account; uncertainty is another key element that a firm must confront as it makes decisions and develops strategies.

The term "force" refers to the broad cluster of events, state of affairs, and/or trends that impact the firm's future. DFs are those significant, underlying "currents" that define and drive events and trends in certain directions. These forces are typically quite broad in scope, long-term in nature, and associated with some degree of uncertainty as to their evolution. Examples of DFs include global population growth, advancing use of technology like the World Wide Web or portable phones, and changes in the global climate.

In order to plan appropriate strategies for change, the forces in the situation must be clearly understood and identified. Understanding the DFs is the first step toward establishing a framework for analyzing critical trends, particularly as they may impact the competitive environment facing an industry. Taking this a step further, Tregoe and Zimmerman saw them as the primary determiners of the scope of future products and markets and a dominant factor that heavily influences major decisions.

Strategic Rationale

Industry conditions change because forces are driving industry participants (competitors, customers, or suppliers) to alter their actions. Some DFs originate from within a firm's industry and competitive environment and can create uncertainty for industry participants—this is always an element present in a competitive environment that a firm can exploit with a well-deployed strategy.

The first task in understanding industry evolution is to look for the DFs of the macro-environment that influence industry structure and competitive behavior; for example, changing government regulations and regulatory regimes. There are also less-obvious external factors. Identifying and assessing these fundamental factors is both the starting point and one of the objectives of scenario analysis.[1]

DFs may seem obvious to one person but be hidden to another; therefore, the identification of DFs should be done in a team environment. It is helpful to run through this common list of categories of DFs: social forces/demographic developments, technological developments, economic developments and events, political developments and events, and environmental developments. Normally, firms have little control over DFs—their ability to deal with them comes from recognizing them and understanding their effects.

DFA also plays a critical role in the larger strategy development process. DFs indicate the external factors likely to have greatest impact on a firm in the near future. The firm must proactively address these forces if it is to achieve success.

Strengths and Advantages

DFA is an essential component of several other analytical techniques, including environment and industry analysis. The first task in building a scenario is to look for DFs of the macro-environment that influence the key industry or customer factors likely to impact the firm.[2] For example, government regulations might influence future competition, but there are also many less-obvious external factors. Identifying and assessing these factors is both the starting point and one of the objectives of the DFA method. DFs are also a key part of doing any industry analysis, which cannot be performed effectively in their absence.

DFs by nature imply change. Understanding them and their impacts requires managers to consider how conditions will evolve in and around their industries and to consider these forces in their decisions and strategy.

DFA tends to receive a higher than average degree of managerial agreement—particularly when the managers are involved in the consensus process used for developing them. Senior managers often have insights developed over time that can provide valuable perspectives in the DFA process. The inclusion of managers and decision makers in the DF identification and prioritization process can be a valuable facet of getting everyone in the firm focused on the type of strategic thinking and competitive learning that tends to serve firms well in the long run.[3]

DFA can be done in a less data-intense fashion than many other techniques and doesn't necessarily require the firm to gather data on a continual basis like many other analytical techniques do. The use of brainstorming, popular group consensus methods, and participative technology facilitates its achievement, and it can be done on a less-frequent basis than required for many other tools while still being effective.

Weaknesses and Limitations

DFA cannot drive strategy formulation alone and seldom specifically answers clients' strategy questions. There are other steps that need to be performed before determining organizational actions (that is, strategies or tactics) even after gaining agreement on DFs. In other words, just recognizing and agreeing upon a critical driving force does not tell decision makers what they need to do, but it does tell them that this driving force will impact their future and that the decisions or strategies that need to be developed must take these impacts into account.

DFs tend to be outside the control of any single firm to change. What can be done is to change how the firm's strategy or tactics takes them into account. Firms do not manage the DFs, but instead must manage their own responses to them.

The process used to perform DFA nearly always needs to be inclusive and participatory. This can be a problem in some firms where key personnel are not available to participate or lack the time to give the necessary consideration to the DF development and prioritization process. Mostly due to organizational structure reasons or internal politics, some firms have experienced great difficulties in generating agreements on the DFs or their prioritization.

DF analysis can suffer from many of the common internal, organizational biases when they are generated using only internal personnel. This is because internal personnel tend to see the world through the same (potentially distorted) organizational lens. As such, it is often useful to employ external resources to reach consensus around the DFs.

Process for Applying the Technique

There are two essential steps involved in performing DFA, each of which includes a number of sub-elements that need to be performed before moving forward. The primary analytical task in performing DFA is to:

1. Identify what the relevant DFs are—this requires separating the major causes of industry change from less important ones.
2. Assess the impact they will have on the industry—this involves identifying the small number of DFs that are likely to have greatest impact on the industry and the firm over the next few years.

Step 1: Identifying an Industry's DFs

Some DFs are unique and specific to a particular industry's situation; nevertheless, most DFs cut across broad swaths of the business environment. They are usually identified by the presence of patterns seen as events and trends, or combinations of trends that combine to create a force. Some of the more common DFs across various industries are shown next.[4]

Common Types of DFs

- Changes in long-term industry growth rate
- Changes in who buys the product and how it is used
- Changing societal concerns, attitudes, and lifestyles
- Diffusion of expertise across more firms and locations
- Election trends, government decisions, and/or shifting regulatory influences
- Growing use of the Internet and its applications
- Important firms that enter or exit the industry
- Increasing globalization of the industry
- Innovation in communication and marketing
- Innovation in processes and products
- Changes in the long-term industry growth rate
- Major changes in customer needs and preferences
- Major changes in production costs and efficiencies
- Prominent changes in uncertainty and business risk
- Technological change and manufacturing process innovation

So how do you discover an industry's DFs? You should start by pruning the generated list of all those DFs that are not relevant to your industry. For example, if you are a wholesaler or B2B firm, you can probably eliminate end-user type forces from the list. After eliminating the obvious ones, determine if there is another driving force that cannot be readily subsumed inside one of those remaining on the list. If the answer is no, then the force should be included.

Another way of trying to understand DFs is to understand how trends (that is, $T_1 \ldots T_n$) or events ($E_1 \ldots E_n$) relate to one another and a potential driving force. This is diagrammed in Figure 20.1. This process helps you to understand the relationship between trends and events and to determine the truly independent driving forces as opposed to overlapping ones.

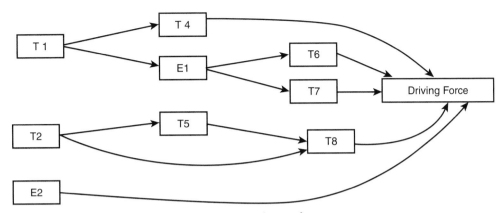

Figure 20.1   Relating trends and events to a driving force

It is a rare analyst or group of managers that can look at their first list and focus in on the key DFs. When these are presented to a group of managers, as most analysts will do in their development of DFs, someone invariably throws cold water on some of the suggested forces and suggests others. Our experience suggests that some of the most constructive debates occur when the DFs determination team tries to identify their relevant set of forces. Of course, it can often get even more interesting once this step is completed and their impacts are discussed.

This list shows the completion of the first stage by a management group of a large, publicly funded university in Canada.

Representative DFs in the Macro-Environment for a Large Public University

Societal and Demographic

- Increased diversity of students seeking university education
- Question over the value of some credentials—particularly relative to experience
- Increasing desire by individuals for lifelong learning
- Concerns over social inequities and fragmentation
- Increasing complexity of social problems
- Continuing aging of population in primary catchment regions
- Changing views regarding the appropriate role of universities

Economic

- Continued globalization
- Growth increasingly powered by entrepreneurship
- Huge increases in participation rate of university students in some regions of the globe—for example, China and Mexico

- Downturn of the economic cycle
- Rising interest rates and impact on student loans

Political

- Uncertainties in direction of public support for universities
- Declining public funding
- Increasing governmental demand for accountability
- Increased student activism due to raised tuition fees

Technological

- Increasing demand for distance learning availability
- Origination of new pedagogical platforms
- Expanded use of information technology in and out of the classroom
- Escalating rates of innovation
- Increasing value placed on knowledge

This list illustrates a typical array of factors to emerge from this step. We recommend that the analyst complete at least one other iteration to reduce these even further, prior to assessing their relative impact in Step 2. At the end of this step, the analyst should have a manageable list of DFs to consider. Our experience suggests that the list should be in the range of five to 10 forces to facilitate the next step of this analysis process.

Step 2: Assessing the Impact of the DFs

Step 2 will require a more intense analytical effort than Step 1 because DFs that remain on the list from Step 1 are all deemed to be important to some degree to the success of your industry and firm. All firms need to offer customers in their target markets products or services that meet their needs in a profitable manner, and the forces already identified impact all rivals in the industry. Now rank these DFs in order of their importance in driving the attractiveness of the industry, the level of profitability that may be achieved in the near future, and provide a context in which strategy changes can be considered and thoughtful decisions made.

The analyst's objective in this second step is to understand the external factors that will shape change in the industry and the difference these factors will make to it. Once the DFs have been identified from Step 1, the analyst needs to ask the following questions:

- Are they valid?
- How do we know?
- How significant are each of them?
- What is their strength?
- Which ones can be altered?
- Which ones cannot be altered?

- Which ones can be altered quickly?
- Which ones can only be altered slowly?
- Which ones, if altered, would produce rapid change?
- Which ones would only produce slow change?
- What skills and/or information are needed and are available to change the forces?
- Can you get the resources/capabilities needed to change them?

There are three common approaches applied at this point.

The first approach is to use a structured ranking approach. With a structured ranking approach, the analyst considers all the DFs listed from Step 1 in pair-wise progression. In other words, take DF 1 and compare it with DF 2, and decide which is more important to the industry and the firm in the determination of strategy, making major decisions, and setting of important policies. Next, compare DF 1 with the remaining DFs, then take DF 2 and compare it with the remaining DFs, and continue the process until all possible comparisons have been exhausted.

As the analyst can quickly calculate, the number of pair-wise comparisons grows rapidly with the number of DFs. For six DFs, there are 15 comparisons; for eight DFs, there are 28 comparisons; and for 10 DFs, there are 45 comparisons. You can readily see the advantages to taking care in selecting the initial DFs.

Our experience using this method is that some of the comparisons will be quickly accomplished, while others will bog down the group in discussion. It ordinarily takes half a day to achieve consensus about the final list of DFs ranked in order of their impact. It is critical that the analyst put in the appropriate effort at this point since it will enhance the quality of any complementary efforts that they subsequently perform, particularly in support of regularly conducted planning activities.

A second approach that many analysts take at this point is to assign a score to each force, from 1 (weak) to 7 (strong). The score is based on the strength of the force and the degree to which it is possible to influence this force. Next, they calculate a total score for each force by adding across the two columns. An example of this is given in Table 20.1 for an operator in the transportation manufacturing industry.

Table 20.1
Ranking Driving Forces

Force	Strength	Ability to Influence	Total (Rank)
a. Consumers seeking more specialized after-sale services.	3	6	9 (5th)
b. Buyers want higher fuel economy.	6	5	11 (2nd tie)
c. Better, safer, roads and highways allow for higher speeds.	2	3	5 (7th)
d. Increased demands for passenger safety.	4	4	8 (6th)
e. New technologies allow more engine and fuel options.	5	6	11 (2nd tie)
f. Demand is increasing mostly in China and India for the product.	7	5	12 (1st)
g. Outsourcing options are growing fast.	4	6	10 (4th)

The third approach is to use a matrix that separates the forces on pre-selected dimensions. The following example uses "importance" and "uncertainty" to distinguish between the set of DFs. Importance rankings can be assigned to each of the DFs in the list with a 1–4 Likert-type scale, with 1 being assigned to the DFs of "lowest importance" and 4 being assigned to the DFs of "highest importance." The same process can be used for "uncertainty," whereas 1 is assigned to DFs with the "lowest uncertainty" and 4 is assigned to the DFs of "highest uncertainty" in terms of their depth, direction, impact. and/or evolution. Those with mean scores above 2.5 in the relevant range are rated "high" in Table 20.2, while those scoring below it are rated as "low."

Table 20.2
Importance Ranking of Driving Forces

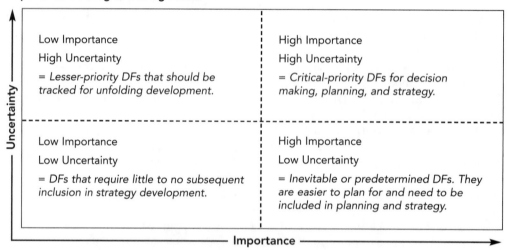

Regardless of which of the three approaches is taken, another key facet of this stage is to determine whether these DFs are acting to make the industry environment more or less attractive; as such, they should be combined with an industry analysis, possibly using the Porter's Five Forces model[5] or the Nine Forces/Industry Analysis (see Chapter 6) or something similar. Four questions related to the DF's impact on the industry environment that must be answered are as follows:

- Are the DFs causing demand for the industry's product to increase or decrease?
- Are the DFs making the bargaining power of other industry participants higher or lower?
- Are the DFs acting to make competition more or less intense?
- Will the DFs lead to higher or lower industry profitability?

The case study provides an illustration of DFA as it is applied to the digital music player industry. This newly emergent industry is an interesting case study for DFA because in 2006, it was still in a relatively early stage of its life cycle relative to the use of players for

MP3 digital file formats, as well as being a spin-off of portable music players that used to play music formatted on CDs, which are in a mature stage of their life cycle.

Once the analysts have performed these steps, their next task is to decide whether (strategic or tactical) actions taken to change the firm's strategy to address the driving force are feasible or not. If so, their goal is to devise a manageable course of action that does the following:

- Strengthens areas where DFs have positive impacts on the industry and firm.
- Creates organizational buffers for areas in which DFs have adverse impacts.
- Creates areas in which neutral DFs may eventually result in benefits.

At this point, it is usually helpful for the analyst to develop another set of tables, one for each of the DFs that has been identified as a priority. For each of these tables, outline in the first column the range of likely impacts that the DFs are expected to have on the industry. In the second column, begin identifying potential solutions that the firm may bring to bear in constructively addressing (that is, minimizing the negative effects and maximizing the positive effects of) the impact. The tables should look similar to what is shown in Table 20.3.

Table 20.3
Impact and Proposed Solutions for Driving Force 1

Force 1: Increasing Environmental Concerns

Impact on Industry	Proposed Solutions
Increasing demand for cars that can run on bio-fuels.	■ Fund and support further research into alternative bio-fuels. ■ Develop new fuel delivery systems for automobiles. ■ Continue development on bio-fuel burning engine materials. ■ Work with existing gasoline suppliers and retailers to develop delivery infrastructure.
Structural materials that can be recycled or will naturally break down at the end of their useful life.	■ Fund and support further research into alternative materials; in particular, bio-degradable ones. ■ Continue development of recycling collection capacities. ■ Work with public authorities to provide incentives to encourage recyclability.
Greater fuel efficiency of vehicles.	■ Continue development of hybrid engine technologies. ■ Provide more engines with partial cylinder managed shut-down capability. ■ Develop lighter materials to reduce weight. ■ Further develop computerized fuel-maximization driving modules.

The next step would require the analysts to work through each of the proposed solutions. They would need to compare these options in terms of costs/benefits, risks/benefits or via a pre-determined set of criteria used for assessing the relative attractiveness and value of the options. Comparing them against the current strategy of the firm is another key task to perform at this point in order to gauge the degree of the change required should the firm adopt the proposed solution, as well as the likelihood that the firm could implement it effectively; and the final task is to analyze and identify the nature of competitor responses that the action may engender.

Summary

Sound analysis of an industry's DFs is a prerequisite to good strategic decision making. What should be noted is that DFs and competitive pressures do not affect all competitors in an industry in the same manner. Profit prospects vary from rival to rival based on the relative attractiveness of their market positions and their strategies in addressing the DFs.

Case Study: The Digital Music Industry

This case study provides an example of DFA as applied to the digital music player industry in 2006.

What are the major DFs affecting the digital music player industry? Are the forces indicating a more or less attractive industry environment from a profitability standpoint?

Growth in levels of demand. Aside from being the most popularly given category of gifts during the 2005 holiday season globally, figures released by the organizers of the Consumer Electronics Show (CES) in Las Vegas, Nevada, in January 2006, showed that sales of MP3 players soared by 200 percent in 2005 to USD$3 billion or £1.73 billion.[6] As these figures, plus related recent sales figures and the media "buzz," will attest, both the digital music player market and the market for digital music are expected to continue experiencing healthy growth. As technological advances spur the enhancement of the devices with more and more valuable features, sales both to new users as well as existing device owners will continue to remain robust.

Product innovation. Frequent product innovation is another characteristic of the industry.[7] This product innovation is largely focused on new product designs; enhanced functionality; and aesthetics that make the products more portable, pleasant to look at (that is, some of these items are viewed as "status symbols" when worn by their owners in some parts of the world), and easier to use. Firms continue to add useful features to MP3 players such as telephone capability, video-playing capacity, appointment schedulers, contact databases, and photographic capabilities. Many of the manufacturers are known for their product innovation capabilities, including Apple, Creative, Microsoft, Samsung, and Sony, among others.

Format war and rights management. There are multiple formats of MP3 digital music files, some of which can only be played on the format owner's own devices. RealNetworks offers its own formats, which also support Apple's basic format of choice, AAC, but does not support the extended proprietary version of AAC, which integrates an Apple-developed digital rights management system called *FairPlay*. Microsoft continues to promote its Windows Media Audio (WMA) standard that it would like to see emerge as the industry standard. Sony music players only work with their proprietary software. Fighting digital piracy and promoting fairness in using files, while making sure artists and music firms are properly compensated for their rights, remains at the heart of an ongoing global regulatory battle.

Convergence. Coupled with product innovation, firms are increasingly working to make MP3 players and other personal electronics more versatile. For example, Apple developed the iPod Photo that allows users to transport and display photos; cell phone makers, such as Sony and Nokia, are developing MP3-compatible sets; and personal digital assistant (PDA) makers, such as HP and PalmOne, have or are developing PDAs with phone, game, MP3 playing, and digital photography capabilities. Most traditional home stereo manufacturers already offer stand-alone players that can play MP3 formats. Finally, MP3 playing capabilities are being increasingly included in new automotive stereo products, adding a different form of portability for playing music (at far higher speeds than while walking).

Growing use of the Internet. The increasing global adoption of broadband Internet service will help drive the market forward by increasing the source of supply and demand for the music to be played on the industry's devices. This also creates a need for a portable method for maintaining one's MP3 collection. This factor could especially benefit the manufacturers whose players are identified with popular subscription services. The ability to download a large amount of music in a relatively short time is a success factor for that segment of the MP3 value chain. Growing use of the Internet will also lead to better informed and more MP3-amenable customers.

Changes in who uses the product and how it is used. An increasingly diverse, global customer base is using the industry's products in more varied ways. The industry's products are moving up the product life cycle from the early adopters to the mainstream; consequently, users are becoming less technologically sophisticated and more demanding on functionality, style, and price. This also changes the nature of tactics and strategies that the major players in the industry will use in order to be successful, particularly around areas like pricing, promotion, advertising, manufacturing, and branding concerns.[8]

The effect of DFs in this market can also be further analyzed by answering the following four questions:

1. **What is the effect of the DFs on demand?**—Virtually all of these changes should increase the level of demand for the industry's products. Increasing product innovation, especially in the area of convergence with PDA or telephone functionality, should lead to higher demand, especially from existing device owners. Growing use of the Internet should also be a demand driver, as it increases the volume of content available, as well as the population of individuals who can potentially use the product.

2. **Are the DFs making the bargaining power of other industry participants higher or lower?**—The resolution of the digital rights issue will clearly empower some players, whether it will be consumers who will have liberalized choice options for their digital music enjoyment, record firms, and/or artists. Also the eventual resolution of the format wars will also clearly empower some industry participants while neutralizing the prospects of others. As such, there remains a high degree of uncertainty surrounding the resolution of this driving trend; however, it will have a significant

impact on some firms, and industry participants will need to develop flexible strategies and contingency plans in case the trends go against their current strategy.

3. **Are the DFs increasing competition?**—There is no doubt that the increased demand for and increasing profitability of products like Apple's iPod will entice new and potentially powerful electronics manufacturers into the industry. The threat of new entrants is a key factor in the rivalry among sellers in the market. The high threat will cause the current players to compete against both each other and possible new entrants, specifically in the area of product innovation.

4. **Will the DFs lead to higher profitability?**—New entrants are expected to arise in the market, which will in turn increase supply. Demand will continue to be increased due to product innovations, market growth, and the increased evolution and advancement in Internet usage globally. It will be interesting to see whether demand or supply will be the stronger force in the coming years. It is reasonable to conclude that profitability will likely be based more on volume than margin in the future. This is a natural occurrence as a market matures. However, the rapid expansion of the market should help to prevent price wars from cutting margins to too great a degree. Because of these factors, the market should still be profitable at least in the short term, especially for firms that can add innovative features to their products that appeal to the more mainstream users.

FAROUT Summary

FAROUT SUMMARY

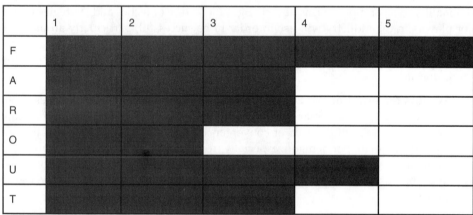

Figure 20.2   Driving forces analysis FAROUT summary

Future orientation—High. The emphasis on continued monitoring and forward-oriented conceptualizations, with its natural links to strategic planning that underlies applications of this tool, infer a future orientation.

Accuracy—Medium. Gaining consensus on the DFs impacting an industry tends to be fairly easy, but determining how to address them is where accuracy will suffer.

Resource efficiency—Medium. Generating the broad and comprehensive range of data needed to identify and gain group consensus of the DFs can be resource intensive, particularly where external experts (futurists, advisors, and custom industry data sets) need to be acquired and organized.

Objectivity—Low to medium. The degree of objectivity will depend on which discovery methods have been used. If an analyst has relied primarily on secondary data or less-experienced respondents, the objectivity will be lower.

Usefulness—Medium to high. The notion of DFs links directly to industry analysis, performance measurement, and strategic planning. DFs emphasize the need to change strategy and resource allocation decisions to reflect changing environmental conditions; as such, decision makers find it very useful.

Timeliness—Medium. The initial process of identifying and determining the importance of DFs can be time consuming, particularly to the extent that broader participation in their determination is sought. Once they are identified, they are quick and easy to use unless the industry environment is undergoing a dramatic change.

Related Tools and Techniques

- Competitive positioning
- Critical success factor analysis
- Event and timeline analysis
- Industry analysis
- Issue management
- Linchpin analysis
- PEST/STEEP analysis
- Scenario analysis
- Strategic group analysis
- War gaming

References

Albrecht, K. (2000). *Corporate Radar: Tracking the Forces That Are Shaping Your Business*. New York, NY: AMACOM.

Fahey, L., and R.M. Randall (1998). *Learning from the Future: Competitive Foresight Scenarios*. New York, NY: John Wiley & Sons.

Fleisher, C.S., and B.E. Bensoussan (2003). *Strategic and Competitive Analysis: Methods and Techniques for Analyzing Business Competition*. Upper Saddle River, NJ: Prentice Hall.

Hermida, A. (2006). "Music players lead digital surge," January 4 on BBC's Web site, found at http://news.bbc.co.uk/1/hi/technology/4580244.stm.

Lewin, K. (1951). "Field theory in social science; selected theoretical papers." D. Cartwright (ed.). New York, NY: Harper & Row.

Marino, L., and K.B. Jackson (2006). "Competition in the digital music industry," c88–109 in Thompson, A.A., Gamble, J.E., and A.J. Strickland. *Strategy: Winning in the Marketplace*, 2nd edition. New York, NY: McGraw-Hill.

Thompson, A.A., Gamble, J.E., and A.J. Strickland (2006). *Strategy: Winning in the Marketplace*, 2nd edition. New York, NY: McGraw-Hill.

Tregoe, B.B., and J.W. Zimmerman (1980). *Top Management Strategy: What It Is and How to Make It Work*, New York, NY: Simon & Schuster.

Tregoe, B.B., Zimmerman, J.W., Smith, R.A., and P.M. Tobia (1989). *Vision in Action: Putting a Winning Strategy to Work*. New York, NY: Simon & Schuster.

Wack, P. (1985). "Scenarios: Shooting the rapids," *Harvard Business Review*, 63(6), pp. 139–150.

Wilson, I. (1992). "Realizing the power of strategic vision," *Long Range Planning*, 25(5), pp. 18–28.

Wilson, I. (1994). "Strategic planning isn't dead—It changed," *Long Range Planning*, 27(4), pp. 12–24.

Endnotes

[1] See Fleisher and Bensoussan (2003), Chapter 18.

[2] Fahey and Randall, 1998; Wack, 1985; Wilson, 1992; 1994.

[3] Fahey and Randall, 1998.

[4] Thompson, Gamble, and Strickland, 2006; Tregoe, Zimmerman, Smith, and Tobia, 1989.

[5] See Fleisher and Bensoussan (2003), Chapter 6.

[6] Hermida, 2006.

[7] Marino and Jackson, 2006.

[8] See Fleisher and Bensoussan (2003), Chapter 23.

21

Event and
Timeline Analysis

Short Description

Event and timeline (E&T) analysis is a group of related techniques that display events sequentially in a visual manner. Event analysis isolates external events and highlights trends, commonalties, and aberrations in competitor or other-actor behavior. When done systematically, E&T analysis can uncover important trends about a firm's competitive environment and serve as an early-warning function by highlighting when a competitor or another market player is straying from its normal course of behavior.

Background

Throughout history, different cultures have displayed diverse beliefs about the nature of time. It can also have an important place in the nature of competition between rivals in the marketplace.

Timelines of historical events (the linking particular units of time with specific events) are graphic representations of how individuals in secular society characterize time. A timeline displays a sequence that points to things that have already occurred, things that are occurring (the present), and things that have not yet occurred (the future).

The direction implied by the timeline says that time and history proceed forward in a line, not in a circle. Portrayed in a line in this fashion, specific events in history are always unique and are never repeated in the same manner. History invariably incorporates change, yet past patterns are often replicated to some degree in the present and future.

The study of events and time in organizations and in economics[1] provides an explanation of the past, present, and future of industries and companies, how and when organizations respond to environmental factors, whether organizational decision makers are impacted adversely by inertia or momentum, and other developmental phenomena. Other common uses for E&T analyses include the deconstruction of criminal events by policing organizations, reasons why accidents have occurred, the ways in which terrorists might attack a sovereign state, and other forms of intelligence applications.

E&T analysis as presented in this chapter is a technique that most analysts probably already employ, though ordinarily not with the rigor and discipline that it requires. E&T analysis entails the systematic charting of events related to the subject in question. The analysis can take the form of a graph, chart, table, or line, among other formats.

E&T analysis is a way to chart the order of how companies perform certain activities, label the information spun off from these activities, and place that information into an analytical framework. Most business processes, including mergers and acquisitions, market entrances or exits, strategic relationship developments, or major market movements, follow a known pattern. These patterns may differ from firm to firm, and even within the firm over time if the patterns are studied and improved; nevertheless, most businesses attempt to document these patterns and improve major processes. They do this to promote learning over time. These efforts are commonly part of knowledge management initiatives and allow firms to seek greater efficiency in the performance of the process as opposed to constantly "reinventing the wheel."

Strategic Rationale and Implications

Even the simplest of tools can help illuminate many competitive analytical issues. When the amount of data and information regarding a specific rival's activities or an event overwhelms an analyst's ability to understand patterns and spot trends, it is beneficial to employ a clear chronology, such as that called for E&T analysis.

E&T analysis helps you to study data in a chronological and evolutionary context. Instead of just seeing "event 3, event 6, event 5, event 9, and so on," E&T assists in establishing a pattern—events 1,2,3, . . . n, and so on. This is particularly helpful since most of the information is gathered in an asynchronous fashion, and much of it, particularly that which is gathered over the WWW, lacks specificity in terms of dates (for example, year, month, season, quarter, or day) or times.

The presence of specific sequences in a timeline, where some events happen before others, can suggest the possibility of cause and effect—events exist in a relationship with one another; that is, in a particular context. Timelines suggest turning points, linear trends, and also progressions. Thus, making a timeline allows one to plot events in a graphic way, to see potential relationships, to help spur memory, and to grasp sequence. In the process, culling certain items from the many possible dates or events sharpens one's appreciation for the dates or events that are necessarily excluded. Simple chronologies of competitive activity within an industry, an isolated look at patterns evident from recent acquisitions, or a geographical representation of competitor activity all make for excellent E&T analysis applications.

Strengths and Advantages

E&T analysis is a basic technique that is most useful in answering "when is (X event) going to happen?" It is nearly always taught to individuals at some point in any basic educational program and, as such, should not require as much training time to master as some of the more sophisticated tools it often complements.

There are a variety of software applications to support the analyst performing E&T analysis. These programs are relatively inexpensive and can usually be mastered quickly. Many project management software applications can also be used by business and competitive analysts in performing this technique. Some applications of E&T analysis allow for a statistical examination of the collected data through time series analysis techniques that attempts to determine correlations between particular events.

E&T analysis is best used when dealing with a large number of discrete events that are spread over a long period of time or are otherwise obscured. It allows you to visualize a sequence of events and more easily see patterns than other more sophisticated forms of analysis. It is one of the best tools available for sorting out and making sense of a large number of events.

Often used as a planning aid, E&T analysis is highly supportive of, and is complementary to, other analysis techniques. When used in combination with other techniques, such as activity flow charts, event flow analysis, linchpin analysis, or the analysis of competing hypothesis process that are not as focused on answering when some event will occur, it can add the evolutionary element that the other techniques overlook.

Used in combination with other techniques for supporting a client's strategic decision, E&T analysis can help you achieve, among others, the following objectives:[2]

- Spot relationships among multiple organizational actors.
- Identify trends and patterns over time.
- Spot discontinuities.
- Differentiate between the analysis of the facts and the resultant conclusions.
- Evaluate the factual basis of possible recommendations.
- Identify matters requiring further analysis and examination—significant event blocks with vague or non-existent causal factors can alert the analyst to the need for additional fact finding and analysis.
- Understand the relationships among primary and secondary forces impacting an event.
- Weigh discrete events.
- Anticipate likely future events.

Weaknesses and Limitations

E&T analysis requires determining which events should or should not be included in the timeline. If this decision is made too narrowly (too exclusive), then important patterns in events may not be revealed. If you are too inclusive, you may be overwhelmed with data that makes it too complex to assess or will require additional time to perform the subsequent pattern deciphering task.

Determining the event constituting the starting point of a timeline can be difficult. You don't want to set the starting event either too early and include extraneous events in your analysis or too late and miss milestone events that should be considered. This difficulty is often addressed through the development of multiple starting points and trial and error.

Non-events (events that did not occur) can often be the most important facets of a timeline and may be overlooked in the process of gathering data. Decisions not made or action not taken can often be just as, if not more, important than those that escaped the analyst's notice in less-sophisticated data gathering or analysis efforts associated with the use of this technique. You must also properly distinguish milestone events from less significant events in the population being studied.

The determination to use E&T analysis tends to be after a key event has occurred so that an analyst and decision maker can deconstruct the pattern of activities that occurred leading up to a critical event. This is done in order to help executives learn from the pattern and to help prevent its reoccurrence. For it to serve a strategic purpose and be of predictive value, E&T analysis needs to be done well in advance of key decisions or events.

It can be difficult to project what will occur in the future, and you need to articulate assumptions clearly when projecting. Conditions, driving forces, and trends are often not captured or not captured accurately in some E&T analyses. You must fight the temptation to extrapolate events along a similar path when conditions or drivers are changing. You must also fight the temptation to be overly optimistic in anticipating that something will happen or to be too pessimistic in predicting that something will occur later than reasonable probabilities would suggest. As in all forms of analysis, you must be careful to weigh the data, facts, and evidence carefully so as to avoid imputing causation where none or little exists, or lack of causation when it does actually manifest itself—that is, avoiding type 1 errors (false positives) and type 2 errors (false negatives).

Process for Applying the Technique

Organization of event data should begin with construction of a timeline. The timeline orders events progressively. Transcribing onto paper what happened and when it happened can provide you with a clear picture for understanding a focal topic and how it evolved. The format of the timeline can be as simple as making a list of what happened and when it happened. Small "post-its" can be used to make a chain of events, with a sentence describing what happened and when it occurred on each post-it. This latter method is preferred since it is more easily expanded. Times and dates of events could also be entered into a computer database, spreadsheet, or word processor and sorted chronologically. This is commonly done in most E&T analysis applications, and the digitalization of this data can make it more effective for future retrieval and sorting. Last, there are tailored programs that are expressly designed for performing E&T analysis and allow for archiving information about the events and for producing visualizations of the eventual product.

In the material immediately to follow, we present several E&T analysis techniques that are used by business and competitive analysts. We begin with the simplest of them—the development of the basic timeline, and proceed to more complex applications like chronological tables, events matrices, and events and causal factors analysis techniques. To finish this section, we provide a case study showing a competitive analysis application of E&T analysis.

Plot the Target Firm's History of Key Events on a Line

Based on our experience, we recommend using the following generic 10-step process for creating the timeline in a graphic format. We also briefly describe how to develop it in a tabular format—otherwise known as a chronological table—at the end of this section. Most of these steps need to be carried out independently for each timeline, although some of these steps may be further consolidated depending on the nature of the question you are examining.

1. Decide what the timeline will show: major events, market expansions, product introductions, events related to a geographic area, randomly chosen events, and so on.

2. Make a comprehensive list of events that you wish to put on the timeline. This will require you or others to gather the population of events that are associated with the subject matter being focused on.

3. Consider how you will choose events to include and exclude from the final timeline. Not all events will be of equal importance in developing an understanding of the evolution of a firm's decisions and/or actions. As such, it is important that you define the rules to use for excluding and including events for consideration. The ultimate criteria employed for this task is that these should be based on the client's critical intelligence needs or topics.

4. Research and note the specific dates when the events that you wish to include occurred. It is a good idea to make a detailed note of your source(s) so that you can later verify the dates or the details of what transpired. As well, background documentation should be maintained in separate files for each event, should further examination or inquiries of the events be required.

5. List the chosen events in a chronology. A chronology is a sequence that starts with the earliest item and ends with the most recent one. Make a special note of the earliest and latest dates that you wish to include. This will also allow you to determine the period of time that their timeline will cover.

6. Decide what units of time you will use (days, months, quarters, years, decades, and so on) to divide the timeline into segments. These decisions may be a matter of trial and error. Calculate the number of segments that your timeline will have.

   1992 to 2007 = 15 years total/1 segment/year = 15 segments

7. Draw a line and divide it into the number of equal segments that you figure you will need.

8. Put the dates on the appropriate segments, from left to right

9. Using the chronology that you made of events and dates, figure out where they would fall on your timeline. It is useful to devise a scheme for how you mark and label them. For instance, you could write certain symbols (for example, $ for acquisitions and * for alliance formations) on the timeline, attach different colored labels, or make a code that refers back to your chronology.

10. If there is no room on your timeline to include all of your chronology, cull some of the dates or make a timeline with larger segments (for example, one timeline for events in the firm's home country and one for events that take place outside its primary market). If your dates can be divided into two or three smaller categories or themes, try making parallel timelines with identical segment sizes. You can then see how the theme develops, and you can also compare two or more themes at a time.

Develop a Chronological Table of Events

"Event flow analysis" is the compilation and analysis of data and information relating to events as they have transpired over time. It allows you to draw conclusions and make recommendations based on your analysis and is commonly used in relation to one specific action or event by a competitive rival, where the important events leading up to the event are noted.

A popular way of performing E&T analysis is in tabular format, typically with three columns that contain the dates that events occurred, basic descriptions of the events, and data indicating the source of information concerning the event. These are often supported by digital files that are searchable on intranets designed for tracking particular competitors or other intelligence targets (see Table 21.1).

Table 21.1
Illustration of a Chronological Table

Date	Event	Source
April 19, 2005	Acquires Jellico Corporation.	Firm press release (see Jellico files)
May 12, 2006	Closing of Warsaw factory and layoff of 420 line workers.	Warsaw media
May 15, 2006	Bankruptcy documents filed for Wafer Fabrication (WFI) business in U.S. federal court.	Court docket (#06.02.000067)
June 3, 2007	Sale of three patents (numbers in attached files) to FabCorp for USD$500,000.	USPTO records (full details contained in patent files on intranet)

Table 21.1 *(continued)*
Illustration of a Chronological Table

Date	Event	Source
June 28, 2007	Rumor of acquisition of WFI by Zenited is circulated at advanced technologies engineering conference.	Mark Owens, Chief Engineer, London office (see e-mailed entry in digital file)

Develop an Events Matrix

An events matrix is particularly useful for looking at multiple rivals, best exemplified by rivals within one's own industry. In this technique, you list the rivals in the first column of the matrix and array the timeline segment across the top. Critical events pertaining to the industry rivals are then put in the cells. This method can be particularly helpful for identifying relationships between rivals and events (see Table 21.2).

Table 21.2
Events Matrix

	2002	2003	2004	2005	2006
Rival 1	Purchases VRS Corp. for $3.4 million.	Introduces new fiber-optic network to Europe.	Replaces 15-year CEO with new hire from Zeptis.	Sells VRS to Xeon for $5.5 million.	Highest profits ever in 1st quarter.
Rival 2	Pulls repeater service from market. Reduces prices on standard service by 15% across the board.	Introduces bundled pricing packages. Enters Chinese market. Announces strategic partnership with Xeon.	Files lawsuit in EU to prevent our use of Teldex name. Wins license for upper band spectrum.	Market share at 30% in the U.S. New alliance with IMB.	
Rival 3	Enters North American market. Introduces new slim handset.	Wins approval for new transmission standard.	Rolls out new ad campaign. Changes subscription terms.	New CEO named.	

Event and Causal Factors Analysis

Experience has shown that major market events are rarely simple and almost never result from a single cause; instead, they are typically multi-factorial and develop from clearly defined sequences of events. You need to identify and document not only the events themselves, but also the relevant conditions affecting each event in an event sequence.

Event and causal factor (ECF) charting is a technique that displays the events sequentially in a visual manner using squares, ovals, and arrows to show the relationship between events important to the problem and potential causes of the problem. It displays the reason why each event occurred.

To accomplish this, a simple straightforward approach can be used that breaks down the entire sequence into a logical flow of events from the beginning of the market event development. It is important to realize that the end point may be defined either as the event itself or as the end of the firm's response phase. This flow of events will not necessarily lie in a single event chain, but may involve confluent and branching chains. In fact, the analyst often has the choice of expressing the event's sequence as a group of confluent event chains, which merge at a common key event, or as a primary chain of sequential events into which causative factors feed as conditions that contribute to event occurrence, or as a combination of the two.

Construction of the ECF chart should begin as soon as the analyst or decision maker begins to gather factual evidence pertinent to the event in question. As already discussed, the events and causal factors will usually not be discovered in the sequential order in which they occurred, so the initial ECF chart will be only a skeleton of the final product and will need to be supplemented and upgraded as additional facts are gathered. Although the initial ECF chart will be incomplete and contain many information deficiencies, it should be started as close to the market event as possible because of its innate value in helping to:

- Organize the event data
- Guide the subsequent assessment process
- Identify and validate factual findings, probable causes, and contributing factors
- Simplify organization of the resultant report
- Validate and confirm the actual event sequence
- Illustrate the event sequence in the report provided to decisions makers

With all its virtues as an independent analytical technique, ECF analysis is most effective when used with other E&T analysis tools that provide supportive correlation or no confirmation. Further, ECF can be the framework into which the results from other forms of analysis are integrated. An appropriate combination of the major E&T analytic tools, including ECF analysis, provides the core for a good, triangulated analysis process.

Figure 21.1 illustrates the conventions of performing the ECF analysis charting technique.[3]

Secondary event sequences, contributing factors, and systemic factors should be depicted on horizontal lines at different levels above or below the primary sequence (see Figure 21.2).

Events should track in logical progression from the beginning to the end of the targeted event sequence and should include all pertinent occurrences. This necessitates that the beginning and the end be defined for each event sequence. Analysts frequently use the focal marketplace action as the key event and proceed from it in both directions to reconstruct the pre-event and post-event sequences. The general format is illustrated in the following section.

Event should be indicated as rectangles, conditions as ovals.

Events should be connected by solid arrows.

Conditions should be connected to each other and to events by dashed arrows.

Events and conditions that are definitive (as indicated by a confluence of data or information pointing in this direction) should be solid. Those that are based on less definitive evidence or presumptions should be indicated by dashed line rectangles or ovals.

The primary sequence of events should be depicted in a straight horizontal line (or lines in confluent or branching primary chains) with events joined by bold printed connecting arrows.

Events should be arranged chronologically from left to right.

Figure 21.1   Process for performing ECF analysis

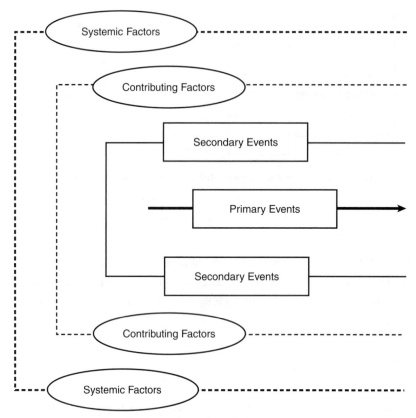

Figure 21.2   General ECF analysis chart format

Suggested Criteria for Event Descriptions

- Each event should describe an occurrence or happening and not a condition, state, circumstance, issue, conclusion, or result; that is, "began accepting subscriptions," not "contracted with electronic retailer to provide retail channel."

- Each event should be a single, discrete occurrence, not combinations of events or multiple occurrences.

- Each event should be described by a short sentence with one subject and one active verb; that is, "Web site accepted subscriptions," not "Web site accepted subscriptions and potential customers received newspaper inserts."

- Each event should be described as precisely as possible; that is, "rival announced they had achieved 100,000 two-year subscriptions in UK marketplace on January 18, 2007."

- Each event should include appropriate quantification if possible (see preceding example).

- Each event should be derived directly from the event (or events, in the case of a branched chain) and conditions preceding it; that is, "firm reduced price on two-year subscriptions" is preceded by "firm received many calls questioning its multi-year pricing policy," which is preceded by "firm tried to discourage one-year sub-scriptions by pricing this term at 10 percent less than two-year term for same options." The idea here is that each event is derived logically from the one preced-ing it. When this is not the case, it usually indicates that one or more steps in the sequence have been left out.

- Conditions differ from events insofar as they: (a) describe states or circumstances rather than happenings or occurrences; and (b) are passive rather than active. As far as is practical, conditions should be precisely described, quantified where possible, posted with time and date where possible, and derived directly from the conditions immediately preceding them.

E&T analysis is a tool that helps you bring logic and order to data, typically in the form of a timeline, chart, or table. The timeline subsequently becomes input and a complement to other analysis techniques. It is also an important part of the analyst's report on the focal firm or event, since it explains what occurred and the sequence of occurrence. Thus, the final timeline must be written clearly and correctly so that the decision makers who use the ana-lyst's report will understand it. Last, but importantly, E&T analysis methods truly are an essential element in any analyst's tool kit and can be employed for a myriad of different analytical purposes.

Case Study

The following case study[4] provides a detailed description of how E&T analysis can be used to answer a question posed by a strategic decision maker. It describes how an analyst iden-tified several months in advance, when and in what quantities, a rival competitor would be releasing a competitive generic pharmaceutical product into the marketplace and how the decision makers used this information in planning tactics to counter and lessen the adverse market impact of the pending introduction.

Timelines in Competitive Analysis

A pharmaceutical company had learned that a competitor received U.S. Federal Drug Administration (FDA) approval for the potential marketing of an over-the-counter (OTC) drug that directly competes with one of its own OTC consumer products. This stage of FDA permission only permits the rival firm to prepare its manufacturing facilities for FDA pro-duction quality inspection, in advance of getting a potential final FDA approval for mar-keting the drug, which is expected within the next year.

The focal firm wanted to know exactly the date of the launch time, as well as the quan-tity of product to be launched. This insight would give the client firm the time and ability to accurately develop a pre-emptive marketing strike, using some responsive advertising and pricing tactics. The client firm stood to lose millions of dollars and market share if its decision makers failed to identify the nature and timing of this introductory window being opened by the rival.

The nature of the problem usually indicates the nature of the analytical solution. In this instance, the client's concern centered around "time." "How long," the client wanted to know, "will it take for the competitor to introduce its product?" FDA approval only signaled a warning, not the actual product launch date. The analysts needed to find a way to link the element of time with the release of information about the competitor. The method they chose to generate a solution was to timeline the situation.

Development of the Timeline

1. Identify Each Process Taking Place

The analyst needed to understand each piece of equipment and how it worked, along with the expertise and personnel required by the rival firm at each major stage of the process. The client took the analyst on a detailed tour of one of its plants. This allowed the analyst to learn about each major piece of equipment and its purpose. The client also introduced the analyst to key employees in its engineering, marketing, and production units. They helped answer the analyst's technical questions. The manufacturing details received during these internal client interviews were what later helped the analyst to project the competitor's production volume up to one year into the future, which was particularly helpful since the rival's plant had not opened yet.

Because the FDA must certify all production equipment for quality control, it was important to understand the machinery being used. These process details were important for the analyst to probe for details on the timing of the expected product launch. Some of the process details and the machinery used are described next.

Table 21.3
Basic Steps in Producing Over-the-Counter Pills

Process Step	Description
Mixing chemicals	A granulator mixes the raw chemical with additives. There are different sizes of granulators. A moderate-sized granulator can produce 400–600 kilograms (k) in just a few hours.
Pressing pills	The mixture outputted by the granulator is put into a pill press. These can produce anywhere from 1k to 3k pills/minute. The client suggested the type of press to be used by the rival would generate about 2k pills/minute.
Coating machine	The pills likely proceed to a machine with a drum that applies the outer coating.
Packaging	This phase consists of several machine-driven steps, including printing the identification codes, filling the bottle, inserting cotton, sealing, capping, labeling, and printing the expiration date.

2. Collect the Data

Data was gathered from a variety of sources, including news, interviews, and FDA documentation. It came in randomly as it was found. Some examples of what was found included the following:

- An estimate from the client of the level of inventory a manufacturer must have in order to prepare for this kind of product roll-out.

- The number of pills expected to be packaged per bottle.
- Three different bottle sizes of 24 pills, 50 pills, and 100 pills would be used as well as the estimated dosage.
- The first shift for the plant was already being recruited.
- A firm estimate of the expected production yield over the course of the start-up period before roll out.
- Equipment manufacturers and, through interviews, an identification of likely key equipment to be used.
- The granulator's capacity.
- The rival's chosen brand name for the product.

The analyst began developing the pattern of activities under the timeline during the data collection phase. This was accomplished by combining the gathered information with the analyst's views and in dialogue with the client.

3. Organizing the Data over Time; Develop the Timeline

The analyst next mapped the sequence of events involving the focal process, particularly which event came first, second, third, and so on. The following describes the timeline sequence for the prospective roll-out.

Table 21.4
Major Steps in the Sequence of a Drug Roll-Out

Step	Event	Reasoning
One	Refitting manufacturing plant	The manufacturer needed enough time to produce and accumulate half a year's volume of pills, the amount needed to meet their roll-out plans. The client's own marketing department had determined, based on other similar roll outs, how many pills the competitor needed to distribute in order to successfully penetrate the market.
Two	FDA approval	The FDA has to approve the equipment directly involved in the drug's manufacture. Various equipment suppliers had suggested that the FDA had already come in and provided the necessary certifications.
Three	Plant visit by packaging supplier	One of the client's purchasing employees had visited a packaging supplier's plant and recalled seeing labels with the drug's name and dosage. This was important data that helped the analyst estimate the amount of raw chemical that had to be processed; consequently, it was easy to calculate the time needed to generate the necessary inventory.
Four	Hiring	The client estimated that it would take 10 weeks for the first shift to produce up to 80 percent yield from each batch—the level required to achieve production efficiency. It would take seven more weeks to train a second and third shift. These additional shifts were needed for the rival to achieve the quantity needed to launch the product.

The analyst had to support the pieced-together timeline with more corroborating data before drawing conclusions. This required additional data gathering in the form of interviews of other industry contacts, such as corrugated box manufacturers, graphic designers, packaging materials suppliers, retail buyers, and trucking/shipping companies, among others. The gathered information became intelligence when the analyst assembled it using the timeline.

4. Draw Conclusions

The analyst was able to project how long it would take for the competitor to stockpile enough pills to launch the product by combining knowledge of the plant's actual FDA certification date and hiring information with the time it would take for the new employees to produce products at a certain yield rate. The intelligence produced by the analyst was an estimated six- to seven-week product launch window, which helped the client to successfully plan a pre-emptive strategy by flooding the market with discount coupons, special institutional promotions, and related sales activity.[5]

FAROUT Summary

FAROUT SUMMARY

	1	2	3	4	5
F					
A					
R					
O					
U					
T					

Figure 21.3   Event and timeline analysis FAROUT summary

Future orientation—Medium to high. E&T analyses array items over time. They are designed to help analysts better understand past events in order to predict the future.

Accuracy—Medium to high. This method is typically more accurate than others because it relies on the analyst using and organizing empirical events. To the extent that the analyst has accurate and verifiable data, the technique should result in higher than average accuracy.

Resource efficiency—Medium to high. Much of the information needed to perform this technique can be found in open, public sources. For more specific purposes, it may also require other forms of data collection, particularly primary collection methods.

Objectivity—Medium to high. This technique does not suffer from potential biases that most other techniques do, in that the only real subjective choice comes from deciding which events to include or exclude from the timeline. The level of objectivity is also lowered when doing advanced applications requiring identification of drivers, conditions, or primary and secondary causal factors.

Usefulness—Medium. Although this technique is complementary to many others, it requires a lot of analytical manipulation to help clients use it "out of the analyst's box."

Timeliness—Medium. The gathering of the data and organization of it underlying this technique, as well as arraying it in a timeline and placing it in easy-to-communicate formats, can be time consuming.

Related Tools and Techniques

- Activity flow charting
- Competitor profiling
- Driving forces analysis
- Event flow analysis
- Event matrix analysis
- Forecasting
- Historiographical analysis
- Indications and warning analysis
- Issue analysis
- Strategic relationships analysis

References

Buys, J.R., and J.L. Clark (1995). *Events and Causal Factors Analysis*. August. SCIE-DOE-01-TRAC-14-95. Idaho Falls, ID: Scientech Inc., Technical Research and Analysis Center.

Fuld, L.M. (1995). *The New Competitor Intelligence*. New York, NY: John Wiley & Sons.

Heuer Jr., J.R. (1999). *The Psychology of Intelligence Analysis*. Washington, DC: Center for the Study of Intelligence.

Kimberly, J.R. and H. Bouchikhi (1995). "The dynamics of organizational development and change: How the past shapes the present and constrains the future," *Organization Science*, 6(1), pp. 9–18.

Krizan, L. (1999). *Intelligence Essentials for Everyone*. June, Washington, DC: Joint Military Intelligence College.

Miller, D., and P.H. Friesen (1980). "Momentum and revolution in organizational adaptation," *Academy of Management Journal*, 23(4), pp. 591–614.

Peterson, M. (1998). *Applications in Criminal Analysis: A Sourcebook*. Westport, CT: Praeger.

Van de Ven, A.H., and M.S. Poole (1995). "Explaining development and change in organizations," *Academy of Management Review*, 20(3), pp. 510–540.

Endnotes

[1] Kimberly and Bouchiki, 1995; Miller and Friesen, 1980; Van de Ven and Poole, 1995.

[2] Buys and Clark, 1995; Heuer, 1999.

[3] Adapted from Buys and Clark, 1995.

[4] Adapted from Fuld, 1995

[5] Adapted from Fuld, 1995, Chapter 12, Case 2.

22

Technology Forecasting

Short Description

Technology forecasting aims to provide information about the direction and rate of technology changes. It uses logical processes to generate explicit information to help industry and government anticipate practical, ecological, political, and social consequences of developments in technology. In government, this information is used to inform policy. In industry, the information can be used to inform strategic improvements to, or replacements of, products and processes and predict changes in markets.

There are four elements in a technology forecast:[1]

- A time horizon (either the time of the forecast or the estimation of time when the forecast should be realized)
- A specific technology
- Some parameters to the technology (characteristics and capabilities gauging level of performance)
- A probability statement about the outcome or range of outcomes predicted

Technology forecasting is performed using a variety of techniques.

Background

Technology is defined in the *Oxford Dictionary* as "the application of scientific knowledge for practical purposes." A forecast predicts or estimates a future event or trend.

For millennia humans have been fascinated by the future and what it might hold. The interest of business in systematically attempting to predict the future is more recent.

There are two broad perspectives that may be taken on what it is that prompts the development of technology. One is that technology will develop in response to scientific and technical opportunity (a technology is discovered, and an application for it is then sought), the other is that technology will develop in response to the need or desire for change (an application is found, and technology is developed for that purpose).

As scientific knowledge changes, so does technology. Change in technology has implications for many aspects of modern business. While some technology change amounts to refinement of existing technology, other change can render existing technology obsolete and can have immediate effects on your ability to compete.

The development of technology experienced an explosion in growth after the Second World War. The defense and space industries were subject to heavy government investment, and research undertaken in these led to many developments that had significant impacts on other industries. For example, the work in the space industry on miniaturizing electronics revolutionized the production of domestic appliances.

Following on the heels of the radical growth in technology development came a major upheaval in the nature of commercial competition. For many decades, economies around the world grew at a fairly steady rate. Change tended to be gradual and the marketplace fairly predictable. However, since the 1970s, markets became much more volatile and unpredictable. Competition became fiercer, and changes in marketplace dynamics occurred much faster than in the past.

Together, these changes, the rate of change itself, and the intensifying of competition in the market, have made looking to the future in terms of technology crucially important to the competitiveness of business and of national economies that is to both the public and private sectors. A change in technology may prompt modification of existing government policy or development of new policy, both of which may have flow on effects for industry; for example, by making tax concessions available for specific areas of research and development or by supporting the setting up of a new industry. Other considerations for industry include that a change in technology could mean a sudden loss of market share as products are superseded or to the loss of a market where a technology is completely replaced—for example, floppy disks and floppy disk readers.

The modern practice of technology forecasting as used in business has, as previously mentioned, its roots in the U.S. space and defense industries in the 1940s and 1950s. It was used by the U.S. as a tool to keep its technology ahead of the Russians during the Cold War.

There exist a variety of methods used to forecast changes in technology. The oldest is expert opinion, and while it is not all that widely used today, refinements of the method survive (for example, the Delphi method) and are discussed later in the chapter.

Probably the earliest systematic technique for forecasting technology change to find its way into business is morphological analysis. The process was developed by an astrophysicist, Fritz Zwicky, in the 1940s as a way to systematically invent solutions to specific problems. The process was first adopted and applied to future studies for use as a corporate learning tool in the 1980s.

In the late 1950s, another important technology forecasting method was developed. The Delphi method originated with and was refined by the RAND Corporation to enhance its ability to conduct business in the defense industry throughout the 1950s and 1960s. It uses the consensus opinion of a panel of experts to explore technology advances.

Over time, technology forecasting techniques have been adopted more generally by business as a tool that makes available information directly relevant to managing a firm's investments in technology. Concepts related to technology forecasting include technology road-mapping and foresight.

"Technology road-mapping" is a term invented by Motorola to describe its method for developing technical strategy. It is a process used by businesses to plan for the projected needs of the marketplace. It provides a plan of action for organizing research and development activities over a course of years (usually no more than 10 years) in order to achieve the stated goal. By focusing on a goal in the future, road-mapping helps a firm to allocate its investment resources and technology capabilities and focus its activities on strategically achieving its goal.

Foresight studies are usually undertaken by a national government to identify and encourage the development of desirable technologies. Foresight studies may play a role in developing the national economy by luring international research and industry firms to set up for business in particular nations.

Strategic Rationale and Implications

As the technology used by business has become more complex and business has become more technology reliant, many firms are actively monitoring their technology requirements and the technologies they rely on to try to stay ahead of the game (or at least keep up).

Technology change potentially has implications for all business. The products a firm markets, the processes a firm uses for production, or the equipment it uses to provide its service may be superseded, thus giving a competitor an immediate advantage in the marketplace.

Technology forecasting can provide information with obvious and immediate applicability and with significant cost implications. For example, the products or services a firm sells are vulnerable to the effects of technology change. Considerable investment is involved in developing a new product and setting up production lines. This will be lost if the product is rendered obsolete by technology developments. It is also possible to gain a price advantage over competitors by investing in more efficient technology production processes.

Figure 22.1 is an example of a traditional business model when compared to the potential impact of an alternative technology.

Additionally, the internal functioning of a business relies on technology. The equipment and software used to conduct administration and distribution processes and the communication methods used in most firms to reach clients are all based on particular technologies. Often this technology will be introduced at great expense and will commit the firm to a considerable substitution cost. For example, consider a situation where a firm installs a new software system to record and track customer service calls. Besides the expense of the software and associated licenses, the firm will have to invest in training for staff. There may also be expenses incurred in migrating earlier records to the new system. A major change or update to a new system will incur expenses all over again.

Historically, there was a lag of around five to seven years (generalizing across industries) between the making of a discovery and the embodiment of the invention into a practical application. There is then a further time lag before the innovation will have an impact on the market.[2] Recently, these times have tended to shorten.

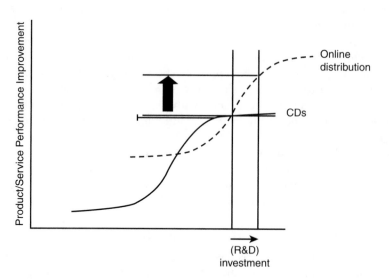

Figure 22.1   Online distribution versus CD technology in the recording industry
Source: Adapted from "Boosting the Payoff from R&D," by R.N. Foster (1982), *Research Management*, 15(1), pp. 22–27.

Technology forecasting aims to extend the time during which a firm may work on its response to a new technology by giving the firm insight into change before it happens or before it has a practical impact. This buys time for the research and development of new products and/or services. It will also give some insight into the likely longevity of investment returns a firm can expect from its investment in a particular technology.

There are a variety of methods used to generate technology forecasts:

- Expert opinion may be sought about likely directions for change. Delphi is an example of a process using expert opinion to forecast likely change. It explores future technology developments by drawing a consensus opinion from a panel of experts.

- Trend extrapolation and growth curves use information from the past to predict developments likely in the future.

- Morphological analysis uses information about current technology to try to find new applications for existing inventions.

- Relevance trees systematically break down a problem as a method for finding a solution.

- Monitoring follows current research and finds links between inventions to predict what practical innovations may arise from them. An example of monitoring is patent analysis.[3]

- Historical analogy picks an analogous technology from the past and plots development in a new technology as following a similar growth trajectory. Historiographical analysis is discussed in detail in Chapter 25, "Historiographical Analysis."

- Scenarios can explore future technology by presenting a series of perspectives on possible futures each involving slightly differing conditions to arise.[4]

Technology forecasting predicts future developments by anticipating the probable characteristics and timing of technology. It will focus on one specific technology outcome and explore the likely attributes of that technology at some nominated time in the future—for example, in 10 years' time. The most useful technology forecast will include some sort of estimate of how the likelihood of its predictions materializing. It should always make explicit the assumptions on which it is based.

While technology forecasting itself is not necessarily concerned with a firm's profits, it should provide sufficient insight to allow a firm to make informed decisions about its investments in technology, which will in turn have a direct bearing on future profitability.

To not undertake any form of technology forecasting is to assume that either technology change is not relevant to a firm or that the technology used is static.

Strengths and Advantages

The greatest strength of technology forecasting is its ability to inform current and future investment decisions throughout a business. Undertaken early in a project, it can provide valuable information about the likely longevity of a technology. It may even indicate the time period over which a widespread (even market standard) technology is probably going to be replaced.

Technology forecasting is a flexible process and can be tailored to investigate the precise area or areas of possible change directly relevant to an individual business or industry. Its usefulness is not limited to highly technical industries and its results are readily comprehensible.

The variety of methods available offers a range of sophistication and allows a firm to choose a method appropriate to its budget. It can be integrated into a firm's regular planning processes or conducted as a one-off process for a particular project.

The individual methods used for technology forecasting all have their own particular strengths.

The Delphi method allows a firm to tap into the expertise of experts across a range of specialized fields while protecting the resulting forecast from the subjective biases or "blind spots" of each individual. The consensus opinion from the panel of experts gives each expert the opportunity to advise on a situation and then to revisit and refine their advice in light of the opinion of their peers.

Trend extrapolation can use available statistical data to assist in the development of indicators and/or inferences about the future rate of change. While this method is often used to predict change in one aspect of a technology, it can be used to pull together information about a variety of aspects and predict a plausible and possible future direction.

Growth curves can also usefully predict when a technology has reached maturity and is likely to be replaced by something new.

Relevance trees are a powerful stimulus for thought. They provide a systematic process for finding a solution to a problem. A relevance tree would identify relationships between parts of a technology or process and its potential development.

Morphological analysis gives detailed analysis of the current and future structure of an industry and shows existing and potential gaps. It leads to explicit consideration of solutions to fill gaps in the market. The process, while exhaustive, is precise.

Monitoring of patents and general research trends can give a firm advance warning of likely new inventions that may be significant for its business.

As can be seen, technology forecasting is a flexible process, providing a range of methods that can be adapted to suit a firm's budget, resources, and timeframe.

Weaknesses and Limitations

As with any form of forecast, the usefulness of a technology forecast is heavily dependent on the quality of the information and the validity of the assumptions upon which it is based. The aspects of technology to be considered in a forecast must be carefully chosen so that important factors are not accidentally missed. The ability to understand what are the important factors driving a particular technology's development may require expertise in that technology that is beyond a firm's own staff. It may be the case that there are shortcomings built into the process as a result of the culture of the firm itself.

The reputation of the individual championing the project or outside consultants presenting the information may sway a firm's willingness to accept and use information and cloud its ability to interpret the complexities of a forecast. For example, a forecast confirming the firm's own preconceptions and emanating from a highly reputable source may be given greater weight in decision making, which is out of proportion with the parameters of the forecast.

Technology forecasts do not provide hard conclusive results. The forecasts will give a prediction of the probable attributes or appearance of a technology at some inexact time in the future.

Technology forecasts involve exercises in predicting probability, which is a notoriously difficult to do. There are several common errors we make when attempting to judge the probability of an event occurring. For example, a memorable event may seem more likely to recur, even though it may be memorable for being unusual in the first place. Generally people tend to overestimate low-probability events (for example, have you ever bought a lottery ticket?) and underestimate high-probability ones (for example, ignoring the very likely negative consequences of one's own pet vices). Human beings are also highly likely to allow their own personal experience or anecdotal evidence to distort their perceptions of reality. In fact, acting on a technology forecast ultimately requires a leap of faith.

Additionally, the individual analytical methods used for compiling a technology forecast all have their own weaknesses.

There are several points at which the Delphi method may fail. The appointment of properly qualified experts is crucial to the integrity of the opinion that results. If the panel or a portion of the panel is not experienced in the area you are investigating, the opinion will not truly be an expert one. Similarly you must be careful that the questions you are asking the experts will answer the specific questions you want answered about the future.

The Delphi method is structured in a way to minimize the impact of idiosyncratic responses; however, there is no way to control the amount of time and care taken by any expert taking part. It is possible that the time-consuming revisiting of questions during the Delphi process may even prompt less time and less care be taken with each round. Whether or not this is the case, the quality of the result depends on the quality of the responses and the range of knowledge of the experts used.

For trend extrapolation and the use of growth curves, the biggest weaknesses are the assumptions underpinning them—that is, the future will follow the patterns of the past. There is also the implicit assumption that change is not sudden.

The processes of trend extrapolation and growth curve plotting are profoundly dependent on the limits chosen for the analysis. Donnelly notes an example where limiting analysis to a particular technology when extrapolating a trend and ignoring other information from the marketplace resulted in disastrously inaccurate predictions. He cites the example of television manufacturers during the 1950s and 1960s. The overall trend was for television sets manufactured in America to become larger and more like a piece of furniture, which led the American firms to concentrate product development in this area. However, at the same time, the Japanese manufacturers were starting to make (and consumers were purchasing) compact sets. The real trend in the market was for greater variety in the size of TV sets, and the American firms effectively locked themselves out of a significant portion of the expanding market by relying on simple trend extrapolation.

Typically, trend extrapolation will look at the future from the perspective of one factor of change at a time. This assumes minimal interaction between different technologies and different technological developments. In fact, it is often the case that change is driven by interaction between aspects of technology.

Relevance trees and morphological analysis are subject to human error and vulnerable to lack of insight on the part of those constructing them. Both can be very time consuming to construct.

Morphological analysis does not take into account factors external to the particular problem or technology in question—for example, costs. It also requires knowledge of all possible solutions to a problem in order to find new applications for the technology (to solve the specific problem you have). Without knowing all alternatives, the analysis is compromised. As all possibilities must be represented, time must be spent in listing many impossible alternative uses for technologies.

Relevance trees are a very general approach for solving a specific problem. It can lead to pursuit of a fundamentally flawed course of analysis, as the flaws may not be obvious until very late in the process.

Each technology forecasting technique including monitoring requires diligence to be effective. Incomplete monitoring may well end up being misleading about likely developments. Similarly, simply monitoring developments, but not analyzing what is found, is worthless.

Process for Applying the Technique

The first step in applying any technique for technology forecasting is to identify as best you can what it is you and your firm's decision makers wish to predict or look for. Are you looking to explore the future for technology change that is driven by pressures of competition and opportunities arising from current technology research? This may be a driver if your firm is seeking to improve its current products to keep ahead of competitors. Or your questions may be more goal-oriented so that you are looking for technology development as a response to some need you have; for example, to fill a gap in your product range or that your clients have. Are you planning to make one technology forecast as a background for a current project? Are you expecting to put a regular process of generating technology forecasts in place?

Whatever the drivers, you and your firm's decision makers need to be clear up front as to the parameters of the analysis. If not, you will be caught in a mire of information, facts, and opinions that will ultimately lead to biases, blind spots, and ineffective analytical outcomes.

Technology forecasting is performed using a variety of techniques, and five common techniques are addressed next.

1. Delphi Technique—Expert Opinion

The Delphi technique builds a technology forecast based on expert opinion. It uses a consensus of opinion to try to minimize the effect of individual bias.

The Delphi process uses a panel of experts, chosen for their knowledge of a particular field or issue in question. If the questions being asked are general, then the panel should have representatives from a variety of disciplines. For example, if your objective is to understand the potential take up of a new technology by society in general, you might approach experts with not only technical backgrounds and industry experience, but those with interests in social areas such as design, cooking, and gardening, to name a few. You may also need to involve a large number on the panel, say in excess of 20.

Where you have specific questions to put to a panel, you are most likely to want experts with specific experience—for example, specialists in the particular technology and possibly experts from outside but relevant areas. Your panel could involve around 10 to 15 experts.

A facilitator coordinates the process and sends a questionnaire or survey to each of the experts on the panel, often in the form of a series of hypotheses about when and which scenarios are likely to occur and seeking responses to them. Often the expert is asked to respond to a scenario by answering a series of questions using a Likert scale (where, for example, circling the number "1" indicates strong disagreement with a statement, "2" indicates disagreement, "3" indicates a neutral response, "4" indicates agreement, and "5" indicates strong agreement). While it is possible to undertake a Delphi process in a face-to-face setting, it is essential to the process that the experts be allowed to respond anonymously. Anonymity is important to prevent pressure being placed on participants to respond in any particular way.

Once the expert opinions are all received, the responses are collated by the facilitator. The results are then sent back to the experts, showing them statistics on points of agreement and conflicting opinion (anonymously) and seeking a further response. Sometimes written arguments may be submitted (anonymously) with a detailed opinion of why some judgment is right or why it is misguided. The experts are invited to respond again to the survey or questionnaire in light of the statistical feedback.

The aim is to find consensus, meaning a majority agreement. Experts who find that their response to a particular question is out of step with majority opinion may choose to revisit it if it was an opinion they felt uncertain of the last time around.

This back and forth procedure will continue for a given number of rounds (usually three, as studies suggest that this gives the best balance between achieving reasonable consensus and not exhausting the goodwill of the panel) in an attempt to build a consensus of expert opinion. The opinion is usually presented at the end of the process as a proportion of experts agreeing to a particular response—say 80% of respondents agreed strongly that such-and-such change is likely to occur in the next five years.

However, the experts are not to be pressured to find consensus if it would compromise their considered opinion. If consensus cannot be reached, final distribution of responses will appear in the forecast with a note that it does not represent a consensus of opinion.

2. Trend Extrapolation

Trend extrapolation requires a forecaster to consider change over a period of time, understand the factors that have driven that change, and predict future change from this knowledge. It is used to forecast change in functional capabilities. This method relies on an assumption that past drivers of change will continue to influence the future and ignores short-term fluctuations in trends as it aims for a long-term forecast. It is useful in an environment where development tends to occur fairly constantly.

Generally, statistics (numeric data about past developments) are plotted onto a graph against time. A line is roughly fitted to the points plotted. It may be straight or curved (for example, showing an exponential growth). The mathematical formula that best explains the shape of the line is then used to predict the position of future points on the line (roughly); that is, over future points in time. See Figure 22.2 as an example of trend extrapolation.

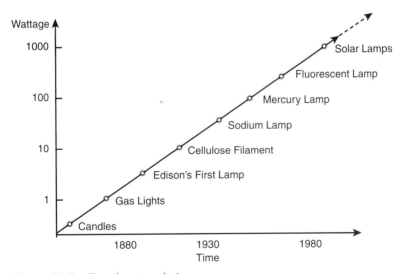

Figure 22.2   Trend extrapolation
Source: Adapted from Lawrence, S.R. (2002). "Technology Scanning & Forecasting," University of Colorado, http://leeds-faculty.colorado.edu/lawrence/mbat6450/docs/schedule.htm.

Limit analysis may then be used to check the utility of a trend extrapolation plot. Limit analysis is based on the fact that all technologies have a limit at some point beyond which there can be no further improvement. For example, improvements to the braking system on a motor vehicle will stop a car more quickly; however, nothing can stop the car instantly (that is, without the elapsing of any time at all). The mathematical plot of the improvement will continue the line (as a theory) beyond the point where any practical improvement is possible. Extrapolation will not yield any useful information if applied to a technology already close to the limit of its potential.

Trend extrapolation may be used to forecast future developments in a technology that has a precursor technology (or several precursors) with a known path of change. The shape of the curve for the precursor (or precursors) is used as a guide for the shape of the technology in question. For example, plotting the efficiency gains in Formula-one car racing engines would give a shape that correlates to efficiency improvements in domestic motor vehicle engines. This process enables more complex predictions to be made.

Trend extrapolation may also examine past developments and predict future ones on the basis of judgment, rather than using statistics and graphs. This will give less precise results than a graph; however, the results may nevertheless be accurate as a forecast. This method is particularly suited to situations where numeric data is too complex to plot into lines, such as where many different factors contribute to the issue being forecast.

3. Growth Curves

The growth of development in technology change is thought to follow an s-curve, similar to the growth of biological life.[5] This shape is regarded as universal and is used extensively in plotting product life cycles (see Figure 22.3).

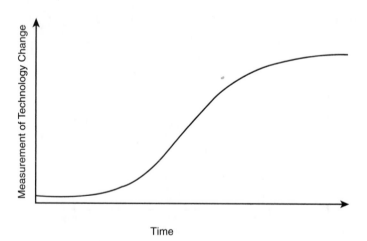

Figure 22.3   Generic s-curve

The s-curve illustrates the gradual process of research leading to a new invention, which is then improved upon (where the line goes most steeply upwards) until the limit of the technology is approached (and the line levels out). See also Figure 22.4.

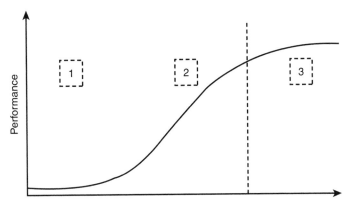

Figure 22.4 S-curve model
Source: Adapted from Foster, R.N (1982). "Boosting the Payoff from R&D,"
Research Management, 15(1), pp. 22–27.

The stages of Figure 22.4 are

1. **Embryonic**—The first few years of R&D yield low returns as the focus is on a wide range of research and knowledge acquisition.
2. **Growth**—Critical Knowledge starts being applied and developed, causing the productivity of R&D to skyrocket.
3. **Maturity**—The productivity of R&D begins to wane as the technology reaches its natural limit.

Plotting the development of a technology over time as an s-curve should give you an indication of whether the technology is reaching the limits of its efficiency and is therefore ripe for replacement.

4. Historical Analogy

Using historical analogy is a very simple and commonly used method for predicting technology change by comparing the path of development followed by an analogous technology—see Chapter 25, "Historiographical Analysis," for an in-depth treatment of this analytical tool.

5. Scenarios

Scenarios are not strictly predictive; however, they are generally considered a good method for technology forecasting—see Chapter 18 in our previous book, *Strategic and Competitive Analysis*, for a detailed approach to this technique.

6. Morphological Analysis

Morphological analysis is sometimes referred to as "organized invention." It starts with a goal you wish to achieve. For example, you may be looking to find the optimal method for packaging an object. It involves the systematic gathering of information about all possible technologies that may achieve a particular purpose. For example, you may be looking at packaging technology, and so you would have to consider any possible material that could be used for packaging—cardboard, paper, plastic, fabric, wood, etc. You also need to list the attributes you seek in packaging. For example, you might be considering attributes like durability, flexibility, being lightweight, protective, recyclable, waterproof, and so on.

The information is then displayed in some sort of graphical form—for example, in a list or matrix—that highlights any gaps. The gaps may represent opportunities for developments. The display of the information gathered may also indicate areas with no potential for development at all.

To make this process work for you, you must be prepared to consider all possibilities and not limit yourself to current possibilities. It requires time and patience and may involve some research to ensure you are aware of all the possible technologies relevant to the problem you wish to solve.

7. Relevance Trees

Relevance trees are detailed hierarchies of methods for achieving a particular outcome. This outcome is the question you want answered by your forecast. It might be something like: How can we reduce energy costs for consumers of our appliance?

A relevance tree divides a broad subject/problem into increasingly smaller and more detailed subtopics. Often, relevance trees are arranged to look very much like an organizational chart or family tree, though they may also be represented with more detailed items radiating out from the central subject.

The items at each level of the tree should provide a complete description of the item to which they are joined. Ideally, there should be no overlap between items in the tree; however, this is often difficult to achieve in practice.

The idea behind a relevance tree is to break down a question or problem into issues small enough to be addressed easily. See Figure 22.5 for a diagrammatical representation.

8. Monitoring

Monitoring is a method for forecasting technology change that does not require a specific question to answer in order to give useful results. There are many forms of monitoring that can predict technology developments. An important one is patent analysis, which is discussed in detail in Chapter 22 of our previous book, *Strategic and Competitive Analysis*.

Monitoring is often based on careful observation of published research results. Published results will be those emanating from research in public institutions and not competitor firms, so these will tend to be results from very early on in the process of a development (before the research is taken up for commercial pursuit). In some industries, this sort of research may not necessarily be available publicly.

Other sources of information for monitoring include industry publications and trade shows. In some industries, there are associations where individuals with an interest in an invention may publicize their work. Observing developing social phenomena may also give insight into areas where technology development is likely to occur; for example, the wide uptake of cellular phones and the concurrent explosion in use of the Internet led commentators to predict phones with Internet capabilities long before prototypes were built.

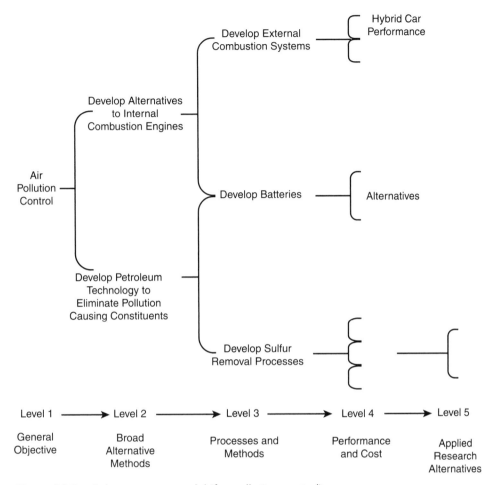

Figure 22.5   Relevance tree model (for pollution control)
Source: Adapted from http://www.wiley.com/college/dec/meredith298298/resources/
addtopics/addtopic_s_02m.html.

   The information gathered by your monitoring activities will only be useful if you can analyze your discoveries and find the links between the various observations you make. It is very easy with monitoring to amass huge quantities of information requiring complex and time-consuming analysis. There are software programs available that facilitate this process. Some search through all the data you have stored, looking for links. Others may actively manipulate the data you have found using processes such as network analysis. Network analysis takes your observations and works through multiple combinations to predict a range of scientific capabilities that may be developed.

Using the Information

Whichever technique you use to construct your technology forecast will be irrelevant if you do not use the output of the analysis in some way to enhance your firm's competitive ability. Care should be exercised when acting on the technology forecast. No forecast is ever going to be 100% true, no matter what you pay for it. It is ultimately a statement of probability.

A forecast is limited by the parameters within which it has been made. The predictive value of a technology forecast is lost when those parameters are ignored. An extreme example is a situation where you perform a trend extrapolation over the next five years, but then use the information to support decisions about the next 10 years (you cannot extrapolate the extrapolation and preserve any accuracy at all).

In the end, as an analyst, you should be as aware of the shortcomings of whatever method of forecasting you use, as you are of its strengths. This does not diminish the value of the forecast; rather, it allows you to get the best value you can from the information you have gathered and by ensuring that any decisions made are fully informed by the output of the analysis.

Case Study: Bell Canada and the Delphi Process

Bell Canada is a telecommunications firm with activities in telecommunications operations, research and development, and manufacturing. In the late 1960s, the Business Planning Group (the Group) within Bell noted a range of factors likely to lead to significant medium- and long-term changes to the business. These included the merging of computer and communications technologies, new competition due to regulatory changes, emerging visual telecommunications markets, anticipated social change, and increasing costs. The Group developed a Delphi study, which they implemented in 1970 and which predicted a span of 30 years from 1970 to 2000.

The Group divided the business into segments: educational, medical, information systems for business, and residential markets. The study aimed to investigate future applications for Bell Canada's business in these areas.

Before preparing the questionnaire it would submit to its panel of experts, the Group undertook an extensive literature review to explore developments foreshadowed in these areas. The aim was to provide some guidance for the experts. The questionnaire was pre-tested on a group of experts already available. This allowed the Group to identify and reword some badly expressed questions and redesign the questionnaire to reduce confusion for panel members. Although this step delayed the process, it ensured that results would be clearer.

The education, medicine, and business questionnaires all started by requesting that the panelists give their personal prediction of change to 10 basic values over the next 30 years in North America (for example, would there be a "significant increase," "slight increase," "no change," "slight decrease," or "significant decrease" in "traditionalism," "authoritarianism," "materialism," etc.). This question was to set the mood and put the experts into the right frame of mind for completing the rest of the questionnaire. Other non-technical areas were also put to the panelists. For example, the education study also addressed evolution in school design and the changing role of teachers over the same 30-year period.

The studies then went on to technologies relevant to each area. For example, the education study examined likely time for introduction of computerized library systems, computer-aided instruction systems, and visual display systems across primary, secondary, and post-secondary education levels. Further questions then broke down these hypothetical systems further and asked for a prediction of when they were likely to be in use.

Similar questions about likely timeframes for adoption of hypothetical technology developments were asked in the medical and business studies. The results of these three studies provided clear and useful information.

The residential use study was different in that it focused on future services and not technologies. An early issue with this study was the problem of identifying which "experts" should make the predictions about future adoption of technology for the residential market; for example, was a housewife more qualified by her experience than an industry insider?

The Group solved this problem by conducting two separate Delphi processes with the same questionnaire: one using a panel of housewives and the other using a panel of industry experts. The issues examined by each panel included their opinion of future acceptance of concepts like electronic shopping from home, remote banking, and electronic security for the home.

The Delphi process ran for three years.

The results of the process were then entered into a database where the forecasts from the experts had been indexed for keywords, abstracted, and stored online. Results of other studies—for example, trend analyses—and from internal research were put into the same system.

The information from the Delphi process has been used in combination with other information for a variety of purposes, including to prepare specific service and business proposals and to prepare "environmental outlook reports," which identify future trends that may affect Bell.[6]

FAROUT Summary

FAROUT SUMMARY

	1	2	3	4	5
F	■	■	■	■	■
A	■	■			
R	■	■	■		
O	■	■			
U	■	■	■	■	
T	■	■			

Figure 22.6   Technology forecasting FAROUT summary

Future orientation—High. Forecasting is by nature future-focused. The extent of the future focus of a technology forecast will depend on the method used and the questions asked to prompt the forecast.

Accuracy—Low to medium. Technology forecasting does not provide hard data. It can be accurate within the parameters of the forecast, but the information is not accurate in the sense that it does not provide precision. Generally the most accurate information will be about the near future.

Resource efficiency—Medium. Some methods for forecasting are very simple and inexpensive (for example, a straightforward trend analysis); others can be very time-consuming (for example, morphological analysis) and/or quite expensive.

Objectivity—Low to medium. The objectivity of a technology forecast will rest on the nature of the questions asked (do they have assumptions built into them?) and on the people undertaking the process to generate the forecast (are they considering all alternatives necessary for the process to work efficiently?).

Usefulness—Medium to high. Provided care is taken not to treat a technology forecast as a statement of inevitability, and the forecast is interpreted in light of the parameters within which it is made, a technology forecast can be a source of very useful information and strategic opportunity.

Timeliness—Low to medium. Most technology forecasting methods are too time-consuming to conduct and yield their most accurate information about the near future.

Related Tools and Techniques

- Historiographical analysis
- Patent analysis
- Scenario planning
- SWOT analysis

References

Ascher, W. (1979). *Forecasting: An Appraisal for Policymakers and Planners* (rev. ed.). Baltimore, MD: Johns Hopkins University Press.

Ayers, R. (1969). *Technological Forecasting and Long-Range Planning*. New York, NY: McGraw-Hill.

Coates, J.F. (1989). "Forecasting and planning today plus or minus twenty years," *Technological Forecasting and Social Change*, Vol. 36, Nos. 1–2, August, pp. 15–20.

Coates, V., Faroque, M., Klavans, R., Lapid, K., Linstone, H., Pistorius, C., and A.L. Porter (2001). "The future of technology forecasting," www.tpac.gatech.edu/papers/techforcast-abs.php.

Day, L. (2002). "Delphi research in the corporate environment," in Linstone, H., and M. Turoff (eds.). "The Delphi method: techniques and applications," www.is.njit.edu/pubs/delphibook/ch3c1.html.

Donnelly, Dr. D. (2006). "Forecasting methods: a selective literature review," www.class.uh.edu/MediaFutures/forecasting.html. Accessed April 2006.

Fleisher, C.S., and B.E. Bensoussan (2003). *Strategic and Competitive Analysis: Methods and Techniques for Analyzing Business Competition*. Upper Saddle River, NJ: Prentice Hall.

Foster, R.N. (1982). "Boosting the payoff from R&D," *Research Management,* 15(1), pp. 22–27.

Frick, Dr. R.K. (1974). "Operations research and technological forecasting," *Air University Review*, May–June.

Lawrence, S.R. (2002). "Technology scanning & forecasting," University of Colorado, http://leeds-faculty.colorado.edu/lawrence/mbat6450/docs/schedule.htm.

Lenz, R.C. (1962). "Technological forecasting," ASD-TDR-62-414, Aeronautical Systems Division, Air Force Systems Command.

Mann, D. (1999). "Using S-Curves and trends of evolution in R&D strategy planning," www.triz-journal.com/archives/1999/07/g/index.htm.

Martino, J. (1983). *Technological Forecasting for Decision Making*. New York, NY: Elsevier Science Publishing Company.

Meredith, J., and S. Mantel (2000). *Project Management: A Managerial Approach,* 4th edition. New York, NY: John Wiley & Sons.

Millett, S.M., and E.J. Honton (1991). *A Manager's Guide to Technology Forecasting and Strategy Analysis Methods*. Columbus, OH: Batelle Press.

Oxford Dictionary. www.askoxford.com/concise_oed.

Schnaars, S. (1989). *Megamistakes: Forecasting and the Myth of Rapid Ttechnological Change*. New York, NY: The Free Press.

Web sites:

http://hops.wharton.upenn.edu/forecast

http://www.wiley.com/college/dec/meredith298298/resources/addtopics/addtopic_s_0 2m.html

Endnotes

[1] Martino (1983).

[2] Meredith and Mantel (2000).

[3] See Fleisher and Bensoussan (2003), Chapter 22.

[4] See Fleisher and Bensoussan (2003), Chapter 18.

[5] See Fleisher and Bensoussan (2003), Chapter 24.

[6] Adapted from Day, L. (2002).

23

War Gaming

Short Description

War gaming is a role-playing simulation of a competitive marketplace used either for general management training and team building or as a tool to explore and test competitive strategies for a specific firm to discover any weaknesses in a plan and to identify possible consequences of adopting such a plan. Teams of players take roles and simulate the dynamics of a marketplace over a period of time. The actions of each team will have an impact on both the effectiveness of current strategies by other teams and future directions for the game. The idea is for participants to gain a perspective of the marketplace from outside their own firm.

Background

Military war games, simulating battle to allow practical training outside the forum of war, probably began since recorded history. The ancient games of chess and Go were developed as war games.

Modern war games are generally considered to date back to the Prussian's Kriegspiel, which is credited with teaching Prussian officers at least some of the skills they needed to win the Franco–Prussian War of 1870–71.

The first recorded non-military war games club was set up in Oxford in the 19th century. In 1913, H.G. Wells published the first book about recreational war gaming, *Little Wars* (full title: *Little Wars: a game for boys from twelve years of age to one hundred and fifty and for that more intelligent sort of girl who likes boys' games and books*). It brought together existing rules for playing with miniature toy soldiers and attempted to codify these rules.

In the late 1960s, the war-gaming society at the University of Minnesota began role-playing their games/wars rather than moving models or counters around on a table top (one of the moderators of these games went on to co-create *Dungeons and Dragons*). Role-playing games became very popular through the 1960s and 1970s and have expanded and developed along with technology (for example, today's MMORGS—massively multiplayer online role-playing games).

The analogy of "business" as "war" is a popular one for capturing the essence of the competitive marketplace. Consider this, for example:

> "It is critical to keep in mind that the [competition] is not an inanimate object but an independent and animate force. [Our competitor] seeks to impose [its] own will on us. It is the dynamic interplay between [its] will and ours that makes [business] difficult and complex."

This is a quote from the U.S. Marine Corps' handbook on strategy[1]—adapted by referring to competition and business rather than the enemy and war. The philosophy translates seamlessly from military strategy to competitive business strategy. It seems logical, then, that the practice of war gaming, long used to explore military strategy and decision making in a risk-free environment, has been appropriated and adapted for use in business.

Since their development in the late 1980s, business war games have become an increasingly popular tool for firms to experience strategic decision making, provide hands-on training to their staff, and see the consequences flowing from the decisions made in a realistic simulation of a dynamic market.

Strategic Rationale and Implications

The basic aim of a war game is to turn information into actionable intelligence by increasing the quality of decision making. Chussil likens the function of war gaming in the context of strategic decision making to that of research and development in the context of product development.

War games today are complex role-playing simulations, which ideally capture the complexity of competitive market dynamics. By running a business war game, a firm can have its participating managers practice strategic decision making in a realistic context.

In many firms, management decisions are guided by quite conservative thinking in which few risks are taken in the hope that this course of action will minimize mistakes. However, taking a conservative approach may in fact end up costing more in the long run than a radical change in strategic direction, as opportunities for profit may be passed up.

In the fast-changing environment of modern business, it is also important for a firm to avoid the trap of endlessly trying to relive its own past success by repeating history. As history unfolds, its course is shaped not just by our own plans and actions, but by many other factors outside our control, such as the strategies of our competitors, new inventions and innovations, and even government policy changes. As new competitors join a market and new products and technologies develop, there can be little wisdom in sticking with what you did yesterday while everyone else has moved on.

A business war game allows experimentation with new strategic directions without incurring real-world costs and so widens the range of strategic planning options a firm may be willing to adopt. It effectively reduces the risk of making mistakes by illustrating the flow on effects of the decision or decisions explored in the war game. It provides a simulation where some of the uncontrollable factors influencing the market can be modeled and their likely affects explored in a risk-free environment.

The action in a war game will span a nominated time period, usually measured in years (though the game itself will last for only a matter of days). This allows the consequences of a particular decision to be tracked into the medium term to thoroughly investigate the reactions of the marketplace. By following the competitive dynamics of the market for a period of time, the war game will uncover either longer-term negative consequences of a decision that may initially deliver profits or show that while a strategy used may offer modest returns in the short term, it will yield much greater profits (than alternative strategies) with time.

The war game situation also forces participants to change their perspective on strategic decision making. Participants are divided into teams that assume roles in the game, simulating a wide variety of players in the marketplace. Teams will usually include several teams representing competitors or customers as well as the host firm. The teams will work in isolation to develop their "move" in the game but then will see the results, not in isolation, but in the context of all "moves" made by all other teams. Managers are no longer making their planning decisions based on their view of the market from their own firm (inside out), but are seeing the effect of their firm's decisions on the whole market from a much wider perspective (outside in).

There are two basic types of war games that can be run for a business. The first uses a generic business scenario to educate managers generally in the process of strategic decision making. It will put the participants in a safe environment in which they can experiment with radical thinking and gain confidence in their own decision-making capacity. The experience will also promote team building among the participants.

The second type of war game is tailored to the needs of a particular firm, mirroring its competitive environment in the war game set up. This type of war game is used to facilitate the firm's strategic planning process. It may be run early in the planning process to indicate strategic directions or, alternatively, it may be run after the strategic plan has been formulated to test it for weaknesses and check what affect it is likely to have on the marketplace. Participants in this type of war game will also gain experience, which will build their confidence in decision making—same as with the generic war game. Similarly, a firm-specific war game will act as a team-building exercise.

Strengths and Advantages

The general development of decision-making skills and team-building effects may be achieved with a relatively cheap generic "off-the-shelf" war game. A tailored war game, however, allows a firm to explore new and different strategic plans for the market in which it competes without incurring real-world costs. The war game is designed around current market and financial conditions and often requires the facilitation by third parties. Competitive intelligence necessary for input into the war game will be provided by the firm. It will use this information, which may already be available, though often not centrally accessible, to create a realistic representation of a particular marketplace. By undertaking a war game, the firm will be gathering together information that may be "owned" by separate parts of the business and integrating it all into a single model from which the firm will be obtaining valuable, low-risk practical intelligence.

One or more strategic plans may then be tested in the game to explore short- and medium-term effects of specific actions in the market. This testing may be carried out at the beginning of the planning process to allow the firm to investigate broad direction change. Or the game may be run after a plan has been developed when it will uncover any weaknesses and/or unintended or undesirable results in the short to medium term.

The successful testing of a strategic plan in a business war game will build support for the implementation of the plan across the firm. Participants from throughout the firm will have had an opportunity to question the strategy and follow it through its rigorous testing. They will be able to communicate their enthusiasm for the successful strategy to non-participants in all areas of the firm.

A tailored war game will give those participating an insight into the future reality of their business environment that is not available to their competitors. It will anticipate future market directions of competitors and their reactions to the host firm's actions. It will contemplate the affects of new products, new competitors, and/or new technology on the market.

After a corporate merger, acquisition, or takeover, a generic war game may be useful to build cohesion between staff who were probably once competitors, while a tailored war game may educate newcomers in the specifics of the firm's situation.

The "after action report" compiled after a war game has run provides an historical record of the scenarios tested and the outcomes of the war game. It is a reference tool for those who took part in the war game and others who did not, to use when formulating strategic plans for the firm.

After a firm has run one war game, any future war games it wishes to undertake will be easier and cheaper to run.

Those taking part in war games will gain confidence in their own strategic decision-making abilities as a result of the experience. They will also have an understanding of "thinking outside the box" and be more willing to consider new and different strategies.

Firms will also find strong cross-functional team building benefits resulting from war games. In many large firms, there is often internal competition between departments or simple lack of communication that hinders the development and/or implementation of firm-wide strategies. Geographic separation of functions, units, or branches of a firm may also make cooperation difficult in practical terms. A war game typically involves teams of players consisting of members from a variety of departments, units, or branches and a variety of management levels. The intense experience of war gaming builds valuable working relationships and open channels of communication between the areas of the firm represented by the members of each team. The feeling of camaraderie resulting from the intense war game experience can also build bridges throughout the firm and increase the chances of successful implementation of future strategic plans.

Weaknesses and Limitations

The design of a war game must be done very carefully, or the game will not run properly, and little or no useful information will result. The major flaw in war gaming is that is requires significant skill and diligence from participants as well as facilitators. The running of a war game itself requires skilled logistical and administrative support. Most firms as such may not have the ability to design and run its own war game.

The design process has multiple points where a mistake or input error will compromise the utility of the war game. For example, choosing the wrong situation to war game may yield accurate but useless information; starting out with an ill-defined scope for the war game may yield information with a big picture focus, but no specific strategic feedback; too narrow a design may rob the teams of any flexibility in how they play the game and give skewed results.

The outcomes of the war game may be easily distorted by having unbalanced teams involved, thereby limiting the actions of the teams. The make-up of the teams must be carefully considered to give a mix from across various functions within the firm and involve different levels of seniority.

When running a war game, the umpires or referees responsible for allowing or not allowing specific actions by the teams may limit the scope of the action with their personal biases or assumptions about the market being emulated. A computer-based umpire may also limit the scope of the game by generating its decisions based on narrow assumptions about market dynamics or finance.

Another potential problem is having the players manipulate the game situation simply to "win." This can happen where a human umpire/referee has well-known preferences for business behavior or narrow views of finance or competition, and teams can use these biases to get approval for their actions at the expense of other teams. Similarly, an unsophisticated computer umpire/referee may allow teams to second guess which strategies will get them furthest in the game situation. When this occurs, no realistic insights will result from the war game.

The quality of generic of "off-the-shelf" war games varies widely. Some can be limited by being based on narrow financial or economic models, which makes the war game scenario react unrealistically to the "moves" of players. Limited modeling of market forces may encourage more conservative strategies by players and limit their learning experience as a result.

A tailored business war game is an expensive and time-consuming exercise for a firm to undertake. The war game can take weeks or months to design. Any staff involved in the design process will need to be trained to do it. Participants will need to have some pre-training to gain the skill level required to take part in a war game. The war game will usually run for several days and will require a dedicated space (often a number of separate rooms) and a network of computers set up for the running of the game.

War gaming in fact takes longer to set up than other analytical techniques.

Process for Applying the Technique

A business war game is a complex exercise to undertake, and there are multiple steps involved in applying a war game to a firm-specific situation. Figure 23.1 illustrates the process and steps involved.

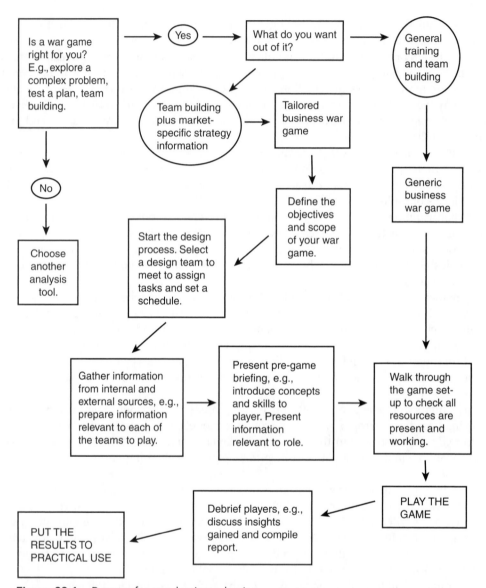

Figure 23.1   Process for conducting a business war game

Step 1: Is a War Game the Way to Go?

The first question to ask when contemplating a war game is whether it is appropriate to your situation. What do you hope to achieve by running a war game? A business war game can be used to encourage bonding between participants or to simply stimulate thinking. It may also be used to rehearse and thoroughly test a specific strategy direction for your firm to ensure that the dollars spent in implementation have the highest possible opportunity for

success—that is, achieving the biggest bang for every dollar spent on a specific strategy—
or to minimize possible risks involved in strategic decision making.

The major disincentive from war gaming for most firms will be the commitment of time
and money required. However, a range of war game styles can be leveraged to suit the
range of outcomes required, from bonding to strategy testing, to varying amounts of both
time and money.

Generic business war games are cheaper because they may be purchased "off-the-
shelf," thus bypassing the long and involved design process required for a tailored war
game. These are useful where a firm wants to deliver staff training and experience in flexible strategic decision making in an intense and hands-on environment, and often last for
only one half to one full day. These types of war games may also give participants confidence to make decisions under pressure and serve as a firm-wide team-building exercise.

On the other hand, there are various levels of complexity that may be incorporated into
a tailored business war game. Some war games may last for only two days, while others
may continue over five days.

A shorter war game may be useful in delivering insights into a changing market and
changing competitive factors, and this may be all that is required to kick start your firm's
strategic planning process.

Longer business war games tend to be used to comprehensively test new plans and
strategies that will require a great deal of a firm's resources. The longer and more involved
the war game, the more complex and expensive the design process will be. However, the
returns may more than compensate for the cost in that risks, unintended outcomes, and
consequences can all be pre-managed for maximum benefit to the firm.

A long tailored war game simulation will, however, be most beneficial for testing a
complex situation, where you face unfamiliar problems, and the cost of any mistake will be
high.[2]

Either way, whether you have a short or long game, a war game will give you creative
insights into your situation and will help to build consensus within your strategy team for
a particular future direction.[3]

Step 2: Getting a Business War Game Off the Ground

Once you decide that a business war game is the right thing for you to do, you will need to
find a powerful and committed sponsor from high within your firm. Your sponsor will be
particularly important where you are contemplating a long and detailed war game, not only
to get the go ahead for the expenditure and hours it will require, but also to champion the
outcomes. For a war game to be successful, you need to be sure that there is a commitment
from senior management in the firm to actually make some practical use of the results.

You will need to select a team to design your war game scenario. Once you have a team
pulled together, the team will need to meet to get the basic war game design settled, including deciding what the objectives/scope will be. They will also need to develop a plan,
schedule, and budget. All the decisions and preparation work from this point on will be
done by the design team.

The design team now needs to buy and/or design the war game.

While all generic war games are bought "off-the-shelf," not all are equal. Research into
the underpinnings of the war game (for example, what sort of modeling is used, what the

processing of input based is on, and so on) is advisable. If a game is cheap because it uses unsophisticated processing, then the strategic decision-making experience may be less than optimal, as decisions will not result in realistic feedback. It may in fact encourage participants to make very conservative decisions. Another consideration is how flexible the game is while being played. Players will not get any useful training in decision making unless they can explore the effects of a variety of actions in each situation. This means you should look for a game that allows players to ask "what if" as they play. Remember that when running a generic war game, the design process will only be relevant to the extent that you need to decide who will be involved and who will be in each team.

On the other hand, the software you use to process information while running a tailored war game should be sophisticated enough to realistically mimic complex marketplace dynamics as teams make their various "moves." It should also be difficult to predict so as to dissuade any rogue players from trying to manipulate the results of the game and allow players to explore "what if."

The design process is crucially important to the success of a tailored war game; however, most firms can obtain assistance for this aspect from a professional war game consultant or facilitator.

By this stage, you will already have considered some of your objectives in deciding what sort of war game you wish to run. Other objectives will be determined by what information do you expect to have in the "after action report" generated after the war game. The next consideration now is what objectives you have for the war game process itself. What sort of experience are you hoping the participants will gain from being involved? Who should be involved? How many teams will you need to play out the war game scenario, and who are they representing? There will always be a team representing the host firm, a facilitator team, and usually an umpire/referee team (or at least someone feeding the information into some umpiring software and giving the results back to the players). There will be at least one competitor, but usually more, and a team representing a particular customer or all customers in the market. Often the war game will include a "wildcard" team representing a new, as yet unknown competitor in the market. Other teams may represent your distributors or retailers.

To an extent, the objectives you choose will influence the scope and domain of your business war game. For example, if you are testing a strategy to move your business offshore, then your war game will have to consider overseas market conditions—but will you need to consider just one or a variety of geographical area and industries? This information is vitally important to the players while they are playing the game as their time will be limited, and they must be guided in what to consider and what not to. It is an important guide for preparation of the briefing material you must supply to all players.

Step 3: Who Should Play?

Together the objectives and scope of the game will point to who should be involved in the war game. You should involve not only management from a variety of levels, but also from different departments within your firm and from different branches as well. How many players should be involved? How many teams do you have, and how many people and what mix of people should be on each?

The facilitator and umpire teams need not be large and may in fact be represented by only two persons. However, those making up the umpire team have a critically important role in the progress of the war game. The umpire decides whether a team will be allowed to take the action it plans to—the umpire is effectively the gatekeeper of what information gets processed, and so any biases the umpire may give in to in playing his or her role will have a direct effect on the integrity of the war game's outcomes.

The number of players in a team should be decided by considering how many people across the firm senior management would like to involve, the number of teams being represented, and what will be a reasonable number for each team to provide a range of input into the team's decision making without having an unwieldy amount of input (from too many team members) to try to integrate.

Each team should be carefully chosen to include members from a variety of areas (departments and offices) and from a range of seniority. Who should lead each team? Mark Chussil notes that some firms have deliberately put more junior staff in charge of war game teams to enhance the sense that team members may speak freely. Some team members may feel intimidated by having to make radical or wildly creative suggestions to a senior manager—and the aim of a war game is to explore exactly these sort of ideas in a risk-lessened environment.

Step 4: Preparing for Your War Game

Players will need comprehensive background information to prepare for the war game and to refer to while they play. Compiling this information from various internal and external sources and ensuring each team gets the information it needs is critical. This is the most time-consuming part of the design process. What information will be needed to give each team the background it needs to realistically play its role? For example, the host firm team will need financial, market share, product (including R&D), and human resources information. Competitor teams will need much of the same sort of information on their own firms, which your design team will need to provide as best as possible. However, the host firm team will only have information about its competitors that it already has. None of the teams will have all the detailed information supplied to each of the other teams. Some information may also be based on rumor in the marketplace. This will all go to reflect the incomplete information used for making real-world decisions.

The design team will have to address the method to be used for teams to communicate their "moves" while playing the game. Often this means designing a template into which decisions can be entered. Information from a standard template should then be easy to transfer into the game-processing software.

Players will need some training before they participate in the war game. War gaming requires a certain level of skill to progress effectively. Players in longer games will generally be asked to attend a half-day or full day pre-war game briefing. Where the game is a generic or shorter tailored game, a short introductory session before the war game and an opportunity to read their background material may be all that is required.

The pre-war game briefing usually occurs a few weeks before the war game proper. Players will be given their background information and be introduced to the processes and concepts of war gaming. They will be told what the objectives of the war game are and what is expected of them. Sometimes the session will include a simple, short war game to give players some direct experience of playing.

Other activities, such as short assignments, which may require further research, may be given to the players to help them get into their roles in the weeks leading up to the war game.

The final important preparation for the running of the game is the physical set up of the space where the business war game will be played. The room or rooms to be used by the various teams and the administrative and technical support staff involved must be furnished with all equipment necessary (for example, whiteboards, paper and pens, computers). It is advisable to have a test "walk through" of the game to double-check last-minute preparations—for example, are all the computers involved recognizing one another on the network?

When you are planning a long war game, it may be necessary to build in some side activities for players to give them a break from the intensity of the war game.

Step 5: Playing the Game

The actual playing of the game can last between one and five days, depending on the game's complexity.

A business war game will run as a series of "rounds," each representing the market after a particular point in time. For example, some war games nominate that each round occurs at three monthly intervals; others may use half yearly (or longer intervals) or a mix of time periods.

Teams go to the area or room assigned to them. Each team will have a set amount of time, usually a number of hours, to prepare its plan for action in the current round based on the latest available information. For the first round, each team will plan its "move" based on the information provided to the players at their pre-game briefing (including any information gathered as a result of any additional research they were asked to do for their specific team).

At the end of the allotted time for the round, the teams will submit their plans to the umpire/referee, who will then decide whether the actions can be allowed in the game context. In some games, other teams—for example, a consumer team—will assess competing strategies and directly reallocate market share. The allowable actions from each team will then be fed into the game-processing software, which integrates plans from all teams and then generates new information about the market—for example, revised market share or profit figures. Each team receives limited feedback about the actions of the other teams mimicking the incomplete information on which business decisions must be based in real life. The new information is used as a basis for making the team's new plan of action for the next round.

While the game is running, it is important to have both administrative and technical support available. The outcomes of the business war game should be recorded (and backed up) continuously to ensure no information or decisions made are lost over the course of the day.

Step 6: After the Game

After the players have finished all the allocated rounds of the game, they need to be debriefed about the experience and reminded of the original objectives. This will give them a chance to reflect on the personal insights and confidence they have gained during the process.

The value of the strategic analysis done during a war game will be lost without follow up after the game has finished. The outcomes that have been recorded by administrative support staff need to be collected and organized into a meaningful "after game report." The tasks involved in putting the report together should be assigned specifically and be subject to a deadline. You do not want the information to "go cold" and interest in the activity to leak away before the outcomes can be put to use.

Once the report is complete, it must be followed up, and the insights gained during the business war game should be acted upon. The learning curve for all the staff involved in a firm's business war game is very steep. However, once there are knowledgeable people in-house, future war games the firm chooses to run will be quicker and easier to prepare.

Case Study

A new CEO with an information technology firm (ITF) found the key division of his firm was facing difficulties. He also discovered the following:

- The marketplace was dominated by one very large competitor (holding nearly 60% of market share) and crowded with about 10 other minor players, including his firm (none of which had more than 8% market share). ITF adopted a strategy of taking market share from the market leader, and this had not been working.
- The products ITF relied on were good, but unremarkable compared to those of competitors.
- Morale was very low.
- ITF had been divested from a larger IT firm some time before, and some of the managers still retained a management style suited to a large firm and not the small one they now found themselves with. There was no consensus among senior staff as to how to turn the firm around.

The CEO decided to conduct a business war game to involve his whole management team and put them in a situation where together they would explore and experiment with the dynamics of the market. He hoped the war game would help raise morale and build agreement in management about a course of action.

Specific objectives were defined. The war game was to include five teams representing existing competitors, one being the market leader. A wild card team would represent a new and as yet unknown competitor with the potential to disrupt the market. Other teams would represent end users and channels (the firms involved in getting the ITF products to the end users). There was also a team for the host firm, a facilitator team, and an umpire team. The war game would simulate the next three years, which would be covered by three rounds of play, each representing a calendar year. The focus was to be on the national market.

A half-day pre-war game briefing was conducted three weeks before the war game.

The teams each worked in separate rooms, preparing for each round. Rounds 1 and 2 required the teams representing the host team and competitors to assess the overall market, anticipate likely competitor strategies, and determine where it would concentrate its efforts. Each team had limited resources to implement their strategies.

The channels and end-user teams had slightly different tasks. It was the role of these two teams to analyze the decisions from each competitor (including the host team) and real-locate market share according to the "success" or otherwise of their strategies.

For round 3, every team took the perspective of ITF and wrote a list of events and trends it saw as likely in the market (including an estimate of the probability that these would occur) at the three-year point, based on the results of the preceding two rounds of play.

A plenary group was chosen to meet and review all of the suggestions arising from the game and developed a grid mapping the events and trends with probability to assess their importance.

The war game indicated that ITF would have to shift its strategy from targeting the market share of the dominant firm to targeting smaller competitors to succeed. The other minor players were all focused on the dominant competitor and not defending their market share from marketing assaults from a similar-sized firm. Success was, however, seen as possible if this new strategy was adopted. The war game also identified strong and weak competitors in the marketplace. The information was taken and used to formulate a new strategic plan.

The war game also had a direct positive effect on team building and morale as contemplated at the outset of the game.

Within four years, the strategy developed through this war game had proved to be so successful that ITF found itself being considered as a major threat by the leader in the market.[4]

FAROUT Summary

FAROUT SUMMARY

	1	2	3	4	5
F	■	■	■	■	■
A	■	■	■		
R	■	■	■		
O	■	■	■		
U	■	■	■	■	■
T	■				

Figure 23.2   War gaming FAROUT summary

Future orientation—High. A business war game is entirely future focused.

Accuracy—Medium. The quality of the outcomes from the game will depend on a number of factors. Flaws in the design of the war game may result in information that is inaccurate for meeting the game's objectives. Inaccurate information provided to players at the outset may skew results. Inability of players to properly understand the role they are assuming and play it realistically will have a negative impact on the accuracy of the outcomes.

Resource efficiency—Medium. Although the investment required to conduct a business war game is high, the returns are also very high. Players will receive valuable training and build relationships within their teams. When analysis of the firm's strategic planning is undertaken, the final plan/s will have been rigorously tested by the war game, and practical advice about future plans will be available.

Objectivity—Medium. The objectivity achieved will depend on the sophistication of software used, the game parameters, the impartiality of the umpire team, and the dedication of the players to the war game process. It is possible to have both very low or very high objectivity—often a result of the quality of the facilitation.

Usefulness—High. Forewarned is forearmed.

Timeliness—Low. To improve the timeliness of the results, a business war game must be undertaken as early as possible in a planning process. The war game itself will require weeks or months to design and prepare, depending on the depth of testing and learning required.

Related Tools and Techniques

- Blindspot analysis
- Competitor analysis
- Financial ratio and statement analysis
- Industry analysis
- Scenario analysis
- Supply chain analysis
- SWOT analysis
- Value chain analysis

References

Center for the Study of Intelligence; CIA (1999). *Psychology of Intelligence Analysis*, Chapter 6.

Chussil, M. (2005). "Business war games," *scip.online*, 1(19), June 23, 2005.

Chussil, M. (2003a). "The seven deadly sins of business war games, part 1," *scip.online*, 1(31), May 8, 2003.

Chussil, M. (2003b). "The seven deadly sins of business war games, part 2," *scip.online*, 1(32), July 10, 2005.

Chussil, M.J., and D.J. Reibstein (1998). "Calculating, imagining and managing. Using war games to leverage intelligence and improve strategy decisions," *The Journal of AGSI*, March.

Fuller, M. (1993). "Business as war," *Fast Company*, Issue 00.

http://en.wikipedia.org/wiki/History_of_role-playing_games

http://en.wikipedia.org/wiki/War game

Kurtz, J. (2002). "Introduction to business war gaming," *Competitive Intelligence Magazine,* November–December, 5(6), pp. 23–28.

Kurtz, J. (2003). "Business war gaming: Simulations guide crucial strategy decisions," *Strategy & Leadership*, 31(6), pp. 12–21.

Kurtz, J., (2005). "Lessons from business war gaming," *Competia*, March 1, 2005.

Reibstein, D., and M. Chussil (1999). "Putting the lesson before the test: Using simulation to analyze and develop competitive strategies," *Competitive Intelligence Review*, 10(1), pp. 34–48.

Underwood, J. (1998). "Perspectives on war gaming," *Competitive Intelligence Review*, 9(2), pp. 46–52.

Endnotes

[1] Quoted by Fuller, 2001.

[2] Kurtz, 2002.

[3] Chussil, 2002.

[4] Adapted from Kurtz, J. (2003). "Business wargaming: simulations guide crucial strategy decisions," *Strategy & Leadership*, 31(6), pp. 12–21.

24

Indications and Warning Analysis

Short Description

Indications and warning (I&W) analysis is a premonitory technique for regularly and systematically tracking key assumptions about the task environment and rivals into the future in order to alert decision makers when the situation changes in a potentially significant and risky way. To anticipate and prevent potentially significant hostile marketplace movements or surprises, I&W analysts try to connect clues gleaned from what could be massive quantities of complex and evolving data. Done well, I&W analysis acts as an alarm to decision makers and reduces the incidence of surprise, uncertainty, and risk. I&W also alerts decision makers to developments that run counter to their planning assumptions and provides them with a critical understanding of the situation in time to take needed actions or precautions.

Background

Traditional I&W methodology has been used for decades by military organizations to determine whether activities by a potential enemy require a heightened state of alert or readiness. Over time, the methodology evolved whereby events that precipitated aggressive behavior were recorded after an enemy had attacked. These events were then studied to develop models to help decision makers understand the specific conditions for a possible attack.[1]

During the Cold War era, both sides of the conflict (NATO and the Warsaw Pact nations) designed systems to alert them of impending aggression by their rivals. This indicator-based approach required intelligence agencies to perform careful and detailed analysis of all actions taken by their rivals and required a determination of the actions that needed to be taken or would likely be taken, in order for one side to move from their current position to an attack mode. The analysis also included constructing a list of a possible rival's actions, determining which actions could be effectively observed or monitored, weighing and prioritizing the actions, and determining a course of action for one's own side based on the indicator being set.

The lessons learned by decision makers during the Cold War have not been entirely lost on firms. Many firms today have systematic methods for monitoring their environment, including the macro-environment, as well as their competitive segments.[2]

These "monitoring" systems are outgrowths of the environmental scanning and tracking systems that became popular in the 1960s, as firms recognized that the broader environment was becoming a more critical part of the business landscape and that it could make or break their fortunes. Whether the importance came from pressures delivered by key stakeholders, unique events, or from seemingly inexorable trends, firms knew that they required better systems to alert them about environmental developments and then integrate them into their strategy development processes.

A very important facet of the environmental monitoring, tracking, and subsequent analysis process is the development and implementation of an indicator and warning analysis system. In developing I&W analysis processes or systems, many commercial firms relied on adapting systems that were standard early warning and risk management practices applied by the intelligence communities at the nation-state level.[3] The public sector I&W analysis practices essentially try to warn the appropriate and relevant government decision makers of impending threats of various natures, whether it be breakdowns in other countries socio-political changes, terrorist activity, pending military actions or critical policy-related developments.

Although I&W analysis initially had more of a premonitory focus, in recent years, its focus has been more on serving defensive purposes. In particular, countries are using the method to warn them of terrorist activities and pending attacks, intrusions into critical digital networks, and how to counter these activities. There are analogies to this more embryonic activity to firms, who can also apply it for counter-intelligence and crisis-response activities.

We believe that competitive firms—particularly those operating across dynamic markets that include uniquely motivated and capable rivals (both current and potential) and a multi-national scope—require a similar system.

However, when it comes to applying this military developed application to commerce, the key issues are less easily defined and more ambiguous. In business and competitive analysis, we often talk about persistent market-related problems rather than impending events, and it's often difficult to identify the specific decision maker that has to be warned. Also there are many instances where a firm can't eliminate or stop a problem; consequently, the analyst must instead focus on dealing with the consequences of a rival's activity. The question for business and competitive analysts is more focused on how to develop a usable methodology in this area that can assist in the refinement of their assessments and provide more robust forecasts. This is where I&W analysis becomes an essential and beneficial technique for an analyst.

Strategic Rationale and Implications

Firms must be prepared to fight and win in the modern marketplace. This is characterized by large numbers of highly capable competitors using a full range of conventional marketing tactics, as well as employing advanced systems along their value chains. In an era of just-in-time processes, shorter product life cycles, fragmented and maturing global markets, thinner profit margins, and intensified competition, time becomes an increasingly important source of competitive advantage. Many firms who recognize this employ time-based competitive strategies.[4] Time-based competitive strategies require firms to strategically use the time dimension related to customers and competitors to improve their relative performance in response time, cycle time, on-time delivery, time to market, just-in-time inventory, and real-time decision making, among others.

The nature (that is, intensity, density, speed, and sometimes even finality) of these marketplace battles makes "quick response" decision making even more difficult at a time when customer-facing employees and managers require more effective direction in order to exploit fleeting market opportunities as well as their rivals' vulnerabilities. Analysts and their systems must be able to provide decision makers with information concerning their rivals, the nature of the threats, the broader STEEP environment,[5] and the effects of each on the accomplishment of the firm's mission. I&W analysis is a method that ensures uniformity in the analysis of rivals and the environment, and the evaluation of the effects of each on their degree of threat, as well as potential collaborative courses of action.

Firms need to shift their focus from the traditional, slow-moving, logical, mature competitive arenas to a new competitive worldview. Many firms lack an I&W capability focusing primarily on the new types of threats that are emerging in global markets. Rivals can still operate "below the radar" in different countries or markets before larger, higher market share competitors realize what is happening. Executives remain concerned over the lack of warning capabilities on market destabilizing events, including new product introductions, major marketing changes, or announcements of key strategic relationships.[6] It is essential that a methodology for studying these preconditions and precipitants of the emerging threats be established.

If a firm's business and competitive strategy must factor in change of a type and speed that has not been seen before, then an analyst's assessments that underpin the developed strategy have got to be equally dynamic. Firms therefore need to have business and competitive analysis systems that can scan and monitor the environment, continually updating the assessments that are put forward to clients. These systems should also help to identify emerging issues in areas that will be of concern to the firm in the future, including those areas that may not be currently in its scope.

A strategic view that includes I&W analysis helps decision makers to be proactive as opposed to simply reactive. It is too easy for firms to be overwhelmed by the unrelenting pace or pressure of events; consequently, it's only while being proactive that firms will have opportunities to stay ahead of rivals. Astute analysts should be producing analytical outputs and assessments that can support proactive marketplace strategies, as opposed to simply defensive or threat-reactive ones.[7]

Strengths and Advantages

I&W analysis forces analysts and decision makers to mutually set business and competitive analysis priorities. This helps firms to overcome the problem of having competitive intelligence staff seeking out "busy work" in the absence of direction or customers' demands and the situation where decision makers ask to "get me everything you can about somebody or something," which can waste the firm's resources.

I&W analysis can reduce the waste of intelligence resources—and save money and scarce time, particularly in the data collection side of the larger business and competitive intelligence process. Data collection, in supporting I&W analysis, is clearly focused on gathering reliable information that can provide a timely and cost-effective warning. The significance of information is predetermined from discussions between analysts and decision makers, thus facilitating the recognition of significant change. If the changes are such that they show that the firm and marketplace are moving in directions notified in an assessment, or that they are moving away from it, or at a different speed, that information can either be used to update the assessment or a warning generated. Many of these changes occur in cycles, requiring analysts and information gatherers to continually feed data into the process, updating assessments, refining warnings, and continually adding to the value that they give decision makers.

Combined with other related environmental scanning or tracking systems, I&W analysis can constitute a powerful set of techniques that will assist strategic competitive analysis units to produce dynamic assessments. I&W analysis should provide insight as a basis for action by strategic decision makers. It should also help analysts to avoid developing "interesting" yet mostly unimportant information for their own sake, but rather, intelligence that is of immediate and beneficial use to decision makers in determining and managing business unit or firm strategies.

I&W analysis also helps to establish a proactive mindset in both analysts and decision making. It gives the firm a better understanding of the current and potential changes that are taking place in the environment and should challenge the "current" wisdom by bringing fresh viewpoints into the decision-making mechanism.

The ultimate value of I&W analysis lies in both the content of the analytical output, as well as the process used to generate it. At the "product level," the outputs of environmental analysis generally consist of descriptions of changes that are currently taking place, indicators of potential changes in the future, and alternative descriptions of future changes (the scenario type aspect). At the "process level," involving decision makers and analysts in determining data-gathering priorities helps to enhance the competitive and competitor learning atmosphere and mindset that many experts claim is increasingly needed today.[8]

Weaknesses and Limitations

Despite the recognition that I&W can serve an important purpose, studies of I&W systems in governmental and military organizations through the years have displayed a disturbing theme. There are a number of recurring problems found in I&W analysis. These impediments include, but may not be limited to, the following:[9]

■ Inadequate recognition by firms of emerging threats, particularly those of low probability but potential great danger—examples of disruption in industries and the frequent inability of market share leaders to properly address them are plentiful.

■ A consequent inadequate collection against such threats—many firms still lack the processes and systems for maintaining $365 \times 24 \times 7$ data and information gathering, and tracking capabilities, even for the critical areas of operations, customers, competitors, or global events.

■ Breakdown of information and communication flows between the various parties assigned tasks in the intelligence and planning process—this can occur particularly among those individuals responsible for gathering important data/information, analysts, and decision makers.

■ Failure by analysts to fully understand rivals and their intentions from the rivals' viewpoints, and removing the built-in biases affecting both analysts and data collectors that impede reaching their objective.

■ Failure by decision makers to heed or give legitimacy to analysts or the minority views.

■ Overwhelmed analysts, analytical systems, and an appreciable lack of proper resources and time to address anomaly indicators in scenarios.

■ Vulnerability to red herrings, deception, and other Trojan horses used by rivals.

It is a complicated task to interpret events or trends that will manifest themselves in some difficult-to-discern ways in the future. This uncertainty may help gain executive commitment to use and sustain I&W analysis, particularly if the predictions for a designated time horizon are not known. Conservative mindsets of either the analyst or decision maker can also weaken the effectiveness of I&W analysis.[10] There is also the risk that decision makers might act too slowly on warnings or that the I&W analyst has provided poor judgments.

I&W analysis is more important in some industries than others. I&W will be highly beneficial in fast-developing industries with high degrees of change. In industries that are mature, exhibit substantially less change, or grow very slowly, there will be less need for I&W analysis.

The huge growth in data and information available on the Web and open sources has been both beneficial and problematic for I&W analysis. The additional data provided through the Web and open sources can potentially contain indicators of competitive rivals' activity or adverse events. The problem with this source of data is that the vast majority of the information captured will be noise as opposed to signals. Being able to distinguish between strong and weak signals, signals and noise, and knowing what thresholds should trigger warnings is difficult to build into automated systems (applications or solutions), and very few commercial firms have acquired the ability to perform this valuable filtering task with consistently high degrees of success.

Effective I&W systems can take many years to develop and to become effective; they often require trial and error, and it helps to test I&W analysis and recommendations in simulations and scenarios to understand the likelihood that they can effectively predict future actions. The most effective I&W analyses are supported by communication and information systems designed to capture and disseminate potential indicators, which most commercial firms have yet to install and institutionalize.

In terms of implementing the technique, it is generally thought that it is more beneficial for analysts to help form a group of executives who have an ongoing interaction with I&W processes. This is, however, often not possible in smaller firms or those that are geographically distant. Unfortunately, experience suggests that most firms have not done a good job at connecting I&W participation with appropriate recognition/rewards, thereby rendering it less effective.

Process for Applying the Technique

There is a presumption of surprise as well as incomplete intelligence underlying I&W analysis that needs to be understood before a firm can initiate the process. These presumptions require you to be involved in what can be exhaustive research in order to build a defensible case underlying the issuance of a specific warning.[11] You need to develop intimate understandings of your rivals, resources, structure, history, capabilities, motivations, culture, blind spots, and biases, among other things. Some of these are easier to understand than others, making the I&W analysis process a more difficult task for analysts.

We recommend following these four basic steps for performing I&W analysis. They include establishing the set of indicators, establishing meaning behind the indicators, validating and ranking the indicators, and determining alternative courses of action.

Step 1: Establish the Set of Indicators

You should collaboratively work with all the decision makers to identify specific actions or events that might potentially signal a strategic attack by a marketplace rival. This step assumes that the decision maker can accurately identify their rivals. For this task, it is beneficial for you and decision makers to collaborate and achieve consensus on an appropriate definition of rivals. This definition must take into account the vision, mission, strategy, scope, and competitive goals of the firm.

Indicators will consist of data or information pointing to those actions or events by rivals that are thought to potentially be a risk to the focal firm and its ability to successfully achieve its marketplace goals. Indicators are signs or suggestions that certain key things may unfold. They are not guarantees that something will happen but are conceptually linked through examination of past significant marketplace actions by rivals.[12] Warnings, which are the eventual manifestations of relationships among the indicators in I&W analysis, are similarly suggestions, hypotheses, or beliefs that some events will transpire.

More specifically, indicators are factors, events (or lack of events), or actions that present a significant clue about the nature of present circumstances and suggests an eventual end result of a series of events. They are measurable, observable, and collectible and signal progression toward a significant competitive action by a rival. Observations of these actions, events, or factors are described as "indications," and information systems should be established to capture them and communicate that a "trigger" has been pulled to analysts and decision makers. Some common indicators that a business and competitive analyst might uncover include those displayed in the following list:

- Filing of shareholder lawsuits
- Wall Street analysts' expectations of a merger candidate's profitability
- Public statements by public officials about a potential firm action
- Rumblings of union dissatisfaction shown in "'sick outs'" and potential strike action
- Increase in insider shareholding transactions
- Sudden and unexpected departures of key executives
- Suddenly increasing "'help wanted'" ads in specific mission-critical activity areas
- Unusual investments in similarly positioned early stage ventures
- Aggressive and unusual asset sales
- Noticeably stepped-up lobbying activity in state or national capitals

Because there is a difference between expectations (indications or warnings) and reality, it is important that you and decision makers come to a realistic shared understanding of the process, its limitations, and its ability to deliver beneficial outcomes. You need to be able to share warnings about actions that may not be popular or desirable to the decision maker, and it is important that you retain your objectivity even in light of the possibility of having to deliver either unpopular or inaccurate predictions.

One of the best means for performing this identification process is to study the past actions of competitors in the marketplace. These actions need to be classified, sequenced, and studied for understanding. The actions may not have all unfolded in linear or logical fashion, creating a need for the analyst to employ different sets of tools to understand the patterns. These tools can include, among other things, performing event and timeline analysis (see Chapter 21, "Event and Timeline Analysis"), decision and event trees, trend analyses, pattern mapping, weighted rankings, probability trees, and other problem-solving techniques.

The historiographical analysis methods (see Chapter 25, "Historiographical Analysis") can also be particularly useful in this task. For example, you can use historiographical analysis as one of the means for answering I&W-related questions, such as the following:

- Did the rival signal a major marketplace battle by first introducing a new product in a particular geographic region?
- Did the rival start a prior battle by systematically lowering prices across a product line shortly before a new introduction?
- Did the rival begin the last set of aggressive actions after a particular event (for example, after a bad quarter or having just replaced a key top executive)?
- Did the rival line up its distribution channel by creating excess capacity before quickly filling it with product?

The key for you performing this step is to determine the pattern of activity that rivals use that signals a major offensive by them in the marketplace and to capture the patterns in the form of indications. At the conclusion of this step, you should have determined a set of indications for the particular rival. Comprehensive I&W systems require the development of these indicators for all rivals, both current and potential.

Step 2: Establish Meaning Behind Indicators

You must consider the following in order to generate insight about the indicators and what they portend for the firm. This "player-oriented intelligence" is tailored for use within I&W analysis. We build upon a concept borrowed from a common formula in criminal analysis, which looks at how criminals might choose and act upon targets. The five areas we suggest the analysis consider include analyzing the rival's motivation, opportunity, capabilities, method, and imminence. Each of these areas is discussed in turn next.

Motivation. It is important for you to try to determine what the rival is hoping to achieve or accomplish by acting or not acting as the indicator portends. Does the rival see a temporary gap in meeting customer's needs in the marketplace? Is it trying to shore up a weak business or product line? Is it trying to achieve some additional cash flow to finance a future expansion? Has it picked a particular point in time to act because it recognizes seasonality or an anomaly in market demand trends that it believes it can exploit?

This is always a tricky facet of the process since predicting rival's intentions requires an intimate understanding of the rival. More often than not, you need to isolate your own biases as well as those of your firm so that you do not color your insights or understanding of the rival. Additionally, you cannot achieve this intimate understanding solely on the basis of collecting, organizing, and synthesizing data. You must literally be able to put yourself in the shoes of the rival. Fortunately, several of the techniques described in other parts of this book can assist you in this task, particularly shadowing (see Chapter 13, "Shadowing"), and war gaming (see Chapter 23, "War Gaming").

Opportunity. In addition to understanding a rival's motivation, trying to gauge what opportunity it is truly aiming to achieve becomes important. It is beneficial for you to determine the actual size of the opportunity the rival seeks to achieve. If it is successful, what would be the increase in sales it expects to achieve and the loss in sales the analyst's firm may experience? How will the "bottom-line" impact be to the rival and the focal firm? How will the rival's success in exploiting the opportunity impact long-term customer perceptions of the marketplace and competitors? Does this indicator suggest some cross-market (multi-point competitive) impacts that make it larger in scope or scale than it represents on the surface?

There is usually a close positive correlation between the opportunity and the rival's likely course of action. The larger the opportunity represented by the indicator is to the rival, the more likely the rival can be expected to fiercely compete for it.

Capabilities. You should try to determine whether the rival has the resources and capabilities to achieve its aims. Using business and competitive analysis tools like functional capabilities and resources analysis, competitor analysis, value chain analysis,[13] and benchmarking (see Chapter 11, "Benchmarking") can help you get to the core of this question.

Determining the rival's capability also means determining who the rival is allying with to accomplish its objectives. You should aim to determine, among other things, the following: Who else is involved? Is this being done only by one party (the rival), or is it being assisted by other collaborators? Does this indicate new strategic relationships that need to be monitored or actively addressed? If it indicates long-standing relationships, what might that indicate about how the action will roll out in the marketplace?[14]

Method. This requires you to understand the range and scope of the rival's action. It usually helps to first determine whether the action indicated is strategic, tactical, or operational in nature. You can also determine which of the marketing levers are being pulled to achieve it—starting with a consideration of the "4Ps" of pricing, place, promotion, and product. Consideration should also be given to some of the generic forms of offensive movement, such as the following:[15]

- Offering equally good or better products for a lower price.
- Leapfrogging all industry rivals to the next generation of product or technology.
- Attacking a competitive vulnerability or weakness of your firm.
- Purposefully attacking or destabilizing segments of the market in which your firm achieves a high proportion of its profits or its fastest growth prospects.
- Using hit and run tactics to quickly take market share or sales from your firm while it is distracted by other events.
- Maneuvering around rivals and focusing on segments of the marketplace that have yet to be contested or have been overlooked.
- Learning from the tactics and successes of other firms and applying them to its offerings.
- Launching a preemptive strike to gain an advantageous position in the marketplace that will discourage or prevent your firm from moving toward.

Imminence. The last key concept for generating meaning is to determine how soon the indicated event might take place. This will require you to consider what other activities or events need to occur before the attack is launched, how much time is needed to launch the attack, how much time is required for the focal firm to prepare its response; and when the consequences of the rival's actions and the focal firm's reactions be manifest in the marketplace and show up in the firm's strategic and financial performance. Obviously, the closer these answers are to the present time, the sooner you will need to accelerate processes so as to give as much advance notice as possible to the decision makers in order that the decisions can be made quickly and actions taken to address the rivals.

Additionally, most marketplace actions that have long-term competitive impacts tend to follow a normal progression, a dynamics of escalation that looks remarkably similar to the life-cycle concepts we have discussed. This concept suggests that there are early, middle, and late stages of any marketplace battles. The most valuable indicators appear early in the roll-out of a market attack, and it is during this stage that analysts must be most vigilant in order to provide their decision makers as much lead time as possible. By the time the rival has rolled out the actual action, the damage is mostly done, and all the firm can do is to try and fire-fight or "crisis manage" the consequences. This result usually means less maneuvering room or discretion for decision makers, a situation the analysts should do their best to help their clients avoid.

Step 3: Validate and Rank Indicators Against Threshold Levels to Determine When Warnings Need to Be Issued

For I&W analysis, it is desirable that, based on the information available, a prediction (the warning) be produced that: (1) indicates the possible causes of the observed information and ranks those causes in order of confidence that they could be a cause; (2) based on those indications, predicts other observable mechanisms and consequences associated with those causes; and (3) provides the means to warn decision makers and other individuals in the firm who will be affected of the actions and potential consequences prior to those consequences being manifested.

It must be remembered that a significant number of indicators are ordinarily required to be present before the I&W system produces a warning. A few events, such as small pricing changes, an increase in hiring, or increasing truck traffic at a distribution center, though possibly important once brought together in the bigger scheme of things, would not necessarily trigger a warning.

As such, there are a number of questions that you must consider in validating the series of indicators you have identified:

- Can you trust the indicator?

- Is it a signal of a pending event or noise (that is, useless information, or even potentially worse, disinformation meant to confuse the analyst and competing organizations so as not to disclose a rival's true intentions)?

- Who (that is, the source of the data or information underlying the indicator) observed the indicator or communicated of its existence? Are these people trustworthy sources?

- Did their observation of the indicators come under stressed or natural circumstances?

It is beneficial that you qualify the indication as being on a continuum ranging from high reliability to low/no reliability. The indications also need to be scored in terms of their imminence, or how quickly the ensuring events might result in significant actions by the competitor. If the pattern or series of indicators are both reliable and imminent, then you may consider issuing a warning to decision makers. You should always remember that there needs to be a high-quality standard for warnings in order to gain and keep the trust and confidence of the decision makers. As such, you need to avoid the "Chicken Little" situation in which warnings are issued for any and every rival action, thereby diminishing the decision maker's will to respond and act, and the firm's readiness to address truly significant concerns as opposed to minor or insignificant ones.

Once a warning is issued, it is provided to decision makers as an estimate of a rival's ability to win a marketplace battle at the given time. This information, coupled with additional data, should allow the decision maker to make informed decisions about the rival's intentions. If the decision maker agrees that the warning of the rival's intentions is valid, they can then take the necessary steps to address the situation before it unfolds in the ways you have suggested.

Step 4: Determine and Recommend Appropriate Firm Responses to the Warning

You should not consider your tasks completed upon the issuance of the warning. Although this will mark the completion of a particular I&W analysis task, it does not end your responsibilities to help the decision makers understand what options are available for the firm so as to maximize the firm's performance in light of the warned-about situation.

You can alert decision makers to the analyzed facts, to their competitive consequences, as well as a potential series of alternative actions, along with well thought-out scenarios of action and reaction, and cause and effect activities that give the decision maker a keener insight into what decisions and subsequent actions might result in the most favorable outcome. You must make sure that your recommendations allow decision makers and relevant firm members the necessary maneuvering room to make decisions and take actions. Even if this maneuvering room is apparently not available and the firm cannot change the inevitable pattern of events about to take place, then at least the decision makers were forewarned of it and can begin the process of setting up the policies, procedures, and structures necessary to deal with the consequences that are ultimately emerging. Additionally, this will reinforce the need for you and the firm to monitor the emerging issues, to gauge the speed, direction, and magnitude of the changes decision makers see as being important, and then to continually refine those forecasts and scenarios so the decision makers can have confidence in the intelligence that you deliver.

Summary

I&Ws are based on a competitive rival's likely preparations for an assault or attack in the marketplace. Conventional I&Ws include several identifiable events: purchasing of media; hiring of specialized employees; new product information being distributed through sales channels; and significant changes in communications patterns with any stakeholder along the value chain. Once observed, these events are then referred to as "indications." You determine how imminent the threat is by the totality of indications and issue warnings to your decision makers at various threshold levels.

However, I&W is normally a methodology restricted to the strategic and operational levels of competition. The new competitive environment requires the development of effective and efficient I&W systems that can separate signals from the noise out of the mass of incoming data. Additionally, they require analysts to work actively and regularly with decision makers in the development of indicators, as well as acquiring the necessary communication, information, and management support needed to maintain this analytical process at effective levels over time. Finally, I&W analysis is not an exact science—predictions can never be issued by analysts without some uncertainty; it means judging the probability that certain events (indicators) precipitated by rivals will lead to significant competitive impacts on the marketplace.

FAROUT Summary

FAROUT SUMMARY

	1	2	3	4	5
F					
A					
R					
O					
U					
T					

Figure 24.1   Indications and warning analysis FAROUT summary

Future orientation—High. I&W analysis focuses expressly on "industry change drivers," pending or imminent competitor activity, and how developments pose potential surprises. This is one of the more useful tools for foreseeing (and hopefully forestalling or minimizing) future crisis situations.

Accuracy—Medium. Constantly monitoring competitor activities, events, and established drivers will enhance the levels of accuracy achieved in the application of I&W. However, it is clearly more difficult to gain a complete understanding and tracking of external factors that underlie indications interact with one another.

Resource efficiency—Medium. Developing appropriate indicators requires study of past data. Monitoring activities, events, and trend information can take significant resources. Public sector organizations (like national military organizations or intelligence agencies) sometimes employ dozens or even hundreds of people to ensure proper utilization. In multinational corporations, I&W can be facilitated through astute usage of software-based solutions and grassroots, informal networks connected through intranets, and related communication facilities.

Objectivity—Low to medium. Dependability rests with I&W analysts and the process they use to arrive at their predictions of rival's future actions. As with many forms of analysis, biases and mindsets may distort true industry shifts in applications of this technique.

Usefulness—Medium to high. In industries with high levels of change and uncertainty, I&W analysis has the potential to save the firm from disaster. Even in less-dynamic industries, this technique can reduce surprises, minimize disruptions, and lessen uncertainty in decision making.

Timeliness—Medium. Gathering information and analyzing and interpreting can take time. Then another team must conjure the scenarios, adding to the timeframe. Once an I&W analysis system is fully operating, triggers in the system can facilitate the analyst's timely warning of activity to their decision makers.

Related Tools and Techniques

- Blindspot analysis
- Early warning analysis
- Industry analysis
- Issue analysis
- S-curve analysis
- Scenario analysis
- STEEP analysis
- War gaming

References

Albrecht, K. (2000). *Corporate Radar: Tracking the Forces That Are Shaping Your Business*. New York, NY: AMACOM.

Campbell, W.A. (1999). "Traditional I&Ws for host-based intrusion detection," presented at the First Annual Computer Emergency Response Team (CERT) Conference, Omaha, Nebraska. Presentation documentation available at http://www.certconf.org/presentations/1999/.

Fahey, L. (1999). *Outwitting, Outmaneuvering, and Outperforming Competitors*. New York, NY: John Wiley & Sons, Inc.

Fleisher, C.S., and B.E. Bensoussan (2003). *Strategic and Competitive Analysis: Methods and Techniques for Analyzing Business Competition*. Upper Saddle River, NJ: Prentice Hall.

Fuld, L. (2003). "Be prepared," *Harvard Business Review*, November/December, pp. 20–21.

Gilad, B. (2004). *Early Warning: Using Competitive Intelligence to Anticipate Market Shifts, Control Risk, and Create Powerful Strategies*. New York, NY: Amacom.

Grabo, C. (2002). *Anticipating Surprise: Analysis for Strategic Warning*. Washington, DC: Center for Strategic Research—Joint Military Intelligence College.

Herring, J. (2005). "Create an intelligence program for current and future business needs," *Competitive Intelligence Magazine*, 8(5), pp. 20–27.

Jones, M.D. (1998). *The Thinker's Toolkit: 14 Powerful Techniques for Problem Solving*. New York, NY: Three Rivers Press.

Sawka, K. (2001). "Warning analysis: A risky business," Competitive Intelligence Review, 8(4), pp. 83-84.

Stalk, G., and T. Hout Jr. (1990). *Competing Against Time: How Time-Based Competition is Reshaping Global Markets*. New York, NY: The Free Press.

Swanson, S.K. (2005). "I&Ws analysis post 9/11: Analyzing enemy intent," *The Vanguard*, Journal of the Military Intelligence Corps Association, 4th quarter, pp. 11–13.

Swanson, S.K. (undated). "I&Ws post 9/11: New strategies for intelligence," retrieved from the Web on March 18, 2006 from http://www.micorps.org/downloads/Swanson_I&W.pdf.

Thompson, A.A., Gamble, J.E., and A.J. Strickland (2006). *Strategy: Winning in the Marketplace*, 2nd edition. New York, NY: McGraw-Hill.

Endnotes

[1] Campbell, 1999.

[2] Albrecht, 2000.

[3] Gilad, 2004.

[4] Stalk and Hout Jr., 1990.

[5] See Fleisher and Bensoussan, 2003, Chapter 17.

[6] Fuld, 2003.

[7] Gilad, 2004.

[8] Fahey, 1999.

[9] Grabo, 2002; Swanson, undated; Swanson, 2005.

[10] Swanson, 2005.

[11] Grabo, 2002.

[12] Swanson, undated.

[13] See Fleisher and Bensoussan, 2003, Chapters 9, 11, and 14.

[14] For help doing this, see Chapter 16, "Strategic Relationship Analysis."

[15] Thompson, Gamble, and Strickland, 2006.

25

Historiographical Analysis

Short Description

Historiographical analysis applies a common research methodology used in history studies to strategy analysis. It attempts to understand strategic issues relative to their origins and evolution in order to more clearly understand the present. Historiography seeks to identify and interpret events that have occurred, as opposed to merely reporting them.[1] By placing the present in an historical perspective, historiographical analysis may also beneficially frame future strategic considerations.

Background

Commonly described as "the history of history," historiography is almost as old as history itself. Since time immemorial, humankind has engaged in communicating and preserving their historical records, first through oral tradition and later through written documentation. Initially, the recording of history was done without any systematic consideration of the *process* of recording history. By the nineteenth century, however, the related field of historiographical analysis was fully articulated to specifically address two issues related to the recording of history:[2]

- The actual process of historical writing
- Methodological and theoretical issues related to this process

Historians inherently ask many questions about the past, and they try to answer these questions through their research. To accomplish this, historians must learn how to read a wide variety of historical records for argument (how to know what other writers are arguing; how to ask historical questions; and also how to uncover, gather, and assess the soundness of historical sources). Historiographers are ever conscious of the "four Cs" of context, causes, continuity, and change.[3]

In the 1960s, Alfred duPont Chandler was one of the first economic historians and strategists to popularly apply historiography to the study of strategic management. Using this analytical approach, Chandler developed a theory of strategy and structure, as well as a theory explaining the rise of managerialism and business enterprise in America.[4]

Since these early developments, advances in the application of historiography to the field of strategic management have been erratic—the majority of research has been directed toward the academic study of management and policy. Nonetheless, historiographical analysis represents a promising analytical process that offers many unique insights into competitive behavior and competition. It can be of good value in developing insights that complement strategic decision making.

Strategic Rationale and Implications

Humans by nature are interested in making progress—they build their cultures with tales from the past of how they have triumphed over adversity, enhanced their conditions and lifestyles, and made advances in technology. Society's focus on constant advancement means that we tend to dismiss or forget the historical perspective. The primary purpose for using historiographical methods for competitive or strategic analysis is to build business theories that revisit the past in order to explain current strategic issues and competitive conditions. Although the technique is neither necessary nor sufficient in the entire strategic analysis or planning process, it can greatly enhance the analyst's understanding of context and activity and provide insights into one's firm or industry.

An important fundamental premise underlies the application of historiography to strategic analysis. This premise is that understanding the origins of strategic issues and their evolution through time provides a foundation from which to guide today's strategic analysis.[5] Historiographical analysis asks the question: *"Why have strategic issues and competitive conditions developed so as to arrive at their current state?"* The answer to this question is essential to properly frame strategic analysis and often provides clues as to optimal courses for present or future action. Often, the underlying forces driving change are closely related to historical precedents. In this way, historiographical analysis can be viewed as a tool that uses knowledge of the past to examine the present as well as to help project the future. For example, understanding the origins and evolution of a path-dependent source of competitive advantage (that is, how the history of a competitive advantage can be explained disproportionately by particular events or actions that occurred in the past) can be greatly facilitated through this type of analysis.

R.S. Goodman and E.V. Kruger have identified several areas where historiographical analysis provides for the rigorous development, critique, or defense of propositions or theories. Although their application was designed for the larger field of academic management research, their work is equally relevant to generating competitive theories for circumstances facing individual firms; therefore, several areas where historiographical analysis can assist the analyst in generating descriptive or explanatory theories at the firm level follow:

- **Research question development**—Historiographical analysis starts with a hypothesis (that is, an in-progress or tentative explanation of some phenomena or problem that can subsequently be subject to investigation and testing) that guides the analysis of corroborating sources of evidence. There is an inherent efficiency in this step that can help you avoid embarking upon a "fishing expedition" through the data and information because, ideally, this will enable you to structure the parameters of the strategic issue before embarking on further research.

- **Variable selection and evaluation**—Analysts using historiographical analysis face similar limitations to those individuals using other related qualitative techniques. This forces the analyst to carefully validate (that is, establish the relative "soundness" of) the sources of information underlying their analysis. Historiographical analysis methodology is premised on the principle of objective skepticism, which suggests that skepticism is driven by external forces rather than internal bias. This is achieved in two ways. First, historiographical analysis removes bias that often afflicts conventional analysis by insisting on *initially* viewing all information as credible and valid. This validity is then confirmed or dismissed *externally* by cross-referencing and triangulation against other evidence generated by primary and secondary sources.

  The breadth of information under the purview of historiographical analysis increases the number and diversity of potential variables that would not normally be considered when using other strategy analysis tools and techniques.

- **Theory construction**—Historiographical analysis also offers a unique approach to theory construction. As opposed to the deductive approach of most analytical approaches, historiographical analysis incorporates an inductive approach that first proposes a general proposition and then searches for confirming evidence. Inductive approaches can be very appealing for analysts within larger, time-pressed enterprises since they are often guided by decision makers who need to be convinced of the facts and shown the underlying logic using evidence they can easily relate to.

- **Hypothesis generation**—Investigating the historical development of strategic issues and competitive conditions encourages a holistic inclusion of all of the relevant factors and their interrelationships with each other. Thorough research requires that your investigative net be cast as wide as possible to allow the diversity of sources to generate multiple hypotheses. This process results in a more complete analysis.

- **Formulation of conclusions**—Based on the corroboration from the various primary and secondary sources, a conclusion (that is, the generalized proposition articulated at the start of the analysis) can be more effectively supported.

Table 25.1 summarizes the strategic rationale of using historiographical analysis to build theories based on the past to explain the present and frame the future.

Table 25.1
Applicability of Historiography to Management Research[6]

Research Stage	Contributions of Historiography
Source evaluation	Helps the analyst identify and critically assess all possible data sources in terms of their content, suitability, reliability, and explanation of context.
Develop the research problem or key intelligence question	Forces the analyst to define a general question to guide research.
	Helps the analyst to avoid the tendency to dredge the data for potentially spurious relationships.
Formulate conclusions	Clarifies the relationship of the research and conclusion in theory.
Generate hypotheses	Requires the analyst to generate multiple hypotheses and multiple variables.
	Helps the analyst to understand the implication of testing chosen hypotheses with selected variables.
Construct a theory	Helps the analyst to develop a theory that reflects the full context of the phenomena being assessed.
Select and evaluate variables	Implicit recognition of data limitations.

Strengths and Advantages

Historiographical analysis broadens the analytical scope of strategic analysis. The diversity of information sources embraced by historiography often presents management with perspectives and insights routinely ignored by other strategy analysis tools and techniques. In this respect, historiography extends the mental envelope of managers by asking new questions or approaching old questions in different ways.

As a refined qualitative method of analysis, historiography provides a richer means for illuminating the relationship between contexts, causes, continuity, and changes. As such, it focuses on explaining important developments in the competitive marketplace by requiring you to study alternative evolutionary patterns of activity and behavior, either topically or chronologically. This keeps you from automatically falling back on their pre-conceived notions or commonly held industry recipes that could limit the development of superior future options for enterprise action.

The analytical development and subsequent managerial decision-making processes are also improved by several positive principles inherent in the historiographical approach, particularly through skepticism and strategic challenge:

- **Skepticism**—Historians, the individuals who most commonly apply this technique, by nature and training accept that history can never be completely recaptured.

Therefore, they exist with competing accounts and interpretations of facts, making them skeptical of the contents and objectivity of different competing sources. Employing historiographical analysis encourages you to adopt the mindset of rigorous objective skepticism.

■ **Strategic challenge**—Historiographical theories cannot be proven in the way we scientifically assess mathematical proofs or related physical phenomena, and that is, ironically, one of the greatest strengths of historiographical analysis. As such, established theories are under constant pressure from newer historiographical theories with greater explanatory power. This critical perspective acts to constantly challenge peoples' assumptions underlying the firm's or competitor's strategy.

Weaknesses and Limitations

One of the primary criticisms of historiographical analysis is its perceived lack of objectivity. Much of the process involves the individual's selection of facts designed to support subjective theories that are not easily amenable to testing through rigorous statistical analysis. In fact, many observers object to referring to the final product of historiographical analysis as theory and instead perceive it to be a close cousin to narrative. However, before dismissing historiographical analysis on this basis, you should consider the confidence that society places on scientific proof; perhaps the only difference between historiographical analysis and other perceptively more robust analyses is the quantification of uncertainty and subjectivity rather than its elimination.

Historiographical analysis is also viewed in many corners as suffering from "prior hypothesis bias." This bias refers to one's tendency to be lulled toward sources or data that support our hypotheses and ignore or minimize data that doesn't. The tendency to act in this way needs to be actively combated, and good historiographers are taught to apply techniques that will lessen this potential problem.

Another weakness of historiographical analysis relates to the dependence its validity has on one's view of history. Several common philosophical views of history include the linear view, the circular view, and/or the chaos perspective. The linear view posits that history is one long continuum of progress with very few points of commonality. Conversely, the circular view suggests that history is a series of overlapping patterns resulting in many points of commonality—it is best described by the karmic phrase "What goes around comes around." The chaos view asserts that history is totally random with no points of commonality. Obviously, one's philosophical view of history will impact his or her evaluation of the worth of historiographical analysis. The circular view would seem to offer the strongest validation of the purpose of historiographical analysis to learn from the past. However, the common occurrence of discontinuities or "disruptions" challenges this view.

Historiographical analysis is sometimes derided for its lack of structure. Indeed, the process approach can appear very loose. Linear thinkers often reject this flexibility, suggesting that the broad scope of induction embraced by historiographical analysis leads to an inefficient and inconclusive analysis. This generalization is also seen as a major flaw of historiographical analysis; that is, the analytical product cannot be used as a universal principle.

A final caution regarding the use of historiographical analysis: Problems can arise if the analyst uses the conclusions to predict the future rather than to better understand the current position. History has demonstrated a tendency to frequently repeat itself, although these repetitions are never perfect or exact to prior occurrences. Business analysts know this from their own experience with technology. Not only do advances in technology change how we do things, it changes what we do now and in the future. For Kodak and Fuji, a historiographical analysis highlighting the importance of film quality could lead these firms astray if it means they fail to recognize that digitization has been rendering their chemically based products obsolete. This weakness is overcome when analysts fully recognize the purpose of historiographical analysis and use it in conjunction with other strategy building techniques outlined in this book.

Process for Applying the Technique

Unlike other more scientific disciplines, historiographical analysis does not begin with a theory from which testable hypotheses are developed. In contrast to the traditional scientific method, historiographical analysis begins with a general proposition and seeks corroborating support from a diverse array of sources using methodologies from many other disciplines. The far-reaching nature of the technique requires that the analyst should attempt to become both widely and well read. The Case Study, for example, provides a sample of historiographical analysis as applied to the retail industry.

Step 1—Develop a General Proposition

The first step, then, in the historiographical process is to develop a general proposition about a strategic issue or competitive condition. Some examples of such general propositions are the following:

- Underlying factors responsible for the prevalence of alliances in a particular industry

- Specific reasons for the industry leader's success with a particular type of technological platform

- Determination of the dependency of certain strategic assets or capabilities that a competitor owns or controls

This short list underscores the broad scope of historiographical analysis. The competitive issues potentially under its purview are very expansive and can incorporate influences from any number of areas.

Step 2—Collect Primary Information

The next step is to seek out primary sources of information. Primary sources include eyewitness accounts and accounts from people who were close to the action along various points of the issue's development. These sources are viewed as the "first draft of history" because of their firsthand nature (that is, they come "straight from the source," not from or through a second source, such as a reporter) and consistency with the oral tradition that started the historiograhical discipline. As such, they are often the most valuable source of information because of the limited potential for distortions. These primary sources may come directly to you from participants or observers, be captured in eyewitness accounts and surveys, be found in published speeches (in written or multimedia formats) by participants at or about the time that the event occurred, or come from experiments or possibly from original photographic records and the like.

Step 3—Collect Secondary Information

Next, you need to seek out secondary sources of information about the issue under analysis. Typical sources of information include newspapers, the Internet, magazines, corporate publications, annual reports, analyst reports, trade publications, academic cases, and so on. These accounts can be considered as the "second draft" of history because they represent the attempt of various individuals to reconstruct the historical evolution of the various issues through their own interpretations and lenses.

Both primary and secondary sources then undergo critical analysis in order to determine authenticity. It is important for you to remain as objective as an historian at the outset of the analysis. This means you must initially assume that all sources are neutral and valid; that is, all of the information gathered from primary and secondary sources is expected at the outset to represent what it purports to represent. This reduces the chances of introducing personal bias into the analysis.

At this point, the distinction between primary and secondary sources can serve as a valuable external and objective legitimacy filter in order to test the validity of the sources. Points of apparent inconsistency can be cross-referenced between primary accounts and secondary accounts. Similarly, different sources within each source category can be checked against each other for accuracy. After this procedure has been completed, you will have answers to several pertinent questions. Is the information authentic? Is it legitimate and known to be true? Are the sources free from any perceived, known, or actual bias?

Step 4—Select the Best Sources for the Third Draft

Next, you select those sources that best address the general proposition developed at the start of the historiographical process. These sources then represent the raw material for the "third draft of history," the analysis of the evolution of an issue developed as intelligence—not for public consumption but as an analytical input to the strategic decision-making process. This requires a critical analysis of all the sources in an attempt to find common threads or continuities in the often-messy web of data that has been culled from the valid primary and secondary sources. These threads are then woven into a theoretical tapestry that sufficiently supports or explains the original proposition.

Step 5—Reporting

Consider this process as the reverse of building a standard logical argument. Normally, arguments are first built on a set of assumptions or premises that support a conclusion. Logic assumes that if premises are valid, then the conclusion that they support is valid. Instead of this standard deductive approach, historiographical analysis employs an inductive methodology. It starts with a conclusion with respect to the general proposition and attempts to secure facts from various sources that satisfactorily explain its origin and historical evolution. Through historiographical analysis, you will gain a much richer appreciation of the

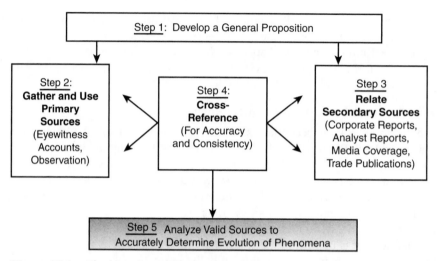

Figure 25.1   The historiographical process

present conditions and characteristics of a strategic issue. As a result, a much wider perspective of possible parameters strengthens the analysis of current and future strategy.

Thus, the process of historiographical analysis can be seen as securing, validating, and, most importantly, understanding facts. The interrelationships between the facts provide the foundation from which to build business theories. This process should be continuous because history is continuous and evolving. After all, any theory is only as good as its explanatory power. A continuous process ensures that theories are revised as conditions change and issues evolve. New theories should be advanced, and old theories should be challenged. Much of this ongoing analysis should be done formally, but a significant amount can also be done informally. Historiographical analysis embraces a wider range of subject areas and analytical disciplines than most strategic management tools.

Hence, you will be well served by reading from as many different sources as possible. Often the most obscure source will provide the most colorful threads needed to weave the theoretical tapestry into the firm's next business idea. In order to increase the possibility of this happening, you should try to gather as many different sources of information, ideas, and perspectives as possible. The resulting mental percolation is often the instigation for unexpected flashes of insight that randomly occur, say, during sleep or while taking the daily shower!

Case Study—Australian Menswear Retailer

Gowing Brothers had been a prominent competitor in the Sydney menswear market since 1868. Its success in the volatile menswear market led two researchers to employ historiographical analysis to answer the question, "What leads to retail success over extended time periods?" After looking at 22 case histories of longstanding North American retailers, three critical success factors (CSFs) (see Chapter 18, "Critical Success Factor Analysis," for more about this technique) were identified for the retail industry. These CSFs were as follows:

1. **Clear market positioning**—This required the outlet to emphasize value, service, and quality in a clearly identified retail segment.

2. **Distinct periods of expansion or modernization**—From 1850–1920, retail expansion focused on larger facilities. From 1915–1935 and 1946–1960, modernization was pursued through new store designs and structural layouts, new technology, improved merchandise management processes, more sophisticated marketing, and improved human resource management.

3. **Strong capabilities allowing excellent operational management of the retail mix**—This included focusing attention on customer, staff, and vendor relationships; technology; finance; human resources management; and sales support.

The two researchers started by analyzing primary and secondary sources of information. The primary sources included interviews with the Director and the Marketing Manager. Some secondary sources included annual reports, ledger accounts, company archives, and newspaper and press clippings. After compiling their data, the researchers put together a detailed chronology highlighting the significant decisions that were made throughout the company's history. The following were identified as the critical decisions (see Figure 25.2).

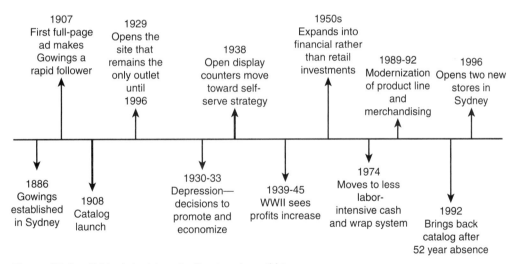

Figure 25.2   Critical decisions in Gowings' retail history

Each of these decisions were put into a historical context relative to what rivals were doing in the same timeframe. They were then used to assess critical success factors 1 and 2, as shown previously. Part of this analysis included the strategic implications of the "road not taken"—that is, the decision *not* to expand into the Sydney suburbs, which were growing rapidly throughout the end of the twentieth century, as several rivals had done at more than one juncture. When it came time to assess CSF number 3, the researchers took a close look at some specific capabilities that fell under the "operations" umbrella, including advertising and promotion, customers, staff and vendor relations, information systems, and financial capability.

After evaluating the fit with the framework, the researchers came to the following conclusion:

- Flexibility as opposed to constancy of market positioning was determined to be a moderate CSF (CSF 1).
- Expansion and modernization were determined to be a strong CSF (CSF 2).
- Operational management was determined to be a medium to strong CSF (CSF3).

As you can see, the framework was found to have a close but not perfect fit to Gowings' experience.

This historiographical analysis also generated some important implications. The study highlighted the significance of a clearly defined market position and the ability to respond to dynamic market conditions. Clearly, many retailers respond too slowly to market conditions. Organizational capabilities related to good relationships with customers, staff, and vendors were also identified, and, last but not least, CSFs specific to retail categories (for example, niche retailer versus budget chain) were identified as several unique capabilities. Even after only one iteration, this historiographical model yielded several significant insights and a formal framework to critically analyze the retail strategy of specific companies.[7]

FAROUT Summary

FAROUT SUMMARY

	1	2	3	4	5
F	■	■			
A	■	■			
R	■	■	■		
O	■				
U	■	■	■	■	
T	■	■	■		

Figure 25.3   Historiographical analysis FAROUT summary

Future orientation—Low to medium. The focus of the analysis is on using knowledge of the past to explain the present. Projecting this analysis to the future is less valid.

Accuracy—Low to medium. Any violations of the critical assumption of recurring historical patterns reduces accuracy. Additionally, this model doesn't handle discontinuity or environmental turbulence very well.

Resource efficiency—Medium. Reliance on secondary sources will significantly increase resource efficiency.

Objectivity—Low. The analysis is heavily dependent on qualitative analysis and selective judgment.

Usefulness—Medium to high. Offers unique insights not offered by other tools and techniques.

Timeliness—Medium. Highly dependent on the complexity of the phenomena and length of time under study. A historiographical analysis can be conducted in a relatively short period of time or can take substantial time when there are a large number of interacting actors and actions to consider.

Related Tools and Techniques

- Analysis of competing hypothesis
- Blindspot analysis
- Critical success factor analysis
- Industry analysis
- Issue analysis
- Linchpin analysis
- Stakeholder analysis
- STEEP analysis
- Strategic group analysis

References

Chandler, A.D. Jr. (1962). *Strategy and Structure: Chapters in the History of the American Industrial Enterprise*. Cambridge, MA: MIT Press.

Chandler, A.D. Jr. (1977). *The Visible Hand: The Managerial Revolution in American Business*. Cambridge, MA: Harvard University Press.

Goodman, R.S., and E.V. Kruger (1988). "Data dredging or legitimate research method? Historiography and its potential for management research," *Academy of Management Review*, April, 13(2), pp. 315–325.

Iggers, G.C. (1987). *Historiography: An Annotated Bibliography of Journals, Articles, Books, and Dissertations*. Santa Barbara, CA: ABC—Clio Inc.

Lawrence, B.S. (1984)."Historical Perspective: Using the Past to Study the Present," *Academy of Management Review*, April, 9(2), pp. 307–312.

Miller, D., and B. Merrilees (2000). ''Gone to Gowings—An analysis of success factors in retail longevity: Gowings of Sydney," *The Services Industries Journal*, January, 20(1), pp. 61–85.

Rampolla, M.L. (2001). *A Pocket Guide to Writing in History*, 3rd edition. Boston, MA: Bedford/St. Martins.

Startt, J.D., and W.D. Sloan (2003). *Historical Methods*. Northport, AL: Vision Press.

Wulf, W.A. (1997). "Look in the spaces for tomorrow's innovations," *Association for Computing Machinery. Communications of the ACM*, February, 40(2), pp. 109–111.

Endnotes

[1] Goodman and Kruger, 1988.

[2] Iggers, 1987.

[3] Rampolla, 2001.

[4] Chandler, 1962 and 1977.

[5] Startt and Sloan, 2003.

[6] Adapted from Goodman, R.S., and E.V. Kruger (1988).

[7] Adapted from Miller, D., and B. Merrilees (2000).

26

Interpretation of Statistical Analysis

Short Description

Statistical analysis involves the manipulation of data using a variety of mathematical formulae and description of situations using mathematical concepts. It enables simple description of complex situations and can give predictive insights.

The interpretation of the statistical analysis is the vital link between the manipulation of data and the practical application of the results to a real-life problem.

Background

Statistics involves summarizing, analyzing, and graphing data. It includes designing strategies for data collection and information extraction, constructing models for describing and forecasting chance phenomena, and using these models for planning and decision making.[1]

Statistical analysis aims to introduce an element of objectivity into the significance attached to information output. In scientific research, statistical analysis is specifically used to objectively evaluate the significance of a set of experimental results or of a series of systematic observations.

Statistics can be thought of as a branch of mathematics involving the collection, organization, and interpretation of data. However, statistical analyses are not purely mathematical exercises. Statistics concern both the analysis of data and the design of systems for extracting data (for example, surveys).

Interpretation is crucial to the value of statistics. The value of the analysis is only as good as the quality of the interpretation. Statistics themselves are not useful and may even be dangerously misleading if not interpreted correctly.

Statistical analysis in its various forms provides a system for reducing uncertainty in decision making by inferring patterns, trends, or tendencies in data (and, by extension, in the real-world situations from which the data comes) and distinguishing these from pure coincidences. It should supplement the experience of decision makers by making available objective information and thereby improving the quality of decisions made.

The design of the data collection strategy and the method of analysis are also crucial to the interpretation of statistics. For example, are the survey questions ambiguous or incomplete? Are the methods being used to conduct the analysis appropriate for the nature of the data? How far can you generalize the results of the analysis?

Strategic Rationale and Implications

Statistics provide systematic analysis of data. Data alone does not help with decision-making in business. Decisions are made on the basis of available information and prior knowledge and experience. Data becomes information when it is relevant to your specific situation. Statistical analysis facilitates the transformation of data into information and so aims to inform the decision-making process.

There is a vast amount of data available in modern business. A wide range of record keeping occurs throughout any firm, from financial records, to mailroom records, customer service, and sales results. Statistics allows for systematic analysis and interpretation of data to collate and organize it into meaningful information.

The ideal way to find inferences is to look at all the past data; however, in practice, you will rarely have access to "all the data" either because it is not available or because there would be too much data to handle. Statistics overcomes this by using a "sample" of data to make inferences about the whole "population." A *population* in statistical terms is the entire set of a particular variable—for example, every sale you have made. A *sample* is a subset of the population. To get an accurate reflection of the population from your analysis, the sample you use should be representative of the entire population and not biased in any way.

A statistical analysis typically arises out of the need to make a decision or answer a question. The first important task in any analysis is the careful formulating of the questions you wish to have answered. Once you have worked out what questions you need to answer, you can start collecting relevant data. The answers you need and the data you collect will also point you in the direction of which statistical method you should adopt to organize the data.

Statistical methods encompass a wide range of activities, from some very simple processes you can easily perform in-house, all the way up to extremely mathematically complex and technical analyses best left to experts.

For example, revenue and cost information is often subject to simple analysis in-house. It is kept and compared with similar information from the previous quarter or year (or other recording period). Often the comparisons will be made in terms of percentage of increase/decrease.

Other statistical analysis may be outsourced to specialist third parties. For example, market research (say, polling or survey research) to investigate opportunities for new products may be contracted out. When these specialists present their results, they will give the numbers and then an interpretation of them. You must be able to interpret the results yourself to be able to use them effectively for your firm.

Interpretation is not only important in relation to complex statistical analyses. Even simple statistics like percentage increases or decreases in revenue may require some interpretation to ensure their usefulness. For example, some firms experience regular seasonal fluctuations in revenue, and so a percentage of increase or decrease at one particular time of year may indicate something quite different from the same percentage change at another time of year.

Strengths and Advantages

Statistical analysis is an extremely valuable tool for a firm as it provides systematic and objective methods for examining data and extracting useful information from its operations.

Statistical analysis can be used to simplify complex problems and provide methods for reviewing and understanding data that can be applied in the future.

The availability of computers makes complex and powerful statistical analysis of data attainable for even small firms. Many widely used standard software packages, such as Excel, include statistical functions that can be applied to databases without having to resort to specialist software.

Statistics can provide insight into trends and tendencies in data that reflect trends and tendencies in a firm's business, both now and in the future.

The inferences made by statistical analysis can also inform decision-making by supplementing their knowledge and experience with objective information. In turn, this contributes to the further development of knowledge and experience.

The results of a carefully designed statistical analysis can provide objective information about a business' performance, its customers, and the marketplace in general. The potential here is the debunking of prejudices and preconceptions that could be limiting the success of a firm in its marketplace.

The neutrality of the mathematical processes used in analysis can additionally remove politics from the results, and with careful interpretation and presentation, the results of statistical analysis can be a very powerful tool and motivator for change.

Weaknesses and Limitations

Statistical analysis is very easy to misuse and misinterpret. Any method of analysis used, whenever applied to data, will provide a result, and all statistical results look authoritative. Careful interpretation is essential both to evaluate the analysis and to apply it, in order to avoid being misled by meaningless results.

Simplifying a problem or real-life situation by selecting limited data to represent it in order to find a solution using statistical analysis can remove the solution from reality, making it less effective (or ineffective) in practice.

The process of designing a statistical analysis is very important and complex. Errors at any point along the way will seriously compromise the value of the exercise. For example, bias in data is fatal to the usefulness of your results. Bias may occur where the design of the analysis is flawed and the data considered is limited systematically.

One of the biggest potential problems with statistical analysis is the quality of the interpretation of the results. Many people see cause and effect relationships "evidenced" by statistics, which are in actuality simply describing data associations or correlation having little or nothing to do with casual factors.

The reputation of the individual championing the analysis or the outside consultants presenting the information may sway a firm's willingness to accept and use information and ultimately cloud its ability to interpret the realities of the analysis. For example, the neutrality of statistical results (largely being numeric) may make them vulnerable to being interpreted in a manner favorable to the preservation of preconceptions. Similarly, a lack of understanding of the concepts behind the results presented may mean that the results are misunderstood and wrongly interpreted.

Another key weakness is that statistics are necessarily backward facing. Analysis is undertaken of existing data, and some assumptions must be built into the process of analysis regarding the continuation (or changing) of business conditions.

Many statistics require the predicting of probability, which is notoriously difficult to do. There are several common errors made when attempting to judge the probability of an event occurring. Generally people tend to overestimate low-probability events (for example, being in an airline disaster) and underestimate high-probability ones (for example, ignoring the greater likelihood that they will crash their car close to home). Human beings are also highly likely to allow their own personal experience or anecdotal evidence to distort their perceptions of statistical data.

Process for Applying the Technique

There is a wide range of techniques available for statistical analysis. Some of the concepts are very simple and easily grasped. Some of the fundamental concepts important in the interpretation of business statistics are described here.

Percentage Changes

Percentages are probably some of the most basic statistics used, and percentage increases and decreases are widely understood and used.

$$p = (x - y)/y \times 100$$

where:

p is the percentage change.

x is the new value.

y is the old value.

Interpretation of percentage increases or decreases can be complicated by a couple of circumstances.

The first arises when you are comparing percentage changes across groups. For example, you might be looking at the percentage change in sales for two branches of the firm over the period of a year. In town A, sales increased from 50 to 65, and in town B, sales increased from 50 to 52. The percentage increase for A is 30 percent, while for B it is 4 percent. Looking at percentage changes only, it is easy to see that the sales team in A deserves a bonus and the one in B needs a shake up.

However, care must be taken when interpreting these sorts of statistics. Returning to the preceding example, it could be interesting to consider population growth in town A and town B to see whether there is more to the story.

What would happen, for example, if the population of town A had increased from 10,000 to 15,000 over the year, and the closure of a major factory in town B led to population stagnation with no change in the population of 8,000. Percentage changes in sales are not usefully comparable in this situation. A more useful measure of the changes would be to compare per capita sales in the two towns.

Per capita rates are generally expressed as a figure per 100,000 and are calculated as follows:

$$c = x/p \times 100,000$$

where:

c is the per capita rate.

x is the value of interest.

p is the total population.

Looking at the per capita sales in A and B, we see that in A, the per capita sales have gone from 500 per 100,000 to 433 per 100,000, while in B sales have gone from 625 per 100,000 to 650 per 100,000. The truth of the situation appears to be that the sales team in B has consistently outperformed the one in A. This would be the case if the competitive environment in both towns were the same; that is, the same competitors are present in each town. The important point to note is that the numbers themselves tell only part of the story and should be interpreted carefully.

The other potential complication for interpreting percentage change is where some other factor has had an influence over the time period, and so an adjustment should be made to the figures. Sometimes these adjustments are seasonal—for example, retail trade figures over Christmas, which are easy to spot and adjust for.

In other circumstances, it may take some research to explain an unusual change. For example, consumption of bottled water is found to have spiked over a couple of months in town C, some distance from head office. While the spike in usage does occur in summer, it is much larger than the usual seasonal increase, so do you rush out to congratulate your sales and marketing teams? A bit of investigation reveals a widely publicized outbreak of Giardia attributed to a particular line of very old pipes in the water supply. The pipes took about six weeks to replace, and people sought out the safer bottled water alternative.

Percentiles and Quartiles

Percentiles are not as widely used as percentages and provide a ranking within a range of data.

Percentiles divide a sample or population into 100 parts. The 10th percentile cuts off the lowest 10 percent of the data. To work out which score represents a particular percentile, you must first arrange your data in increasing order. You can then work out which score by multiplying n (the total number of data points) by $P/100$ (that is, the number of the percentile divided by 100). The percentile will occur at m, the nearest whole number greater than or equal to $n \times P/100$ (either the mth value in the list of the mean of the mth and the $(m + 1)$th values).

Quartiles divide data into four parts after the data has been arranged in increasing order. The lower quartile cuts off the bottom 25 percent of the data, and the upper quartile includes only the top 25 percent. In between the upper and lower quartiles is known as the inter-quartile range or mid-spread (and consists of 50 percent of the data). The second quartile, in the middle of the inter-quartile range, occurs at the point known as the median (see later in the chapter for further explanation on the median).

To work out the quartiles for a sample of numerical data, after arranging the data in increasing order, you need to consider $n/4$, where n is the sample size. The lower quartile will be at point m, where m is the first smallest whole number equal to or greater than $n/4$. Therefore, where n is not a multiple of 4, the lower quartile is the mth value in the ordered data. If n is a multiple of 4, the lower quartile is the mean of the mth value and the $(m + 1)$th value.

Normal Distribution and Bell Curve

Distribution refers to the pattern of distribution of measurements for x (along the horizontal or x-axis) against the number of instances, or the frequency of the measurements (vertical or y-axis).

A normal distribution has only one peak. The mean appears in the middle of the peak, and the tails slope away symmetrically on either side. The curve is bell-shaped and commonly referred to as a "bell curve."

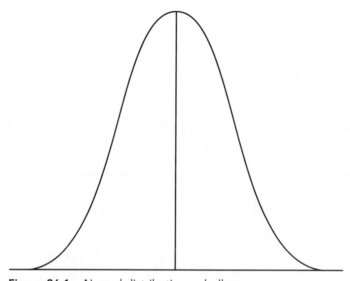

Figure 26.1   Normal distribution or bell curve

Calculation of an accurate mean and standard deviation for data assumes that the data spread approximates a bell curve.

Summarizing Data with One Value—Central Tendency

There are three ways to characterize the "average" of data: mean, median, or mode. Each is useful in a different situation.

Mean—The mean is a measure for the average value of a set of numeric data. To find the mean of a variable, you add each observation you have of that variable together and then divide the total by the number of observations you had. In reality, you would not use every single instance of a variable but would choose a smaller sample to make your calculation.

$$x_{mean} = (x_1 + x_2 + x_3 + \ldots x_n)/n$$

where:

x_{mean} is the mean value of the sample.

n is the total number of values you are looking at in your sample.

x_1 is the first data point, x_2 is the second data point, and $\ldots x_n$ is the last data point.

For example, say you wanted to find the average delivery time for an order. You decide to use a sample of 5 delivery times: 2 days; 4 days; 3 days; 3 days; 2 days. You add 2 + 4 + 3 + 3 + 2 to get a total of 14. Divide 14 by 5 (the number of delivery times you added together to get the total of 14) to find the average of 2.8. (Note that, in reality, your customer will not experience 2.8 days as their delivery time: They will experience this as 3 days.)

A mean is useful because it can be used in a variety of other mathematical formulas—for example, standard deviation. However, the use of a mean to describe the "average" measure in a set of data assumes a normal distribution of values. In fact the mean can be misleading where your data includes one or a few very high or very low values—that is, data falling outside a normal curve. These very high or very low values are called "outliers."

You could consider another example using delivery times. Say you were looking at much the same delivery times as previously. The first four times were identical, but the last period you were looking at was 13 days (say, being the time taken to deliver to an international customer). Your new delivery times are: 2 days; 4 days; 3 days; 3 days; 13 days. The mean delivery time is now (2 + 4 + 3 + 3 + 13)/5, which is 5. Five days is not a delivery time experienced by any of your customers—it is a lot longer than most of the local deliveries and much shorter than the international delivery—and so the mean is not a useful measure here.

One method for overcoming the problem of an outlier (or several outliers) in your data is to calculate a mean that does not include them. When this is done, the exclusion of the outlier values must be noted when the mean is discussed.

Returning to the second set of delivery times, you might work out your mean using the first four times ((2 + 4 + 3 + 3)/4 = 3) and note that 3 days is the mean time for local delivery and that this was calculated excluding an international delivery time of 13 days.

Median—The median is not a calculated average. The observations you have made are arranged in order of magnitude, and the median is the central point in the array. If the central point is between two data points, the median is the mean of the two points.

For example, when using the first set of delivery times mentioned previously, arranging the observations would give: 2, 2, 3, 3, 4. The central value is 3 (there are 2 observations below and 2 above the first 3 listed), which is the same value given by calculating the mean in this situation.

The median is not a measure that can be used in further calculations. It can only be used to summarize your set of data.

However, the median can be very useful where your data ranges over a wide set of values, some of which are very large or very small compared with most—that is, the exact sort of data that makes a mean misleading. In the second set of delivery times, when you arrange the new values in order (2, 3, 3, 4, 13), the median is still 3 and so gives a better indication of "average" delivery time than the mean and without having to exclude any values.

Mode—The mode is the most frequently recorded value for an observation. You can have more than one mode in a distribution. The mode is not generally used to summarize numeric data, but is very useful as a single value summary with categorical information.

An example of this could also be taken from delivery data; however, looking at the destination for the goods rather than the time taken. Say the five deliveries are being sent to New York, Washington, New York, Boston, and Los Angeles. The mode of this data set is New York, which tells you the "average" destination (or destination of the "average" order).

Standard Deviation

The standard deviation gives a measure for the distribution or spread of measures within your sample in relation to the mean. As is the case where you are using the mean to describe the "average" value of your data, the standard deviation assumes a normal distribution of data.

The standard deviation is measured in the same units as the mean. So, for example, where you are examining order sizes coming into your business in terms of dollars, the standard deviation will be expressed as a dollar amount.

Standard deviation is calculated from the residuals, or differences, between each data point and the mean. Each residual is squared before they are all added together. The total is then divided by the number of data points in the sample. The square root of that value is your standard deviation. The formula can be written as:

$$\Sigma = \sqrt{((x_1 - x_{mean})^2 + (x_2 - x_{mean})^2 \ldots (x_n - x_{mean})^2)/(n-1))}$$

where:

Σ is the standard deviation for the sample you are looking at.

n is the total number of values in the sample.

x_1 is the first data point, x_2 is the second data point, and . . . x_n is the last data point.

x_{mean} is the mean value of the sample.

Standard deviation is usually calculated by entering all of your data into a software program and getting the program to do the number crunching for you rather than manually working out each residual and squaring it, etc. An example is the STDEV function in Excel, which works out the standard deviation over a range of cells in a worksheet (for example, = STDEV(A1:Z99)).

In a normal distribution, sixty-eight percent of observations of value x will appear within one standard deviation on either side of the mean (within the band stretching from one standard deviation above the mean to one standard deviation below the mean). Ninety-six percent of observations occur within two standard deviations of the mean and over 99 percent within three standard deviations of the mean (see Figure 26.2).

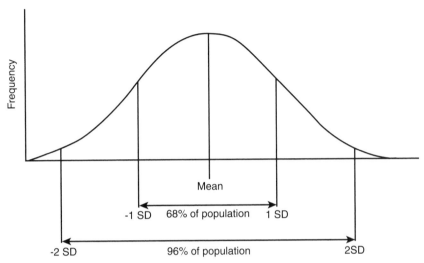

Figure 26.2   Normal distribution showing standard deviation

Whether the standard deviation is considered a large amount or not is dependent on the quantities being compared and not on the numeric amount, per se. If the standard deviation is close to the amount of the mean, then it would be considered high and indicate that your data was widely spread out. For example, if your standard deviation when looking at order size is $122, this might be a high standard deviation if the mean order size were $200 (68 percent of orders fell between the values $78 and $322), but not if the mean order size were $2000 (68 percent of orders fell between $1878 and $2122).

A high value for the standard deviation indicates a wide spread of values in the data set. A low value indicates that most of the data points are clustered closely around the mean, and a graph of the data would show a steeply sided bell curve.

Comparing Data

Statistics are often used to test whether there is a real (significant) difference between two groups or circumstances or conditions. This sort of test can be used to measure the effectiveness of some change made to one of the groups prior to measurement. An example would be to test whether a marketing campaign had successfully increased awareness of a new product. Another use for this sort of test is to investigate whether the same group or circumstance has changed over time (so the same thing is measured on two occasions). An example of this would be to test whether your attrition rate among your customers had changed over time or had not.

These sorts of tests require a null hypothesis. A *null hypothesis* proposes that there is no difference between two groups or circumstances or that something has had no effect.

The test used to compare means of two groups is called the *t-test*. It investigates whether two samples are likely to have come from the same population (and are, therefore, not different from one another statistically).

t = (mean$_1$ – mean$_2$)/standard error of the difference between the means

Calculation of the standard error of the difference between the means uses the sample size (n) and the standard deviations of each sample. It is a measure of the variability or dispersion of the two groups.

The t-score resulting from the test is then compared with a table of t-scores, which will say whether the t-score obtained indicates a significant difference between the groups or that there was no significant difference. The significance of the difference is expressed using a p-value (see "P-Values" later in the chapter for further explanation).

Regression Analysis

Looking at two instances of the same value or factor can be useful for investigating changes in it over time. Other comparisons can be used to investigate relationships between two different factors or properties (measured at the same time).

A simple example of two properties that might be related would be height and weight for a sample of people. You could display the results as a scatter plot, showing each person on the plot represented by a point indicating their height (in centimeters on the y-axis in Figure 26.3) and their weight (in pounds on the x-axis in the figure). The convention is that the value or factor you want to predict appears on the y-axis, so Figure 26.3 would be used to predict approximate height of a person from the population the sample came from, given a specific weight.

Relationships between the two properties or values plotted on a scatter plot are summarized by a line. This is called *regression analysis of the data*.

There are several methods for investigating the strength of a linear relationship between properties.

Straight Lines

Where a scatter plot displays data with points approximating a straight line, you can draw in a line approximately fitting the data, as shown in Figure 26.4.

The line gives you a rough method for predicting a value for y given a particular value for x.

A point on a straight line is represented by the formula:

$y_{predicted} = a + bx$

where:

$y_{predicted}$ is the value you are predicting.

a is the intercept (where the line would cross the y-axis at y = zero).

b is the slope of the line.

x is the known value.

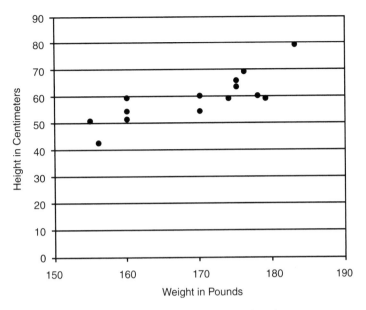

Figure 26.3   Scatter plot of weight against height
Source: Adapted from McNeil, D., Middledorp, J., Petersons, M., and P.
Shaw (1994). *Modern Statistics: An Introduction*, Macquarie University.

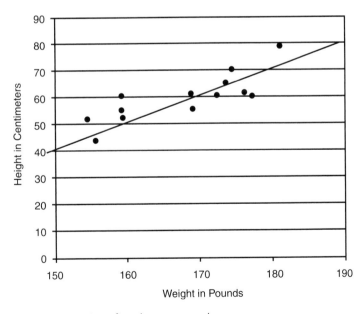

Figure 26.4   Line fitted to scatter plot

The value of a and b for any line can be calculated using the coordinates of any two points on the line; the coordinates for the points are x_1, y_1 and x_2, y_2.

$$a = (x_2 \times y_1 - x_1 \times y_2)/(x_2 - x_1)$$
$$b = (y_2 - y_1)/(x_2 - x_1)$$

Using the example in Figure 26.4, we can see that the value of y predicted by the line for the point where x=160, is 50 (the point on the line is 160,50). Similarly, where x=170 we can see the line predicts y=60 (the point on the line is 170,60). Substituting into the formula for a and b, we get the following:

$$a = (170 \times 50 - 160 \times 60)/(170 - 160) = -1100/10 = -110$$
$$b = (60 - 50)/(170 - 160) = 10/10 = 1$$

For predicting data along the line in Figure 26.4, the formula is: $y_{predicted} = -110 + 1x$

Goodness-of-Fit

When you draw a straight line through data, you are predicting a value for y for each value for x. The actual measures you have for y values will differ from the predicted values for y by an amount called a *residual*.

The "goodness-of-fit" of your data to the line tests the accuracy of the formula for your line in predicting new values for y by finding the standard deviation of the residuals, or more precisely from the sum of squares of the residuals:

$$S_{residuals} = (y_1 - y_{1 \text{ as predicted by formula}})^2 + (y_2 - y_{2 \text{ as predicted by formula}})^2 \ldots + (y_n - y_{n \text{ as predicted by formula}})^2$$

There is also an actual standard deviation, which is calculated using the same formula as for $s_{residuals}$ but uses the mean of the y values rather than the y values, as predicted by the formula for the linear relationship.

The standard deviation of the residuals is then used to calculate r^2:

$$r^2 = 1 - s_{actual \ residuals}/s_{residuals}$$

The r^2 value will be between 0 and 1, and the closer to 1, the better is the fit and the more accurate the formula for the linear relationship is at predicting y values for a given x value.

Lines That Are Not Straight

Sometimes data distribution will approximate a line, but not a straight one. A common example of this is an exponential curve (see Figure 26.5).

Here, the relationship is represented by the formula:

$$y_{predicted} = a + b \times x^2$$

Data may also reverse this sort of curve where there is a different proportionate relationship between the values x and y.

A relationship resulting in a curved line, whether exponential or hyperbolic (as shown in Figure 26.6) or another curve will not be simply fitted over your data using your eye and a ruler. It will result from a complex analysis of your data by a statistical software application.

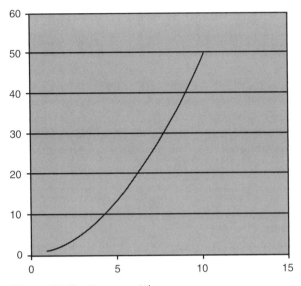

Figure 26.5   Exponential curve

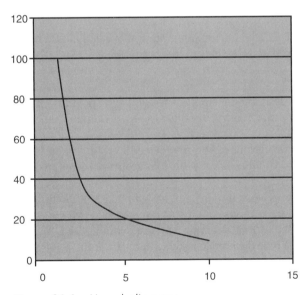

Figure 26.6   Hyperbolic curve

Interpreting Relationships Found by Regression Analysis

Note that these linear relationships cannot be used to approximate values for *any* possible value of *x* and should only be used over the range of the original data. Care must be taken not to extrapolate outside the range or to interpret any extrapolation *very* carefully.

Data points outside the original range may be inaccurate or even absurd. For example, consider the point on the line in Figure 26.4 where *x* is zero: No one has a weight of zero any more than they may have a height of –110.

Another important point is that a formula for a linear relationship does not imply that changes in *x* cause changes in *y*. The formula is simply a method for predicting new *y* values.

Correlation

Correlation is a form of regression analysis. It is mentioned separately because it is such a widely used concept. As with all regression analysis, correlation gives an indication of the tendency for one thing to occur in relation to the tendency for another to occur.

The correlation coefficient calculated for the data indicates the strength of the association between the two properties. It will be a number between –1 and 1. The closer the absolute value of the correlation coefficient is to 1, the stronger the association.

Note that as was the case when discussing relationships previously, a high correlation coefficient does not prove the existence of a cause and effect relationship between two events.

The correlation coefficient is the same r that was calculated when calculating the goodness-of-fit of a line to data (it is the square-root of the r^2 value).

P-Values

P-values are used to describe the significance of a statistical finding. They relate in part to the number of observations used to reach the conclusion and the magnitude of the observations.

A statistical test is often based on the idea of a null hypothesis. A null hypothesis proposes that there is no difference between two groups or circumstances or that something has had no effect.

For example, if you wished to investigate whether a marketing campaign was successful, you might compare responses to a survey from two groups of customers—one group who had been exposed to the campaign and one who had not. The null hypothesis would be that there should be no difference in the responses of the two groups.

Where a p-value is given as 0.05, this means that if the null hypothesis is true (and there is no difference between the two groups you are testing), you would only have a 5 percent chance of getting the results from a sample group that you in fact got. In other words, if you found a statistical difference between the groups, then saying the difference was significant at p=0.05 indicates that the chance that the difference arose purely by coincidence is only 5 percent.

FAROUT Summary

FAROUT SUMMARY

	1	2	3	4	5
F	■				
A	■	■	■	■	
R	■	■	■		
O	■	■	■		
U	■	■	■		
T	■				

Figure 26.7   Interpretation of statistical analysis FAROUT summary

Future orientation—Low. Statistics are generated using existing historical data. The analysis provided may guide decision making about the future but is based on an extrapolation of historical data.

Accuracy—Medium to high. The accuracy of the statistical analysis performed will depend on the accuracy of the data used and also on the care taken in deciding what tests to perform on the data. Interpretation of the data analysis may also be subject to biases.

Resource efficiency—Medium. Resource efficiency will depend on the nature of the questions and on the design of the analysis. Where carefully chosen samples of data are used, efficiency is greatest. Using very large sets of data (for example, to avoid bias) will reduce efficiency.

Objectivity—Medium. The objectivity of the actual statistical analysis should be high if unbiased data is used. However, bias in data and then bias in interpreting the results of analysis can be very difficult to avoid in practice.

Usefulness—Medium. Statistical analysis is very useful as a method for organizing and understanding vast amounts of data. However, the usefulness may be compromised very easily by using biased data for analysis, designing the analysis poorly, or by misinterpreting the results (for example, by assuming a cause and effect relationship where none exists).

Timeliness—Low to medium. Statistics are always generated after the event and often analyze data from several years previously. The vast amounts of data may make organizing of the data cumbersome, and the skills required to analyze this data may be quite complex.

Related Techniques

- Benchmarking
- Competitor cash flow analysis
- Financial ratio and statement analysis
- Patent analysis

References

Dr. Arsham's Statistics site. Accessed at http://home.ubalt.edu/ntsbarsh/Business-stat/opre504.htm.

Levin, R., Rubin, D., Stinson, J., and E. Gardner (1989). *Quantitative Approaches to Management*. Singapore: McGraw-Hill International Editions.

McNeil, D., Middledorp, J., Petersons, M., and P. Shaw (1994). *Modern Statistics: An Introduction*, Macquarie University.

Endnotes

[1] McNeil et al, 1994.

27

Competitor Cash Flow Analysis

Short Description

Cash flow is often described as the "life blood" of a business. While profit is a reasonable measure of performance (due to the "matching concept" of accrual accounting), it is a very poor measure of viability. Cash flow is the prime measure of viability and also is a major determinant of operating flexibility—the ability to fund new initiatives and to defend against competitive attacks.

This chapter considers both historic and future cash flow analysis. While historic cash flow analysis adds a little to our understanding of a business, its underlying strength, and the ability of management to cope over the business cycle, it is future cash flow that is the most valid in determining viability and future flexibility. Naturally, any consideration of the future will be subject to the validity and reasonableness of the assumptions made. Hence, forecasting cash flows requires a current analysis of a business and its environment, as shown in other analytical techniques throughout this book.

Cash flow analysis is not sufficient in itself to understand a business or its competitors—it only provides a partial view of the environment. However, it can significantly enhance the overall analysis and provides a useful cross-check on the reliability of other analytic techniques.

This chapter discusses the various definitions of cash flow. It does not address the simplistic and commonly used definitions of earnings before income tax (EBIT) and earnings before deducting interest, tax, depreciation, and amortization (EBITDA). Rather, a proper analysis needs to consider the cash effects of balance sheet items—changes in working capital and capital expenditure needs.

Background

Strangely, there has been little study of cash flow analysis, certainly in comparison to the wealth of studies on profit analysis.

The "statement of cash flows" was the last of the major accounting statements to be added to firm annual reports in the early 1990s. This was largely in response to the spate of corporate disasters during the global recession. Banks and other investors had been misled by reported profits to believe that companies were viable. To highlight the difference between profit and cash flow, the statement of cash flows was added. It is the only information in the financial statements that is not based on accrual accounting. It is divided into three sections—operations, investing, and financing.

Early attempts at cash flow analysis were still largely based on accrual accounting statements. One of the first determinants of viability was deemed to be the current ratio—the ratio of current assets to current liabilities. However, even as far back as 1919, Alexander Wall found that the current ratio could be volatile and was not necessarily a good predictor of failure—its changes were driven by factors other than failure.[1]

Research carried out by Winaker and Smith found that the benchmarks for ratios were industry-specific; that is, adjustments needed to be made for "good" or "bad" results depending on the industry.[2] So we begin to see that cash flow analysis cannot be done in isolation of a single firm; we need to benchmark and understand the industry in order to make sense of cash flow analysis.

Nonetheless, the current ratio remains one of a handful of favorite ratios used by bankers and appears in loan document covenants for both large and small firms, and across industries.

In 1966, William Beaver published a seminal paper that focused attention on cash flow, albeit still limited to accounting ratios. Beaver's preference was to use ratios that give some indication of cash flow: "Cash flow ratios offer much promise for providing ratio analysis with a unified framework."[3]

Following the corporate disasters of the 1991–1992 global recession, cash flow analysis gained more prominence and "Cash is King" became a popular catch cry.

Investors such as Warren Buffet (see the Berkshire-Hathaway annual reports) declared their preferences for cash flow:

> "In the long run, managements stressing accounting appearance over economic substance usually achieve little of either."

> "Our acquisition preferences run toward businesses that generate cash, not those that consume it . . . However attractive the earnings numbers, we remain leery of businesses that never seem able to convert such pretty numbers into no-strings-attached cash."

At the same time, cash flow analysis (specifically, discounted cash flow (DCF) analysis) became the dominant and theoretically preferred method of valuation, gradually supplanting simplistic capitalization ratios, such as price/earnings multiples. The use of DCF analysis and "net present value" has not been as dominant as could be expected, largely because of the complexity of the analysis (and thus the scope for calculation errors) and the poor environmental analysis used to check the reasonableness of the assumptions.

However, in 2001, McKinsey and Co. published a revised document on valuing dot.com companies following the spectacular collapse of the overvalued bubble companies. The opening line to the document is, "Investment values always revert to a fundamental level based on cash flows. Get used to it."[4]

Most investment banks use DCF analysis as their major valuation technique for acquisitions and even theoretical share values. Several investment analysts use "long-term cash flow" as the prime determinant of a firm's value.

Finally, banks are attempting to become "cash flow lenders"; that is, the prime decision is made on whether the borrower can generate sufficient "free cash flow" to service the debt (pay the interest and meet the loan repayments).

Today, while the principles of cash flow are well recognized, the practice still has far to go. When BHP bought the Magma Copper assets in the U.S. in 1995, it paid A$3.2 billion. The value was largely based on the amount of copper reserves and the price of copper. Due diligence apparently failed to discover that Magma Copper had little in the way of copper reserves (as CRA had found earlier, when it walked away from a Magma Copper purchase). Also the copper price used in the model was at an all-time high, assisted by price manipulation by one rogue trader in Sumitomo Copper. When the copper price collapsed shortly after and the lack of copper ore became apparent, BHP wrote off more than A$2.5 billion of its investment.

Strategic Rationale and Implications

Cash flow analysis is not just about firm viability.

First, free cash flow is a major determinant of financial flexibility. Does the firm have the scope to make new investments or to take new strategic directions? Free cash flow, or at least access to further cash resources, also determines the firm's ability to undertake major investments that do not have early payback.

The classic measure of the dot.com companies when determining if their strategic plans were viable was their rate of "cash burn" and their level of cash reserves. Certainly, many of the dot.coms burned cash at unsustainable levels.

Second, free cash flow is a major strategic strength. Strong cash flow in some business units allows a firm to commit to implementing strategies in other business units.

This was recognized in a simplistic fashion in the Boston Consulting Group (BCG) matrix of stars, cash cows, problem children, and dogs.[5] The idea is to have enough cash cows to support the stars through their growth (but cash negative) phase and perhaps to move problem children across to star status. However, the BCG model is over simplistic in that there are many more factors involved in determining cash flow than a reliance on market share.

Cash flow analysis provides an additional financial viewpoint of a business.

Despite the obvious link between cash flow and viability, surprisingly, historic cash flow does not show a significant correlation to failure. The difficulty lies in the ability of companies to stave off failure, at least in the short term, by falling back on sales of assets, tapping other sources of finance, and so on.

Ward, for example, argues for a cash flow theory whereby firms need to maintain cash flow stability (between operations, investing, and financing) to achieve financial health and stability. An event such as declining sales or rising costs can cause financial stress on the firm. How management responds is critical to the restoration of equilibrium.

Foster and Ward argue that an examination of the interactions between the operating, investing, and financing cash flows can indicate at what stage of financial stress the firm is in and provides information on management's actions for correction.

Certainly, examples can be found to support this assertion (see the Burns Philp case study later in this chapter). However, many more examples can be found where a firm is not in distress but where similar interactions are occurring in its cash flows.

The findings in numerous studies—by Godbee, Casey, and Bartczak, and other researchers—show that historical cash flow analysis by itself does not prove to be a good predictor of distress.

Proponents also point out that cash flow analysis is less susceptible to the manipulations of creative accounting.

Certainly, there is more scope with "creative accounting" to dress up both the "income statement" (the profit and loss statement or statement of financial performance) and the balance sheet (the statement of financial position). Capitalizing expenses, deferring expense recognition, bringing forward revenue recognition, and ignoring some accruals are just a few of the means to manipulate accrual accounts.

Cash is cash, and it is less amenable to be manipulated on the timing issues. For example, in the six months before Enron went bust, it reported an accrual profit of some US$800 million (much of which was recognition of revenue on long-term contracts that would not be realized for up to 20 years). On the other hand, operating cash flow was negative in the amount of US$1,300 million—the reality of cash versus the window dressing of profits.

This does not mean that cash flow is immune to manipulation. WorldCom demonstrated this by switching cash flows between operating and investing categories. However, the scope for manipulation is much more restricted.

Cash flow also highlights the style and goals of management. An example was the Australian firm, David Jones, when controlled by the Adsteam Group. According to all the statements and public announcements, David Jones remained a conservative, high-end retailer. However, a check of the statement of cash flows gave a very different picture. Over 70 percent of the cash flows for David Jones had nothing to do with the conservative business of retailing. The cash flows showed that most of the activity was high-risk share trading (apparently trading in shares of other members of the Adsteam Group).

The breakdown of cash flow according to operations, investing, and financing provides further detail on the sustainability of a business and its strategies.

Australian retailer Brash Holdings is an example. Founded in 1862, it floundered more than 130 years later due to a flawed strategy and operating performance. Although the operating margins (for example, sales margins) and gearing ratios were steadily deteriorating, the funds analysis stressed that the strategy was not sustainable and could not wait for improvement. (Funds analysis was the forerunner to cash analysis until the more accurately timed cash flow statements became available.)

From 1989 to 1991, the firm invested well over A$100 million in stock, equipment (shop fittings) and goodwill on acquisitions as it pursued its strategy of 30 percent per annum growth—the sole articulation of its strategy was to become the fourth-largest retailer in

Australia by 1996. But where was the money coming from? Only 16 percent was coming from operations—and more than half of that was leaking out again in the form of high dividend payments. Suppliers were funding over 42 percent of the business, and debt was the other main source of funding. Such funding was only sustainable until suppliers and banks ran out of patience.

A refinement of this analysis is the "sustainable growth rate" calculation.[6] Robert Higgins introduced and defined this concept in 1977. It is a measure of how fast a firm can grow its sales without blowing out its target gearing ratio. Stripped to its bare essentials, the rate is determined by four factors: the required asset level to support sales; the sales margin; how much profit is leaked out of the firm in the form of dividends; and the gearing level. To grow faster, the business must either adjust one of these parameters or inject more equity.

In the example of Brash Holdings, its deteriorating performance and high dividend payments meant the sustainable growth rate was less than 5 percent per annum. While there were some equity injections, the plummeting share price eventually cut off this source of funds. Rather than face reality, the firm continued to blow out its gearing, particularly by stretching its creditors beyond reasonable limits. Reality eventually hit.

Strengths and Advantages

Cash is cash, and cash flow analysis provides greater insight into the financial viability of a business. Further, cash flow analysis is less susceptible to the manipulations of creative accounting due to the timing issues of cash in and out of the business.

The breakdown of historic and future cash flows according to operations, investing, and financing provides detail on the sustainability of a business and its strategies, and highlights the style and goals of management.

However, future cash flow analysis is the most valid tool for assessing a firm's viability. Thus, for bankers, it is also the most valid decision-making tool for lending, especially to large corporations where security, typically, will be only 40 percent or less of the loan value.

Cash flow modeling provides a virtual laboratory model of the business and its environment—the business has a forecast of what cash surpluses or shortages will be available in future years. Some analysts now refer to such surpluses as "strategic cash flow"—it is cash surplus that can be used for new investments, returns to shareholders, or reducing liabilities.

A well-crafted cash flow forecast model not only provides a forecast of the cash flows, it allows the business situation to be tested. Typically, sensitivity analysis asks "what if" questions. What happens to cash flows if sales rise or fall by 10 percent, if collection of debt slows down, or if additional capacity is required, and so on? Several "what if" conditions combined form a scenario analysis. For example, if a new competitor enters the market or a price war breaks out, the model can calculate the effect on sales, prices, and so on, and show the resulting effects on cash flow.

As such, cash flow forecasting is one of the major tools for assessing the severity of risks. Calculation of the probability of an event occurring is a separate aspect that requires environmental and competitive assessment.

Weaknesses and Limitations

Sadly, cash flow analysis is done rarely and poorly. The main reasons for this are not conceptual, but practical. Complex future cash flow modeling is difficult, time-consuming, and prone to error.

Modeling of a major project, such as opening a large coal mine or infrastructure project, may require six months or more to research the inputs and build the model. Large models also may have thousands of lines of equations, and the scope for error is considerable, especially when running sensitivity analysis. Some organizations attempt to use audited templates, but the "one size fits all" method usually results in a behemoth of a model that mimics the human genome project—some 90 percent of it is redundant and unused.

Building a model from scratch provides much greater insight into a business, but this requires more skill and usually more time.

Finally, the validity of any model rests on the validity of the assumptions on which it is built. The old computing saying of GIGO (garbage-in, garbage-out) applies. A seemingly small difference in assumptions can have enormous ramifications.

As a consequence of the skills needed, the time and cost involved, and concerns over the scope for error, cash flow forecasting for investment or strategic purposes is not done as widely as it deserves; this is despite the ready availability of computing power and software such as Excel. Instead, we see companies and banks falling back on simple (but invalid) measures such as EBIT and EBITDA. These measures can be calculated in a matter of seconds, but they are really quite some way from the real free cash flow of a business. Even making adjustments, such as deducting capital expenditure from EBIT, does not provide much of a refinement.

Cash flow forecasts are still done in detail for liquidity planning purposes. However, despite the detail, such models are usually constructed using little more than a listing of revenues and expenses, and with limited calculation. When properly designed and used, the models can be powerful tools. For example, if there were only two major domestic airlines in a country, complex modeling of your competitor's airline could provide simulation of the effects of price movements, route changes, and even the introduction of a third airline without the expense of trial and error in the market.

Processes for Applying This Technique

The basics of cash flow analysis are not just quantitative (How much cash is there?) but also qualitative (Where is the cash coming from and going to, and is it sustainable?).

The basic cash flows in a business are depicted in Figure 27.1.

Note that the central box of "operations" is represented in the financial statements by the income statement (statement of financial performance). While a major determinant of cash flow, it is only part of the story. Beyond operations and sales, there are another seven boxes on the diagram that also affect cash flow, and several can be larger than the operations. These boxes are represented by the balance sheet (statement of financial position). It is a reminder that we must look beyond just operations if we are to understand cash flows. Profitable companies can fail!

The diagram also highlights the inadequacy of using EBIT or EBITDA as surrogates for free cash flow.

Cash Flow for a Practice
(Simplified)

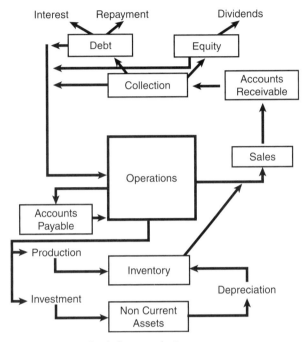

Figure 27.1   Cash flow analysis

As previously mentioned, historic cash flow analysis traditionally looks at the sources and uses of the cash. The prime delineation is provided within the statement of cash flows—operating, investing, and financing.

For an established firm, we like to see strong positive operating cash flows. In terms of risk, stable operating cash flows from year to year are desirable. A further breakdown of analysis would determine if these operating cash flows are coming from normal ongoing business operations or whether they are from one-off events.

In the case of the airline Qantas, it is in a risky industry, and its financial gearing is also high, with debt usually matching equity to give a high debt-to-equity ratio of 1:1 or 100 percent. Yet Qantas is one of the few major airlines that has maintained an investment quality credit rating. This is largely achieved by careful management of its operating cash flow. Despite issues with terrorism, wars, SARS, and other external events, Qantas can generally achieve an operating cash surplus of around A$1 billion each year.

We understand that start-up companies may have negative operating cash flow during their start-up period. Ideally, such shortfalls would be funded mostly by equity investors. To determine the viability of the start-up's business plan, we need to know the rate of their cash burn and how much cash they hold in reserve.

We also understand that growing companies, both start-ups and established firms, will generally have negative net investing cash flows. There are a few exceptions, such as Woolworths, which has limited capital needs for expansion and can fund much of its expansion in sales from the positive net working capital management it achieves. We become concerned, though, if the investment cash flows are hugely negative compared to the operating cash flows, especially if this continues for several years in a row.

Finally, we like to see a balance of funding from financing activities. If the firm is growing and needs to raise capital, both equity and debt need to grow proportionately in order to maintain a stable gearing ratio.

In the case of Qantas, it was in the middle of a major capital investment program, a number of years ago, to refurbish its fleet of aircraft. Consequently, cash flow from investing activities have been (and should continue for a few years) running negative by several billion dollars a year. Due to the difficulty in raising the share price, most of this investment has been debt funded. By 2003, Qantas' already high debt-to-equity ratio had risen from its normal 100 percent to 121 percent. By that stage, ratings agencies would have been watching it. During the next few years, Qantas changed its operational tack, slowing reinvestment in its fleet and increasing its operating cash flow surplus to nearly A$2 billion a year. The excess cash was used to repay debt. Added to retained profits, the debt ratio fell back to 100 percent in 2004 and to 86 percent in 2005. Qantas found it necessary to adjust its operating strategy to recover its financial strategy—that Qantas management was able to adjust to these needs would have been favorably viewed by the investment community.

The relevant ratios on Qantas are shown in Table 27.1.

Table 27.1
Financial Ratios for Qantas

Ratio	2002	2003	2004	2005
Gearing (L/E)	247 percent	226 percent	201 percent	182 percent
Debt Ratio	104 percent	121 percent	101 percent	86 percent
Sales Margin	3.9 percent	3.1 percent	5.7 percent	6.0 percent
Return on Investment	2.9 percent	2.0 percent	3.7 percent	4.2 percent
Return on Equity	10.1 percent	6.6 percent	11.1 percent	11.9 percent
Asset Turnover	$0.74	$0.67	$0.64	$0.70

Of course, analysis of a firm's historical cash flow is improved if it is compared, if not actually benchmarked, against its industry peers.

Future Cash Flow Analysis

Future cash flow analysis begins with building a model that is a reasonable (but not precise) approximation of the operations of the business. It is used for strategic analysis, valuation, and risk assessment. A precise model would take too long to build, would be unwieldy, and would be costly in terms of effort and time.

Apart from spreadsheet modeling skills, the prime skill of the analyst is to understand the business. This will not only assist in constructing the approximation of the business, but will also help to determine the reasonableness of the assumptions. Hence, before the model can be constructed, considerable background work must go into gaining knowledge of the business and its competitive environment.

Finally, the model needs to be built with flexibility. This will include many conditional statements and links between variable factors. Otherwise, the model will not be suitable for one of its prime purposes: the conduct of sensitivity analysis.

Tip Sheet on Cash Flow Analysis

For both historic and future cash flow analysis, the key word is *sustainability*. Can the cash flows be sustained to pay bills and/or fund growth?

Historic Cash Flow Analysis

1. Are the numbers reasonable? If you believe the numbers are "fudged" or manipulated, there is little point in spending time analyzing them. You run your eye over for anything that looks strange. This might be an unusually large number or a number that bucks the trend over the past few years or one that just seems too odd. In the case of Burns Philp, Profit after Tax was higher than Cash Flow from Operations. Since profit has large accrual items such as depreciation and amortization deducted from it, normally operating cash flow is 1.5 to 2.0 × the profit after tax figure. Further investigation of Burns Philp showed that the effective tax rate was less than 20%, suggesting that the cash flow figure was more "true" than the profit figure. (Indeed, Burns Philp was capitalizing many expenses: treating them as assets not expenses.)

   Another aspect of Burns Philp was generally declining operating cash flow over the years—a very worrying sign. Then, cash flow slightly rose in 1995. But a check of the items found that the turnaround was solely from the one-off inclusion of a refund from the Superannuation Fund on the basis that the company had been overpaying for many years and had now suddenly discovered this overpayment. Back that number out of the cash flows, and the declining trend was continuing.

2. What is the major source of cash flow, and how steady is it over the years? For a start-up business, we expect it to make losses in the early years, and so the major source of cash flow may be equity injections.

   However, once a business is established, we expect the main source of cash flow to be from operations: selling products and services to customers at a premium to what they cost to deliver. There may be odd years where major expansion or acquisition means that financing sources (debt or equity) may exceed the cash from operations, but these should be rare.

3. We are concerned at the use of "risky" sources of funds. In the case of retailer Brash Holdings, the major source of funds was suppliers (trade creditors), which was more than four times the cash from operations. A check of the days payable ratio showed that the creditors were being stretched out on their payment terms—a risky and short-lived strategy.

4. We are also concerned if most of an expansion strategy is being debt financed. There should be a balance between debt and equity (to maintain gearing ratios). Debt financing is even more deadly if there is an overly generous dividend payout policy so that too much cash from operations is "leaked" out of the business to the shareholders. A debt-funded expansion strategy, particularly through aggressive acquisitions, is one of the highest correlating factors for corporate distress.

Future Cash Flow Analysis

1. Again, sustainability is the big issue. Have the cash flows come from ongoing, sustainable operations or are they from one-off items that cannot be guaranteed? That is where Newscorp ran into difficulties in the early 1990s. The business changed from a fairly stable newspaper publisher in Australia, Britain, and America into a satellite broadcasting start-up in Britain as well as purchasing Fox movie studios, to try to establish Fox as a new TV network in America. Cash flow became volatile while costs and debt-servicing commitments remained steady.

2. If presented with a cash flow forecast especially in a spreadsheet form, again you need to test if the forecast is correctly calculated before going into detailed analysis. Look for strange numbers that are unusually large or buck the trend when looking across time periods. Are the calculations correct?

3. Is everything included in the forecast? A common mistake is to leave out the effect of growth on working capital needs. When Power Brewing trebled its production capacity, the spreadsheet used by its bank did not include the extra stock and debtors required to service such an expansion. This neglected some $10 million of funding needed to support the business.

4. Next, with a cash flow forecast, are the assumptions reasonable? Projections always look good on paper—how many companies are going to show a declining business or cash flow? But do the assumptions tie up with the numbers today, and what can be expected going forward? Remember, you cannot reasonably have four suppliers in a market, with each claiming 60% market share.

   To assess the reasonableness of assumptions, the analyst had to understand the industry, the competitors, and the business. Cash flow forecasts should not be pulled "out of thin air" but are rather the embodiment of several pieces of background analysis.

5. Finally, the real power of cash flow forecasts, especially in a computer spreadsheet, is sensitivity and scenario analysis. The model can be used to assess the impact of risk events. What if a competitor starts up a price war; or if a major customer defaults; or if the equipment suffers a major breakdown; and so on? Combining several of these sensitivities will develop a scenario as with Power Brewing.

Cash flow analysis is not normally complete in itself but is rather a good tool to combine several analytic techniques and to be used as a cross reference to other techniques.

Case Studies

Because this chapter has considered both historic and future cash flow analysis, a short case study on each aspect is provided next.

Historic Cash Flow Analysis: Burns Philp

Burns Philp was incorporated in 1883 and operated as a diverse group in shipping (one of the long-standing South Seas Traders), retailing, insurance, and trusteeship.

Burns Philp became involved in yeast manufacture in the 1980s when it bought a long established Australian producer, Mauri Bros. In the 1990s, Burns Philp made a series of expensive acquisitions in the herb and spice business—mainly in America, but also in Germany, the Netherlands, and Britain.

Burns Philp then encountered more severe competition than it had when it had expanded globally in yeast. There were entrenched competitors who would not (indeed, could not) yield market share to Burns Philp. McCormick Foods in particular proved to be an entrenched and determined competitor. For McCormick, defending its retail spice business was a matter of life or death.

When Burns Philp's investment in the spice business was written down by the auditors by close to A$1 billion in 1997, it nearly wiped out its entire equity. The firm was in breach of its loan covenants, and its life was only maintained by the banks not foreclosing on it.

The share price plunged from A$1.50 to just 6 cents in a matter of weeks. Most commentators focused on the sudden fall of Burns Philp. Ian Horton of the Investment and Financial Services Association was quoted in February 1998 as saying that Burns Philp was a business "going from being a very successful one to a basket case in a very short space of time." Certainly, most equity analysts and corporate investors had not realized the desperate situation of Burns Philp when they made their stock recommendations or large investments a few months earlier.

How much of Burns Philp was a surprise? The benefit of hindsight unearths the clues, but were they evident before the event? Most commentators focused on the profits and the grand international growth strategies. At least one analyst, Helen Cameron, had a different view (perhaps aided by a stint as strategy planning manager in Burns Philp). When asked well before the crash why she had left Burns Philp, she simply commented: "Look at the cash flows."

The financial statements (balance sheet, profit and loss statement, and statement of cash flows) reviewed are from 1992 to 1995. These statements cover a period of two to five years before the crash.

Objective analysis shows some issues of great concern in a supposedly strong firm. For a start, we are concerned about the reliability of the reported profit figures. The profit and tax figures for 1993 to 1995 are tabled next.

	1993	1994	1995
Profit before tax ($m)	147.8	155.6	131.4
Tax ($m)	−27.6	−21.3	−9.1
Profit after tax ($m)	120.2	134.3	122.3
Tax as a percentage of profit	18.7 percent	13.7 percent	6.9 percent

Yet the corporate tax rate in these years was over 30 percent. We can understand the actual tax rate being less than the nominal rate in some years due to timing differences with accrual accounting, but such large differences year after year lead us to suspect that the taxable profit was far less than the reported firm profit.

At least part of the explanation seemed to lie in how Burns Philp was treating slotting expenses. These were payments made to supermarkets in the U.S. just to get their spices on the supermarket shelves. It seems Burns Philp paid huge amounts (several hundred million dollars) several years in advance! Rather than treat this as an expense, they argued that under accrual accounting concepts, they should be amortized over the period in which they helped earn income. Unfortunately, the competitive reactions by McCormick meant there never were any profits.

By capitalizing these expenses, Burns Philp removed them from the profit and loss statement and instead had them treated as assets in the balance sheet. On the other hand, the cash flow was still negative—it was cash going out. The 1995 Burns Philp Annual Report states:

> "Slotting fees are the upfront multi-year payments to retailers for contracts related to shelf space in supermarkets. While a traditional feature of doing business with supermarkets in the United States and some other countries, an escalation in slotting payments was used during 1994 and 1995 as a competitive reaction to our increased presence in the world spice market. This situation seems to have abated with new contracts being negotiated at more realistic levels."

> "Burns Philp incurs costs ('slotting allowances') in connection with shelf space contracts for certain of its consumer food products. Where these contracts extend beyond a one-year period, the slotting allowances are deferred and amortized over the life of the contract. Costs which relate to future periods are disclosed as other assets in the balance sheet."

The cash flow statements offer more items of interest and concern. In summary form, cash flows were as follows:

	1993	1994	1995
Net from Operations ($m)	151.6	101.1	113.9
Net from Investing ($m)	–483.3	–432.8	–200.3
Net from Financing ($m)	250.8	186.6	188.2

The firm was obviously on a growth binge.

A more intense analysis unearths the concerns. The operating cash flows have fallen from over A$150 million to just under A$114 million. At least the 1995 results were slightly up from 1994; however, the 1995 results were "fixed up" by the old trick of looking at the superannuation fund controlled by the firm and deciding that it had made excessive payments over the years and that this should be refunded in 1995. Removal of this one-off bounty of A$20 million plunged operating cash flows below A$100 million.

The drop in the negative investing cash flows in 1995 was only due to the sale of Burns Philp's last cash cow, its BBC Hardware retail chain, for nearly A$500 million. Without this cash injection, investing cash flows would have been negative by about A$700 million. Like the superannuation fund refund, this was a one-off item that would not be there in future years.

Finally, the financing cash flows show most of the funding was coming from debt issues, as Burns Philp increased its debt levels by *over* A$200 million each year.

This showed a firm with declining operating cash flows despite a massive investment program that was debt funded. This was a recipe for disaster. Add some operating failures such as the spice business (plus others), and Burns Philp came close to failure.

In the end, it survived because the banks could see little value in a wind up, and the major shareholder, Graeme Hart, and a few fellow investors tried to save their investment by putting another A$300 million into the firm to try to turn it around.

Objective cash flow analysis shows the disaster in the making several years before the supposed "sudden collapse." Strategic competitor analysis would also have given some cause for alarm, but the hardest evidence was in the cash flow statements. As a leading financial commentator has said, Burns Philp's survival was dependent on the actions of Robert Lawless, CEO of McCormick Spices in the U.S. One would suspect that Lawless took one look at Burns Philp's operating cash flows, cost structures, and high gearing and decided to "put the shaft in so hard he just brought them right down."

Future Cash Flow Analysis: Power Brewing

In the early 1990s, banks were just starting to learn about becoming objective cash flow lenders. Computer-based cash flow modeling was in its infancy.

Leading Australian businessman, Alan Bond, had taken over the State of Queensland's own beer: the Castlemaine Brewery. He did the same in New South Wales with Tooheys. This followed his acquisition of the small Western Australian brewery, Swan.

In no time, Alan Bond had alienated his distributors (the pub owners) and his consumers (the drinkers). Trading terms were tightened, goodwill components in pub leases were ignored, and the packaging was changed to read brewed by Swan Brewery, Perth (Capital of Western Australia).

Bernie Power was one of the largest pub owners in Queensland and had been toying with the idea of opening a brewery. Suddenly, Alan Bond had tapped the keg of his idea. Bernie Power launched Power Brewing. It quickly claimed status as Queensland's real beer, and soon the brewery was selling at capacity with a 20 percent price premium, so keen were drinkers to avoid the Alan Bond beer brand. Power Brewing quickly achieved a 10 percent share of the Queensland market.

If you are at full capacity, the next obvious step is to triple capacity.

So, Power Brewing (by then a public company) borrowed some A$48 million from the bank to triple its capacity.

The bank developed a spreadsheet to look at future cash flows. The base case model showed generous future cash flows as tabled next. Year 1 was negative due to the capital investment in the expansion. The cash flow shown is free cash flow after all operating items and capital expenditure.

Year 1	Year 2	Year 3	Year 4	Year 5	Year 6
−A$40.7m	A$24.9m	A$27.5m	A$28.7m	A$29.6m	A$30.4m

Unfortunately, the spreadsheet had an error. Working capital movements were ignored. Since the firm was tripling production and sales, working capital would also approximately treble, especially as Bernie Power offered reasonably generous payment terms to his fellow publicans. The effect was an additional negative A$10 million in the first year of expansion.

Of even greater concern was that the assumptions were simplistic and not reasonable. Prices were deemed to rise with inflation (which historically had not happened) and, even more illogically, the 20 percent price premium was expected to be maintained despite now saturating the market. Other assumptions included the plant running at 99.98 percent capacity each year and that all production would be sold.

Worse still, the model was quite inflexible, with little calculation within the model, making it very difficult to conduct a sensitivity analysis on the model.

This was regrettable. The tripling of output meant that Power Brewing was signaling to its competitors that it intended to move from 10 percent market share to 30 percent market share. At this stage, Power Brewing would need to have taken market share not just from Alan Bond's Castlemaine Brewery but also from the other rival, Fosters.

The response was foreseeable: a price war.

So how do the future cash flows look under a price war? Several sensitivity analyses are tabled next, and in the last case, we have a scenario of a fall in prices and volume, including the effect of the working capital change.

	Year 1	Year 2	Year 3	Year 4	Year 5	Year 6
Sales volume down 10 percent after year 1						
	−$40.7m	$13.3m	$14.4m	$14.7m	$14.6m	$14.4m
Sales volume down 20 percent after year 1						
	−$40.7m	−$1.6m	−$1.7m	−$1.6m	−$1.4m	−$1.3m
Prices down 10 percent after year 1						
	−$40.7m	$12.1m	$17.3m	$18.0m	$18.0m	$18.0m
Prices down 20 percent after year 1						
	−$40.7m	−$6.5m	$4.4m	$4.9m	$5.5m	$6.2m
Scenario: Prices and volumes down 20 percent, working capital included						
	−$43.3m	−$28.2m	−$23.8m	−$25.2m	−$26.7m	−$27.5m

Obviously, such negative cash flows are not sustainable, especially for a fledging brewer with no operation in other markets. With the share price falling and its bank concerned, Power Brewing was happy to form a joint venture under Fosters' terms to share the new brewery. A few years later, Fosters bought the remaining half of Power Brewing.

The case shows that a well-constructed model with reasonable assumptions and sensitivity testing would have shown the strategy and business plan to be fatally flawed. Alternative strategies could have then been considered, such as stay small, form an alliance with other small regional brewers, or sell to Fosters when in a stronger bargaining position.

However, the error in the model (neglecting working capital), the unrealistic assumptions, and the lack of flexibility all led to self-delusion.

FAROUT Summary

FAROUT SUMMARY

	1	2	3	4	5
F	■	■	■	■	
A	■	■	■	■	
R	■				
O	■	■	■		
U	■	■	■	■	■
T	■	■			

Figure 27.2   Competitor cash flow analysis FAROUT summary

Future orientation—Medium to high. The future cash flow model is the synthesis of all techniques to look at the future.

Accuracy—Medium to high for the historic cash flow analysis. It is more accurate or at least more reliable than the other accounting statements. For future cash flow analysis, accuracy would be medium. Models require a very good understanding of the business and its environment as they often require considerable modeling and business skill.

Resource efficiency—Low. Some information can be gained from public documents, but much detail on operations requires internal analysis of the business and can require cross-functional understanding of marketing, engineering, operations, and taxation.

Objectivity—Medium. Historic analysis is quite high. The use of many assumptions in forecasting can be influenced by political influence or "rose-colored glasses." There are tools for testing the reasonableness of assumptions, such as historic trends, engineering estimates, and break-even analysis.

Usefulness—High. Well-crafted models have enormous usefulness for strategic and business assessment and for the analysis of competitive situations and alternative strategies.

Timeliness—Low to medium. Historic cash flow analysis can be done quickly with public domain information. Complex forecasting models can take considerable time to build and use.

Related Tools and Techniques

- Competitor analysis
- Cost/benefit analysis
- Financial analysis
- Historic trend analysis
- Industry analysis
- Market forecasting
- Sustainable growth rate

References

Beaver, W.H. (1966). "Financial Ratios as Predictors of Failure," Empirical Research in Accounting: Selected Studies, *Supplement to Journal of Accounting Research*, 5, p. 80, pp. 71–111.

Berkshire-Hathaway annual reports.

Casey, C.J., and N.J. Bartczak (1985). "Using Operating Cash Flow Data to Predict Financial Distress: Some Extensions," *Journal of Accounting Research*, 23(1), pp. 384–401.

Fleisher, C.S., and B.E. Bensoussan (2003). *Strategic and Competitive Analysis: Methods and Techniques for Analyzing Business Competition*. Upper Saddle River, NJ: Prentice Hall.

Foster, B.P., and T.J. Ward (1997). "Financial Health or Solvency? Watch the Trends and Interactions in Cash Flows," *Academy of Accounting and Financial Studies Journal*, Vol. 1, No. 1, pp. 33–37.

Godbee, G.J. (2004). "The Leap to Failure: Distinguishing Between Corporate Distress and Failure Prediction," Unpublished Thesis, Macquarie University.

Higgins, R.C. (1977). *Financial Management: Theory and Applications*. Chicago, IL: SRA.

Horrigan, J.O. (1968). "A short history of financial ratio analysis," *Accounting Review*, 4, pp. 284–294.

Koller. T.M. (2001). "Valuing dot-coms after the fall," *The McKinsey Quarterly*, March 22, 2001.

McCaffrey, R.. "The Limits of EBITDA," retrieved from the Web on August 25, 2006 at http://www.fool.com/news/indepth/telecom/content/ebitdalimits.htm.

Wall, A. (1968). "Study of Credit Barometrics," reprinted in Horrigan, J.O. (ed), *Financial Ratio Analysis: An Historical Perspective*. New York, NY: Arno Press.

Ward, T.J. (1995). "Using Information from the Statement of Cash Flows to Predict Insolvency," *The Journal of Commercial Lending*, 77(7), March, pp. 29–36.

Winaker, A., and R. Smith (1930). "A Test Analysis for Unsuccessful Industrial Companies," *Bureau of Business Research*, Bulletin No. 31, University of Illinois.

Endnotes

[1] Horrigan (ed.), 1968.

[2] Winaker and Smith, 1930.

[3] Beaver, 1966.

[4] Koller, 2001.

[5] See Fleisher and Bensoussan (2003), Chapter 4.

[6] See Fleisher and Bensoussan (2003), Chapter 27.

28

Analysis of Competing Hypotheses

Short Description

Analysis of competing hypotheses (ACH) is a multi-variable, qualitative technique that aids judgment on important issues requiring careful weighing of alternative explanations or conclusions. ACH requires an analyst to explicitly identify all the reasonable alternatives in a particular situation and have them compete against each other for the analyst's favor, rather than evaluating their plausibility one at a time. This can help an analyst to combat bias and cognitive distortions that often reduce the quality of the analysis process or the outputs generated by it.

ACH is grounded in basic insights from cognitive psychology, decision analysis, and the scientific method. ACH provides an analytical philosophy that uses the scientific method to provide order and structure to a mass of data and how the analyst addresses it.

Background

ACH was first revealed to competitive intelligence analysts in Richards Heuer's, *The Psychology of Intelligence Analysis*, and as mentioned previously, ACH provides an analytical approach that uses the scientific method in a unique way to provide order and structure to the mass of information collected and how an analyst should attend to this information (see Figure 28.1 for an illustration of a generic ACH process).

But why would this approach be of importance? An example from the U.S. intelligence community, which arguably is far more professionalized in an institutional sense than business, and competitive analysis is in the private sector, may answer this question.

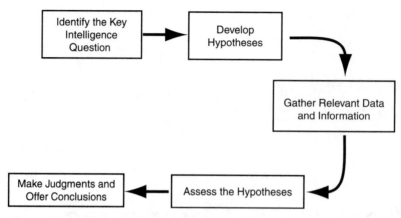

Figure 28.1   Illustration of a generic ACH process

Studies are carried out in a post-mortem fashion by various commissions following many well-publicized (and even some not well-publicized) failures of intelligence in the U.S. One of these was performed following the 9/11 attacks of 2001. The *Report of the Commission on the Intelligence Capabilities of the U.S. Regarding Weapons of Mass Destruction—WMD, 2005 (WMD Report)*, identified a number of weaknesses involving a lack of consideration of alternate hypotheses associated with parts of intelligence analysis by analysts that resulted in the destruction of the Twin Towers in New York City. For example, the WMD Report stated that analysts "have a difficult time stating their assumptions up-front, explicitly explaining their logic, and, in the end, identifying unambiguously for policy-makers what they do not know." It also stated that, "As much as they hate to do it, analysts must be comfortable facing up to uncertainty and being explicit about it in their assessments." In order to address these issues, the WMD Report recommends that analysts in the intelligence community encourage "alternative hypothesis generation."

Doing analysis to inform decision makers about the future is a demanding task. As we discussed in Chapters 1 through 5 of this book, business and competitive analysts employ a variety of analytical processes designed to objectively study data and information to enhance decision makers' understanding of events and issues. Whatever the process, the analyst must employ a systematic logic in coming to conclusions. Part of this systematic logic process will include making assumptions about why things are as they are and what is and isn't happening.

Individuals make many assumptions about what they understand and assume to be true and valid. Sometimes, these assumptions are made explicit and communicated to decision makers; at other times, they remain implicit and are not communicated. Because these assumptions can greatly influence the quality of an analysis, it is critical that they are given proper recognition in the analysis process. The ACH process described in this chapter is designed to serve this important role.

Strategic Rationale and Implications

What is so helpful about ACH for the business and competitive analyst is that it is a process for refuting hypotheses. This is in contrast to the more commonly practiced process of gathering evidence that confirms pre-existing beliefs. Analysts typically perform their tasks by choosing what they intuitively suspect is the most likely answer to a client's question and then examine the gathered information to see whether it supports this answer. Analysts typically stop their examination when the evidence appears supportive of their favored hypothesis. If the evidence is unsupportive of their chosen answer, they can either reject the evidence as misleading or develop another hypothesis and repeat the procedure. This is called a "satisficing strategy," which means choosing the first solution that seems satisfactory, rather than exhaustively considering all the possibilities to identify the best or most ideal solution. The problem with this is that there may be several seemingly satisfactory solutions, but there is only a single "best" solution.

Analysts can be led astray with this common approach when they focus on confirming a hypothesis they think is likely to be true and which is accompanied by a large amount of evidence supporting their view. In this situation, they will typically overlook the fact that most of this evidence is also consistent with, and supportive of, alternative explanations. In these cases, these other alternatives are typically not properly refuted.

The management of intelligence analysis should encourage the application of techniques that allow clear delineation of assumptions and chains of inference; the specification of the degree of uncertainty about the evidence and resultant conclusions; and the elaboration of alternative perspectives and conclusions.

People tend to avoid cognitive dissonance. Most people are also uncomfortable when their belief systems are challenged. The ACH technique allows for a procedural loosening of dominant thought processes just as a scientist has to loosen his expectations of whether or not a particular experiment will verify or disconfirm his hypothesis.

Strengths and Advantages

ACH is an effective process that keeps individuals from falling prey to common analytic pitfalls. Because of its thoroughness, it is particularly appropriate for controversial issues when analysts want to leave an audit trail to show what they considered and how they arrived at their judgment. In these cases, the decision maker can quickly scan how conclusions were arrived at and the foundations for the judgments. In the same way, it also serves as an effective logic double-check for the analyst.

In the intelligence literature, ACH is promoted as an effective analysis aid for two reasons. First, it is seen as a helpful tool to assist an analyst's judgment on issues that require a careful evaluation of alternative explanations or conclusions. It helps to guard against some of the common biases and perceptual distortions mentioned in Chapter 3, "Avoiding Analysis Pitfalls," by compelling the analyst to account for all the alternatives.[1] Second, ACH provides a convenient and visual means for indicating the specific area in which there may be dissenting views. If another analyst or the decision maker disagrees with the original analyst's judgment, a matrix (shown in Table 28.1) can be used to highlight the precise area of disagreement. Subsequent discussion can then help the stakeholders to focus on the ultimate source of the differences.

In addition, Sawka suggests that ACH has the following three key strengths:

1. **ACH compels a systematic examination of all hypotheses**—Analysts tend to "satisfice" in their day-to-day work and halt their evaluation process once a considerable amount of evidence supports their favored hypothesis. For example, an analyst who concludes that her first hypothesis has adequate evidentiary support will not be likely to bother evaluating the remaining hypotheses under consideration. The problem here is that the data may actually support one or more of the unevaluated hypotheses as strongly as the chosen hypothesis.

2. **ACH illuminates the analyst's logic to their customers**—ACH helps decision makers to understand why a chosen course of action was superior to others. ACH also allows analysts to illustrate logically why their recommendations may even prove to be superior to those that the decision makers might have held going into the analysis; as such, it provides added legitimacy to analysts that otherwise might not be earned in the normal conduct of their work.

3. **ACH ensures that the analyst properly considers the data and information they have gathered**—Consider how each key piece of information supports, is against, or is unrelated to, all of the competing hypotheses. It will be impossible for a single piece of evidence to be in support of competing hypotheses. The process helps focus on problems (contradictions, deficiencies, and discrepancies) in the analysis process and data sources used. In many cases, it can help identify gaps in data that can lead the analyst to solicit further evidence gathering.

By generating the set of hypotheses in advance of collecting data and evaluating it, ACH becomes a systematic process that benefits the analyst personally in the form of a self-review, tightening logic and checking the rationale for arriving at judgments, and by providing additional legitimacy in the eyes of the decision makers. This can enhance the trust that decision makers have in their analysts and hopefully encourage them to give greater credence to the analyst's recommendations.

Weaknesses and Limitations

Getting analysts to regularly employ the ACH process is likely to be an uphill battle. The eight steps associated with the most common version of ACH are cognitively draining and difficult for many analysts to regularly perform. Also the entire process is time consuming compared to the prospect of quickly delivering a response that answers their client's question.

Stech and Elasser suggest that a problem with using ACH is that most people lack the capability to consider the sheer volume of evidence that can go into developing and analyzing a set of competing hypotheses. These alternatives grow exponentially if the possibility of deception by a rival is also involved. They suggest that many individuals will overlook the possibility of deception because of the difficulty in managing all the details that are associated with this added complexity and uncertainty.

Most analysts recognize that the possibility of deception occurs on a daily basis, but systematic methods for recognizing it are lacking, at least in part because common reasoning aids the deceivers. Deception detection depends on two reasoning skills in which humans are particularly weak: reasoning about negative or absent evidence and false evidence. For these reasons, Stech and Elasser focus their research on developing computerized tools to help analysts identify deception. The development of automated applications for performing methods like ACH should eventually help analysts to employ the process more efficiently and effectively, but these applications remain embryonic in their current level of development and deployment in the business community.

Another related possible limitation is that ACH can actually increase the likelihood that the analyst will be deceived. In particular, Heuer's "Draw Tentative Conclusions" step (see Step 5 in the section, "Process for Applying the Technique") recommends weighing hypotheses in light of evidence, a process that already promotes reasoning errors arising from "everyday irrationality." The problem with the relative assessment of competing hypotheses, in light of evidence, is that it neglects the individual base rates of both evidence and hypothesis in conventional analysis and fails to provide an evidentiary false-positive rate in counter-deception situations.

Process for Applying the Technique

The following eight-step process is adapted from the standard one recommended by Heuer. His approach is the most commonly employed in intelligence agencies and has been demonstrated to be effective in a variety of different contexts. It is easy to adapt for most applications in business and competitive analysis.

Step 1: Identify the Possible Hypotheses to Be Considered

Step one of ACH is to develop alternate hypotheses about the decision maker's key intelligence question. This step is intended to help the analyst consider alternate explanations and avoid prematurely making conclusions based on a few salient observations or preconceptions.

At this early hypothesis-generation stage, it is very useful to bring together a group of analysts with different backgrounds and perspectives. Conducting brainstorming in groups stimulates the imagination and can generate possibilities that individuals would not generate on their own. The key is to generate as many hypotheses as possible, without performing any judgments of their credibility or viability at this point. Heuer suggests that as a general rule, analysts should consider more alternatives when there is a higher level of uncertainty surrounding the question being examined or the potential impact of the conclusions will be greater.

Wait for all the possibilities to be identified before considering them. The goal in this stage of assessment is to select the hypotheses to be examined in greater detail in a subsequent analysis. Try to keep the number of hypotheses manageable; Heuer suggests that about seven will serve as a good target because this shouldn't overwhelm the analyst.

Designate the hypotheses not to be analyzed as unproven (that is, there is no evidence that suggests they are correct) hypotheses. Other hypotheses may indeed be disproved, whereby positive evidence does suggest they are incorrect. Also consider the possibility that a rival company is trying to deceive your firm from knowing what they are actually doing.

Step 2: List the Significant Evidence in Support of and Against Each Hypothesis

Begin this step by listing the general evidence that applies across all the listed hypotheses. Evidence in this step refers to all the factors that impact your judgments about the hypotheses. Evidence doesn't need to be firm at this point to be included.

Be careful to note the absence, as well as the presence, of evidence. To encourage thinking about absent evidence, ask, "If this hypothesis is true, what should I expect to see or not to see?" What is missing and not seen may represent the need for additional data collection efforts. Recognize that each hypothesis requires asking different questions and, therefore, seeking out other evidence.

Assumptions about your competitors' intentions, goals, or standard procedures also need to be included. These assumptions can produce strong preconceptions as to how likely a hypothesis may provide the sought-after answer. They need to be included in the evidentiary list since these assumptions may heavily impact the final judgment.

Then consider each hypothesis individually, listing factors that tend to support or contradict each one.

Step 3: Prepare a Matrix with Hypotheses Across the Top and Evidence Down the Side

This step may be the most crucial one in this process and is the one that is likely to be done incorrectly, thereby leading to the diminishment of the benefits that could otherwise be generated by the ACH process. It is also the step that differs most from the natural, intuitive analysis approach typically used in the absence of ACH.

Combine the hypotheses (from Step 1) and the evidence and arguments (from Step 2). This information is then placed into a matrix format, with the hypotheses across the X-axis and evidence and arguments down the Y-axis (that is, side). The matrix provides a visual perspective of all the key facets of the intelligence question (see Table 28.1).

Table 28.1
Sample ACH Matrix

	Hypothesis 1	Hypothesis 2	Hypothesis 3	Hypothesis 4
Evidence 1	+	–	+	–
Evidence 2	+	+	+	+
Evidence 3	NA	–	+	–
Evidence 4	–	–	+	–
Evidence 5	?	–	+	–
Evidence 6	+	?	+	?

Next, consider how each item of evidence relates to the hypotheses. Differing from the typical process, which is to examine one hypothesis at a time, this step requires the simultaneous/concurrent assessment of the relationship between evidence and hypotheses. Take one item of evidence at a time and consider how consistent it is with each hypothesis. In Step 5, you will work down the columns of the matrix, examining one hypothesis at a time to see how consistent that hypothesis is with all the evidence.

To fill in the cells of the matrix, take the first item of evidence and ask whether it is (a) consistent with (+ or C for consistent), (b) inconsistent with (– or I for inconsistent), or (c) irrelevant (? or NA for not applicable) to each hypothesis. A notation should be made in the appropriate cell under each hypothesis in the matrix. The key point is to provide a shorthand representation of the complex reasoning behind how the evidence relates to each hypothesis.

Using a matrix format helps you to weigh the diagnostic value of each evidentiary item. This is a major distinction with traditional analyses. To use an automotive analogy, a high temperature light on the dashboard may have great value in telling a driver that their vehicle has a problem but relatively little value in determining what the source of the temperature gain is. Because a high-running temperature is consistent with so many possible hypotheses about the car's problem, this evidence has limited diagnostic value in determining which hypothesis is the more likely one.

Evidence is diagnostic when it influences your judgment on the relative likelihood of the various hypotheses identified in Step 1. If an evidentiary item appears consistent with every hypothesis, it is likely to have little to no diagnostic value. Analysts commonly realize that most of the evidence supporting what they believe to be the most likely hypothesis is not very helpful; this is because that same evidence is also consistent with other hypotheses. By identifying the items that are highly diagnostic, the analyst can have greater confidence in their eventual judgment. These items should also be re-examined for accuracy and considered for alternative interpretations, as discussed in Step 6.

Step 4: Refine the Matrix

The way the hypotheses are worded is crucial to drawing conclusions from the analysis. As such, it will often be appropriate to reconsider and reword the various hypotheses. This may lead to the addition of new hypotheses or the replacement of existing hypotheses with finer distinctions made to them in order to consider all the significant alternatives. Two hypotheses may be better combined into one when there is no evidence that distinguishes two separate hypotheses.

Attempt to delete evidence and arguments that are unimportant and/or have no diagnostic value. These items should be saved in a separate list or file as a record of information that was considered. Essentially, you are establishing an audit trail for your work. If others disagree with your assessment, they can be provided with this separate list.

Step 5: Draw Tentative Conclusions About the Relative Likelihood of Each Hypothesis by Trying to Disprove It

This step is the adjunct to Step 3. In Step 3, you worked across the matrix, focusing on a single item of evidence and examining its relationship to each hypothesis. In this step, you work down the matrix, looking at each hypothesis. The matrix format gives an overview of all the evidence supporting or opposing all the hypotheses. In this fashion, all the hypotheses can be examined together in order to determine which one is most likely.

Begin by looking for evidence that enables you to reject hypotheses or at least to determine which ones are unlikely. Proceed by rejecting or eliminating hypotheses, while tentatively accepting only those hypotheses that cannot be refuted. Although the scientific method cannot be entirely applied to intuitive judgments, it is useful to disprove hypotheses rather than confirm them.

No matter how much information is consistent with a given hypothesis, one cannot prove a particular hypothesis is true because the same information may also be consistent with other hypotheses. Alternatively, a single evidentiary item inconsistent with a hypothesis may be sufficient to allow for rejection of that hypothesis.

Humans have natural tendencies to focus on confirming hypotheses they already suspect to be true. They ordinarily give more weight to information that supports a hypothesis than to information that weakens it. Because this distorts the results, it is preferred that you do just the opposite; consequently, this step means you will have to go against your natural tendencies.

Closely observe the minuses in your matrix. Hypotheses with the most minuses are the ones to which you should give the most consideration. It is useful to spend more time on these least-likely hypotheses. The one that is most likely is usually the one with the least evidence against it, not the one with the most evidence for it.

This initial ranking ordered by the number of minuses is only a rough ranking. This is because some evidentiary items will be more important than other evidence. Degrees of inconsistency cannot be adequately captured by a single notation. You can better judge how much weight to give it by reconsidering the full nature of the relationship between the evidence and the hypotheses.

Steps 4 and 5 are where the ACH process is heavily susceptible to bias—of failing to weigh the impact of evidence by its false positive rate and misestimating prior probabilities. It is also worth noting at this point that the matrix should *not* dictate conclusions; instead, it should accurately reflect the analyst's judgment of what is and is not important and how these important factors relate to the probability of each hypothesis. The matrix is an aid to thinking and analysis, to ensure consideration of all the possible interrelationships between evidence and hypotheses, and the identification of those few items that really swing the analyst's eventual judgment.

Step 6: Analyze How Sensitive Your Conclusion Is to a Few Critical Pieces of Evidence

This is the step in which you must question the few linchpin assumptions (see Chapter 29, "Linchpin Analysis," for more about linchpin assumptions) or evidentiary items that really influence the analytical outcome in one direction or the other. Analysts should ask the following kinds of questions at this point:

- Are there questionable assumptions underlying your interpretation?
- Are there alternative explanations?
- Could the evidence gathered and used be incomplete and/or misleading? This will especially be problematic in cases where a market rival is purposefully trying to throw you off the true path for what they are doing.

You always need to determine which assumptions merit additional questioning. ACH is useful because it helps you to identify what needs to be rechecked. It may be appropriate at this point to reassess original source materials as opposed to relying on others' interpretations. It is always desirable to identify in your report the critical assumptions that led to the interpretation and conclusions because they are dependent upon the validity of these assumptions.

Step 7: Report Conclusions

Because analytical judgments cannot be made with certainty, decision makers should know the relative likelihood of all the alternative possibilities. Decision makers need to make decisions on the basis of a full set of alternative possibilities, not just the single most likely alternative. Analysts should offer contingency plans in case one of the less-likely alternatives turns out to be true.

It is helpful to quickly review what it means for a hypothesis to be likely. A hypothesis that is probably true could mean anywhere from a 55 percent to an 85 percent chance that future events will prove it correct, leaving anywhere from a 15 percent to 45 percent possibility that decisions based on this judgment will be based on faulty assumptions and turn out to be wrong. This is why it is important for analysts to communicate how confident they are in their recommendation and what it would take for them to raise this confidence level.

The report produced for decision makers should provide a comparative evaluation of competing hypotheses. Although this is not common practice because it adds length and is sometimes viewed to be superfluous to the primary argument being made, it is still an important part of the analytical product and should be included in one form or another.

Step 8: Identify Milestones for Future Observation That May Indicate Events Are Taking a Different Course Than Expected

Any conclusion the analyst provides to the decision maker should always be regarded as tentative. This is because the situation may materially change or new data may come in to alter the interpretation. Because of this, analysts should identify things in their report that would alter their situation appraisal. In other words, specify in advance what it would take for them to change their minds. This is also helpful for the analyst because it will make it more difficult to rationalize such developments, if they occur, as not really requiring any judgmental modifications.

Summary

Heuer notes that three key elements distinguish ACH analyses from conventional intuitive analysis:

- ACH begins with a full range of alternatives rather than with a most likely alternative that the analyst seeks (and usually manages) to confirm. This step ensures that all alternative hypotheses receive balanced consideration.

- Like many common statistical rules that require a researcher to be discriminatory in how they consider evidence, ACH helps the analyst to distinguish the precious few evidentiary items that have the highest diagnostic value in assessing the relative likelihood of the alternative hypotheses. In conventional intuitive analysis, explicit consideration is rarely given that key evidence may also be consistent with alternative hypotheses.

■ ACH requires the analyst to identify evidence that refutes, as opposed to confirms, hypotheses. The most probable hypothesis is usually the one with the least evidence against it, unlike conventional analysis where it would be the one with the most evidence in favor of it.

ACH is a powerful method for assisting and enhancing many of the other techniques detailed in this book. It is one of the approaches that every individual pursuing a career in business and competitive analysis should gain competence in applying.

FAROUT Summary

FAROUT SUMMARY

	1	2	3	4	5
F	■				
A	■	■	■		
R	■	■			
O	■	■	■	■	■
U	■	■	■		
T	■	■			

Figure 28.2   Analysis of competing hypotheses FAROUT summary

Future-orientation—Low. ACH is intended to help the analyst evaluate competing hypotheses, not to generate better hypotheses about the future. There is nothing in the application of the technique that compels the analyst to be future focused in their generation of alternative hypotheses.

Accuracy—Medium. The systematic application of the scientific method as indicated by ACH should cause analysts to tighten any gaps in their logic and to identify when evidence does and does not support competing hypotheses. Where accuracy suffers is in the generation of the competing hypotheses themselves, as well as the interpretation of how the evidence correlates to the hypotheses and in judging which hypotheses are the most likely.

Resource efficiency—Low to medium. ACH usually requires the analyst to work with others in generating hypotheses or in serving as sounding boards to help evaluate their interpretation of the matrix. It can also require additional data gathering to fill in evidentiary holes.

Objectivity—High. Based closely on the precepts of the scientific method, this process compels analysts to be rigorous in their analyses and leaves them much less open to challenge than most other analytical aids.

Usefulness—Medium. ACH helps to provide additional support for the analyst's judgment and/or recommendation, but is less helpful in delivering actionable outputs that can be quickly acted upon. It is useful in supporting the outputs of other tools that provide more decision-ready analysis products.

Timeliness—Low to medium. ACH requires time to compile and complete. Even the decision maker's review of the ACH evidence will take time and usually requires interpretation by the analyst.

Related Tools and Techniques

- Assumptions analysis
- Linchpin analysis
- Scientific research approach
- Statistical analysis

References

Dawes, R.M. (2001). *Everyday Irrationality: How Pseudo Scientists, Lunatics, and the Rest of Us Systematically Fail to Think Rationally.* Boulder, CO: Westview Press.

Fishbein, W., and G. Treverton (2004). "Making sense of transnational threats," Occasional Papers, 3(1), October, Washington, DC: The Sherman Kent Center for Intelligence Analysis.

Fleisher, C., and B. Bensoussan (2003). *Strategic and Competitive Analysis: Methods and Techniques for Analyzing Business Competition.* Upper Saddle River, NJ: Prentice Hall.

George, R.Z. (2004). "Fixing the problem of analytical mind-sets: Alternative analysis," *International Journal of Intelligence and Counter-Intelligence*, 17(3), Fall, pp. 385–405.

Heuer Jr., J.R. (1999). *The Psychology of Intelligence Analysis.* Washington, DC: Center for the Study of Intelligence.

Sawka, K. (2003). "Competing hypotheses analysis (CHA)," *Competitive Intelligence Magazine*, 6(2), pp. 53–54.

Stech, F.J., and C. Elasser (2004). "Midway revisited: Deception by analysis of competing hypothesis," MITRE Corporation, Tech. Rep. Available online at http://www.mitre.org/work/tech papers/tech papers 04/stech deception.

Stern-Dunyak, A. (2004). "Fooled again: Developing counter deception decision support," *The MITRE Digest*, May. Available online at http://www.mitre.org/news/digest/advanced_research/05_04/ar_counter_decision.html.

WMD (2005). *Report of the Commission on the Intelligence Capabilities of the U.S. Regarding Weapons of Mass Destruction*. Washington, DC. Full report available at http://www.whitehouse.gov/wmd/.

Endnotes

[1] Fishbein and Treverton, 2004.

29

Linchpin Analysis

Short Description

Linchpin analysis is a highly adaptable, logic structuring technique that is intended to minimize mistakes and promote clarity even with complex arguments containing variables about which there is a high degree of uncertainty. It is driven from basic assumptions that an analyst would include regarding the competition and a rival's proposed actions. To develop predictions with a high degree of confidence, careful attention is required when selecting the factors deemed most likely to drive and determine the outcome of a situation on which there is a dearth of strong empirical evidence.

Background

Individuals are compelled by their circumstances to make dozens of assumptions on a daily basis. The rigorous and systematic testing of assumptions has long been an essential part of the intelligence trade. It has also been a longstanding part of defense or military intelligence practice, particularly for assessing the consistency of forecasts or predictions under differing assumptions. J.R. Heuer, Jr. notes that analysts need to question their assumptions because failures occur when faulty assumptions go unchallenged. Experience also suggests that when analytical judgments are shown to be incorrect, it's usually because the data or information gathered was wrong.

The problem is that analysts, or any other busy individuals, do not have the time to question every one of their assumptions. This leaves them with the issue of where to focus their attention. They should focus on the linchpins underlying their analysis. Linchpins are essential central pieces on which an argument balances. Linchpin analysis helps analysts to identify the key assumptions that could make or break their view of a focal situation.

U.S. Government intelligence officials use linchpin analysis when gauging the military capabilities and likely actions of opposing countries. But prior to the first war in the Persian Gulf in the early 1990s, the U.S. Central Intelligence Agency (CIA) did not regularly use this technique—both intelligence analysts and policy makers were caught off guard by Iraq's invasion of neighboring Kuwait. At that time, many CIA strategists believed that Iraq was not in a position to attack another country. They assumed this because Iraq was supposed to be recovering from its lengthy war during the 1980s with neighboring Iran. Many U.S. policy makers regarded this assumption very highly, and little effort was put into advancing alternative arguments or reasons for why it may not have been accurate.

Until the early 1990s, the CIA had predominantly used "post-mortem" analysis to review events viewed as intelligence failures. These post-event reviews did not prove to be very effective in providing intelligence or policy-making officials with much in the way of proactive measures they could take in order to prevent similar incidences in the future.

Because of the shortcomings recognized to have occurred over the Iraqi invasion of Kuwait and similar events, the CIA and other intelligence organizations have since focused more actively on developing an enhanced strategic warning capability. Part of this enhancement led to the inclusion of linchpin analysis into the standard intelligence development process, both to identify a wider range of alternatives and to prepare a wider range of alternatives and actions if and when linchpin assumptions are altered. Careful attention to selection and testing of key assumptions to deal with substantive uncertainty is now well established as the doctrinal standard for most intelligence analytic processes and is a key part of instruction for new analysts in the professional curriculum of the CIA's Sherman Kent School.[1]

Most studies of analytical tools have not shown linchpin analysis being regularly used by business and competitive analysts or in the development of strategic plans.[2] By compelling analysts to consider the linchpin assumptions underlying their views and results, linchpin analysis can improve the quality of results produced, ensure greater consistency in analytical logic, and help decision makers to better envision a variety of possible futures associated with a competitive situation.

Strategic Rationale and Implications

The business and competitive analyst's generic role is to help decision makers make decisions today that can better position their enterprises for succeeding in a risky and uncertain future. Unfortunately, no person has perfect knowledge or full certainty about the future; consequently, analysts use an array of processes and techniques to help them to better understand and hopefully reduce the uncertainty or perceived risk about the future. That process is a key premise underlying this book and our prior book.[3]

Sometimes, an analyst tries to guess what might happen, and decision makers subsequently apply that information as a basis for their planning or decision making. Such guesses are otherwise known as assumptions, and these are an important source of uncertainty and risk for businesses. Assumptions are propositions or statements that the analyst treats as either true or false. An assumption is a way of dealing with an uncertain future when there are a number of possible alternatives.

For example, an analyst might assume that a firm's suppliers will deliver the right order on time, that a rival CEO will continue to compete through a wide range of outsourcing initiatives, or that a firm will continue to support a new product with highly aggressive pricing tactics. But what happens if the analyst has assumed incorrectly and the actions that ensue are dramatically different from the ones assumed? Assumptions come associated with risk. What makes things more difficult for the analyst is that this risk is often taken unwittingly. In its simplest form, an assumption is a view about how to proceed on the basis that one alternative will turn out to be valid and the others will be incorrect.

A competitor's or your decision maker's assumptions may be based on a number of factors, including any of the following:

- Beliefs about competitive position
- Past experience with products, customers, suppliers, or rivals
- Geographic factors
- Market and industry trends
- Heuristics/rules of thumb

Any of the preceding items can be subject to the various forms of bias that were described in Chapters 1 through 5 of this book. A thorough competitive analysis always includes the assumptions that a competitor makes about its own competitors and tries to make a determination as to whether that assessment is accurate.

Most forms of business and competitive analysis require identifying the key drivers or linchpin assumptions regarding a rival that will eventually lead them to pursue a specific pattern of action guided by their competitive strategy. Any assumption is debatable, and there is a degree of uncertainty about its validity. Analysts must validate their reasoning and logic by providing defensible evidence of their assumptions.

For our purposes, there are two key forms of assumptions—(1) explicit (stated, transparent, and subject to challenges) or (2) implicit (made subconsciously and not open to challenge or scrutiny). Implicit assumptions are the riskier form and one reason why a technique like linchpin analysis deserves a special place in the analyst's toolkit. Most analytical processes require the analyst to explicitly identify his assumptions, not only for the purpose of ensuring that the analyst recognizes what they are, but also so that the decision maker understands them and their resultant impact on the subsequent analytical reports.[4]

In many incidences, a false assumption would lead to problems since people usually tend to assume that things will go the way they expect and prefer. Additionally, not all assumptions will have equal weight in the analyst's considerations. Some assumptions may prove to be false without having any significant effects on the overall actions taken, but there are others that could have serious consequences.

Business and competitive analysts may describe their firm's competitors as being fierce rivals, threatening, fast moving, and often more successful than they are. The assumptions that your firm and your rival's managers hold about their firms and industry sector help to define the kinds of competitive moves that will be considered or undertaken. For example, if in the past a major competitor in your industry introduced a new type of product that failed, the firm's and rival firms' managers may assume that customers don't want or need the benefits offered by the product and that there is no market for it. These assumptions are not always accurate and may present lucrative opportunities if they are empirically invalid.

Such assumptions and perceptions can be helpful in quickly characterizing a competitor's behavior, since they make the analysis process quicker and more efficient; nevertheless, they can become dangerous if allowed to persist unchallenged for too long. This occurs because an analyst's basic premises about a competitor or the competitive environment inhibit the analyst from interpreting the rival's actions differently and can cause the analyst to misread an adversary's true competitive intentions.

The inhibited analytical frame they apply raises the level of risk attached to the situation being analyzed, thereby creating further difficulty for decision makers and others in the firm that operate under the inaccurate premises supplied by the analyst.

Analysts' views are also commonly clouded by unchallenged assumptions when making judgments about the competitor's behavior in the marketplace. For example, new entrants may have opportunities to introduce a product similar to a previously unsuccessful one without retaliation because incumbent companies may not view this as a serious threat. In the early 1960s Honda, at the time a successful maker of small engines used in lawnmowers and related products, was able to enter the U.S. motorcycle market with a small motorbike. This occurred at least in part because the past experience of major U.S. manufacturers with smaller motorbikes had led them to assume that there was no market for the seemingly underpowered and undersized Honda products.

Linchpin analysis requires the analyst to evaluate the competitor's behavior, temporarily under the assumption that their product introduction plans are the opposite of what the analyst believes them to be. Alternative explanations of these plans are then generated. These explanations and the assumptions underlying them become clear to the analyst, but they may have been missed if the analyst had remained stuck in their paradigm of the competitor.

Analyses of potential developments are based on assessments of factors that together would logically bring about a future without uncertainty. These factors are the drivers or linchpins of the analysis. If one or more of them should change, be reversed, removed, or turn out to have been wrong, the basis for the forecast or prediction would no longer be supported. Identifying the role of these factors is a fundamental requirement of sound analysis and forecasts. Policy makers need to know the potential impact of changes in these linchpins. It is also the professional obligation of analysts to inform their decision makers when the evidence is thin for any of these linchpins, there are high degrees of uncertainty, or empirical evidence supporting them is absent. They must also make it clear when the assumptions are based primarily on past practice or on what appear to be logical extensions of what is confidently known.

How sensitive is the ultimate judgment to changes in any of the major variables or driving forces in the analysis? The linchpin assumptions that drive the analysis are the ones that need to be questioned and scrutinized. Analysts should ask themselves what could happen to cause any of the assumptions to be out of date and how they can know that this has not already happened. They should try to disprove their assumptions rather than confirm them. If an analyst cannot think of anything that would cause a change of mind, her mindset may be so deeply entrenched that she can no longer objectively see the conflicting evidence. One advantage of the competing hypotheses approach (discussed in Chapter 28, "Analysis of Competing Hypothesis (ACH)") is that it helps to identify the linchpin assumptions that swing a conclusion in one direction or another.

Strengths and Advantages

The quality of analysts' logic and their systematic applications of analysis methods and techniques will be directly associated with the long-term consistent effectiveness of analysis performance. Many analytical techniques do not have built-in checks and balances to ensure the quality of analysis being conducted. Linchpin analysis is a technique that essentially requires analysts to systematically think through and assess their assumptions, thereby ensuring that alternative possibilities are considered.

Linchpin analysis is valuable in challenging conventional wisdom, staying away from stereotypes, and mitigating against groupthink and other bureaucratic practices that inhibit analysis. It is a technique that constantly challenges the analyst to carefully consider all the competitive possibilities and explanations for competitor or other actor behavior, and prevents analysts—and their intelligence consumers—from being locked into single, narrow views of an industry actor.

Linchpin analysis is highly beneficial when analysts observe that their executives are operating on false, out of date, or overly optimistic or pessimistic perceptions of rivals or a competitive situation. This can be tough for the analyst to discern and possibly made even more difficult if they need to confront decision makers with their beliefs that the executives' views are inaccurate or otherwise unhealthy. Internal clients will typically welcome the use of linchpin analysis if the analyst has developed a good degree of trust and confidence in their relationships. A good sign is when the analyst or a decision maker struggles to explain a series of rival's moves. Properly used, linchpin analysis can provide a beneficial contrast to an out-of-date view and provide an objective reality check to competitive analysis.

Weaknesses and Limitations

Linchpin analysis requires the analyst and/or the decision maker to identify the key assumptions or driving forces associated with their analytical logic. This is not easy for anybody to do, particularly for those not used to having their assumptions and logic challenged; as such, linchpin analysis can be rendered ineffective if the linchpins themselves are not elicited.

Linchpin analysis does not lend itself well to situations that require a very timely turnaround. Ideally, it requires the testing of the entire set of alternatives, hypotheses, and alternative hypotheses that underlie a description of the future, plan, or potential recommendation. To the extent that there are many hypotheses to examine, linchpin analysis can require a substantial amount of time to conduct.

Linchpin analysis does not generate forecasts or predictions. That requires other techniques (for example, scenario analysis, war gaming, and forecasting). Once those techniques have been employed, linchpin analysis can be used to test their veracity. As such, it will not ordinarily provide an answer to a decision maker's questions, but will help to increase analysts' confidence in the recommendations they provide using other methodologies.

Finally, the technique requires analysts to have confidence in their own analytical capabilities. Many analysts do not conduct linchpin analysis, and many decision makers will not ask for it because they are apprehensive of having their analysis shown to be deficient. As such, it is often good practice to have the technique mandated within the organization, as was done in some public sector intelligence agencies so that analysts understand its importance and are encouraged to perform it as a means for improving their analytical outputs and results.

Process for Applying the Technique

The linchpin analysis process is fairly simple, although it requires a lot of experience and insight to perform effectively. The basic process for how the process works consists of the following five steps:

1. List all the underlying assumptions that were accumulated about a competitor or competitive situation. This can be done best by having the analyst and others who had been involved with the process "step back" from the focal process. One way of collecting these assumptions is to list them via a worksheet similar to the one we provide in Table 29.1. In addition to being helpful in eliciting the assumptions themselves, the worksheet also requires the analyst to list the evidence that was used in supporting the assumption, as well as some source data to provide for further assessment.

Table 29.1
Analyzing Assumptions Worksheet

Linchpins	Reason/Data	Unstated Assumptions
Sony Corporation's next-generation version of its PlayStation will be a multimedia, Internet-ready, BluRay-based game player.	■ Patents were filed in 2005 for each of these capabilities. ■ Preview versions showed several capabilities. ■ They are betting on PlayStation as the center of tomorrow's living room.	■ The unstated assumption for this claim is the belief that Sony's CEO cannot afford to lose another format war or he will be let go. ■ Sony is unwilling to relinquish this market to Microsoft.

2. Develop judgments and hypotheses about a recent competitor decision or their marketplace action against those assumptions.

3. Take one key assumption (that is, a linchpin) and, for the sake of argument, either eliminate it or reverse it.

4. Re-evaluate the evidence in light of this changed or deleted assumption and generate a new set of hypotheses and judgments.

5. Re-insert the assumption that was eliminated or reversed and determine whether the new judgments still hold accurate.

Linchpin Assumption Sensitivity Analysis

Linchpin assumption sensitivity analysis (LASA) is another method for using this approach. LASA requires the analyst to consider the impact of their results against changes to the degree (as opposed to entirety) of the linchpin assumption. The analyst achieves this by varying the assumptions against several pre-established threshold values.

For example, if the linchpin assumption is (1) that the rival will introduce the new product on February 15, (2) that its introductory price will be €50, and (3) that it will be supported by €100,000 worth of local advertising, the following assumptions, among others, could be considered:

- The introductory date will be 30 January. The other two variables remain the same.

- The introductory date will be 30 March. The other two variables remain unchanged.

- The introductory price will be €42. The other two variables remain unchanged from the original.

- The introductory price will be €58, while the other two variables remain unchanged.

- There will be only minimal advertising support of €10,000; the other variables remain the same.

- There will be extremely heavy advertising support of €200,000 in advance of the introduction, while leaving the other two variables unchanged from the original values.

Obviously, further multiple combinations can also be queried through this method. By employing spreadsheets or other software applications, the analyst can quickly and carefully test the sensitivity of these assumptions. This should allow them to consider a wider range of alternatives, as well as a larger number of contingency situations for planning purposes.

Process for Using Linchpin Analysis in Assessing Risk

All assumptions, and especially the linchpins, carry some degree of uncertainty and risk. There is another simple process for assessing how risky assumptions might be and for including them in the analyst's process when appropriate.[5] This again requires the analyst to explicitly list the linchpin assumption or assumptions. A simple "*if . . . then*" statement can be written for each of the analyst's linchpin assumptions in the following form:

"*If* this assumption is proved to be false, *then* the effect on the matter will be . . ."

The *"if"* side tests how likely the linchpin assumption is to be invalid, while the *"then"* side tests whether it actually matters. Another way of describing this is to see the *if* statement as reflecting probability, whereas the *then* statement is about impact. Probability and impact are two essential dimensions in most determinations of risk. This simple approach can be used to turn the analyst's assumptions into risks. Where an assumption is assessed as likely to be false and/or it could have a significant effect on one or more recommendations, that assumption should be considered a major risk that will require the analyst to explicitly identify it and then provide alternatives or contingencies to the decision maker.

This type of linchpin analysis is a powerful way of exposing risks since it addresses the particular assumptions made about a given situation. There are, however, two dangers with this technique.

First, this approach can only consider explicit assumptions that have been consciously made and openly communicated. There are, however, many implicit or hidden assumptions that people make every day, some of which can turn out to be highly risky.

Second, this approach tends only to identify so-called "downside" risks—threats that a particular assumption may prove false and become a problem for the project. This form of linchpin analysis is not good at identifying opportunities because some analysts' assumptions tend to be optimistic by nature (that is, the "glass half full" versus "glass half empty" analyst).

The first shortcoming can be overcome by a facilitated approach to identifying and recording assumptions, using someone who is independent and external to the analysis to challenge established thinking. For the highest effectiveness, this analysis technique requires comprehensive disclosure.

For opportunity identification, this method can be extended to address and challenge constraints—these are restrictions on what the rival can or cannot do and how it must or must not proceed. But some of these constraints may not be as fixed as they first appear; indeed, some of them might be assumed as constraints. In fact, it might be possible for a constraint to be relaxed or perhaps even removed completely. In the same way that assumptions can be tested to expose threats, a similar *"if . . . then"* test can be applied to constraints to identify possible opportunities—*"If* this constraint could be relaxed or removed, *then* the effect on the project would be . . ."

Instead of making assumptions about the future or accepting that stated constraints are unchangeable, analysts can employ this method to be better prepared to challenge assumptions and expose constraints as either significant threats or opportunities through this analytical process.

Linchpin analysis provides analysts with a means for testing the accuracy of their assumptions, the sensitivity of their logic, and the consistency of their arguments; as such, it is a widely applicable tool that can be used in combination with many of the methods and techniques of business and competitive analysis described in this book. It should be a routine part of the analyst's assessment process, and with experience, it can be done more quickly and effectively.

FAROUT Summary

FAROUT SUMMARY

	1	2	3	4	5
F	███	███	███		
A	███	███			
R	███	███	███		
O	███	███	███	███	
U	███	███	███	███	███
T	███	███			

Figure 29.1   Linchpin analysis FAROUT summary

Future orientation—Medium. Linchpin analysis is used to test assumptions about events or actions that are expected to take place; it does not generate forecasts or predictions on its own behalf.

Accuracy—Low to medium. Linchpin analysis relies heavily on properly identifying assumptions and their potential impacts on alternative hypotheses or scenarios. Accuracy is enhanced to the extent that the analyst accurately and comprehensively identifies all assumptions and can determine their potential impacts. It is impacted by state, effect, and response uncertainties.

Resource efficiency—Medium. The application of linchpin analysis requires inputs from results generated by other techniques. It can require additional information to be gathered, particularly if it uncovers gaps in the logic of the original techniques it is being used to examine.

Objectivity—Medium to high. Linchpin analysis is designed to enhance analytical objectivity by forcing analysts to consider the impact of various alternatives and assumptions on outcomes.

Usefulness—High. Linchpin analysis can be applied across a broad/wide range of analytical situations, improve the quality of results produced, and ensure greater consistency in analytical logic.

Timeliness—Low to medium. Analyzing a large number of assumptions, alternatives, hypotheses, and their impacts can be highly time-consuming.

Related Tools and Techniques

- Abduction
- Alternative competing hypothesis (ACH) analysis
- Analogy
- Assumptions analysis
- Blindspot analysis
- Opportunity analysis
- Scenario analysis
- Sensitivity analysis

References

Davis, J. (1992). "Linchpin analysis," *Analytical Tradecraft*, 7(4), pp. 8–9.

Davis, J. (2002). "Improving CIA analytic performance—Strategic warning," CIA Sherman Kent School for Intelligence Analysis, Tech. Rep. 1. Available online at http//www.odci.gov/cia/publications/Kent Papers/pdf/OPNo1.pdf.

Fleisher, C.S., and B. Bensoussan (2003). *Strategic and Competitive Analysis: Methods and Techniques for Analyzing Business Competition*. Upper Saddle River, NJ: Prentice Hall.

Gib, A., and R. Gooding (1998). "CI tool time—What's missing from your toolbag?," pp. 25–39 in the *Proceedings of the 1998 international conference of the Society of Competitive Intelligence Professionals*, Chicago, IL.

Heuer Jr., J.R. (1999). *The Psychology of Intelligence Analysis*. Washington, DC—Center for the Study of Intelligence.

Hilson, D., and R. Murray-Webster (2005). *Understanding and Managing Risk Attitude*. Hants, England: Gower Publishing.

Marrin, S. (2003). "CIA's Kent School—Improving training for new analysts," *International Journal of Intelligence and Counter-Intelligence*, 16(4), pp. 609–637.

Morgan, M.G., and M. Henrion (1990). *Uncertainty—A Guide to Dealing with Uncertainty in Quantitative Risk and Policy Analysis*. New York, NY: Cambridge University Press.

Rigby, Darrell (2003). *Management Tools 2003*. White Paper. Boston, MA: Bain & Company, Inc.

Sawka, K. (1997). "Linchpin analysis," *Competitive Intelligence Review*, 8(3), pp. 85–86.

Sawka, K., and S. Marceau (1999). "Developing a world-class CI program in telecoms," *Competitive Intelligence Review*, 10(4), pp. 30–40.

Endnotes

[1] Davis, 2002; Marrin, 2003.

[2] Gib and Gooding, 1998; Rigby, 2003.

[3] Fleisher and Bensoussan, 2003.

[4] Morgan and Henrion, 1990.

[5] Hillson and Murray-Webster, 2005.

Index

Q

FT Press
FINANCIAL TIMES

In an increasingly competitive world, it is quality
of thinking that gives an edge—an idea that opens new
doors, a technique that solves a problem, or an insight
that simply helps make sense of it all.

We work with leading authors in the various arenas
of business and finance to bring cutting-edge thinking
and best-learning practices to a global market.

It is our goal to create world-class print publications
and electronic products that give readers
knowledge and understanding that can then be
applied, whether studying or at work.

To find out more about our business
products, you can visit us at www.ftpress.com.